Computers and Human Language

Computers and Human Language

GEORGE W. SMITH

New York   Oxford
OXFORD UNIVERSITY PRESS
1991

Oxford University Press

Oxford   New York   Toronto
Delhi   Bombay   Calcutta   Madras   Karachi
Petaling Jaya   Singapore   Hong Kong   Tokyo
Nairobi   Dar es Salaam   Cape Town
Melbourne   Auckland

and associated companies in
Berlin   Ibadan

Published by Oxford University Press
200 Madison Avenue, New York, New York 10016

Oxford is a registered trademark of Oxford University Press

Library of Congress Cataloging-in-Publication Data
Smith, George W. (George William), 1941–
Computers and human language / George W. Smith.
p. cm. Includes bibliographical references and index.
ISBN 0-19-506281-7 (cloth).—ISBN 0-19-506282-5 (paper)
1. Computational linguistics. I. Title.
P98.S6 1991 410'.285—dc20 90-39032

9 8 7 6 5 4 3 2 1

Printed in the United States of America
on acid-free paper

For Laura Feugill Smith

Preface

What do you know when you know a language? Why is it that words form sentences in certain combinations but not others? How do words and sentences mean? What takes place in the instant needed to comprehend an utterance? This book is about computational approaches to such questions, approaches that have emerged over four decades of lively research. Sometimes computers play their familiar role, gathering and organizing and analyzing linguistic information so that properties of languages might be better understood. Or they employ linguistic knowledge to structure and retrieve information couched in language. But computation has also stimulated new ways of thinking about language and cognition. Computers now emulate, even simulate processes by which we understand sentences or interpret extended discourse.

Although the sequence of chapters ascends the traditional ladder of linguistic components from small structures to large, they divide and merge topics to reflect major lines of computational inquiry:

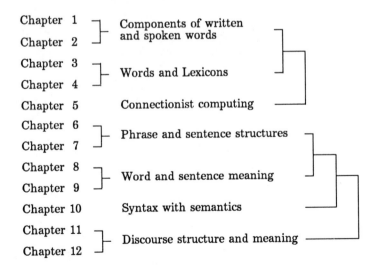

The first four chapters explore the sublexical and lexical levels of language, where most of the practical applications of computers to language are currently to be found. These early chapters also introduce computational structures and processes, preparing readers with little or no experience with computer programming for the chapters which follow. Chapter 5 presents an alternative paradigm of computing with applications that for now are also on the sublexical and lexical levels. Chapters 7 through 12 explore the highly developed computational approaches to syntax, semantics, and their integration as well as linguistic and more broadly conceptual approaches to extended discourse. The objective of this work in computational linguistics is to model aspects of human cognition and eventually to enable computers to understand language. Supporting the discussion is empirical evidence about the acquisition, storage, recognition, comprehension, and production of language.

Most chapters proceed as the thinking has proceeded by proposing series of hypotheses. Successive proposals recast their predecessors, retaining what helps explain the nature and functioning of language and rethinking what is not helpful, until something close to the present view is reached and motives for current research become clear. The emphasis, especially from Chapter 6 onward, is on general principles, rather than on the details of particular implementations. At every step, however, processing examples illustrate the hypotheses and methods under discussion, and these are fundamental to the exposition. The reader is urged first to walk through them, then experiment with fresh words or sentences and with extensions to the relevant structures and rules.

For their help in shaping this text, I am grateful to the students in my courses on language and computers. Students of computer science, linguistics, cognitive science, and the humanities, they gladly taught each other and taught me. I wish also to thank Neal Bruss, Glenn Flierl, Chuck Meyer, and Louise Z. Smith, who carefully read portions of the draft and offered valuable advice, as well as Susan Hannan of Oxford University Press, on whose expertise I relied as I prepared the camera-ready copy.

University of Massachusetts at Boston   G.W.S.
August 1990

Contents

12. Knowledge about Discourse

Anaphora and Segmentation, 407

Discourse Segments and Structure, 419

Computers and Human Language

Chapter 1

Components of Words

Section one: Symbols and Computation

1.1 Languages as symbolic systems

Symbols are familiar, convenient ways of representing information; we encounter them every day. A **symbol** is a cipher, an entity with no inherent meaning, that has been assigned a meaning by a user of symbols or a community of users. Symbols often participate in systems of symbols. The red, yellow, and green of traffic lights are symbols, each with a unique meaning; they convey "stop," "caution" and "go" quickly and without ambiguity. In combination, they constitute a system of symbols, albeit a very simple system, but the three meaning-ful alternatives guide the behavior of hundreds of millions of people. The decimal numeral system is another system of symbols, a system of great range and versatility. Employing the ten numerals 0 through 9, together with an agreed-upon notation in which a numeral's value depends on the column in which it occurs, the decimal system affords an infinite number of possible symbols and can represent sequence, quantity, and countless other mathematical abstractions. Musical notation with its clefs, staffs, notes, dots, bars, measures, signatures, and other symbols is another rich symbolic system, collectively capable of representing the complexity of music and its infinite creativity.

Language is yet another symbolic system, though we may not think about it that way. Much as the red of a traffic light is a color that symbolizes a command, the sequences of sounds or graphic shapes that constitute words and sentences of a language function as symbols to signify the meanings or intentions of a speaker. Much as numerals take on new meanings when they enter into combinations (10 signifies a different quantity than the sum of 1 and 0), so words combine to form a potentially infinite number of different phrases and sentences where their meanings are modified and expanded by the presence of other words.

Like mathematical operations, language use is rule-abiding behavior. Rules determine what arrangements of sounds or characters constitute words, what arrangements of words constitute well-formed phrases and sentences, and what arrangements of word, phrase, and sentence meanings constitute intelligible expressions. Our minds are organized in such a way that we can acquire these rules and follow them without being fully conscious of what they are. Finally, much as musical notation affords physical existence and permanence to what would otherwise be ineffable and quite transitory, so language is entitative and, once recorded or written, permanent. More versatile than numerals or musical notation, the symbolic system of language permits us to express perceptions, images, situations, memories, beliefs, feelings, hypotheses, indeed anything that we can think about our immediate circumstances and surroundings or about any other states of affairs, real or imagined.

Computers are processors of symbols, equally capable of working with numerical or linguistic symbols. Computer memory can store language in enormous quantities and make it available to very rapid searches. Computers can also help in studying properties of language and of language cognition. Their processes can carry out any linguistic rules that can be made explicit. Presently they can recognize or generate legitimate sentences of a language, produce acceptable paraphrases or translations of language, and make inferences and discover explanations. The range of human capabilities that cannot be successfully emulated by manipulating symbols is steadily shrinking.

Whether computers will eventually understand language or think using language are controversial questions that hinge on what more is meant by "understand" and "think" than can be accomplished by identifying, categorizing, combining, and otherwise manipulating symbols. Later, we will encounter the "representation hypothesis" which holds that word and sentence meanings are represented in the mind by a symbol system of mental entities and relations and that what we ordinarily call understanding or thinking consists of manipulating these symbolic representations. Some people disagree with the hypothesis, arguing that symbol manipulation does not involve such mental phenomena as consciousness or intentionality and is therefore only part of what it is to think and understand. If mental entities and processes can be made fully explicit, and if the representation hypothesis is borne out, then by the process of elimination we should have a much clearer idea of what else is meant by understanding and thinking than we have at present. To explore the progress made thus far, we need to begin with the discrete and quite arbitrary nature of language symbols, necessary attributes if language is to be represented in a different medium with no loss of information.

1.2 Symbols are arbitrary and discrete

Language symbols can be represented in various media, though two are primary: speech and writing. Spoken languages choose a limited number of contrasting sounds from the continuum of possible sounds that the vocal chords, lips, and tongue can produce. According to a code shared by speakers of the language, these sounds combine to form symbols that are words or, sometimes, phrases. Thus the distinct five sounds /f/, /k/, /s/, /w/, and /i/ may form the phrase that is pronounced /kwik fiks/ and means a rapid and perhaps temporary repair. Written language employs a code of contrasting graphic shapes to accomplish the same purpose, so that the characters c, f, i, k, q, u, x, plus a space, spell the phrase *quick fix*. Neither the distinct sounds nor the graphic characters have any syntactic role or meaning in and of themselves. The smallest unit having a meaning is a word, such as *quick* and *fix*, or sometimes an affix, such as the *-ly* in *quickly* or the *-es* in *fixes*, or an idiomatic phrase, such as *kick the bucket*, where the meaning cannot be deduced from the constituent words. Their significance is in the meaningful combinations they form.

When spoken or written language is represented in secondary media, where neither the sound of the word nor its graphic shape is reproduced, little or no information is lost. Many forms of shorthand translate spoken words and phrases into graphic symbols. Morse code substitutes for each character of written language a distinctive pattern of long and short energy pulses to communicate electronically, and Braille substitutes patterns of raised dots to communicate by touch. Computers also encode language, employing a system that resembles Morse and Braille. Languages can be encoded in these various media, without loss of information, because language symbols are almost entirely arbitrary.

Most words do not function by resembling their meanings in either sound or physical shape: neither sound nor shape links them to semantic or grammatical roles. Instead, the link is entirely a matter of convention and social agreement; communities of language users arbitrarily associate certain strings of sounds or graphic shapes with meanings. Thus in written English a single-bladed utensil for cutting is a *knife*, in written German it is *messer*, and in Spanish knives are *cuchillo*. Though a few characters in written Chinese and Japanese do resemble their meanings, the resemblance is not strong enough to communicate the meanings directly; the resemblance is apparent only if the meanings are known, and synonyms are not represented in these systems by similar characters. As for spoken languages, though they have onomatopoeic words, such as *bang*, *growl*, and *swish*, where the sound resembles the meaning, they are few and they too differ from language to language. *To giggle* in English is *kichern* in German and *reirse tontamente* in Spanish. Nor do individual sounds appear to have any associated meanings. Despite repeated efforts to find statistical correlations between, say *i* with words that have as part of their meaning sharpness or shrillness or smallness or *gl* with words related to sight, no such correlation appears to exist. Many examples come to mind, but with them come so many counter-examples that the generalization fails. Further evidence that language symbols are arbitrary comes from other kinds of languages. American Sign Language uses hand motions, facial expressions, and body language. It represents the animal for which English has the word *dog* with a word formed by a snap of the middle finger against the thumb then a slap against the thigh.

The arbitrary nature of the symbols affords language its versatility and expressive power. Though the channel by which languages communicate is limited to sounds, shapes, and gestures, this does not constrain the topics of discourse to auditory and graphic phenomena. If words had to resemble meanings, finding spoken words for sounds and sources of some sounds might be possible (though what would be done about radio or phonograph is hard to imagine) and written words might specify physical objects and spatial relations. But these hardly exhaust the meanings for which we need symbols. Sensations other than sound and sight require symbols, as do emotional and aesthetic feelings, personal and social relations, ethical and moral choices, abstractions of every kind, and a host of other meanings. An arbitrary system of symbols can readily represent the indefinitely large quantity of such meanings.

For the most part language symbols are also discrete or "digital," operating by the presence or absence of sounds or characters, not their presence in varying degrees. Two symbols that are only minimally different from one another may have quite dissimilar meanings and usually they do, witness *lit, lid, bit, bid, bet,* and *bed.* With these six words, a difference in one character is an absolute difference. This is an important advantage in that context can help identify words that are not written or spoken clearly. Context in *I slept on the* — allows only one plausible choice from among the six similar words. If similar meanings had similar symbols, context would not be nearly so useful. Even tonal languages, which distinguish words by pitch, present discrete alternatives rather than a gradual scale; in one dialect of Chinese, *pan* means "class" when spoken at a steady high pitch and "half" when spoken with a falling tone. Though much of our experience is of analog phenomena–size, color, temperature, sound, texture, speed, emotion, intelligence, conformity, motivation, and exertion–all vary by degree, the vocabulary by which we communicate that experience consists only of discrete symbols: *hot, cool, cold* express states that, though not precisely defined, are discrete. Even the intensifiers and hedges, sometimes used to convey, gradations are discrete: *very hot, somewhat cool, not at all cold.*

For representing language within computers, the discrete nature of language symbols is almost as important as their being arbitrary. Because two symbols are different absolutely and not by degrees, any medium for representing them need only register that they are distinct. Language symbols do not require any measuring of degrees of similarity and difference. This is an advantage, because modern computers are also fundamentally digital, consisting at the most basic level of a vast number of on/off switches. Computers are capable of working with analog phenomena, but only with some difficulty, using techniques of approximation and sampling. The code by which information is represented within computers is digital, registering states of high or low voltage in a series of tiny cells. Thus language and computers are, by virtue of the discrete nature of language symbols, remarkably compatible. Translating sounds or characters into the computer code is a matter of substitution; no measurements or approximations are needed. To be sure, there are sometimes difficulties in recognizing the language symbols (especially sounds), but once they are recognized the translation is straightforward and quite simple.

Section two: Beginning with Written Language

2.1 Some attributes of written language

Both in the history of languages and in their acquisition by children, written language is subsequent to spoken language. Most of the world's major languages employ alphabetic character sets in which characters represent or once represented contrasting sounds. Languages like Czech, Finnish, and Spanish come much closer than English does to having each alphabetic character represent one and only one sound. When alphabets do not have sufficient symbols to distinguish all the sounds of a language, some languages employ diacritics, such as the Spanish tilde (*señor*) or the German umlaut (*männer*); others use pairs of characters called digrams, which may have a special orthography or may simply be written as separate characters (*th*, *ch*, *sh*, and *ng* in modern English). Whatever the method, alphabetic symbols represent symbolic sounds.

Many ancient languages and a few living ones have writing systems that are not alphabetic. Some use syllabaries or sets of characters that symbolize clusters of sounds. Japanese, for example, employs two syllabaries: *hiragana* is used for native words and *katakana* for loan words and special effects. Each has forty-six characters (called *kana*), and with the help of diacritics they suffice to represent the approximately one hundred distinct units of sound in spoken Japanese. Still other languages use ideographs that represent meanings directly, not mediated through speech. (An ideograph is a stylized version of what originally was a mnemonic picture used in writing; Roman keyboards have at least one ideograph, the % which portrays the division for percentages.) In the People's Republic of China, which has eight mutually unintelligible dialects of the majority Han language and as many as fifty other "national minority" languages, these symbol systems provide a *lingua franca*. Speakers in the south of China (for example) associate Cantonese pronunciations with ideographs; speakers in the north associate their different Mandarin pronunciations with the same ideographs; thus Cantonese and Mandarin speakers, as well as speakers of other dialects, can communicate in ideographic writing.

For the most part, computers store, manipulate, and analyze written rather than spoken language, though this is beginning to change. The hegemony of written language is partly because the earliest applications of computers to language called for written language, and mainly because it is extremely difficult to automate the recognition of continuous speech and hence to translate spoken language into computer code. Although intonation (the systematic varying of loudness, pitch, and duration) allows spoken language to convey information that is either absent from written language or unsubtly conveyed by punctuation and italics, written language does have some important advantages. Because it lacks not only intonation but also the gestures, facial expressions, and prospect of immediate feedback that assist spoken language, writing tends to be more fully explicit and less ambiguous than spoken language. Not only are syntactic and semantic relationships are usually clear, but written sentences tend to be structurally complete and free from the slips of the tongue, false starts, and other erroneous and extraneous matter that proliferate in spontaneous speech.

Although typing is slower than speaking (about 60 words per minute for a competent typist versus 150 for moderately paced speech), reading is considerably faster than listening. An average reading speed for college students is about 360 words per minute, and many readers are much faster. With spoken language the mode of transmission is serial: one word after another strung through time. Written language is also serial, but access can be random when we want it to be, because the entire text is simultaneously available. We can scan the text, skipping over lines or paragraphs or larger chunks, and seek out the information we need. With the advent of computers and electronically stored text, we can search out key words or phrases, leaving it to the machine to scan the text very rapidly and missing nothing. Computers also support **hypertext**, a nonlinear, interactive form of electronically represented print. Hypertext deploys information (either text or graphics) in modules, and links the modules to form a huge web of information, which may be hierarchical, associative, or both. When hypertext is displayed on a video screen, the words or phrases linked to other modules are marked by highlighting or icons. By choosing one of the marked items, the reader can "jump" to relevant information in another module. A hierarchical hypertext might at the highest or entry level provide a general account of the history of the United States. Should the reader want more about the colonial era, she can descend a branch of the hierarchy to an amplified account. If it is actually colonial architecture she is after, she descends yet another branch to an overview of that topic and other choices of periods and regions.

Written language has other advantages. It is usually normative. Though pronunciations of words vary from region to region and change from time to time, spellings remain stable over time. What variation there is (as, for example, between American and British English: *color / colour*; or with compounds *match box / match-box / matchbox*) is highly predictable. Spellings of the word endings that make syntactically important distinctions are consistent whereas their pronunciations vary. The *-s* by which English distinguishes plural from singular is pronounced /s/ in *dogs*, /z/ in *cats* and /is/ in *horses*; the *-ed* that marks the past tense is pronounced /d/ in some words (*shoved*) but /t/ in others (*talked*). Though such inconsistencies mean little to us and we have no trouble deciding what is meant, getting the number and tense right can be important to many computer applications. Spellings also link the common stems of related words (*real, reality; human, humanity*) that have come to be pronounced quite differently. Finally, though some words are distinguished only by their pronunciations (verb-noun pairs such as *import / import, subject / subject* are particularly nettlesome), spellings differentiate a great many words that are pronounced the same (*to / too / two; four / fore; bred / bread*). Given these advantages and the availability of devices that expedite the handling of written language, including text editors, word processors, desktop publishing programs, spelling checkers, modems, fax machines, high-speed printers, and automatic typesetters, the fact that written language is the primary and easiest language for computers is probably for the best.

2.2 Encoding written language

Information is represented within conventional computers by a code that has just two units, usually designated by the symbols 0 and 1. Though we are usually insulated from this level of detail, because displays and printers translate the code into language (a process of symbol substitution), it is helpful to know something of the properties of computer code and the circuitry that manipulates it. Within the computer's circuits, the two units register as states of low and high electrical force (or voltage). If pairs of circuits represent elements in a numerical code, four distinct arrangements are available, enough to represent the space and the first three characters in the Roman alphabet: 00 for the space, 01 for *A*, 10 for *B*, and 11 for *C*. (It may seem strange to think of the space as a character, and indeed it was not until about the tenth century that writing began to delimit words with spaces. But the space carries information: *at one* has a different meaning from *atone* or *a tone*.) By substituting codes for characters, we can represent a simple phrase in terms of 0's and 1's:

A   C   A   B

01 00 11 01 10

Notice that each code unambiguously represents a character, and that nothing is lost in the translation because the code simply substitutes one discrete unit for another. Computer codes operate in just this way, except, of course, that several circuits must be linked so as to afford enough different arrangements of 0's and 1's to represent all the characters in the alphabet in both upper and lower case, the marks of punctuation, and so on.

Employing just the two states, without gradations, makes for reliability in moving and storing information, because each electronic circuit needs only register the binary distinction between high and low. In this respect, the method of representing information resembles the traffic lights with their sharply contrasting red and green messages. Given the volume and bewildering complexity of the information processed by modern computers, the reliability of binary is a crucial property.

Other properties of the code can best be illustrated by comparing it with Morse code, which until the advent of computers was probably the most widespread convention for electronically encoding language. Like computer code, Morse is binary. Its units are a long pulse and a short pulse of energy, written as a dot and a dash. Contrasting sequences make up each character:

Q   U   I   E   T

— — • — • • — • • • —

But there are important differences between Morse and the codes that computers use. Designed for efficiency and speed, Morse takes advantage of the fact that some letters in the alphabet are more frequent than others. (As the story goes, Samuel F. B. Morse worked out the code by visiting a printing shop to count the elements of type available for each character.) Morse assigns short, simple codes to the more frequent letters of the alphabet and longer, more complicated sequences to those that are less frequent. Compare the codes for *E* and *T* in *QUIET* with the code for *Q*. Such efficiency is not necessary with computers, where the processing and storing of code is managed by tens of thousands of circuits etched on tiny slices of silicon and capable of exchanging information at rates measured in nanoseconds, or billionths of a second. (A vehicle traveling at one foot per nanosecond would make fifteen thousand round trips between Boston and San Francisco every hour.) Their thousands of circuits and high speed afford the luxury of a large and orderly code, which in turn facilitates computer operations that sort and search for information.

Each character is represented in a computer code by a set of (usually) eight binary digits. Thus E is 01000101, Q is 01010000, the space between words is 00100000, and so on. In our familiar decimal system, columns represent powers of ten, whereas in binary they represent powers of two. Thus the sequence of binary numerals runs 0, 1, 10, 11, 100 and so on, with every second step carrying a 1 to the next column on the left. Here is an example that converts binary to decimal:

0	1	0	1	0	0	0		
128	64	32	16	8	4	2		
x 0	x 1	x 0	x 1	x 0	x 1	x 0		
	64	+	16	+	4	=	84	

For a little more practice with binary, consider the method called "parity checking" for assuring that any error in the transmission of binary code will be caught. Say we are using nine binary digits. The first eight will represent information in binary code, and the ninth or "parity bit" will be either 0 or 1 depending on whether the last digit of their total is 0 or 1. (In mathematics parity is the comparative odd or even relationship between two integers.) If the first eight digits are 01010001 and the ninth is 0, something has gone wrong. Adding three 1's and five 0's produces 11, and the information will need to be retransmitted. Error-checking schemes, only a bit more complicated than this can do even better, not only revealing that an error has occurred, but also giving its location. Though computers can perform arithmetic with them, it should be noted that binary codes are not numbers, but rather numerals–symbols for numbers. Despite their reputation as number crunchers, computers manipulate symbols rather than numbers and perform addition or other mathematical operations by manipulating those symbols according to rules.

The numerical aspect of computer code offers a decided advantage over Morse, because numerals can also represent sequence, range, and interval. In the first place, numerical sequence can represent the collating sequence of characters. Nearly every written language has a collating sequence. For English it is alphabetical order; for Chinese and Japanese, collating sequences are based on the number and kinds of strokes that form a character. Within the code for our Roman alphabet the twenty-six lower case letters occupy one range of numerals; their upper case counterparts occupy a separate range of

A	01000001	(65)	a	01100001	(97)
B	01000010	(66)	b	01100010	(98)
C	01000011	(67)	c	01100011	(99)
D	01000100	(68)	d	01100100	(100)
E	01000101	(69)	e	01100101	(101)
F	01000110	(70)	f	01100110	(102)
G	01000111	(71)	g	01100111	(103)
H	01001000	(72)	h	01101000	(104)
	* * *			* * *	
X	01011000	(88)	x	01111000	(120)
Y	01011001	(89)	y	01111001	(121)
Z	01011010	(90)	z	01111010	(122)

Figure 1. Binary codes for some upper and lower case characters.

numerals. Thus filtering a text to eliminate everything but words is merely a matter of specifying a range of codes. (Figure 1 gives the sequences of binary codes for portions of the Roman alphabet.) Given the fixed interval between lower and upper case versions of any character, converting one to the other is a simple matter of addition or subtraction by 32. Then the computer can alphabetize by comparing codes for words and swapping those that are out of order. Once a list is in alphabetical sequence, it is easily searched. One method of searching compares the target word with the middle word in the list; if the code is lower than of the middle word, then the target is compared with the middle of the first half, and so on, with each step narrowing the search. Thus the numerical code allows computers both to create order and to search ordered information. Recognizing this capacity, a French term for computer is *l'ordinateur*.

Eight binary digits provide a total of two-hundred fifty-six codes, more than enough to represent the upper and lower case alphabets, marks of punctuation, some diacritical marks (usually the caret, circumflex, acute accent, grave accent and tilde), as well as a selection of the symbols used in various systems of notation (∞ for infinity, for example, and $\equiv$ for logical equivalence). All characters for which a given system has codes are said to belong to its character set or typeface. Different systems use different codes and slightly different character sets, although the American Standard Code for Information Interchange (ASCII, pronounced "ask' ee") is the most common, and it is the code given above. A competitor to ASCII is EBCDIC (eb' sih dic'), which runs on certain large computers. Computers represent text and nearly everything else (including spreadsheets and data bases) in ASCII or EBCDIC. Only executable instructions to the machine are repre-sented in a different format.

That computer codes are based on the binary numbering system explains some computer jargon. The 0 or 1 that occupies each column is a **bit**, short for binary digit. A collection of eight bits constitutes a **byte**, (pronounced 'bite', but with the 'y' for better contrast with bit). As we have seen, each character of a text is usually stored as one byte of computer code. The processing capacity of computers, that is the number of columns of binary code that can be processed at once, is measured in bits; microcomputers manage eight, sixteen, or thirty-two bits. Larger computers process "words" of sixty-four bits or more. The amount of memory possessed by a computer is measured in multiples of a thousand, a million, a billion, even a trillion bytes: kilobytes, megabytes, gigabytes, and terabytes. Kilobyte derives its prefix from the Greek *khilio* for thousand, but the higher numbers required some inventive prefixing. They derive from the Greek *megas* or "great," *gigas* or "giant," and *teras* or "monster." For some idea of what these numbers mean, consider that an ordinary double-spaced typewritten page occupies about two kilobytes of computer memory, the second edition of the *Oxford English Dictionary*, now available in computer-readable form, has about three-hundred and fifty megabytes of definitions and citations, and the eighty million or so books in the Library of Congress contain more than ten thousand gigabytes of text.

Besides assigning numerical codes to the upper and lower case characters, numerals, punctuation, and common notation, ASCII and EBCDIC also have codes for "control characters," so named because they control the operation of video displays, printers, typesetters, and communications equipment. Although these are not characters in any ordinary sense of the word, they are encoded numerically just as the alphabetic characters are, and they are embedded within the stream of text. That instructions and text can be mingled in this manner reflects the symbolic nature of computer operations. The meaning of any given code is an assigned meaning and may just as easily be an instruction as a character. Looked at another way, all codes are instructions; the code for the upper case *A* instructs the display or printer to draw slanted lines with a crossbar. In all, ASCII has thirty-two control characters. The tab has its code (numeral 09) as do the line feed (10), which moves the print position down one line, and the carriage return (13) which directs the display or printer to return to the left margin. Thus the sequence of codes for a formatted text would look something like this in computer storage:

```
01001000 01100101 00100000 01110011 01100001 01110111 00001101 00001010
    H        e      space      s         a        w       Line    Carriage
                                                           feed     return

00010011 01001000 01100001 01110111 01100101 01100101 01110100 00010011
  start      H        a        w         l         e        t       stop
underline                                                         underline
```

Notice that underlining is also managed by control characters; the byte 00010011 instructs the computer to start underlining and to continue

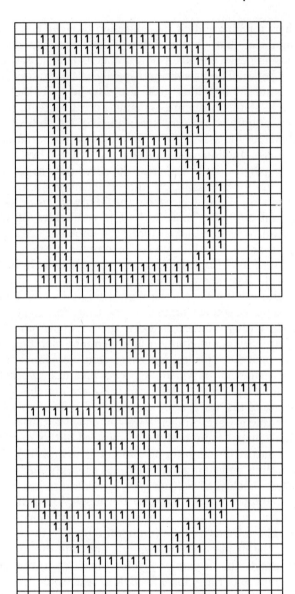

Figure 2. Bitmaps for upper case B and
a Chinese ideograph for "word."

until that byte occurs again. In essentially the same way, embedded
control characters can instruct printers to switch fonts (sizes and styles
of type) so that certain passages are printed in italics, in the Helvetica
typeface rather than Century Schoolbook (used in this book for the
headings and text, respectively) or perhaps in a condensed mode with
fifteen rather than the usual ten or twelve characters to the inch.

Printers and video displays translate the character codes as graphic shapes by substituting a symbol that is a pattern of ink or light for a symbol that is a pattern of electrical states. Descriptions of the characters may be **bitmaps**, two-dimensional arrays of bits (Figure 2), or they may be numerical **vectors**, specifying straight and curved lines and their coordinates. In either case codes are translated into descriptions of characters whether of the Roman alphabet or Greek (α β γ δ η ξ), Cyrillic (Д Ж И Ч Э Ю), or Hebrew (א ב ג ד ה ם) alphabets–even Hiragana (あ え え お け え). On the screen or printed page, the characters are of a standard height (measured in "points" 1/72.27th of an inch) and may be of a fixed width or proportionally spaced. Fixed-width characters were invented to accommodate the mechanical limitations of typewriters, but are awkward for an alphabet with characters as different as the *i* and the *w*; proportional spacing goes back to the scribes, is less wasteful of space, and can be easier and less tiring to read.

Working in the opposite direction, optical character readers substitute computer codes for printed shapes. First, the shape is digitized by superposing an appropriately sized grid, then turning on every cell that contains a line segment. The resulting bitmap can then be compared to a library of bitmaps for known characters. Since bitmaps contain more information than is actually required to identify characters, each character in the library can be represented in terms of features that distinguish one character from another. Upper case B for example, differs from upper case P in that it has two loops instead of one, and it differs from 8 in that a straight line intersects the left side of the double loops. Recognition by "feature extraction" superposes bitmaps of features over the appropriate portions of the character, in effect substituting the relevant features for the entire bitmap. When very large amounts of information are to be stored, especially large amounts of text (and one commercial databank is adding about sixty million words of text a week), it makes sense to conserve memory by giving up the luxury of one byte per character. Again, there is opportunity for substitution. Compression routines replace ASCII bytes with another more succinct code just before the text goes into storage:

Text 8 bit	compress ⇒	Storage 6 bit	decompress ⇒	Text 8 bit

A simple routine looks up the byte in a conversion table and substitutes a corresponding, say six bit, alternative (A six bit code allows for 2 to the 6th power or 64 distinct characters, enough for the upper and lower case letters and for punctuation.) Using six rather than eight bits reduces the storage requirement by one quarter. Looking for something even better, we might employ variable length codes, assigning as few as three bits to eight very frequent characters (space, *e, t, o, a, i, n* and *s,* which comprise nearly eighty percent of the characters in any stretch of text in English) and longer, six bit codes to characters that are less frequent. A different strategy exploits the very high frequency of certain combinations of two or three characters: digrams or trigrams. (The twenty-six character alphabet of English plus the space and the apostrophe yield 28 × 28 or 784 digrams and 28 × 28 × 28 or 21,952 trigrams, but fewer than 600 digrams and 6000 trigrams actually occur in English words. Some are very common (*th, in, er*), others are rare (*q* followed by any character but *u*), and frequencies of occurrence are well established. Digram coding assigns unused codes (for example, the ASCII codes above 128) to frequent pairs (*th in er re an he en ti te* and *at* are the ten most frequent in English). Compression methods in actual use are far more efficient than any of these simple expedients. Adaptive Huffman coding, for example, uses the frequencies of characters in the text to determine variable length codes. Because differences in frequency are extreme (a given character is about a hundred times more likely to be *e* than *j, q* or *z,* and spaces are still more frequent), the average number of bits per character is less than four and a half. Whatever the method, the important point is that compression codes, and indeed all computer codes, simply substitute one unique symbol for another. As long as the symbol remains unique, the process can be reversed and information is preserved.

2.3 Working with encoded strings and lists

A sequence of characters of any kind and extending to any length that can fit in computer memory is a **string**. The term is apt because, although a string may be a linguistic entity, it need not be; and unless specially instructed, the computer "knows" only that the characters are contiguous, not that they spell out a word or a sentence. Converting a long string that is a text to a series of short strings constituting a list of the words in the text is a necessary preliminary to many procedures for working with language. Another preliminary is selectively to convert upper to lower case letters, so that the word list can be alphabetized. The two can be merged into a single procedure, which will illustrate methods of working with strings of character codes, as well as a few of the difficulties, especially those that derive from ambiguities in the character set. The procedure works its way through the text character by character, making decisions as it goes.

Figure 3 gives an algorithm for the decision making. An **algorithm** is a specification of a process, written in ordinary language. A computer program could implement the algorithm but would be written in artificial programming language used for instructing the computer. Programming syntax is very precise and unforgiving; a small mistake

#1   IF the character code is end of file marker

THEN stop

ELSE input a new character, and obtain its ASCII code.

#2   IF the code is 46 (a period) OR 63 (a question mark)
OR 33 (an exclamation point) OR 13 (a carriage return)

THEN change the code to 32 (space), set NEW-SENTENCE to
yes, and continue.

ELSE continue.

#3   IF the code is 32 (a space) AND the length of the present
word is greater than zero.

THEN store the present word, prepare for a new one and
loop to #1

ELSE continue

#4   IF the new character's code is greater than 64 AND less
than 91 (that is, an upper case letter)

THEN   IF NEW-SENTENCE is yes

THEN add 32 to the code, substitute the character
with the new code for the present character, set
NEW-SENTENCE to no and continue.

ELSE concatenate the character to the present
word and continue.

ELSE continue.

#5   IF the new character's code is greater than 96 AND less
than 123 (that is, a lower case letter) OR 44 (apostrophe)

THEN concatenate that character with the word and loop
to #1

ELSE loop to #1

Figure 3. An algorithm for converting text to word list.

can halt the program or (worse) produce unreliable results. To be
useful, algorithms must have the same precision, specifying what is to
be done in what sequence with everything stated in a way that is
unambiguous and sufficiently explicit to be readily translated into a
program. Notice that every significant condition must be anticipated,
including one that we might think self-evident, the end of the text.

Within the algorithm, decision making is accomplished by a series
of conditionals: if the conditions stipulated by the IF. . . statement are
true, the actions specified in the THEN. . . statement are performed. If

not true, the actions specified in the ELSE. . . statement are executed. Every language for instructing computers has some version of the conditional (several use the formulation IF, THEN, and ELSE), and the conditional is fundamental to computation in that it frees the computer from an immutable schedule of actions and permits flexible responses to the input or to the result of some previous operation. Instructions are in sequence so that after executing either the THEN or the ELSE, the computer goes on to the next IF. Sequence is important. In this case, the computer cannot append a character to the word it is forming (which it does in steps #4 and #5) before it has made a series of decisions. The decision making is strictly binary. Either the condition is met or it is not; either the THEN statement executes or the ELSE executes. Some decisions, however, are more complicated:

□ If multiple conditions must be met, they can be linked with AND (which means both).

□ If either condition or both permit the action, they can also be represented by OR.

□ If alternative conditions permit an action they can be linked with XOR (one but not both).

These are known as Boolean operators, for George Boole who first worked out the binary logic of these connectives. If a given decision requires a prior decision (as in step #4), a second conditional can be inserted (or "nested") within the first.

Examining characters one at a time, the procedure assigns them to the present word via steps #4 and #5 for upper and lower case letters, respectively. By specifying two ranges of admissible codes, the instructions filter out punctuation and control characters. Left to their own devices, steps #4 and #5 would merrilystringtogether all the letters they encounter; therefore prior instructions must separate the words. Since most words are delimited by spaces, step #3 responds to a space by ending the present word and beginning another. Again there are problems. Sometimes there will be more than one space between words, hence step #3 must make sure that the present word has at least one character (for example, *I* or *a*). Also, the interval between paragraphs or between lines of poetry may contain a carriage return and perhaps a tab, but not a space. The solution is to identify marks of terminal punctuation and convert them to spaces (in step #2). The extra step exacts no great cost because the procedure will also use terminal punctuation in deciding what upper case letters to convert to lower case.

Conversion to lower case is managed by step #4, which subtracts 32 from the codes for upper case characters. But step #4 must operate selectively, converting only those letters that are upper case to begin a sentence, not those that begin proper names. Thus, when step #2 encounters a mark of terminal punctuation, it records a yes at a memory location for NEW-SENTENCE, so that step #4 can consult NEW-SENTENCE to determine whether the upper case character begins a sentence. If it does, the character is converted to lower case and NEW-SENTENCE is reset to no. Again there is an ambiguity in the character set. The upper case character at the beginning of the sentence may also be the first letter in a proper name. There is no ready way of resolving the ambiguity short of providing a "stop" list of proper names that would be consulted for every word that follows a mark of terminal punctuation and begins with an upper case letter.

2.4 Multilingual representation

ASCII or EBCDIC provides for the Roman alphabet, but what about the alphabets of other languages and the ideographic systems and syllabaries of China and Japan? Living languages employ about fifty different alphabets and these vary greatly in appearance and in historical descent. Most of the alphabets have twenty to thirty characters, although some have as few as a dozen (Hawaiian, for example) and others have as many as fifty (Singhalese, the language of much of Ceylon). To sort properly, to search, or to perform other internal operations, the computer requires a code that accommodates characters employed by various languages and registers their sequence. For many languages this is accomplished by twelve codes in ASCII that can differ from country to country; so that, for example, the Scandinavian countries can complete their 29 and 30 character alphabets within a system designed for the Roman alphabet. That is only an expedient, not a full solution. Although bytes are convenient units for computers, they afford only 256 characters, and the fifty alphabets in common use require several times that many codes. Using sixteen columns or two bytes per character suggests itself as a possible solution. Two bytes would accommodate 65,536 characters, and each language would be using less than a byte to represent its characters and their sequence.

Embedded instructions offer a more satisfactory solution. Recall that instructions, such as the control characters that turn underlining on and off, can be inserted within text. An international agreement, designates the byte 11111111 as an instruction to shift alphabets, with the byte that follows to designate the alphabet. Thus the sequence 11111111 00100110 means shift to the Greek alphabet, and a subsequent 11111111 00100111 means change to Cyrillic, the Slavic alphabet which in modified form is used by Russian, Bulgarian, and other languages. (The Roman alphabet used for English and other languages is 00000000.)

This takes care of all the phonetic alphabets, but the Chinese and Japanese scripts remain. Numbering in the tens of thousands, Chinese ideographs require a two byte code; so a double shift signal (11111111 11111111) instructs the computer that what follows is ideographic with each pair of bytes representing a character. For convenience, the code represents only the 6,763 most commonly used ideographs and further divides these into two classes. (This does not solve the problems of entering and displaying characters; some keyboards have as many as four thousand characters and others use special shift keys to select among several "pages" of character sets.) Two-byte codes are also required for Japanese, which may be the most complex of the living scripts. Although the entire Japanese language can be written using the two syllabaries (hence in a one byte code), many of the kana have multiple meanings; *ka*, for example, has over two hundred. For this reason, Japanese employs a hybrid of kana and ideographs (dervived from the Chinese and called *kanji*). Verbs are commonly represented as *kanji*, and their many inflectional markings (for tense and the like) are *kana*. The language of South Korea also uses ideographs derived from the Chinese, supplemented for inflectional markings by alphabetic characters.

Writing conventions also differ from language to language and some present special challenges. The computer, coupled with a graphics display and printer or with modern photo-typesetting equipment, can meet most such challenges. The sequence of bytes is stored in the order in which the text is spoken, regardless of conventions for writing the text. Though the spoken and written orders coincide in most European languages, in some other languages they do not. Written Hindi, for example, moves certain vowels out of phonetic sequence, with the exact order depending on what constituents are being combined; the spoken word *hindi* is written as if it were *ihndi*. The vowel character in Thai may have several parts that are written so as to surround consonants, and Korean words are written in one or more square syllabic clusters. None of these conventions present insuperable difficulties. Most can be managed by storing characters until the full word is known, then invoking rules to rearrange characters or parts of characters.

Except when two languages are combined in the same document, the direction of writing poses no special problems, whether the script is Chinese or Japanese, written in vertical columns, Korean, with characters grouped in square shapes that reflect syllable structure, Hebrew, written from right to left, or Arabic, also written from right to left but in descending curlicues. The language is encoded in its spoken order, and the video display or printer orients the text in whatever shape and direction is required.

A great many languages, including Arabic, Persian, Sanskrit, and to some extent Greek, draw characters differently depending on their context. For Arabic, the graphic shape of every consonant symbol is potentially affected by all other consonants in the word, and Greek characters have special forms if they occur at the ends of words. These contextual variations require that the computer read the surrounding characters (including the following space for Greek) and decide the character's shape on the basis of what it finds. In that it can carry out these various conventions, modern technology offers a flexibility not readily available with the typewriter and difficult even for the printing press, which are constrained to using manageably small fonts of characters and to printing only within the physical boundaries of a piece of metal type. The wonderful repertoire of graphic shapes in Arabic, for example, would require a font of more than a thousand pieces of type to represent just twenty-eight consonants and a few vowels, and even a complete font would fail to capture the graceful flow of one character into the next.

Section three: Minimal Units of Meaning

3.1 Morphemes and word formation

Many words are formed either by combining words as segments of longer words (for example, *blue* and *bird* in *bluebird*) or by combining **stems** and **affixes**. The word *unbending*, for example, consists of the stem *bend* and the affixes *un-* and *-ing*. An affix, such as *un-*, which precedes the stem is a **prefix**, and an affix following the stem, such as *-ing* is a **suffix**. Most stems are word segments, which (like *bend*) also exist as free standing words, but affixes cannot and must be "affixed" to stems. The affixes of a language belong to a small closed set, which is augmented or changed only slowly over time; English now has about seventy-five prefixes in everyday use and somewhat more suffixes. Some languages, including Arabic and many of the languages of Southeast Asia, also have **infixes** or affixes inserted within words. A sequence of consonants in an Arabic word represents the stem, and infixes are vowels or vowel-consonant combinations inserted discontinuously among the stems. (This method of affixing resembles the way English forms the past and perfect tenses of a few "irregular" verbs, such as *sing, sang, sung*). Certain other languages– Turkish, is an example–do not have segments comparable to words and instead compose their sentences entirely of word segments that resemble affixes.

Free standing words, stems, affixes, and other word segments, including those forming compound words, are termed **morphemes** or (more recently) **formatives**. Although most of the discussion in this section illustrates principles of morphology with the stems and affixes of English, the broader concept is more nearly adequate because it applies to all languages, whether they form words and sentences in the manner that English does or employ some other method. Morphemes or formatives are minimal syntactic and semantic units: the smallest units that have grammatical functions, that convey meanings, or that do both. In this respect they differ from the distinct sounds and characters that, although they combine to form words, are not themselves significative units. The study of morphemes and the criteria by which morphemes are identified and classified, as well as the word-formation rules that govern which morphemes may combine in what order to form words is known as **morphology**. Although sometimes associated with human or machine lexicons and with the storage and retrieval of words (to be explored in Chapter 3), morphological analysis of languages has emerged as a major field of inquiry, deserving separate treatment.

Because many applications of computers to language require bulky lexicons, one obvious motive for morphological analysis is to eliminate redundancy and thus reduce the memory required for machine lexicons and minimize the time needed to search them. For some languages, such as German, which routinely strings together several words to form compound words (*schadlingsbekamfungsmittel*, for example, is composed of words for insect, combat, and means), morphological analysis would also include analysis of compounds. For languages like English, there is more profit in focusing on stems and affixes. Morphologically sophisticated routines would permit all words with the same stem to be stored as a single lexical entry along a list of permissible affixes or, better yet, rules for determining which affixes are permissible. An ordinary desk dictionary, for example, includes more than a thousand adjectives formed with the suffixes -*able* or -*al* and several thousand adverbs formed by adding -*ly* (*month/monthly, high/ highly*).

Without some method of stripping affixes, a spelling checker based on that dictionary would need separate entries for the stems plus the derived words. Not all suffixes produce as many new words as -*able*, -*al*, and -*ly*, but one commercially available word processing program manages a spelling list of more than ninety thousand words using about thirty thousand word entries, together with a series of routines that handle about forty prefixes and thirty of the most easily dealt with suffixes. Programs that check spelling can even exploit preposterous derivations (such as *leg + ible = legible, leg + al = legal* or *for + est = forest*) as long as they produce correct spellings. At present, most routines for stripping affixes are handcrafted and linguistically naive (as the false derivations indicate), but the strong practical motive, together with recent advances in morphology, promise systematic and more reliable analysis.

3.2 Informative affixes

For other applications, especially those that analyze syntax or interpret meanings, identifying stems and **derivational affixes** can yield useful information about the lexical categories and meanings of words. For English and other Indo-European languages, derivational prefixes help determine the meaning of the word (*co-chair* = *chair* plus *co-* or "mutually chair," *preview* = *view* plus *pre-* or "view before"), derivational suffixes do the same (*worker* = *work* plus *-er* = "one who works"; *booklet* = *book* plus *-let* "small book"). Derivational suffixes help determine the lexical category as well (*-ness* converts an adjective or adverb to a noun: *quickness*; *-ous* does the opposite: *dangerous*). Not all languages employ derivational affixes; Chinese, for example, has words like English *hand* which can be either a noun or a verb depending on the context, or *plastic* which can be either an adjective or a noun.

A program equipped with a list of stems, a list of affixes, and information about the affixes can obtain valuable information about words. Consider the distinction between *fast runner* which means one who runs fast and *handsome runner*, a runner who is handsome. If morphological analysis uncovers the stem *run* and the lexicon identifies it as a verb, then the fact that *fast* ordinarily modifies verbs can help get at the correct meaning. In like manner, correctly identifying the antecedent of the pronoun *he* in *Though they had been Nixonites, but they decided he should be impeached* requires that the suffix *-ites* be removed to reveal a male stem to which *he* may refer.

Programs that "tag" words with their lexical categories often apply morphological analysis, together with lists of very common words and positional constraints, to analyze large corpora of text, an onerous task if done entirely by hand. Programs for detecting grammatical errors (such as the failure of subjects and verbs to agree in number) and diagnosing stylistic tendencies (bureaucratese and the like) also rely on position and morphology. Like the spelling checkers, some tagging programs observe the precept that whatever works works, using some endings that, though not suffixes, nevertheless identify the lexical category. It happens for example, that almost all English words ending *-ine* are nouns and almost all ending *-lit* are adjectives.

Though derivational affixes can provide useful information, the information gleaned from affixes alone is not always reliable. Sometimes the lexical category of the derived word or the meaning of the suffix depends on the category of the stem. Thus *-er* added to a verb forms a noun (*maker*) and added to an adjective forms an adjective (*larger*). As for meanings, *-able* added to a verb means susceptible, capable or worthy of the action of a verb; whereas *-able* added to a noun stem means "possessing" or "fitted to be" or "behaving like" the noun.

Occasionally affixes are entirely ambiguous as to meaning (*inaction* = lacking action, *inset* = set within) and as to lexical category (*affectionate* = adjective, *pollinate* = verb), or unambiguous affixes combine in more than one order to form an ambiguous word (*unlockable* = *un* + *lockable*: not capable of being locked or *unlock* + *able*: capable of being unlocked). But programs for syntactic and semantic analysis must frequently cope with ambiguity, and they reach decisions using several sources of information. Since an entirely unknown word could belong to any lexical category or have any meanings, morphological analysis can usefully narrow the range of choices. This does not mean that the meaning of a word is necessarily the sum of the meanings of its stem and affixes. The meanings of derived words commonly become more specialized than their derivations would suggest; and sometimes derivations are entirely misleading. Thus *-al* added to a noun stem often means "pertinent to or connected with" as in *musical*, but *fatal* means "deadly"; similarly, *-ee* refers to a person acted upon (*draftee*), but not in *escapee*. Words such as these in which the morphology is misleading must be listed separately in the lexicon, and the entries for *fate* and *escape* must block morphological analysis.

Many languages also have **inflectional affixes**. Though English once had a great many inflectional affixes–nouns, pronouns, verbs, even adjectives had affixes–only a few survived the transition from Old English to Middle English. (One reason is that most were suffixes, and when English came to stress the first syllables of words, the suffixes were not emphatically pronounced.) The surviving inflectional suffixes include markers for plural nouns (*-s* or sometimes *-en*), for third person singular verbs (*s*), for possessives (*-'s* or *-s'*), for the past tense of many verbs (*-d* or *-ed*), for present (*-ing*) and past participles of verbs (*-ed* or *-en*), and for comparative and superlative forms of adjectives and some adverbs (*-er* and *-est*).

Unlike the derivational affixes, most of which combine selectively, joining with some stems of a given word class and not with others (*brotherhood*, and not *friendhood*), each inflectional suffix combines with nearly every member of a very large class of words. Hence the few English affixes occur very frequently. All are suffixes in modern English. None changes the lexical category of the stem, and in any sequence of suffixes, the inflectional suffix will come last (*relationships*, *nationalized*). Other languages differ widely in what lexical categories have inflectional affixes and in the kind of affixes that indicate inflections. In Japanese only verbs are inflected; Swahili and other Bantu languages have several classes of nouns, each with its own singular and plural prefixes; Arabic and Hebrew have inflectional prefixes and infixes. Some languages, such as Chinese and Vietnamese, have no inflectional affixes at all.

Whereas the derivational affixes participate in syntactic and semantic relations within words, inflectional suffixes typically indicate syntactic or semantic relations between words in a sentence, and some participate in systems of agreement. For English, the chief rules require that subjects and verbs agree in number (*a dog barks*, *dogs bark*) and allow only certain auxiliary and main verbs to combine in certain sequences (*must have been giving*, for example, not *must have being gave*). Using both constraints, a syntactic analyzer could decide that *water* is the subject and *can spill* the verb sequence in the sentence *the water can spill*. Other languages, even languages closely related to English, have more extensive sets of inflectional affixes, and English itself once had a more inflections. Some languages systematically vary affixes to accomplish what English does with a few affixes and a selection of auxiliary verbs. Their affixes distinguish more tenses than do the English affixes, and quite often they discriminate gender, mood (expressing facts or requests or uncertainty) voice (active or passive) of verbs, as well as aspect (completed or continuing).

As for nouns, English has inflectional affixes only for number, but many languages use affixes to distinguish person, gender, case (actor, acted-upon, beneficiary, instrument, and so on, for some of which English uses prepositions), and even kinds of plurals (two versus three or more). In these languages, more lexical categories may have inflectional endings and the rules for concord may be more elaborate; notice in the following German sentences that not only the nouns and verbs but also the articles and adjectives participate:

Vor	dem	Fenster	stehen	die	vier	kleinen	Baüme.
Before	the	window	stand	the	four	small	trees.

Vor	den	Fenstern	steht	der	kleine	Baum.
Before	the	windows	stands	the	small	tree.

More extensive sets of affixes entail more extensive rules for agreement and therefore offer more guidance to a program that must recognize syntactic relationships in order to analyze sentence structures, to interpret semantic relationships, to decide what word or phrase a pronoun refers to, or to perform other higher-level functions. Although inflections can themselves be ambiguous and some of the highly inflected languages tend to exercise fewer constraints on word order, the syntax of inflected languages can be much easier to analyze than is English syntax.

3.3 Stemming and spelling adjustment

The basic strategy for morphological analysis is quite simple: match the beginning and the end of the word against a list of prefixes and suffixes, then, upon identifying a potential affix remove it and attempt

IF the word ends -ly
THEN   remove the -ly and
       IF the remaining string does not end -i
       THEN   IF string doesn't match a stem
                THEN add -le and
                       IF string matches a stem
                       THEN yes!
                       ELSE end
                ELSE yes!
       ELSE change -i to y and
            IF string does not match a stem,
            THEN end
            ELSE yes!
       ELSE   IF string matches a stem
                THEN yes!
ELSE end

Figure 4. An algorithm for stripping the affix -ly.

to match the resulting string with a stem listed in the lexicon. If the
lexicon contains a matching word, then the analysis succeeds. A few
complications arise. Some affixes contain sequences of characters that
may be mistaken for other affixes (_counter-_, _inter-_, _under-_, _-ular_, _-ness_);
thus a procedure which looks for affixes must consider the longer
possibility first. Also, affixes can pile up; an extreme example is
deinstitutionalization, a word of recent coinage. It consists of a stem
with a prefix and four suffixes.

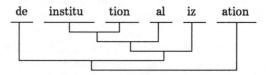

Institution and _institutional_, are words of long standing and _institution-
alize_ emerged in the nineteenth century; recently certain patients have
been _deinstitutionalized_ to community settings in a bureaucratic policy
known as _deinstitutionalization._ When removal of one affix does not
expose the stem, the routine must look for a second suffix or a prefix,
and at each point along the way check the lexicon.

   Spelling changes in either the affix or the stem must also be
considered; often these are dictated by phonological considerations,
how the result is pronounced. The prefix _in-_, for example, becomes _il-_
preceding an _l_ (_illogical_), _ir-_ preceding an _r_ (_irrespective_) and _im-_

preceding *b*, *m* or *p* (*impossible*), and each of the variant spellings must therefore be listed among the affixes. With suffixes, changes occur in the stem, and this means that once the suffix is removed, spelling must be adjusted before any attempt is made to match the stem. Illustrating the kinds of adjustments that need to be made, Figure 4 gives an algorithm for removing *-ly* and adjusting the resultant stem. The algorithm accommodates four possibilities: that the suffix can be removed with no change to the stem (*mainly / main*), that a final *i* in the stem must be changed to *y* (*easily/easy*), that a final *le* must be supplied (*ably / able*), that *-ly* is not an affix (*rely, belly*).

Usually, it is not necessary to write separate procedures for each affix; generalized procedures are possible. For instance, most inflectional suffixes and many derivational suffixes begin with vowels; a procedure for stripping them would change a final *i* in the stem to *y* (*tri + ed / try*) and would supply a final *e* is supplied when the stem ends in a consonant (*leav + ing / leave*). Another adjustment rule would take care of the doubled consonants, which sometimes must be deleted (*runn + -ing / run*). A half-dozen generalized routines suffice for the frequently occurring spelling changes in English, but adjustment rules must be sensitive to special cases. The double consonants *ll*, *zz*, or *ss* may be part of the stem (*roll, kiss, buzz*), which should be sought in the list of stems before the second consonant is deleted. Similarly, the final *e* is added when a potential stem ends in two vowels followed by the consonant *c*, *g*, *s*, *v* or *z* (*piece, gauge*), but not for other consonants. Even when adjustment rules are quite sensitive, some exceptions remain and these require a special "stop" list to be consulted before attempting to strip affixes or adjust the spelling. Spelling adjustment can be even more complicated in other languages. Turkish, for example, has an elaborate system of vowel harmony which adjusts the spellings of suffixes to make them harmonize with stems.

3.4 Analysis by word formation rules

Procedures which strip suffixes, match stems, and adjust spellings are sufficient for many purposes such as spelling checkers and thesaurus programs where the premium is on swift analysis and efficient storage, but more sophisticated systems–those that parse syntax and analyze meaning–benefit from a more exacting process of morphological analysis based on **word formation rules**. Evidence is accruing from many languages that the formation of words from stems and affixes does not occur at random, but is instead a systematic rule-abiding process, capable of being incorporated in a computer program as a series of conditions.

The challenge is to identify the many different factors that determine the formation of words. Conditions may have to stipulate the position of the suffix (i.e., is it the first in a series or last), the phonology of the stem (does it begin with a vowel or certain consonants), the stem's lexical category (is it a verb, noun, adjective, adverb), and the morphological, syntactic, or semantic features of the suffix. Phonological features, which are determining factors in many spelling adjustments, stipulate various classes of vowels and especially consonants, stress, and other features of the sounds contained in stems and affixes. Morphological features include such matters as whether a verb forms its tenses in a regular or irregular manner (*watch - watched - watched* versus *do - did - done*) and whether a stem or suffix is latinate (i.e., of Latin or Greek origin). A syntactic feature might be whether a verb can or cannot take an object. Informally, transitive verbs are verbs (such as *watch*) that are capable of having objects–persons or things acted upon; an intransitive verb (such as *sleep*) does not take an object. Semantic features would include whether a noun is animate or inanimate (for example, *dog* versus *rock*) and whether it is abstract or concrete (*nation* versus *island*). To be sure, exceptions emerge, both lexical gaps, such as the failure of *salute* to form *salution* by the same rule that forms *dilution* and *pollution* from *dilute* and *pollute*, and derived words whose apparent stems do not exist (for *actor* there is *act* and the same rule applies for numerous other noun-verb pairs; for *doctor*, however, English has no *doct* and for *author* it has no *auth*).

Though this would be an excessive amount of information to keep track of were the purpose only to identify the stems of words, morphological procedures that use such detailed information have two important virtues. Having access to complex and sometimes idiosyncratic information especially about stems, they are more reliable than procedures that simply match stems and affixes, and then adjust spellings. Since a simple morphological mistake can thwart the processes of syntactic and semantic analysis, reliability is an important property. The second virtue is that such procedures yield the lexical category and features of a derived word–information that can prove useful in the syntactic and semantic stages of processing. And the information can be about newly coined words that have not yet reached any dictionary, that perhaps have just been coined by the author, a frequent occurrence in scientific literature. In turn, by experimenting with rules, linguists seek to elicit better rules and to resolve the many uncertainties–even controversies–that have arisen about word formation in English and other languages.

The rules for eight suffixes, given in Figure 5, illustrate the kinds of information that are required for analysis based on word formation rules, as well as information that can be derived by the analysis. Boundary restrictions specify where the suffix may appear in a string of suffixes, and they can yield valuable phonological information. (Since we have not yet looked at spoken language, however, we will exclude the phonological portions of rules.) Suffixes designated plus (+) cannot

Affix	Boundary	Pattern	Condition	Assertion
abl	#	able 4 *e* sible 5 d* able 3 te*	verb transitive	adjective latinate
ed	-	ed 2 *e*	verb not irregular past participle	verb past/
ion	+	ation 5 *e*	verb	noun singular abstract
ist	+	ist 3 *e* / y*	noun	noun human
ity	+	ity 3 *y*	adjective latinate	noun singular
ize	+	ize 3 *e* / y* noun	adjective/ transitive/ intransitive	verb

Figure 5. Word formation rules for some common suffixes.

be followed by other derivational suffixes. Suffixes designated minus (-) must come last in any string of suffixes, and those designated with the number symbol (#) may precede the other two types.

Patterns specify spellings, much as the spelling adjustment rules do, except that they permit spellings that are idiosyncratic of a particular affix or group of affixes. Notice the stipulation that when -*ing* is added to words ending in -*y*, the -*y* is not changed to *i* or deleted. The notation specifies sequences of steps. For instance, 3 *e*/y* for -*ize* instructs the computer to remove the last three letters, then check for the stem (where it would find *legal* for *legalize*). If a match fails then add *e* and look up the result (*sterile* for *sterilize*), and if that fails add *y* (*jeopardy* for *jeopardize*). The conditions and actions specify lexical category and features of the word before and after the suffix is added. Lexical category plays a role in all the rules; notice, for example, that the rule for -*est* specifies adjectives or adverbs and prevents the false derivation from verbs of *digest* and *interest*. And features further restrict the derivations, as for example when the morphological feature requiring a regularly inflected verb for the *-ed* prevents the false derivations as *seed* from *see*.

For multiple affixes, one rule can use information derived via another; thus *drinkability* is possible because the latinate suffix *-abil* intercedes between the non-latinate *drink* and the *-ity*. Information-asserted for each derived word is reliable. For example, an *organist* is indeed a human being that plays the organ, but *relist* is not a human being who relies (because *rely* is not a noun). Similarly, *idealization* and *urbanization* are abstract nominalizations and thus appropriate targets for a program that analyzes style, but *onion* is not an abstraction for the act or process of becoming *one*. Even the boundary restrictions can be informative. Suffixes of the class designated + have predictable effects on the pronunciation of words that can be turned over to a system for synthesizing or understanding speech; the suffix *-ee*, for example, usually shifts the main stress in the word to the suffix (*add<u>ress</u>* - *address<u>ee</u>*).

Thus a process that seems relatively straightforward, separating affixes from stems, requires knowledge of multiple and cooperative kinds. A stemming routine that operates simply by matching characters makes frequent mistakes. Spelling adjustments improve its performance and listing potential stems also helps. For reliable morphological analysis, however, formation rules, with their derivational, phonological, syntactic, and semantic knowledge, are required. As word formation rules become more and more sophisticated (which usually means that they are supplied with more and more kinds of knowledge), their reliability steadily improves. Though there must always be "stop lists" containing exceptions, the goal of fully automatic analysis for all words containing affixes is within reach. Work is also proceeding on systems that, given as data the affixes and words of a language, together with lexical categories, derivation, and pronunciation, will elicit or refine word formation rules for that language. Some of the systems rely chiefly on brute force, grinding through large samples of the language to ferret out rules more or less by trial an error. Others proceed in the manner of a descriptive linguist, employing the heuristics and discovery procedures that reduce the number of false hypotheses.

Exercises

1. One symbol system that section 1.1 does not mention is the prisoner's tally: ///// for five, /// for three, and so on. Comparing it with the system of binary numerals, what would be the advantages and disadvantages of the tally for representing language?

2. The algorithm presented in Figure 3 is incomplete in that it does not provide for words and sentences enclosed in parentheses. Using the codes, 40 and 41 for opening and closing parentheses revise the algorithm to accommodate them. The algorithm also fails to provide for single and double quotation marks; do they pose any difficulties not posed by parentheses?

3. What is the minimum number of binary digits required to represent the twelve characters of the Hawaiian alphabet? One commonly used character set for Japanese has ninety-two characters. How many binary digits would its code require? Demonstrate your answers.

4. Words are composed of syllables; in turn each syllable is composed of a vowel (a, e i, o, u, and y) or vowel cluster, preceded, followed, or both, by characters representing consonants. Many words have more than one syllable, of course, and many syllables recur in many words: *discover*, *discard*, *cardboard*. Because English has a finite number of possible syllables, each could be assigned a code. What would be some advantages of using syllables rather than characters as a basis for computer encoding of language? What would be the disadvantages?

5. To what lexical category would a computer program with knowledge only of derivational suffixes (not of stems) assign each of the following words: *steamship, family, conflate, local,* and *priest*? Why would knowledge of a verb stem be misleading in the case of *priest*? What kind of information would help with *priest*?

6. Using the algorithm in Figure 4 as a model, devise a routine for removing the suffix *-est* from words such as *fastest, biggest,* and *largest*. The routine should assure that the resulting stem is correctly spelled.

7. Specify a word formation rule that would generate the words in list 1 below, but not the words in list 2. Your rule should be as informative as you can make it both about the stem and about the derived word. Also, you might consider whether there is any other group of words with the same suffix.

List 1:	List 2:
addressee	plannee
appointee	respondee
assignee	speakee
deportee	spendee
endorsee	stopee
employee	workee

8. It has been remarked that much language computing involves pattern matching and that the challenge is to represent linguistic patterns explicitly and unambiguously. Based on what you have seen thus far, does that seem accurate? Explain.

Further reading

For provocative discussions of symbol systems and cognition, see Newell and Simon (1972) and Johnson-Laird (1988). On writing systems, see Sampson (1985) and Coulmas (1989), and for the methods of representing alphabetic, syllabic, and ideographic character sets, see Becker (1984) and the papers in *Computer Processing of Chinese & Other Oriental Languages*, I (1984). Matthews (1974) offers a comprehensive, highly readable discussion of morphology. The simple stemming procedure is derived from Winograd (1972), which shows how the processes for identifying several endings can efficiently be integrated in a single routine; Lovins (1968) describes similar routines in detail. Greene and Rubin (1971) discuss procedures that determine the lexical category of a word from the final few characters of a word (which may or may not be suffixes). On morphology and word formation rules, see Adams (1973), Aronoff (1976), and Selkirk (1982); on the computer implementation of word formation rules, see Byrd (1983), Karttunen (1983), Karttunen and Wittenburg (1983), and Bear (1986).

Chapter 2

The Challenge of Spoken Language

Section one: Systems of Speech Sounds

1.1 Phonemes and phonotactics

Acoustically, speech consists of small, rapid variations in air pressure, generated when air from the lungs flows past the vocal folds within the larynx and then through the vocal tract. Some variations pulse at a regular rate or frequency, which we hear as a sonorous stable tone. The faster the vibrations the higher the pitch. These are the **vowel** sounds, produced by positioning the vocal folds so that the flow of air sets them in vibration. American English has three groups of vowels. **Short vowels**, as the adjective suggests, are of shorter duration than **long vowels**, which can be analyzed as consisting of an initial loud pitch followed by a softer vowel-like sound. **Reduced vowels** are so weakened that it is often uncertain whether they are phonemes at all. Other variations in air pressure come in a hash of multiple frequencies. These noise-like sounds, the **unvoiced consonants**, are actually turbulence, created in the air flow by constricting it at one point or another along the vocal track. The **voiced consonants** consist partly of steady voiced sound and partly of noise. Finally, there are the **semivowels**, produced without voicing, but with so little obstruction of air that they resemble vowels. Vowel sounds are more easily distinguished than are consonant sounds, which have much less acoustic energy, which is curious since English and many other languages have many more consonants to be distinguished than they have vowels.

Within categories, the acoustic properties that distinguish individual sounds are subtle, sometimes very subtle. That the sounds can be distinguished at all is due to their being part of a sparse system of sounds. Each language uses only a small subset of human language

Voiced consonants:

b   bit fibber
d   din sadder shoved
g   get ghost exact
ð   then bathe
v   vat of nephew
z   zap roses scissors buzz
    xerox exact
ž   azure treasure beige
ǰ   judge suggest gin
m   mut dummy dumb
n   note sign knee
ŋ   finger anxious

Unvoiced consonants:

p   pit slipper hiccough
t   tin talked Thomas
k   kit quit crack scheme
f   fit tough Philip
s   sip psychology receive
    whistle science fix (fiks)
š   ship nation machine
    special ocean passion
θ   thin bath ether
h   hip who
č   chest pitcher nature

Semivowels

l   late sell
r   rig furry rhythm
w   win quit choir
y   you few muse

Vowels:

I   bit been women pretty
E   let says lead friend
    said many
æ   fat plaid laugh
a   father heart sergeant
    park (in New England)
U   put could soot wolf
^   putt among flood tough
α   hot yacht water
    taught bought

Reduced vowels:

ə   workmen possible just
ɨ   worry alley

Long vowels:

ay bite sight dye die buy
    aisle choir eye island
aw down doubt
oy boy soil
ow rote boat bow beau
    doe dough sew
uw shoe food sue crude
    through two too dew
ey fate bait steak vein
    they bay air freight
iy be feet feat retrieve
    receive ravine people

This is the notation usually employed by American linguists. To provide a unique symbol for each phoneme, it uses characters from the Roman alphabet and from other sources (θ is the Greek theta; ð is the Old English eth). In the text, references to specific phonemes use these symbols, enclosing them in slashes.

Figure 1. Phonemes and their spellings.

sounds and requires only that the contrast among those sounds be produced and perceived. The contrasting sounds are known as **phonemes** for that language. Thus, though the medium of spoken language is analog in that duration, volume, and pitch are continuously variable, the phonemes are discrete or "digital." To distinguish, say, the words *pad* and *bad*, speakers need only produce a /p/ that is enough different from the /b/ for listeners to perceive the contrast. The distinction may or may not be reflected in writing. The difference between the words *either* and *ether* is between two phonemes both spelled *th*, but the *ei* and *e* are different spellings of the same phoneme. Thus it is the contrast with other phonemes in the system that is meaningful or, put another way, a phoneme is a unit of meaningful sound.

American English has the twenty-four consonant phonemes listed in Figure 1, and about sixteen vowels, though the precise number of phonemes, as well as their pronunciations, differ from dialect to dialect (the /a/ is particularly hard to pin down). Contrasts drawn in one language are not necessarily drawn in others. Some languages do not, for example, distinguish /p/ and /b/, and the language user may regard them as the same phoneme. Monolingual speakers of such languages would have great difficulty distinguishing the sounds and might suppose *bad* and *pad* to be the same word. Pronouncing unfamiliar pronouns also presents problems. The "th" phoneme in *ether* (and in *this* and *bath*) is another example. Because it does not exist in French, some native speakers of French have trouble producing a *this* which does not sound like *zis*. Similarly, the phonemes the semivowels /l/ and /r/ are not contrastive in Japanese.

Phonemes combine to form syllables, but not all combinations are possible in a given language. A **syllable** is a unit of sound consisting of a vowel preceded and/or followed by consonants. In many languages, the most common syllable has a vowel as its nucleus, preceded and perhaps followed by a consonant (*ham/let*), but two or three consonant clusters (*green/sward, sprinkle*) and other configurations also occur. Much as context controls the formation of words from morphemes, allowing only certain combinations of stem and affix, context also determines the ways in which phonemes combine to form syllables and words. The clusters of phonemes that can appear at the beginnings of syllables, for example, are highly constrained. If a syllable begins with three consonant phonemes, the first must be /s/ and the second must be /p/ or /t/ or /k/. If the second consonant is /p/ then the third must be /r/ or /l/ or /y/. Third consonants following /t/ or /k/ are similarly constrained. Of the approximately fourteen-thousand possible combinations of one, two, or three consonants in the word initial position, fewer than sixty occur in English. Among those excluded are several that occur in other languages: for example /k v/ as in the Yiddish *kvetsch* and /m b/ as in the Bantu name *Mbutu*.

Formulated as **phonotactic rules**, these constraints will correctly divide the words *system branches*, rather than mistaking *syste-* for *cyst*, and thus avert any fruitless searching for *mbranches* in the lexicon.

Men's room presents a similar case, because /sr/ does not occur word initially. For *card room*, however, lexical knowledge would be required; because although /dr/ can occur word initially, *droom* happens not to be a word. Consonants appearing before a vowel can also exercise constraints on those appearing after the vowel. If, for example, the syllable begins /s/ followed by /k/ or /p/ or /l/ then a vowel, the consonant following that vowel cannot be an identical /k/ or /p/ or /l/. Syllables such as /s k e k/ and /s p e p/ and /s l e l/ are not possible in English. Phonotactic rules specify these constraints on the combining and ordering (tactics) of phonemes.

Rules also specify the "transitional" probability that a given phoneme will appear in sequence with another phoneme and the "positional" probability of a given phoneme's appearing at the beginnings of words or the ends. The transitional probability that /r/ will follow /t/ is, for example, high, but the probability that it will follow /s/ or /š/ is very low. Among positional probabilities, the phoneme /b/ has a relatively high probability of appearing at the beginnings of words and a very low probability of appearing at the ends; in contrast /d/ has a high probability at the beginning and an even higher probability at the end.

1.2 Translating speech symbols

Since components of speech belong to a family of symbols that function systematically and abide by rules governing their distribution, it might seem that the translation between spoken language and computer code should be nearly as straightforward as the translation of written language. After all, speech technology can reproduce or detect the subtlest of speech phenomena, and computers can exercise rules that manipulate symbolic entities. The technology would produce speech by concatenating discrete phonemes, each fully and separately articulated, into strings of spoken words, phrases, and sentences. It would translate speech to text by segmenting the stream of speech into its constituent phonemes, referring any uncertainties to special computational procedures that apply phonotactic constraints and probabilities, and consulting a lexicon with paired phonetic and orthographic words to adjust spellings. It ought to be that straightforward, but it is not.

Commercially available **text-to-speech synthesis** programs generate from text with an unrestricted vocabulary synthetic speech that is sufficiently intelligible for listeners to identify more than ninety percent of the constituent words. The speech is not entirely natural sounding, however, because the technology reproduces only crudely the contours of intonation that systematically vary pitch, loudness, and duration, to convey the grammatical structures of a sentence and overlay such attitudes as doubt and surprise. Computational **word recognition** identifies words separately spoken with distinct pauses, and by a method that does not identify their constituent phonemes. Progress has also been made on **speech recognition**, the more challenging task of identifying the constituent words in the flow of continuous speech. But the best systems have small vocabularies, only a thousand or so words (whereas an educated adult might recognize forty-thousand, many with similar acoustic properties). They are limited in the syntax they can work with, and in the subject matter as well. They deal almost exclusively with speech that is read or spoken at a steady pace and carefully pronounced. Spontaneous speech (which speakers compose as they talk) with its false starts, hesitations, prolonged syllables and ungrammatical constructions, is far beyond their abilities.

Though these are substantial accomplishments, they are limited, not because the research has not been attempted, but because speech technology–especially speech recognition–presents a very difficult challenge. The research has both theoretical and practical motives. By modeling aspects of human performance, especially overt performance such as speech production and recognition, researchers can gain insight into complex and sometimes very subtle ways that the mind operates. The task of understanding fluent speech is especially well suited to computer modeling since it appears to integrate several different kinds of knowledge, including knowledge of speech acoustics, phonology and intonation, of words, and of sentence structure and meaning.

The practical motives are equally compelling. Speech technology promises easier, faster, more spontaneous interaction with computers. Circumventing the keyboard is especially desirable, because typing requires special skills and is slow, clumsy, and tiring. A touch typist might average about sixty words per minute, but that requires considerable skill; fully intelligible speech can reach five times that rate or more. Speech systems benefit those whose eyes or hands are needed for other tasks, as in a cockpit, stockroom, or laboratory. They also provide assistive technology for the physically handicapped. With optical character readers and text-to-speech synthesis, for example, sightless persons (most of whom do not know Braille) can read. Other applications take advantage of the telephone, using touch tones for input and synthesized speech for output, to take orders or to report airline schedules or stock market quotes.

1.3 The acoustics of speech

To see just what is required for speech synthesis and recognition, we need to look more closely at the acoustics of speech. For vowels and voiced consonants, the vocal chords produce a "fundamental" frequency; a bass speaker produces a fundamental of about 110 cycles (vibrations) per second. For a treble speaker the cycles come faster, hence the fundamental frequency is higher. The fundamental is accompanied by vibrations at higher frequencies, called overtones. After leaving the vocal chords, the sound passes through the oral cavity, which acts as a resonator, much like the voice box on a guitar or violin, diminishing or canceling some overtones and intensifying others. Which overtones are intensified depends on how we shape the oral cavity by positioning the lips, and especially the tongue.

The intensified overtones, or bands of relatively high amplitude at certain frequencies, are **formants**, and it is the formants that differentiate vowels and help identify consonants. Each vowel has several parallel formants, ordinarily lasting about 300 milliseconds. The intervals between formants, especially between the two lowest, which are also the most intense, distinguish the vowel sounds from one another. The interval for /ɛ/ (as in *bed*) is less than for /iy/ (*bead*), and the interval for /ɪ/ (*bid*) is narrower still. Higher formants, those above 3000 cycles per second, are heard primarily as qualities that give individuality to voices, but are not essential to intelligibility. (Ordinary telephone lines, designed for intelligibility rather than high fidelity, have a bandwidth of 300 to 3300 cycles per second.) Because the relative frequencies of formants remain stable regardless of the fundamental, we recognize an /a/ spoken in falsetto or deep growl as the same vowel. We are attending to an interval rather than an absolute sound.

The acoustic properties of consonants are diverse and often quite subtle, as the "stop" consonants /b/ /d/ /g/ and /p/ /t/ /k/ will serve to illustrate. Stop consonants are produced by briefly closing off the flow of air, then releasing it, yielding a period of relative silence followed by a burst of sound spread over multiple frequencies, but with some formants. With /b/ and /d/ and /g/ the formants appear as soon as the burst of sound begins, but with /p/ /t/ and /k/ the formants are delayed for as much as 50 milliseconds and when they appear they are decidedly weaker. Thus the two groups (sometimes called voiced and voiceless stops) differ in the timing and intensity of formants, and the voiced stops are more like vowels than are the voiceless stops. Other consonants can be either voiced or unvoiced. Voicing is the only difference between the phonemes /θ/ and /s/, which are unvoiced, and /ð/ and /z/, but that difference distinguishes both the phonemes and the words that contain them: *ether* from *either* and *price* from *prize*.

Voicing or the lack thereof distinguishes otherwise similar phonemes, and often words, and is therefore a linguistically significant attribute of the phoneme. Such attributes are called **features** or **distinctive features** of phonemes. Another feature is the hissing sound or high-frequency turbulence that accompanies the six English "sibilants": /z/ /ž/ and /ǰ/ (which are voiced) and /s/ /š/ and /č/ (unvoiced). In all, about sixteen different features combine, in one way or another, to distinguish phonemes in English. Each of the features is binary, either present or not present; and phonemes are bundles of features. The phoneme /b/, for example, consists of the features +voiced +consonant +labial +anterior. That is, /b/ is formed with the obstruction of the vocal tract as characteristic of consonants (+consonant); the constriction is partly by the lips (+labial), but there is further constriction by the tongue placed in front of the alveolar ridge located just behind the teeth (+anterior).

Features are important because they provide systematic ways of generalizing about phonemes and groups of phonemes. For instance, features often determine whether phonemes can be juxtaposed in words or at certain positions in words. The past tense of regular verbs in English offers an example. It not a single phoneme, but is instead pronounced /t/ /d/ or /ɨd/ depending on the context. The voiceless /t/ follows voiceless phonemes (*hooked*, *roped*), whereas the voiced /d/ follows voiced phonemes (*nagged*, *robbed*).

Experience with speech recognition has shown that some features are more readily recognized from acoustic data than are others. Sibilants, for example, and voiceless stops have distinctive acoustics. Though it is not easy to distinguish, say, the stops /p/ and /t/ or the sibilants /s/ and /z/, recognizing that the sound is a voiceless stop or a sibilant reduces the number of possibilities.

Making matters more complicated, speech sounds are not like letters in the alphabet, each spoken separately and distinctly. If they were, speech and speech comprehension would not be nearly so fast as they are. Rapid speech can produce twenty to twenty-five phonemic segments per second, and the human brain cannot distinguish even half that many separate sounds per second. Instead, speech sounds are part of a stream in which segments overlap. Vowel formants are affected by adjacent consonants, and often the acoustic properties of the vowel identify both the vowel and a consonant that precedes or follows it. Thus the voiced stops differ from one another in having different effects on the formants of subsequent vowels. The leading edge of vowel formants is slightly curved, representing a brief transition period in which frequencies are rapidly changing up or down to the formant frequency. Depending on the consonant, they change systematically. For /b/, the transition frequencies of the lower two formants rise; for /g/, both fall; and for /k/ the lower formant rises while the upper formant is falling. Consonants following the vowel have a similar effect on the trailing edge of the vowel formants. In effect the leading and trailing edges of the formants are **coarticulating** the vowel and the consonant, simultaneously conveying information about both. Coarticulation helps explain why speech can be so fast–much faster than a string of discrete sounds can be produced, faster than a string of letters can be typed or a string of discrete Morse codes can be keyed.

A now classic set of experiments dramatized the psychological reality of coarticulation. Tape recordings were made of words containing certain phoneme sequences, then cut and spliced to other sequences taken from other words. Subjects consistently misperceived the result. When, for example, the /sk/ from *ski* was joined to /ul/, most subjects heard a different stop consonant, /p/ rather than /k/, and therefore *spool* rather than the expected *school*. When the /sk/ was spliced to /ar/ almost all heard *star* rather than *scar*.

That formants, leading edges, and other linguistically significant acoustic phenomena are very subtle raises an important question: How is it that we can be so acute as to register slight differences in frequency and duration? Studies of newborn infants suggest a startling answer. We may be innately disposed to perceive and attend to sounds and particular properties of sounds that are linguistically significant. The infants were supplied with special pacifiers that measured the rate of sucking, since it is generally the case that infants respond to new events in their environment by increasing the sucking rate. First they were presented with computer-generated sounds with a short delay before the onset of the formants, thus approximating a voiced consonant. As they became accustomed to the sounds the sucking rate slowed. Then the babies were presented with sounds in which the delay, though extended only slightly, was enough for an adult to perceive an unvoiced consonant. The sucking rate suddenly increased, suggesting that either alertness to phonemic categories or at least the ability to distinguish distinctive features is innate. Innate predisposition is only part of the story, however. Interpretation of speech sounds depends also on learning; systems of phonemes and phonological rules must be acquired through experience with spoken language.

1.4 Allophones and phonological rules

Phonemes are not invariant sounds. For example, the /p/ in *pan* is aspirated with a small puff of air, but the same phoneme in *span* is not. Vowel phonemes exhibit similar variations. Vowel sounds are held longer when they precede certain consonants than when they precede others; compare *bead* with *beat* and *bid* with *bit*. Aspiration and lengthening are not features in the English sound system because they do not distinguish phonemes. The aspirated and unaspirated /p/ and the shorter and longer vowels are called **allophones** (literally, divergent sounds): variant acoustic realizations of the same phoneme. What are only phonetic variations in one language may be phonemes in another. The aspirated and unaspirated variations of /p/ in English are different phonemes in Thai and in Hindi, aspirated and unaspirated /k/ are different phonemes.

How is it that native speakers are able to recognize that the /p/ in *pan* and *span* or the /ı/ in *bit* and *bid* are allophones of the same phoneme? It seems unlikely that we measure for similarity (though

computational approaches sometimes do). What is likely is that we
know what allophonic variation can appear where. Aspiration and
vowel lengthening are very predictable. The /p/ is aspirated only when
it begins a word (or syllable) and is followed by a stressed vowel; and
aspiration occurs not only with /p/ but also with the other unvoiced
stop consonants (/t/ and /k/). The same generalizations apply if we
invent new words: the /p/ will be aspirated in *pukel* and not in *spukel*.
Lengthening is equally regular. It occurs when the vowel precedes a
voiced consonant and does not occur when it precedes an unvoiced
consonant. Because aspiration, lengthening, and similar allophonic
variations generalize both as to context (word beginnings, followed by
stressed . . .) and to classes or subclasses of phonemes (vowels,
unvoiced stop consonants) and they hold for invented as well as
existing words, they provide phonological rules resembling the rules
that specify what phonemes can be juxtaposed and which will be
coarticulated. Thus our knowledge of speech sounds consists not of
invariate sounds that are phonemes, but rather of mental representations and rules that specify their allophonic variations:

Though acoustic events may be different (aspirated or not aspirated, for
example) their underlying phonological representation is the same, and
it is for this reason that we understand the /p/ in *pan* and *span* to be
the same phoneme.

Without invariate sounds to reproduce or identify, speech synthesis
and recognition become more challenging, but at first blush the
existence of phonological rules seems promising. After all, rules can be
incorporated into computer programs. Speech synthesis would apply
one or more phonological rules to select the appropriate allophone to
fit a context. Thus we might have rules in the form

IF x A y   THEN A'

That is, phonemes of class A occurring in the context x y will be
pronounced as the allophones in the corresponding class A' or, to cite
a specific rule, voiceless stops occurring at the beginnings of words will
be aspirated voiceless stops. Speech recognition would use rules to
confirm the allophones identified by acoustic analysis (is an aspirated
voiceless stop plausible at this point?) or to yield new information,
perhaps identifying the often murky boundary between words (distinguishing, for example *Jane's pins* from *Jane spins*). Although there is
as yet no complete system of rules or complete theory of speech
production and perception, much is known and has been incorporated
into linguistically sophisticated systems for speech synthesis and
recognition.

To be sure there are complications. Some rules are optional. For example, semivowels, though ordinarily voiced, are sometimes devoiced when they follow unvoiced consonants as /s/ or /p/. But only sometimes. Worse, one variation (such as the devoicing of semivowels) can precipitate others, extending the relevant context over several phonemes and considerably complicating the task of identifying them. Computers excel at very complicated analyses, however. As long as mandatory or optional rules and their interactions can be made fully explicit, these complications are not insurmountable. What follows is more problematic.

The variations we have seen thus far preserve the contrastive nature of phonemes. The range over which a /p/ varies does not overlap the range of variation for a /t/ or any other phoneme. However, when variation attenuates the acoustic energy of the phoneme, overlapping many occur and it may not be possible to recover the phoneme. In fluent speech the vowels are susceptible to a phenomenon known as **reduction**, which shortens their duration from approximately three-hundred milliseconds to as little as twenty-five or thirty milliseconds and affects the shapes of the formants as well. For example, the /ɛ/, especially if it is in an unstressed syllable (as in *awareness*), resembles the feeble "uh" sound in *the*. That sound, known as the schwa (the symbol is / ə /), has formants somewhere between those of *bade* and *bid*, though its formants are much weaker and less well defined. Not only is the unstressed *e* pronounced as a schwa, but nearly every other unstressed vowel, including the *a* in *workable*, the first *i* in *divide*, the *o* in *major*, and the *u* in *industry*, can be and usually is pronounced the same feeble way. For this reason, the schwa (from the Hebrew for "emptiness") is by far the most common sound in English.

Something similar to the reduction of vowels happens with certain consonant phonemes. When /d/ or /t/ is preceded by a stressed vowel and followed by an unstressed vowel, it can lose some of its acoustic energy and become a "flap" (so-named because the sound is produced by quickly flapping the tongue against the bony ridge behind the upper teeth). Thus many speakers of American (but not British) English pronounce *writer* and *rider* as if they were homonyms.

Other contextual variations delete constituent sounds: usually single phonemes, but sometimes phoneme clusters. Like reduction and flapping, these deletions are irreversible, and although quite common, they are not readily predictable because they depend on the rate of speech and the speaker's articulation. Vowels are often deleted when they come between two voiceless stops (*p'tassium*), when followed by a resonant or vowel-like consonant (chiefly /l/ and /r/), or when preceded by a consonant and followed by a stressed syllable (*d'stroy*). Stop consonants are sometimes deleted following a nasal (*kin'ness*) and almost always deleted if the following vowel is a schwa (*twen'y*). Stops at the ends of words are often deleted following /l/ or /s/ (*tol'* for *told*, *mos'ly*), and sometimes entire syllables disappear (*crim'nal, choc'late*). There are even situations in which speakers manage to add phonemes to words. An optional rule inserts stop consonants between /m/ /n/ or /ŋ/ and a voiceless consonant. The rule produces *leng<u>k</u>th* and *dream<u>p</u>t*, and it causes *sense* to be pronounced as if it were *cents*.

Vowel reduction, flapping, and deletion can be simulated for speech synthesis, but being irreversible, they present a severe challenge for speech recognition. No phonological rule can say which vowel became a schwa or whether it was a /d/ or a /t/ that became a flap. Because the phoneme is not uniquely recoverable, the schwa or flap is ambiguous. Deletions also produce ambiguity: was there something there or not, a speech sound or ambient noise? The only way to resolve such ambiguities is to apply morphological and lexical knowledge (*-able* is a common affix and will combine with verbs such as *work*; *mosly* is not a word, but *mostly* is). As we will see, sometimes even that is not enough; especially for continuous speech, knowledge of sentence structure and meaning is also required.

Section two: Speech Synthesis and Recognition

2.1 Word recognition by templates

The first word recognition system, built in the 1950s, recognized phonemes, but almost none has since. The system recognized the four vowels in *watermelon*, and because that sequence of four vowels is unique, it could readily differentiate between *watermelon* and other words. The "watermelon box" recognized only the one word, however, and was not extendable. Because of the subtle acoustics of phonemes and their contextual variation, recognizing words by identifying their constituent phonemes is very difficult. Instead, most word recognition systems create **templates** or mathematical patterns that capture acoustic characteristics of the words. A few systems sample shorter segments, sometimes called **labels**, consisting of a syllable or perhaps demisyllable (a consonant and the leading or trailing edge of a vowel).

With either templates or labels, the procedure is the same. The intended speaker (for speaker-dependent systems) or a group of speakers (for speaker-independent systems) pronounces the set of words that will become the system's vocabulary. Some systems handle as many as a thousand words. One or more templates are created for each word, sometimes using mathematical clustering techniques to obtain a representative or prototypical pronunciation. When the system is put to use, it makes templates of words spoken to it and compares them with the templates in its vocabulary, recognizing those words for which there is a sufficiently similar template.

Templates are created by sampling the sound at regular intervals, a technique that digitizes sound, converting the continuing or analog waves of changing air pressure into a series of numbers based on either amplitude or frequency. Time-domain sampling measures 256 gradations of amplitude, that is, where the sound wave is in its rise or fall, every, say, eighth of a millisecond, or at a rate of 8000 samples per second. (These are the gradations and sampling rates used by the telephone system to digitize speech.) Frequency-domain sampling measures at intervals of 10 milliseconds perhaps, the number of waves coming in each of, say, 16 selected frequency bands–that is, the number coming at the rate of 200 per second, at 300 per second, and so on. With either method the infinite number of possible values of the analog waveform is changed to a finite set of values represented in bits. Though it might seem that sampling ignores valuable information, the state of the analog speech signal between samples, it is possible to reconstruct almost exactly the voice sound from the samples; only the higher formants, those which help individuate speakers, are lost.

Sampling collects huge amounts of information. Consider that if an ordinary word takes about one-third of a second to pronounce, then we would have 2666 samples (8000 divided by 3), each with 8 bits worth of information (256 values), or a total of 21,333 bits per word. Less frequent sampling might miss linguistically significant information, including such cues as the timing of formant onset that helps distinguish voiced and unvoiced stops, and the rapid changes in transition frequencies that help distinguish between the voiced stops. And the sampling rate is not nearly so frequent as it could be. To achieve the accuracy of a compact disk or a digital audiotape, both of which also digitize by sampling, would require 16 bits of information for each of about 30,000 samples or 480,000 bits per word. By way of contrast, assuming an average word length of 5 characters, the same word in writing would require only 5 bytes or 40 bits. Speech is not as profligate as those figures suggest. In addition to conveying words and sentences, it also conveys the speaker's feelings and something of her personality. Nevertheless, the difference between 40 bits and more than 20,000 to communicate the same information is staggering.

The large volume of acoustic information produced by sampling must somehow be condensed to form a reasonably compact template. One answer is to include only significant information in the template, eliminating any redundancy. This is the essential insight of **linear predictive coding**, currently the most popular method of compressing and decompressing speech signals. To see how this might be done, look at the waveform in Figure 2, then consider what can be predicted about sample i if the amplitude at sample h is known to be +4. With

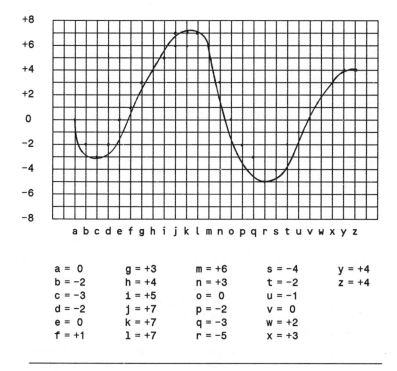

a = 0   g = +3   m = +6   s = -4   y = +4
b = -2   h = +4   n = +3   t = -2   z = +4
c = -3   i = +5   o = 0   u = -1
d = -2   j = +7   p = -2   v = 0
e = 0   k = +7   q = -3   w = +2
f = +1   l = +7   r = -5   x = +3

Figure 2. Sampling to digitize sound.

such frequent sampling, the waveform becomes a gently rolling curve with only slight increases or decreases from sample to sample. So sample i will be somewhere in the range of, say, +2 to +6 and will not suddenly plunge to -6. The predictions employed in linear predictive coding are somewhat more sophisticated, founded on the sum of several previous samples (with each given a different weight), on whether the energy source is a vowel pulse or consonant noise, and so on. But the principle is the same. Now suppose that we have a compression device that makes that prediction, compares it with the actual value at h, and records the difference between the predicted and actual values. Since the amounts will be small, the difference can be measured on a scale with fewer than the 256 gradients afforded by 8 bits (or the 65,000 afforded by 16 bits). About 16 gradients (4 bits) would do. Of course, we will need a device to decompress the signal, using the same predictions and the recorded differences.

Once the system's vocabulary is stored as a library of templates, it is ready to recognize words. For each word spoken to the system, a template or set of labels is formed and compared with those in the template library. Slight differences in pronunciation mean that an exact match is highly unlikely, so the system looks for the lexical entry most nearly resembling the input, using mathematical techniques for measuring closeness of fit, as well as "accept thresholds" that specify how close is close enough. One very effective technique is **dynamic programming**, a path-finding algorithm that seeks the best alignment between two similar patterns. (Dynamic programming has several other linguistic applications; it has, for example, been used for probablistic analysis of morphology and syntax.) Let's say we have the following templates:

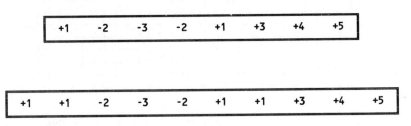

(Actual templates would, of course, have many more values.) The templates match in most values, except that for the second the word was pronounced slightly slower, dawdling twice at +1. This is a common problem, because it is very difficult to pronounce a word twice at exactly the same rate. If the first template is simply superposed on the second, the distance between them can be determined by subtracting the lower from the higher, but the misalignment will obscure their similarity. We would like to compare a given sample in the template with two or more consecutive samples in the library template, but we need to know which library samples.

This is where dynamic programming comes in, manipulating time to align the two templates. First the differences are obtained between each value in the first template and each in the second (that is, between +1 in the first template and + 1, +1, -2, and so on in the second and repeat this for the second -2, -3 and those following). These values are arrayed as the rows and columns of a table (see Figure 3). A path of minimal differences from the beginning of the templates at the lower left to the end at the top right indicates a match. In the example, the bracketed 0's, show that two templates correspond exactly (except for the duration). The same technique will identify similar pronunciations if values in the templates differ only slightly (a differential of 1, say, rather than 0).

Recognition accuracy with template matching can be 90% or better when the vocabulary is small and words have distinctly different pronunciations. (It is helpful to have polysyllabic words.) This is enough to be very useful. There is of course no pretense of psychological plausibility, it being unlikely that we do linear predictive coding or

+5	4	4	7	8	7	4	4	2	1	[0]
+4	3	3	6	7	6	3	3	1	[0]	1
+3	2	2	5	6	5	2	2	[0]	1	2
+1	0	0	3	4	3	[0]	[0]	2	3	4
-2	3	3	0	1	[0]	3	3	5	6	7
-3	4	4	1	[0]	1	4	4	6	7	8
-2	3	3	[0]	1	0	3	3	5	6	7
-1	[0]	[0]	1	2	1	0	0	4	5	4
	+1	+1	-2	-3	-2	+1	+1	+3	+4	+5

Figure 3. Path finding by dynamic programming.

dynamic programming in our heads. Though the motive is practical rather than linguistic, speech recognition by way of templates has some affinity with one theory of speech perception. Motivated in part by the prevalence of contextual variations, gestalt theory holds that a syllable, word or phrase constitutes a "gestalt," a unified physical and symbolic configuration having properties that cannot be derived from its constituents. According to the theory, gestalts are basic units of language perception and no intermediate recognition of its constituent phonemes need occur.

Word recognition via templates is feasible only for separately spoken words. Words spoken in isolation from one another tend to have stable auditory characteristics, and without that stability, template matching would not succeed. In continuous speech, however, pronunciations become less stable, changing to fit the environment of continuous sound. Applying the techniques of sampling and pattern matching, though it is possible, is not feasible for a vocabulary of any size or for any but the most rudimentary syntax. Every conceivable sentence for the vocabulary and syntax has to be anticipated, as does every plausible pronunciation of those sentences. This plethora of alternatives must then be delicately woven into a word network with phoneme sub-networks, reusing as many identical stretches as possible, so as to reduce the number of fruitless searches and to avoid overloading the memory. Such labyrinthine structures have been built and, especially when they incorporate dynamic programming, they perform well. But they are exceedingly difficult to modify for new vocabulary or to extend for new syntax. Other, more flexible systems employ matrices of word pairs or triplets to determine what words can plausibly follow an already recognized word; some use probabilities. But only with limited vocabularies (a few hundred words) are any of these techniques feasible. Substantially increasing the vocabulary would result in a huge network or matrix, far too large to be searched in a reasonable length of time. Though they are engineering triumphs, these expedients do not meet the challenge of continuous speech.

2.2 Text-to-speech synthesis

Speech synthesis comes in several forms. Some applications require only that the computer recite words and stock phrases from a small vocabulary. These applications can use templates, resembling those used for word recognition, or a phonetic transcription of the words. All that is required are devices for converting the digitized sound back to analog sound waves: electronic oscillators generate the vowel tones and consonant noise, and filters select frequency bands to produce the formants. Other applications require text-to-speech synthesis; that is, the computer converts text with an unrestricted vocabulary into intelligible, natural-sounding speech. From a library, the synthesizer could gather templates or phonetic transcriptions representing each of the words in the sentence and concatenate them into sentences. But two problems would emerge. Templates, even with linear predictive coding, require a substantial amount of memory, several hundred megabytes for a small library (remember that each separate word form, singulars and plurals, present and past tense, and so on would require a separate template.) Worse, templates or transcriptions represent separately sampled words, spoken in a neutral context. Stringing them together without attention to the contextual influences of one word on another would hardly produce natural-sounding speech; and unless issued at a plodding pace, they would not be very intelligible. Thus it is that the best speech synthesis does not employ templates, but is instead electronically fabricated.

Fabricating speech has proved an interesting challenge, and the past several years have seen a substantial amount of progress. Current systems either use allophones as basic units of sound or nominate for each phoneme one allophone to serve for all contexts. Allophones, of which there are about 240 in English, are preferable because the appropriate allophone can be selected to suit the phonological context. Working at a finer grain, as with the silence, burst of noise, and weak formants that characterize stop consonants, though it has been attempted, may not be worth the effort, because what we perceive as a phoneme is not a precise sound, but instead a sound that falls within a permissible range of sounds. Some experimentation goes on with molecular sounds, either diphones (the span of sound from the midpoint of one allophone to the midpoint of the next) or demisyllables. These avoid many of the problems with contextual variation. However, working with a thousand or more units in the case of demisyllables or with the nearly fourteen hundred diphones is cumbersome; and because artificial techniques of modulating from one allophone to the next have been developed, molecular techniques offer no great advantage.

Dramatic improvements in speech synthesis have come from work with **speech prosody**, the systematic variations in intensity, pitch, duration, and timing that are characteristic of natural-sounding speech and that assist with communication. Prosody has not received nearly the attention that phonemes, allophones, and features have; and although some prosodic rules have been discovered, they are not as well understood as the phonological and phonotactic rules. Prosody is, however, more than an added but inessential grace. It assists communication in several ways. In the first place, unnatural-sounding speech distracts listeners from the message, and empirical evidence shows that listeners are predisposed to thinking that what does not sound natural will not be fully intelligible. More important, speech prosody assists communication by parceling the sentences into shorter units for easier perceptual processing. It signals syntactic boundaries and transitions, distinguishes kinds of sentences, and in general clarifies the structure of the message. Prosody also accentuates new or important information by giving it stress *(she bóught a computer* versus *she bought a compúter)* and occasionally disambiguates sentences *(she left diréctions for Joe to follow* versus *she left directions for Joe to fóllow)*.

Like the phonological rules that select among phonemes, prosodic rules adjust pronunciations to contexts. Rules for the prosody of words are easier to specify than those for phrases and sentences, because the relevant context (the syllable and strings of syllables) is bounded and readily defined. Among prosodic qualities, the most prominent is the **stress** given to vowels and therefore to the syllables they dominate. Stressed vowels have a slightly longer duration and are slightly higher in pitch (or sometimes slightly lower) than unstressed vowels. Rules governing stress can be thought of as working backwards through the word, taking into account the vowels and consonants in the final syllable, the syntactic category of the word, and the number of syllables in the word. The phonological constraints are as follows:

- □ If the final syllable ends with two consonants, then its vowel will receive the stress *(exíst, revólt, adópt)*.

- □ If the final syllable ends with a single consonant, stress will fall on the penultimate syllable *(éxit, ímage, práctice)*.

▫ If the final syllable has a long vowel, then stress will fall
on that vowel *(eráse, deplóy, retriéve)*.

With verb-noun pairs, the verb follows these rules and the noun does
not *(recórd-récord, suspéct-súspect)*. Similar rules apply to words of
three or more syllables, although they are more complicated.

Differences in duration will be most prominent with the stressed
syllable, but other factors vary the duration, including the position of
a phoneme (initial consonants have a greater duration than medial
consonants), the adjacent phonemes (vowels have a slightly greater
duration following stop consonants), and the length of the word
(phonemes in polysyllabic words have shorter durations than those in
monosyllables. These rules are complicated, and additional complications arise when rules interact, but they are sufficiently explicit to be
implemented in a speech synthesizer, where they help supply the
rhythms of natural-sounding speech.

When words combine to form sentences, the prosody of sentences
is superimposed, subtly modulating the patterns of stress, duration, and
pitch within individual words and blending the words together.
Although sentence prosody depends on meanings, intentions, and other
factors that are not readily systematized, a speech synthesizer supplied
with a minimum of syntactic information (such as could be incorporated in a small dictionary and a few dozen rules), can make the
pronunciations of a sentence seem more nearly natural. What is more
important for quick, reliable communication, the prosody can offer
perceptual cues to the structures of sentences and the functions of their
constituents.

Some of the syntactic information concerns the kinds of words that
receive stress. Negations, modal verbs *(will, may, should)*, quantifiers
(many, few, some), and interrogative words *(what, who, why)* receive
more stress than do non-modal verbs, nouns, and adjectives. Articles
(an, the), prepositions *(in, of)*, and other function words receive the
least stress. The difference is considerable. For instance, the initial /t/
in a noun such as *top* will last about 70 milliseconds, whereas the
duration of the /t/ in *to* will be less than 45 milliseconds. Convenient-
ly, the lexical categories requiring the most stress and those requiring
the least stress have very few members (whereas there are many
adjectives, nouns, and verbs), hence a small dictionary can list them all.
The same small dictionary, together with some simple routines for
determining lexical category from suffixes, can help segment the
sentence into noun groups, verb groups, prepositional phrases, and
other phrasal constituents, instructing the synthesizer to mark the ends
of segments, as human speakers do, by lengthening final syllables,
slightly raising the pitch, and briefly pausing.

Another important aspect of sentence prosody is the **pitch contour**,
which distinguishes kinds of sentences. With the numeral 2 indicating

"normal" pitch, and 1 and 3 to indicate lower and higher levels, assertions and some questions exhibit the following pattern:

2   3   1
The man bought a paper.

Actually, the pitch modulates up and down depending on syllable stress; so if the contour were plotted on a graph, it would present a squiggle but would rise at the midpoint of the sentence and then descend to a pitch lower than that with which the sentence began. Other constructions have different contours, drawn from a small inventory of possibilities: a gradual decline in pitch followed by an abrupt rise, an abrupt fall, and so on. Without some attention to pitch contour of the sentences it is producing, the synthesized speech will seem odd: as if the synthesizer is speaking with confidence a language that it does not know.

However, using rudimentary syntactic analysis–enough to identify sentence types and to locate sentence constituents–a synthesizer can produce a pitch contour that is creditable enough not to distract the listener from the message. The synthesizer would produce the gradual rise and descent for assertions, but assign distinctly different contours to questions that invite a yes or no answer and to imperatives:

2   2   3
Is the man leaving?

3 2 1
Pick it up.

Very little information about word order and punctuation is required to identify these sentence types. Both yes/no questions and imperatives begin with a verb, and punctuation distinguishes one from the other. Also, a speech synthesizer might use paired commas or parentheses to identify parenthetical expressions and appropriately drop the pitch:

2   1 1 1   1   3   1
Joe, as I told you, bought a paper.

Rudimentary syntax will not suffice for other syntactic phenomena. When two assertions are combined by a conjunction or as subordinate and main clause, pitch holds very steady from a word or two before to a word or two after the junction.

2   2 3   2 2   1
When the man left, he crossed the street.

2 3   2   2 3   1
He bought a paper and he read the headline.

However, these constructions are challenging even for sophisticated programs that analyze syntax, and speech synthesizers will not be getting them right any time soon. Nor will they be interpreting the speaker's intention to incorporate the distinctive contours by which we voice contradictions, for example, or express surprise.

2.3 Continuous speech and juncture

For speech recognition, the greatest challenge involves **juncture**, the transition from one word to the next. As we listen to speech in a language we know, we have the experience of separately spoken words. That is only an illusion, however, arising from our facility at analyzing the physical continuum of sound into lexical units. Without that facility, which employs several kinds of knowledge, we might find baseball in the Book of *Genesis* (in the beginning/in the big inning.) For some idea of what we are actually confronting, recite the nursery rhyme that most people have trouble segmenting:

> Mares eat oats and does eat oats and little lambs eat ivy.
> A kid'll eat ivy too, wouldn't you.

What we do not hear, though we suppose we do, are pauses between words. Examination of speech waveforms reveals continuous stretches of sound, broken by the short periods of silence that precede the stop consonants and a few others (such as /c/ and /j/). Speech recognition is s_pee¯chre_co_gni_tion.

Occasionally word boundaries will have acoustic cues. Some languages, Czech for example, regularly stress the first syllable in a word; other languages, Turkish among them, stress the last syllable; and for others, such as French, there is a fluctuation in the fundamental frequency. Some promising new evidence suggests that English speakers hypothesize the start of a new word when they hear "strong" syllables (those containing unreduced full vowels). However, most of the cues in English sentences—a slight lengthening of the first consonant, perhaps, or slightly increased stress on the final syllable—are subtle, ambiguous, and not very dependable. Without reliable boundaries, picking individual words out of the continuous stream of speech can be very difficult. Moreover, spurious "ghost" words will emerge. With some splitting and merging, it is not hard to construct an entire sentence of the ghosts that bedevil automated speech recognition:

> the sad poet remembers a long ago time.
> thus add poetry members along a goat I'm.

The challenge posed by juncture is compounded by contextual variations that carry over from one word to the next. When a word that ends with a vowel is followed by another beginning with a stop consonant, the vowel formants will anticipate the stop consonant; the /ɨ/ in *fuzzy bear*, for example, or the /u/ in *blue top*, both anticipate the /b/. Formants for the same vowels in *fuzzy hair* and *blue lagoon* will be different. If one word ends and the next begins with the same sound (*talk quietly*, *some more*), the common sound is usually not repeated and the two words are compressed into one as in "s'mor." Worse, assimilation will sometimes change the acoustics of one phoneme making it easier to pronounce in conjunction with another. One may be changed, so that *it is* comes to be pronounced "idiz," or the two phonemes may transmute into a third: *did you* is "diju" with /d/ and /y/ becoming /ǰ/. Similarly, *what's your* becomes "hwatsur" with /s/ and /y/ combining to form /š/. Deletion and reduction are also common. A stop consonant at the end of a word is either deleted when followed by another stop consonant (*best buy*, *just great*) or the silence is prolonged then followed by a single burst of noise. Thus it is hardly surprising that when individual words are delicately snipped from conversations (using an electronic "gate" that does not change their acoustic properties), most are unrecognizable. Only when the gate is made wide enough to admit portions of neighboring words do the words become recognizable.

The problems mentioned so far derive from the analog nature of speech and its quick pace. Unplanned speech presents additional problems. False starts, hesitations (often with voicing), prolonged syllables, and slurring of sounds are frequent when speakers compose their ideas while they speak. If the speech takes place in an unquiet place, as in a busy office or a airplane's cockpit, sound must be filtered by procedures intelligent enough to distinguish linguistically significant parts of the speech signal from environmental noise, some of which may itself be speech.

We succeed in recognizing words despite so many obstacles because we are very good at guessing. Using whatever information can be gleaned from the acoustic signal and our familiarity with words, we seek the best fit. This has been demonstrated by several empirical studies. In one experiment, sounds intermediate between related phonemes were artificially created. One artificial sound, half way between the phonemes /g/ and /k/, was attached first to /ɪ s s/ and presented to listeners, who identified the word as *kiss*. However, when the same intermediate sound was grafted to /ɪ f t/, the listeners heard *gift*. In neither case did they report a sound they could not identify. Clearly, they were matching what they heard against words in their mental lexicons and were choosing in each case the only plausible candidate.

The question arises whether perceptual processes operate autono-mously. Or do they employ knowledge of sentence structure, and of word and sentence meanings, perhaps even knowledge of the context of the utterance and of the world? Theories of language perception divide on the question of autonomy and interaction:

□ The most strict version of autonomy holds that only phonological and lexical knowledge are required, and that once words are recognized they are handed along to other language modules for further processing.

□ A weaker version of autonomy holds that although information about syntax and meanings assists in word recognition, extra-linguistic knowledge of the context and the world does not.

□ Interactive theories maintain that word recognition can use any relevant knowledge, but differ as to when the knowledge comes into play (before or after the word is perceived) and whether that knowledge can propose candidate words or merely choose between those proposed by the perceptual and phonological processes.

The several theories make very different predictions about the time and manner in which linguistic and extralinguistic knowledge can influence word recognition. To test the predictions, "on line" experimental techniques investigate recognition as it takes place. Though the issue is by no means decided, the preponderance of the evidence now suggests that lexical information (that is, knowledge from the human lexicon about what are words) can influence how we perceive the sounds making up the words. Knowledge of syntactic sequences and semantic plausibility enter at a later stage in the processing to adjudicate among candidate words but do not ordinarily interact with phonological and lexical knowledge.

Higher-level knowledge almost certainly intervenes when (as frequently happens) the speech signal is degraded or lost. Listeners choose the word or words that seem most plausible in the context. Evidence on the sublexical level comes from a series of experiments that presented subjects with sentences from which segments as long as a syllable were replaced by a coughing sound. Asked whether anything was missing from the sentence, most said the sentence was complete; and though most reported that they heard the sound they could not accurately place it. When silence (potentially a meaningful lack of sound) was substituted for the cough, most subjects were able to locate it within the sentence. Shadowing experiments, which ask subjects to repeat quickly what they have just heard, offer additional evidence. Perceiving what they expect to perceive, subjects tend to correct mispronunciations and other errors, but they are not conscious of what they are doing. When asked to expect errors and to repeat them, the subjects cannot perform that conscious task with anything like the reliability with which they unconsciously make corrections. Another experiment asked subjects to repeat first a normal sentence, then a syntactically well formed, but meaningless sentence, and finally a randomly ordered, nonsensical string of words. Subjects had little trouble repeating the normal sentence, but their performance began to suffer with the lack of meaning, and they made mistakes with nearly half of the random strings of words. Yet another experiment demonstrated that listeners were able to identify words in sentence context after hearing only an initial syllable or so, even though the same syllable might occur at the beginnings of many other words. As in the repetition experiments, this ability degraded with ungrammatical sentences and with random strings.

2.4 Speech recognition

Though modern acoustic technology is subtle and precise, machines are less adept than human listeners at identifying speech sounds. Many current systems for continuous speech take an interactive approach, allowing several knowledge components to exchange hypotheses on words that might be present, and then collectively arrive at a decision. These systems do what human listeners do, with the difference that humans use higher level knowledge only when the speech signal is faint or distorted, but computational speech recognition requires it for nearly every word.

Phonemes or possible phonemes are hypothesized from parametric analysis of the speech signal (frequencies and amplitudes and how they change over time). These hypotheses are then tested to determine whether they make sense in the developing context of a word or a sentence. When parts of signals are incomplete or unrecognizable, higher-order forms of knowledge propose likely candidates, which are tested for consistency with the speech signal. Proposals can come from any of several knowledge components. From knowledge of the English lexicon, the missing phoneme in /kɑmpuwt-r/ can be proposed, because English has no other word with those phonemes in that order. Often, however, there is so much uncertainty about phonemes that the lexical component proposes multiple candidate words, as many as twenty words for a short stretch of sound. Syntactic knowledge of possible verb sequences can propose that the missing word in *I have — reading a book* is *been*, because only *been* fits that context in the verb sequence. In other circumstances, however, syntactic proposals are much less specific; consider for example all the different kinds of words with which a sentence might begin. To fill the gap in *the very old — spoke softly*, the semantic knowledge that *spoke* is restricted to human subjects, selects among a number of similar-sounding nouns (*man/ban/ham*).

Some systems also use information about the current state of the discourse and about its domain, though this can be risky because the computer will sometimes find what it expects rather than what is actually there. One system for recognizing spoken chess moves, anticipating that the player would make the best move available, managed to mistake *king* for *queen* despite their very different vowels. None of the several knowledge sources can succeed working alone, but the strength of the interactive approach is that they can cooperate, sharing information in a timely manner.

If several sources of knowledge are to participate in the recognition process, they need to have some way of exchanging information. HEARSAY II, an early and very influential speech-recognition system, had them share a computational "blackboard" as a locus for opportunistic and incremental processing. Communications were structured as condition-action rules, resembling IF THEN conditionals. Conditions described the situations in which the knowledge source could contribute to the collective decision making, and actions offered the proposals or constraints. In the parlance of computation, the blackboard allowed for both "data driven" and "goal driven" processing. Knowledge sources need to communicate with each other, of course, so the blackboard was partitioned into regions of local concern. Despite the partitioning, processing was complex and therefore slow. And the system required a very large working memory for sharing information and tentative construals, so large that the blackboard scheme is probably not a plausible model of human cognition.

For some idea of how the knowledge-based approach recognizes words in continuous speech, consider what would be required to recognize the eight words in *bring me a lettuce salad and ice tea*. The sentence would perhaps be spoken /brɪŋmɨ lɛdˆzæl-d?naystiy/ with a brief pause (as for thought) following the first six phonemes. Some phonemes would be deleted, including the /d/ from *and*. Others would be reduced: the unstressed /a/ in *salad* to a schwa and the schwa in *and* to a murmur. (Long vowels, such as the /ay/ in *ice* and the /iy/ in *tea* fare better and are usually somewhat easier to identify.) The /s/ at the end of *lettuce* and beginning of *salad* would almost certainly be assimilated. The semivowel /l/ will be easier to recognize in *lettuce* than in *salad*, because consonants at the beginnings of words are more fully articulated. The pitch contour shows a downward drift but is steady across the conjunction from /d/ through /ay/.

Acoustic analysis would divide the utterance into phonemic segments and propose phonemes, yielding a lattice of possibilities like that in Figure 4. Acoustic analysis is usually more reliable at segmentation, which is determined by periods of rapid change in the waveform, than it is at identifying phonemes, though it will miss some

p	l	ə	m	y	iy	a	y	æ	g	ʌ	ž	a	y	ʌ	p	ʔ	ŋ		ž	b	ɨ
p	y	ɪ	ŋ	w	ɨ	ə	r	ɨ	t	ɨ	z	aw	l	ɨ	d	æ	ʔ	ɨ	z	d	ɪ
b	r	ɨ	n	m	ɪ	ʔ	l	ɛ	d	ə	s	æ	r	ɛ	t	ə	n	ay	s	t	iy

| bring | | me | a | lettuce(s)alad | | | and | ice | tea |

Figure 4. Phonemic representation of fluent speech.

boundaries between phonemes and it will shift others. For our sentence, none of the phonemes has been identified for sure, and there is indecision about whether certain sounds are phonemes or only noise (indicated by question marks). Acoustic analysis suggests three possibilities for each phoneme or suspected phoneme. Though this may not seem very many choices, the combinatorial possibilities are great. The six phonemes before the pause can enter into 3^6 or 729 possible combinations, and the eighteen beyond the pause can enter into 3^{18} or 387,420,489. This extreme proliferation of alternatives, aptly called a "combinatorial explosion," rules out any approach that proceeds by brute force, matching sequences of phonemes against phonemic spellings in the lexicon.

Much of the work of the recognition system consists in narrowing the number of possible words to be matched against the phoneme sequences in the lattice. Thus, the discourse component, which possesses knowledge of the task at hand, takes the initiative, offering a hypothesis. Since the system is designed to receive orders, the first word may begin a request. The syntactic component proposes that if the sentence is a request, it is likely to be voiced either as a command, beginning with a notional verb like *bring* or *give*, or as a yes/no question beginning with an auxiliary verb. The prosodic component opts for a command, based on the downward drift of the pitch contour. Only a few notional verbs would serve to make requests, and their phonetic spellings are retrieved from the lexicon. One of the spellings of *bring* matches four successive phonemes in the lattice. Tentatively deciding that the first word is *bring*, the system calls upon the syntactic component for patterns of words that can follow the category of verbs to which *bring* belongs. Syntax suggests four patterns, ranked in the order of their usefulness:

	Example:
VERB then BENEFICIARY then OBJECT	*bring me ice tea*
VERB then OBJECT	*bring ice tea*
VERB then OBJECT then *for* BENEFICIARY	*bring ice tea for me*
VERB then OBJECT then *to* BENEFICIARY	*bring ice tea to me*

(Other verbs would have different patterns; *sleep*, for example, does not ordinarily have either an OBJECT or a BENEFICIARY.) Although almost any noun group or pronoun could qualify as OBJECT, a BENEFICIARY must be an animate being and, if a pronoun, may be in the object case. Because there are only a few such pronouns, they are tried first. Among them is *me* with phonemes matching the next two in the lattice.

What follows the BENEFICIARY will be the OBJECT or OBJECTS, but that is not much help because any item on the menu or combination of items can be OBJECTS. Phonology has two known word boundaries, but *tea* offers a better target than *a lettuce*, which begins with two phonemes that are difficult to pin down. Moreover, because people usually order the beverage last, the discourse component can propose that the beverage words be consulted first. Again the strategy is to constrain the number of possible words. Moving backwards from *tea*, there is a noise or slight pause (actually it's the schwa from *and* reduced almost to extinction) preceding /n/, so the lexicon is consulted and indeed *nice* is a word. That mistake might persist or perhaps the system, taking a suggestion from the syntactical component, might look for the *and* which usually comes between the last two items in a list. The lexicon would provide alternative phonetic spellings /æ n d/ and /æ n/, and failing to find a match for either in the phonemes preceding nice tea, the grouping /ʔn ays/ would be considered, matching the two words *and* and *ice*.

Again moving backwards through the sentence /s æ l ɛ d/ matches an item on the menu. Since there are phonemes preceding *salad*, the discourse component would be consulted for the usual attributes of a salad. *Green*, *chef's* and *small* do not promise a match, but *lettuce* will fit if a juncture rule allows the insertion of an *s*. The schwa remains, the only word it matches is *a*, syntax allows an *a* to precede the singular *lettuce salad*, and all eight words have now been recognized.

Actual processing would entail much more trial and error. Lower-level procedures tend to be undiscriminating, offering not only multiple phonemes but also multiple words with approximately the same pattern of sounds. Problems of juncture are so severe that most systems must relax the criteria for recognizing phonemes at suspected word boundaries, or they do not even attempt to segment an utterance into words until analysis is well underway. Because they must encompass the infinitude of ways that we have of expressing ourselves, higher-level procedures will either make false suggestions or stubbornly postpone decisions. The most efficient procedures appear to be those in the middle, which look for local contexts, consisting of more than one constituent but not necessarily a syntactically well-formed phrase. These small "islands of reliability" give the lower-level procedures firm boundaries within which to work and give the upper-level procedures foundations for plausible inferences.

As with morphological procedures, interpreting continuous speech requires both active reading of context and linguistic knowledge of multiple and cooperative kinds. These are not isolated instances. The word "intelligent," when used to describe computational procedures or human behavior, usually implies the sensitive reading of context and predictive application of knowledge. Seemingly intractable problems yield to their combined force. Sensitivity to context and predictive knowledge will be a recurring theme in the chapters which follow, to be sounded again in the discussions of lexical searching, syntactic parsing, semantic interpretation, co-operative syntactic and semantic analysis, and the linguistic and more broadly cognitive approaches to discourse. The challenge is to discover what context and what information is relevant, and to integrate procedures which use them into a smoothly functioning whole.

Exercises

1. Criticizing the English system of spelling, George Bernard Shaw claimed that a possible spelling for *fish* is *ghoti*. Explain.

2. Formulate a set of phonological rules that predicts the pronunciation of the plural morpheme *s* (s or z or iz) from the phoneme that precedes it. Your rules should recognize three groups of preceding phonemes: the sibilants (/s/ /z/ /š/ /ž/ /č/ and /ǰ/) and the remaining voiceless consonants (/p/ /t/ /k/ /f/ and /θ/), as well as the voiced consonants and vowels. Cite examples to demonstrate that each of your rules succeeds.

3. Given the way they are generated and matched, what would be an additional, potentially useful application for word templates? Explain.

4. Using dynamic programming, determine whether the following patterns match:

+3	+2	+1	-1	-3

+3	+2	+1	-1	-1	-4	-4

5. How does the pronunciation of the underlined vowel change when each of the following verbs is converted to a noun?

expl<u>ai</u>n	explan<u>a</u>tion	comp<u>e</u>te	comp<u>e</u>tition
an<u>a</u>lyze	an<u>a</u>lysis	organ<u>i</u>ze	organ<u>i</u>zation
ded<u>u</u>ce	ded<u>u</u>ction		

Formulate an optional rule that would predict the change from an aspect of the intonation, and find other examples that obey your rule.

6. Explain how one might arrive at an interpretation of the following complete sentence. Two possibilities, rated as to their likeliness, are offered for most of the phonemes; a question mark indicates that the sound may be ambient noise. Knowledge of the subject of discourse is not needed.

2nd choice	t	aw	ŋ	c	ɨ	r	a	n	ə	g	ɨ	t
1st choice	d	ow	n	č	ə	l	ay	?	?	k	I	d
intonation		2			2	3			1			

7. Suppose that someone developed a system for continuous speech recognition that used only the acoustic signal. Devise some sentences that severely test the system, and explain what makes your sentences challenging.

Further Reading

For a clear introduction to the complex subject of phonology, see Ladefoged (2nd ed. 1982); somewhat more advanced are Anderson (1985) and Kaye (1989). On the relationship between phonology and other aspects of language, Jakobson (1978) is especially valuable. On speech production, see Catford (1988) and Levelt (1989), and on speech sounds and their physical properties, see Fry (1976) and Handel (1989). Also see the special issue of *Cognition*, Volume 25 (1987), Numbers 1 and 2. On intonation and speech prosody, see Cruttenden (1986) and Grosjean and Gee (1987).

For accounts of human speech perception, see Harris and Coltheart (1986), Allport, MacKay, Prinz, and Scherer (1987), Hyman and Li (1988), Aitchison (1989) and Altmann (1990). Research on how spoken word recognition is aided by the syntactic and semantic context includes Schatz (1954), Miller, and Isard (1963), Warren (1970), Forster (1976), Ganong (1980), Grosjean (1980), Salasoo and Pisoni (1985), and Marslen-Wilson (1985 and 1989). See also Seidenberg, Waters, Sanders, and Langer (1984). There is disagreement as to precisely when context can begin to influence recognition: when some sensory information becomes available (Grosjean, 1980; McClelland and Elman, 1986), when a word has been hypothesized (Forster, 1976; Tanenhaus, Carlson, and Seidenberg, 1985), or when the word is to be integrated into the representation of the sentence (Marslen-Wilson, 1985; Norris, 1986).

On approaches to speech synthesis, see Witten (1982) or Linggard (1985); Allen, Hunnicutt, and Klatt (1987) describe a highly developed text-to-speech system. Extensive accounts of highly developed systems for computer under-standing of speech are given by Walker (1978) and Erdman, Hayes-Roth, Lesser, and Reddy (1980); other systems are described in Lea (1980), Fallside and Woods (1985), and Waibel and Lee (1990). Arguing against the approach by way of syntax and semantics, Church (1987) demonstrates that information about allophonic variations and syllable structure can be instrumental in speech recognition; Waibel (1988) makes a similar case for the role of prosodic information.

Chapter 3

Words and the Lexicon

Section one: Lexicons and Lexical Entries

1.1 Ubiquitous lexicons

From the most rudimentary to the most ambitious, nearly every application of computers to language involves a lexicon. The application may compile a lexicon for some purpose (investigating the vocabulary of an author or an era, perhaps, or automatically indexing a text), or it employs a lexicon as a repository of words and knowledge indexed to words. As applications become more ambitious, they require more and still more lexical information. We have already seen some examples. The simple stemming procedure described in Chapter 1 needs only a list of plausible stems, but more reliable analysis by word formation rules requires detailed morphological features and boundary rules for each stem, together with its lexical category and semantic properties. Similarly, word recognition requires only a set of acoustic templates, but systems for interpreting continuous speech, which must cope with problems of juncture and incomplete articulation, require not only acoustic information, but also information about phonological, syntactic and semantic properties of words and groups of words. Several decades of experience in devising computer programs that recognize syntax, interpret meaning or analyze discourse have led researchers to conclude that these activities also require substantial amounts of knowledge, most of which either resides in the lexicon or is accessed via a lexical index.

Researchers working outside the computational paradigm have reached much the same conclusion. Recent theories of language production and comprehension stress the mental lexicon as a vital bridge between word shapes or sounds and the structures and meanings of sentences. Lexical entries provide not only the syntactic and

61

semantic attributes of particular words (and perhaps phrases) but also the structural frameworks on which interpretations of sentences are built. Thus the lexicon, human and computational, as well as the representation of lexical information, has emerged as a productive field of inquiry.

1.2 Word forms as lexical keys

Access to individual items in a lexicon is typically via labels for the lexical entries, called **keys**. Much as we would consult the index of a book, computers retrieve information by first searching for the key. Word recognition systems use acoustic templates as keys, and systems for continuous speech use sequences of phonemes or other representations of acoustic information. Spelling checkers may use "similarity keys," strings of characters derived from the spellings of words in such a way as to minimize the effect of common misspellings. Systems that convert sentences of predictable wording into formal database queries use frequently co-occurring words and even brief sentences as keys, thus reducing the need for syntactic and semantic analysis. For most applications, however, the keys are spellings of word forms, or sometimes word stems, with all inflectional and some derivational suffixes removed. ("Word forms" because two or more words may have the same spelling.) As we will see, spellings make convenient keys, though they are not ideal.

Arriving at a satisfactory formal definition is difficult, but a **word** can be provisionally defined as the smallest linguistic unit that, in most languages, exhibits internal stability and positional mobility. Internal stability means that the constituent morphemes usually combine in one and only one way. The morphemes *quick* and *-ly* combine as *quickly*; they do not combine as *quickly* sometimes and *lyquick* at other times; similarly *background* is never *groundback*. As for positional mobility, consider the shuffling of *boy*, *friend*, and *parents* in these sentences:

> The boy introduced his friend to his parents.
> His friend introduced the boy to his parents.
> His parents introduced the boy to his friend.

Quickly and a few similar words have even more potential locations in sentences:

> * he * wrote a letter * and * mailed it *

Given their internal stability and positional mobility, it is convenient to regard words as basic entities and the building blocks of larger units. Certainly we think of words as having independent existence, and even for those languages that have never been committed to writing, native speakers intuitively grasp what constitute words. Words can stand alone in speech and sometimes in writing (as in the dialogue "What?" "Scram." "Alright"). They are capable of particular grammatical employment (as subject of a sentence, for example, or as modifier) and have particular meanings (so that no two words are in all respects exactly synonymous.) Also, words are of convenient size to be swapped from place to place in sorting the lexicon or to be scanned in the process of search. About ninety percent of the words in a typical stretch of written English have eight or fewer characters; fewer than one-half percent have more than twelve, and the average is between four and five characters. Spaces clearly mark the boundaries between words in many written languages (though not in Japanese, Thai and a few others), whereas the boundaries of phrases and of clauses that are not sentences, can be hard to ascertain.

Though access to the mental lexicon is via phonological representations of words, written words (spellings) are far easier to work with than spoken words. Unlike pronunciations, spellings are sequences of reliably identifiable units. Characters are readily entered using a keyboard, and optical character readers reliably interpret typed or printed text. Experimental systems manage even to read handwriting. Spellings are normative, whereas pronunciations vary from region to region and speaker to speaker; and spellings differentiate many homonyms, words that have very similar or the same pronunciations: *soul* and *sole* for example. (Recent research suggests that spelling is not, as once was thought, merely a defective technique for transcribing speech, but instead is rule-abiding when the interaction of phonological and morphological influences is considered. Rules combine basic units–either characters or such clusters of characters as *sh* and *ch* –into regular, predictable patterns.)

Working with words and their spellings does, however, present a few problems. Spellings occasionally obscure the connection between morphologically related words (*go - went*; *bad - worse*; *goose - geese*. This phenomenon, known as suppletion, occurs in many languages, but in no language does it involve many words, and with few words to consider, linking the suppletive forms to a single key (in a vocabulary study, for example, or for machine translation) can easily be done by hand or with a simple "stop" list of special cases. Spellings can also suggest false word formations. Without some care in the morphological analysis, certain words may be assigned to the wrong key: *understand*, for example, does not mean "stand beneath" and *concur* does not mean "with dog."

Problems of lexical ambiguity and idiomatic phrases are more formidable. Ambiguities include **homographic** word forms which, though spelled the same, have entirely different etymologies, meanings and sometimes lexical categories (*bat* as a wooden stick and a nocturnal flying mammal); and **polysemous** words, which have multiple related meanings (*neck* as part of a body, part of a bottle, a narrow strip of land, and so on) or multiple lexical categories (*delight* as verb or noun, *green* as noun or adjective). A few other words, such as *that* and *it*, are ambiguous in that they have meanings in some constructions, but not in others (*it is clear that he is coming*). Because the spelling (or pronunciation) will not reveal which homographic word is meant or which meaning or lexical category (a notorious example is *as*, which can function as any one of six lexical categories or subcategories), the lexicon must provide multiple entries, leaving the choice among them to syntactic and semantic procedures which use context in making decisions.

Much as some words require multiple entries, some groups of words function as wholes and deserve single entries. Such phrases as *look after*, *bring to light*, or *get it over with*, are idioms, their meanings not predictable from the meanings of their constituent words.   Their syntactic behavior may also be unpredictable. *Rather*, for example, though usually an adverb (*rather large*), becomes a verb when preceded by certain auxiliaries (*had rather*). Conversely, *touch* is usually a verb, but conjoining it with *go* produces an adjective (*touch and go*). Perhaps four to five thousand idioms are in everyday use, and although empirical research shows that humans treat idiomatic phrases as if they were single words and experience no difficulty in processing them, computational projects require preprocessors that recognize idioms (often by looking for them in a list of idioms) and mark them for special handling.   All these problems–spelling irregularities, suppletion, misleading word formations, lexical ambiguity, and idiomatic phrases–must be coped with, but the spellings of words remain the best available candidates to be lexical keys.

1.3 Lexicons as repositories of information

A lexicon can readily supply several kinds of information, either directly by incorporating the information in the lexical entry or indirectly by serving as an index to information stored elsewhere. When the purpose is to analyze structures of sentences or their meanings, that information concerns not only the word itself but also the likely contexts of the word. Such contextual information, introduced briefly here and considered in more detail later, includes lexical categories and syntactic features which determine the grammatical combinations into which the word may enter; as well as semantic features, cases and prototypes, all of which help establish the meanings of words and groups of words. Also, the lexicon may include or (more likely) index the "scripts" and "plans," which supply the common knowledge human beings use in interpreting sustained discourse. Far from being simple collections of words, computational lexicons (and perforce the human lexicon), are repositories of detailed and vital information.

Lexical categories, most of which go by the names we learned in school as "parts of speech," are of two kinds. Some are small, stable groups of words, while others are large and constantly changing. Stable categories for English include predeterminers (for example, *all, both, half*), determiners (*a, the, any, either, much*), prepositions (*of, to, in, for*), coordinating conjunctions (*and, but, or*), conjuncts (*hence, however, similarly*), subordinators (*that, if, when*), personal pronouns (*he, they, her*), indefinite pronouns (*everyone, someone*), demonstratives (*this, those*), relatives (*that, which, what*), forms of the auxiliary verbs *to be* and *to have* (*is, was, had, having*), and modal auxiliaries (*would, can, should*). Sometimes the list of stable categories is expanded to include a hundred or so time and place adverbials (*near, above, again, soon*). Languages seldom invent new members for any of these categories or borrow members from other languages. Their pertinacity was such in English that they survived the period 1100 to 1500, when the lexicon profoundly changed, with borrowings first from French and then from Latin, and when prepositions came to replace many inflectional affixes. Most such words are more important for their grammatical functions than for their meanings, functions that some other languages accomplish using inflections. Indeed some (such as *to* in *I want to go*) have hardly any meaning. They are therefore known as **function words** or **grammatical words**.

Open categories for English are nouns, verbs, adjectives and adverbs. Unlike the function words, members of these classes change over time as words are borrowed or new words are coined, and others fall into disuse. (Open categories in some languages, however, may be closed in others; the Ghanaian language, Akan, has a small group of adjectives and conveys through its verbs much of what English conveys with adjectives.) Because these words carry much of the meaning or semantic content of sentences, they are often called **content words**. Though native speakers might be hard pressed to come up with a fully explicit definition of *adjective* or *noun* (linguists also have problems), "test frames" will usually establish the lexical category of a given content word. These exploit our grasp of what words to select for what contexts.

for verbs:	You —— well.
for nouns:	The —— is/are good.
for adjectives:	The —— one is.

In the first frame, only verbs (such as *do, eat, think*) will fill the gap; in the second frame only nouns (*act, food, idea*), and in the third only adjectives (*busy, spicy, smart*). Members of each group share the ability to occupy other positions: all nouns, for example, can be objects of certain verbs (*I forgot the act / food / idea*) or prepositions (*for the act / food / idea)*; and following certain verbs, adjectives may complete the sentence *(it is busy / spicy / smart)*. The only category not readily identified is the adverb, which tends to be a catch-all category for several diverse groups of words not readily assigned to any other: words that modify adjectives; those that modify verbs or entire sentences by specifying time, place and manner; a few that connect sentences *(however, therefore, nevertheless)*; and a heterogeneous assortment of other words.

As the test frames suggest, syntactic categories are selectional. We are guided in selecting the words that we combine into sentences by the categories associated with those words in our mental lexicon. We are further guided by syntactic **features** of words. Number is a familiar feature: singular nouns or pronouns when they are subjects require singular verbs. Similar features include person and gender, which assure agreement between a pronoun and the word to which it refers. Perhaps less familiar are the features count and non-count, though we observe them as if by instinct. A singular count noun (such *dollar* or *apple*) must be preceded by a determiner: *I have a dollar for the apple,* but a non-count noun *(money, corn)* can go without: *I have money for fruit.* As these examples suggest, part of our knowledge of a word consists in information about the contexts in which that word may appear.

Verbs in English, and many other languages, exhibit an interesting set of features which govern the structures of sentences in which the verbs participate. *Arise, enjoy, eat, present, donate, become,* and *think* are all verbs, but the following test frames reveal important differences:

> You —— .
> You —— one.
> You —— one to/for her.
> You —— her one.

Only the first frame will accept *arise*, only the second will accept *enjoy*, but both will accept *eat*. *Arise* has the feature intransitive, meaning that it does not take a direct object (in this case *one*), *enjoy* has the feature "transitive" and the object is obligatory, whereas *eat* has both features. As these first three examples suggest, verb features predict sentence structures, and such predictions prove invaluable in identifying syntactic structures.

The system of verb features in English is extensive and remarkably subtle. Consider the remaining four verbs. *Donate* and *present,* despite their similarity in meaning, share only the third frame. Like *enjoy, become* fits only the second frame, but with a difference. What follows *become* is not an object but a complement that renames and describes the subject *you.* (Try substituting a word like *red* or *actors* for the uninformative *one.*) *Give* and *donate,* despite their similarity in meaning, have different sets of features, allowing *give* to occur in all four frames but restricting *donate* to the first three. Finally, consider the difference between *present* and *think*: *you present her one* is a shortened form of *you present one to her* and *you think her one* is short for *you think she is one*. With *present*, *her* is the indirect object, a beneficiary; with *think*, *her* is an object complement renaming the direct object. Other lexical categories exercise similar constraints. For example, the adjectives *glad*, *fond*, and *hopeful* govern the constructions that can follow them: *glad* can take a prepositional phrase, a clause or neither (*he was glad for her*, *he was glad that she won* or simply *he was glad*); *fond* must take prepositional phrases (*she is fond of doing it*, but not *she is fond* or *she is fond that she does it*); and *hopeful* does the opposite (*she is hopeful that she can do it* but not *she is hopeful of doing it*).

The mental lexicon also contains information about the meanings of words, phrases, and sentences. Though approaches to the study of meaning (semantics) are less well developed than approaches to syntax, many represent the meanings of content words in terms either of **superordinating words** or of **semantic features**, drawn in either case from a manageably small collection of superordinates or features. Superordinates are words whose meanings are included in the meanings of more specific words. Semantic features are primitive concepts whose meanings are included in words. Though the features may correspond to words, they need not do so and therefore have an advantage over superordinates in that they promise linguistic universality. Thus *woman* would have the superordinates *being*, *human*, *adult*, and *female* or the semantic features CONCRETE, ANIMATE, HUMAN, ADULT, FEMALE. Other lexical categories also have their superordinates or features; the verbs *see*, *hear*, *taste* have the superordinate *perceive*. *Kiss*, *touch*, *collide* have *contact*, and *walk*, *bring*, *migrate* have *move*.

Some lexical entries may also provide structural information about how meanings combine. One sense of *drive*, for example, predicts several relationships: a HUMAN (and only a human) does the driving, a VEHICLE is necessarily the instrument, other HUMANs may be passengers, OBJECTs or SUBSTANCEs are freight, PLACEs or DIRECTIONs serve as origins, paths, and destinations. Thus the lexical entry for *drive* would provide for these relationships and leave slots for the particular driver, vehicles, destinations, with each slot constrained to a particular filler. The entry for one sense of *drive* might stipulate:

[OPERATE]   ←(agent)− [HUMAN, ADULT]
             ←(instrument)− [VEHICLE]
             ←(origin)− [PLACE]
             ←(destination)− [PLACE]

Other verbs may be less demanding; *sit*, for example, requires only PHYSICAL OBJECT for a constituent to qualify as that which sits. The verb's entry may also carry instructions for locating appropriate fillers, specifying that drivers are usually subjects of sentences and vehicles are direct objects. Some computational systems go even further, supplying world knowledge that is not fully explicit in the sentence. An entry for *buy*, for example, would specify two causally related TRANSFERs: a buyer transferring currency or the promise of currency to a seller, thereby causing the seller to transfer legal ownership of property to the buyer.

The representations for semantic structures are derived from the graph notation developed by Charles Sanders Peirce as a graphical representation of symbolic logic. Brackets enclose semantic features or superordinates and may represent any entity, state or action. Parentheses enclose the relations that link concepts and arrows orient the relationship. Similarly, the graph:

[ANIMAL] ←(part)— [SKIN]

expresses the fact that all animals, whether human or non-human have skin as one body part.

When the components of a word do not fully define them, the lexicon may supply additional information in the form of lexical **prototypes**. A prototype gives typical attributes, usually formulated as series of relationships, much like the roles associated with verbs. The prototype for *professor* might include among others the following relations:

professor ←(role)— [teach]
         ←(role)— [research]
         ←(education)— [postgraduate]
         ←(affiliation)— [college or university]
         ←(discipline)— [unknown]
         ←(specialty)— [unknown]

Some of these attributes are only typical and may not apply in every case, and they are replaceable or (in computer jargon "defaults"). Not all professors divide their time between teaching and research, and not all are affiliated with colleges or universities. When the context offers evidence to the contrary, as in the phrase *the unemployed professor*, the default can be removed or replaced. A prototype may also have slots left vacant for particulars that are expected but unknown. About professors, for example, we know that they belong to one discipline or another; they are necessarily professors of English, biology or some other discipline, but the word itself does not convey which.

Taking this one step further, a lexicon may also contain or index information about subjects of discourse. What one encounters in visiting a restaurant or attending a class is often stereotypical, and because we can assume that someone we are conversing with knows about restaurants and classes, we say only as much as we need to say in order to be understood. The rest is implicit. If a computer program is to interpret the discourse, it must be supplied with the implicit information. Associated with the word *class* in one of its senses it would have information about a typical classroom session: what instructors do, how students participate, the duration, physical layout, and so on. Such stereotypical accounts, especially when they contain a substantial narrative component, are called **scripts**. The scripts offer extended accounts of typical sequences of events, with emphasis on the causal and other connections between events; they allow particulars to be filled in or supplanted. Scripts by their nature tend to be inflexible, and therefore psychologically implausible. It can also be difficult to select the relevant script from those available, to keep track of what portion of the script is currently relevant, and to cope with unstereo-typical twists and turns in the discourse. Rather than matching the discourse against a script, **plan**-based systems work with smaller pieces, attempting to infer the causal and enablement connections that pertain among states, expressed goals, and actions, thus to stitch together the pieces of the discourse to interpret it as a coherent narrative.

Section two: Sorting and Sorted Word Lists

2.1 Collating sequences and sorting

The most widely used method of organizing lists is to sort them by the **collating sequence** of their characters. For English and other alphabetic languages, the collating sequence is alphabetical order. For ideographic languages, such as Chinese and Japanese, collation is based on the number and kind of strokes used in forming a character. Colla-ting sequences go back to antiquity, when they served mainly as an aid to memory; the verses of many biblical psalms follow a strict sequence in which the first verse begins with *aleph*, the second with *beth*, and so on. But sequence also facilitates searching and was used for that purpose at least as early as the first century A.D., when Apollonius Sophistica compiled a verbal index to Homer's poetry, sorting his list by the first two characters in each word. This method of using the alphabet for a rough grouping (resembling a thumb index) persisted until the late middle ages, when alphabetizing finally came to be based on the spellings of entire words. In his preface to the *Catholicon* (1286), Giovanni di Genoa must explain full-word sorting, then he adds "I beg of you, therefore, good reader, do not scorn this great labor of mine, and this order as something worthless."

Nowadays, we take it for granted that a list of any considerable length, an index, a dictionary, perhaps a concordance, will be fully sorted; and we can usually assume that the "great labor" was done by computer. Computers make it feasible to undertake projects that would be unthinkably laborious if done by hand. One of the first to recognize their potential was Father Roberto Busa, who in 1949 set out to compile a concordance to the entire corpus of Saint Thomas Aquinas: some eight million words in all with another few million of collateral writing; Busa's computer-assisted concordance occupies more than sixty volumes. Ease of sorting means that electronic dictionaries used (especially in Europe) by foreign language translators of technical writing need not await periodic major revisions as do ordinary printed dictionaries. They can be updated weekly, even daily, and thus keep pace with new terms, generated by the hundreds of thousands every year. (For perspective, an "unabridged" general-purpose dictionary of the English language, nearly a foot thick in printed form, has about four hundred and fifty thousand entries.)

Similar considerations led to the electronic version of the new second edition of the *Oxford English Dictionary*. Although the OED has "only" about five hundred thousand headwords, it quotes two and a half million brief passages, from as early as the twelfth century and as recently as the 1980s, to illustrate changes in meaning and usage. The electronic edition not only makes frequent updating feasible but also makes information more accessible by indexing the citations by date, source, and author. No longer is it necessary to plod through all twelve volumes of the printed OED (as one scholar did a few years ago) in order to establish that Shakespeare is the source of 1,904 main citations. Sorting is also instrumental in finding new words to incorporate in dictionaries. A lexicographer can have the computer sort large text files into alphabetical lists then compare the alphabetical lists with existing dictionaries, automatically compiling a list of new words together with their sources and brief excerpts from the context to clarify their use.

Most sorting procedures compare words or phrases character by character until they find a discrepancy, then decide whether to exchange them. Thus a sorting routine might determine that because the ASCII code for the third character in *bat* (116) is greater than the code for the third in *bag* (103), the words should be exchanged or that *bat* should be inserted in the position following *bag*. If an entry consists of a word together with information about the word, say its lexical category and pointers into a hierarchy of components, semantic network, or structure of frames, the sorting can be based on the word only or (to keep homographs together) on the word and the information about the word.

Sorting will not, of course, bring together such suppletives as the alphabetically far-flung forms of the verb *to be* (*am*, *be*, *is*, *was*, and the rest) or establish that *likes* and *liking* are both forms of the verb *like*. To group diverging word forms under a single head word (which lexicographers call a **lemma**), special lemmatization routines are necessary. Though it should eventually be possible to employ sophisticated morphological analysis, the commonest method at least for now is to lemmatize one text manually, use it to lemmatize a second text, manually adding lemmata for words not found in the first, and so on to gradually compile a dictionary of words and lemmata.

Ordinarily, when two entries are the same, they are left in place; but a sorting procedure can be made to delete one of the identical items, thus producing a conflated list of unique word forms or **types**. Each instance of a type is a **token**. (Thus the preceding sentence contains seven types, and the type *a* has two tokens.) Or the procedure can associate a counter with each type and increment the counter with every repetition, thus counting the number of tokens of each type. Once the counting is done, the procedure may re-sort the list using the count rather than the collating sequence to determine the order. Thus sorting procedures can produce a sorted list of all tokens, a sorted list of types, a list of types in collating sequence and their counts, or a list of types and counts in the order of word frequency. Each kind of sorted list has its uses, some of them surprising, but first let's look in somewhat more detail at the sorting process itself.

2.2 Sorting strategies, especially quicksort

A major difference among sorting procedures is in their methods of selecting items to be compared, and the efficiency of the procedure usually depends on the method selected. A simple exchange sort compares successive items in the list, the first item with the second, the second with the third and so on, swapping those that are out of order and making repeated passes through the list until no further swaps can be made. An insertion sort works through the list item by item, comparing each with the remaining items on the list until it finds an item with a smaller value, whereupon it inserts the first item to follow the second. For a randomly ordered list of five hundred words, such brute force methods might entail a hundred to a hundred and fifty thousand comparisons, many involving the same pair of words, and forty to sixty thousand swaps. (Exact numbers would depend on the degree of disorder in the list.) With each comparison or swap taking only a few nanoseconds (billionths of a second), the exchange and the insertion methods both work well enough for short lists or lists that are very nearly in order. But nanoseconds add up, and for a list of any considerable length the exchange and insertion sorts will be painfully slow.

First pass:

```
ME an so we up be us if in to he on as go by no
ME an so we up be us if in to he on as go by no  swap
by an so we up be us if in to he on as go ME no
by an so we up be us if in to he on as go ME no  swap
by an ME we up be us if in to he on as go so no  swap
by an go we up be us if in to he on as ME so no  swap
by an go ME up be us if in to he on as we so no  swap
by an go as up be us if in to he on ME we so no  swap
by an go as ME be us if in to he on up we so no
by an go as ME be us if in to he on up we so no  swap
by an go as he be us if in to ME on up we so no
by an go as he be us if in to ME on up we so no  swap
by an go as he be ME if in to us on up we so no
by an go as he be ME if in to us on up we so no  swap
by an go as he be in if ME to us on up we so no
by an go as he be in if ME to us on up we so no
```

(by an go as he be in if) me (to us on up we so no)

Second pass:

```
BY an go as he be in if               TO us on up we so no  swap
BY an go as he be in if               no us on up we so TO  swap
BY an go as he be in if  swap         no TO on up we so us  swap
be an go as he BY in if               no so on up we TO us
be an go as he BY in if  swap         no so on up we TO us  swap
be an BY as he go in if               no so on TO we up us
be an BY as he go in if  swap         no so on TO we up us
```

(be an as) by he (go in if)   (no so on) to (we up us)

Third pass:

```
BE an as  swap    GO in if      NO so on      WE up us  swap
as an BE          GO in if      NO so on      us up WE

(as an) be        go (in if)    no (so on)    (us up) we
```


Fourth pass:

```
AS an swap    be go    IN if swap    no    SO on swap    US up swap    we
```

Sorted list:

```
an  as  be  by  go  he  if  in  me  no  on  so  to  up  us  we
```

Figure 1. Quicksort in operation.

    A much more efficient method, **quicksort**, employs a simple binary strategy that many use for sorting index cards. Developed in the course of early linguistic research on machine translation, quicksort (sometimes called partition exchange) is perhaps the best general-purpose sorting routine yet devised. For index cards, the strategy is simply to sort the cards into groups on either side of a pivot; if card M is the pivot, cards A-K go in one group and M-Z in the other. Then each of the smaller groups is split in two groups, and on and on until the cards are sorted. Quicksort applies the binary strategy to lists, creating successively smaller and smaller sublists, and employing a simple stack to keep track of the boundaries. (See Figure 1, where the pivotal word for each pass is capitalized and the word to be compared and perhaps swapped with it is underlined.) At each step, the list reflects any action taken in the preceding step; thus at the third step *ME* and *by* have been swapped. At the end of the first pass, words above and below the pivot have been separated into two subgroups; at the end of the second path, each of the subgroups has been divided in two, and so on. The virtue of this procedure is that, once a lexical entry is assigned to one of the sublists generated by each pass, it needs never be compared with entries assigned to a different group. The potential number of comparisons is greatly reduced. Quicksort's index card strategy requires just ten passes to sort a list of five-hundred and twelve items, eleven passes for one-thousand twenty-four items, twelve for two-thousand forty-eight, and so on, steadily increasing in efficiency as the list grows longer.

Other sorting strategies cope with special situations. One commonly occurring situation is that the list to be sorted is too big to be manipulated in the confines of computer memory. If the problem is that each item occupies too much space (the citations and other information associated with entries in the *Oxford English Dictionary* can go on for several printed pages), the solution is to index the list, associating with each keyword a pointer to the location of the full entry in mass storage. If the problem is that the list has too many items (a common occurrence in literary and linguistic computing when all words in a text or several texts are to be sorted), a merge sort is preferable. In this variation of the index card strategy, a large list of words is arbitrarily split into several manageable sublists, each of which is then sorted in reverse alphabetical order. These sublists are then merged into a final list, built from the bottom up by comparing the top word in the reverse-sorted sublists. As the sublists are being merged, only a small portion of them and of the merged list needs to be in memory at any one time; the rest can be stashed away in mass storage.

Volatility also poses problems. If a list is constantly being updated with deletions and insertions, keeping it fully alphabetized may not be feasible. One answer is partial alphabetizing, employing the principle of the thumb index. Words are assigned to subgroups, called "buckets," by their initial characters: *aa-* through *ag-* for the first bucket, *ah-* through *an-* for the second, and so on to *wa-* through *wh-* and *wi-* through *zy-*. Thus *airplane* would be assigned to the second bucket and *zoning* to the last bucket. Partial alphabetizing can be particularly effective with active memory. Each bucket can be assigned to a separate processor, allowing multiple concurrent searches. The buckets would need to be of nearly equal size, both for convenience in allocating memory and for efficiency in searching through their contents. To the rescue come the cryptographers, who (in aid of code-breaking) have computed statistics for every combination of characters in every position within commonly occurring words. The frequencies vary widely. Some combinations, such as *kv* and *mb*, never occur word initially in English, primarily for phonetic reasons; while others such as *an* and *th* are quite common. Partial alphabetizing quickly focuses the search on a relatively short list of words, and though not nearly as efficient in narrowing the search as a simple binary method for fully alphabetized lists, may be efficient enough.

Recently a new kind of computer has emerged, capable of carrying out processes in parallel. With parallel processing, different considerations arise. Whereas quicksort achieves its efficiency by minimizing the number of comparisons on each pass–comparisons that conventional computers must carry out in sequence–efficiency is gained in an opposite way with parallel processing, particularly with "fine-grained" parallelism, in which thousands of simple processors execute the same operation simultaneously. (The alternate, "coarse-grained" parallelism, employs a few very powerful processors; such machines do better with tasks that cannot readily be reduced to many, very simple, autonomous operations.) With fine grained-parallelism, any procedure, even a brute force procedure, which maximizes the number of comparisons on each pass, will necessarily be more efficient. If the number of passes can also be minimized, so much the better; but because the number of passes even in a relatively inefficient routine is insignificantly small, sorting with parallel processors is virtually instantaneous. Programs need not delay sorting until a list is complete or unlikely to be changed; instead sorting can be interleaved with processes that acquire or modify data.

2.3 Verbal indexes and concordances

Verbal indexes and concordances were among the earliest applications of computers to language and remain among the few unqualified successes, accomplishing in a few hours what scholars, from the times of Apollonius Sophistica until the late 1940s, took months, even years, to accomplish by hand. A **verbal index** is an alphabetical list of the word tokens in a text or corpus of texts with an indication of where each word occurs; a **concordance** adds the context, usually excerpts of the passages in which the tokens occur, and sometimes the speaker, the kind of speech (whether dialogue, soliloquy, or whatever) and or information about the context, and the like. Indexes and concordances are invaluable for locating words in a text or vaguely-remembered passages. They fully come into their own in the search for patterns of words or thoughts, a practice that goes back to the Renaissance, when verbal indexes were used to locate parallel passages in the Bible, particularly parallels among the four gospels. Concordances would reveal Shakespeare's repeated linking of Romeo and Juliet with brief flashes of intense light, "like the lightning, which doth cease to be / Ere one can say it lightens" or Milton's association of evil with multiplicity and divisiveness.

Computers make it feasible to undertake tasks of greater particularity, revealing such subtle phenomena as, in *Antony and Cleopatra*, the Roman's contemptuous use of unspecific determiners (*a, another,* etc.) for Cleopatra and respectfully specific determiners (*the, this*) for Antony. Computers also make it possible to undertake huge projects. For example, the computer-generated *Thesaurus Linguae Graecae* includes all extant texts written in Greek up to A.D. 200 and a selection from the next four hundred years. In a still larger undertaking, computer-generated concordances of sixteen-hundred complete works, representing the spectrum of writing in French since 1789 have been generated as raw material for the *Trésor de la Langue Française*, a huge historical dictionary of the French language.

Procedures for building indexes and concordances have been standardized and are incorporated in software packages, readily available through university or other computer centers and quite easy to use. The procedures assist in entering text (and sometimes automate the process using optical character readers), convert the text to a word list, record the location of each word, select the context to be quoted, perform limited morphological analysis, sort the list, then format and print the result. Some packages, designed for on-line concordances, facilitate "boolean searches" in which the computer looks for specified combinations of words within a given span. Others provide routines for determining the frequencies of words, the diversity or richness of the vocabulary, the degree of variance between texts, and virtually any other needed statistic. Some provide for manual pre-editing to distinguish homographs and to link suppletive forms and variant spellings. Among the more versatile packages are the OCP, which runs on several kinds of computers) and the CLOC (especially good for investigating co-occurring words). Lately there has been some attempt to provide for the segmenting of sentences into syntactic or semantic units, so that the computer can use more sophisticated criteria than punctuation or simple word counts in selecting the points at which to begin and end passages for quotation.

In addition to the standard indexes and concordances, a variety of special-purpose tools is available to linguists and literary scholars, and techniques for indexing and concording have applications in other fields. Among the special tools are the "reverse" indexes, which sort words by the alphabetical order of their endings. Originally devised for tracing the morphological evolution of Middle High German, a highly inflected language, they are now used to study the syntax of highly inflected languages, to investigate the complex interplay of morphological, syntactic, and semantic features that governs the suffixing of words, and to explore the subtle prosodic rules governing rhyme patterns in poetry. An example of the application of concording to non-literary tasks is the keyword in context (or KWIC) technique for information retrieval employing partial concordances. A refinement of ordinary indexing schemes that is especially useful when keywords cannot be very specific or are ambiguous, KWIC systems extract the content words surrounding preselected significant terms from titles, abstracts, and sometimes texts. They sort these entries in the order of the keywords, store the resulting list in computer memory, and permit search queries which specify the key word together with one or several contextual words.

Concording techniques also facilitate the identification and study of **collocations**, that is, words that frequently co-occur with one another. *Much prefer* and *juvenile delinquency* are collocations; *much reject* and *adolescent delinquency* are not. One method of identifying collocations splits text into pairs of words (*text might, might be, be split*), then alphabetizes the pairs. Since co-occurrences may not be adjacent, all the words within a given span of a specified word may be gathered then alphabetized. The latter method has proven useful in studying phrasal verbs (*put on, put over, put up*), because other words may intervene between the verb and its preposition. Phrasal verbs are of interest in English (particularly American English) because they continue to be formed at a extraordinarily rapid rate. Relatively little is known about collocations and the logic of their formation, which can sometimes be perplexing. (Why not *adolescent delinquency* or *much reject*?) Only with the advent of computers has it become feasible to collect and study them on a large scale.

Collocational research may shed light on important cognitive phenomena such as our perceptual span in listening to or reading language. Our eyes do not plod through a written line one word at a time, but instead jump from one point to another then on to another. This chunking of language occurs in listening as well. Reliable information about the span, syntactic composition, and semantics of idiomatic phrases and other frequently recurring collocations may lead to a better understanding of the units in which language is perceived and stored in short-term memory until comprehension takes place. Collocational research also plays an important role in linguistic semantics; words that co-occur with significant frequency to constitute "fields" yield insight into the semantic organization of the language. The research has more immediate benefits as well–in foreign language and bilingual instruction, for example; in automated text-indexing; and in lexicography. For lexicography, collocations play a role in identifying homographic and polysemous words: if *bank* co-occurs with *river, water, flow*, it is one word; if it co-occurs with *money, account* or *deposit*, it is another. Such information, applied to cases more subtle than the two senses of bank, has been used in the compilation of the *Trésor de la Langue Française*. Phrasal dictionaries are also essential for computer systems that interpret syntax and semantics, because idioms by their very nature violate the rules and other generalizations on which such systems depend. Some semantic systems go further; an example is PHRAN, the PHRasal ANalyzer developed by Yigal Alon and Robert Wilensky, which matches text strings against phrasal templates.

2.4 Corpora of written and spoken language

Compilation and analysis of large representative collections of text, known as **corpora**, represent another application of computers to language. The first to be compiled was the one-million word Brown University Corpus of written American English. It consists of five-hundred representative samples of informational and imaginative prose, all published in 1961. The samples, each containing 2000 words of consecutive text, were drawn from such diverse sources as newspaper reportage, government documents, and popular fiction. Words were sorted, conflated, and counted, then re-sorted in the order of the counts to produce lists in order of frequency. Subsequently, words in the Corpus were tagged with their lexical categories and subcategories, and these also were sorted, counted, and ranked to afford insight into the syntactic properties of English and of the several genres.

Since the Brown Corpus, other computer corpora have been compiled. The Lancaster-Oslo/Bergen (LOB) Corpus of written British English replicates the categories and sampling methods of Brown. For spoken British English, the London-Lund Corpus has six major categories, among them spontaneous conversations, interviews and debates and planned speeches. Among the corpora that are currently underway, some are designed for special purposes; the International Corpus of English, for example, will explore some twenty national varieties of English. Others are to be much larger than the corpora currently available, because many important linguistic phenomena do not crop up very often even in a million words of text. The Birmingham University Corpus, designed for lexicographic and other purposes, and comprised of several sub-corpora, totals some twenty-million words; and the Data Collection Initiative, already consists of thirty-million words and is projected to grow to several hundred million. Unlike the corpora selected to be representative of particular genres, the Initiative is opportunistic, incorporating whatever becomes available.

In addition to these corpora, many texts and collections of texts are available in computer-readable form. Major collections include LIBRI, the Literary and Information Bases for Research and Instruction (classical and other literary text), the Oxford Text Archives (literary and other text in several languages), the International Computer Archive of Modern English, and the Centro Nazionale Universitario di Calcolo Elettronico (text in Italian). Though many of the texts in these collections are of incompatible formats, a set of standards has emerged, based on Standard Generalized Markup Language (SGML), to simplify the interchange of text among computing system or applications. The standards also provide a way of marking linguistic phenomena that does not presuppose any one view of language and will therefore be usable by linguists of many different theoretical persuasions.

Corpora that are collected through careful sampling are particularly important for research on language variation. They can reveal differences between spoken and written language, differences between genres or other subgroups (scholarly versus popular writing, say, or spontaneous versus scripted speech), and differences in linguistic usage between language communities (for example, English as spoken in Australia and England). Indeed what may be learned by comparing subparts of a corpus (comparing the style of popular fiction with the style of government documents would be an extreme example) is often more revealing than data about the corpus as a whole.

Though corpora have little to say about what potentially can occur in spoken or written language (corpora are finite, after all, and our own intuitions can tell us what is possible), very large corpora provide reliable statistics on occurrence and co-occurrence of lexical categories and word senses. These permit the testing of linguistic hypotheses in areas where attested data is more reliable than intuitions. Very large corpora will also yield to mathematical models of language systems, automatically constructed. If, in turn, the models can be used to create probablistic methods of recognizing syntactic structures or interpreting sentence meanings, corpus research offers the intriguing prospect of computer programs that autonomously learn languages.

Section three: Variation and Statistical Analysis

3.1 Tokens, types, and word frequencies

When a sorting procedure conflates multiple instances of the same word to produce a list consisting only of word types, the result can be startling. The text of the present chapter, excluding the figures, consists of about thirteen-thousand tokens representing just 2427 types. In the choosing of words, writing is a highly repetitive endeavor. To explore the nature of the repetition, the same sorting procedure can be made to count tokens as it conflates them, and again the result is startling. In the one-million word Brown Corpus, six types account for 205,961 tokens or somewhat more than one-fifth of the total. The six are, in order of frequency, *the, of, and, to, a,* or *in.* Although frequencies drop off rapidly below the top six, word tokens are by no means evenly distributed. The one-hundred and thirty most frequent types in the Corpus account for more than half the total number of tokens, while over fifty-thousand types comprise the remaining half. The list is slightly different in spoken language; the pronoun *I* occurs nearly as frequently in spoken English as *the* does in writing, and demonstrative pronouns are also more frequent in speech where they reduce the frequency of articles. The extreme variation between the most frequent words and the rest is by no means a phenomenon of English alone. Most languages, ancient and modern, iterate a few to a few dozen words at exceptionally high frequencies.

If types from a large sample are ranked in the order of decreasing frequency, the rate of decrease for all but the most frequent words is a constant. This phenomenon, known as Zipf's law, is one of the few mathematical regularities that language exhibits. It may suggest an equilibrium between unwillingness to exert mental energy in coming up with words (assuming that words, once used, are more readily available to be used again) and the need for words specific enough to express the meaning. Or it may suggest that, as an efficient channel of communication, language obeys laws of probability determined by the number of available word choices.

Word repetition has practical implications for many programs that process text. In generating verbal indexes and concordances, the computer is usually instructed to ignore the most frequent words or to represent them only by cumulative totals. (An exception that illustrates the wisdom of this policy is the original published version of a concordance to Shakespeare which devotes more than five hundred and thirty double-column pages to *the, of, and, to, a,* and *in.*) Some procedures for text compression practice similar economies by replacing very frequent words with one-byte codes, then restoring the words when the text is retrieved. Word frequencies also have implications for the time required to process a text. For example, programs which screen for misspellings or typographical errors usually consult dictionaries of as many as a hundred-thousand words to determine whether each spelling in the text exists. Because a separate search for every token would consume an exorbitant amount of time, it can actually be more efficient to sort and conflate the text into a list of types, consult the dictionary for each type, and either list suspected mistakes or return to the text to search for and highlight them.

Among the statistics generated from lexical counts, word frequency is the most common. The average frequency of a word is calculated by dividing the number of tokens of that word by the total number of

Chapter 3 Section 1		Chapter 3 Section 2		Chapter 4 Section 1		Brown (section J)		Brown (entire)	
4.4	the	6.9	the	6.4	the	6.9	the	7.8	the
3.7	of	3.9	of	4.3	of	3.6	of	4.6	of
3.5	and	3.3	a	3.3	a	2.9	and	2.6	and
2.4	words	2.8	and	2.6	and	2.6	to	2.5	in
2.2	a	2.5	in	2.4	in	2.3	a	2.5	to
2.2	to	2.3	to	2.2	to	2.1	in	2.2	a
2.1	in	1.6	is	1.4	or	1.1	that	1.5	is
2.0	as	1.5	be	1.4	is	1.0	is	1.0	that
1.7	or	1.4	with	1.3	that	1.0	was	1.0	for
1.2	for	1.3	list	1.2	be	1.0	he	.8	be
1.2	are	1.2	for	1.2	can	.9	for	.8	as
1.1	that	1.0	sorting	1.2	as	.9	it	.8	by
1.0	is	1.0	on	1.0	are	.7	with	.7	was
.9	word	.9	that	.9	information	.7	as	.7	with
.8	have	.9	each	.8	by	.7	his	.7	it
.8	information	.8	as	.8	with	.6	on	.6	are
.8	lexicon	.8	by	.8	nodes	.5	at	.6	this
.8	be	.7	word	.8	items	.5	by	.6	on
.8	which	.7	can	.7	lists	.5	I	.6	or
.7	with	.7	or	.7	for	.5	this	.5	which
.7	not	.7	words	.7	they	.5	had	.5	from
.7	lexical	.6	are	.7	an	.5	not	.5	not
.6	some	.5	index	.6	not	.4	are	.5	at
.6	more	.5	sorted	.6	pointers	.4	but	.4	were
.6	but	.5	one	.6	links	.4	from		
.6	spellings	.5	thus	.6	networks	.4	or		
				.6	tree	.4	have		
						.4	an		
						.4	they		
						.4	which		

Samples from this text consist of the first 2000 words in each of the three sections of this chapter (excluding figures); the Brown Corpus consists of 500 samples of 2000 words, to which section J contributes 80 samples.

Figure 2. Sample word frequencies.

word tokens then multiplying by one-hundred or one-thousand. Figure 2 gives the frequencies of the most common words in samples from several portions of this book and, for comparison, the frequencies for the most common words in the entire Brown Corpus and in the section of the Corpus most nearly corresponding in genre (consisting of writing from the natural and social sciences, medicine, mathematics, engineering, and the humanities). Notice that function words, and for the most part the same function words, appear near the top of each of the lists.

On all five lists the most frequently occurring lexical categories are determiners and prepositions. In the three sections, content words begin to appear at a frequency of about 1/100, and those that appear reflect the subjects of sections. For a few content words, high frequency is attributable both to the subject and to the unavailability of synonyms. *Words* and *word* are an example; *term* and *expression* are not exact synonyms and *lexical item* is clumsy; only occasionally in the first section is it appropriate to use *spellings* (.6/100) or entry/entries (.3/100 combined). Subject matter can also dictate tense; note the slightly higher frequencies of *is* and *are* in this text and the absence of *was* and *were* (which are very infrequent in the samples from this text). Computational linguistics presents few occasions to employ the past tense. The frequency of other words is governed by genre. The personal pronouns *he, his,* and *I* are among the most frequent words in the Brown Corpus (of which about a fifth is fiction and other kinds of imaginative prose), but personal pronouns are infrequent in this text and in the scholarly writing of category J.

Another common statistic is the **type/token ratio**, computed by dividing the number of tokens by the number of types: the lower the result, the greater the diversity of words in the sample. The type/token ratios for the three samples are 2.9, 3.1, and 2.9, respectively. Type/token ratios indicate density of information and precision of lexical choice; they tend to be much lower in written language than in conversational speech, because choosing the exact word requires time that conversations do not afford. Used cautiously, the ratios offer a rough measure of the richness or diversity of an author's vocabulary.

Both word frequencies and type/token ratios can be so easily obtained that they are often byproducts of procedures that sort words; concordance programs and even some spelling checkers generate them. As with any other statistics, however, both can be misleading. Consider *of*, the second most frequent word in the Brown Corpus. Its frequency in the Corpus as a whole is about 36/100, but closer inspection reveals that *of* varies in frequency from highs of 4.9/100 and 4.6/1000 in subdivisions containing government documents and learned writing to a low of about 2/100 in several categories of fiction. (It is important to remember that word frequencies are averages: if we add the numbers, 1, 2, 8, and 9 then divide by 4, we get an average of 5, a number quite different from any of the others.) Type/token ratios can also be misleading, because the relationship between types and tokens is not linear; many words in, say the first 2000 tokens will be repeated in the next 2000. Therefore sample sizes must be the same. The ratio for the 6000-word text created by merging the three 2000-word samples (each around 3.0) is 4.1. Such problems can be solved, however. For word frequencies, several samples are better than one, and the simple χ^2 (chi-square) test will determine when differences are statistically significant. In place of type/token ratios, the "K characteristic," based on average frequencies and the fluctuation of averages among several samples, is more reliable.

Some purposes call for more sophisticated techniques, particularly multivariate techniques for simultaneously investigating multiple samples each with multiple variables. Studies of language variation, for example, must classify and organize samples so as to determine distribution patterns of vocabulary, pronunciation, and the like. In textual criticism, degrees of similarity or dissimilarity can establish the genealogical relationships among manuscripts of the same work or determine which of several passages were written by the same author. For these purposes, **cluster analysis** can generate a dendrogram or "similarity tree," which like most computational trees is upside down. At the bottom, branches represent the several samples. At the next level up, the most similar samples combine, then the most similar of the combined samples combine, and so on up to the top, where all samples combine into a single root. Or the purpose may be to determine significant co-occurrences among word frequencies or the frequencies of lexical categories in each of several samples. Do certain words or categories co-occur more frequently in speech than in written language, in poetry than in prose, in the work of one author than in that of another? **Factor analysis** uncovers associations consolidating a large array of variables to a smaller group of composites called "factors." It reveals which variables are associated in that a high incidence of one co-occurs with a high incidence of the others and which are associated in that a high incidence of one means a low incidence of the others. In one study, for example, a relatively high type/token ratio co-occurred with a high frequency of modifying "that" and "which" clauses; apparently the clauses compensated for the lack of specificity in word choices.

3.2 Function words, attribution, and style

Nearly all of the very frequent types are function words: words whose primary role is to manage the tense and mood systems for verbs, to signal the constituents of sentences (as *an*, *a*, or *the*, for example, signals that a noun follows), and the like. It is no great trick to compose a sentence containing two dozen function words or more:

> **Because all of the** dogs **had been** waiting **for a very** long time,
> **they were just** beginning **to** strain **at their** leashes **and I** knew
> **that I could not** expect **them to** do **what I** wanted.

English is not alone in constantly iterating *and*, *I*, *in*, and the rest; French has *et*, *je*, *a*, German has *und*, *ich*, *auf*, Russian has *i*, *ya*, *v*; many languages have function words, and they are almost always among the most frequent words of the language. One reason for their frequency is that most have few or no synonyms or partial synonyms; we can replace *walk* with *stroll, march, stagger, strut, saunter, trudge, ramble, traipse, pace* and a host of other words, but most of the function words cannot be replaced without changing the syntax. Another reason is that languages rely on function words to serve purposes that recur in nearly every sentence. In spoken language where they crop up just as frequently, most are unstressed monosyllables and many have schwas for vowels. Thus they pose severe problems for speech recognition.

As children begin to speak utterances of more than two words, they omit most function words. Though their sentences are structurally quite similar to those spoken by adults, the sentences are telegraphic, consisting primarily of message bearing content words. Thus a two year old might say *[The] baby [is] play[ing with a] bear*. Subsequently and only gradually are the function words added (together with the closely related inflectional morphemes). Acquired only slowly, facility with function words can also be lost or impaired as a result of highly localized damage to the brain. (The condition is called aphasia.) If the anterior part of the brain's left hemisphere has been injured, perhaps by a tumor, stroke or gunshot wound, the ability to use and recognize certain categories of function words is often diminished, but facility with content words is impaired only slightly if at all. Patients may omit certain function words (determiners, for example) and mistake others, such as *in, be* and *may*, for their content word homophones *inn, bee* and *May*. Inflectional morphemes, close relations to the function words, may also be omitted. Damage to certain other locations has different linguistic consequences, leaving the function words unimpaired. Phenomena of acquisition and impairment, such as these, are especially interesting because they bear on the questions (for the most part unanswered) of how we manage to acquire syntactic knowledge and how language is stored and retrieved within the brain.

With their high frequency, function words necessarily contribute significantly to style. Style, which not only expresses the writer's message but also individuates the writer, is the cumulative result of a great many local choices of words and syntactic constructions. Some choices express intentions and are carefully made; others, especially the frequently recurring choices among function words, are matters of individual preference and habit. They resemble the whorls, arches and other distinctive features by which fingerprints differ in that they do not necessarily reveal the character of the writer or his work, but they can differentiate one writer from another. Many of these are choices of function words. A writer may prefer certain connectives (perhaps the curt *so* rather than the more florid *therefore* or *consequently*) or certain sentence structures (complex sentences with subordinating conjunctions such as *although* and *because* rather than compound sentences with their coordinating conjunctions). Certain sequences of lexical categories may be habitual for the writer: sentences beginning with prepositions then determiners (*of the* . . .) perhaps.

Inevitably, many investigations of style focused on function words and on sequences of lexical categories in which function words play a major role. Among the most dramatic studies are those that seek to establish the authorship and integrity of texts: was the text written by the putative author and has it been corrupted by other hands? The high frequency of function words makes for statistically reliable sampling, and frequencies tend to remain stable from sample to sample of an author's work. In an early and very successful case, Frederick Mosteller and David Wallace set out to establish whether Alexander Hamilton or James Madison wrote twelve disputed *Federalist Papers*. Among function word frequencies computed from the authors' works and from the disputed pamphlets, those for *while, enough, upon*, and a few others, satisfied statistical tests for reliability as discriminators. All favored Madison's authorship, and the evidence is so strong that the question appears to be settled.

Subsequently, stylistic analysis has been focused on such questions as did Chettle forge *The Groatsworth of Wit* to capitalize on Robert Greene's posthumous popularity (very likely), was the book of *Isaiah* the work of a single author (probably the work of three), was there a single "*Pearl* poet" who composed five of the most important fourteenth century poems (almost certainly not), what was Shakespeare's contribution to *Henry VIII* and *Sir Thomas More* (still the subject of lively debate), was Fielding the author of several anonymous essays in the *Craftsman* (probably), and did Hemingway write *The Old Man and the Sea* shortly before it was published (probably much earlier). Not all cases can be resolved. Alternative candidates may not be present or samples may be too small for reliable statistics; sometimes an author's style will be too variable for reliable results or two discriminators may point in opposite directions; but given the right circumstances, statistics of style can help resolve difficult questions of attribution.

Other questions can be addressed by investigating the frequencies of function word categories. Propelled in part by the national concern about illiteracy–as many as twenty-three million adult Americans lack appropriate reading and writing skills–researchers have investigated the syntax of spoken language and its relationship to written syntax. The prevailing view had been that, because speakers have little time to plan and revise their sentences, spoken language is not syntactically complex and that, in particular, it is not very cohesive. Frequency studies of connectives have shown otherwise. Cohesion in spoken language is simply achieved by different means. Rather than using writers' densely informative noun phrases or participial and infinitive clauses functioning as nominals, speakers gradually elaborate their ideas, using *that, which*, and *who* clauses, and causative and conditional conjuncts (such as *because, unless*). Such information is invaluable to those who design the curricula by which adults acquire proficiency in reading and writing.

3.3 Content words and vocabulary studies

Words that do not belong to the small, closed classes of function words are content words: nouns, verbs, adjectives, and most adverbs. Content words vastly outnumber the function words in any lexicon, and the vocabulary of content words in English has grown especially large. With a word defined as a dictionary entry (with suppletive and inflected forms and some derivational forms combined under the same entry), English has as many as sixty-thousand content words in general use, and is growing by about five-hundred words a year. Specialized English vocabularies, especially in the sciences and technologies where English has become the *lingua franca*, have tens of thousands more. Turnover is constant, as old words lose favor and new words are coined or borrowed to refresh the language, accommodate social changes, and express new knowledge. The most productive sources of new words, once humanistic writing and especially literature, are now science, business, and North American slang. Unless a researcher could somehow contrive to sample many hundreds of millions of words of text and continually update the sample, the absolute frequencies of content words have little significance, but the relative frequencies of one word or group of words compared with another proves useful in descriptive and applied linguistics and in content analysis.

For the descriptive linguist interested in the nature of linguistic change, relative frequencies of content words can reveal trends in usage and trace changes in vocabulary. Modern Turkish affords an excellent opportunity.   Since the Turkish alphabet was romanized in 1928, vocabulary has been undergoing a massive transformation.   Words coined from old Turkish roots or borrowed from European languages, primarily French and English, have been replacing words of Persian and Arabic origin;   hence the language offers a laboratory for those interested in linguistic change. By careful sampling, then obtaining frequencies of both old and new words, linguists have been studying the nature of the change, the channels through which it proceeds, and varying rates of diffusion.

Content word frequencies also play a role in applied linguistics. Increasingly, word frequency guides the compilation of dictionaries and selection of readings for foreign language courses, as well as for the burgeoning bilingual and second language curricula. For readings, they ensure sufficient repetition of words and pace the introduction of new words. Computers generate cumulative vocabulary lists for potential sets of readings: one list for the first reading, one for the first two, and so on. These lists of words and their frequencies measure the rate at which words are introduced and repeated. Sometimes word frequencies help tailor foreign language courses to the needs of specialists. Samples from major publications of a scientific or technical field (usually) determine the utility of specific words. For language learners' dictionaries, content word frequencies not only guide the selection of words to be included, but also the headwords under which lemmata are listed.

3.4 Sequence and co-occurrence in tagged text

Tagging associates with each word in a text or corpus of texts a **tag** identifying its lexical category and sometimes its subcategory or syntactic features. The Brown, LOB, and London-Lund corpora are available in tagged form, as is the Penn Treebank, a 4.5 million word selection of texts from the Data Collection Initiative. There is also the York Computer Inventory, a representative sampling of literary prose from the seventeenth through the twentieth centuries, compiled by Robert Cluett and his associates. Tagging can to some extent be automated. For most word types, the lexical category is assigned by consulting a computerized lexicon, which may simply be a list of types and their lexical categories from an already tagged lexicon. That leaves the approximately five percent of word types that are ambiguous between lexical categories; some are so frequent that as many as twenty percent of the tokens in corpus many be ambiguous. Some of these yield to special heuristics that identify the word's category from its immediate context. One heuristic determines whether an *-ing* word is functioning as a verb, an adjective, or a noun *(I am walking, the walking horse, walking is fun)* by considering first the prior context then the subsequent context:

- □ If it is immediately preceded by an article, demonstrative, quantifier, numeral, or possessive pronoun; then it is either an adjective or a noun.

- □ If it is not a verb and is followed by an adjective or a noun, then it is an adjective.

- □ If it not a verb and is followed by a preposition or a verb, then it is a noun.

Fair enough, but not enough. In many constructions, ambiguous types cannot be resolved by heuristics, and until recently these had to be tagged by hand: a laborious process prone to error. Now, however, "stochastic" algorithms promise reliable disambiguation of the stubborn cases. The algorithms operate somewhat as the heuristics do except that they apply probabilities derived from the number of times a target word is of a given lexical category and the number of times it is followed by one or more words of given lexical categories. Dynamic programming computes from these numbers the most likely assignment. The probabilities are high and, as better statistics become available, they are constantly improving. Highly reliable automated tagging is in the offing. Collateral work is underway on automated processes that identify prosodic segments and assign intonation contours for spoken language, with most of the effort focussing on scripted rather than spontaneous speech.

Tagged texts provide an abundance of information: not only the relative frequencies of all the lexical categories and subcategories, but also, what is often more revealing, the sequences of lexical categories (readily counted in tagged texts). Consider again the problem of attribution. In one celebrated case, the question was whether, as Alexander Solzhenitsyn and others have alleged, the Soviet Nobel prize-winning Mikhail Sholokov plagiarized *The Quiet Don* or parts of it from a minor Cossack novelist, Fedor Kryukov. Most of the simpler discriminators pointed toward Sholokov, but none decided the issue, so the texts had to be tagged. Frequencies of certain lexical categories favored Sholokov, but what clinched the case was word order. In the heavily inflected Russian language, word order is quite free. The researchers needed only use sequence of three lexical categories, because thousands of different such sequences are possible; and extensive sampling demonstrated that their frequencies are very reliable discriminators. *The Quiet Don* was not plagiarized.

A similar application, though less successful, is computational stylistics. A branch of literary criticism, stylistics investigates the verbal properties of literary language. That literary periods (such as the Renaissance), artistic movements (the Baroque), individual authors, or specific works have characteristic styles is beyond dispute, so it should be possible to describe them in terms of recurring choices among alternate possibilities offered by the language. Milton's poetry, for example, contains the recurring sequence, learned from Italian: adjective - noun - conjunction - adjective: *"sad task and hard*," and Jonathan Swift obsessively begins his sentences with connective words and phrases. Precise, systematic, objective descriptions of literary styles are scarce, however.

Some researchers believed that computational stylistics would set on a firm footing what hitherto had been "impressionistic." Their governing assumption was that a characteristic style represents a deviation from some norm. Norms, however, proved difficult to establish. Rigorous methodology requires many small samples, but samples exhibited too much variation. As for the characteristic styles, phenomena that proved statistically significant were usually obvious, needing no counts, whereas more interesting qualities either proved subtle, eluding identification, or did not occur frequently enough for reliable quantification. Then comes the difficulty of interpreting verbal properties in a way that is neither circular ("a high frequency of initial connectives suggests concern for transitions") nor arbitrary ("the diversity of sentence patterns argues a creative mind").

Although computational stylistics has enjoyed no dramatic successes, certainly nothing on the order of Mosteller and Wallace's, it has generated a wealth of information about macro-phenomena of language, particularly long-term trends in prose style. Among these trends is the steady rise of the attributive adjective, those preceding the noun. It began in the seventeenth century and continued until late in the nineteenth century when it was eclipsed by an explosive increase of attributive nouns. In either case information that might in an earlier prose style have occupied a subordinate construction following the noun is pushed to the front. Styles of individual writers also evolve over time, and computational projects have explored them, demonstrating for instance William Butler Yeats' style changes in ways that are primarily lexical rather than (as critics had supposed) syntactic. Comprehensive studies have been undertaken of writers as diverse as Jonathan Swift, Jane Austen, and Sylvia Plath.

Corpus research has also provided important information about the syntactic variation among genres of spoken and written language. One recent study, by Douglas Biber, investigated sixty-seven variables in twenty-three genres mainly from the LOB and London-Lund corpora. The genres included varieties of spoken English, both spontaneous and scripted, and a comparable range of written genres. Variables were frequencies of lexical categories and subcategories, as well as the frequencies of some tagged constructions. Factor analysis revealed patterns of co-occurrence among those variable that differed significant-ly from the norm. Patterns included high or low frequencies that occur together and those that co-vary in a complementary fashion so that a high frequency of one occurs systematically with a low frequency of the other. Several independent patterns emerged, most of them readily interpretable. One distinguishes between genres (mostly written) with a high density of information tightly integrated and interactive genres whose purpose is often affective rather than informative. Another distinguished those that integrate ideas and those that more gradually elaborate them. Rather than exhibiting sharp oppositions between speech and writing, genres occupied a continuum for each pattern with considerable overlap between written and spoken genres. Genres were differently grouped from pattern to pattern, independently varying along several dimensions. Thus Biber's study demonstrates that stylistic variations, though systematic, are multiple, complex and not readily reducible to dichotomies.

Exercises

1. The English verb system has three different kinds of auxiliary ("helping") verbs: forms of *to have* (*had, has, have, having*), of *to be* (*am, are, been, is, was, were*), and modals (*can, could, may, might, must, ought, should, would* etc.). Though the verbs are few enough to list, they could also be distinguished using test frames. Devise three test frames, each identifying members of one of the three groups. Trust your intuitions about what is and is not an allowable sequence of verbs.

2. To what lexical category would you assign each of the italicized words from Lewis Carroll's "Jabberwocky"? Which appears to be ambiguous as to lexical category? In each case, explain your reasoning.

> 'Twas *brillig* and the *slithy* toves
> Did *gyre* and gimble in the *wabe*;
> All *mimsy* were the borogroves,
> And the mome *raths* outgrabe.

3. Using the following semantic features and relations, as well as the graph notation, assemble lexical entries that would distinguish two senses of the verb *eat*:

> ANIMATE   [ ] ←(agent)– [ ]
> CONCRETE   [ ] ←(object)– [ ]
> CORROSIVE   [ ] ←(instrument)– [ ]
> EDIBLE
> UTENSIL

4. Describe a simple computational procedure that would list words in a text in such a way as to bring together many rhyming words. What would be required to bring together all rhyming words?

5. Explain the ambiguity in each of the following sentences. Then for each sentence, write another sentence or two the context of which would eliminate the ambiguity.

> The fisherman was the sole owner.
> I don't think he is that kind.
> The chicken was too hot to eat.
> Old women and men can enter first.
> He saw that gasoline can explode.
> Jen left directions for Nancy to follow.
> Landing airplanes can be dangerous.

6. One frequently cited statistic is the ratio of attributive adjectives (i.e. adjectives that precede the nouns they modify) to verbs, the supposition being that a verbal style is more vigorous, less florid than a style that relies heavily on adjectives. For several reasons, however, the statistic can be misleading. What would some of those reasons be? What information in addition to the adjective/verb ratio would you want to have?

Further reading

For an exhaustive account of the lexical categories in English, see Quirk, Greenbaum, Leech, and Svartvik (1985). On the mental representation of lexical information, see Aitchison (1987), and Evens (1989). On the problem of lexical disambiguation, the papers in Small, Cotrell, and Tanenhaus (1988) present a sampling of linguistic and computational approaches. Further discussion of superordinates and semantic features, case grammar and lexical stereotypes is provided in Chapters 8 and 9; and readings are given there. On collocations, see Mitchell (1971), Berry-Rogghe (1973), Mackin (1978), Cruse (1986), and Smadja and McKeown (1990). On aphasias see Kean (1978) and Caramazza and Berndt (1982).

Hockey (1980), Oakman (1984), and Butler (1985) discuss concordancing, attribution research, and other applications of computers to literary and linguistic research. Hockey and Marriott (1980) describe the OCP and Reed (1977) describes the CLOC. On the 2nd edition of the OED (Simpson and Weiner, 1989), see Hultin and Logan (1984), Weiner (1985), and the papers in *Information in Data* (1985). On attribution, see Mosteller and Wallace (1964) and Kjetsaa, Gustavsson, Beckman, and Gil (1984). Leech and Short (1981) and Burrows (1987) are excellent examples of the helpfulness of computers for rhetorical and thematic analysis of literary texts. For the York Inventory, see Cluett (1976); studies of individual authors include Milic (1967), Butler (1979), Jaynes (1980), and Burrows (1987). Potter (1988) offers a perceptive account of the difficulties encountered by computational stylistics. The journals *Computers and the Humanities*, the *Bulletin of the Association of Literary and Linguistic Computing* and its successor, *Literary and Linguistic Computing*, publish original research as well as review articles in the field.

On corpora, their compilation, analysis, and value, see Johansson (1982), Aarts and Meijs (1986), Meijs (1986), and Garside, Leech, and Sampson (1987) as well as the proceedings of the International Conference on English Language Research on Computerized Corpora and *ICAME News*, published by the International Computer Archive for Modern English. Descriptions of the corpora include: London-Oslo-Bergen Corpus: Johansson and Hofland (1989); the London-Lund Corpus of spoken British English: Svartvik and Quirk (1980); the International Corpus of English: Greenbaum (1990), the Birmingham Corpus, Renouf (1987) and the Data Collection Initiative: Liberman (1989). Aarts and van den Heuvel (1985), Atwell (1987), Garside (1987), Church (1988), and DeRose (1988) describe methods of tagging corpora. On the compilation of lexicons for natural language processing, see Ritchie, Pulman, Black, and Russell (1987), as well as the papers in the special issue of *Computational Linguistics* (Vol 13, Numbers 3-4, 1987) devoted entirely to the lexicon; also see the papers in Gellerstam (1988) and in Boguraev and Briscoe (1989). On SGML, see Coombs, Renear and DeRose (1987) and Meyer (1988). Frequency counts of the words in the Brown Corpus are reported in Francis and Kučera (1967); for frequencies of lexical categories, see Kučera and Nelson (1982). Johansson and Hofland (1989) provide frequency counts for lexical categories in the LOB corpus, as well as frequencies of preceding and following lexical categories. Woods, Fletcher, and Hughes (1986) and Butler (1985) discuss the opportunities and dangers presented by statistical analysis. Biber (1988) reports on the corpus study described in section 3.7; see also Biber (1989b).

Chapter 4

_____

Structure and Search

Section one: Lexical Information in Computer Memory

1.1 Memory and structure

Conceptually quite simple, computer memory resembles a vast chalkboard on which a grid has been painted, dividing the board into many thousands of tiny cells. Information can easily be written on the chalkboard and just as easily erased or changed. Again like the chalkboard, memory is passive, merely a series of locations capable of holding information. Each cell has room for a single byte; adjacent cells accept strings of characters, with the first cell specifying the string's length. Each cell has a numerical address, indicating its location within the grid. To fetch an item, only the first cell's address need be known. Called a **pointer**, the address points to a specific location in the grid. Using the pointer, together with the number of adjacent cells occupied by the item, the central processor has direct access to any item or list of items in memory.

Lists may have embedded in them additional pointers leading to noncontiguous addresses so that discrete pieces of information need not be adjacent in order to be associated with one another. Embedded pointers, as we will see, also afford protean flexibility, arranging information in structures that range from the elegantly simple to the most complex. Structures built of pointers can represent any relationship among words or any linguistic system of information.

Any scheme for representing a collection of discrete items such as a list of words is a **data structure**. The various structures–stacks and queues, lists and trees–incorporate straightforward relationships among items, chiefly sequence or categorization. But the primary purposes of data structures are to store self-contained, individual items and to facilitate their retrieval. They differ in this respect from methods of **knowledge representation**, where the aim is to represent entities in a context of relationships and the relationships have at least as much prominence as the entities. Thus in a data structure, components of a building might be represented either alphabetically in a list, or by categories in a tree:

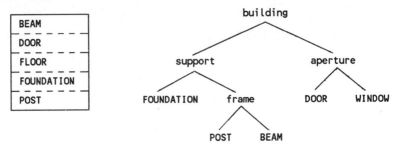

Represented as a fraction of our knowledge of walls and the relationships among their parts, the terms might look more nearly like this:

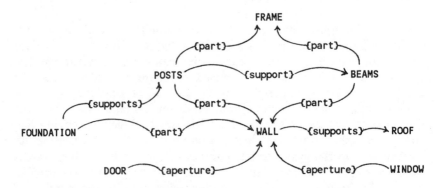

Notice the multiple interleaved relationships among constituents: the FOUNDATION, BEAMS and POSTS are all parts of WALL, and the FOUNDATION supports POSTS which in turn support BEAMS. To express these relationships adequately requires the more complicated network of links. Although the object is always to represent information in the most concise and perspicuous manner possible, expressive adequacy is even more important. For this reason, knowledge representation has become a major field of inquiry and a challenge.

1.2 Linear and linked lists

The most rudimentary information structure is the linear list, which simply places items in adjacent memory locations so that the sequence of their arrival is the only organizing principle. The list may simply

Stack: Queue: Circular queue:

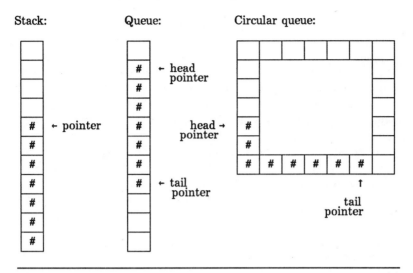

Figure 1. Linear data structures.

pile one item atop another in a **stack**; the spring device for stowing cafeteria trays illustrates the principle, and the operation is called a "push" (see Figure 1). A stack requires only one pointer giving the address of the topmost item. When the item is pushed on the stack, the single pointer is incremented by a number representing the number of cells occupied by the item. When an item is removed, as when trays are dispensed (an operation known as "pop"), the pointer is decreased by the same number. The essential property of a stack is that the last item added is the first removed, and thus a stack can be used to reverse the order of any list. That property lends itself to place-keeping functions; the quicksort procedure in the preceding chapter employs a stack as does the depth-first traversal described below. As we will see, the recursive transition networks and "shift reduce" will employ stacks to navigate the hierarchal structures of sentences. Stacks also afford a natural representation for the idea of recency; the topmost item is the most recent, the next is the next most recent, and so on. Recency plays a considerable role in linguistic analysis; for example, we will encounter stacks for holding potential antecedents for pronouns and for suspended segments of discourse.

Queues resemble stacks, except that they reverse the order of retrieval: a pointer at the head indicates where items should be added and another at the tail indicates the first to be retrieved. Since queues will migrate through memory as items are repeatedly added and removed, they can be made circular. After an allocated number of memory locations has been filled, the head pointer returns to where it began. If items are also being removed, the head chases the tail. Or the head may be allowed to overwrite items at the tail, maintaining a short, continually updated list of the most recently used words, for example, or the most recent choices among ambiguous senses of a word or phrase.

Much more flexibility can be obtained with **linked lists**, in which each item has stored with it one or more pointers leading to other items or lists of items occupying **nodes**. Pointers can be generated on demand and need not specify adjacent locations in memory; hence there is no need to decide ahead of time how long a list will be and to allocate an appropriate amount of space. Inserting a new node to follow an existing node requires only that the existing node's link be transferred to the new node and replaced by the address of the new node: there is no need to trundle nodes from place to place in physical memory.

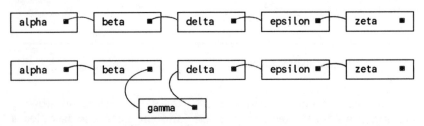

To facilitate the deleting of nodes or the rearranging of lists, each node can be supplied with two links, one pointing back to the previous node and the other pointing forward to the next. A doubly-linked list can be alphabetized simply by swapping the pointers of those words that are out of order.

Special header nodes make it possible to incorporate sublists within lists. Marked with tags (- in the example below) to identify them, headers consist only of pointers.

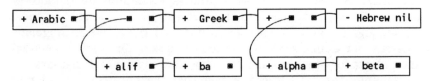

Because they are dynamic—able to grow, shrink or change shape in ways that need not be predictable at the outset—and because they can readily be updated or rearranged, linked lists are favored for many linguistic purposes. Even better, linked lists can represent the internal organization of information, its **logical order**, which (as we will see) need not be linear. Most programming languages can work with linked lists, and some, notably the favored language for work in artificial intelligence, LISP (an acronym for **list** processing), automate the management of pointers, making the lists themselves basic structures.

1.3 Hierarchical structures

By adding sublists to lists, we are moving in the direction of hierarchical structures. As useful as they are, one-dimensional linked lists are best suited for representing sequences of items, and many kinds of information are more accurately represented in two dimensions. Hierarchies group related items or gradually refine the distinctions among items. Trees may represent words in a thesaurus, structures of sentences, constituent meanings of words. There is even evidence that much discourse has an inherently hierarchical structure. The primary data structure for hierarchical relationships is the **tree**. A tree consists of one node (called the **root**) with no predecessors and one or more subsidiary nodes, each having one predecessor. Linking the nodes are pointers called branches. (By convention, trees are usually drawn with the root at the top and with branches extending downward from the root and other nodes.) One, two, or several branches extend downward from nodes, so that some trees or portions of trees are thin and others are bushy. The number of branches is known as the **branching factor**, a measure of the difficulty of search and other procedures and the time they will consume.

In a **binary tree**, nodes have at most two branches, offering a simple this-or-that choice, convenient for decision making. As it happens, many linguistic phenomena can be captured in binary trees. The tree in Figure 2 presents the ←(is a)− relations between semantic features as a hierarchy of alternatives. To proceed downward in the tree is to encounter increasingly more specific choices, each of them binary. Thus something is either located in space and time or is an ABSTRACTION. If it is located, it is either a PHYSICAL OBJECT or a SITUATION. SITUATIONs divide into TEMPORAL and STATIC, TEMPORAL divides into ACTs (breathing, walking) or EVENTs, and EVENTs divide by whether their outcomes are ACCOMPLISHMENTs (building or writing something) or ACHIEVEMENTs (arriving, destroying).

Such hierarchical arrangements can support the **inheritance**, with each node inheriting not only from its parent node but also from all nodes above it in a direct line of ascent. Thus HUMAN implies ANIMAL, ANIMATE, and SOLID and any attributes associated with those features. Inheritance makes for efficiency of representation in that a given attribute need be specified only once, at the highest appropriate level, and can be inherited by all superordinates. In the late 1960s, M. R. Quillian suggested that the human lexicon is organized to support inheritance of attributes. Evidence supporting his hypothesis comes

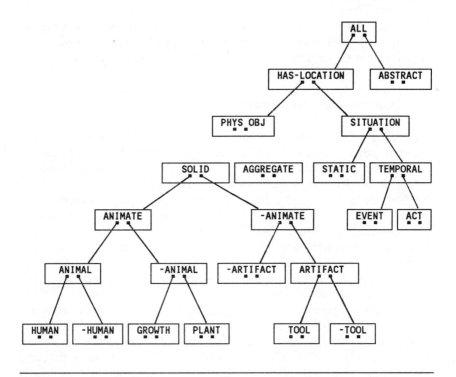

Figure 2. Semantic features as a binary tree.

from experiments in which subjects are asked questions like: Do canaries sing? / Do canaries fly? / Do canaries breathe? designed to elicit information from successive levels of an inheritance hierarchy. Response time is about a tenth of a second longer with *fly* than with *sing* and is longer still with *breathe,* suggesting that information in the mental lexicon is in part at least hierarchically structured:

$$
\begin{array}{ll}
\text{ANIMAL} & \leftarrow(\text{has part })-[\text{skin}] \\
& \leftarrow(\text{capable of})- [\text{movement}] \\
| & \\
(\text{is-a}) & \\
| & \\
\text{BIRD} & \leftarrow(\text{has part})-[\text{wings}] \\
& \leftarrow(\text{capable of})- [\text{flight}] \\
| & \\
(\text{is-a}) & \\
| & \\
\text{CANARY} & \leftarrow(\text{color})-[\text{yellow}] \\
& \leftarrow(\text{capable of})- [\text{singing}]
\end{array}
$$

Since it takes time to move up the hierarchy, response time is longer for attributes associated with superordinates. But problems quickly

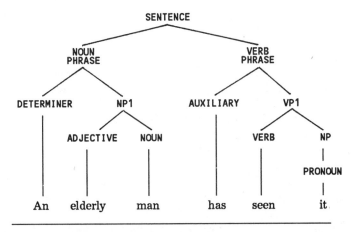

Figure 3. A phrase structure tree.

emerged with Quillian's theory, especially its explanation of response times. The effect could as easily be caused by habitual associations, and there was little difference in the time required to go one step up the hierarchy or two steps. A complicating factor is that, in addition to following existing links, comprehension actively computes new links to go with those already present. Nevertheless, vertical links supporting inheritance probably do have a role in human memory, where they combine with horizontal links of several kinds.   Certainly tree structures with inheritance have proved useful in computational semantics (and in nonlinguistic computation as well) for the efficiencies of storage and retrieval that they afford.

Information that is not inherently binary can often be represented in a binary tree by using place markers. For simplicity in stating grammatical rules, linguists often treat the structures of sentences as if they were binary and employ trees like the example in Figure 3, where NP1 and VP1 can be read "the rest of the phrase." Though binary structure is convenient, nodes in a tree may contain any arbitrary number of keys and of pointers, either to accommodate categories or subcategories that come in groups of three or more or to achieve efficiency in maintaining and searching the tree.

1.4 Networks and semantic networks

For some information, the most natural form of representation is a network. Yet another structure built using embedded pointers, a **network** is an assemblage of nodes attached either directly via links or indirectly via links and intermediate nodes, but connected in such a way that, potentially at least, there can be several paths between any two nodes. Paths may return eventually (or "cycle") to the node at which they began. Networks represent pieces of information that do not coalesce into a single uniform pattern (such as a tree), but are nevertheless associated. An example is the interwoven clusters of synonyms in a thesaurus, where one word is associated either directly or indirectly with an indeterminate number of others. Though networks afford a useful measure of freedom, the linking of nodes does not in itself express much information. Recall that a tree implies a hierarchy of specificity (whether of wholes and parts, classes and members, or whatever) and that hierarchy gives a meaning to each downward link. Unless some particular relation is specified, each link "means" only that items are associated, and that is not good enough, even for a thesaurus. A thesaurus can incorporate more information by assigning a weight to each link, giving the strength of the association: *newspaper* would be associated with its near synonym *tabloid* by a weight of +4, with *magazine* (also printed and appearing periodically) by +2, and with *book* by +1. Networks of weighted links have many applications, and the underlying idea, that links might be differentiated, has many more.

If links can specify different weights, they can also specify different relationships. A simple example is the **object-attribute-value** triplet used in many expert systems and some linguistics application. The triplets have two kinds of links: an ←(is)– link associates a specific value with the attribute and a new kind of link ←(has a)– attaches the attribute or property of an object to that object. The object may be any kind of entity, either physical or conceptual, and its attribute is some property or characteristic that it possesses. We might represent as an attribute of words its belonging to a lexical category:

[WORD] ←(has a)–[CATEGORY] ←(is)–[VALUE]

[give] ←(has a)–[CATEGORY] ←(is)–[verb]

Once we begin specifying different kinds of links, of course, we must specify procedures for interpreting them. It would not do, for example, to confuse ←(is a)– with ←(has a)– or ←(is)– because only the former supports inheritance. Despite this added complexity, labeled links are invaluable. For computational linguistics they form semantic networks, where the links carry fully as much information as do the nodes, and transition networks where links carry all the information and nodes are way stations.

"Semantic" refers to the labeling of links, not to linguistic semantics, though it was Quillian who first developed semantic networks to model his theory of the human lexicon. The links, drawn from a finite vocabulary of links, specify recurring propositions. For example, the fragment ←(part)–[binding] expresses the (true) proposition that the

a. network representation of the verb *sell*.

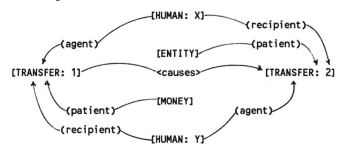

b. fragment of a definitional network.

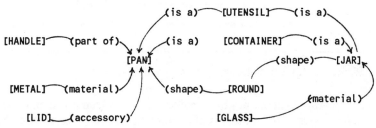

c. semantic representation of *With his nose the dog pushed his bowl.*

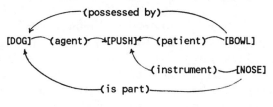

Figure 4. Semantic networks.

---

binding is part of a book. Information in a semantic network resides not only in its nodes and labeled links but also in the structure that they compose. Thus, [bindings] ←(part)–[book], which reverses constituents, expresses the false proposition that bindings have books among their parts.

Semantic networks come in many forms, small and large; see Figure 4. Sometimes it is natural to represent and manipulate linguistic information in manageable pieces (which psychologists refer to as "chunking"). Associating the several cases with each verb is an example. For each verb, the lexicon would contain a small semantic network representing its meaning in terms of expected cases. Alterna-

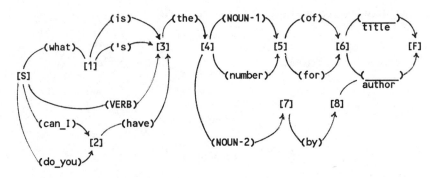

VERB = give, show, print, find, retrieve

NOUN-1 = author, authors, writer, writers

NOUN-2 = book, books, volume, volumes, edition, editions

Figure 5. A transition network for predictable inquiries.

tively, the lexicon might consist of a vast semantic network which defines each word in terms of a constellation of other words. Networks can also incorporate the results of syntactic or semantic analysis of a sentence. Notice that the sentence network has two cycles leading from *dog* back to *dog*, one by way of ←(possessed by)– and the other via ←(is part)– relations, because identification of both *nose* and *bowl* depends on *dog*. When ←(is a)–relations connect members of a group to a group (as in the definitional network), they can support inheritance. Each member inherits the relationships that define the group; thus *pan* can share the attributes of UTENSILS and CONTAINERS.

Transition networks represent sequential patterns and recognize them step by step. The patterns may include optional, alternative, or repeatable elements. An example of such a pattern is the configuration of syntactic and (sometimes) semantic elements that constitute well-formed sentences, even the constituents of stereotypical discourse or conversation. Consider the network in Figure 5, which has the humbler purpose of recognizing predictable queries to a library's card catalog. It consists of a series of numbered nodes, called **states**, linked to other states by one or more outgoing **arcs.** Arcs specify words, phrases, or (in upper case) categories of words to be compared with the user's sentence. Beginning at the initial state, each outgoing arc is tried in turn, and if there is a match, that arc can be traversed to a new state. To traverse the entire network from the initial to the final state is to recognize the query and identify whether it is a title or author. Though there are other ways of representing information and of controlling procedures, transition networks have the advantage that they do both and in a straightforward, entirely transparent manner.

1.5 Frames and systems of frames

Many linguistic applications call for an especially adaptive form of knowledge representation known as a structured object or **frame**. Frames can be visualized as small networks with labeled slots (or "roles") at the nodes. Some slots contain information that is necessarily true. Others have easily displaced defaults that encode expectations or typical attributes (such as those in a lexical prototype) and sometimes allow processing to proceed even in the face of missing information. Still other slots may be vacant, indicating only the potential for information of a given kind. The essential idea (usually credited to Marvin Minsky) is that frames represent typical instances or routine events and situations, schemata for representing lexical prototypes, as well as the scripts and plans for sequences of routine or causally related events are linguistic examples.

The frame in Figure 6 gives a prototype for *professor* that might serve as a lexical entry. It stipulates that only two pieces of information are certain: a professor is necessarily a person and is engaged in an occupation. That he or she teaches, does research and has a college or university affiliation are likely enough to serve as defaults. No prediction can be made about the professor's discipline or specialty within that discipline, except that constraints govern the vacant slots, limiting potential fillers only to those that are appropriate. Thus frames provide four kinds of knowledge: that which is certain, that which is typical, that which constrains, and that which can be inferred. Knowledge of all four kinds, as we will see, is often essential for linguistic applications.

Not all the information given in a frame is declarative. Frames gain much of their expressive power by incorporating procedural information as well. Attached to some of the slots are small, self-activated procedures, called **demons**, whose purpose is to fetch information or make inferences. If, for example, only the specialty of a given professor is mentioned, his or her discipline can usually be inferred. The demon would first establish whether the slot for specialty is filled. Finding there a Chaucerian, it could then consult a table giving English literature as the discipline. (Alternately, if the slot were empty and *Chaucerian* appeared in a sentence being interpreted, a morphologically knowledgeable demon might react to its suffix by consulting the table, then fill the slot.) Since frames typically belong to hierarchies of frames (thus PROFESSOR descends from PERSON and OCCUPATION frames), an important role of demons is to fetch information from other frames. Occupations, for example, have salaries; by consulting OCCUPATION, a demon could explicate a reference to the "professor's salary." Sometimes demons undertake tasks of greater complexity. They can, for example, analyze syntax so as to resolve ambiguities, establishing perhaps that a mention of George Washington refers to the professor's

$$
\left[
\begin{array}{l}
\text{PROFESSOR} \\
\text{\textleftarrow(is a)-}\;\; \big[\;\text{HUMAN}\;\big] \\
\text{\textleftarrow(instance)-}\;\; \big[\qquad\qquad\big] \\
\text{\textleftarrow(identified by)-}\;\; \big[\;\text{OCCUPATION}\;\big] \\
\text{\textleftarrow(function)-}\;\; \big[\;\text{constraint: research and/or teach}\;\big] \\
\text{\textleftarrow(affiliation)-}\;\; \Big[\;\text{constraint: college or university or institute or none}\;\Big] \\
\text{\textleftarrow(discipline)-}\; \left[\begin{array}{l} \big[\;\text{constraint: academic discipline}\;\big] \\ \big[\;\text{procedure: if (specialty) filled, consult discipline/specialty list}\;\big] \end{array}\right] \\
\text{\textleftarrow(specialty)-}\;\; \big[\;\text{constraint: academic specialty}\;\big]
\end{array}
\right]
$$

Figure 6. Prototype frame for the word *professor*.

specialty rather than his institution. In that they incorporate both knowledge and methods for obtaining knowledge, frames join in a single structure two modes of representation, the declarative and the procedural, which though complementary, have historically been in competition.

Systems that employ frames in modeling language comprehension assume that human memory is not a huge network of nodes, but is instead partitioned into smaller chunks functioning as wholes with inheritance and other links between chunks. This assumption has sound basis in theory and is supported by some empirical evidence. It has been widely adopted, not only in computational linguistics but also in psychology and the other cognitive sciences. Chunking of information, though there is much to recommend it, also raises difficult questions. What information does the frame contain? Is the information primarily linguistic or could it include anything that we know about, say, professors? How detailed is the information? Though very comprehensive, very detailed frames would predict that sentences contain much less information than in fact they do; principled ways of determining what should be included and what excluded have proved elusive.

1.6 Contents addressable memory

All the structures discussed in the preceding sections and others even more elaborate can be implemented with a conventional computer. But a single processor governing one large bank of memory (a design that goes back to the earliest days of computing) can be very inefficient, especially with semantic networks and with structures of frames. Accessing memory typically takes longer, much longer than making decisions, so the central processor spends much of its time waiting idly for something to do while information is shuffled in and out. As a consequence, knowledge-hungry applications, which include many linguistic applications, run very slowly.

Recent advances in computer architecture promise a solution. Whereas conventional memory is passive, capable only of holding information, not seeking it out, active memory consists of several thousands, even tens of thousands, small, simple processors each governing a small collection of memory cells. Each processor operates individually matching the content of the request against the content of its memory cells. To distinguish it from memory that is addressed by locations, active memory is often called **content addressable memory**. Processors are wired together so that search requests can be passed from one to another and, when a search is successful, a signal sent through the memory at a rate faster than the request cancels it. Multiple linked processors mean that several areas of memory can be searched simultaneously or several searches for different pieces of information can proceed concurrently.

Since the goal is to gain speed without sacrificing flexibility, the configuration of processors is very important. One possibility is to be wire processors in a loop, with each processor linked to two immediate neighbors. Loops make it simple to pass requests, allow a search to proceed on clockwise and counterclockwise paths simultaneously, and permit separate concurrent searches. But within a loop each search proceeds sequentially from one processor to the next, and since it takes time for a processor to receive a request and pass it along, loop structures entail too much delay. At the opposite extreme, each processor could be wired to every other processor. A fully inter-connected network would not necessarily be more efficient, however, because message passing consumes time and the first processor would be sequentially passing messages to each of the others. Better would be a configuration that minimizes the number of messages passed by each processor while maximizing the number of processors at one remove, two removes and so on.

The intriguing geometry of the "n-cube" or hypercube does just that. First visualize an ordinary three-dimensional cube or 3-cube. It would have eight processors corresponding to the cube's eight vertices, with each processor wired to three others as if along the three edges of the cube. Now imagine a four-dimensional "hypercube" or 4-cube with sixteen processors, each connected to four others. (The geometry, of course, is only conceptual; it is simulated physically by wiring processors together.) A 5-cube has thirty-two processors, each connected to five others, a 6-cube has sixty-four, and so on up to the twelve or more dimensions of commercially available systems. Paths through a hypercube are optimally short (the most distant processor is only N removes away) and the number of connections supported by each processor (also N) is reasonable. Because each of the multiple processors can be individually instructed, active memory is extraordinarily flexible. Memory can be configured (by selectively disabling connections) to match the inherent structure of the data: whether it's a tree or a tangled hierarchy (that is, a tree that also has connections going sideways and upward).

Hypercube

Neighboring processors can govern groups of associated words, and a processor can "prime" its neighbors, instructing them to take precedence in responding to any subsequent search request. Abundant empirical evidence suggests that something very much like this takes place when human beings retrieve words from their mental lexicons. Chapter five describes a method of searching that simulates lexical priming in a network that resembles the neuronal structure of mammalian brains. Active memory can accomplish even more. Processors assigned to each sense of every word in a sentence might be supplied with syntactic and semantic contexts into which the word sense can enter, then instructed to search out feasible combinations with other words. Eventually arriving at a combination that accounts for every word, they would in effect explicate the syntactic and semantic structure of the sentence. This is one of several research applications of parallel processing to the problem of sentence comprehension, and we will return to it after a closer look at the structures of sentences.

Section two: Lexical Search and Retrieval

2.1 Motivations

In most language applications, computers spend more time locating and retrieving information from memory than they spend on all other activities combined. From the earliest days of computing when an inventor of the computer also invented a elegant method of searching an alphabetized list, to the recent development of connectionist networks capable of spontaneous learning, search has proved to be a challenging, fruitful realm of inquiry and has become one of the most highly developed fields of computer science.

All things being equal, it is easiest to search an alphabetical list (consider the prospect of looking in an ordinary telephone directory for a number rather than a name), but sometimes alphabetizing is not appropriate. The reason may be that a list is volatile, so constantly changing that re-alphabetizing in order to search it is not feasible. The structure of information may be meaningful and must be preserved, as in a syntactic tree, a semantic network or, for that matter, in ordinary text.

Sometimes the information to be located mitigates against alphabetical searches, as when the object is to find similarly spelled words (so that a spelling checker can suggest corrections). Other possible search targets include similarly pronounced words, semantically associated words, or co-occurring words (in an index to documents, for example). Sometimes search strategies improve on the speed of alphabetical searching by taking advantage of such properties of language as the extreme variations in word frequency or the special capabilities of parallel processing computers. No one method of searching is best for all situations, and new solutions are constantly emerging. A particularly dramatic example occurred in the late 1970s when, after nearly thirty years of ploddingly slow, character-by-character text searches, a fast and reliable method was discovered that literally skips through texts.

2.2 Binary search for an alphabetical list

Less than two years after he and J. Presper Eckert built the first digital computer, John Mauchley described an elegant and remarkably efficient algorithm for **binary search** of an alphabetically ordered list. His method and variants of it are still in daily use. A close cousin to quicksort, binary search achieves its efficiency in much the same way; it successively divides the search area until the object of search is found or proved to be absent. (Figure 7 gives the simple algorithm.)

For an idea of how binary searching achieves its efficiency, think of a series of sixty-three words as if they were arranged in a tree, where the middle word occupies the root, the middle words of each half occupy the two branches from that root, and so on (see Figure 8.) Now consider the task of finding *run*. The procedure would begin by comparing *run* with *low*, the middle word of the sixty-three word list. Discovering that *run* and *low* do not match and that run comes later in the alphabet, it compares *run* with *saw*, which is in the middle of

#1 Find the middle word of the list

#2 IF the middle word is equal to or greater than the target

    THEN   IF the middle word does not equal the target

        THEN   IF words remain in the list

            THEN   set the boundaries of the list to extend from the beginning to the word preceding the middle word and go to #1

            ELSE   report failure.

        ELSE report success.

    ELSE   set the boundaries of the list to extend from the word following the middle word to the end and go to #1

Figure 7.   An algorithm for binary search.

the second half of the list. The procedure continues, comparing *run* with *one*, *per*, and *red* until eventually it finds a match. Only six comparisons are needed to find the forty-seventh word on the list. And *run* is one of the worst cases: four comparisons find *air*. If the list is increased to one hundred and twenty-seven words, only one more comparison is needed for the worst case. The thirty- to sixty-thousand English words in common use would require sixteen or seventeen comparisons, the four hundred and fifty-thousand words in an unabridged dictionary of English would require twenty comparisons, and a census of the five- to six-billion people currently inhabiting the earth would require only thirty-five. The longer the list, the greater the efficiency.

2.3 Search trees

To use binary search, it is necessary to maintain the list in alphabetical order; this means that for each addition or deletion the list must be sorted. If the list is volatile, with many additions and deletions, the frequent moving of words from place to place becomes burdensome. One solution is the **binary search tree**. The alphabetical list is structured as a tree with each word occupying a node. Each node also contains at most two pointers, a "left" pointer to a word preceding it in the alphabet and a "right" pointer to a word following it. (See Figure 9, top.) Adding words is merely a matter of searching the tree for an appropriate parent node, then adjusting pointers. Words already in the tree do not need to be moved. Though deleting words is somewhat more complicated, it too can be accomplished without shifting words.

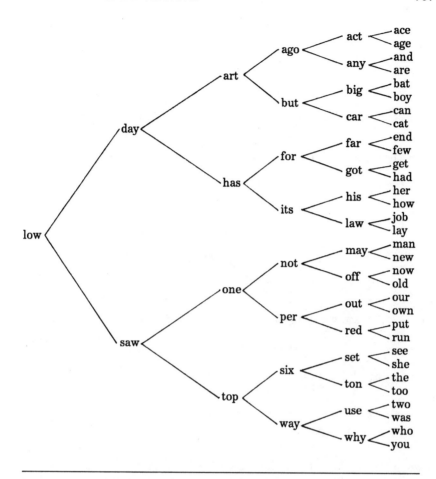

Figure 8. Tree representation of binary search.

Once words have been added or deleted, the tree will no longer be optimal, but as long as it remains reasonably balanced, searching will be efficient. The method of searching resembles binary search. At each step the target word is compared with the word at the present node. If it does not match, either the left or the right pointer is pursued depending on whether the target alphabetically precedes or follows the word at the node.

   If a binary search tree becomes asymmetrical with the lowest leaves at many levels, the tree loses its efficiency and search times degenerate especially for the worst case. One popular answer is the balanced or **B tree**, a non-binary (or "multi-way") tree that has become the workhorse for data storage including lexicons of all sorts. B-trees store multiple keys at each node as well as pointers to more than just the two descendants of a binary tree. Failing to find *cat* at the highest

Binary tree fragment

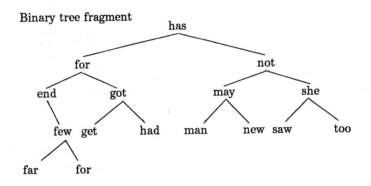

B-tree fragment

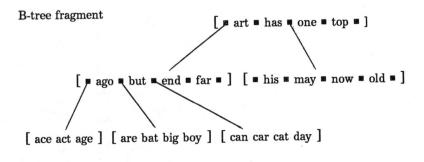

Figure 9. Search trees.

node in Figure 9 (bottom), the search would follow the pointer between *art* and *has*; failing to find *cat* at the second level it would follow the pointer between *but* and *end*. The effort required to search the tree and the time required to reorganize it (when insertions and deletions are made) are minimized by restricting the number of keys and the branching factor at each internal node to vary only within mathematically defined optima. Once the limits are exceeded, the tree is reorganized (an automated procedure), but they are sufficiently broad that reorganization does not become too frequent. Limits also guarantee, of course, that the tree never becomes so unbalanced as to require inordinately long searches and in particular they constrain the worst case. This underlying strategy is so effective that the B tree has spawned many variants, each suited to a particular purpose. Some applications, for instance, require that data also be available for retrieval in sequence, so that it is possible, say, to generate an alphabetical list of the words in a lexicon or a dictionary. In a **B+ tree**, the internal nodes consist only of pointers, and the keys are in leaf nodes where a single left-to-right scan will retrieve them in order.

2.4 Accommodating frequency and recency

Is there any order other than alphabetical that yields faster access to words? In particular, is there any way of minimizing the number of times that search must go deep into the tree? Because all its words are at the deepest level of the tree in Figure 8, the six words of *man can see the new age now* actually requires more comparisons, three more, than the eight words of *but one day art may not top its old act.* Abundant empirical research suggests that the speed with which humans retrieve words from their mental lexicons (averaging less than a fifth of a second) is substantially affected by recency and word frequency. The more recent our last encounter with the word or the more frequent the word, the more quickly it is retrieved. The two are, of course, related in that the more frequent a word, either in the language at large or in the subject at hand, the more likely that it has been used recently.

Frequency and recency have obvious implications for search routines, because the efficiency of a routine such as binary search assumes equally frequent queries for each word. The list of sixty-three words given in Figure 8 contains *are*, *the*, and *was*, three of the most frequently occurring words in the language, with a combined frequency of about 108/1000 words. Each would require six comparisons, whereas the three words requiring the fewest comparisons, *low*, *day*, and *saw*, have a combined frequency of only about 1/1000 words: not a satisfactory state of affairs. We could take refuge in Zipf's law that the Nth most common word occurs with a frequency inversely proportional to N and in the resultant probability that sequentially searching a list ordered by frequency will require about fifty percent as many comparisons as searching the same list in random order. However, that would mean giving up the efficiency of binary search, because the keys would no longer be in alphabetical order; and for a list of more than a few items, binary searching provides much more than a fifty percent savings.

A better solution employs nodes and pointers to build a search tree that minimizes the number of comparisons needed to find frequently occurring words, while preserving at each step the simple choice of whether to go higher in the alphabet or lower. Algorithms for building such trees weigh the implications of each choice-point in terms of the frequency of words on either side, starting with the smaller subtrees and working back toward the major branches. **Weighted binary search trees** come into their own when the frequency of words within a subject domain is known (the frequency of most content words in the language at large is too low to justify the expense), when the lexicon will not require frequent updating and memory is sufficient to accommodate not only words but a structure of pointers. If those conditions are not met, a weighted binary search tree can be the first

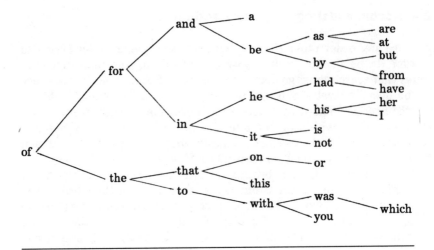

Figure 10. A weighted binary tree.

of two or more tiers in a lexicon that would separate them from recent
words and from still others that are neither frequent nor recent:

weighted binary tree for the most frequent words	→	circular queue for the most recent words	→	general dictionary

This tiered approach, though without the refinement of the recency
queue, has been proposed as a model for the human lexicon. The
model has the most frequent words, which are also those learned
earliest, occupying a special section allowing the quickest access.

Restricting the weighted binary tree to only the few very common
words would exploit an important exception to Zipf's law: with the
very most common words, frequency declines not gradually but
precipitously. Thus the weighing of choices makes the most difference
for these words; for the thirty-one most common words, it would
produce an unbalanced, but nevertheless binary tree. (See Figure 10.)
If the target word does not appear on this first list, the procedure
might consult a circular queue consisting of several dozen words used
most recently. For lexicons that include the word class of each word,
the queue might be limited to content words, since they are more likely
to come in clusters. Failing to find the word in either the frequency
tree or the recency queue, the procedure would then enter a binary
search of the alphabetically ordered general dictionary which constitutes the third tier. The tiered approach is, of course, independent of
the method of searching at any one tier. The spelling checker of one

popular word processor looks first in a dictionary of twenty-five hundred common words, then in a supplementary list compiled by the user. Only if the word occurs in neither list is the main dictionary, consisting of more than a hundred thousand words, consulted.

Another efficient way of representing function words and other small lists of very frequently occurring words is the **trie** (derived from re*trie*val, but pronounced to rhyme with *pie* in order to distinguish it from *tree*). Applied to language, trie searching would represent the spellings of words in a tree structure with branches that diverge where the spellings diverge. The following fragment of a trie, for example, represents the words *the, then, that, than, to, we, when, whom, when,* and *where:*

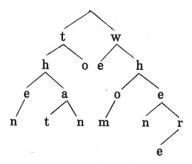

Trie searching for these spellings is efficient because at most only two characters, rather than entire words, need be matched at each decision point—a significant savings for frequently searched lists. But efficiency rapidly degrades as the branching factor increases, so some tries represent only the first few characters in words as branches, supplying the remainder of each word at the nodes. When more than a few hundred words must be represented, however, some other method (usually a B tree) will be more efficient.

2.5 Traversing trees and networks

Searching an alphabetically ordered structure such as the weighted binary tree is self-directing; comparing the target word with the word at each node determines whether to go lower in the alphabet or higher. As we have seen, however, trees may represent non alphabetic methods of ordering information. The hierarchy of features is a binary tree with gradually narrowing categories (ANIMATE, HUMAN, and so on), and a tree-structured thesaurus clusters words of similar meanings within a non binary tree that is shallow and quite bushy. When the search cannot be self-directing, it is necessary to **traverse** the tree, visiting the nodes in an arbitrary, predetermined sequence:

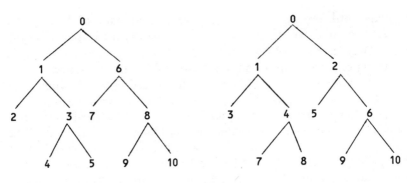

Depth-first traversal   Breadth-first traversal

For binary trees, **depth-first traversal** begins at the root, takes left turns when available, takes right turns where it cannot turn left, and moves up one level and to the right when no downward course is open. (Giving precedence to left turns is merely a convention and the order could just as easily be the reverse.) The effect is to plunge rapidly to the bottom of the tree then slowly wind back upward. **Breadth-first traversal** does the opposite, visiting all nodes at each level from left to right and gradually working its way down through the tree. Either method assures that every node in the tree will, if necessary, be visited. When thoroughness is the only objective, depth-first traversal is preferred, because easier to design.

The ordering of nodes in a tree, however, is itself important information and the order of traversal is therefore significant. There may, for example, be reason to give priority to the lower or higher nodes. If words are arranged in the order of decreasing frequency, a breadth-first search would be in order. For trees of increasing specificity–words and their superordinates, for example– breadth-first search would give priority to the superordinates. Even the process of analyzing the structures of sentences turns out to be a matter of traversing a hierarchy, for which there are depth-first and breadth-first parsing strategies. Though these are basic orders, each with many applications, other possibilities exist, including methods of traversing trees from the bottom upward. Document retrieval systems, for instance, often consult a keyword thesaurus in order to convert some of the specific words in a user's query into the more general "preferred terms" by which the documents have been indexed. An initial stage in the search would restrict itself to the lowest levels only, below the preferred terms; then, upon encountering the user's word, probe upward through the hierarchy to discover the preferred term under which it is subsumed.

For some idea of what a traversal can accomplish and how it is done, consider Figure 11, where the task is to search for the minimum common supertype of two lexical features and (in the example) to learn

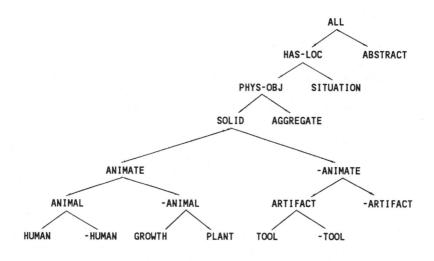

Action:	Content of stack:
Descend to HAS-LOC	ALL
Descend to PHYS-OBJ	HAS-LOC ALL
Descend to SOLID	PHYS-OBJ HAS-LOC ALL
Descend to ANIMATE	SOLID PHYS-OBJ HAS-LOC ALL
Descend to ANIMAL	ANIMATE SOLID PHYS-OBJ HAS-LOC ALL
Descend to HUMAN	ANIMAL ANIMATE SOLID PHYS-OBJ HAS-LOC ALL
	└─ copy stack
Ascend to ANIMAL	ANIMATE SOLID PHYS-OBJ HAS-LOC ALL
Descend to −HUMAN	ANIMAL ANIMATE SOLID PHYS-OBJ HAS-LOC ALL
Ascend to ANIMAL	ANIMAL ANIMATE SOLID PHYS-OBJ HAS-LOC ALL
Ascend to ANIMATE	SOLID PHYS-OBJ HAS-LOC ALL
Descend to −ANIMAL	ANIMATE SOLID PHYS-OBJ HAS-LOC ALL
Descend to GROWTH	−ANIMAL ANIMATE SOLID PHYS-OBJ HAS-LOC ALL
Ascend to −ANIMAL	ANIMATE SOLID PHYS-OBJ HAS-LOC ALL
Descend to PLANT	−ANIMAL ANIMATE SOLID PHYS-OBJ HAS-LOC ALL
Ascend to −ANIMAL	ANIMATE SOLID PHYS-OBJ HAS-LOC ALL
Ascend to ANIMATE	SOLID PHYS-OBJ HAS-LOC ALL
Ascend to SOLID	PHYS-OBJ HAS-LOC ALL
Descend to −ANIMATE	SOLID PHYS-OBJ HAS-LOC ALL
Descend to ARTIFACT	−ANIMATE SOLID PHYS-OBJ HAS-LOC ALL
Descend to TOOL	ARTIFACT −ANIMATE SOLID PHYS-OBJ HAS-LOC ALL
	└─ compare stack with copy

Figure 11. Traversing a tree to locate minimum common supertypes.

what *I* with the feature HUMAN has in common with my *computer* (TOOL). Each of these features implies others (thus HUMAN implies ANIMAL, ANIMATE and so on) and the minimum common supertype of HUMAN and TOOL is the most specific feature implied by both. Thus the traversal will not only locate HUMAN and TOOL, but will also establish the relationship between them. In effect, finding a path between two features will retrieve information that is implicit in the ordering of nodes in the tree.

This mildly challenging task has a straightforward solution. Assume a tree with pointers leading downward, together with an ancillary stack for help in negotiating the tree. (Often it is possible to dispense with stacks by reversing the links or by following "threads," special pointers that lead from one segment of the tree to another; but our procedure for finding supertypes will have a second reason for using a stack.) The depth-first traversal plunges rapidly downward, then moves laterally. At each step the stack keeps track of addresses that have been visited so that each time the traversal reaches a dead end, it can recover by retrieving the address atop the stack. Upon encountering the feature of either word (in the example, HUMAN is encountered first), the procedure copies and saves the addresses presently on the stack. The search resumes, looking now for the feature of *computer*. The traversal then scours the lower levels of the tree, looking for TOOL among the most specific features. Once TOOL is located, the addresses on the stack are compared with those in the copy, following the last-in, first-out order of retrieval. The first match is the minimum common supertype.

Breadth-first and depth-first traversals are thorough, sometimes too thorough. If the tree to be searched is very deep or the branching factor is large, the search space must be limited to those portions of the tree most likely to contain the target. What is known about the target will suggest limits. For example, primitives that serve as constraints (as when *drive* requires a VEHICLE as object and a PLACE as destination) are by nature inclusive; thus a search for them should not descend very deep into the tree. The answer is a **bounded** search that prevents the traversal from going deeper than some arbitrary level before reascending to explore collateral branches. To prevent traversal from straying too far from some a particular node or descending path, lateral boundaries can also be stipulated. Sometimes it is useful to specify costs of exploring alternative paths and use these to constrain the search. A large semantic network may offer multiple ways of reaching a goal, some of them via (let's say) very general concepts, others via specific concepts. Each link would have an associated cost. If the path is likely to be shorter via the general concepts, the links that join them would have lower costs than the links leading to specific concepts. At each step in the traversal, the processor chooses the alternative with the least cost.

2.6 Marker passing for concurrent searches

The search for the minimal common supertype was unilateral. Starting from the root node, it found one type, then the other. Next it consulted the stack to determine the minimal common supertype. Bilateral concurrent traversal is also possible and, in searching for connections between two distant nodes in a network, is usually more efficient. Imagine two search processes, each moving outward from separate locations in the network. (With a conventional computer, concurrence would be simulated by alternating between the processes.) As each visits a node, it marks it and provides a reverse pointer backward in the direction from which it has come. Eventually, one will come upon a node that has been marked by the other and will have a complete path (via the reverse pointers) between the two locations in the network. It may not, however, be the shortest path between the two network locations, so the traversals may continue, eventually finding multiple paths, some of them reasonably direct, others more circuitous. There must, of course, be some point at which paths are abandoned (usually a set number of nodes); otherwise the process would continue until all nodes in the network were marked. This is the essential idea behind **marker passing**. If concurrent search processes mark all nodes adjacent to the nodes at which they begin, and then all nodes adjacent to those, gradually radiating outward, marker passing simulates a theory of how human memory operates by **spreading activation**.

Marker passing and spreading activation have several linguistic applications. Programs for understanding discourse build "plans" for a causal or whole-substep relation between two actions. Let's say, for example, that it has reason to suppose a relationship between *going to the store* and *preparing supper*. Associated with *store* are various subtypes: hardware stores and boutiques, pharmacies and super-markets, as well as the several actions one performs in stores, the viewing, querying, selecting, paying, receiving change and more. Associated with supermarkets are food and potables and everything else that a supermarket sells. Associated with *supper* are preparing food, eating food, and so on. The task of a marker passing algorithm is to discover the step-by-step relationship between going to the store and preparing supper.

Spreading activation may play a role in recognizing words in the stream of continuous speech and in disambiguating words with multiple senses. For word recognition, the idea is that any perceived portion of an incompletely articulated word activates all words containing a similar sequence of phonemes or set of phonemic features. For lexically ambiguous words, there is strong evidence that all senses of the word are activated, at least for a short time, even in biasing contexts. One experiment demonstrated that hearers activated both the "insect" and "electronic listening device" sense of *bug*, even though the context strongly favored the entomological sense. If a vocabulary of word meanings is represented in a large semantic network with conceptual nodes (such as PHYSICAL OBJECT, HUMAN, –ADULT) and relational links (is a, has part, and so on), or if related words are closer to one another than are unrelated words, finding the shortest paths between the incompletely articulated word or the ambiguous sense and other words or concepts in the immediate context will select one possibility and reject the others. In effect, multiple words or word senses compete to find the shortest path to the contextual words. Consider the two meanings of *ball* in *the plastic ball* and *the masked ball*. The search might radiate out in several directions, some of them inappropriate, but eventually it would establish that *ball* in *the plastic ball* is the physical object. The path would be much shorter from *ball*, a sphere that is a physical object, to *plastic*, a material of which physical objects can be composed, than the roundabout path from a *ball*, a dance via event, not a physical object, an entity.

Marker passing and spreading activation are not entirely new ideas, though they are drawing increased attention now that parallel processing computers are available. They derive from Quillian's original proposal for semantic networks, have been implemented for conventional computers and have proved feasible if the search space is not overly large. (It helps that related concepts are often near one another.) What makes marker passing and spreading activation especially interesting now is the advent of massively parallel computers. The computer might have one processor for each memory cell or a small cluster of cells, with all of the processors–hundreds, even thousands of them–linked to form a vast network. Processors simply send messages to neighboring processors, which forward them to their neighbors and so on, propagating the search throughout the network. Because processors would be acting autonomously, the time required to find the shortest path would depend only on the length of the path; any other paths than the shortest would not be relevant to the search time. Thus marker passing by spreading activation would be an optimal method of searching a parallel processing network.

Section three: Special-Purpose Searching

3.1 Hashing and surrogate keys

By expending a small amount of time to make calculations as items are added to a list, **scatter storage** (commonly known as **hashing**) results in rapid searches, sometimes faster even than those using the binary method, and it does not require that the list be alphabetized. The idea is to set up a table that stores the items, to give item in the table addresses by which the computer can gain direct access, and (here's the interesting part) to generate those addresses by extracting information that uniquely identifies each item. The extracted information reduces or "hashes" the item to a number. To search the list for a given item, the computer can extract the same information, thereby generating the address and gaining direct access to the item. Let's say the task is to compile a list of frequent collocations, such as *by and large* and *catch sight of* and their meanings. We can extract two pieces of information from each item: the first character's position in the alphabet (2 for *b*, 3 for *c*) and the number of characters (12 and 14, including spaces), then add the numbers together, yielding 14 for *by and large* and 17 for *catch sight of*.

Those could be our addresses, but an additional step will yield a more compact table. For simple arithmetic, the total size of the table will be nine and thus 14, 17, and other numbers higher than 9 should systematically be converted to numbers between 0 and 8. One way is to divide the numbers by 9 and use the remainder for our address, since that remainder will necessarily be a number between 0 and 8. (This peculiar idea of dividing in order to obtain, not the quotient, but a remainder is modulo arithmetic.) Dividing 14 by 9 yields a remainder of 5, which will be the address for *by and large*; for *catch sight of* the address is 8. This entire process, from extracting the information to constructing the table, would be programmed; we would only supply the collocations. Figure 12 gives a hash table containing our two phrases and a few others. Now we can search the table. Does an entry explain the meaning of *on hand*? The computer calculates its potential address by adding 15 for *o* to 7, the length, dividing the total by 9, and obtaining the remainder 4 as the place to look.

This calculating of addresses may seem too good to be true. Binary search, for all its efficiency, usually entails some trial and error, whereas hashing promises direct access, obviating any need to search. Hashing cannot guarantee unique addresses, however. The first character's position in the alphabet and the length of the phrase, together with the modulo arithmetic, provide reasonable scatter for a short table. By extracting more information, we would do even better, but almost inevitably there will be cases in which hashing provides the same address for two different phrases. The present method, for example, yields 8 as the address for *strike a bargain*, but *catch sight of* already has that address. This is known as a **collision**. Except for very sparsely occupied tables, the probability of collision is rather high. Consider von Mises' "birthday paradox": invite to a party twenty-three people chosen at random and despite the 365 possibilities, chances are slightly better than even that two of them will have the same day and month of birth; invite eighty-eight people and the chances are that three will share a birthday.

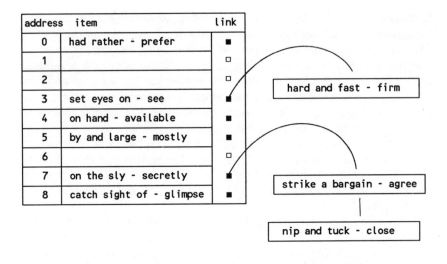

Figure 12. Hash table of collocations and their meanings.

Even if collisions were just possible (rather than probable), they must be dealt with. The simplest strategy creates "buckets" for multiple items at each address and has them searched sequentially. A different strategy provides for *ad hoc* linking of items, as shown in Figure 12; the link is simply an address in a predefined overflow table. Yet another strategy, known as "open addressing," attempts to fill empty ("open") addresses in the hash table by mathematically permuting the hash address into a sequence of new numbers, which become potential addresses for the item. Though open addressing conserves memory, it necessarily entails some degradation in speed. Researchers are working toward sets of "minimal perfect" hashing algorithms, which for lists of predetermined sizes allow no collisions and conserve both memory and time. There is no free lunch–not yet.

Hashing also makes it possible to merge several keywords into one set of numbers, creating a surrogate key in which each keyword can be recognized separately. The method is useful for creating a signature for each document in a database and for other applications requiring multiple keys to a single entry. This time we will use the position within the alphabet of the first three characters plus the word length, and divide each number by 19 to obtain a set of four numbers between 0 and 18.

Shakespeare	s	=	19th in alphabet	mod(20) =	0
	h	=	8th in alphabet	mod(20) =	4
	a	=	1st in alphabet	mod(20) =	5
length		=	11 characters	mod(20) =	15

The next step creates a signature consisting of a sequence of twenty binary digits (bits) arrayed in a "bit table." Initially, all are 0s and we register the code for Shakespeare by changing the 1st, 12th, 19th and 9th bits to 1 (in computer parlance, the bit is "set" or "turned on").

	00	01	02	03	04	05	06	07	08	09	10	11	12	13	14	15	16	17	18	19
Shakespeare	1	0	0	0	1	1	0	0	0	0	0	0	0	0	0	1	0	0	0	0

Now let's say we want a signature for a document about Shakespeare and three of his contemporaries, a signature synthesized from all four names:

	00	01	02	03	04	05	06	07	08	09	10	11	12	13	14	15	16	17	18
Shakespeare	1	0	0	0	1	1	0	0	0	0	0	0	0	0	0	1	0	0	0
Jonson	0	0	0	1	0	0	0	1	0	0	0	0	0	0	1	0	0	1	0
Spenser	0	0	0	0	0	0	0	0	0	0	0	0	0	0	0	0	0	0	0
Donne	1	0	0	0	0	0	0	1	1	0	0	0	1	1	0	0	0	0	0
Signature	1	0	0	1	1	1	0	1	1	0	0	0	1	1	1	1	0	1	0

The signature registers 1 if any of the four authors' bits has been set to 1. To search for an article concerning Spenser, we would generate a bit table for his name, compare it with signatures, and if the bits set for Spenser are also set in a signature, the procedure retrieves that document. On the other hand, the bit table for Marlowe (not among the four authors) does not correspond, because the bits for 02 and 07 are not set in the signature.

Signature	1	0	0	1	1	1	0	1	1	0	0	0	1	1	1	1	0	1	0
Marlowe	0	0	0	0	0	0	1	0	0	1	0	0	0	1	0	0	1	0	0

Since bit tables take up very little room in computer memory and are easily compared, a large number of such signatures could be very quickly searched. Collisions will occur, of course; in this case Dostoevsky would yield a false positive. Their frequency can be reduced with a hash function that includes more information: it might incorporate characters and include their positions within the word.

Boolean searching for specified combinations, say for Donne AND
Jonson, is also possible:

Jonson	0	0	0	1	0	0	0	1	0	0	0	0	0	0	0	1	0	0	1	0
Donne	1	0	0	0	0	0	0	1	1	0	0	0	1	1	0	0	0	0	0	
Combined	1	0	0	1	0	0	0	0	1	0	0	0	1	1	1	0	0	1	0	
Signature	1	0	0	1	1	1	0	1	1	0	0	0	1	1	1	1	0	1	0	

Since all bits set for Jonson AND Donne are also set in the signature,
the query finds a match. Variants on this technique allow other
Boolean searches: for Donne OR Jonson, for Donne AND NOT Jonson,
for Shakespeare AND either Donne OR Jonson, and so on.

3.2 Searching for similarly spelled words

Surrogate keys also play a role in searching for items similar, but not
identical to some specified item. Our example will concern similarity
of spelling. Upon encountering *he wsa tired* or *beleif*, a reader might
mutter "proofread!" or "*i* before *e* except after *c*." But neither the
typographical error nor the misspelling would obscure the writer's
intention. For a computer, however, the spelling is the word; without
assistance, its search for either misspelled word would come up empty.
Surveys show that as many as one in ten database queries fail to find
some of the relevant documents because of spelling mistakes either in
the query or in the database index. Thus systems that check spelling
are more than mere amenities for writers.

If the object is chiefly to catch typographical errors, digram or
trigram analysis is effective. Trigrams can be especially useful in
catching errors near the beginnings of words where certain combinations of consonants cannot occur, thus *_tl*, *_dl*, *_pw*, *_fw* (_ indicates
the leading space). The first step is to sort the text alphabetically and
conflate tokens so as to avoid separate searches for all instances of all
words. Then each type is divided into digrams or trigrams. Thus,
pwoerful, produced by hitting the *o* and *w* keys in the wrong order
would yield the trigrams *_pw*, *pwo*, *oer*, *erf*, *rfu*, *ful*, and *ul_*. Each of
these is sought in a list of trigrams and their frequencies. Any word
with a trigram not on the list is necessarily a misspelling. If all
trigrams in the list, the average of their frequencies is computed,
yielding an "index of peculiarity," then tokens are sorted by this index
to produce a list in which peculiar (though not necessarily incorrect)
spellings converge and offending digrams or trigrams are highlighted.
The list may also suggest, again on the basis of frequency, some

corrections. Searching by digrams or trigrams works reasonably well for typographical errors and for some errors of suffixing (for example, the failure to change *y* to *i* before adding a suffix beginning with a vowel). It will not help with such phonetically induced misspellings as using the wrong letter for the schwa (*seperate, tendancy*), failure to double letters (*accomodate, necesary*) or unwarranted doubling (*ommitted, familliar*), and various insertions and deletions (*atheletic, privlege*).

For general-purpose spelling checkers, the usual method is to consult a general spelling dictionary and perhaps one or more specialized dictionaries. If the word does not appear, the spelling is suspect. Though one might suppose that the bigger the dictionary the better, an unabridged dictionary does not necessarily supply the best general-purpose word list. Aside from the time required to search through a half million words, unabridged dictionaries contain too many likely spelling or typographical errors that are also words (*fo* is obsolete for *few* and *od* is an imprecation).

If spelling assistance is to be truly useful, however, it should not only identify suspect words but also suggest corrections. Spelling correction poses an interesting challenge: how to find a word in the dictionary if you do not know its spelling? The challenge is not quite as difficult as it seems. Better than nine of every ten mistyped or misspelled words have only one fault; and the fault is necessarily one of four kinds: a wrong letter (*existance*), a missing letter (*begining*), an extra letter (*priviledge*), or a pair of transposed letters (*recieve*). Among the several methods of finding plausible corrections, some compute the lengths of substrings shared by the misspelling and dictionary entries. A first search would list all dictionary entries that match a significant number of successive characters read from the beginning of the word, with significance depending on the length of the word; a second search would do the same, beginning at the ends of words and reading backwards. Comparing the lists generated by these two searches will yield one or more dictionary entries which share with the misspelled word significantly long substrings. If the searches yield several entries, the entries are ranked according to the summed length of the shared substrings.

Another method, perhaps the most promising, converts words into **similarity keys**. A similarity key is a relaxed version of a word that retains some but not all of the word's characteristics. In a sense, a hash address is a similarity key in that it records the identity and position of one or more characters together with the word length, and these constitute identifying characteristics of the word or of a group of similar words. Some systems for spelling correction do use hash addresses plus "bucket" storage to find plausible corrections. For example, a hash address computed from the positions of the first two characters in each word plus the length would yield (among others) the following groups of words for the misspellings *necessery*, *necesary*, and *neccessary*.

ne- 8 chars

nebulous	negative	neophyte	nepotism	neurosis
necklace	negligee	neoprene	nescient	neutrino
needless	neighbor	nepenthe	neuritis	newscast

ne- 9 chars

necessary	neediness	neologism	neuralgia
necrology	negotiate	nephritic	neurology
nectarine	neolithic	neptunium	newspaper

ne- 10 chars

neapolitan	needlework	negligence	neutrality
necromancy	neglectful	negotiator	newfangled
needlefish	negligible	neoclassic	newsletter

Hashing the first misspelling leads to the bucket of words beginning *ne-* and consisting of nine characters. The system might simply report those possibilities to the user or, because the fault may be a missing or extra character, it could report all three groups of words. Alternatively, it could edit the suspect spelling in an attempt to find an exact match. If the word can be made to match a dictionary entry by substituting one character or transposing a pair of characters, the entry is probably the intended word. For the spelling *necessery*, substituting *a* for the second *e* would supply a match. If no match is found, the possibility of missing letter must be considered. Thus, *neccessary* would lead to the ten-letter words, but fail to discover an incorrect letter or a transposition. Then the nine-letter words would be considered; successive letters in the suspect word would be deleted, and eventually a match would be found.

Hashing gets us on the right track, but a better similarity key would suppress characteristics involved in many misspellings while retaining enough information to limit plausible corrections to a manageable number. For example, a key can be formed by collocating the first character of the word, then the remaining unique consonants, and finally the remaining unique vowels. (Thus $n+csr+ey$ and both *neccessary* and *necesary* would yield $n+csr+eay$). The rationale for this method is fairly simple. The first character is retained because, though it may be involved in typographical errors, it is seldom implicated in misspellings. Consonants precede vowels partly because there are more of them and they therefore distinguish more words and partly because mistakes with the schwa vowel account for a great many spelling errors. (Systems that must cope with poor voice transmission, such as the Soundex system used in taking airline reservations, go even further, omitting all vowels plus *y* and *w*, which are produced with so little obstruction of air that they sound like unstressed vowels.) Only unique characters are retained so as to suppress the numerous spelling faults that double or fail to double characters. A problem with this method is that it relies heavily on the early consonants in the suspect word, and a few common misspellings (such as *aquaint* for *acquaint* and *accend* for *ascend*) omit early consonants. Each dictionary entry consists of the similarity key then the correct spelling, and entries are sorted into the alphabetical sequence of the keys. To find plausible corrections for a suspect word, the system derives its similarity key then retrieves from the dictionary all words with keys that are the same or quite close.

Misspelling:	Key:	Correction:	Key:	Words with same or similar keys:	
seperate	s+prt+ea	separate	s+prt+ea	separation supersonic sprout	sprite support
begining	b+g+e	beginning	b+g+e	began beginner begonia began bygone	begging begone begun bugging

Having retrieved a plausible correction or group of corrections, the system eliminates corrections that are more than one character too long or too short, then undertakes the process of editing and matching.

3.3 Searching intact text

As an aid to editing, word and text processing programs usually provide a facility for searching intact text, and until recently scanning was slow, slow at least in comparison with other automated methods of searching. Text scanning requires two operations: one to superpose characters of the text and the target word or phrase, the other to compare them. This usually meant trudging through the text, character by character, a maddeningly slow process for a text of any length, until R. S. Boyer and J. S. Moore devised a surprisingly simple method that reduces the total number of operations by as much as two-thirds, hastening the search.

Illustrated in Figure 13, Boyer/Moore search begins by aligning the keyword with the beginning of the text, then comparing the final character of the keyword with the corresponding character in the text. Should they not match, the keyword is shifted forward so as to align

Trudging method: Boyer / Moore method:
The furrow follows free   The furrow follows free
↑   ↑
free   free
  ↑   ↑
  free   free
    ↑   ↑
    free   free
      ↑   ↑
      free   free
       ↑↑   ↑
       free   free
        ↑   ↑
        free   free
                                                    ↑↑↑↑
                                                    free

[11 more moves; 15 more comparisons]

                    ↑
                    free
                    ↑↑↑↑
                    free

To determine the forward movement, Boyer/Moore search maintains a table, giving the distance from the last letter in the word to the most recent occurrence of each letter in the word, or if the target word does not contain that letter, the table gives its length. For *free* the table would be:

a 4	f 3	k 4	p 4	u 4
b 4	g 4	l 4	q 4	v 4
c 4	h 4	m 4	r 2	w 4
d 4	i 4	n 4	s 4	x 4
e 1	j 4	o 4	t 4	y 4

Figure 13. Two methods of full text search.

the text character with the last occurrence of that character in the keyword. If the keyword does not contain the text character, then the keyword is moved forward to a position one character beyond the text character. In this way, the search can proceed by more than one text character at a time, and search times are radically reduced. Thus after *free* is superposed on *furr* in the example, it is moved ahead by two characters aligning the *r*'s. Similarly when *free* is superposed on the four characters (space) *f r e* for the penultimate comparison, the text *e* matches, but the *r* does not, so the target word is moved forward by one character, as specified under *e* in the table. For the other superposings, the target word does not contain the text character, so it is moved ahead by its entire length. The result is a search that moves much faster than the character-by-character method, but with no risk of missing the target word.

3.4 Automated indexing and abstracting

A torrent of text is published every year, much of it highly specialized. The flood is growing at a compound rate of at least five percent annually, partly because of the increasing amount of new information generated each year, but mainly because information is now being disseminated more widely. Most of the text is in computer-readable form at one stage or another in its production, and huge numbers of texts or passages (in the tens of millions) are collected in computer databanks. String searching, even when it is as efficient as the Boyer/Moore method, is not feasible for locating relevant texts or passages.

Access must be via indexes, most of them compiled manually. Manual indexing is expensive and time consuming, but what is worse, even when experts do the indexing, they are individually making judgments and tend to be inconsistent. Categorized lists of terms and "scope notes" guide the experts; these improve consistency, but at the expense of flexibility. Any *a priori* system of categories, however frequently it is updated, will necessarily impose an arbitrary structure on a body of information that is constantly evolving and mutating. These problems have prompted efforts to develop inexpensive, fast, and consistent methods of automatic indexing, based on *a priori* categories, but on a selection of the vocabulary actually used in the text. To be effective these methods need to be reasonably exhaustive, identifying most of the texts relevant to a user's query, and reasonably discriminating, so that texts it does identify are usually relevant.

The first step is to filter out words that do not discriminate content. These include function words, and words (such as *introduce, discuss,* and *consider*) that refer to the discourse rather than its content. A morphological routine then converts each of the remaining words to a base form. Thus *speak, speaks, spoke, spoken, speaker, unspoken,* and so on would be converted to the base form *speech.* The base forms are sorted, conflated, counted, and arranged in order of descending frequency. Indexing terms will be selected from among the most frequent, in part because these reflect the content of the text and in part because infrequent words in the text tend also to be infrequent in users' queries.

Figure 14 gives the most frequent base forms in the section on morphology from Chapter 1 and the entire Chapter 2. Each list contains a half-dozen terms that would be useful for the index, but how do we winnow these from the majority that are not useful? The answer is to select terms that are moderately frequent in specific texts, but of low frequency elsewhere. Asterisks mark words that are frequent in the Brown Corpus; plus signs mark words that are also frequent in this book. Since a collection containing texts on morphology and speech recognition is likely to contain other texts on language,

Section on morphology: Chapter on spoken language:

word+	noun+	speech	syllable
affix	adjective+	word[+]	template
stem	form*	phoneme	formant
verb+	information*	sound*	stress*
meaning*	example*	vowel	acoustics
English+	program+	consonant	distinguish*
language+	combination*	recognition	*variation*
suffix	entire*	knowledge*	sample*
lexicon+	spelling	sentence+	stop*
derivation	add*	voice	language+
inflection	prefix	different*	high*
analysis*	list+	system*	syntax+
category*	subject+	rule*	synthesis
morphology	segment	follow*	frequency*

+ frequent in the collection   * frequent in the language

Figure 14. Candidates for automatic indexing.

linguistics, and computation, frequencies for the collection are apposite. Mathematical calculations based on the frequency of a term in the text and the inverse of its frequency in the collection produce "significance values" for determining whether the term should be incorporated in the index or how that term should be weighed. A different but related set of numerical values can be derived from "signal to noise" calculations: noise words are evenly distributed through the collection, whereas the best signals are those words that recur in clusters. In either case, if the value for a given term exceeds a preset threshold, the term is included in the index. Not all of the terms collected in this way will be useful (*segment*, for example, is frequent in the morphology section, but not in the text as a whole), but the preponderance will be germane to the content of the text.

An indexing scheme based solely on word frequencies encounters several problems. One problem is that words with very specific meanings, though useful in discriminating the contents of texts, tend to be of very low frequency. Notice, for example, that the list of frequent words from the chapter about computational approaches to spoken language contains little of the technical vocabulary of acoustics or phonology, and about computation. Yet the cumulative effect of many words such as *waveform, coarticulation, algorithm,* and *digitize* surely characterizes the subject matter. The solution, especially for indexing technical documents, is to substitute thesaurus headings for the specialized vocabulary. Headings include words that are likely to

Compiled form:

	computer	acoustics	morphology	phonology	affix	discourse
text 1	yes	yes	no	yes	no	no
text 2	yes	no	yes	no	yes	no
text 3	no	yes	no	yes	no	no
text 4	yes	no	no	no	no	yes
text 5	no	no	yes	no	yes	no
text 6	no	yes	no	yes	no	no

Inverted form:

	text 1	text 2	text 3	text 4	text 5	text 6
acoustics	yes	no	yes	no	no	yes
affix	no	yes	no	no	yes	no
computer	yes	yes	no	yes	no	no
discourse	no	no	no	yes	no	no
morphology	no	yes	no	no	yes	no
phonology	yes	no	yes	no	no	yes

Figure 15. Construction of an inverted index.

appear in users' queries. Thus, for example, *computer* might be substituted for *algorithm, byte,* and *subroutine*; and *phonology* for *coarticulation, sibilant,* and *diphone*. In this way the specialized vocabulary will bulk large enough to be reflected in the index. The same technique can compensate for the unequal distribution of synonyms in the language. For some words, there are many others with the same or nearly the same meaning, and words with multiple synonyms will necessarily appear less frequently than words with few synonyms. Unfortunately, no similar provision can be made for pronouns. Though each pronoun should count as an occurrence of the antecedent to which it refers, procedures for reliably discovering their antecedents require an immense amount of lexical, syntactic and semantic information and are not yet feasible.

Indexing a collection of texts produces a large number of terms, each identifying a specific text. These must be searched very rapidly while the user waits at a computer terminal. The usual solution is an **inverted index**. First, the vocabulary of terms is represented as a series of columns in an array and, proceeding text by text, the index terms for each text are recorded (see Figure 15). Next the array is inverted so that each row lists texts indexed to particular terms. In effect, the row become an index to be manipulated independently in response to a user's query. If, for example, the user specifies *computer* and *phonology*, Boolean AND merges the corresponding lists and produces a list consisting only of texts that are indexed to both terms:

	text 1	text 2	text 3	text 4	text 5	text 6
computer	yes	yes	no	yes	no	no
phonology	yes	no	yes	no	no	yes
AND =	yes	no	no	no	no	yes

A user interested in noncomputational approaches to components of words might stipulate *phonology* OR *morphology* AND NOT *computer*:

	text 1	text 2	text 3	text 4	text 5	text 6
phonology	yes	no	yes	no	no	yes
morphology	no	yes	no	no	yes	no
OR =	yes	yes	yes	no	yes	yes
computer	yes	yes	no	yes	no	no
AND NOT =	no	no	yes	no	yes	yes

The techniques for automatic indexing can be extended to generate abstracts of texts. Automatically generated abstracts are not coherent, readable summaries; rather they are aids to retrieval, reflecting enough of the contents of a text to let the user determine if it is relevant. First a list is compiled of indexing terms frequent in the text and infrequent in the collection. Next a "weight" is computed for each sentence in the text, or sometimes in each paragraph. Sentence weight is computed from the number and significance value of the indexing terms in the sentence, from its position in the paragraph (first sentences often give the paragraph's topic), from the presence of discourse verbs (*discuss, present, describe, explore, investigate,* and the like), and from such cue phrases as *this paper, our research, to summarize,* or *in conclusion.* An arbitrary number of sentences with the highest weight are chosen for inclusion in the abstract together with any preceding or following sentences linked to those chosen are linked by such connectives as *therefore, similarly* and *besides.*

Exercises

1. Of the following methods of representing information, which are best classified as data structures and which are forms of knowledge representation? In each case, briefly explain your reasoning.

an alphabetized list	a transition network
a semantic network	a character trie
a weighted binary tree	a frame
a document signature	a hash table
a phrase structure tree	a text
a set of similarity keys	a B tree or B+ tree

2. A dictionary and a thesaurus represent different solutions to the problem of organizing information for efficient retrieval. Describe them as data structures, give some advantages and disadvantages of each structure, and briefly sketch a computational hybrid that would offer some of the advantages of both structures.

3. How might the properties of a stack be used as part of a program for counting the number of English words with a particular derivational suffix?

4. Devise a transition network and lexicon that will recognize these frequent queries about my sheepdog:

Can he see me?	Do sheepdogs make good pets?
May I pet him?	Does he have a tail?
Do sheepdogs like small kids?	May I walk him?
Will he bite me?	Does he have eyes?

The network in Figure 5 can serve as a model, but you should be able to get by with fewer arcs.

5. Devise an efficiently searched structure for representing the 24 most frequent words in the Brown Corpus (given in Chapter 3, Figure 2).

6. Given the feature hierarchy in Figure 11, what is the minimum common supertype of a horse [-HUMAN] and a house [ARTIFACT]? Demonstrate your answer using a stack and depth-first traversal.

7. Critique the method of automatic indexing described in section 3.4. In what ways is it less satisfactory than manual indexing?

Further reading

For a comprehensive and highly readable discussion of data structures and search algorithms, see Knuth (1968) and (1973); also see Aho, Hopcroft, and Ullman (1983) or Standish (1980); and on search in artificial intelligence, consult Winston (1984), Charniak and McDermott (1985) and Kanal and Kumar (1988). On the issues and methods of knowledge representation, see the collected papers in Findler (1975), Brachman and Levesque (1985), Cercone and McCalla (1987), Brachman, Levesque, and Reiter (1990), and Reichgelt (1990). On the role of recency and frequency in lexical retrieval, see Foss (1969) and Scarborough, Cortese, and Scarborough (1977); on semantic networks, see Quillian (1968), Evens (1989) and Sowa (1984, 1990). On the detection and correction of misspellings, see Peterson (1980) and Pollock and Zamora (1984). The chapters on syntax and semantics, which follow, have further references to research on knowledge representation. Extended discussions of indexing and other procedures for maintaining and searching text databases can be found in Salton (1989), Teskey (1982), Salton and McGill (1983), and in the annual *Proceedings of the American Society for Information Sciences* and *Information Technology: Research and Development.*

Chapter 5

Sublexical and Lexical Processing in Parallel

Section one: Toward a New Kind of Computing

1.1 Serial versus parallel processors

Recently, a new kind of computing has emerged, known as **parallel distributed processing** (PDP). PDP systems are parallel in that many very simple processors operate collaboratively, and they are distributed in that the information possessed and manipulated by the system is spread over a network of interconnections. Though very different from the conventional design, PDP systems are computers. What makes them especially interesting is that they succeed with certain applications that are difficult for conventional computers. Among their present linguistic applications, most are at the sublexical and lexical levels. PDP systems excel at perceptual processing where a large volume of information must be assessed simultaneously, and they do proximate pattern matching where the patterns to be matched are not identical but merely similar. For example, PDP systems can recognize characters printed in a variety of typefaces and fonts and decipher some handwriting; they manage creditable text-to-speech synthesis and may soon improve the recognition of allophones and intonation in spoken language.

On the lexical level, PDP systems efficiently store and instantly retrieve associated but unstructured collections of words or other data, and thus plausibly simulate certain behaviors of human lexical memory, notably the phenomenon of priming, by which retrieval of one word facilitates the retrieval of related words. Most remarkably, they exhibit a capacity for self-organization that resembles inductive learning. Presented with multiple, slightly different examples of a pattern, they learn how to recognize the pattern. They can then recognize it in examples they have not encountered before. Though it

130

Central processor: Bus: Addressable memory:

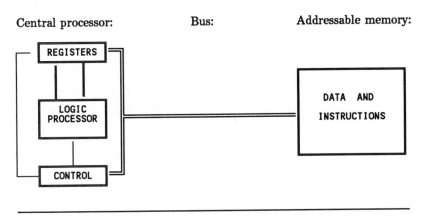

Figure 1. The architecture of a serial computer.

is unlikely that PDP systems will replace computers of the conventional
design, computers of the future may well contain PDP and conventional
subsystems, the former for recognition and associative tasks, the latter
for manipulating symbolic structures.

Before considering parallel distributed processing and its advantages
for sublexical and lexical processing, it is useful to know something
about the design of conventional serial computers and some of the
parallel processing alternatives. Serial computers have a single central
processing unit connected to an addressable memory (see Figure 1).
The processing unit obeys rules and instructions that manipulate
symbols; they perform the logical and arithmetic operations of the
computer. Processors operate sequentially, executing one instruction
at a time. A control unit synchronizes the operations of the central
processor in its interactions with addressable memory and with devices
such as the keyboard, video display, and long-term memory.

A series of communication channels, collectively called a bus,
transfers data and instructions to and from memory, together with
memory addresses and control signals synchronizing the transfers. The
bus also carries data to permanent storage and to or from input and
output devices, such as a keyboard and a video display. Thus the bus
resembles a busy highway. When data or instructions are required for
a particular operation, a request is sent along the bus to memory.
Once the data or instruction is located, it travels back via the bus to
the central processor. If the operation requires more than once piece
of data (as for example to compare them), there may be separate
requests, separately responded to.   Request-response cycles are
sequential, so that each new request must await the completion of its
predecessor. Also, once the operation is performed, its result may be
sent back to memory, occasioning further congestion on the bus.
Though processors maintain several stores of short-term memory,

called registers, for immediate input and output, every step in every procedure requires access via the bus for instructions and data. The bus becomes a serious bottleneck forcing the very fast central processing unit to spend much of its time waiting.

Moreover, many procedures, particularly those that emulate human cognitive processes, call for parallel processing. Either the procedures require concurrently executable subtasks or they rely on collective decision making. Concurrent or collective tasks can be performed by a single processor with sequentially fetched instructions and data, and in theory a conventional computer can perform any computable procedure, indeed designs for parallel processing computers–even PDP networks–are often explored by simulating their operation on serial computers. But the processing is exceedingly awkward and slow. The single processor switches rapidly back and forth, executing substeps in "pseudo-parallel." Pseudo-parallelism is seldom an efficient or natural application of conventional computers.

Some parallel processing computers are direct descendants of conventional computers. Their processing units are similar to and in some cases the same as those used by serial computers: they simply have more processors. The computers vary in the degree to which control over the processors' operations is centralized. For procedures that can be executed concurrently, some parallel computers operate several processors in tandem (see Figure 2). Their concurrent operation makes for greater speed and efficiency. However, the procedures must be largely independent of one another, and coordinating tandem processors so that each will have the data it needs but does not interfere with the operation of other processors poses a difficult challenge for the programmer. For procedures in which the same series of substeps is repeated for many items in a stream of data, it is more efficient to have a pipeline of simpler, less powerful processors each performing one or more substeps then handing the data along to another processor in assembly-line fashion. Supercomputers achieve much of their incredible speed from processor pipelines. In other respects, however, tandem and pipeline computers resemble conventional computers; processors are carefully synchronized and a computer program choreographs their operations.

"Dataflow" architectures decentralize control. A dataflow computer consists of wired network of processors that can be configured (by switches) to carry out the decision making and other operations required for a complete procedure. Each processor node becomes a specialist at some logical or arithmetic operation or series of operations; it receives input from other nodes and can act as soon as it has the requisite data for its operation. Thus the flow of data through the network determines the sequence of operations. A variant of the dataflow approach is demand-driven processing, in which the operation at a given node is performed only if its output is required by some

Tandem processing: Pipeline processing:

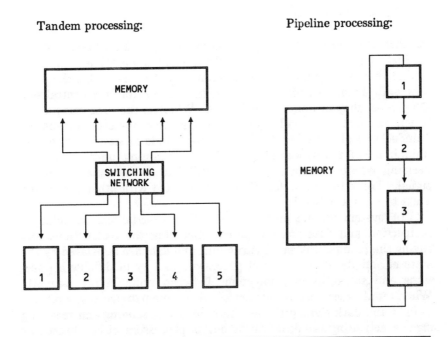

Figure 2. Alternatives to the conventional computer architecture.

other node. Because processors are responsive to one another, dataflow and demand-driven computers do not require synchronization and centralized control.

Even if the quest for efficient computation did not demand it, there is one other reason to consider parallel alternatives to conventional computing. The most successful known computing device, the human mind, does parallel processing at several levels. Though most of our conscious experience is serial, we can perform one set of operations consciously (generating sentences, for example) while we perform others without conscious attention (driving a car, perhaps, or typing). At a finer grain, the operations themselves involve parallelism: slow-motion studies of fast typists show that as one finger is pressing a key, other fingers are moving toward subsequent keys to be pressed. Many other cognitive processes exhibit degrees of parallelism. When we encounter an ambiguous word, for example, all of its meanings are separately activated; within a short time the most plausible is selected and the others fade away. At a still finer grain, our eyes, ears, and other senses simultaneously process vast amounts of information in parallel. The retina of the eye presents nearly a million distinct signals to a portion of the optic nerve where they are concurrently and almost instantaneously processed.

1.2 Collective decision making

Parallel distributed processing systems are distant cousins of the parallel computers. They resemble the tandem and pipeline computers in that they employ multiple processors. And they resemble the data-flow and demand-driven computers in that control is decentralized. Otherwise, they are entirely different. Whereas the processing units of conventional and parallel computers execute complicated operations founded in logic, the hundreds, even thousands of simple processing units in a PDP network are capable only of summing input signals and deciding whether their strength is sufficient to warrant an output signal. These units are densely interconnected with other processing units to form a network.

PDP systems do not process information in serial fashion, fetching instruction and data from memory, executing the instructions and saving the results. Instead, instructions and data are registered by the state of activity or inactivity of processors and by modifiable connections and strengths of connections between units in the network. When input processors are presented with some pattern (say, a bitmap of light and dark elements), they become active, sending and receiving signals, activating and deactivating output processors, either directly or via intermediate processors. Eventually, when signals have been propagated throughout the network, it settles into a new state of equilibrium, and the result of the computation (for example, the identity of the pattern) can be read from the output processors. Decisions are made as if by a committee: member processors can express differing opinions, be influenced by the opinions of others, change opinions, and eventually reach a consensus.

The basic operation of the processors is straightforward. They receive excitatory and inhibitory signals and obtain their sum. When the sum of the inputs to a receiving processor exceeds a specified threshold, that processor itself becomes active, producing output signals, which in turn contribute to the activating and restraining of still other processors. The destination of the output and its strength are determined by connections that mediate between processors or groups of processors. One common configuration conjoins two input signals so that C will activate only if A and B are active and propagating excitatory signals. If, for example, A and B are activated by light detectors that determine whether individual cells in a bitmap are dark or light, a "hyphen detector" might respond to two appropriately located active cells.

Both A and B have minimal thresholds (t = min.) and an activation level of +1. The connection strengths of their channels to C are +.5. The signal strength reaching C is the sum of the products of activation times connection strength or (+1 times .+5) + (+1 times .+5) = +1 and since the excitatory +1 is greater than C's threshold (t= +.7), C will activate. To represent inclusive disjunction (either this or that or both), the threshold of C can be lowered to a value (below +.5) that allows it to be activated by either A or B or by both A and B. Inhibitory relationships, including A and NOT B, can also be represented:

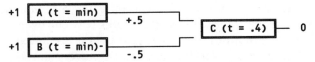

The negative connection strength inverts the signal from B, so that the activation level of A exceeds the threshold for C, if and only if there is no counteracting signal from B.

In effect, knowledge about AND and AND NOT is encoded as connection strengths between processors. It may be helpful to imagine a simple application. Let's say we have a series of eight input processors connected to a series of output processors in such a way that if we present the ASCII value of a lower case character (01100001 for *a*, 01100010 for *b*, and so on) to the input processors, the network will yield their upper case codes (01000001, 01000010, and so on). The two sets of codes are, respectively, **input** and **output vectors**. (Though the term vector derives from geometry, any ordered array of independent numbers, including a binary code, is a vector.) As we will see, PDP network learn by modifying connection strengths in such a way that patterns of active input processors come to be associated with patterns of active output processors. Because PDP networks represent knowledge as connections between processors and the strengths of those connections, study of the networks, of their properties and capabilities is sometimes called "connectionism."

Simple linear networks consisting only of input processors linked to output processors have important applications, but they are severely handicapped in that they cannot represent all logical relationships. They can manage this AND or AND NOT that, as well as this OR that OR both. But exclusive disjunction (XOR): this OR that AND NOT both is beyond their capabilities and requires an intermediate processor:

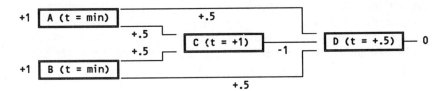

Processor D may receive three signals: one each from A and B and another that combines A and B via the intermediate processor C. If A or B is active but not both, it sends signals to C and D. The signal to C does not exceed the threshold so it remains inactive, but the signal to D is sufficient to activate it. If A and B both activate, each sends a signal of strength (+1 times +.5) directly to D, but they activate C (by the same formula), which sends an inhibitory signal -1. The sum of +1 and -1 is 0, which does not meet the threshold for processor D, so D does not activate.

PDP networks consist of many processors linked in these basic ways, with the topography of the network depending on the application. Some networks have excitatory or inhibitory links between every input processor and every output processor. Other networks are hierarchical, with every processor on a given level connected to every processor on an adjacent level so that signals may be sent back and forth between levels, but with processors on the same level either not connected to one another or connected only via inhibitory links.

1.3 Neurally inspired computation

The inspiration for PDP processors comes from structures found in mammalian brains. These neural structures consist of small energy-producing elements, called **neurons**, which participate in dense networks of millions of neurons. Each neuron consists of a nucleus from which extend a great many short branching fibers, called dendrites. Most also have a stalk-like axonal path, extending some distance out from the nucleus and ending in more branching fibers. Dendrites carry excitatory and inhibitory energy to the nucleus, which combines them. If the result exceeds the neuron's threshold, it becomes active and "fires," sending an energy spike down the axonal path and through the fibers to junctions called synapses, where it triggers the release of a chemical neurotransmitter. The chemical migrates across the synapse to receptors on the dendrites of other neurons, where it causes a chemical reaction. As a result of that reaction, excitatory or inhibitory energy traverses the dendrite to the nucleus. Because both dendrites and axonal paths have multiple branches, the firing of one neuron (or more typically several neurons) can excite or inhibit many others, these can excite or inhibit others, and so on. Also, axons projecting from one group of neurons to another often have matching axons that project back to the first group, so that the originating neurons may also receive feedback that modulates their activation levels. Only that much of the vastly more complicated electrochemical operation of neurons and neuronal systems is imitated in PDP networks. The primary focus is on networks of uncomplicated neuron-like processors and on the emergent, often useful properties of those networks.

Although PDP networks are sometimes used in investigating mental activities and are often, though misleadingly, called "neural networks," they are simplifications, not models, of the brain. There are many differences. Though PDP networks with as many as a thousand nodes have been developed (most are much smaller), they are dwarfed by the brain, which has in excess of 10^{11} neurons, and neurons have on the average a thousand or so axonal and dendritic connections. Though neurons resemble PDP processors in that they either fire or do not fire, the chemical reactions at the synapses do not behave in an all-or-nothing fashion. Axons release varying amounts of chemical neurotransmitters, dendrites have varying amounts of the receptor, synapses can delay the transmission of signals, and the presence of certain enzymes can influence activation levels and the propagation of signals. Also, some neurons fire spontaneously. Making matters still more complicated, neurons are not all alike: in some, the axons also receive signals or dendrites also propagate signals or neighboring dendrites can influence one another. The number and strengths of synaptic connections can change over time by a still-mysterious process that is presumed to result in learning.

Neurons participate in circuits of neurons, circuits participate in neuronal systems, and it is from the circuits and systems that cognitive behavior arises. Computational simulations have clarified the processing circuits for sight and hearing, and plausible models of the human retina and cochlea have been developed, but very little is known about the organization of neuronal activity in the cerebral cortex, the site of memory, language activity, and thinking. Most neuroscientists concentrate on the physiology and behavior of neurons and the simpler circuits, refusing even to speculate on the operation of larger neuronal systems.

Of more immediate relevance than neuroscience to the design of PDP networks is the mathematics of complex systems. When many processors are combined with particular connection strengths, each will influence and be influenced by the others in a complex dynamic. But the result is mathematically constrained. The progress from initial activity to an eventual stable state, as John Hopfield has shown, resembles a physical system whose energy is decreasing, and the mathematics of decreasing computational "energy" can therefore guide researchers in developing predictably functioning networks. Imagine, as Hopfield suggests, a heavy rain falling unevenly on a terrain of hills and valleys. For a time, water will flow down the hillsides and through the valleys, sometimes sloshing over a small hill from one valley to the next, but eventually an equilibrium will be reached: when water is no longer flowing from place to place. So it is with the computations of a neural network. If the network is to recognize a single input pattern from among a number of possible patterns represented as connections and connection strengths, it will usually–like the water flowing into the valleys–reach a stable state representing the nearest match. Though there is some danger that the network will get stuck at local minima (shallow valleys) though there are deeper valleys nearby, this can usually be averted by subjecting the network to a brief spike of energy–the equivalent of subjecting the flooded landscape to an earth tremor. Much as the behavior of the water can be mathematically predicted, given sufficient information about the rainfall and the topography, so the emergent behaviors of the PDP networks can be reduced to mathematics. Not only has Hopfield given PDP researchers a clear understanding of the mathematical properties of the networks, he has also shown that they are capable of solving certain intractable problems, particularly problems involving optimization of resources. What is not yet clear from the mathematics of PDP networks, however, is the power the networks might have: what kinds of problems they can and cannot solve within a reasonable length of time.

Section two: Distributed Processing and Memory

2.1 PDP networks for perceptual processing

In perceptual processing, both visual and auditory, parallel distributed processing has several advantages over conventional computing. One reason is that perceptual processing must cope with a great many discrete pieces of information arriving simultaneously or nearly so: the light and dark cells of a bit-mapped character, for example, or the partially parallel transmission of speech sounds. This is difficult for a serial computer, which must make the many decisions in sequence, one at a time. Perceptual processing must also evaluate such extraneous background noise and smudges on the page, and arrive at an identification that overrides this discrepant information. At the same time a perceptual processor must also cope with indistinct or missing information–incompletely drawn characters and reduced or elided phonemes–by finding the best possible fit between the input and the patterns it recognizes. This is something that humans do especially well; we experience little difficulty in recognizing the face of a friend before and after a haircut or identifying the voice of that friend even over a bad telephone line. Again, this is difficult for conventional computers, and though a great many methods of proximate pattern matching have been explored, they are cumbersome and quite slow.

Rather than processing in serial fashion each piece of information, a bit of character, for example, or a significant variation in the frequency or amplitude of sound, as would a conventional computer, a PDP network processes many small pieces of information concurrently. Consider, for example, optical character recognition, an application for which PDP networks have already proved their value. Each character (or a portion of a character) is projected on a bitmap of light detectors. Responding to the pattern of light and dark that forms the character, the light detectors generate as an input vector a two-dimensional array of values. The input vector will determine the signal sent by the input processors. It might send an excitatory +1 signal or an inhibitory -1 or it might refuse to respond. Thus we have a method of registering a large volume of simultaneously arriving information.

The next step is to provide for proximate pattern matching. Most character readers are trained to the details of specific fonts, such as Times Roman or Helvetica, and particular typefaces, Roman or boldface or italics. They would be more useful could they as we do recognize the character whatever the font or typeface:

A   A   A   A   **A**   *A*   A

One solution, developed by David Rumelhart and Jay McClelland, is to recognize first that, much as allophones are composed of phonological features, typefaces are composed of graphic features, and second that a small collection of such features composes the characters of a given character set. The Roman character set uses about a dozen features. The uppercase A, for example, has left and right slanting lines and a short crossbar. The letter N shares the left slanting line and has two vertical lines; H has the vertical lines, together with the cross bar. This suggests that instead of looking for complete characters, the network should look for features:

Right slanting line: Left slanting line: Crossbar:

-1	0	+1	+1	+1
0	+1	+1	+1	0
0	+1	+1	+1	0
+1	+1	+1	0	0
+1	+1	+1	0	-1
+1	+1	0	-1	-1
+1	+1	0	-1	-1

+1	+1	+1	0	-1
0	+1	+1	+1	0
0	+1	+1	+1	0
0	0	+1	+1	+1
-1	0	+1	+1	+1
-1	-1	0	+1	+1
-1	-1	0	+1	+1

-1	-1	-1	-1	-1
0	0	0	0	0
+1	+1	+1	+1	+1
+1	+1	+1	+1	+1
0	0	0	0	0
-1	-1	-1	-1	-1
-1	-1	-1	-1	-1

The numbers for each cell represent connection strengths; thus the crossbar detector responds to horizontal lines at close to the middle of the bitmap. Since patterns will seldom be exactly the same, the object is to identify the feature most nearly resembling the input.

To find enough evidence of the feature to distinguish it from similar features but tolerate unpredictable discrepancies, including faintly drawn lines or extraneous marks, context should be allowed to influence decision making. Very faint evidence of, say, a horizontal line should be given more attention if it appears between two vertical lines or left and right slanting lines than if it appears in a context that suggests an O or a Q. Thus we need two interactive levels, one for nodes that recognize characters and the other for nodes that recognize features.

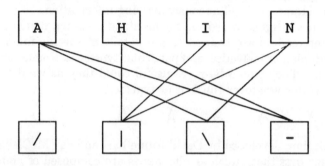

Excitatory connections (indicated by solid lines) associate a feature with each character that contains that feature; inhibitory connections (broken lines) disassociate features from characters that do not contain them. Character nodes will both receive information from feature detectors and provide them with feedback, sometimes supplying information that is obscured or missing in the input. Ideally, there would be yet another level for words with excitatory or inhibitory links between characters and the words that do and do not contain them. Abundant empirical research suggests that knowledge of possible words plays a significant role in character recognition. When groups of characters are presented very rapidly, as by a tachistoscope, the characters composing random strings are less quickly and less reliably identified than are those composing words or pronounceable non-words. For optical character recognition, however, it is simply not feasible to store and attempt to match the several hundred thousand words that the system would need to recognize.

Processing begins when nodes at the lowest level become active and propagate excitatory signals upward. Not all the nodes for a given feature will activate and some nodes belonging to other features will become active. A Roman typeface, for example, with the left leg of the A slanting at 130°, might activate more cells than the italic A with a slant of 140°. At times competition will arise between alternative possibilities: is the line slightly slanted or vertical? The collaborative

relation among processor nodes and levels of nodes will eventually lead
to a resolution by propagating excitatory and inhibitory signals.
Uncertainties and ambiguities may be resolvable at the feature level if
enough cells are activated. Or there may be an appeal to the character
level. Finding / creates the presumption that the character is A or X
or Z. If the feature node for – is also active, the two nodes will have
activated the processor for A, which will reinforce the evidence on the
feature level for \. Information propagated downward from the character to the feature level facilitates recognition by constraining the
number of possible features. If / and – are identified, then the remaining feature must be /. Thus features identify characters and
partially identified characters help identify additional features.

The same basic strategy has been applied to the more difficult
challenge of recognizing spoken words, and although the PDP systems
do not solve the problem, they do offer a plausible architecture for its
solution. Picking out the subtle and short-lived acoustic phenomena
that distinguish allophones requires frequent sampling and generates
huge amounts of data. Networks can cope with the abundance of
acoustic data by processing multiple samples of multiple features in
parallel. Multilevel networks can apply linguistic knowledge as
constraints: higher levels in the network contain knowledge of what
features combine to form allophones, what phonemes combine to form
diphones, and so on. One such system takes as its input representations of acoustic features (rather than actual speech), sampling eleven
times for each phoneme. Each of seven feature dimensions has nine
possible values, so each phoneme is represented at the lowest level of
the network by 11 times 7 times 9 or 693 nodes. Feature nodes are
linked interactively via excitatory and inhibitory connections to
phoneme nodes, and phoneme nodes are similarly linked to a small
vocabulary of word nodes.

Multilevel PDP networks also simulate speech production and speech
errors. Nodes are linked to form a hierarchy with feature, phoneme,
syllable, and word levels:

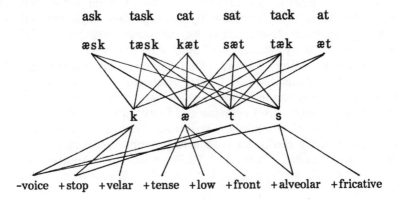

Nodes are also connected so as to represent the sequencing of constituents. If activation begins at the phoneme level, each active phoneme excites all of its features and all of the syllables of which it is a constituent. Activation also spreads to nodes that are not directly relevant (though it is weaker there); occasionally, for example, activation spreads down to the feature level then up to other phonemes with the same feature. Eventually the network achieves one of several possible stable states, which represent not only correctly pronounced words but also occasional errors in just the locations that humans also err. For instance, initial phonemes or syllables are transposed to produce Spoonerisms: *preach seduction* for *speech production*.

2.2 Associative and reconstructive memory

PDP networks have other special capabilities. Notably they support associative and reconstructive memory. Instead of storing separate pieces of information at particular memory addresses, they distribute the information in patterns of connections among processing nodes. Additional related pieces of information are added simply by overlaying them using the same nodes and connections, but different strengths of connection. When the network is presented with partial information, it reconstructs the rest. These capabilities have several linguistic applications. PDP networks can be taught to associate groups of semantically related words, for example, cooking terms such as *oven, fry, bowl, pare, spatula, stir,* and *wok*. All talk about the same field of endeavor. (Such groups are sometimes called semantic fields.) PDP networks also offer a plausible simulation of episodic memories, clusters of events that occurred together in time. In either case, the network would simulate priming: when one word is remembered, other associated words become more readily accessible; when one event is evoked, the rest of the experience comes flooding back.

Distributive memory is also very durable. Conventional computers associate pieces of information by linking them with pointers into chains that form trees, networks, or other structures. Though computer circuitry is very reliable, any chain of information is vulnerable to being broken. One missing link means that any information beyond that link is lost. Associative networks do not run this risk. If one connection or even several fail, information can be reconstructed from what remains and is usually not lost.

To see how information is distributed through a network and how it is overlaid, we can begin with a very simple network consisting of two pairs of nodes, {A,B} and {C,D}, that are connected so as to provide four channels, from A to C and A to D and from B to C and B to D:

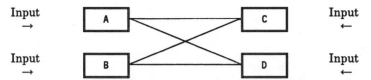

Input   ┌─────────┐   ┌─────────┐   Input
  →   │   A   │   │   C   │   ←
               └─────────┘   └─────────┘

Input   ┌─────────┐   ┌─────────┐   Input
  →   │   B   │   │   D   │   ←
               └─────────┘   └─────────┘

Now we present two items we want to associate; let's say they are parent-offspring relationships with the participants coded as numerals. Coding resembles binary coding except that it employs the three values +1 , -1 and 0 which correspond to three connections, excitatory, inhibitory and neutral. If the vector encoding *mare* is +1 -1 and the vector for *foal* -1 +1, these values will be the activation levels of the units:

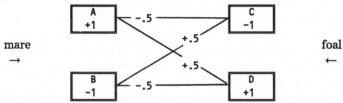

mare   foal
  →   ←

To associate *mare* with *foal*, we need to adjust the weights of the connections between units in such a way that each unit's level of activation is the sum of the activation levels times connection strengths for the two units connected to it. Obtaining the activation of A at +1 requires that the connection strengths are -5 between A and C and +.5 between A and D. That is: (+1 times +.5) plus (-1 times -.5) = 1. The same procedure yields a connection strength of +5 between B and C and -.5 between B and D. Once the connections and their strengths are established, the network remembers the association. If, with the four units inactive, we activate A and B to correspond to the code for *mare*, C and D will assume the levels of activation for the code for *foal*. And the association holds in either direction. Activating C and D for *foal* causes A and B to register the code for *mare*. What we have so far is not especially useful; we could accomplish as much with a conventional network merely by establishing pointers. With a connectionist network, however, multiple associations can be overlaid so that all are retrievable when individual units are appropriately activated.

Overlaying a second association on the first requires that the new connection strengths be separately established, then simply added to those of the first. Thus *cow* (+1 +1) and *calf* (-1 -1) will have the connection strengths:

$$A \rightarrow C \quad -.5 \qquad\qquad B \rightarrow C \quad -.5$$
$$A \rightarrow D \quad -.5 \qquad\qquad B \rightarrow D \quad -.5$$

Adding these to the connection strengths already in the network yields a network with connection strengths that represent both sets of values:

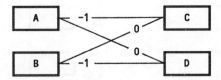

Either pair can now be obtained by activating one pair of units and reading the result from the other. Thus +1 +1 (for *cow*), multiplied by the connection strengths yields:

$$
\begin{array}{llll}
(+1 \text{ times } -1) & \text{plus} & (+1 \text{ times } 0) & = -1 \\
(+1 \text{ times } 0) & \text{plus} & (+1 \text{ times } -1) & = -1
\end{array}
$$

What we have is a device that reliably converts any one of a set of input vectors into a uniquely corresponding output vector. Assuming a sufficient number of interconnected input and output processors, any set of patterns that can be represented as vectors can be overlaid. For example, each of the input vectors representing the feature detectors for optical character recognition could be associated with a code for the corresponding feature, and these could be overlaid, yielding a single network that recognizes all twelve features.

2.3 Simulating lexical priming

An experiment that elicits the well-established psychological phenomenon of priming might present subjects with a word such as *team*, then a second stimulus, and ask if the stimulus is a word or a nonsense string (see Figure 3). If the second stimulus is a word belonging to the same semantic field and therefore associated with the prime, as *score*, for example, is associated with *team*, the subject will take less time to decide that it is not a nonsense string than if the second stimulus is, say, *yogurt*. Priming has been explained in various ways. One theory holds that priming reflects paths and locales within the mental lexicon. Semantically related words are located near one another, so that once that path to a locale has been taken once, it is easier to take it a second time and find a neighboring word. Another theory holds that the lexicon consists of a vast web of words interconnected in such a way that any activity involving one triggers those words that have the most connections with it. The first theory corresponds roughly to the method of retrieval in conventional computer memory; the second corresponds to an associative PDP network.

If processors represent words, and if excitatory and inhibitory connection between processors reflect associations and dissociations among words, a network can simulate priming. Let's say that we have eight words that belong variously to the three domains: drama, music, and sport:

	team	swing	hero	score	actor	theme	pitch	playbook
drama	no	no	yes	no	yes	yes	no	yes
music	no	yes	no	yes	no	yes	yes	no
sport	yes	yes	yes	yes	no	no	yes	yes

Pitch and *score* are associated in three ways in that each belongs to music and sport and neither belongs to drama, whereas *pitch* and *theme* are dissociated in two domains and associated only in one, music. The network acquires each of the three vocabularies in turn. Processors assigned to the associated words activate, spontaneously establishing excitatory and inhibitory connections with other processors. Each pair of yes's or pair of no's counts as an excitatory connection and each pair with a yes and a no forms an inhibitory connection, though (since excitatory and inhibitory connections cancel each another) the network need only represent the net number of connections. Thus, for example, one excitatory connection plus two inhibitory connections yields one inhibitory connection. As soon as the network digests each set of associations, it reaches a stable state and can go on to overlay the next set until eventually it has them all.

Now for the priming. If the network is presented with partial information, say the words *theme* and *hero*, the processors corresponding to those words will become active and send excitatory or inhibitory signals to each of the other processors, activating or restraining them. Signals propagate through the network until eventually it reaches a state of equilibrium, with the sum of the excitatory and inhibitory inputs to each processor determining whether it is active or inactive. In the example, *theme* and *hero* belong to the domain of drama, and processors associated with the remaining words belonging to that domain (underlined) are active and therefore primed. To do any useful work, of course, the network would need to be large enough to overlay vocabularies several thousand times bigger than our eight-word example, but if each processor is assigned a word and the network is then exposed to the patterns of association and disassociation in the vocabulary, it will spontaneously establish the pattern of excitatory and inhibitory connections that constitutes knowledge about those words.

2.4 Categorization and hidden units

In the network for priming, each node is directly connected via excitatory and inhibitory links to all of the other nodes. For any word this configuration represents particular associations and disassociations, but does not explicitly represent the notion that words are included in

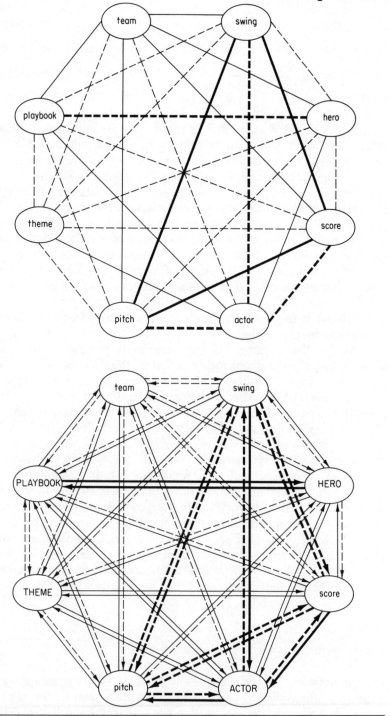

Figure 3. PDP network before and after priming.

or excluded from categories of words. All associations are word to word and no processor or group of processors represents each of the domains drama, music, and sport. That they do not categorize is an important limitation of the kinds of networks we have encountered thus far. If people did not learn to categorize, learning to treat different entities as instances of the same category, each mental entity would be unique, and thinking would not be possible.

When networks are provided with one or more layers of nodes intermediate between the input and output processors, however, particular configurations of active and inactive processors can represent categories. Nodes that are intermediate between input and output are called **hidden units,** because they cannot be activated directly; instead they are activated or deactivated as a result of the activation of input and output processors. If every input processor is connected to every hidden processor and every hidden unit is connected to every output processor, the input and output collaborate to determine stable states of the hidden units. For the priming example, we might have a network consisting of eight input nodes that excite or inhibit three intermediate nodes; in turn the intermediate units excite or inhibit eight output nodes:

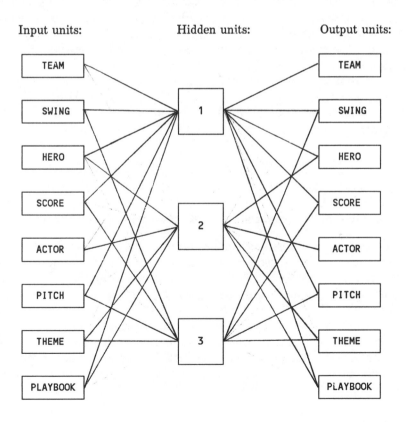

Heavy and light lines give net excitatory or inhibitory connections between nodes). The network is so configured that each hidden unit represents one of the three categories, but it is not necessary to determine beforehand the number of categories and allocate one to a node. Categories or any clusters of associated constituents can be (and usually are) represented by combinations of active nodes. For example, one network, trained on a thousand samples sentences to recognize the sequences of lexical categories that constitute well-formed sentences in English, developed clusters of active hidden units for representing members of the noun group (determiner, adjective, noun, and so on) and other clusters for representing the verb group.

Section three: Connection Strengths and Learning

3.1 Toward spontaneous learning

The associative network learns associations in a way that resembles rote memorization, but PDP networks are also capable of a more sophisticated kind of learning. Repeatedly exposed to examples, they compute the statistical correlation between input and output, discern regularities, and apply them to new cases. For instance, one PDP network has learned from examples the several ways in which English forms the past tense of verbs: not only the regular suffixing (/t/, /d/ or /id/) as determined by final consonant of the stem, but also the classes of irregular or "strong" verbs that form the past tense in other ways:

1. hit – hit, spread – spread	5. speak – spoke, choose – chose
2. bleed – bled, meet – met	6. ring – rang, stick – stuck
3. bend – bent, feel – felt	7. blow – blown, take – taken
4. flee – fled, have – had	8. rise – risen, write – written

The network passes through stages reminiscent of those that children pass through as they acquire verb forms: learning distinctions (from 420 stem-past tense examples), then overgeneralizing (*hitted, bringed, goed*), and finally mastering the regular and irregular forms and their subclasses. When the network is given stems to which it has not previously been exposed, it returns the correct past tense.

All of this is accomplished by a two-level pattern associator using a simple "convergence procedure" that modifies the connection strengths between input and output processors and the thresholds of the output processors. The procedure begins with connection strengths set to random values (representing meaningless "noise"). The network is presented with an input vector symbolizing phonological properties of stem. The phonological properties include both the relevant sounds and their contexts; thus the input vector for *beg* would be derived from the triples: #be, beg, and eg#. In turn, the input nodes activate the output nodes in a particular vector. That vector is compared with the desired output (symbolizing the properties of the past tense form). If a given output node is inactive but should be active, the strengths of connections leading from the active input processor to that output processor are increased, and the threshold for the output processor is decreased slightly. If an output node is active but should be inactive, the procedure is reversed; connection strengths are lowered and the threshold is raised. If the output vector is as it should be, no changes can be made and, paradoxically, the network does not learn by that example. It can only learn from discrepant values. The same procedure is followed for a new example, and so on through the entire set of 420 examples. Then the procedure begins again with the first example, and eventually cycles a few hundred times through the full set of examples.

Gradually, the network begins to distinguish the pairings of inputs and outputs, then it generalizes (and overgeneralizes), and eventually it produces the appropriate output for each of the input stems. It has not just memorized the examples, however, matching inputs to outputs. Any input node that participates frequently in a input/output pairing will play a major role in the final configuration of the network. It is activated in many iterations of a class of examples, it stands in a recurring relationship to a pattern of active output nodes, and its influence is therefore repeatedly amplified. So there is no difference between "memorizing" what outputs go with what inputs, on the one hand, and acquiring generalizations about what output properties go with what input properties on the other hand. The network is able to recognize the properties of a novel stem and produce the appropriate form for the past tense.

3.2 Learning by back propagation

Simple convergence procedures suffice for networks with only input and output nodes, but networks with hidden units require more sophisticated procedures. Though the connection strengths for inter-mediate and output layers do not correspond in any simple way to the individual patterns that the network is learning, their connection strengths must somehow be adjusted if the network is to learn. Procedures have been developed, however, by which the network automatically apportions blame for mistakes and makes consequent adjustments in connection strengths. The most widely used and best understood of these procedures is **backward error propagation**, or **back propagation** for short.

Back propagation requires processors with variable levels of activation (not just active or inactive) and a network with at least three levels: an input level from which activation flows through an intermediate level to an output level. The network is hierarchical in that every input processor is connected to every intermediate processor and every intermediate processor to every output processor, but processors at each level are not connected with one another. Intermediate and output processors do not have thresholds to determine their all-or-nothing behavior, but instead have special input processors that are always active and serve (via negative connection strengths) to reduce the sum of their inputs and hence control whether they will become active. It is possible to modify the strengths of connections between input nodes and hidden nodes, between the special processors and their hidden or output nodes, and between the hidden nodes and the output nodes.

Back propagation calculates an error signal from the discrepancy between the actual and desired activation of the output processors. It uses the error signal to modify the connection strengths leading to output processors, making them either more or less likely to become active. Then it does the same for connection strengths leading to hidden processors, in effect propagating information about the error backward through the network. Often error signals need to be moderated to slow the rate of change and thus prevent the network from oscillating wildly among states and lessen the chance that it will prematurely settle into a less than optimal stable state.

Any recurring property of the input/output pairing will play a major role in the development of the connection strengths to and from the hidden processors. Learning by back propagation resembles learning by humans in that the acquired connection strengths are generalizations. Rather than simply memorizing individual cases, networks with hidden processors form categories. Again optical character recognition offers an example. Consider how written characters might be learned if such a network were repeatedly presented with many slightly different examples of the letter E and made to associate them with the ASCII value for E. Any property of the E (one cell in a bitmap or a group of cells) that persistently recurs with E and not with other characters would come to be more strongly associated with the ASCII code than other properties that occur only occasionally. Once the network has several such properties, it could recognize not only E shapes that it had encountered among the examples, but new cases as well.

The number of input and output processors depends on the application. In this case the network will associate digitized alphabetic characters with the digital ASCII values for those characters. The task

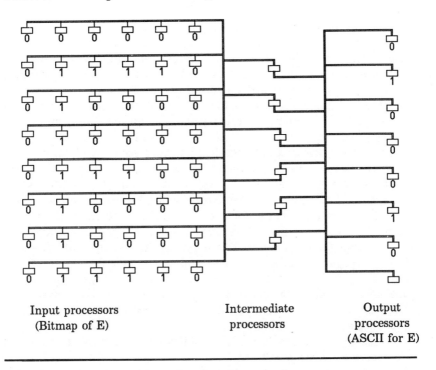

Input processors	Intermediate	Output
(Bitmap of E)	processors	processors
		(ASCII for E)

Figure 4. Learning ASCII values for character shapes.

requires forty-eight input processors, each corresponding to a cell in a
six-by eight-bitmap, and eight output processors, corresponding to the
eight digits of an ASCII value. (See Figure 4, where the heavy lines
represent multiple separate connections among processors;   for
simplicity the special processors are not shown.) The intermediate level,
or more precisely the modifiable strengths of the connections leading
to and from the intermediate level, represent the regularities.   The
exact number of intermediate processors is not important, though there
are limits. With too many processors at the intermediate level, in this
case eight or more, the network simply memorizes the associations
between input and output rather than extracting and giving weights
to significant regularities.   Six intermediate processors afford three-
hundred and thirty-six connections (6 × 48 plus 6 × 8), more than
enough for accurate recall.

Training proceeds very much as with the simple pattern associator.
A vector corresponding to the bit-mapped pattern is presented to the
input processors, and each activated processor propagates a signal to
every intermediate processor.   In turn each intermediate processor
computes a level of activation according to a formula that first adds the
values from the input processors (less the signal from the special
processor), then multiplies that value by the connection strengths and

by a function that assures continuously increasing or decreasing levels of activation between +1 and 0. Receiving signals from the intermediate processors, each output processor also computes a level of activation using a similar formula. (All of this occurs automatically.) In the second stage, activation levels of the eight output processors are compared with the ASCII codes for the character, and an error amount is computed. No complex calculation is required; one method is simply to subtract the level of activation from the ASCII code.

From the error amount together with the strength of connections between intermediate and output processors, new connection strengths are computed for each pair of intermediate and output processors. Using the old strengths between output and intermediate processors to correctly apportion "blame" for errors, together with the intermediate processor's former activation level, the network computes a new level of activation for each intermediate processor. Next, using the new "back propagated" activation level and the old activation level, the network computes an error amount for each intermediate processor, and this is used to calculate new connection strengths between the input and the intermediate processors. The procedure begins again at step one, and the cycle of spreading activation then backward error propagation continues until the activation levels of the output processors converge on the ASCII code.

Though back propagation resembles human learning in that it discerns regularities and forms categories of instances, it is in other respects an unlikely model of human learning. In the first place, though recall is instantaneous, learning by back propagation is so slow as to be psychologically implausible. Hundreds, even thousands of iterations of the training cycle are necessary before connections are learned. Moreover, there is no guarantee that regularities discerned by a network will be important. With bitmaps and ASCII codes that makes little difference, because both are arbitrary symbols and connections between them are equally arbitrary. However, human learning is founded on understanding and is therefore evaluative; we learn to distinguish important relationships from incidental correlations.

Nevertheless, what has been accomplished using hidden units with back propagation or similar learning schemes is remarkable. Another PDP network, NETalk, developed by Terrence Sejnowski, has learned to translate from written to stilted spoken English and has mastered both the highly regular correspondences between spellings and phonemes (save, gave, rave) and the exceptions (have). Trained with spellings of sentences as input and phonological transcriptions as output, NETalk begins by producing random sounds, then learns the distinction between vowels and consonants and, somewhat later, the significance of spaces between words, until eventually it is able to translate not only training sentences but also sentences it has not encountered before.

NETalk has an input "window" seven characters wide, so as to register the pronunciation of each character in sufficient context; for each of the seven, there are 29 input nodes, each corresponding to a letter of the alphabet, a punctuation mark, or a space. There are 26 output phoneme nodes which, after the network is trained, are used to control a phoneme-to-sound synthesizer, so that NETalk actually speaks aloud. Connecting the input to the output nodes are 80 hidden nodes. These come to represent the pronunciations of characters and combinations of characters, and when their activity is probed some interesting patterns emerge. Sixteen or so units are active for each character in context and they work in groups. One group tends to be active when NETalk is pronouncing vowels and another when NETalk pronounces consonants. The two groups spontaneously organize themselves in different ways. Within a vowel group, which must cope with the several pronunciations of each vowel, is a subgroup specializing in the ways of pronouncing the characters; *a* has one subgroup, *i* has another, and so on. For the more numerous consonants, subgroups form for similar pronunciations: *c* and *k*, for example.

PDP networks may yield new insights into human cognition and human languages. For the present, they succeed where each piece of information is discrete, related to other pieces by co-occurrence and therefore association. That much is inherent in the networks and their operations. Unlike conventional computers, they do not explicitly represent structure or rules that create structures. The difference is roughly the same as between a collection of atoms and a molecule. Though both have atoms as their constituents, a molecule is something other than the sum of its parts and is the simplest unit possessing all the chemical and physical properties of a compound. Most current theories of syntax and other, higher-level language components operate on the molecular level. They posit the existence of symbolic structures and rules that operate on those structures rather than on their constituents. (The next chapter shows how this occurs with syntax.) Structural approaches have been very productive. They help explain why language is as it is, and that is their justification. Though it is unlikely that connectionist approaches will supplant the current structural approaches, they may offer a second, compatible level of explanation. The latter is possible since connectionist networks can in theory implement structural approaches, though without making explicit the structures and their manipulation. The difference would be of the adequacy and perspicuity of alternative explanations. Some phenomena would be best explained on the connectionist level and modeled using PDP networks or some future evolution of them. Other phenomena would be best understood on the structural level and modeled using conventional computers or their parallel processing descendants.

Exercises

1.   The inclusive OR (this or that or both) is frequently required for phonological and other linguistic rules.   Devise a configuration of two processors which would conjoin two input signals in such a way that the output processor would register inclusive OR.

2. If a hyphen were represented as two consecutive cells in a bitmap and a dash were four consecutive cells, configure a set of simple processors, like those in section 1.2, to distinguish hyphens from dashes.

3. Extend the optical character recognition network described in Section 2.1 to accommodate the uppercase L, T, and Z.

4.   What would be required to add another parent-offspring pair to the associative network in section 2.2?   More processors?   Additional vectors? Demonstrate your answer.

5. Some of the following word forms are verbs, some are nouns, and some can be either. Using the network in section 2.4 as your model, devise a network that represents the words as input and output units and represents their categories as hidden units.

drink	meal	snack
food	bite	soup
dine	munch	salad

6. Is it likely that by exposure to many examples a PDP network could learn how to make the necessary spelling adjustments when suffixes are stripped from English words? Explain.

Further reading

On parallel processing, see Kowalik (1988) or Krishnamurthy (1989).   On connectionist networks, the primary source is Rumelhart and McClelland (1987 and 1988); also see Hopfield (1982), Feldman and Ballard (1982), Cowan and Sharp (1989), and the papers in Khanna (1990). Cotrell (1989) offers a highly developed connectionist approach to word sense disambiguation.   Also see McClelland and Rumelhart (1981), Rumelhart and McClelland (1982), Dell (1986), Rumelhart and McClelland (1986), Sejnowski and Rosenberg (1987), Hinton and Anderson (1989), Pao (1989) and the special issue of the *Journal of Memory and Language* 27, 2 (1988). On lexical priming, see Meyer and Schvaneveldt (1971), Collins and Loftus (1975), and Forster (1976).   On cognitive modeling, see Arib, Caplan and Marshall (1982), Durbin, Miall and Mitchison (1989), Levine (1989), and Churchland (1986); McGregor (1983) gives a detailed historical account, and most of the seminal papers are collected in Anderson and Rosenfield (1988); Fodor and Pylyshyn (1988), Pinker (1988), and Lachter and Bever (1988) offer critiques of this work. The journal *Neural Computation* publishes research in the field.

Chapter 6

Approaches to Syntax

Section one: Sentences and Sequence

1.1 Linguistic intuitions

Native speakers of English, or any other language, have strong intuitions about the way words combine to form phrases and sentences. With suffixes and word order as our only guides, we can find a familiar pattern in a string of nonsense words. *Ralous dscrumpers anselted ubitions* has a pattern that we know intuitively: it is the pattern of *famous leaders created nations*, or without the suffixes, *young people made fudge*, or without the words: describer - actor - act - acted upon. We know, tacitly at least, a great many such patterns, and these constitute the **syntax** of the language. For now, syntax can be defined as the arrangement or patterning of words, though we will refine that definition as we go along.

We can apply our extensive store of patterns quite flexibly, as we spin out sentences and permutations of sentences: *John made a present for Jane* becomes *a present was made for Jane by John* then perhaps *John made Jane a present* or *it was John who made a present for Jane*. We do this effortlessly and without much conscious thought. We know that superficially different sentences such as these four are synonymous, that under no imaginable circumstance can one of the four sentences be true and another false. We also know that a superficially similar sentence may, and in the case of *John made Jane the leader* does, convey a quite different relationship among the parts.

We refrain from using sentences that are not among our store, though we may have no explanation for avoiding them. In sentences such as *John made Jane it* or *Jane was given and Jill a present*, for example, something has gone awry. Though they may be related to the well-formed sentences and the meaning may be clear in context, they seem odd or unfamiliar because they do not exhibit a pattern we know. Further, we can perceive that certain sentences offer two or more

conflicting patterns–sentences such as *She drew the man with a pen,
Both parents of the boy and the girl arrived simultaneously* or *Flying
planes can be dangerous*. Who has the pen? How many people
arrived? Is it *to fly planes* or *planes that fly*? We are very alert for
patterns, so alert that we are occasionally startled by "garden path"
sentences. In *the horse raced past the barn fell*, the first three words
offer one pattern, as inviting as a garden path, but it happens not to be
the pattern of the sentence: *the horse [that was] raced past the barn
fell*.

Very little is known about how we store the patterns always at
ready or how we go about applying them as we proceed word-by-word
through the sentence. The patterns themselves are on display in the
sentences we produce or recognize, but whatever representation of
those patterns we carry around in our minds is not open to introspection. Nor are we conscious of the procedures we employ in that instant
it takes to produce or recognize a sentence.

Questions of representation and procedure must, however, be
addressed, whether the motive is to theorize about human cognition or
to devise workable syntactic components for computer systems. From
intuitions about what does and does not conform to the patterns we
know, linguists can hypothesize about the regularities of language.
They then work out conjectural representations and procedures, which
implement their hypotheses, and encode these as knowledge structures
and computer programs. Computers are well suited to the task in that
they excel at recognizing patterns, their algorithms and data structures
can implement most linguistic hypotheses, and programming exerts a
useful discipline requiring that everything be made fully explicit, with
nothing left vague or unconsidered.

When structures and programs are designed to investigate cognition,
they are often called **models**. Computational models, whether of
weather systems or the economic consequences of monetary policies,
are not what we usually think of as models, small-scale replicas
authentic in every detail. Instead they are simplifications, embodying
only those features that interest the researcher. In this chapter and
the next, the most important simplification is that syntactic processing
is autonomous, though almost certainly it is not. Syntactic processes
probably interact with processes that manage word recognition and
lexical retrieval and other processes that determine word and sentence
meaning. Once the computational model is built, it can be tested. Will
it generate or recognize the sentences of a language? Only those
sentences? Will it be momentarily misled, as we are, by garden path
sentences, and how does it cope with syntactic ambiguity? Failures
are often as informative as successes, yielding unanticipated insights
and strongly suggesting what the researcher should consider next.

For both theoretical and practical purposes, the governing assumption is that the best model is the least complex. A byword for research

is Occam's razor: "Entities should not be multiplied beyond necessity." Rather than employing the full power of the computer to organize and manipulate data, researchers attempt the least complicated form of representation consistent with linguistic phenomena and the most constrained procedures consistent with human performance. It is not hard to see why. To be psychologically plausible, theoretical systems must (eventually) account for the speed at which native speakers produce and comprehend sentences, and they must explain in a principled manner how finite brains cope with the infinite variety of language. For practical systems, the concerns are similar. They must conserve memory and impose no unreasonable delay between input and response. They must also be sufficiently straight-forward to be readily modified and extended.

The readiest way to understand current thinking is to consider various models for sentence recognition. Beginning with a very simple linear model, we will proceed to a hierarchical model and then to an augmented model, at each step retaining what is valuable and supplementing or reformulating the model to make it more nearly adequate. A fully adequate model should incorporate our intuitive knowledge of what is and is not a sentence and our grasp of the syntactic and logical relations among sentence constituents.

1.2 Beginning with word order

For modern English and for many other languages, a pattern consists most obviously of the arrangement of words in a significant order. Sentences expressing the relationship actor – act – acted-upon in modern English employ only two of the six possible arrangements:

	They chose Joe.	?	Chose Joe they.
?	They Joe chose.		Joe they chose.
?	Chose they Joe.	?	Joe chose they

Other modern languages employ different orders. Japanese, for example, places the acted-upon second and the act third; Hebrew and Welch place the act first, then the actor and the acted-upon.

Whatever the sequence, word order is important, because the sequence of words helps identify their functions. Thus, although either *they* or *Joe* is capable being the actor, its position immediately preceding *chose* identifies *they* as the actor in an English sentence. Even when languages have additional indicators of function, word order may not be entirely free. Japanese, for example, uses the markers *ga* for actor and *o* for acted-upon: *John ga hon o mita* means *John saw the book*, but word-order remains actor – acted-upon – act. English also has its indicators: *they* and *who* are actors; *them*, and *whom* are

acted-upons. *Joe* and *president* can be either, however, and word order
alone distinguishes the meaning of *Joe saw the president* from that of
the president saw Joe.   To be sure, some languages do not use
word-order to identify function.   Latin and Old English, for example,
have extensive morphological systems to distinguish among actor, act,
and acted-upon (as well as other more subtle functions) and word order
serves mainly to control the focus.   (The orders *they chose Joe* and *they
Joe chose* are not synonymous in Latin;   the word to be focussed on
goes last, thus *they chose Joe* answers the question *whom did they
choose?* and *what did they do to Joe?* elicits *they Joe chose.*)

Among modern languages, English is unusually dependent on word
order.   Word order distinguishes the statement *John has seen the book*
from the question *has John seen the book*, and if there is no "has" (or
other auxiliary verb) to invert, English sentences supply one: *John
saw the book* becomes *did John see the book.*   (By way of contrast,
Japanese retains the normal word order, and adds the marker *ka* to
indicate a question: *John ga hon o mita ka.*)   Even with the lesser
components of sentences, word order in English can be crucial.   Thus
my *book case* is different from a lawyer's *case book.*   And whether
crucial or not, word order in English tends to be fixed:

John   could   have   been   seeing   the book.
          1   2   3   4

John saw the   first   five   red   recipe   books.
                  1   2   3   4

Note that the order of the numbered words (verbs in the first sentence,
modifiers in the second) cannot be altered without producing a
sentence that sounds odd or changes the meaning.

Given the stringency of word order in English, our capacity to create
or understand sentences might be modeled by a **finite-state device**.
Derived from a branch of mathematics known as automata theory,
finite-state devices provide for step-by-step processes in a way that has
long been thought pertinent to linguistic processing.   The easiest way
to think of such a device is as a finite set of **states** connected by **arcs**
to form a **transition network**, plus a processor that controls the
transition from one state to the next via the arcs.

I   S   S   S   S   F

For a linguistic model, each arc would represent a word, a phrase, or
a category of words or phrases. (Which of these it represents depends
on the theory of syntax that is modeled.) When we create or recognize
a sentence, we are traversing the network from the initial state (I) to
the final state (F) via the four intermediate states (S), with the
sequence of arcs dictating the order in which we proceed.   Thus

recognizing a sentence would involve pattern matching. The processor compares the word, phrase, or category in the sentence with the word, phrase, or category specified by the arc, and a match permits the processor to traverse that arc. In its most restricted form, this is all that the processor can do.

Following the dictum of Occam's razor, we should ask if this is enough. Is such a device sufficient to create or recognize all the sentences of the language and only those sentences? If it is not enough, automata theory provides ways of systematically enhancing the processor; these in turn constitute a way of measuring its power. Enhancements include the ability to look back or to look ahead, to leave the present state, execute a sub-procedure, and then return. The ability to leave and return is inherently more powerful than the ability to look ahead. Once we have decided which of these enhancements are necessary to create or recognize sentences, we have in effect a blueprint for implementing the device via the data structures and algorithms of a computer. For the time being, our device will simply recognize sentences that belong to the language, making no attempt to describe or analyze them.

1.3 Sentences as strings of associations

That sentences consist of word sequences suggests that nothing more is required than the simplest of finite state devices, a collection of nodes and branches constituting an **associative network** of words. The network would specify all sequences that constitute sentences. Thus the network in Figure 1 would represent a fragment of our knowledge of sentences beginning with *dogs*. Along the way, states may offer a choice of words or phrases, or the opportunity to end a sentence with punctuation or a pause (represented as #). In all the network generates nine sentences, among them *dogs go first* and *dogs chase cats*, and can easily be expanded to contain hundreds more. The network also exercises constraints. It will not allow the non-sentence, *dogs go cars*, because no outgoing arc from *go* leads to *cars*. Nor will it allow the incomplete expression, *dogs go with*; no arc following *with* leads to a final state. Networks that generate sentences will also recognize them. The first word or phrase in the sentence is compared with the first in the network. A match permits entry into the network. From that point on any arc consumes the present word or phrase and permits a transition via that arc to a new state, until eventually the entire sentence is consumed and the network has been traversed.

The proposal that our knowledge of language consists entirely or in part of networks of words arose with behaviorism, a school of psychology that flourished in the first half of this century. In the view of some behaviorist psychologists, particularly those who founded their

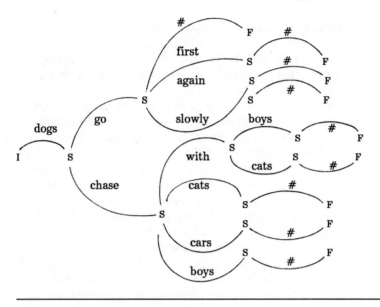

Figure 1. An associative network of words and phrases.

theories on associationism, the networks of words provide a complete
and satisfactory model of the mental representation of language. They
theorize that the networks are built through a process of conditioning.
If we frequently hear one word or phrase followed by another, we come
to associate them in sequence, forming "arcs" in a mental network.
Sequences that we hear less frequently are less strongly associated, and
the relationship between two or more outgoing arcs from a given state
can be expressed as probabilities. Given the word or phrase preceding,
say it is *chase*, there is a certain probability that the next word will be
cats, a lesser probability that the next word will be *cars*, and so on.
Sequences that we never experience do not form arcs, hence the
absence of a given arc expresses a constraint in the language. Lacking
an association between *with* and *slowly*, we are constrained from saying
the dogs go with slowly.

Associative language learning provides a better account for some
phenomena than for others. That to comprehend a sentence is merely
to follow a string of associations would explain how we manage to
compose or recognize a spoken sentence in approximately the time it
takes to speak it. No interval is required for analysis or synthesis.
Also, prior association would explain our predilection for idioms and
other frequently recurring collocations, where word seems automatically
to follow word.

However, associative networks offer no explanation for certain of
our linguistic abilities. In the first place, how could we ever learn
enough sentences? One estimate has it that to learn most of the

possible sentences of twenty words or less would require a childhood lasting a century and the capacity to learn at the rate of about 3,000,000,000,000,000,000 sentences per second. Clearly, we create sentences that we have never heard before, creating new paths at will; but the associative network offers no explanation of how we might do that. Nor can a finite number of paths through a network explain how we cope with infinity. Although any particular sentence is finite in length, the set of all possible sentences is infinite and no longest possible sentence exists. We can, for example, count in sentences: *this is the first one, this is the second one*, through *this is the one billion and first one* and so on infinitely, because numbers are infinite. Similarly, we can iterate certain patterns into infinity: from *I knew* to *he knew that I knew* to *I knew that he knew that I knew*, and onward with nothing to stop us except good sense.

How then do brains that are finite, capable of making a large but not unlimited number of connections, handle language that is infinite? The examples provide a clue. Notice that the sentences in the first set are identical except for the number. Thus they could be represented as *This is the* —— *one*. Notice also that other words can substitute for the numbers in the now-empty slot. We can substitute colors *this is the red one* and on through green, brown, purple and the rest; then shapes *this is the round one*, then sizes, textures, and so on through a large category of words that we call adjectives. Words from other categories, however, violate our sense of what is a sentence: ?*this is a cup one*; ?*this is a speak one*; or ?*this is a slowly one*. In turn, words from those other categories have their slots: *cup* and other words from the category of nouns fill a slot in *The* —— *was there*. Our tacit knowledge of categories of words and of a finite number of patterns in which those categories can be combined to constitute sentences may explain how finite brains can create or recognize an infinite number of sentences. This comes at a cost; the associative networks can integrate knowledge about syntax with knowledge about the meanings of words (semantics). But to focus only on patterns of lexical categories is to select one component of human cognition and to assert that the principles by which that component operates can be stated to a significant degree independently of the principles by which other components operate.

1.4 Sequences of lexical categories

The associative network of words is a way of enumerating all the sentences in a speaker's knowledge of the language. It offers little insight into the nature of the language or its internal organization and concerns itself only with how sentences might be acquired and stored. Once we substitute lexical categories for words and begin specifying sequences of categories, however, we are beginning to venture generalizations about the language, creating a syntactic **grammar**. Grammar has two meanings, which for our purposes will coincide though they need not. It describes that knowledge which permits us to speak a language and it constitutes a way of speaking about a language. A grammar of syntax attempts to account for all strings of words that users of the language would accept as sentences and distinguish them from strings that are not, in effect, establishing criteria for membership in the set of possible sentences of a language.

The grammar is **generative** in that it will generate those sentences. By formulating grammars of particular languages, linguists can determine what is (and is not) possible in a grammar of a human language. Until recently most of the theorizing was based on highly detailed descriptions of English, less detailed information about French, and isolated phenomena from other languages; but the presumption was that studying the grammars of particular languages should lead to general principles, a "universal grammar" that would describe the properties shared by all languages. The goal, the linguist's holy grail, is an understanding of that still mysterious faculty that enables all humans to acquire and use the grammars of their native languages.

Linguists devise grammars by compiling sets of descriptive hypotheses called **rules**. These should not be confused with prescriptive rules for correct or elegant prose, some of which (such as the restrictions on using *shall* and *will*) are matters of convention or taste, not grammar. A grammar for a subset of English, consisting only of NOUN – VERB – NOUN sentences, might have three rules specifying steps by which a sentence can be generated:

$$S0 \rightarrow NOUN \quad S1$$
$$S1 \rightarrow VERB \quad S2$$
$$S2 \rightarrow NOUN$$

These are **rewrite rules**: the first reads "S0 can be rewritten as NOUN then S1" and means that a sentence may be of the pattern NOUN followed by S1, with S1 to be specified by a subsequent rule. (For consistency, we can think of the lexicon as containing rules such as NOUN → *dog* and VERB → *talk*.)

Formulated in this way, rewrite rules serve two purposes. Since they generate all possible sentences of the language and only possible sentences, they constitute a generative grammar of the language. They can also be applied one-by-one to guide the process of recognizing sentences. For now, the grammar is still linear, accommodating one word at a time in sequence. (Because grammars of this kind treat sentences as strings of words, they are sometimes called string grammars.) Each rule corresponds to an arc in the associative network of words, except that now the rules specify categories instead of words.

The equivalent transition network simply merges the three rewrite rules and adds a destination:

In keeping with Occam's razor, our conception of language structures and language processing remains very simple. The processor belongs to the class of computing devices (technically, finite state automata) so restricted that it "knows" only its present state, instructions indexed to that state (such as the instruction to attempt a match), and the symbol it is to process. It cannot consult symbols that it has already processed, look ahead to determine what is coming, temporarily abandon a state to perform a sub-procedure, or in any other way alleviate its myopia. The idea is to see what can and cannot be accomplished with no more power than this, and then to supplement it only to the extent necessary to accomplish what we need.

Thus far our very simple grammar allows sentences of only one pattern; by adding rules for determiners and adjectives, we can easily expand its repertoire. The rules will specify that determiners and adjectives are optional, that determiners (if present) precede adjectives, and that adjectives in turn precede nouns. Four configurations can now precede the verb: NOUN, DET NOUN, ADJ NOUN, and DET ADJ NOUN. And the same four can follow it. Counting all combinations, we have expanded our repertoire from one sentence pattern to nine. Equally important, we have retained the constraints that mold English sentences. For example, the grammar excludes sentences that do not have verbs, and it requires that determiners precede rather than follow their nouns.

Figure 2 specifies the expanded grammar first as a series of rewrite rules and then as a transition network. (Some computer systems use rules, others employ networks. For now we can treat them as equivalents, though some important differences in their efficiency will emerge later.) Notice that the network pairs DET and JUMP arcs to provide for optional determiners. Thus at state SO the procedure will attempt to match the lexical category of the first word in the sentence with the category DETERMINER. If that match succeeds, the word is consumed and the arc traversed. Should the match fail, the procedure traverses the JUMP arc without consuming the word. In effect the pairing of arcs permits the merging of partially similar networks. Similarly, the bracketed rewrite rules also express options. Thus SO can be rewritten either as DET S1 or as S1, meaning that we can have either a determiner followed by the rest of the sentence or, failing that, we can have the rest of the sentence. For adjectives, the procedures are the same. Notice, however, that there is no way to traverse the

Transition network:

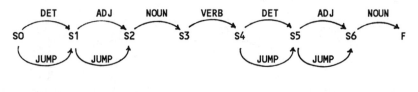

Rewrite rules:

$$
\begin{array}{llll}
\text{S0} & \rightarrow & \text{DET S1} & \quad\quad \text{S4} \rightarrow \text{DET S5} \\
 & & \text{S1} & \quad\quad\quad\quad\quad\, \text{S5} \\[6pt]
\text{S1} & \rightarrow & \text{ADJ S2} & \quad\quad \text{S5} \rightarrow \text{ADJ S6} \\
 & & \text{S2} & \quad\quad\quad\quad\quad\, \text{S6} \\[6pt]
\text{S2} & \rightarrow & \text{NOUN S3} & \quad\quad \text{S6} \rightarrow \text{NOUN} \\[6pt]
\text{S3} & \rightarrow & \text{VERB S4} &
\end{array}
$$

note: when two or more rules apply to the same state, they
are conflated as above; thus for state 0, the pair of rules:
S0 → DET S1 and S0 → S1 present alternative possibilities.

Figure 2. A linear grammar of lexical categories.

transition network without taking arcs 2-NOUN-3, 3-VERB-4 and
6-NOUN-F; the sentences in our subset of English must still have those
minimum ingredients and in that order. Nor is there any escaping the
three corresponding rewrite rules; the only way of obtaining S3, for
example, is via S2 → NOUN S3. This ignores the so-called "intransitive"
verbs, such as *sleep* and *behave*, which are not usually followed by the
determiner – adjective – noun sequence.

For now, we need not complicate the grammar by providing for
these and other phenomena of English sentences. Most present no
great obstacle. Intransitive verbs, for example, require a JUMP arc
extending from state S4 to state F, and at state S3 the rewrite rules
would stipulate separate treatment of the two kinds of verbs:

S3 → TRANSITIVE VERB S4   S3 → INTRANSITIVE VERB.

When two or more arcs depart the same state, a **schedule**
determines the order in which they are attempted. Scheduling entails
some inefficiency in that the procedure is looking for what might
possibly be present rather than simply responding to what is present.
Thus at S0 the procedure attempts a match on the determiner arc
before taking the jump arc, then at S1 it looks for an adjective before
taking the noun arc. Scheduling also requires caution. Reversing the
schedule at either of the states would cause the procedure to ignore the

Current word:	Arc:	Rewrite rule:
Painted	0-JUMP-1	S0 → S1
	1-ADJ-2	S1 → ADJ S2
covers	2-NOUN-3	S2 → NOUN S3
hide	3-VERB-4	S3 → VERB S4
the	4-DET-5	S4 → DET S5
damage	5-JUMP-6	S5 → S6
	6-NOUN-F	S6 → NOUN

Figure 3. Recognition of *Painted covers hide the damage.*

possibility of determiners and adjectives in the sentence. Similarly, when an adjective and a noun both serve as modifiers of a noun, the adjective normally goes first: *the green math book*, not *the math green book*. If the schedule reverses this order, sentences with modifiers in the normal order will not be recognized. The more complicated the syntax the more crucial is the scheduling. When we come to provide for phrases and clauses serving as modifiers within noun phrases, improper scheduling would misinterpret the syntax. Prepositional phrases such as *with glasses* always precede relative clauses such as *that I saw* when both modify the noun as in *the man with glasses that I saw*. Reversing that order means that the prepositional phrase modifies a constituent of the relative clause.

Figure 3 traces the recognition of *painted covers hide the damage*. The sentence is especially challenging because every word except *the* belongs to more than one lexical category. The procedure must disambiguate as it goes along, and it can. The lexicon would list *painted* as a verb or an adjective. Neither possibility is matched by the first arc in the transition network or the first rule in the set of rewrite rules. But arc 2 or rule S0 → S1 permits an advance to the next state, where arc 3 or rule S1 → ADJ S1 matches adjectives.

Sometimes a single pass is not sufficient. For example, if the sentence were *plastic hides the damage*, the procedure would identify *plastic* as an adjective and *hides* as a noun, then fail for want of a verb. Since a very large number of words belong to two or more lexical categories, this is not an uncommon occurrence. Somehow the procedure must look for the alternative in which *plastic* is correctly identified as a noun and *hides* as a verb. One solution is to provide for **backtracking**. The procedure maintains a record of its choices among locally feasible alternatives. If its decision at any choice point does not subsequently pan out, it can return and attempt another. For a grammar more complex than ours that allows more choices, the procedure might backtrack several times before it negotiates the entire sentence.

For one adjective   For infinitely iterated
and one noun: adjectives:

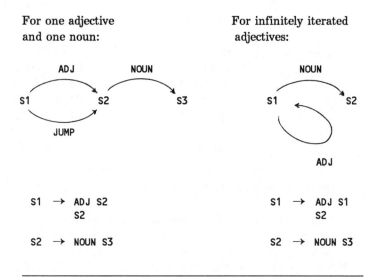

$$S1 \rightarrow ADJ\ S2 \qquad\qquad S1 \rightarrow ADJ\ S1$$
$$S2 \qquad\qquad\qquad\qquad\qquad S2$$

$$S2 \rightarrow NOUN\ S3 \qquad\qquad S2 \rightarrow NOUN\ S3$$

Figure 4. Two methods of accommodating adjectives.

1.5 Iteration and embedding

Thus far the grammar allows for only one adjective preceding each
noun. Nouns in English can have two or more adjectives, sometimes
several more. Providing for two adjectives before each noun will
expand the repertoire of sentence patterns to thirty-six; providing for
three expands the repertoire to sixty-four. The arithmetic is attractive,
but what about the cost? For every potential adjective, we must add
two states (one preceding each noun) and either two rules or four arcs.
Say we provide for three adjectives preceding the first noun and for
three more preceding the second noun. That would mean that more
than half of the rules or arcs are looking for adjectives, only because
they might be there. That is hardly an efficient state of affairs.
Sentences have on average only about 1.3 adjectives, according to the
Brown Corpus, and not all of them precede nouns. Also, sequences of
more than three adjectives do occur, so the procedure will not recognize
all well-formed sentences. And it is by no means clear that we can
justify any limit to the iteration. What evidence can be cited for the
negative proposition that more than X number of adjectives cannot
occur in sequence?

Looked at differently, the problem is not in the matching of
adjectives, but in the definition of a sentence as a series of states. We
have said that a given noun may or may not have a determiner, and
that it cannot have two. A sentence such as *I went to a the school* is
not well-formed. This suggests that for determiners, we need to specify

an opportunity (a state) and the passing of that opportunity (a change of state). For adjectives, we need only an opportunity, and we should not specify that the opportunity has passed until (subsequently) the procedure finds a noun. This much we can accomplish by providing arcs and rules that match words without advancing the state; the arcs or rules will match as many adjectives as a sentence contains (see Figure 4.) Notice that the arc for adjectives executes a loop returning to the state from which it began. Similarly, S1 → ADJ S1 will repeat as long as there are adjectives to be found; whereupon S1 → S2 takes over. Thus we can accommodate some forms without abandoning a linear conception of syntax or much complicating the model.

Our inability to specify limits surfaces again with embedded structures, and for these the problem is not so easily solved. English has **embedded constructions** in which what looks like a sentence or part of a sentence modifies a noun: *the small spark the old man struck started the big fire.* Such a construction could be accommodated in the transition network by an appropriate sequence of states and arcs following the nouns plus a jump arc to bypass that sequence for sentences in which it does not occur. As for the rewrite rules, we could specify the rules

$$S2 \rightarrow \begin{array}{l} \text{DET S3} \\ \text{ADJ S3} \\ \text{NOUN S4} \\ \text{VERB S5} \end{array}$$

(The state numbers are arrived at simply by counting out the number of states in a sentence with an embedded sentence, such as *the small spark the old man struck started the big fire.*) As with adjectives, however, no rule constrains the number of such embedded constructions that may occur in sequence. Thus we would have to continue *ad infinitum* specifying sets of states for the embedded construction, and we cannot specify VERB S5 or any numbered state at which the matrix sentence resumes. Because adjectives are single words, they could be accommodated with no changes of state. With embedded constructions, however, we need what amounts to a repeatable subprocedure with states for the determiner, noun, and verb.

Students of computer science may recognize this problem and know a solution. Finite state devices can handle simple iteration (as occurs with the adjectives), but cannot handle rules requiring subprocedures with internal changes of state. Having no inherent way of recording where they left off so they can return after executing the subprocedure, they require some form of memory external to the device. For multiple layers of embedding, the most recently stored state must be returned first. This final requirement suggests that memory take the form of a stack: its "last-in must be first-out" property precisely fits the requirements. See, for example, Figure 5 where processing on the sentence network is twice interrupted at state 2 to seek the embedded sentences

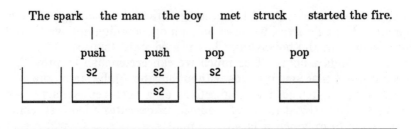

Figure 5. Place-keeping with a stack for multiple embedding.

---

the boy met and *the man the boy met struck*. Once those sentences are recognized, control is returned to the network.

Supplementing the finite state grammar in this manner does not violate Occam's razor. To be sure, the stack is another entity, but some temporary store operating on the last-in/first-out discipline is necessary to accommodate the embedded constructions. That would be sufficient justification for adding the stack, but as the next section demonstrates, the stack has other uses. It permits a major reformulation of the grammar, and the new formulation efficiently captures regularities of the language that are ignored by the linear grammar.

Section two: Hierarchies of Phrases

2.1 Context-free phrase structure grammar

One motive for moving from associative networks of words to the linear grammar of lexical categories was to capture as generalizations useful regularities in language. Words belong to categories, and well-formed sentences exhibit certain sequences of categories and not others. We could continue identifying sequences and writing rules that incorporate them until the grammar, grown fat and quite ungainly, recognized all sequences that can occur in English. For some idea of how ungainly, consider that the full complement of a noun's modifiers looks something like this:

```
the   first   four    old     water    skis  with straps  that you find
 |      |       |       |        |        |        |            |
     ordinal cardinal adjective attributive head prepositional relative
                                   noun            phrase       clause
```

The pattern is quite regular and can be captured by a linear grammar, but the grammar would have to repeat the rules for each of these constituents in almost every context (and there are many) where a noun can occur.

That rules must be repeated, however, suggests a different kind of regularity, which we can use in much the same way we used the existence of categories. We can specify categories of phrases and use those categories to create a lean, more efficient set of rules. We can begin by noting that the sequence of categories preceding the verb is precisely the same as the sequence following the verb. This sequence is the **noun phrase** (NP). For evidence that such an entity exists consider the behavior of pronouns:

NP		NP
The skilled mechanic	repairs	foreign cars.
He	repairs	them.
? The skilled he	repairs	foreign them.

Notice that pronouns can substitute either before the verb or after and that they replace not just the noun, but the entire sequence and cannot, for example, be modified by adjectives or prepositional phrases. That *he* and *the skilled mechanic* are entities of the same kind is confirmed by the fact that they can be conjoined. That is, we can say *he and the skilled mechanic,* but not (for example) *he and repairs foreign cars.* The two tests, substituting and conjoining, identify other entities. For example, *repairs foreign cars* is a verb phrase (VP), which consists at the minimum of a main verb and may contain entities of other kinds, including (as in the example) noun phrases. Verb phrases also can be substituted for other verb phrases (*the skilled mechanic fixes problems*) or conjoined with them (*the skilled mechanic fixes problems and repairs foreign cars*).

That noun and verb phrases (and other similar entities) exist and that their behavior can be captured by small sets of rules offers presumptive evidence that the phrasal structures play a role in human cognition. Empirical evidence suggests that they serve as planning and perceptual units in the production and comprehension of language. Speech, though it is linear, uttered one word at a time, contains errors that suggest we do not select one word from our mental dictionary, say it, select another word, say it, and so on, chaining them together. Transpositions of phonemes between phrases that are otherwise intact (*let me sew you to your sheet*) or transpositions of the phrases themselves (*he sliced the knife with his finger*) suggest that we plan utterances in chunks, composing phrases and structures of phrases before a word is uttered.

A now classic series of "click" experiments, conducted by Fodor and Bever, suggests that phrases serve as perceptual units during sentence recognition. Subjects were presented with a spoken sentence and, at some point during the sentence, a brief clicking sound. The researchers knew from numerous findings in perceptual psychology that perceptual units are quite resistant to interference from outside (such as a click) and that clicks between sentences are much more likely to be remembered than clicks within sentences. They hypothesized that the same would hold true for phrases if, like sentences, the phrases serve as perceptual units. Their hypothesis was confirmed. More interesting, when the subjects remembered clicks within phrases, they tended to locate them at or near major boundaries (for example, the boundary following the first noun phrase). When the click occurred before the boundary, subjects reported hearing it later; When it occurred after the boundary, subjects reported hearing it earlier. In either case the subjects were relocating the click to a position closer to the boundary. These findings and the results of further experiments strongly suggest that the comprehension of sentences is broken into subprocedures that correspond to the structure of phrases in the sentence.

A **phrase structure grammar** describes the hierarchical manner in which words combine to form phrases and phrases combine to form sentences. Note that a phrase may be a word or group of words, and structure refers to the nesting or hierarchy of parts. That is, a sentence consists of a noun phrase and a verb phrase, a verb phrase consists of a verb or verbs and optionally a noun phrase, and so on.

A phrase structure grammar is **context free** if its rules apply regardless of context. Thus the composition of subphrases (such as the NP and VP immediately under S) is entirely independent, and rules specifying, for example, an NP will be the same for NPs preceding the verb, those following the verb, and those occurring in other contexts. Context-free grammars are sufficient to describe many of the sentences occurring in English and other natural languages, and they are restricted enough to guide efficient processes for recognizing those sentences. (Indeed the "languages" for instructing computers have context-free grammars.) Most languages are not entirely context free, however. English, for example, constrains the choice of pronouns preceding the verb to one form (*he, they*) and those following the verb to another (*him, them*), it requires agreement in number between the verb and the noun phrase that precedes it, and it has several other contextual constraints. But the idea is to approach languages as if they were context free and later to augment certain rules to make them sensitive to context.

Figure 6 gives a simple phrase structure grammar that accommodates the various observations we have made so far. AUX stands for auxiliary verb, a form of *be, do, have*, or one of the modals (*will, could*, etc.). Though auxiliary verbs are also subject to contextual constraints, we will for now treat them as if they were context free. As with the linear grammar, symbols on the right side of each rule can be substituted for the symbol on the left side. Figure 7 traces the recognition of a sample sentence. The stack is still tracking progress

S	→	NP VP		VP	→	AUX VP1
						VP1
NP	→	DET NP1				
		NP1		VP1	→	VERB NP
		PRONOUN				VERB
NP1	→	ADJ NP1				
		NOUN				

Figure 6. A phrase structure grammar.

through the sentence, but progress is now measured in terms of what remains to be found, with the topmost symbol on the stack guiding the procedure. Most of the rules replace the symbol for a phrase or part of a phrase with symbols for its immediate constituents; but when the lexical category of a word to be recognized matches the topmost symbol, that symbol is removed. Recognition is successful if the procedure reaches a state at which all words have been consumed and the stack is empty. Recognition fails if a prediction remains with no word to satisfy it or if a word remains with no prediction to accommodate it. Thus recognition would fail if the sentence ended with *repairs*, because the prediction of an NP would be unfulfilled, or if *cars* were followed by another noun, because an empty stack provides no cue as to how the parsing might continue.

2.2 Parsing and structural representations

Thus far we have been concerned only with the recognition of sentences. Now that structure is something more than sequence, however, representation becomes important. The process of recognizing a sentence and simultaneously building a representation of its structure is **parsing**. A device (actual or conceptual) which performs this process is a **parser**. (These terms sometimes refer to other processes as well, especially those that interpret sentence meaning using some syntactic information.) A parser partitions a sentence into its constituent phrases, subphrases, and lexical categories, labels all these constituents, and builds a hierarchical representation of their structure. Representation can take the form of a list with nested sublists or a tree:

S → NP VP   (S (NP VP))

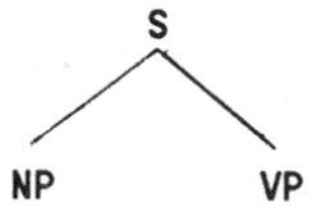

The relationship of rules to structure is always isomorphic. As each rule executes, it builds a corresponding level in the representation, a

[start]				S		
S	→	NP VP		NP	VP	
NP	→	DET NP1		DET	NP1	VP
DET	→	the		NP1	VP	
NP1	→	ADJ NP1		ADJ	NP1	VP
ADJ	→	skilled		NP1	VP	
NP1	→	NOUN		NOUN	VP	
NOUN	→	mechanic		VP		
VP	→	AUX VP1		AUX	VP1	
AUX	→	is		VP1		
VP1	→	VERB NP		VERB	NP	
VERB	→	repairing		NP		
NP	→	NP1		NP1		
NP1	→	NOUN		NOUN		
NOUN	→	cars		[empty]		

Figure 7. Phrase structure recognition.

nested bracket or a node with branches. Thus the rule for an NP (an NP would be atop the stack once S → NP VP executes) would produce the following result:

NP → DET NP1   (S (NP (DET NP1)))

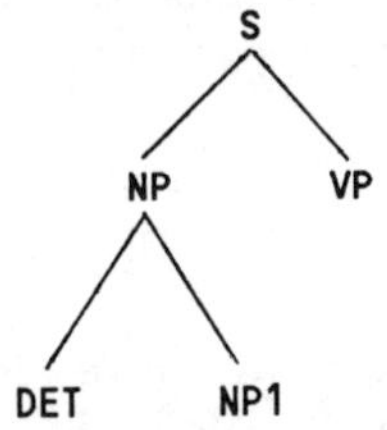

After a few rules execute, the nesting of brackets becomes almost unreadable, so from now on we will use the tree diagrams, which are known as **phrase markers**. The phrase marker in Figure 8 corresponds to the parse in Figure 7; each node corresponds to the constituent on the left of a rewrite arrow.

Phrase markers are convenient for describing structures and thinking about processes, but a caution is in order. It is not necessarily the case that any structural representation is built in the process of sentence comprehension. Though empirical research suggests that we create mental representations of the propositional content of sentences, persistent efforts have found no trace of a purely syntactic representation. It may be that we indeed do build representations of sentence or phrase structure to pass along to processes that subsequently extract meaning; but it is equally possible that interpretation of meaning is concurrent with parsing and that syntactic structures simply guide the interpreter.

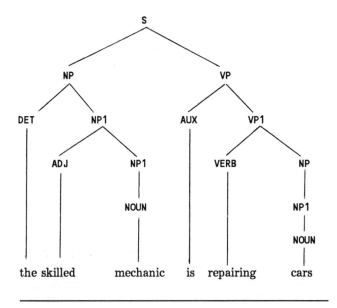

Figure 8. A phrase marker.

The first noun phrase of a simple sentence such as the one represented in Figure 8 is traditionally referred to as the **subject** and the second NP as the **direct object**. Though these terms play a significant role in linguistic analysis, they are intuitive and quite difficult to define. On the one hand, they describe functions of phrases: thus in a sentence with a verb expressing an action (*repair* is an example), the subject is the doer of the action and the direct object undergoes the action. If the verb expresses a state of affairs, the functions are quite different: *Connie resembles a famous entrepreneur.* On the other hand, the notions of subject and object play a role in descriptions of constituent structure. Thus we can describe a yes/no question in terms of the inversion of a subject and the first auxiliary verb. Consider, for example, a sentence that has two NPs preceding the verb sequence:

The women that Jane knows are trying to sell the car.

Women is the subject of is *trying*, and to form the question, the auxiliary is moved to a position preceding it and not perchance the other noun phrase:

Are the women that Jane knows trying to sell the car?

The subject also agrees in number with the verb (in this case both are plural), and if a tag question is added, its subject agrees in person, number and gender with the subject of the sentence:

> Jane is thinking about buying it, isn't she?

In the sentences considered thus far, the functional and structural definitions apply to the same noun phrases. However, consider this sentence:

> The car was purchased by Jane.

Functionally, *Jane* is the subject and *car* is the direct object, but structurally *car* is the subject and *Jane* the object of a preposition. For now, we will consider subjects and objects only for the place they occupy in constituent structures.

2.3 Recursion and rewrite rules

How useful is a phrase structure grammar? Certainly the noun and verb phrases are there, and specifying the grammar in terms of phrases eliminates some redundancies. We have also the evidence that phrase structure plays a role in comprehension. Were that all that could be said for the grammar, it would be of considerable interest. What clinches the case for phrase structure grammar is that the diverse and sometimes intricate syntactic structures of English and other languages consist of only a few kinds of phrases, combined and recombined. These phrases, in turn, require only a small set of simple rules. Although some structures and some relationships between structures resist analysis into phrase structure rules, the elegant simplicity and descriptive range of phrase structure grammars make them basic components of most modern theories of syntax.

An important reason for the elegance and economy is that the grammar has **recursive** rules. That is, a phrase structure grammar can define phrases in terms of simpler versions of themselves. To see how recursion lends economy, consider that noun phrases can contain prepositional phrases, and that, as with adjectives, no constraint limits the number of prepositional phrases that can be strung together:

> The mechanic from the garage on the corner by the statue in the center of town repaired the puncture in the tire on the left front of the car.

That sentence, with its monstrous total of eight prepositional phrases, seems complicated, but our simple grammar will recognize it if we add only two rules:

> NP → NP PP   PP → PREP NP

Notice that the second rule allows us to reuse (recursively) the NP rules we already have; a prepositional phrase is simply a preposition plus a noun phrase. The embedded noun phrase may in turn have a preposi-

S	$\rightarrow$	NP VP	NP	VP		
NP1	$\rightarrow$	NP PP	NP	PP	VP	
NP	$\rightarrow$	DET NP1	DET	NP1	PP	VP
the	$\rightarrow$	DET	NP1	PP	VP	
NP1	$\rightarrow$	NOUN	PP	VP		
PP	$\rightarrow$	PREP NP	PREP	NP	VP	
PREP	$\rightarrow$	from	NP	VP		
NP	$\rightarrow$	DET NP1	DET	NP1	VP	
DET	$\rightarrow$	the	NP1	VP		
NP1	$\rightarrow$	NOUN	NOUN	VP		
NOUN	$\rightarrow$	garage	VP			

Figure 9. Recursive application of rewrite rules.

tional phrase. (The mechanic is *from the garage*, but it is the garage that is *on the corner*.) This recursive structure of noun and prepositional phrases means that alternating the rules for NP and PP will account for an infinitely long sequence of prepositional phrases. Figure 9 traces the recognition of the first part of the sample sentence.

So far the grammar specifies only three contexts in which noun phrases may occur: they can precede or follow the verb or occur within prepositional phrases. Noun phrases also appear in other contexts, within the noun phrase, for example:

Attributive: [NP The [NP antique car] mechanic] loves old cars.
Possessive: [NP [NP The mechanic] 's work] pleased the owners.

Brackets show the nesting of noun phrases. Attributive noun phrases immediately precede the noun. For present purposes, we can postulate the simple rule NP1 → NP NP1, though in a working parser we would need to avert the left recursion so that this rule and NP → NP1 will not endlessly cycle. The new rule is directly recursive in that the category on the left of the arrow is repeated on the right and the rule can be applied to its own "output." Possessives, on the other hand, precede any adjectives and take the place of determiners. *Carol's old car* is a well-formed sentence, *the Carol's old car* is not well formed, and in *old Carol's car*, the adjective modifies *Carol's*, not *car* (that is, it is part of the possessive NP). Possessives can be recognized by two additional rules in which the symbol POSS for stands for possessives and MARK for the suffixes *'s* and *s'*,

NP → POSS NP   POSS → NP MARK

To accommodate adjacent possessives (*Jane's father's illness*) requires a third rule, NP1 → POSS NP1. The rules for both attributive and possessive NPs produce **left-branching structures**; they extend nodes

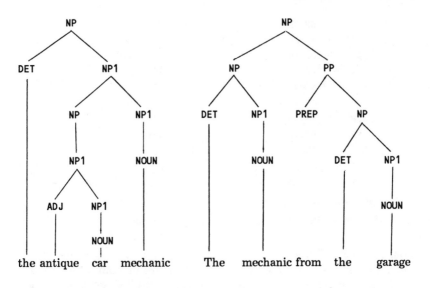

Figure 10. Recursive noun phrases.

to the left of the matrix NP. Figure 10 contrasts a left-branching attributive NP with a **right-branching** prepositional phrase. This distinction will become important when we consider parsing strategies.

Besides noun and prepositional phrases, two other kinds of phrases occur frequently, and both involve recursion. A verbal phrase may serve either as a right-branching modifier (*the mechanic repairing foreign cars quit the job*) or as a noun phrase (*repairing foreign cars annoyed the mechanic*). Since verbal phrases derive from verb phrases, they can be accommodated by adding just two rules to the grammar:

NP1 → NOUN VP1   NP → VP1

See Figure 11 for the structure of a sentence containing a verbal phrase as modifier. The other commonly occurring construction we have already encountered; it has a sentence serving as a phrase. Since nearly every constituent has multiple uses, it is hardly surprising that sentences should contain substructures that are sentences. As the following sentences illustrate, they may be subjects of verbs or their objects, and like pronoun NPs, they cannot be preceded by determiners or adjectives.

That he knew it astonished me.
The mechanic knew that the man owned the car.

They can be of any length; in the following sentence everything past the second word belongs to a single sentential NP:

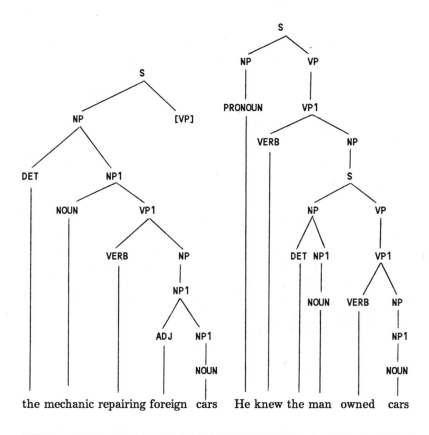

Figure 11. Verbal and sentential phrases.

> I know that if the people we saw on the bus were aware
> of the problem they would probably tell the driver and
> he would pull over to the curb to correct it.

Sentential noun phrases can be recognized by reusing the rule for sentences (S → NP VP), together with the rules:

NP → S   NP → COMP S

COMP is short for complementizer, usually the word *that*.

Somewhat more complicated rules would be necessary to explicate fully the relationship between *knew* and *mechanic* in the first of the sample sentences, to insist on complementizers for subject NPs and make them optional for objects, and so on. But those are details. The point remains that almost every rule of a fully developed phrase structure grammar has multiple applications. There exist only the few basic kinds of phrases, and these few kinds appear and reappear, performing various functions. Whereas the linear grammar requires about a dozen rules for a repertoire of only nine sentence patterns (not counting the infinite iteration of adjectives), a phrase structure grammar consisting of fewer than two dozen rules has a repertoire of several hundred sentence patterns if we count the various combinations of prepositional, verbal, sentential phrases, plus attributives and possessives. Though such phrase structure rules cannot account for all syntactic phenomena (as we will see) and therefore require special augmentations, they do serve as a basic component for most modern grammars.

An extension of phrase structure grammar, known as **X-bar theory**, captures additional regularities of English, and because these also describe syntactic structures in many other languages they may offer a glimpse of a universal grammar that underlies all. Consider first that our phrase structure rules allow NP1 to be rewritten as a noun and an optional PP or S (*delight in her success, delight that she succeeded*) and VP1 to be rewritten as a verb and an optional PP or S (*he sent for help, he knows that help will arrive.*) In the notation of x-bar theory, these rules would be formulated as follows:

$$N' \rightarrow N \ S$$
$$N' \rightarrow N \ PP$$
$$V' \rightarrow V \ S$$
$$V' \rightarrow V \ PP$$

N and V are the heads of the phrases they occupy: N' and V' (called N-bar and V-bar). Heads are so distinguished because they share with their phrases certain important properties; if, for example, N is plural, N' is necessarily also plural. A rule (called a "schema") generalizes these rules, rewriting the phrase structures and lexical categories as the variables X and X' and the optional structures as (complement):

$$X' \rightarrow X \text{ (complement)}$$

In effect the schema generalizes the four rules, but at a higher level of abstraction. Now consider the possibility of an adjective phrase, consisting of an adjective followed by either a PP or an S (*proud of her success, proud that she succeeded*), which affords two additional rules that are generalized by the schema:

$$A' \rightarrow ADJ \ PP$$
$$A' \rightarrow ADJ \ S$$

An additional generalization can be captured if we note that an adjective phrase may begin with a degree word followed by the adjective (*very proud, somewhat proud*) and that the degree word serves as a specifier, much as a determiner specifies for an NP. Thus we have the abstract rules:

$$\text{A}' \quad \rightarrow \quad \text{(DEGR) A}'$$
$$\text{N}' \quad \rightarrow \quad \text{(DET) N}'$$

which, in turn, can be captured by a second schema employing the variable X" (X-double bar):

$$\text{X}'' \quad \rightarrow \quad \text{(specifier) X}'$$

In effect the two schemata substitute for eight phrase structure rules, generalizing the structures of verb, noun and adjective phrases. Moreover, the two schemata appear to be linguistic universals, describing an abstract category of specifiers and complements, which, though languages realize them in different ways, exist in all grammars. Though X-bar theory operates at a level of abstraction much higher than the grammar we have been considering and has had little influence on computational approaches, it does suggest that phrase structure grammars are on the right track and it may hold the promise of linguistic universals.

2.4 Recursive transition networks

A phrase structure grammar is readily implemented in a set of recursive transition networks, plus extensions to handle prepositional phrases. Figure 12 presents network versions of the basic grammar specified in Figure 6. As before, arcs in the networks correspond to rules in the grammar. Thus, for example, the sentence network specifies that a sentence must consist of a noun phrase followed by a verb phrase and is therefore equivalent to the rule S → NP VP. The network differentiates several kinds of arcs. The **cat arcs** match the lexical categories of words, performing the same function that word arcs in the linear grammar perform.

Seek and **send arcs** are new and they manage the recursion. When the processor encounters seek NP or seek PP, it suspends operation on the present network and pushes the location of the calling arc onto the stack, so that it can resume operation once the phrase has been matched. (For this reason, terminology is sometimes used for seek and send arcs: "push NP" and "pop NP".) Also, notice that the sentence network has its own send arc and thus can be called recursively, in much the same way that the PP and NP networks are called. The NP network has a separate send arc for pronouns, in order to enforce the constraint that pronouns are never modified by prepositional phrases. Extending a transition network to handle such

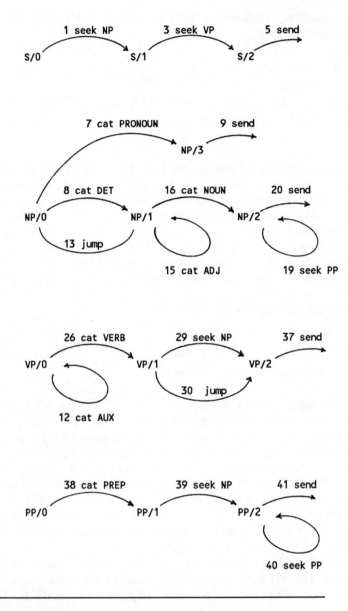

Figure 12. Recursive transition networks.

phenomena as attributive and possessive NPs (via recursive calls on the
NP network), as well as verbal and sentential phrases (which entail
recursive calls on the sentence network), poses no great difficulty and
can be deferred until section 3.3.

	State	Arc	Recognizes	Resulting stack		
1	S/0	1 seek NP		S/0		
2	NP/0	8 cat DET	the	S/0		
3	NP/1	16 cat NOUN	mechanic	S/0		
4	NP/2	19 seek PP		NP/2	S/0	
5	PP/0	38 cat PREP	from	NP/2	S/0	
6	PP/1	39 seek NP		PP/1	NP/2	S/0
7	NP/0	8 cat DET	the	PP/1	NP/2	S/0
8	NP/1	16 cat NOUN	garage	PP/1	NP/2	S/0
9	NP/2	20 send		NP/2	S/0	
10	PP/2	40 send		S/0		
11	NP/2	10 send				
12	S/1	3 seek VP		S/1		
13	VP/0	26 cat VERB	repairs	S/1		
14	VP/1	14 seek NP		VP/1	S/1	
15	NP/0	13 jump		VP/1	S/1	
16	NP/1	15 cat ADJ	foreign	VP/1	S/1	
17	NP/1	16 cat NOUN	cars	VP/1	S/1	
18	NP/2	20 send		S/1		
19	VP/2	37 send				
20	S/3	5 send				

Figure 13. Transition network parsing.

Figure 13 illustrates the operation of the transition networks for *the mechanic from the garage repairs foreign cars*. Notice that the parsing becomes recursive at step 5 when the NP network is called a second time to parse an NP that is a constituent of a PP, which is, in turn, a constituent of an NP. States from which attempted seek arcs depart are on the stack, allowing the parser to wind its way gracefully back to the sentence network (via the sequence of send arcs in steps 9 through 11). Notice that because the seek arcs have succeeded, the parser's return is to the state following.

2.5 Bottom-up parsing

The parsers we have considered so far operate in a **top-down** fashion. They begin with a rule (or network) for the sentence, then proceed down the hierarchy through phrases and lexical categories to words. The most common alternative is **bottom-up** parsing. As that term

Word	Action	Stack
The	Shift DET	DET
automobile	Shift NOUN	NOUN DET
	Reduce with NP1 → NOUN	NP1 DET
	Reduce with NP → NP1	NP DET
mechanic	Shift NOUN	NOUN NP DET
	Reduce with NP1 → NOUN	NP1 NP DET
	Reduce with NP1 → NP NP1	NP1 DET
	Reduce with NP → NP1 DET	NP
from	Shift PREP	PREP NP
the	Shift DET	DET PREP NP
garage	Shift NOUN	NOUN DET PREP NP
	Reduce with NP1 → NOUN	NP1 DET PREP NP
	Reduce with NP → DET NP1	NP PREP NP
	Reduce with PP → PREP NP	PP NP
	Reduce with NP → NP PP	NP
is	Shift AUX	AUX NP
repairing	Shift VERB	VERB AUX NP
foreign	Shift ADJ	ADJ VERB AUX NP
cars	Shift NOUN	NOUN ADJ VERB AUX NP
	Reduce with NP1 → ADJ NOUN	NP1 VERB AUX NP
	Reduce with NP → NP1	NP VERB AUX NP
	Reduce with VP1 → VERB NP	VP1 AUX NP
	Reduce with VP → AUX VP1	VP NP
	Reduce with S → NP VP	S

Figure 14. A bottom-up parse.

suggests, parsing begins with words and their lexical categories, combines them into phrases, combines phrases into higher-level phrases, and those into sentences. Because it is guided by words in the sentence, it is data driven, whereas top-down parsing is goal driven or hypothesis driven, the goal being a complete sentence.

One method of bottom-up parsing employs a **shift-reduce parser,** a refinement of the parser we used in section 2.3. As it proceeds through the sentence, the parser either shifts the next word (or its lexical category) to the stack, displacing downward what is already there, or reduces by substituting other categories using rules of the grammar, or combines the top most items. It places the result of each reduction on the stack, and when the only item left on the stack is an S the parse has succeeded. Figure 14 traces the parse of *the elderly mechanic from the garage repairs foreign cars.* Notice the reduction of

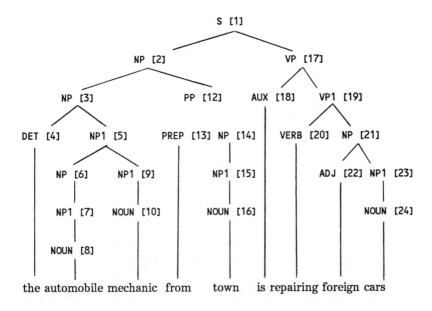

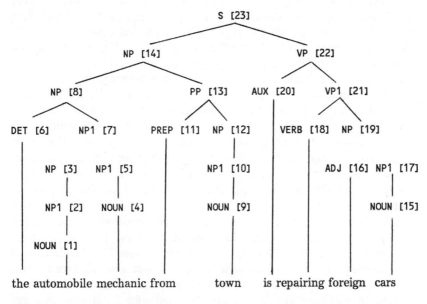

Figure 15. Traversal orders for top-down and bottom-up parsing.

DET and NP1 to NP. A top-down parser would do the opposite,
"expanding" the NP to DET NP1.

The relationship among constituents in the phrase marker offers a
way of thinking about the sequence in which to execute rules. Figure

1	S → NP VP	NP	VP		
2	NP → DET NP1	DET	NP1	VP	
3	DET → the	NP1	VP		
4	NP1 → NOUN	NOUN	VP		
5	NOUN → automobile	VP			
6	VP → VP1	VP1			
7	VP1 → VERB NP	VERB	NP		
	[backtrack]				
2	NP → NP1	NP1	VP		
3	NP1 → NP NP1	NP	NP1	VP	
4	NP → DET NP1	DET	NP1	NP1	VP
5	NP1 → NP NP1				
	[left recursion]				

Figure 16. Top-down parse with backtracking.

15 contrasts the top-down and bottom-up orders of traversal. Numbers in brackets give the sequence in which constituents are removed from the stack. Notice that top-down parsing corresponds to a depth-first traversal. For certain structures, notably those that branch to the left, bottom-up parsing can be very efficient. Notice in Figure 14 that the parser handles with aplomb the left-branching attribute noun *automobile*. For the same sentence, as Figure 16 demonstrates, a top-down procedure would conclude at step five that *the automobile* is a complete NP and pursue its false conclusion until the parse fails for lack of a verb at step 7. (If the word following *automobile* were ambiguous between noun and verb (*repair*, for example, or *garage*) the parse would proceed even further before failing.) After some flailing around, it would discover that by discarding much of what it had already done and applying a different rule at step two, it would be able to proceed further.

Then it would encounter a worse problem, endlessly recycling the rules for NP (which rewrites to include an NP1) and NP1 (which rewrites to include an NP). This is **left recursion**, the Achilles' heel of top-down parsers. If we parse from right to left, the rules for certain right-branching structures will endlessly cycle. Though there is a solution (providing rules for a longer context), for languages that are consistently left-branching (Japanese is an example), bottom-up parsers have a decided advantage. However, the bottom-up design encounters problems with some right-branching structures, prematurely reducing constituents then needing to backtrack. And, as we will see in the next chapter, they also have difficulty with certain sentences in which constituents have been moved.

Otherwise there exists no decisive reason for preferring either approach. Ambiguities of lexical category (*can* or *bank* as noun or verb, *green* or *English* as noun or adjective) create problems for bottom-up parsers, because they must consider all possibilities for each word, including those that would never lead to a well-formed sentence. Top-down parsers are more discriminating; at any point in the parse, they consider only categories that could legally appear in the context at hand. However, with grammars more complete than the rudimentary set of rules we have thus far, top-down parsers must spend consider-able time rewriting rules at the upper levels of the phrase marker before eventually getting to the words of the sentence; much of that processing may be discarded should the sentence prove unobliging.

Other considerations may favor the bottom-up method of building upward through the hierarchy of phrases. As discussed in Chapter 10, bottom-up parsing allows the incremental pairing of syntactic with semantic rules and hence allows for the timely application of semantic constraints. Bottom-up parsing can also be instrumental in speech recognition, where it is often difficult to identify every words. Clearly enunciated words (often content rather than function words) afford small "islands of reliability." Beginning from these islands of identified words, a bottom-up parser can work backward in the sentence and forward; it can use partially completed syntactic structures as evidence for predicting what the unidentified sounds may represent.

Section three: Ambiguity, Preferences, and Modeling

3.1 Coping with non-determinacy

Parsers employing either the top-down or the bottom-up approach (or any other) must be able to backtrack or otherwise cope with **local ambiguity**-the unhappy fact that at some points where a choice must be made, available information will be insufficient to determine which alternative is correct. Context-free grammars are locally **non-determi-nistic** in that at any moment, more than one rule may be applicable with nothing to determine which it should be. Both top-down and bottom-up parsing, therefore, will build structures that do not ultimately prove viable. What is worse, many words are ambiguous as to lexical category. Consider *a German car mechanic works hard*. Is *German* an adjective or a noun, and if an adjective, does it modify *car* or *mechanic*? If a noun, is it an attributive or the head of the phrase? Is *car* an attributive? For that matter, is *mechanic* an attributive and *work* the head noun? Information necessary to make those decisions is near the beginning of the sentence, but sometimes the necessary information is a distance away:

Is the man standing on the corner your friend?

       | |

    choice: modifier   answer: modifier
    or main verb?

Do the assignments that I have given you conflict?

| |

choice: command or question?   answer: question

Careful scheduling can lessen the number of false paths, either *ad hoc* scheduling methods, which give priority to rules for frequently occurring constructions, or principled scheduling, which may emulate the efficient processes by which human beings comprehend syntax (so far as they are known).

Complicating matters, some sentences are ambiguous when taken as a whole, and for them the parser cannot be satisfied merely to find one successful path. Prepositional phrases, for example, often have more than one possible attachment. With *he completed the work at noon*, the final phrase can attach in either of two ways (NP1 → NP1 PP or VP1 → VP1 PP). Sequences of prepositional phrases compound the problem, because the number of potential attachments increases exponentially with the number of phrases. The ambiguity is most obvious when semantics cannot resolve it: *I saw the man on the hill with the telescope*. Does *with the telescope* explain how I saw him or identify which man or specify which hill? Similar problems arise in determining the scope of conjunctions: what does *or* connect in each of the following sentences?

I'll have bread or rolls and coffee.
I'll have bread or coffee and cream.

These are **global ambiguities**, a rather grand term but intended only to distinguish them from ambiguities that are local and hence resolvable. No syntactic information will resolve global ambiguities; hence a parser cannot decide. Nor would we necessarily want it to. We might want the parser to simulate non-determinacy, recognizing unresolved ambiguity in the syntax and building representations of the alternative structures, perhaps offering them up in the order human beings prefer.

Given all this ambiguity, both local and global, it is strange that humans do not experience uncertainty in comprehending sentences. Seldom are we conscious of ambiguities. We have no memory of examining locally feasible alternatives, of pursuing one possibility and then another; and the very rapid pace of speech comprehension (better than four words a second) gives us little or no time for decision making. With global ambiguities, we usually reach a single construal, and unless we reexamine the sentence, we are not aware of the others.

That our comprehending of syntax is swift and sure, whereas computational parsing tends to be halting, has made ambiguity a central issue in syntactic processing. It has prompted researchers to develop expedients for recovering from unavailing paths or to avoid them. Models for human sentence processing make ambiguity their agenda and investigate computationally the mechanisms and strategies that human beings may use to cope. Though the syntax presented so far is not complete, we have enough to consider some expedients used in working parsers and to explore competing models that emulate human performance.

3.2 Backtracking and chart parsing

To cope with local ambiguities and to simulate non-determinacy for globally ambiguous constructions, the parser must at least be capable of recovering from paths leading to local failure. Failure occurs when the parser reaches a state from which no rule (or arc) allows it to proceed further. The parser is blocked before the sentence is finished. A parse can also fail if the end of the sentence is reached, but expected constituents remain on the stack. The sentence is finished, as it were, before the grammar will allow. The optimistic thinking about these problems is not that the parser has failed, but that it has eliminated a possibility. (Unavailing paths are so frequent in knowledge-based search processes, in computational theorem-proving, in problem-solving and expert systems that trial and error is accepted practice, as long as it is guided by heuristics and thus is not entirely blind.) Therefore, much work, for parsers and other devices, has gone into methods of recovering from errant paths.

For practical parsers and for some that are linguistically motivated, a common solution is backtracking, particularly **chronological backtracking**. The parser keeps a running record of rules or arcs that might apply at any point, but that were not chosen. By maintaining the record in a stack, the parser can backtrack to the most recent choice point (hence the method is chronological). If no alternative there leads to a successful path, the parser has the next most recent choice point atop the stack, and so on.

Though chronological backtracking consumes little memory, it can consume too much time, trudging the same paths over and over again. The usual solution is to maintain a record of structures already recognized. For every position in the sentence, the record specifies all well-formed substrings that begin or end at that position. For convenience the record is in the form of a **chart**, an abstract geometric structure consisting of vertices connected by edges. Vertices represent a series of states corresponding to constituents in the sentence. Each time the parser executes a rule (or an arc), it extends an edge between the appropriate vertices to specify the constituent it has succeeded in

After parsing an NP:

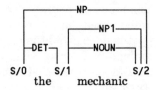

After parsing an NP containing a PP:

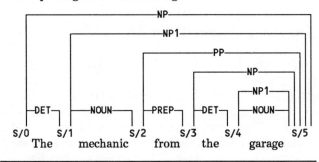

Figure 17. Two stages of a chart.

recognizing. When it must backtrack, it can consult the chart at each state, retrieve well-formed constituents, and thus avoid reparsing them.

This is to take advantage of the context independence of rules and the constituents they recognize. The same rule and constituent may participate in the recognition of quite different structures. For example, when the parse of *the mechanic from the town repaired it* failed, it had already recognized the determiner and noun and can retrieve these from the chart (see Figure 17). Since the parser had only gotten a short way into the sentence, the rules and constituents are few. But consider that following the prepositional phrase the possibilities have more than doubled (second stage of the chart). Since no possibility is ever discarded, the parser can backtrack and, without redoing any work, explore a different path through the grammar.

An **active chart parser** takes this idea one step further, representing as edges not only completed constituents, but also partially completed rules. It can therefore use the chart to manage the parse and never duplicate any of its work. Figure 18 shows the parse of a simple, but locally ambiguous sentence. The aim is to create an active edge that spans the entire sentence. For the first word, a determiner, the chart has active edges for the two rewrite rules that require a determiner. (The new rule NP → DET \ADJ NOUN is a convenience for this example.) The portion of the rule following the backslash represents what remains to be found. With *fellow* (ambiguous between

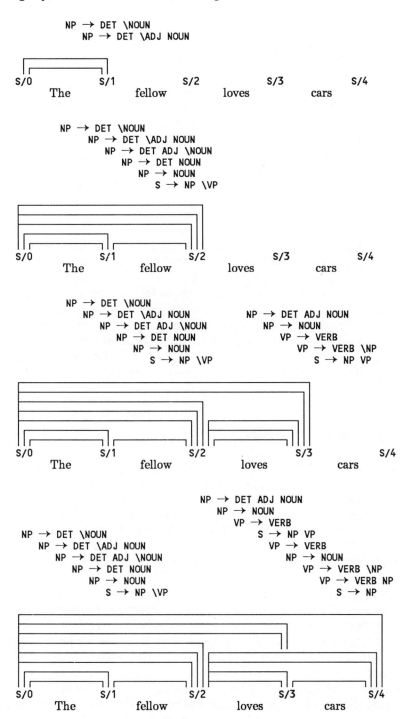

Figure 18. An active chart parser at work.

a noun and an adjective), we have completed NP → DET NOUN (which becomes an "inactive edge") and a new active edge with NP as the first constituent for the sentence rule. In this case, *the fellow* is a complete NP, but in a different sentence it might be incomplete *(the fellow worker)*. Notice that at S/3 the parser entertains the possibilities that *the fellow loves* either is an NP (via NP → DET ADJ NOUN) or a sentence (via NP → DET NOUN, VP → VERB and S → NP VP). Neither analysis is correct, but because edges are never removed, there is no need to reparse. When *cars* is recognized as an NP, it contributes to a VP (via VP → VERB NP) and that VP, in turn, merges with the NP, *the fellow*, (via S → NP VP) to complete the one correct parse spanning the four words.

Active chart parsers have become very popular, mainly for their efficiency. Never repeating any work, they are among the fastest parsers developed to date. They are not difficult to construct and are very adaptable. They demand no special grammar, and the method of parsing can be bottom-up (as in our example) or top-down. Active chart parsers can even combine methods for still more efficiency. For example, a noun phrase might be proposed top-down, based on the position in the sentence, then built bottom-up. Because they allow complete flexibility in the order in which rules are attempted, active chart parsers are useful in modeling human performance; they can simulate preferences that arise in processing sentences.

3.3 Parsing preferences

When confronted with certain structural ambiguities, usually global ambiguities but sometimes local ambiguities as well, human beings exhibit preferences. The preferences are unconscious, but strong and quite consistent. We prefer one analysis to another, though both are equally possible according to the grammar, and we often fail to notice that a different construal is possible. These tendencies are highly systematic and can be categorized into two families of preferences, right association and minimal attachment, with preferences of each family arising in certain arising in certain generalized structural circumstances. The preferences are therefore presumed to offer evidence of how the human sentence processor operates.

Right association attaches a word or phrase to the lowest existing node to the right in the phrase marker, even when a different attachment is feasible. For a predominantly right-branching language like English, this means that new constituents tend to be interpreted as being part of the constituent that is being parsed rather than as part equally possible according to the grammar, and we often fail to notice that a different construal is also possible. These tendencies are highly

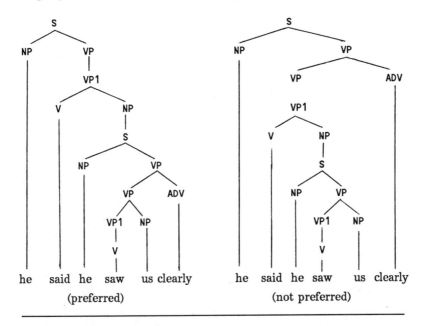

Figure 19. Right association.

systematic and can be categorized into two families of preferences, right association and minimal attachment, with preferences of each family potential for ambiguity arises in sentences containing embedded verb phrases. The prepositional phrase *for you* could attach to either verb phrase in *he wanted the table we found for you,* and *with thin legs* could attach to either of the two most recent noun phrases in *the boy on the stool with thin legs.* Also, *clearly* can attach to either verb phrase in *he said he saw us clearly* (see Figure 19). In each case, right association attaches the modifier to the constituent immediately to the right; thus clearly attaches to the verb phrase dominated by the head *saw* rather than that dominated by the head *said.* Similarly, *for you* attaches to the lower right (with *found*) rather than the upper left (with *wanted*), and *with thin legs* attaches to *the stool.* Where there is lexical ambiguity, right association can create garden paths, as in *without her help would be unavailable,* where ambiguous *her* allows *help* to be incorporated into the PP, and *the granite rocks during earthquakes,* where the ambiguities of *granite* and *rocks* conspire to create an apparent NP.

The preference for **minimal attachment** builds the structure containing the fewest nodes compatible with the input (see Figure 20). Consider, for example, that because prepositional phrases can attach either to a VP (as we have just seen) or to an NP, two analyses are possible for *Joe read the book on the floor.* Minimal attachment prefers the analysis in which *on the floor.* Joe was standing, sitting,

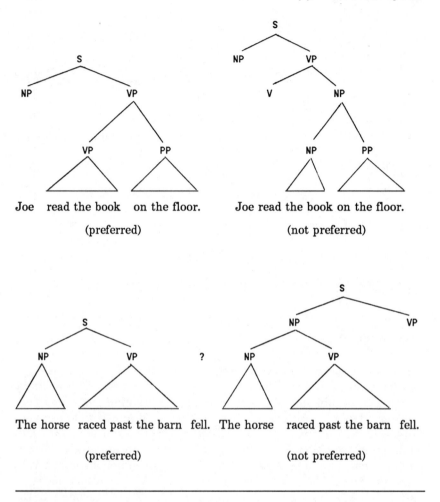

Figure 20. Minimal attachment.

or lying on the floor as he read. The preference is so strong that it overcomes right association which would attach the phrase at the lower right, as a modifier of *book*. Like right association, minimal attachment also accounts for the garden path effect in *the horse raced past the barn fell*, for example, or *Joe told the boy the dog bit the doctor would help him*. Recognizing a VP following an NP, in the first sentence, we anticipate the simplest analysis, which would have the VP attach immediately below the S and complete S → NP VP.

Both right association and minimal attachment are only preferences, however, and they can be overridden by syntactic constraints and by considerations of meaning. Minimal attachment may be overruled when verbs constrain the kinds of structures that can follow them;

chose is such a verb and it allows only non-minimal NP attachment, as in *I chose the book on the floor*. (Compare *I put the book on the floor*.) In *he wanted the table that we saw for you*, the meaning of the verb overrides right association; *for you* is attached to *wanted* (rather than to *saw*), because *saw* does not ordinarily have a beneficiary. Thus preferences should be understood as "defaults" that come into effect when no syntactic or semantic factors override them. That they are indeed defaults is confirmed both by studies that measure the time and difficulty of deciding an attachment and by delicate eye-tracking experiments that determine which bits of text are being fixated at a given moment.

3.4 Computational modeling of preferences

The parsing preferences afford a test of computational model for human sentence processing. The model should meet three require- ments. First, it should consistently emulate what is observable in human behavior, in this case regularly producing the attachments (those low and to the right or with a minimal number of nodes) that humans prefer. Second, that behavior should arise from design principles rather than from *ad hoc* manipulations. Right association and minimal attachment are general preferences, and it would not do to have them built in separately for each kind of phrase and for each context in which the preferences occur. No Rube Goldberg device of separately tailored arcs or rules would be very convincing. Third, modeling the preferences should lead to some explanation of why the parser is as it is and perhaps how that came to be.

As it turns out, principles of scheduling, either for transition network arcs or for rules used by a shift-reduce parser, guarantee the preferences and the principles are of the same order of generality. Thus both the transition networks and the shift-reduce parser meet the first two requirements for an adequate model. Because graph notation makes the choices and their schedule clearer, we will use the networks to illustrate. Figure 21 gives a set of recursive transition networks that have been extended to accommodate the structures in our examples and to model the preferences. To parse the adverbs and prepositional phrases that modify verb phrases, the VP network has two new arcs (16 and 17). A new sequence of arcs (6 and 10) in the NP network handles verbal phrases (as in *the horse raced past the barn*), and a new arc (7) parses sentences that function as NPs (*he said he saw us*).

Scheduling send and jump arcs to follow all others at a given state ensures right association. The parser will attempt to incorporate the next word or words within the current phrase before moving on. For example, at state 2 of the verb phrase network, the send arc will

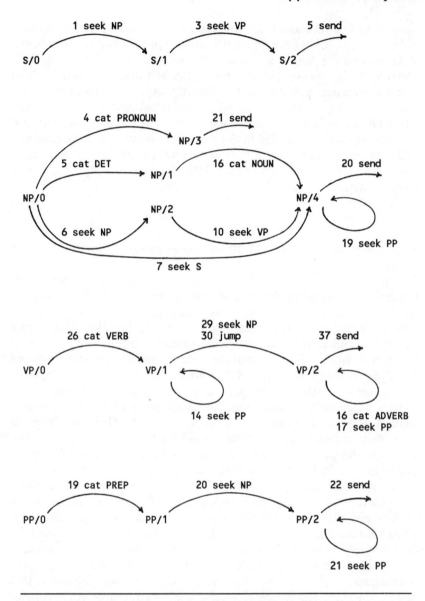

Figure 21. Extensions to the recursive transition networks.

execute only after the arcs for adjectives and prepositional phrases are tried. This assures that, before departing the network, the parser will attach any adverb or prepositional phrase to the VP (in our example, the embedded sentence). In the trace in Figure 22, the parser seeks the VP network for the matrix phrase at the fourth step, then at the

	State	Arc	Recognizes	Resulting stack
1	S/0	1 seek NP		S/0
2	NP/0	7 cat PRONOUN	he	S/0
3	NP/3	21 send		
4	S/1	3 seek VP		S/1
5	VP/0	26 cat VERB	said	S/1
6	VP/1	29 seek NP		VP/1 S/1
7	NP/0	7 seek S		NP/0 VP/1 S/1
8	S/0	1 seek NP		S/0 NP/0 VP/1 S/1
9	NP/0	7 cat PRONOUN	she	S/0 NP/0 VP/1 S/1
10	NP/3	21 send		NP/0 VP/1 S/1
11	S/1	2 seek VP		S/1 NP/0 S/1
12	VP/0	12 cat VERB	saw	S/1 NP/0 S/1
13	VP/1	29 seek NP		VP/1 S/1 NP/0 S/1
14	NP/0	7 cat PRONOUN	us	VP/1 S/1 NP/0 S/1
15	NP/3	21 send		S/1 NP/0 S/1
16	VP/2	15 cat ADVERB	clearly	S/1 NP/0 S/1
17	VP/2	37 send		NP/0 S/1
18	NP/4	11 send		S/1
19	S/2	5 send		

Figure 22. Right association in *he said she saw us clearly*.

eleventh recursively seeks the VP network for the embedded sentence. After entering the VP network for the second time, it does not depart that network until the adverb is parsed. For a shift-reduce parser proceeding bottom-up, the same principle applies. Since reductions conclude the parsing of phrases, it follows that shifts are given preference over reductions whenever both are possible.

Scheduling seek arcs to follow the cat or word arcs at a given state will ensure minimal attachment, forcing the parser to explore all possibilities within the present network before exploring possibilities offered in a subnetwork. As Figure 23 shows, minimal attachment pre-empts right association. When, at the seventh step, the parser takes the cat arc 6 rather than the seek arc 11, it is committed to minimal attachment (of *the man*). Because it then has no path to arc 19 for *with a feather*, the possibility for right attachment of the latter has been preempted. It cannot be attached to *the man*. Implementing the same principle with a shift-reduce parser requires non binary rules (VP1 → VERB NP PP, in this case) and a schedule that resolves reduce - reduce conflicts in favor of the reduction that consumes the larger number of levels of the stack. If the stack contains PP NP and V, for example, that non-binary rule would have precedence over NP → NP PP, thereby favoring right association over minimal attachment.

	State	Arc	Recognizes	Stack
1	S/0	1 seek NP		S/0
2	NP/0	7 cat PRONOUN	she	S/0
3	NP/3	21 send		
4	S/1	3 seek VP		S/1
5	VP/0	12 cat VERB	tickled	S/1
6	VP/1	29 seek NP		VP/1 S/1
7	NP/0	6 cat DET	the	VP/1 S/1
8	NP/1	16 cat NOUN	man	VP/1 S/1
9	NP/4	11 send		S/1
10	VP/2	19 seek PP		VP/2 S/1
11	PP/0	38 cat PREP	with	VP/2 S/1
12	PP/1	39 seek NP		PP/1 VP/2 S/1
13	NP/0	6 cat DET	a	PP/1 VP/2 S/1
14	NP/1	16 cat NOUN	feather	PP/1 VP/2 S/1
15	NP/4	11 send		VP/2 S/1
16	VP/2	41 send		S/1
17	S/2	5 send		

Figure 23. Minimally attached *with a feather*.

What we have so far fulfills two of the criteria for an adequate
model, but not the third. The parser consistently emulates observed
human behavior, and the generalized principles of scheduling result
directly in generalized preferences. The parser does not, however,
fulfill the third criterion. It offers no explanation of why the schedules,
and therefore the preferences, are as they are. The sequence of
decisions do, however, offer a hint. Notice that in all cases the
preferred analysis attaches the word or phrase more quickly than the
non preferred analysis. In the example of right association, it is the
next arc that attaches the adverb, whereas the non-preferred analysis
would send the parser back to the calling network which could then
attach it. In the example of minimal attachment, the non-preferred
path requires a second seek of the NP network before *the man* and
eventually *with a feather* can be attached (via arcs 6 and 19).

That the attachment which can be reached more quickly is preferred
suggests a revision that would exploit the evident preference for speed.
Instead of the sequentially scheduled arcs, what if the parser were
capable of a limited kind of parallel processing? All arcs leaving a given
state would be pursued simultaneously, and the processing would
continue along multiple paths until one of those path succeeded in

recognizing the current word or phrase. At that point all other paths would be abandoned, and parallel parsing would begin again from the state achieved by the successful path. In effect, this pursuing of multiple paths becomes a race, and preferred attachments are the winners.

3.5 Toward a deterministic parser

Intuitively, human parsing seems deterministic, or very nearly so. At any choice point, we seem to have information sufficient to determine an inevitable path through the grammar. We are aware neither of backtracking (except on garden path sentences) or of pursuing multiple analyses simultaneously. Intuitions can of course be unreliable, but they are worth pursuing. So the question becomes, what kinds of information would be sufficient to guide our choices. One answer, explored in Chapter 10, is that information about the meanings of words and sentences is available during the parse to resolve syntactic ambiguities. That would not, however, explain the parsing preferences, which appear to be syntactically motivated. An exploratory model for human parsing, developed by Mitchell Marcus and appropriately called PARSIFAL, pursues a different answer. When confronted with a choice, PARSIFAL looks a limited distance ahead in the sentence and considers the possibilities.

That the distance be limited is crucial. Since the parser is applying rules as it looks ahead, there is little difference between looking ahead as far as necessary to see which of two alternatives will pan out and choosing one path until it fails then returning to pursue another. By looking ahead just three constituents (usually words), PARSIFAL never needs to change its analysis of structures and never pursues false paths. Moreover, its behavior exhibits the human preferences for right association and minimal attachment, and both arise from the design of the parser.

PARSIFAL employs two data structures, a stack containing proposed and partially completed constituents and a three-cell buffer, which affords the look ahead into the sentence. Each node in the stack has associated rules, which are active only when the node is at the top of the stack (thus NP → PRONOUN and NP → DET NP1 would be active when an NP is atop the stack–the packet of rules that are active at any one time corresponds roughly to arcs at any given state in a transition network.) Constituents enter via the buffer where they occupy sequential cells (showing word order) when an active rule asks for the category of currently empty cells. Thus the stack contains structures in need of constituents and the buffer contains constituents in need of a structure. (The buffer can also temporarily store already parsed structures until a larger structure of which they are to be constituents is present on the stack.) Parsing takes place by applying to the buffer's contents, rules that change or add to the stack. The parser has three options:

□ Create one or more nodes atop the stack to hold expected constituents.

□ Extract a constituent from the buffer and attach it to the top node on the stack.

□ Drop the top node from the stack to the first cell in the buffer, allowing the parser to reexamine that constituent and attach it elsewhere.

To illustrate these operations we can use the sentence *he will have said we saw her clearly*, which requires right association and adds some pesky local ambiguities (see Figure 24). PARSIFAL uses "situation-action" rules that are quite different from rewrite rules, and it has a more advanced grammar, but neither difference is important to the basic operation of the parser, so we can use rewrite rules and assume our grammar.

The parser begins by postulating an S and an NP. Thus step 1 shows the incomplete [S . . .] and above that the NP. The first cell of the buffer contains the pronoun *he*, which is attached and the now-complete NP is dropped into the buffer. The second step attaches that NP to the incomplete S, which is now atop the stack. In this way the interaction of stack and buffer is reminiscent of the shift-reduce parser, but without the reduction step. Instead of shifting an NP onto the stack and later reducing it to the S node with the rule S → NP VP, the parser simply attaches the dropped NP to the S which still lacks a verb phrase.

To decide what structure to build on the stack, the parser can examine the three cells of the buffer. Since *will* and *have* can be either auxiliaries or main verbs (*they will have a house, they will their possessions*), an ordinary parser would need scheduled rules, based perhaps on relative frequency, and would necessarily make the wrong choice some of the time. By consulting the buffer, however, PARSIFAL can determine that *will* and *have* are auxiliary to the following *said* (see Figure 24). Using rules such as

AUX → AUXS   VP → AUXS VERB NP

the parser can work its way through the sequence of verbs. (As shown in the next chapter, such rules would need to be more specific about what verb forms can participate, and in what order.)

```
Stack:        [NP]
         1    [S . . . ]
Buffer:       ┌──────────────┐ ┌──────────────┐ ┌──────────────┐
              │ PRONOUN he   │ │              │ │              │
              └──────────────┘ └──────────────┘ └──────────────┘

         2    [S . . . ]
              ┌──────────────┐ ┌──────────────┐ ┌──────────────┐
              │ NP he        │ │              │ │              │
              └──────────────┘ └──────────────┘ └──────────────┘

         3    [S [NP [PRONOUN]] . . . ]
              ┌──────────────┐ ┌──────────────┐ ┌──────────────┐
              │ AUX/VERB will│ │              │ │              │
              └──────────────┘ └──────────────┘ └──────────────┘

         4    [AUXS]
              [VP . . . ]
              [S [NP] . . . ]
              ┌──────────────┐ ┌──────────────┐ ┌──────────────┐
              │ VERB/AUX will│ │ VERB/AUX have│ │ VERB said    │
              └──────────────┘ └──────────────┘ └──────────────┘

         5    [AUXS [AUX]]
              [VP . . . ]
              [S [NP] . . . ]
              ┌──────────────┐ ┌──────────────┐ ┌──────────────┐
              │ VERB/AUX have│ │ VERB said    │ │              │
              └──────────────┘ └──────────────┘ └──────────────┘

         6    [AUXS [AUX] [AUX]]
              [VP . . . ]
              [S [NP] . . . ]
              ┌──────────────┐ ┌──────────────┐ ┌──────────────┐
              │ VERB/AUX have│ │ VERB said    │ │              │
              └──────────────┘ └──────────────┘ └──────────────┘

         7    [VP . . . ]
              [S [NP] . . . ]
              ┌──────────────┐ ┌──────────────┐ ┌──────────────┐
              │ [AUXS]       │ │ VERB said    │ │              │
              └──────────────┘ └──────────────┘ └──────────────┘

         8    [VP [AUXS]. . . . ]
              [S [NP] . . . ]
              ┌──────────────┐ ┌──────────────┐ ┌──────────────┐
              │ VERB said    │ │              │ │              │
              └──────────────┘ └──────────────┘ └──────────────┘

         9    [VP [AUXS] [VERB] . . . ]
              [S [NP] . . . ]
              ┌──────────────┐ ┌──────────────┐ ┌──────────────┐
              │              │ │              │ │              │
              └──────────────┘ └──────────────┘ └──────────────┘
```

Figure 24. Parsing the verb sequence.

The look-ahead procedure also helps with the sentential NP, *we saw her face clearly*, although this time it will only confirm the analysis (see Figure 25). An NP is expected, but *she* cannot be the object of *said*. Looking ahead to the following word, a verb, helps the parser select an appropriate rule (NP → S) at step 10. The parser then accepts *we* as the subject of the embedded S and posits a VP (steps 12 and 13).

```
10    [NP]
      [VP [AUXS] [VERB] . . . ]
      [S [NP] . . . ]
```
PRONOUN we		

```
11    [NP]
      [NP [S . . . ]]
      [VP [AUXS] [VERB] . . .]
      [S [[NP] . . . ]
```
PRONOUN we	VERB: saw	

```
12    [NP [S . . . ]]
      [VP [AUXS] [VERB] . . .]
      [S [[NP] . . . ]]
```
[NP [PRONOUN]]	VERB: saw	

```
13    [VP]
      [NP [S [NP [PRONOUN] . . . ]]]
      [VP [AUXS] [VERB] . . . ]
      [S [[NP] . . . ]
```
VERB: saw		

Figure 25. Parsing the sentential NP.

The buffer comes into play again at step 13 when the parser must look ahead to the word beyond *her* in order to interpret that pronoun. The recursive transition network, using the schedule set for right association, would go astray here, preferring the cat PRONOUN arc for a simple object to the seek NP arc for possessive NPs and would then fail to account for *face* and need to backtrack. When the parser reaches the adverb, *clearly*, it makes the attachment preferred by right association. Both the matrix s and the embedded s are on the stack, but because the latter is atop the stack, it alone is accessible and the adverb is attached to *we saw her face* rather than its matrix *he will have said*.

The three-cell look-ahead has handled ambiguities with no difficulty so far, but what about garden path sentences? If the parser is to be psychologically plausible, three cells should prove insufficient and the parser should derail. In fact it usually does, even for very short sentences such as *have the people paid tomorrow*, where the word necessary to decide whether *have* indicates a command or a question, is exactly four words away, one too many. For other garden path sentences, including the classic *the horse raced past the barn fell*, look-ahead succeeds only if the buffer contains a simple, non-right-recursive phrases. (A noun phrase could occupy one cell, but not a prepositional

14   [VP [VERB] . . .]
      [NP [S [NP [PRONOUN]] . . .]]
      [VP [AUXS] [VERB] . . .]
      [S [[NP] . . .]]

      | PRONOUN her | NOUN face | |

15   [POSS-NP]
      [NP . . .]
      [VP [VERB] . . .]
      [NP [S [NP] . . .]]
      [VP [AUXS] [VERB] . . .]
      [S [[NP] . . .]]

      | [POSS-NP] | NOUN face | . |

16   [NP]
      [NP [POSS-NP] . . .]
      [VP [VERB] . . .]
      [NP [S [NP] . . .]]
      [VP [AUXS] [VERB] . . .]
      [S [[NP] . . .]]

      | NOUN face | ADV clearly | . |

17   [NP]
      [NP [POSS-NP] . . .]
      [VP [VERB] . . .]
      [NP [S [NP] . . .]]
      [VP [AUXS] [VERB] . . .]
      [S [[NP] . . .]]

      | [NP [NOUN]] | ADV clearly | . |

18   [NP [POSS-NP] [NP [NOUN]]]
      [VP [VERB] . . .]
      [NP [S [NP] . . .]]
      [VP [AUXS] [VERB] . . .]
      [S [[NP] . . .]]

      | [NP [NOUN]] | ADV clearly | . |

19   [VP [VERB] [NP [POSS-NP] [NP [NOUN]] . . .]]
      [NP [S [NP] . . .]]
      [VP [AUXS] [VERB] . . .]
      [S [[NP] . . .]]

      | [VP] | ADV: clearly | . |

20   [NP [S [NP] [VP [VERB] [NP [POSS-NP] [NP [NOUN]]] . . .]]]
      [VP [VERB]. . .]
      [S [[NP] [VP [AUXS] [VERB] . . .]]]

      | [NP] | ADV: clearly | . |

21   [VP [VERB] [NP [S [NP] [VP [VERB] [NP [POSS-NP] [NP [NOUN]]]
      . . .]]
      [S [[NP] [VP [AUX] [VERB] . . .]

      | ADV: clearly | . | |

Figure 26. Assuring right association.

phrase containing a noun phrase.) Beginning at the point where the
initial NP has been parsed:

```
[VP . . . ]
[S [NP] . . . ]
```

VERB raced	PREP past	DET the

```
[VP [VERB] . . . ]
[S [NP] . . . ]
```

PREP past	DET the	NOUN barn

Notice that *fell* is not in view when the crucial decision is made to
parse *raced* as the main verb; and when it comes into view, it is *too
late*.

```
[NP]
[PP [PREP] . . .]
[VP [VERB] . . .]
[S [NP] . . . ]
```

DET the	NOUN barn	VERB fell

Once the VP has been successfully parsed, no rule in the grammar will
accommodate it.

```
[S [NP] [VP [VERB] [PP [PREP] [NP]]]]
```

VERB: fell	.	

Thus the parser performs much as we do with garden path sentences,
eventually reaching a state from which it cannot proceed. The limited
look-ahead causes problems with over other sentences that humans
find difficult: for example, sentences that move noun phrase far from
their ordinary locations: *Midori, I enjoy having conversations with.*
Garden path sentences and those with moved constituents should cause
the parser to stumble, but there should also be some way of recovering.
Chapter 10 explores as one possibility interleaving semantic assistance
that allows the parser to recover.

Exercises

1. Identify any recursive constituents in each of the following sentences.

> That the elephant escaped was dangerous.
> The young fellow's life was in danger.
> Prospects for his survival were minimal.
> The job involved catching elephants.
> The elephant was moving very slowly.

2 . Using the rewrite rules in Figure 6, trace the recognition of *Politics makes strange bedfellows*. Include any backtracking.

3. Using the transition network in Figure 13, trace the parse (or parses) of *A line is a length without breadth*.

4. Among the full complement of noun modifiers given in section 2.1 are ordinal and cardinal numbers. Adapt the transition network in Figure 13 to recognize such sequences as *five dogs, the first dog, the first five dogs* and *the first forty five dogs*. What difficulties might you encounter if you wanted also to recognize the pattern in *two-hundred and five dogs*?

5. The usual word order in about half the world's languages places the direct object before the verb. Japanese is an example and Japanese also places a preposition's object before the preposition. If English were such a language, *Bob the dog saw noon at* would be a well-formed sentence. Rewrite the phrase structure rules given in Figure 6 to accommodate sentences in such a language.

6. Give three different phrase markers that would be generated by the following rewrite rules:

$$S \rightarrow a \ b \qquad\qquad c \rightarrow \text{eat}$$
$$a \rightarrow \text{people} \qquad\quad b \rightarrow \text{b and c}$$
$$b \rightarrow \text{eat} \qquad\qquad c \rightarrow \text{eat and c}$$

7. Given the sequence of rules in Figure 6, at what points would an ordinary parser be forced to backtrack with *The old hand waves*. Now assume a parser that is equipped both with a stack and a buffer, trace the parse of the same sentence.

8. For someone designing a parser, what problem is posed by the fact that each of the following sentences is well formed?

> I knew the solution immediately.
> I knew the solution was correct.
> He told the man that he was right.
> He told the man that he met.

Further reading

For a full introductory account of syntax, see Radford (1981). Akmajian and Heny (1975), Chomsky (1980 and 1986), and McCawley (1988) are more advanced. On computational approaches to syntax, indispensable sources are Winograd (1983) and Allen (1987). See also Moyne (1985) and the useful collections of papers in King (1983), Dowty, Karttunen, and Zwicky (1985), Bolc (1987), and Reyle and Rohrer (1988). On coping with ambiguity, see Tomita (1986) and Small, Cotrell, and Tanenhaus (1988). Reports of recent research regularly appear in the journals *Linguistic Analysis, Linguistic Inquiry,* and *The Linguistic Review.* For recent work on computational parsing, consult the journals *Computational Linguistics, Cognitive Science,* and *Natural Language and Linguistic Theory*, as well as the published proceedings of the annual conferences of the Association for Computational Linguistics and the American Association for Artificial Intelligence and the biennial International Joint Conference on Artificial Intelligence.

For surveys of the empirical studies, see Foss and Hakes (1978) and Garnham (1985). On the early "click" studies, see Bever (1970) and Fodor, Bever and Garrett (1974). Bever (1970) proposes that whereas grammaticality is determined by rules, the parsing of sentences is constrained by heuristics that arise from properties of the human cognitive system. On right association, see Kimball (1973, 1975), and on minimal attachment, Frazier and Fodor (1978). They present a hypothetical parser that exhibits both minimal attachment and right association. Wanner and Maratsos (1978) and Wanner (1880) show how parsing preferences can arise from the principled scheduling of an ATN; Fodor and Frazier (1980) respond that the ATN makes certain false predictions; Wanner (1987) presents the parallel ATN, which is critiqued by Altmann (1988). Shieber (1983) and Pereira (1985a) employ shift-reduce parsers to capture the preferences.

For debate on whether such structural principles guide the parser's decisions, see Clifton and Ferreira (1989) and Steedman and Altmann (1989). Chapter 10 explores the relationship between parsing preferences and knowledge of semantics and discourse. Marcus (1980) describes the look-ahead parser and motivation for it; see also Briscoe (1983) and Milne (1986); Johnson-Laird (1983) demonstrates that some topicalizations will defeat the look-ahead procedure.

Chapter 7

Augmented Parsers and Modern Grammars

Section one: Achieving Sensitivity to Context

1.1 Context-free grammar and structural restrictions

The phrase structure parser described in the preceding chapter accepts several hundred sentence patterns and can be extended for patterns of greater and still greater complexity. It accepts many constructions that are not part of the language:

> ? The dog bring his bone.
> ? The dog drank a water.
> ? The dog licked I.
> ? The dog bring.
> ? The dog wanted I give him a bone.

Each of these violates a **structural restriction** in English. The first sentence violates a restriction of number: subjects and verbs can be either singular or plural but must agree in number.   The second sentence illustrates an extension of the system for agreement: a count determiner (used for countable entities) is incompatible with a non-count noun (substances or composites).   In the third sentence, the restriction is of case. Pronouns in English have three cases: subjective, objective, or possessive; and the subject of a verb must be in the subjective case. The fourth sentence violates a transivity restriction: a verb such as *bring* must have an NP direct object. For other verbs, such as *glow*, the situation is opposite; they cannot take objects. The sentence shows that additional restrictions govern direct objects. A sentence can be an NP, but only certain verbs (such as *believe*) permit sentential direct objects. *Want* does not. Number, count, case, transivity and other inherent properties of words that are implicated in structural restrictions are known as **syntactic features**.

Syntactic features are as much a part of our knowledge of language as are the lexical categories. If a parser is to emulate human performance, accepting all possible constructions and boggling at those that are not possible, then its rules must recognize features and incorporate the structural restrictions. There is a highly practical motive as well. Consider the following scenarios. In parsing *the car repair was finished*, the parser can decide that *repair* is not a verb, because it does not agree in number with *car*. With *visiting relatives is/are pleasant*, the number of the verb determines whether the initial NP is an NP (the act of visiting relatives) or a noun modified by a verbal (relatives who are visiting.) In parsing *a wheat farm. . .*, it could decide immediately that because *a* requires a count noun, *wheat* is only an attributive, hence *farm* must be a noun rather than a verb. Finally, because *he* is a subject pronoun and *knew* allows a sentential NP, the parser can negotiate *he knew she bought it* without backtracking. A parser that can recognize structural restrictions will often resolve local ambiguities and thus avoid false paths.

To enforce structural restrictions, the parser must be made sensitive to context. At first glance this seems simple enough. Transitivity, for example, could be handled by specifying that verbs marked intransitive in the lexicon can complete a verb phrase and that those marked transitive will be followed by an NP.

$$\text{VP1} \rightarrow \begin{array}{l} \text{V-intransitive} \\ \text{V-transitive NP} \end{array}$$

But now consider what would be required for sensitivity to number. Whereas the restriction that pertains between verbs and direct objects involves a dependency between sister nodes and is easily implemented, the restriction for number involves nodes that are not sisters:

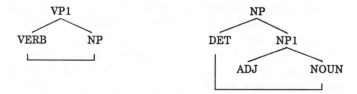

To enforce the restriction between a determiner and its noun requires that we make parts of two rules dependent on one another:

$$\text{NP} \rightarrow \text{DET-number NP1} \qquad \text{NP1} \rightarrow \text{ADJ NOUN-number}$$

It would therefore be necessary to propagate the singular-plural distinction throughout the rules that connect determiners and nouns, subjects and verbs, and so on, replacing each context-free rule with two or more rules that are sensitive to context. Rule after rule would be

duplicated until the parsimony of phrase structure grammar is lost in
a welter of partial redundancies:

S	→	S-sing	S	→	S-pl
S-sing	→	NP-sing VP-sing	S-pl	→	NP-pl VP-pl
NP-sing	→	DET-sing NP1-sing	NP-pl	→	DET NP1-pl
NP1-sing	→	NOUN-sing	NP1-pl	→	NOUN-pl
VP-sing	→	AUX-sing VP1	VP-pl	→	AUX-pl VP1
VP-sing	→	VP1-sing	VP-pl	→	VP1-pl
VP1-sing	→	VERB-sing	VP1-pl	→	VERB-pl

Other constraints between subject and verb require additional rules.
For example, used with pronouns, the present tense singular forms of
the verb *to be* depend on the person: *I am, you are, he is.* Other
constraints pertain to structures following the verb. Though some
involve dependencies within rules (such as the difference between *is*
and *hit*), for others the dependency is between rules, each of which
would need to be duplicated.

The usual method of avoiding redundancy is to employ some form
of record keeping for transivity, number and other features. The
record is created, updated, and consulted by special instructions
associated with rules or arcs. Parsers that are so equipped are said to
be **augmented**. To add record keeping is to add yet another component and again to risk violating Occam's razor, but the situation is
much as it was in adding the stack for recursive parsing: these
augmentations serve the present need, and other considerations will
make them seem inevitable. They will help implement necessary
additions to the phrase structure grammar: the transformational
component of transformational grammars or the special rule-generating
rules and structure-generating equations in more recent grammars
(sections 3.2 and 3.3 describe these).

1.2 Conditions, actions, and registers

An **augmented transition network** employs conditions, actions, and
some form of record keeping, usually registers, to hold the results of
the parse. **Registers** are alterable data structures, built of nodes and
pointers and capable of being added, deleted, or modified on demand.
They can be linked hierarchically to form register structures, and the
those structures can either mirror the phrase structure of sentences or
record the functional relation among such constituents as the subject,
direct object, and so on. Some parsers, equipped to recognize them,
even build structures of semantic cases.

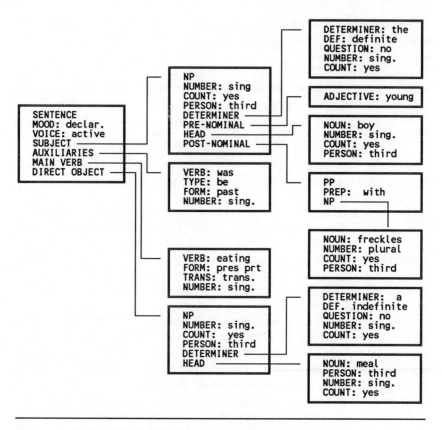

Figure 1. A structure of registers, representing the sentence
The young boy with freckles was eating a meal.

Figure 1 illustrates a structure of registers built for a sample
sentence. It makes fully explicit the form of the sentence, the functions
of major constituents, and the features of all constituents.   The
left-most bracket is the sentence register. It specifies MOOD (declarative, interrogative or imperative) and VOICE (active or passive), features
that can be inferred from the sentence structure. It also specifies the
functions of major constituents of the sentence.   Pointers in the
sentence register (represented by the lines with arrows) link these
functions to the constituents performing the functions. Each major
constituent has its own register, which contains features and may have
additional pointers to registers containing words. In all, the register
structure includes a large amount of syntactic information, but it is
needed for one or another purpose. For example, the distinction
between definite and indefinite (which applies to determiners and
certain pronouns), would be used by a discourse component to
determine whether the NP refers to some previously occurring NP. *The
boy* has been referred to earlier, but *a boy* has not.

Conditions associated with arcs in the network check such features as the number, count, case, and transivity, allowing the arc to execute only if the appropriate features or combinations of features are present. The relevant feature may be of the current constituent, of a constituent already parsed, or both. Conditions specify what circumstances must hold at the current state of the parse in order to execute an arc.

Actions build registers and record features as the parse proceeds. Whenever an arc matches a constituent, an action associated with that arc will create the appropriate register and assign to it the matched constituent. Thus an action on the SEND arc of the NP network would create an NP register and assemble a table specifying the features of the NP; actions on the first NP arc of the S network would assign that NP to the SUBJECT register. Once a verb is encountered, conditions associated with the VERB arc would check to see whether that verb agrees in number with the NP in the SUBJECT register; if it does, the VERB register can be incorporated into the structure of registers. Conditions, actions, and registers (or register structures) make the parser sensitive to context.

Now we need a parser that can build the register structure and a lexicon that specify features. Figure 2 presents a set of transition networks based on those in the last chapter, except that new arcs in the NP network accept sentential noun phrases. The conditions and actions given in Figure 3 set registers and handle agreement in number, count, and case. An action on arc 6 replaces the default value UNMARKED in the NP network's COUNT register with "yes" for determiners (such as the articles *a* and *an* and the quantifiers *each* and *most*) that agree with a count noun. (By tradition, the asterisk refers to the present constituent and is pronounced "star.") The condition associated with the arc for head noun (16) assures agreement.

A similar method assures agreement in number and appropriate case, with special provision (arc 25) for sentential noun phrases, which are always singular. Notice that the NUMBER is handed upward from the noun or pronoun arc that will supply an NP HEAD to the NP network and eventually to the S network. Because conditions are checked and actions execute only if arcs otherwise succeed, timely conditions are an efficient way to avoid backtracking. For example, the condition on the verb arc checks S-NUMBER; there is no waiting for the entire verb phrase to be built.

1.3 Sensitivity to prior context

Because they are reflected in the morphology of words, case and number are familiar restrictions to native speakers of English. However, English and other natural languages observe many other less obvious structural restrictions, including many restrictions that require

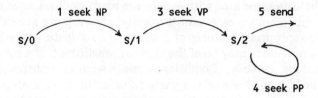

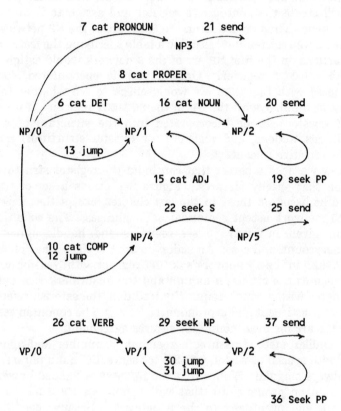

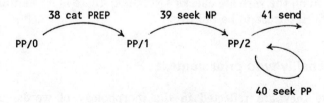

Figure 2. Augmented transition networks.

Arc:

1	seek NP	Condition:	case of * is not OBJECT
		Actions:	assign * to SUBJECT
			set S-NUMBER to NUMBER of *
3	seek VP	Condition:	NUMBER of * = S-NUMBER
6	cat DET	Action:	set NP-NUMBER to NUMBER of *
			set NP-COUNT to COUNT of *
			assign * to MAIN VERB
7	cat PRONOUN	Action:	set NP-CASE to CASE of *
			assign * to NP-HEAD
16	cat NOUN	Condition:	NUMBER of * = NP-NUMBER
			COUNT of * = NP-COUNT
			assign * to NP-HEAD
26	cat VERB	Condition:	NUMBER of S = NUMBER of *
		Actions:	assign * to MAIN VERB
32	seek NP	Condition:	CASE of * is OBJECT or NONE
			NUMBER of * = S-NUMBER.

Lexical entries:

(*a*   DET (COUNT = yes))

(*boys*   NOUN (NUMBER = plural) (PERSON = 3rd.)
          (CASE = unmarked) (COUNT = yes))

(*he*   PRONOUN (NUMBER = sing.) (PERSON = 3rd.)
          (COUNT = yes) (CASE = subject))

(*much* DET (COUNT = no))

(*talk*   VERB (NUMBER = plural) (FORM = infinitive))

(*water* NOUN (NUMBER = singular) (PERSON = 3rd)
          (COUNT = no) (CASE = unmarked))

Figure 3. Augmentations for number, count, and case.

sensitivity to prior context. For these, we can begin by distinguishing three groups of verbs. The first consists of verbs that do not ordinarily take direct objects. Sometimes called intransitive verbs, they include *talk, laugh, sleep, pause, stand, sit, go, rest, glow,* and not very many others. They require the jump arc (30), which extends from VP/1 to VP/2 and thus bypasses the arc that parses direct objects. If the verb

Arc:

10	cat COMP	Condition:	SUBJECT is empty or SUBCATEGORIZES = <u>say</u>
12	jump	Condition:	SUBCATEGORIZES = <u>say</u> SUBJECT is empty or SUBCATEGORIZES = <u>say</u>.
22	seek S	Action:	Set SENTENCE-TYPE to DEPENDENT
		Added to arc 26: Action:	Set SUBCATEGORIZES to SUBCATEGORIZES of *
19	seek NP	Condition: Action:	Case of * is not SUBJECT SUBCATEGORIZES = <u>talk</u> or <u>ate</u> or <u>put</u> Assign * to SUBJECT
30	jump	Condition:	SUBCATEGORIZES is <u>talk</u> and not <u>put</u>
31	jump	Condition: Action:	SUBCATEGORIZES is <u>eat</u> and not <u>put</u> Assign [Someone/something] to DIRECT OBJECT
39	seek NP	Condition: Action:	Case of * is not SUBJECT Assign NP to PREP-OBJ

Figure 4. Augmentations for transivity and sentential noun phrases.

belongs to one of the other groups, the condition (SUBCATEGORIZES = *talk*) will prevent the parser from taking that arc (see Figure 4).

> The young boy slept   on the bed.
> (1 (6 15 16 20)   3 (26 30 36 (38 39 (6 16 20) 41) 37) 5)
>
> (Numbers refer to arcs; parentheses enclose operations within a give network.)

Subcategorizations (which we will name using representative verbs) are syntactic constraints on what constituents can combine, in this case constituents that combine with a verb in forming a verb phrase. They do not depend on the meanings of words, though semantics also has a separate set of constraints, known as selectional restrictions, which require, for example, a human subject for *talk* and a message as direct object for *say*. Because some intransitive verbs do occasionally take direct objects *(this room sleeps four people)*, conditions on the arc for direct objects do not exclude that possibility. Verbs in the second group have a functional direct object, but do not require that the object be explicitly stated. We can say either *we ate apple pie* or *we ate*. Other examples of this large group of verbs include *read, watch, drive, hear,* and *understand*. The arc for direct objects will execute following these verbs, but if there is no direct object, the jump arc (31) supplies a dummy. Finally, there are the verbs that must have a direct object, among them *put, admire,* and *love.* Following these verbs (SUBCATEGORIZES = *put*), the parser is prohibited from either of the jump arcs and must find an NP.

He   brought Jim

(1 (7 21) 3 (26 29 (8 20) 37) 5)

When we consider indirect objects (in section 2.4), we will need to make further distinctions within this last group to specify whether the indirect object can immediately follow the verb or appear as the object of the preposition *to* or *for.*

Verbs subcategorize in several other ways as well. Certain verbs (*put* is an example) require locative word or phrase in addition to direct objects, whereas others, such as *brought,* permit but do not require the locative:

? She put the box.   She brought the box.
She put the box there.   She brought the box there.
She put the box on the shelf. She brought the box to the shelf.

Or consider *want, enjoy, expect,* and *regret*; although all require direct objects, they are not interchangeable in the following pairs of sentences:

I want to go there.   I enjoy going there.
I expect to go there.   I regret going there.

Thus we might have the subcategorization <u>want</u> for verbs that permit an infinitive phrase as direct object and <u>enjoy</u> for verbs that permit a participial phrase.

Some verbs can be followed by more than one adjacent NP, with the subcategorization of the verb determining the function of those NPs. Compare, for example,

They gave the woman a book.   They elected the woman president.

With *gave* and similar verbs, the first NP is an indirect object, serving as recipient or beneficiary and the second is the direct object. With *elected,* the first NP is a direct object undergoing a change of state and the second, an object complement, gives the result of that change. Though subcategorization is most extensive with verbs, nouns and even adjectives can exercise restrictions. For example, the adjective *fond* allows a following prepositional phrase but not a sentential noun phrase; *hopeful* does the reverse, and *glad* allows either:

I am fond of her.   I am hopeful that she will come.
He is glad of that.   He is glad that she will come.

Syntax can sometimes impose multiple restrictions, and these can be significant because they collaborate to reduce ambiguity. For example, as the following sentences suggest, sentential noun phrases are highly constrained:

> That he went home pleased everyone.
> Everyone knew that he went home.
> ? Everyone admired that he went home.
> ? Everyone pleased he went home
> ? He went home pleased everyone.
> ? We were aware of that he went home.

To parse sentential noun phrases in a way that more fully reflects what we know about them requires conditions that specify four different kinds of restrictions. First, though sentential noun phrases can usually serve as subjects, only certain verbs (including *believe, say, expect)* permit them as direct objects. Thus we need to restrict the arcs that parse them with the disjunctive condition either "SUBJECT is empty" or "SUBCATEGORIZES = say." Second, when a sentential noun phrase serves as an object, it need not be preceded by a complementizer (usually *that*), but if it is the subject, the complementizer is mandatory. Thus two arcs (10 and 12) lead to seek S, but 12 (a jump arc which permits passage without *that)* executes only if the subject has already been parsed. A third restriction prevents sentential noun phrases from being the objects of prepositions; thus we need a condition on arcs 10 and 12 which will block them if the NP network is called from the PP network. Finally, not all sentences types can function as NPs; commands and questions are disallowed. Thus seek S sets the sentence register for SENTENCE-TYPE (declarative, interrogative, imperative or dependent) to DEPENDENT, and arcs for parsing questions and commands must carry conditions which check that register before executing.

> That　　he　　complained　　　　surprised me.
> (1 (10 22 (1 (7 21) 3 (26 30 33 37) 5) 25) 3 (26 29 (7 21) 33 37) 5)

> I　　　knew　　　Joe　　disliked it.
> (1 (7 21) 3 (26 29 (12 22 (1 (8 20) 3 (26 29 (7 21) 33 37) 5) 25) 33 37) 5)

1.4　Sensitivity to subsequent context

The restrictions that we have considered thus far require sensitivity to the context established by some prior constituent. For subject-verb agreement, which ordinarily is enforced when the verb is encountered, the prior constituent is the subject NP. Other restrictions, notably those operating within the verb group, require sensitivity to subsequent context. In English, the verb group consists of the notional or main

modal:	form of have:	form of be:	main verb:
			goes
		is	going
	has		gone
	has	been	going
should			go
should		be	going
should	have	been	going

Figure 5. Verb groups in English.

verb, with any preceding auxiliary verbs. Some auxiliaries combine with forms of the main verb to indicate tense: the time of the verb's action or state of being, and whether the action or state is continuing. Thus: *he has gone, he will go, he is going, he will have been going.* Others, known as modal auxiliaries, indicate the speaker's attitude toward that action or state of being, whether it is possible, desirable, necessary, and the like: *he could go, he should go, he must go.*

As Figure 5 demonstrates, sequence is highly constrained. Modals must come first in any sequence in which they appear, and main verbs must come last; any form of *have* in the sequence must precede any form of *be*. All auxiliaries precede the main verb. The verb following a modal must be in the untensed or infinitive form (that is, the verb form in *to go* or *to believe*). The verb following *have* must be a past participle *(gone, believed)*. Except in passive constructions, of which more later, the form following *be* must be a present participle *(going, believing)*.

These restrictions are part of our knowledge of English and should therefore be incorporated in the augmented transition network, where they offer the side benefit of resolving some local ambiguities. Ambiguities arise because present and past participles can also modify nouns, and the modals *might, can, need* and *dare,* can all be mistaken for nouns, as can many untensed verbs, including *regret, spill,* and *fear.*

		verb sequence?
They	regret broken	promises
They	regret	broken promises
The	can will spill	
The can	will spill	
They	fear snow	
They	fear	snow

None of these sentences is globally ambiguous, but without the restrictions, each would generate more than one parse. On the other

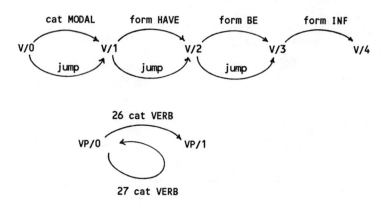

26 cat VERB

Condition: NUMBER of S = NUMBER of *

Actions: Assign * to MAIN VERB
                  Set SUBCATEGORIZES to SUBCATEGORIZES of *

28 cat VERB

Condition: If FORM of * is UNTENSED
                      and TYPE of MAIN VERB is MODAL
                      or TYPE of AUX is MODAL
                  If TYPE of * is MODAL
                      and TYPE of MAIN VERB is not MODAL
                  If FORM of * is PAST PARTICIPLE
                      and TYPE of MAIN VERB is "have"
                      or TYPE of AUX is "have"
                  If FORM of * is PRESENT PARTICIPLE
                      and TYPE of MAIN VERB is "be"

Actions: Append MAIN VERB to AUX
                  Assign MAIN VERB to *
                  Set SUBCATEGORIZES to SUBCATEGORIZES of *

Figure 6. Two ways of parsing the verb group.

hand, the restrictions would not block legal parses in a globally
ambiguous sentence, such as *they observed that water can leak* (where
can may belong either to the noun or the verb phrase.)

Verb group restrictions suggest a sequence of cat arcs, with
conditions on all but the first to check its predecessor. (See Figure 6,
top.) If we put this in terms of rules, we are expanding the two rules
VP → AUX VP1 and VP1 → VERB into four, sacrificing some of the
parsimony of the grammar. The simplest kind of sentence with only

one main verb (*she slept*) would occasion three tests before it is finally parsed by the fourth. Also, since forms of *be* and *have* and several modals can be main verbs, the network must do some backtracking.

One way of approaching this problem is to think of the parser as making tentative decisions as it proceeds left to right through the sentence, then occasionally revising its decision in light of subsequent context. Thus we might have the two arcs shown in Figure 6. Arc 26 parses the first verb in the sentence as if it were the main verb (which often it is) and assigns it to the register for the main verb. If arc 28 encounters a second verb and the several conditions allow, it shifts the putative main verb to the register for auxiliaries and substitutes the new verb. In effect the parser is made sensitive to subsequent context, reinterpreting a verb in view of what follows it. For a fully populated verb group, the register contents would be shifted as follows:

present word	AUX	MAIN VERB
He <u>could</u> have been going	could	
He could <u>have</u> been going	could	have
He could have <u>been</u> going	could have	been
He could have been <u>going</u>	could have been	going
arc 26 28 28 28		

Arc 28 is scheduled first at VP/1 so as to parse only adjacent verbs, and this has a useful side effect. When confronted with globally ambiguous sentences like *they are frightening animals*, we prefer to interpret *frightening* as part of the verb sequence rather than to attach it as a modifier to *animals*. The ordering of arcs does the same, producing the psychologically more popular parse first.

Incorporating tentative decision making in a parser that has been augmented presents no difficulty. Registers are by definition alterable data structures, and actions can as easily change registers as set them. By avoiding some backtracking, the parser becomes more efficient; and reducing the number of arcs (or rules) to the minimum necessary preserves the parsimony of the grammar. The decision making is not very different from what occurs in the look-ahead parser, which must build structures in order to judge whether they are feasible. On the other hand, we are giving the parser additional capability; and if that addition were only to handle verb groups, it would not have sufficient justification.

Other phenomena require sensitivity to subsequent context. For example, English has phrasal verbs, consisting of a verb and either a particle or a preposition:

He looked the situation over.   He looked into the situation.

Both *look over* and *look into* are phrasal verbs; because it cannot follow the object *situation*, *into* is a preposition, whereas the particle *over* can. Phrasal verbs are especially frequent in American English, which readily accepts them from slang: *tune in, turn on and drop out.* Some common verbs *(put, take, turn, get, make)* combine freely with particles or prepositions, and there is even a phrasal verb that functions as a modal *(have to).* What requires sensitivity to subsequent context is that the presence of a particle or preposition can alter the syntactic behavior of the verb, converting an intransitive verb into a transitive verb *(look* with *over* or *into)* or vice versa *(give* with *in).* To accommodate phrasal verbs, the parser treats the verb as it would any other until it encounters the preposition or particle. Then it checks the lexicon for a phrasal verb, appends the particle to the verb, and (if necessary) resets the subcategorization register. As we will see, verb groups and phrasal verbs are not isolated instances; it is often necessary in the course of a parse to change the contents of registers or alter their structure.

1.5 Rule-based parsers and unification

Rule-based parsers can also be augmented, simply by adding actions and conditions to the rewrite rules. They create and consult registers just as with transition networks. The rules in Figure 7 assure subject verb agreement and manage the verb group. (A more concise formalism might employ NP1-number and VP1-number registers to store the number temporarily as the NP and VP are being built.) However, such augmentations reduce the parser's flexibility, because it becomes necessary to assure that information specified in a condition will be available when a rule executes. Stipulating that the reduction consuming the most constituents be tried first–a provision we want anyway to assure minimal attachment–is helpful but not sufficient. The parser would still have to proceed through the sentence in a strict left to right order, and the highly efficient algorithms for parsing context-free grammars, which prohibit rigidly scheduled rules, could not be used.

One popular solution employs **unifications** of features, allowing registers to be filled in any order. Features are specified as sets of values. Two sets of values unify by creating a set representing their intersection (i.e., the values they share). If values are specified for one but not the other, those values are copied; however, if the intersection of sets is empty, unification fails. For example, the lexical entry for each number-bearing word would specify the possible values:

(a DET {singular})	(several DET {plural})
(slept VERB {singular plural})	(runs VERB {singular})
(dog NOUN {singular})	(cats NOUN {plural})
(fish NOUN {singular, plural})	(the DET {singular, plural})

NP → DET ADJ NOUN	(Condition:	DET-number = NOUN-number
	Actions:	assign DET ADJ and HEAD registers
		set NP-number to NOUN-number)
NP → DET NOUN	(Condition:	DET-number = NOUN-number
	Actions:	assign DET and HEAD registers
		set NP-number to NOUN-number)
NP → ADJ NOUN	(Actions:	assign ADJ and HEAD registers
		set NP-number to NOUN-number)
NP → NOUN	(Actions:	set NP-number to HEAD-number
		assign NOUN register)
VP → VERB VP1	(Actions:	assign MAIN VERB register
		set VP-number to VERB-number)
VP1 → VERB VP1	(Condition:	[verb sequence conditions]
	Actions:	append MAIN VERB to AUX
		assign VERB to MAIN VERB)
S → NP VP	(Condition:	NP-number = VP-number
	Actions:	assign NP to SUBJ
		assign VP to PRED)

Figure 7. One portion of an augmented phrase structure grammar.

Associated with the rule NP → DET NOUN would be the unification equation:

$$\text{NP-NUMBER} = (\text{DET-NUMBER} = \text{NOUN-NUMBER})$$

which we can paraphrase "unify DET-NUMBER and NOUN-NUMBER then unify the result with NP-NUMBER." Thus *the cats* would unify {singular plural} and {plural} yielding {plural}, *the fish* would unify {singular, plural} and {singular, plural} yielding {singular, plural}, and either will unify with NP-NUMBER, for which no values are given. But *a cats* or *several dog* would yield only an empty set { }, and unification would fail. With unification, registers can be filled in any order.

Unification can also be applied to the categories specified by rules and the structures they build. Say the constituent NP can have the values:

(NP {PRONOUN, PROPER, (DET NOUN) (DET ADJ NOUN)})

If the parser builds the structure (DET NOUN) for *the man,* unification would yield (NP (DET NOUN)). The great advantage of **unificational grammars**, as they are known, is flexibility, especially when implemented with a parser that is equally flexible, an active chart parser perhaps. Recall, for example, that a bottom-up parser would ordinarily need to build an entire VP before attempting to merge it with the subject NP via S → NP VP. That means that the check for subject-verb agreement, useful in disambiguating sentences, would wait until the final step in the parse. With a unificational grammar, it is possible to build three separate structures, representing the subject NP, the verb group, and the remainder of the verb phrase. The first two could be unified into a structure that leaves the SUBCATEGORIZATION register unchanged. The discussion that follows will focus on augmented transition networks, because their graph notation makes for clearer exposition of linguistic issues, but we will encounter unification again in section 3.2 below and in Chapter 10.

Section two: Augmentations for Transformed Structures

2.1 The deep-structure hypothesis

The grammar we have thus far will analyze a large number of sentence patterns, and an augmented parser based on that grammar, but made sensitive to context, will correctly handle most structural restrictions. The next step is to expand the grammar to comprehend more of English syntax. If we proceed *ad hoc*, however, hanging rules on rules to accommodate new constructions, we are in danger of obscuring fundamental relationships. Consider the following sentences:

The nurse gave that newspaper to the elderly man.
   1   2   3

That newspaper was given to the elderly man by the nurse.
     2   3   1

The nurse gave the elderly man that newspaper.
   1   3   2

That newspaper the nurse gave to the elderly man.
    2   1   3

It was the elderly man that the nurse gave that newspaper to.
     3   1   2

Though superficially different, the five sentences paraphrase one another; they are virtually synonymous. Each has the numbered NPs performing the same function; and if one of the sentences is true, all five must be true. A grammar that fully expresses our linguistic knowledge should make explicit the relationship among such sentences and explain their synonymy.

The deep-structure hypothesis offers an explanation: the five sentences, though they have different **surface structures**, share the same **deep structure**. The first is in the "active voice" (the initial NP, *the girl* acts) and its structure, which can be generated by ordinary phrase structure rules, corresponds to the deep structure of all five:

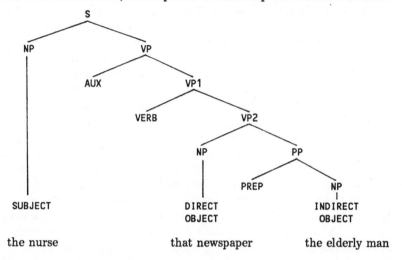

In English, though not in all languages, the structural subject is the first NP under the S node, making that NP the focus or theme of the sentence. The first NP under the VP node is the structural direct object, and the object of *for* or *to* under the VP node is the structural indirect object. In the active sentence, these correspond to functionally defined constituents. There is a functional subject that performs an action or exists in a state specified by the verb, as well as a functional direct object that receives the verb's action. The functional **indirect object** either receives possession or control of the direct object or is otherwise the beneficiary of an action (*he sold it to me*; *he did it for me*).

As for the other surface structures, note that the correspondences do not necessarily hold. The second of the sample sentences has undergone **passivization**, which shifts focus to *the newspaper* by moving it to the position of subject in the phrase structure; it must agree in number with the verb, and if it is a pronoun, it must be in the subject case: *?the newspapers was given ?them were given*. (Though some have taken movement quite literally as describing a mental process, it should be understood as a metaphor describing the relationship between two structures.) The remaining sample sentences also dislocate functional constituents. The third sentence has undergone dative movement, relocating the indirect object (or dative) *the elderly man* to a position preceding the direct object; in the fourth, the direct object has been "topicalized," moved to a position preceding the subject (presumably for emphasis). In the fifth, a "cleft construction," the deep structure sentence is embedded within another (which has *it* as its structural subject), and within the embedded sentences the indirect object has been moved to the front.

Assuming that a deep structure exists, what reason do we have for supposing that it corresponds to the structure of the active sentence and not, for example, to the passive? Perhaps the passive is more basic and the active construction has undergone movement. The reason is that the circumstances in which the passive can occur are limited. An active sentence can have one, two, or three functional NPs, but the passive sentence must have at least two. Also, a subcategorization of verbs (including *have, resemble,* and *weigh)* cannot participate in the passive: *my sheepdog resembles a rug* but not *a rug is resembled by my sheepdog.* Similar restrictions apply to the other examples.

To apply our phrase structure rules to passive sentences (which they will parse) would be to ignore its underlying synonymy with the active sentence. For the others, we would need to add phrase structure rules for the successive NPs following the verb in the third sentence and preceding it in the fourth, as well as rules for the addition of *it was . . . that* in the sixth. New rules would generate quite different phrase markers, further obscuring the close relationship among the five sentences.

The examples we have considered thus far all move NPs, but other constituents can be moved as well. We have already seen one example. The particle of a phrasal verb can be moved to a position following the direct object (but not the indirect object) so that *he looked over the work for his friend* becomes *he looked the work over for his friend.* Another example is the yes/no question that moves the first auxiliary verb to a position preceding the subject: *he is working* becomes *is he working?.* If the sentence has other auxiliaries, they remain in place *(should he have been working?)* and if the sentence has no auxiliary, a form of *do* is supplied *(does he look over the work?)* This curious phenomenon, known as *do* support, is a relatively recent addition to English grammar, dating from Shakespeare's time or thereabouts.

Figure 8 gives additional examples of the changes between surface structure and the hypothesized deep structure and illustrates some of the diversity that is possible in English. The changes have various motivations. Some, for example, place the focus on constituents by moving them to the initial position in the sentence; focus, as we will see, is a phenomenon of discourse and its segmentation. There are even sentences which, though superficially similar, have quite different deep structures, for example, *he is eager to please* and *he is easy to*

Subject raising:	It seems that he is sad. ⇒ He seems to be sad.
Object raising:	It is easy to fool me. ⇒ I am easy to fool.
Adverb preposing:	I will finish it today. ⇒ Today I will finish it.
Participle preposing:	A boy was acting up. ⇒ Acting up was a boy.
PP preposing:	He relied on them. ⇒ On them he relied.
Locative inversion:	A box sat on the rack. ⇒ On the rack sat a box box.
Extraposition:	A dog yelping loudly fell. ⇒ A dog fell yelping loudly.
Heavy NP-shift:	Joe sent books he found ⇒ Joe sent to his pal the in Paris to his pal. books he found in Paris.
There insertion:	A man entered. ⇒ There entered a man.
Equi-NP deletion:	I asked Ted (Ted to go). ⇒ I asked Ted to go.
Wh-question:	He said what. ⇒ What did he say?
Relative movement:	I had dogs (he fed dogs). ⇒ I had dogs that he fed.
Clefting:	I need a shovel. ⇒ It is a shovel that I need.
Pseudo-clefting:	We need a shovel. ⇒ What we need is a shovel.
Topicalization:	I like airplanes. ⇒ Airplanes I like.
Comparative deletion:	He is older than Al is old. ⇒ He is older than Al.
Conjunctive deletion:	He walked and he talked. ⇒ He walked and talked.

Figure 8. Sentences illustrating movement and other variations
between deep and surface structure.

please. The difference in deep structures explains why they are not
synonymous: *he wants (he please someone)* and *he wants (someone
please him)*.

Most modern grammars either offer some version of the deep-
structure hypothesis or provide some systematic way of relating such
variant structures as actives and passives. (The grammars discussed
in sections 3.2 and 3.3 illustrate the latter approach.) Working parsers
follow suit, either by building deep structural phrase markers or by
creating register structures that reflect the corresponding functions or
cases.

2.2 Transformational grammars

The distinction between deep and surface structures derives from generative transformational grammar, a very influential approach to linguistic description developed in the late 1950s by Noam Chomsky and his associates.   Generative theories seek to characterize what a language user knows about his or her language by devising rules that generate phonological, morphological, or syntactic structures. In their approach to syntax, phrase structure rules (closely resembling those that we have been using) generate deep structure; then different rules, known as **transformations** operate on descriptions of deep structure to generate descriptions of surface structure. Over the years, generative transformational grammar has gone through several reorganizations and renovations: "standard theory," "extended standard theory," "revised extended standard theory," and more recently "government and binding theory."   Among the changes, some of the most important involve the transformational component.

To describe exactly the relationships between deep and surface structures, theorists sought a parsimonious set of transformations, able to add, delete, modify and move constituents. A rule for passivization, for example, specifies the relevant portion of the deep structure (SD), with each constituent indexed by a number, then it specifies the transformed structure (SC):

	SD:	NP	AUX	VERB	NP
		#1	#2	#3	#4
⇒	SC:	#4	be + en	#3	by + #1

The double-shafted arrow can be paraphrased "is transformed to." AUX is here an abstract category which includes any auxiliary verbs plus the tense and other attributes of the main verb. All sentences have a subject NP (#1), a verb, and tense (#s 2 and 3), but notice that the structural description restricts passivization to deep structures containing an NP direct object (#4). The structural change moves the direct object to the subject position and the subject to a prepositional phrase where it is the object of *by*. It adds a form of *be* and converts the verb to a past participle (past participles usually have the suffix *-ed* or *-en*).

By specifying in algorithmic detail the derivation of surface from deep structure (which is in turn specified by exacting phrase structure rules), transformations offer straightforward, very precise descriptions of surface structures. Though generative grammar has subsequently reduced the descriptive role of transformations and parsers do not recover deep structure simply by reversing them, the comprehensive inventory of surface structures, produced over several decades of very careful analysis, remains invaluable.

As generative transformational grammar evolved, focus began to shift to overgeneration and constraint. For certain phenomena, it was very difficult to formulate transformations that captured generalizations, but did not generate surface structures that are not part of the language. For example, English has wh-questions which ask for the specification of the person or thing incompletely specified by a question word or phrase appearing at the beginning of the sentence:

> Who is knocking at the door?
> Which book does he want?
> For whom did he make it?
> Who(m) is he going with?

To describe wh-questions, we could postulate a series of very specific transformations, such as the following, which would correctly handle the second of the sample sentences.

SD:	Q	NP	AUX	VERB	NP
		#1	#2	#3	#4
⇒ SC:	wh + #4	#2	#1	#3	

The transformation moves the direct object to the beginning of the sentence and inverts the subject and auxiliary verb. Other transformations would describe the other sentences in which the question word is the deep-structure subject, the indirect object, and the object of *with*. Writing separate transformations for all four would ignore the similarity that all four sentences place the question word or phrase first, "fronting" it. The alternative is to propose a very general transformation specifying that wh-questions move NPs to the beginnings of sentences:

SD:	Q	X	Wh + NP	X
	#1		#2	#3
⇒ SC:	#2	#1	0	#3

The variable X indicates the presence of syntax that is not involved, and 0 indicates a constituent that has been deleted. Now we have an opposite problem. Though the transformation is sufficiently general to describe all wh-questions, it will overgenerate, producing surface structures that do not occur in English. The solution is to look for principled constraints that apply to many structures or many transformations and that might reveal something of how our knowledge of language is organized in the mind. Elaboration of constraints meant that transformations can be further simplified; indeed one theory, government and binding linguistics, replaces the wh-movement transformation and others like it with the single transformation, Move alpha, which means move anything that is not constrained from being moved.

226   Augmented Parsers and Modern Grammars

Principled constraints offer explanations, and without them grammars cannot do more in explaining linguistic relationships than the "finagling factor" (that quantity which when added to or subtracted from your answer gives the right answer) does in explaining mathematical relationships. Generalized constraints would help explain the learnability of languages by reducing the particularity of rules and by restricting the kinds of grammar that the child may try out on the data of his or her native language. Many generalized constraints have been proposed: constraints on the kinds of structures that can be transformed, constraints on the kinds of structures that can be created, and constraints on the kinds of rules that can be employed or the sequence in which rules apply. Though some progress has been made, constraints that are not merely arbitrary or *ad hoc* are not easy to find.

Another motive for investigating constraints is the processing power of transformations. Power is an important criterion by which grammars are evaluated, and it is measured by the capabilities they assume in a processor. The goal is to find the weakest possible processor capable of describing the phenomena of natural language. Transformational adding, deleting, moving, and modifying require a processor far more powerful than is required by a context-free phrase structure grammar. Indeed the class of transformational grammars assumes the equivalent of a "Turing machine," a computing mechanism so powerful that it can execute **any** process that can be precisely defined. That is like saying that in planting a garden, one digs with a trowel much of the time but needs geologists, surveyors, and bulldozers for some of the seedlings.

Worse, a processor that powerful can simulate the operations of transformational grammar even if the structures on which transformations operate are generated by nothing more than the rudimentary linear grammar. There is no need for a context-free grammar and recursion, and we would have no explanation of why so much of the language obeys phrase structure rules or why phrase structure appears to play a role in sentence comprehension. Worse still, there is no theoretical assurance that the processing will always halt, that the processor can always decide that a given string is or is not a well-formed sentence. Though that question is decidable for human beings, an unconstrained processor could go on forever deleting, moving, and changing constituents, to explore a limitless number of possible constructions.

Among the proposed constraints are several that prevent the extraction and movement of any constituent from within certain kinds of structures. In the following questions, the word *what* is moved to the beginning of the sentence, but only the first question is well formed: in the others movement is blocked by constraints that prevent the extraction of constituents from within relative clauses, from subjects of sentences, and from coordinate structures:

> What did they ask for?
> ? What subjects do you like to read books that are about?
> ? I know who that Joe was elected pleased
> ? What did he order a hamburger and?

Ideally constraints should be even more general than these, and some are. Consider, for example, the following pairs of sentences, which appear to be similar:

> Jack saw Ann with a telescope.
> What did Jack find Ann with?

> Jack heard the song by Paul Simon.
> ? Who did Jack hear the song by?

In both cases, an NP is moved from a prepositional phrase, but with the second something has gone wrong. A difference between them may be familiar from the discussion of parsing preferences in Chapter 6. In the first, an example of minimal attachment, the prepositional phrase from which the NP is extracted is attached to the VP *(find Ann)*. In the second it is attached to and therefore within an NP *(the song by Paul Simon)*. That difference suggests that the transformation may be constrained from moving a constituent from within a constituent of the same kind. Now assume that we have a rule for modifying them with sentences:

NP → NP1 RELATIVE-CLAUSE

RELATIVE-CLAUSE → RELATIVE S

Although these rules will produce the sentences below, each of which has NPs within NPs, a wh-question cannot extract either of the embedded NPs:

> Jack saw the man who owned the dog
> ? What dog did Jack see the man who owned?

When we see that the same constraint prevents the extraction of a sentence from within a sentence or a prepositional phrase from within a prepositional phrase, we begin to glimpse a generalization. And the generalization becomes more interesting when it prevents other transformations. For example, extraposition can extract prepositional phrases from within noun phrases and move them to a position later in the sentence:

> A book about Bach's cantatas has just been written.
> A book has just been written about Bach's music

Extraposition cannot, however, extract a prepositional phrase from within a prepositional phrase:

? A book about cantatas has just been written of Bach.

Another general constraint stipulates that no transformation can result in a structure that cannot be generated by the base phrase structure rules, which explains why the passive, for example, generates *the book was found by John* instead of wild work like *John by was the book found*.

2.3 Parsing and psychological plausibility

How would one go about constructing a parser to accommodate passive sentences, wh-questions, and other surface structures that transformations describe?   On this point, the theory is deliberately silent.   A generative grammar describes a native speaker's linguistic knowledge, his or her **competence** in the language, and it reflects principles by which all languages are organized, a universal grammar. It does not claim that native speakers employ transformations (or their equivalents) in the **performance** of language, executing them to produce sentences or reversing them to comprehend sentences.   Transformations describe structural relationships, not cognitive processes. Nor is there any convincing psychological evidence for processes that mediate between deep structure and variant surface structures.

Nevertheless, the precision of the earlier, algorithmic transformations encouraged researchers to develop parsers that execute those transformations in reverse. The processing proved cumbersome and very slow.   A transformational parser must begin by forming a description of the surface structure. For a sentence of any complexity, no set of rules will yield a single description;   instead, rules yield multiple descriptions, most of them spurious. Each must be tested by applying reverse transformations then comparing the result with legitimate deep structures. Since a surface structure can be the result of applying several different transformations and repeating one or more rules, transformational parsers must try all possible sequences of transformations, and this means that the number of proposed deep structures will increase exponentially.   Other problems, including notorious difficulties in recovering deleted constituents, emerge along the way.

Another motive for the current reassessment is to find psychologically plausible grammars. Though generative grammar is a theory of competence only and not of performance, some relationship ought to obtain between the knowledge of language and the processes by which it is produced and comprehended. Clearly enough the phrase structure component plays a role;   the "click" experiments, as well as other studies, have demonstrated its functioning. However, repeated efforts have turned up no evidence of mental processes analogous to transformations or intermediate forms of representation resembling deep structures.

Several empirical attempts have been made to correlate the difficulty of understanding a sentence (as measured in time or memory load) and the number or complexity of transformations that generate it. Recall that transformations occur sequentially; for example, indirect object movement might be followed by passivization, then *there* insertion:

> Someone is giving too much candy to the children. ⇒
> Someone is giving the children too much candy. ⇒
> The children are being given too much candy. ⇒
> There are children being given too much candy.

All that adding, deleting, changing, and moving should exact some cost, and even if the several operations within each transformation occur in parallel (so that in passivization the NP is being moved at the same time that the verb sequence is being rewritten), one transformation is feeding another. You may guess the results just from reading the thrice-transformed sentence. Though a few early experiments suggest a correlation, subsequent research has failed to confirm it, and researchers are now agreed that no correlation exists.

Failure to find a correlation where one is expected is suggestive, though hardly conclusive. But there is more evidence against transformational processing. Recall that many transformations operate "globally," manipulating entire phrase structure trees after they have been constructed, and that what a transformation does with a given constituent may depend on the existence or form of another constituent some distance ahead in the sentence. This should argue that entire sentences are heard before comprehension begins. However, our behavior with garden path sentences and other local ambiguities suggests little delay between the beginning of the sentence and the onset of processing. One estimate, based on the apparent capacity of short-term memory, is that we can work with only "seven, plus or minus two" items at a time. (Short-term memory is a mental antechamber where bits of unstructured information await interpretation for a few milliseconds; it differs from what we ordinarily call memory, which may store structured information for a few seconds or a lifetime.) "Monitoring" experiments, which ask listeners to identify words of a given lexical category in normal, in meaningless, and in syntactically scrambled sentences suggest that processing begins as soon as enough words are available to constitute a phrase.

More dramatic evidence comes from "shadowing" experiments, in which a recorded sentence is played to a listener, who is asked to repeat what he is hearing after as short a delay as possible (usually about five syllables). Any spontaneous mistakes tend to be congruent with prior syntax, and when the recorded sentences contain mispronounced or nonsense words, these also are interpreted in such a way as to make them congruent with prior syntax. The available evidence all suggests that sentence processing is entirely local, not global; and many post transformational grammars are founded on that assumption.

Additional "shadowing" experiments that introduce semantically anomalous words or constructions suggest that semantic analysis may be interleaved with phrase-by-phrase syntactic analysis: once the syntax of an NP, let's say, has been identified, that analysis is handed over to a semantic component without waiting for information about the entire sentence. A functional component designed to recognize the functions of NPs (subject, object, etc.) and of certain other words and phrases may intercede between interleaved syntax and semantics. Or the syntactic, functional, and semantic processing may take place in parallel. We will return to the question of whether syntactic processing and semantic processing are autonomous, interleaved or parallel; but it is worth noting that some modern grammars (including those in sections 3.2 and 3.3 below) allow for interleaved semantics.

The difficulty of building transformational parsers led to the development of augmented parsers able to recover functional and other deep-structural relationships directly from the surface. In their manner of operation, these resemble the phrase structure parsers, except that they employ actions to achieve uniformity of representation and a hold facility for temporary storage. Though augmented parsers can implement various grammatical theories and do not necessarily assume a transformational account, they benefit from the exact algorithmic descriptions of sentence structure, and especially from research into constraints. Meanwhile, theorists have been developing computationally more tractable grammars. These also cleave to the phrase structure approach but have special mechanisms for sensitivity to context and certain "transformed" structures. We can begin with the augmented parsers and generalized parsing strategies for bounded movement, unbounded movement, and deletion, each of which occurs in several contexts with various kinds of constituents.

2.4 Accommodating bounded movement

As we have seen, the logical subject of passive sentences appears in a prepositional phrase, and the logical direct object takes its place in the surface structure. With dative movement the indirect object appears, not as the object of *to* or *for*, but in a position preceding the direct object. These are examples of bounded movement in that exact locations can be specified. They could be parsed by new networks for the passive and for the moved indirect objects, but that would bring on a now-familiar problem. We would need a new network for every new construction. The alternative is to employ the strategy we used for

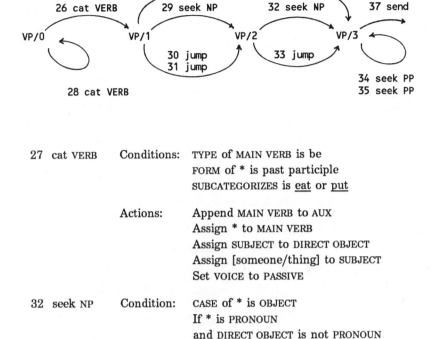

27 cat VERB	Conditions:	TYPE of MAIN VERB is be
		FORM of * is past participle
		SUBCATEGORIZES is eat or put

Actions: Append MAIN VERB to AUX
Assign * to MAIN VERB
Assign SUBJECT to DIRECT OBJECT
Assign [someone/thing] to SUBJECT
Set VOICE to PASSIVE

32 seek NP Condition: CASE of * is OBJECT
If * is PRONOUN
and DIRECT OBJECT is not PRONOUN

Action: Assign DIRECT OBJECT to INDIRECT OBJECT

34 seek PP Condition: * is "to" or "for"

Action: Assign PREP-OBJECT to INDIRECT OBJECT

35 seek PP Conditions: * is "by"
VOICE is PASSIVE

Action: Assign PREP-OBJECT to SUBJECT

Figure 9. Accommodating dative movement and passivization.

verb groups in section 1.4: have the parser assume an active sentence with the indirect object appearing as a prepositional object, but allow the parser to revise its decisions when evidence emerges of passivization or a moved indirect object. Thus we have more justification for the augmentations, particularly the alterable registers.

For indirect object movement, the parser should accept both *the nurse gave that newspaper to the elderly man* and *the nurse gave the elderly man that newspaper* and should create the same register structure for both, with *the elderly man* occupying the indirect object register. For the first sentence, we need a PP arc following the arc for direct objects. (See Figure 9.) A condition on PP arc 34 restricts it to the two prepositions and an action builds a register for indirect objects, assigning to it the object of the preposition. The second sentence, however, presents a small problem. An NP immediately following a verb is more likely to be a direct object than an indirect object, and for efficiency that should be the presumption. If a second NP follows, the presumed direct object should be moved to the register for indirect objects. The actions employed by an augmented parser can make these exchanges, and the need to make them–not only for indirect-object movement but for other transformations as well–offers a further justification for the actions. With this strategy, the parse would proceed as follows:

State:	Arc:	Result:
S/0	1 seek NP	Assigns *The nurse* to SUBJECT
VP/0	26 cat VERB	Assigns *gave* to MAIN VERB
VP/1	29 seek NP	Assigns *the elderly man* to DIRECT OBJECT
VP/2	32 seek NP	Moves *the elderly man* to INDIRECT OBJECT
		Assigns *that newspaper* to DIRECT OBJECT

What we have thus far permits many false parses, however, because the arcs or rules are insufficiently constrained. For *she drove him to the store*, they would correctly identify *him* as the direct object, but mistake *store* for an indirect object. For *she drove him home*, they would err with both NPs, mistaking *him* for an indirect object and *home* for a direct object. As with transivity, the relevant information is in the verb and there are at least six categories, each governing a particular configuration:

SUBCATEGORIZES is *like*	DO (no indirect object)
SUBCATEGORIZES is *produce*	DO (for) IO
SUBCATEGORIZES is *buy*	IO DO or DO (for) IO
SUBCATEGORIZES is *dedicate*	DO (to) IO
SUBCATEGORIZES is *tell*	IO DO or DO (to) IO
SUBCATEGORIZES is *bring*	IO DO or DO (to/for) IO

By adding to the arcs or rules for direct and indirect objects conditions that constrain them to operate only when the verb is appropriate, we can make parsers sensitive to prior context, blocking false paths. One additional constraint derives from a more generalized constraint on where pronouns may appear and is reflected in the unacceptability of sentences such as *I gave him it*. It stipulates that if arc 32 proposes a pronoun as direct object, the indirect object cannot be a pronoun.

A similar parsing strategy succeeds with passivization, where the object is to produce the same register structure for passive and active constructions. An augmented parser would assume an active sentence, until it encounters the characteristic verb sequence of the passive (a form of the verb *to be* followed by a past participle). (See Figure 9.) An action associated with arc 27 reassigns the phrase currently in the SUBJECT register to the register for direct objects and replaces it with the dummy phrase [someone/something]. The subsequent arc 35, which allows only prepositional phrases beginning with *by*, can replace the dummy phrase with the deep-structural subject. The parse of *That newspaper was given to the elderly man by the nurse* resembles a game of musical chairs:

State:	Arc:	Result:
S/0	1 seek NP	Assigns *That newspaper* to SUBJECT
VP/0	26 cat VERB	Assigns *was* to MAIN VERB
VP/1	27 cat VERB	Moves *was* to AUXILIARY
		Assigns *given* to MAIN VERB
		Moves *That newspaper* to DIRECT OBJECT
		Assigns [dummy] to SUBJECT
VP/3	34 seek PP	Assigns *the elderly man* to INDIRECT OBJECT
VP/3	35 seek PP	Assigns *the nurse* to SUBJECT

Again the parser needs to be constrained, because some sequences of *to be* plus the past participle are not passives (try converting *he is gone* to the active). Arc 27 should accept only verbs that take direct objects and hence can be passivized and exclude those few that do not participate (?*campuses are resembled by beehives*). As the example suggests, arc 35 needs to be further constrained to accept only potential subjects.

English has several other kinds of bounded movement. One of them we have already noticed in a different context. Particles can move from a position immediately following the verb to a position immediately following the direct object and preceding any sentence-final indirect object:

He looked up the word for me. ⇒ He looked the word up for me.
                                ? He looked the word for me up.

Another example is the method of forming questions, which inverts the subject and first auxiliary verb:

He will have gone home. ⇒ Will he have gone home?
He has done what.   ⇒ What has he done?

Yet another is "*there* insertion" which moves the subject of a sentence to follow immediately after the verb, leaving in its place the word *there*:

A commotion arose. ⇒ There arose a commotion.

Similarly, when the subject of a sentence is itself a sentence, it can be moved to the end of the matrix sentence, and the word *it* is substituted:

That he came amazed me. ⇒ It amazed me that he came.

Lengthy direct objects can be moved to the end of the sentence:

I saw an old friend from my college days last week.
⇒ I saw last week an old friend from my college days.

These and similar phenomena yield to the basic parsing strategy we used for dative movement and passivization: arcs create registers then change register contents as subsequent context becomes available.

2.5 Unbounded movement and the hold facility

Not all forms of movement have strictly constrained origins and destinations. Other well-formed constructions exhibit **unbounded movement**: constituents are moved an arbitrary distance and their function is no longer evident from their position in the word order. As we have seen, the formation of wh-questions moves the question word or phrase from one of several positions in the sentence:

You are doing what. ⇒ What (are you doing   )?
                                                gap

He is doing it for whom. ⇒ For whom (is he doing it   )?
                                                    gap

In each case, movement leaves a syntactic gap. Similarly, topicalization can move nearly any constituent to the beginning of the sentence:

They relied on him. ⇒ On him (they relied   ).
                                         gap

I never wanted that job. ⇒ That job (I never wanted   ).
                                                    gap

We must work. ⇒ Work (we must   ).
                               gap

Relative clauses offer another example. They resemble sentential NPs, but with some important differences. Relative clauses can function either as NPs or as modifiers (*I saw someone who climbed the hill*) and they begin with relatives (*what, who, which*, etc.), sharing only *that* with the sentential NP. What is most important for present purposes,

the sentence following the complementizer in sentential NPs is complete
(*I saw that he admired her*), whereas the sentence following a relative
features a gap from which the relative has been moved:

Subject of the relative clause:
I know who gave it to you.   ⇒ I know who (gave it to you).
                                                gap

Direct object:
I know she gave what to you. ⇒   I know what (she gave   to you).
                                                                 gap

Indirect object:
I know she gave it to whom. ⇒ I know whom (she gave it to   ).
                                                                 gap

Not only can the gap appear in any constituent that requires an NP,
but it can also be any arbitrary distance away. Consider for example,
these entirely legal (if progressively less plausible) sentences in which
the relative clause is modifying a noun:

I know the woman whom (you saw   ).
                                    gap

I know the woman whom (they said (you saw   )).
                                               gap

I know the woman whom (it is likely (they said (you saw   ))).
                                                             gap

I know the woman whom (he claims (it is likely (they said (you saw   )))).
                                                                        gap

Thus we have wh-questions, topicalizations, relative clauses and
other forms of unbounded movement all yielding to the same analysis.
Additional support for the analysis comes from selectional restrictions.
With relative clauses, for example, the case of the relative (*who* or
whom) reflects its role at the gap: *I know who saw you* versus *I know
whom you saw*. And subject verb agreement is preserved: *I saw
several people that know him* versus *I saw several people that he knows*.
Transivity requirements are also satisfied; for example, the verb *put*
requires a direct object, and that requirement is satisfied by a fronted
relative:

I know he put *it* on the table.
I know *what* he put on the table.
? I know he put on the table.

All is as usual, except for the word order.

That unbounded movement presents the parser with a constituent
followed by a gap suggests a simple parsing strategy: the parser should
place the constituent in temporary storage and await an appropriate
gap in the syntax. For this purpose, augmented parsers have special

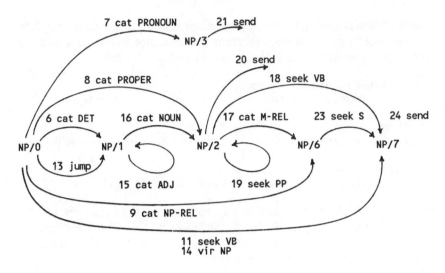

9 cat NP-REL	Actions:	Set TYPE to NP
		Assign RELATIVE to *
		Block HOLD
14 vir NP	Condition:	HOLD is NP
	Action:	Retrieve HOLD
17 cat MOD-REL	Actions:	Set TYPE to MODIFIER
		Assign RELATIVE to *
		Block HOLD
23 seek S	Initialize:	If RELATIVE-TYPE is NP
		assign RELATIVE to HOLD
		If RELATIVE-TYPE is MODIFIER
		assign HEAD to HOLD

Figure 10. Accommodating relative clauses.

hold registers, as well as **virtual** rules or arcs that treat constituents
on hold as if they occupied the gap.

The new cat arc 9 matches relatives that can introduce NPs (the
pronouns *who, whom, what,* and *which* and their compounds formed
with *-ever,* together with a few adverbs, including *where* and *why*). The
"initialization" instructions for the following seek S arc puts the relative
on hold. As the term suggests, initializing a network presets registers.
Once a constituent is on hold, it is available to the first NP arc that
fails to find an NP in the sentence; that is, it fails to get beyond NP/0
by any means other than arc 6. Thus we would have:

I   saw   what   happened
(1 (7 21) 3 (26 29 (9 23 (1 (14 24) 3 (26 30 33 37) 5) 24) 33 37) 5)
          ↑   ↑
          places *what*   retrieves *what* as
          on hold   subject of relative clause

Marie   knows whom he   wrote   to
(1 (8 20) 3 (26 29 (9 23 (1 (7 21) 3 (26 29 33 34 (38 39 (14 24) 41) 37) 5) 24) 33 37) 5)
     ↑   ↑
     places *whom*   retrieves *whom* as indirect
     on hold   object of relative clause

The new arc (17) matches those pronouns that can introduce relative clauses serving as NPs (*that* and *whose, who, whom,* and *which*), and the initialization for arc 23 does slightly better than that with the relative clause NPs: it places the pronoun's antecedent on HOLD.

I   read the book that Rus   wrote.
(1 (7 21) 3 (26 29 (6 16 17 23 (1 (8 20) 3 (26 29 (14 24) 33 37) 5) 24) 33 37)
5)   ↑   ↑
                      places *book*   retrieves *book*
                      on hold   as direct object

Because every call on the S network to parse a relative clause creates a separate HOLD, the augmented transition network can recursively parse right-branching relative clause modifiers of any length, even if it extends to improbable lengths: ... *that milked the cow that tossed the dog that worried the cat that killed the rat that ate the malt that lay in the house that Jack built.* To avoid mismatching constituents and to enforce constraints, the parser must at certain points in the parse be prevented access to what is already on hold. For example, a condition on the two arcs for relatives should deny access to any constituent currently on hold. In this way the parser would be prevented from misparsing *what do you like to read books that are about,* which violates the constraint against extracting constituents from relative clauses.

Postulating the hold register as another entity required for parsing does not violate Occam's razor if that entity is indeed necessary. This seems to be the case for computable grammars, and empirical evidence suggests that something of the sort plays a role in human cognition. Experiments that measure memory load during the interval when constituents are on hold should show a heavier load, and the load should be especially heavy because we do much better at remembering integrated linguistic structures than at remembering unintegrated words or phrases. The experiments interrupt subjects while comprehending sentences and ask them to perform unrelated memory tasks. Error rates for interruptions made during the interval are much higher than those for interruptions made elsewhere in the sentence, indicating that the comprehension of surface structures generated by unbounded movement places a considerable burden on short-term memory. These results are consistent with the hypothesis that moved constituents are put on hold until they are needed.

This strategy employing a hold facility and virtual constituents will not, however, work with rule-based parsers proceeding bottom-up. The problem is not in formulating the rules; we can imagine "rewriting" VIRTUAL and HOLD, simply treating them as if they were lexical categories:

$$
\begin{array}{ll}
\text{NP} \rightarrow \text{DET NOUN S'} & \text{S'} \rightarrow \text{RELATIVE S} \\
\text{S'} & \\
\text{VIRTUAL (NP)} & \text{RELATIVE} \rightarrow \text{HOLD (NP)}
\end{array}
$$

But how are we to prevent the first rule from supposing a gap any time an NP is called for, filling the supposed gap before subsequent context reveals there is none? That bottom-up parsers cannot allow gaps is their Achilles' heel. It is as problematic as left-recursion for top-down parsers, and several solutions have been proposed, including counsel of despair: abandon purely bottom-up processing and constrain virtual rules using a predictive, top-down component.

2.6 Recovering deleted constituents

As one would expect, deletion can occur only when the deleted constituent is uniquely recoverable. There must be sufficient redundancy in the sentence so that no information is lost. The redundancy may be between grammar and structure. As we have seen, for example, dative movement can delete *to* or *for*, because those are specified in the rule and hence are recoverable. Similarly, passivization can delete a dummy subject, producing a "reduced" passive:

[someone/thing] broke it ⇒ it was broken.

Because the verb requires a subject, the dummy is implied. Another example, is the imperative construction with which English issues commands:

You will get the bicycle ⇒ Get the bicycle.

One way to see exactly what is deleted is to append a tag question, which makes explicit the subject and first auxiliary verb *(he did it, didn't he)*; for the imperative *get the bicycle*, the tag question is *will you*. Since imperatives delete specific words, they are recoverable. Imperatives can be parsed simply by bypassing the subject arc in the sentence network and entering the verb phrase network at VP/1, beyond the arc for auxiliaries (see Figure 11). If that arc succeeds in

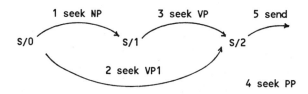

2 seek VP1   Condition: FORM of * is UNTENSED
                              SENTENCE-TYPE is DECLARATIVE

                  Actions: Assign PRONOUN "you" to SUBJECT
                              Assign MODAL "will" to AUX
                              Set SENTENCE-TYPE to IMPERATIVE

Figure 11. Parsing imperative constructions.

finding a verb phrase, the actions fill the SUBJECT and AUXILIARY registers of the S network:

Get   the bicycle.
(2 (26 29 (6 16 20) 33 37) 5)

Deletion can also occur if the deleted constituent is recoverable from the immediate context. For example, the first noun phrase may be deleted from an embedded sentence if that phrase is co-referential (both refer to the same entity) with an immediately preceding noun phrase in the matrix sentence.

Joe had Tom (Tom open the door). ⇒ Joe had Tom open the door.

We can bring back the missing *Tom* by converting the embedded sentence into the passive: *Joe had (the door opened by Tom)*. A similar deletion occurs with *for/to* complements when they follow verbs such as *want, arrange,* or *like* and certain adjectives:

Jack arranged (for Jack to go).   ⇒   Jack arranged to go.
Jack wants (for Tom to go).   ⇒   Jack wants Tom to go.
Joe is eager (for Joe to please).   ⇒   Joe is eager to please.
Joe is tough (someone to please Joe). ⇒   Joe is tough to please.

Similarly, relative clauses are sometimes "reduced" by deleting of the relative pronoun and (when they are passive or contain a present participle) deleting a form of the verb *to be* as well:

The bat which he used broke.   ⇒   The bat he used broke.
The jack which was used   ⇒   The jack used by the
  by the mechanic broke.   mechanic broke.
The man who is visiting us agreed.   ⇒   The man visiting us agreed.

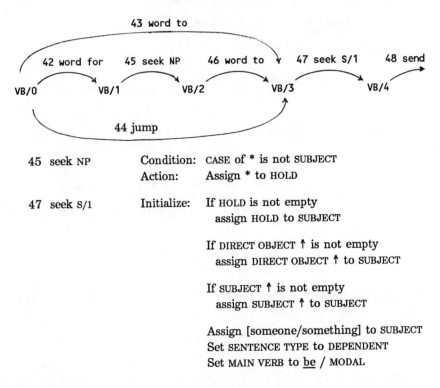

45 seek NP   Condition: CASE of * is not SUBJECT
                       Action: Assign * to HOLD

47 seek S/1   Initialize: If HOLD is not empty
                                       assign HOLD to SUBJECT

                                    If DIRECT OBJECT ↑ is not empty
                                       assign DIRECT OBJECT ↑ to SUBJECT

                                    If SUBJECT ↑ is not empty
                                       assign SUBJECT ↑ to SUBJECT

                                    Assign [someone/something] to SUBJECT
                                    Set SENTENCE TYPE to DEPENDENT
                                    Set MAIN VERB to be / MODAL

Figure 12. A verbal phrase network.

By some analyses, other constructions also undergo deletion. Objective complements follow change of state verbs and certain others in English, and they either specify the new state of the direct object or they describe the object.

We elected her (she became chair).   ⇒   We elected her chair.
We considered (she was electable).   ⇒   We considered her electable.

By a different analysis, such object complements as *chair* and *electable* are constituents following the verb like direct and indirect objects, and not the residue of reduced sentences.

To accommodate deletions, the parser enters the sentence network at a point subsequent to the initial state and presets registers with a copy of the deleted constituent taken from the register structure of the matrix sentence. For/to clauses and reduced relatives are examples. To isolate these operations, we replace the NP network's seek VP arc with the separate verbal phrase network shown in Figure 12. The symbol ↑ points to the register structure for the matrix; thus arc 47 looks first to the hold register (for a sentence such as *Audrey wanted for Joe to go*), then to the direct object register *(he saw Joe walking down the street)* and finally to the subject register *(Joe enjoyed reading books)*.

He   enjoyed   building chairs
(1 (7 21) 3 (26 29 (11 (44 47 (3 (26 29 (13 16 20) 33) 37) 5) 48) 24) 33 37) 5)
                  ↑   ↑
        makes *he* the subject   returns *he [is] building
                                            chairs* as direct object

Chuck wanted   for   Joe   to   go
(1 (8 20) 3 (26 29 (11 (42 45 (8 20) 46 47 (3 (26 30 33) 5) 48) 24) 33 37) 5)
          ↑   ↑   ↑
   places *Joe* on hold   makes *Joe*   returns *Joe
                          subject   [does] go* as
                                           direct object

Not all forms of deletion can be handled so cleanly. When two or more constituents of the same kind are joined by conjunctions, what they have in common may be deleted:

> Nancy liked reading novels and Jen liked reading novels.
> ⇒ Nancy and Jen liked reading novels.

> I gave Nancy *Tom Jones* and I gave Jen *Wuthering Heights.*
> ⇒ I gave Nancy *Jane Eyre* and Jen *Wuthering Heights.*

> Nancy enjoys reading eighteenth century fiction and Jen enjoys reading nineteenth century fiction.
> ⇒ Nancy enjoys reading eighteenth century fiction and Jen nineteenth century.

> The novel is easy to read and the novel is easy to discuss.
> ⇒ The novel is easy to read and discuss.

As these examples attest, it is by no means easy to determine what has been deleted. All parsers have trouble with these constructions, and comparatives pose even worse problems: *Nancy liked the book more than Jen.* (Than she liked Jen? Than Jen liked the book?) Simply asking the parser to derive from the grammar some account of what is necessary following *and* to complete a well-formed sentence would not suffice. Instead the parser would need somehow to incorporate the constraint that conjoined structures must be parallel before deletion, perhaps by interpreting *and* as a signal to start parsing some phrase of a kind that has appeared in the immediately preceding context. So far, however, the parser has needed to match input only against rules, not against register structure; the latter would require extensive new facilities, could consume an implausible amount of time, and might never reach a decision.

Section three: Current Reassessments

3.1   Shifting the burden

The past fifteen years have seen a widespread reassessment of syntactic theory, much of it focusing on problems with the transformational component of generative grammar–its excessive power and psychological implausibility. As we saw in section 2.2, one idea was to simplify that component and investigate principled ways of constraining it. There are many other possibilities, among them two promising new grammars, which we will survey in this section. Rather than relying on constraints, they take a different tact, shifting the descriptive burden of transformations to other components:

- □   Generalized phrase structure grammar eliminates the need for transformations by placing the entire burden on the phrase structure component. Though the rules remain context free, they are enhanced to accommodate features and are supplemented with rules that, on demand, generate additional rules.

- □   Lexical-functional grammar, as its name suggests, transfers some of the burden to the lexicon and the rest to a new functional component, which exploits subcategorizations by verbs and incorporates functional constituents such as subject, direct object, indirect object, and so on. The grammar is context-sensitive.

These are not sketchy theories; both are fully developed grammars and describe a substantial portion of the syntax of the English language. Unlike grammars that depend on transformations to describe phenomena such as passivization and unbounded movement, neither appears to be overly powerful. Both grammars are plausible psychologically, and offer predictions that can be empirically tested. They have been implemented in parsers and prove computationally tractable. (Indeed portions of lexical-functional grammar were inspired by earlier work on sentence comprehension using augmented transition networks). Like the grammar developed in this chapter, both lexical-functional grammar and generalized phrase structure grammar allow for the interleaving of semantic rules with syntactic rules. Relying on the lexical or phrase structure components is not the only possible solution, however. Chapter 10 discusses the possibility of placing most of the burden to the semantic component and using only a rudimentary context-free grammar to assist the semantic interpreter.

3.2 Generalized phrase structure grammar

Recursive phrase structure grammars have important advantages; they are simple and parsimonious, and their rules are isomorphic with tree-structure representation.   They are sufficiently flexible to be implemented through top-down, bottom-up, and mixed-mode parsing strategies. When phrase structure grammars are expanded, however, they quickly lose their capacity to express generalizations. As we saw at the beginning of this chapter, specifying restrictions within rules means replacing one rule with several. s → NP VP expresses the generalization that all sentences contain subject and verb phrases, but a series of rules of the format

$$S(\text{sing.}) \rightarrow NP(\text{1st pers. sing. subj.}) \quad VP(\text{1st per. sing})$$

sacrifices generality in order to enforce subject-verb agreement. Rules proliferate even further when the grammar is expanded to describe structures generated by transformations. Each structure requires a set of several rules, and the fact that transformed surface structures paraphrase the corresponding deep structures is entirely lost.

Generalized phrase structure grammar, as the name suggests, copes with transformed structures and recovers the underlying deep structure without sacrificing the advantages of a context-free grammar and without increasing its formal power. Developed by Gerald Gazdar and his associates, the grammar consists of phrase structure rules, together with schemata and meta-rules. Schemata and meta-rules express the relationships between phrase structure rules in such a way as to prevent unnecessary proliferation.

Schemata collapse sets of rules with some common property into single statements.   They are especially useful for expressing the generalizations that features would obscure. For example, one schema describes sentences:

$$S \rightarrow NP[f] \quad VP[f]$$

where $\underline{f}$ stands for a combination of agreement features (such as 1st sing.); thus the schema abbreviates as many phrase structure rules as there are possible values of $\underline{f}$. (There is an analogy here with the augmented parsers, which also distinguish rules from features. Schemata resemble rules or arcs, and features are relegated the conditions associated with each rule or arc.) Such is the power of schemata that some can express principled constraints that have no direct expression in a transformational grammar. For example, the schema

$$c \rightarrow c \text{ } and \text{ } c$$

stipulates the constraint that only like constituents can be conjoined (*he saw the man and the woman*, but not *he saw the man and walking down the street*).

Given the special handling of features and the structural constraints that use them (such as subject - verb agreement), generalized phrase structure grammar is context-free. Thus it has the advantage of requiring less power than the context-sensitive grammars discussed in section 3. There remains some uncertainty about whether, such structural constraints aside, natural languages are context free. As we saw in Chapter 6, the inability to specify limits on embedding is one important motive for constructing recursive context-free grammars. In any context-free grammar, rules generate pairings as follows:

$$P \rightarrow a\ b \qquad\qquad P \rightarrow a\ P\ b$$

Such rules can generate any number of embedded structures, but they cannot generate unlimited numbers of overlapping pairs:

a   a   b   b   a   a   b   b

embedded   overlapping

Grammatical sentences in some languages, notably Dutch and Mohawk, have overlapping pairs in which each member is dependent on the other. If those overlapping dependencies are unlimited, as the embeddings are, then the languages cannot be generated by a context-free grammar. Even English may have a few such constructions, though they are rare:

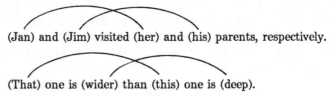

(Jan) and (Jim) visited (her) and (his) parents, respectively.

(That) one is (wider) than (this) one is (deep).

In the first sentence, *respectively* appears to require agreement between *Jan* and *her* and between *Jim* and *his*. But does it? Proponents of generalized phrase structure grammar, citing such well-formed sentences as *they visited his and her parents respectively*, suggest that agreement is not required and that *respectively* has only the semantic (as opposed to syntactic) role of specifying the order in which they are expressed. In the second sentence, it appears that English either requires different words (*deep* rather than *wide*) or requires deletion; thus ?*that one is wider than this one is wide* may not be well-formed. Whether the overlapping in English, Dutch, and Mohawk is indeed unlimited and whether there exists any other evidence that language is not context free remain open questions. If the answer is no, then generalized phrase structure grammar is sufficient. If the answer is

Rules: Derived rules:

VP → V[1]

VP → V[2] NP   VP[pass] → V[2, past part] (PP[by])

VP → V[3] NP PP[to]   VP[pass] → V[3, past part] PP[to] (PP[by])

VP → V[4] NP PP[for]   VP[pass] → V[4, past part] PP[for] (PP[by])

VP → V[5] NP NP   VP[pass] → V[5, past part] NP (PP[by])

VP → V[6] S   VP[pass] → V[6, past part] S (PP[by])

Lexicon:

| bring 2,3,4,5 | dedicate 2,3 | produce 2,4 | understand 1,2,6 |
| buy 2,4,5 | imitate 2,4 | sleep 1 | |

Figure 13. Corresponding rules for active and passive constructions.

yes, then the grammar, though it helps describe linguistic performance, is not sufficient to describe linguistic competence.

The next challenge is to provide for dative movement, passivization, and other forms of bounded movement without sacrificing parsimony. For these, generalized phrase structure grammar employs meta-rules. Borrowed from computer science where they abbreviate the grammars of certain computer languages, **meta-rules** systematically create new rules from rules that already exist. In a sense they resemble transformations, except that they operate on rules rather than structures. For example, a phrase-structure grammar has a series of rules (Figure 13, left-hand column) that specify verb phrases in the active voice. To reflect the structural constraints, each rule includes as a verb-feature, the category of verbs to which the rule applies, and categories are numbered to match entries in the lexicon. Also, rules that specify prepositional phrases have features to distinguish *to* and *for* indirect objects.

If we now expand the system of rules to include passives, we need five additional rules (Figure 13, right-hand column) to accommodate the various configurations in the passive. Moreover, simply to add rules is to ignore the relationship between active and passive versions of a sentence, as well as the generalization that all passives are formed in essentially the same way. Both, however, can be captured by a single meta-rule to represent our knowledge of the relationship between the active and the passive voice:

Rules:	Derived rules:
S → NP VP	S /PP[at] → NP VP /PP[at]
VP → V PP	VP /PP[at] → V PP /PP[at]
S → NP VP	S /NP[wh] → NP VP /NP[wh]
VP → V PP	VP /NP[wh] → V PP /NP[wh]
PP → PREP NP	PP /NP[wh] → PREP NP /NP[wh]

Figure 14. Corresponding rules for topicalized prepositional phrases and for wh-questions.

If there is a rule:	then there is a rule:
VP → V[f] NP W	VP[pass] → V[f, past part] W (PP[by])

where [f] refers to any feature or complex of features and W designates any non-pertinent word or string of words. Applied to the rules in the left-hand column, the meta-rule creates the rules in the right-hand column, all of which are phrase structure rules and capable of being implemented in a parser. Notice that the antecedent (or <u>if</u> portion) of the meta-rule excludes intransitive verbs by stipulating an NP, and that the consequent (<u>then</u> portion) provides for the optional prepositional phrase containing the logical subject. Thus meta-rules accomplish what transformations accomplish, but by modifying rules instead of operating on structures. They succeed with the other forms of bounded movement: with the inverted subjects and verbs of questions (*he is coming* ⇒ *is he coming*), for example, and the relocation of indirect objects (*he gave a present to me* ⇒ *he gave me a present*).

What about the more difficult challenge of unbounded movement? Can schemata and meta-rules cope when deep-structure locations are not predictable? They can. Recall the descriptions of unbounded movement in section 2.4: a sentence with a topicalized prepositional phrase consists of a prepositional phrase plus a sentence that lacks a prepositional phrase. Similarly a wh-question consists of a wh- NP plus a sentence lacking a wh- NP. Many theories of syntax share this method of describing the result of unbounded movement; Gazdar and his associates incorporate it directly into their schemata by employing **slashed categories** that explicitly represent the gaps. They propose the following schemata for the surface structures resulting from topicalization and wh-movement:

S → PP[f] S /PP[f]   S → NP[f] S /NP[f]

where the feature [f] is a specific preposition or a wh- NP, and the "slash category" S /PP[prep] means "a sentence lacking one prepositional phrase containing the preposition [prep]." Rules such as these function much as do the hold registers (and associated actions and conditions) of an augmented parser. In effect the PP[f] and NP[f] put constituents on hold, and the slashed categories prepare for their retrieval. Accommodating relative clauses would be the rules

NP → NP-REL[f] S/ NP-REL[f]   NP → NP M-REL[f] S /M-REL[f]

and generating these schemata are meta-rules of the general form,

If there is a rule   then there are also the rules

A → B C   A/P → B/P C and A/P → B C/P

where P stands for a phrase that can be displaced, and the notation /P refers to a structure that lacks such a phrase. For the topicalized PP and the wh- question, the meta-rules will create the rules in Figure 14. A small set of meta-rules will accommodate all the surface structures previously consigned to the transformational component, and in a fully articulated version of the grammar, the rules and meta-rules are associated with rules for semantic interpretation.

3.3 Lexical-functional grammar

An alternative to letting the phrase structure component of the grammar take over the descriptive role of transformations is more fully to exploit the lexicon and especially the lexical entries for verbs. As we have seen, both passivization and indirect object movement are lexically governed in that certain verbs allow them, while others do not:

He admired the actor.	⇒	The actor was admired by him.
He resembled the actor.	⇒	? The actor is resembled by him.
He handed the work to us.	⇒	He handed us the work.
He transferred the work to us.	⇒	? He transferred us the work.

We can think of these as patterns; in one pattern, *admired* must have a subject and an object. Lexical-functional grammar incorporates such patterns in the lexicon. The six legal sentences given above have the following patterns:

admired   (↑PRED) = = 'admire ⟨ (↑SUBJ) (↑OBJ) ⟩'

admired   (↑PRED) = = 'admire ⟨ (↑BY OBJ) (↑SUBJ) ⟩'

resembled   (↑PRED) = = 'resemble ⟨ (↑SUBJ) (↑OBJ) ⟩'

handed   (↑PRED) = = 'hand ⟨ (↑SUBJ) (↑OBJ) (↑TO OBJ) ⟩'

handed   (↑PRED) = = 'hand ⟨ (↑SUBJ) (↑OBJ2) (↑OBJ) ⟩'

transmitted   (↑PRED) = = 'transmit ⟨ (↑SUBJ) (↑OBJ) (↑TO OBJ2) ⟩'

(Ignore for now the up arrows, which help merge patterns with phrase structure rules.)   A major advantage of storing all patterns in the lexicon is that retrieval is presumably easier than processing (as by transformations). Thus the grammar predicts (what appears to be the case) that actives and passives can be dealt with quickly; the time and effort required to comprehend them should be about the same. That passivization appears to move NPs and make other changes would be only a mirage arising from the alternative surface forms.

Though each pattern is separately stated, the patterns are not unrelated. The paraphrase relationship between actives and passives (an important argument for transformations) arises from the fact that different surface forms have the same underlying semantic relationship. (PRED identifies these as predicate-argument structures compatible with the formal semantics discussed in the next chapter.)   The order of functions makes the translation reasonably straightforward:

(↑ PRED)   =   'admire ⟨ (↑ SUBJ)   (↑ OBJ) ⟩'
                                agent   patient

(↑ PRED)   =   'admire ⟨ (↑ BY OBJ)   (↑ SUBJ) ⟩'
                                agent   patient

The patterns are also related by rules resembling the meta-rules in generalized phrase structure grammar:

active/passive   (SUBJ) → (BY OBJ) or 0   (OBJ) → (SUBJ)

indirect object   (OBJ) → (OBJ2)   (TO OBJ) → (OBJ)

The first passivization rule offers the option of changing (SUBJ) to (BY OBJ) or deleting it; the second mandates a change of (OBJ) to (SUBJ). The rules differ from meta-rules in that they do not execute when sentences are produced or comprehended, but instead operate when the verbs first enter the lexicon. Expressing the generalization that many verbs allow active and passive patterns or that some verbs allow two locations for the indirect object, they simplify the grammar and hence the child's task of acquiring it.

The patterns are stated, not in terms of NPs and other constituents of the phrase marker, but in terms of the functional structures, subjects, direct objects, and indirect objects. Functions have important advantages. They are readily interfaced with semantics (especially, as we will see in Chapter 9, with semantic cases) and they appear to be language universals, found in all languages, though their phrase structure realization may differ from language to language. (Thus in English the subject is realized as an NP preceding the verb, whereas in Arabic, Irish, and Welsh it follows the verb.) Languages with elaborated morphologies give more prominence to functions than does English, which has subject and object forms only for a few personal and wh-pronouns.

The schemata associated with lexical entries for verbs (and other words) are matched against schemata that augment certain phrase structure rules:

$$\text{S} \rightarrow \quad \underset{(\uparrow\text{SUBJ})==\downarrow}{\text{NP}} \quad \underset{\uparrow==\downarrow}{\text{VP}}$$

$$\text{NP} \rightarrow \left[\,\text{DET}\,\right]\ \text{NOUN}$$

$$\text{VP} \rightarrow \underset{\uparrow==\downarrow}{\text{VERB}}\ \left[\underset{(\uparrow\text{OBJ})==\downarrow}{\text{NP}}\left[\underset{(\uparrow\text{OBJ2})==\downarrow}{\text{NP}}\right]\right]\left[\underset{(\uparrow\ (\downarrow\text{pcase}))\,)==\downarrow\ )}{\text{PP*}}\right]$$

$$\text{PP} \rightarrow \underset{}{\text{PREP}}\ \underset{(\uparrow\text{OBJ})==\downarrow)}{\text{NP}}$$

These resemble ordinary phrase structure rules, except that they are somewhat looser, designed so as not to exclude any well-formed sentence. Bracketed constituents are optional. Thus a VP can consist of a verb that takes no objects (*fall*), or a verb that takes only a direct object (*admire*), or a verb that takes NP indirect and direct objects (*hand*). Starred constituents can be repeated any number of times including none; thus the PP rule specifies dative *to* phrases, passive *by* phrases, and any other prepositional phrases. The rules will generate a phrase marker (called a **c-structure**) in precisely the way we have seen before (see Figure 15). Such loose rules will generate some phrase structures that are not well formed; these will be blocked when the associated schemata have no matching schemata in the lexical entries. Thus the VP rule will generate sentences as eccentric as *the man falls a friend the book to a boy by a person*, leaving it to the schemata for *falls*:

$$\text{'fall}\ \langle\ (\uparrow\ \text{SUBJ})\ \rangle\ \text{'}$$

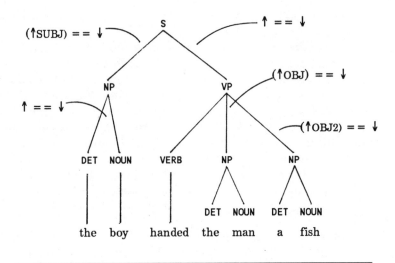

Figure 15. A c-structure with unification equations.

to disallow everything following the verb. The rules are context free, permitting a parser with highly flexible scheduling and interleaved semantics.

Whereas the phrase structure rules build phrase markers, the schemata working independently build functional structures. The up and down arrows are variables, pointing respectively to parent and present nodes. In the S rule, (↑ subj) means "subject of the parent S" node and the following ↓ arrow points to the present NP node, thus the equations correspond to pointers in the phrase marker. (See the tree above.) The equations assert that the constituents unify if values for the variables in one are not inconsistent with those in the other. Thus the unification equation (↑ subj) == ↓ can be paraphrased: the subject of the structure S unifies with the structure of the NP. The unification equation ↑ == ↓ which appears under the VERB in the rule for VP and under VP in the rule for S passes a verb's functional description from VERB to VP and from VP to S. Unification also handles subject-verb agreement and other context-sensitive phenomena. The lexical entries represent features as schemata:

a	DET	(↑ definiteness == indefinite)
		(↑ NUMBER == singular)
boy	NOUN	(↑ NUMBER == singular)
		(↑ PRED == 'boy')
handed	VERB	(↑ NUMBER == singular or plural)
		(↑ TENSE == PAST)

When lexical entries are unified with functional structures, the TENSE of VERB becomes the TENSE of the VP (unless the tense of an AUX blocks it) and therefore of S, and NUMBER for *a* unifies with the identical NUMBER for *boy* and with the not inconsistent NUMBER for *handed*. When all unifications are complete, the result is a **functional structure** or **f-structure**, which is entirely independent of the **c-structure** and quite shallow, resembling the structure of registers built by an augmented transition network.

Loose phrase structure rules also work in concert with schemata to manage unbounded movement. Wh-questions require a second S rule that provides for a fronted NP that must be a question word, as well as a rule that marks the subsequent gap by allowing an absent NP:

S →   NP   AUX   NP   VP
          ↓ == ↓np   (↑subj) == ↓   ↑ == ↓
          (↓q-word) == yes

NP →   0
          ↓ == ↑np

Left unconstrained the NP rule could do considerable mischief, generating empty NP nodes at every position that allows an NP. Though unbounded movement (unlike passivization and dative movement) is not governed by the verb, the necessary constraint is supplied indirectly by the verb's schemata. The verb *admire*, for example, requires an NP direct object:

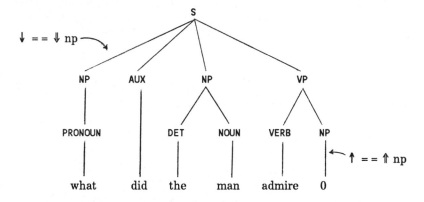

The variables ↑np and ↓np bind the question word to the empty NP node. Whereas the single-shafted arrows point to parent and child nodes along a single line in the c-structure, the corresponding double-shafted arrows make long-distance connections within some bounded space. For wh-questions, the bounded space is the S; for relatives, it would be the embedded S.

Exercises

1. As noted in section 1.3, predicate adjectives can sometimes restrict the constructions that may follow them. Add an arc to the sentence network that would accommodate such predicate adjectives as *fond*, *glad* and *hopeful* and add conditions to the NP and PP networks that would block a sentential NP following *fond* and a prepositional phrase following *hopeful*, but allow either following *glad*.

2. Provide sample lexical entries and a unification equation (for the relevant rule) to assure the appropriate parsing of count and non-count nouns.

3. With well-formed sentences in English, will the hold facility ever contain more than one relative pronoun? If the hold is used for both relatives and question words, will it ever contain one of each?

4. Each of the following sentences appears to contain an incomplete constituent. Using the notation for transformations, describe what has happened.

> This administrator is difficult for us to work with.
> That program is impossible for him to interpret.
> This project is disagreeable for me to work on.
> This schedule is inconvenient for Joe to follow.
> This window is too dirty for her to see through.
> That promise is burdensome for me to fulfill.

5. Rather than appealing to the notion of subject and direct object NPs in parsing passive sentences, we might imagine a rule that, upon recognizing the "signature" verb sequence, exchanges the first noun in the sentence with the last noun. Give some reasons why this simple expedient would not work.

6. Explain the difference between the constructions preceding and following the verb *is* in the following sentence and, using the ATN in the appendix to this chapter, trace the parse of the sentence:

> What he does know is that she will arrive in time.

7. One form of movement is the inversion of the subject NP and the first auxiliary verb to form yes/no questions: *they are leaving* → *are they leaving*? Consider whether this would require the HOLD facility, a change in the methods of assuring subject - verb agreement. or both. Add to the networks in the Appendix whatever is required to handle the inversion.

8. What has been deleted from the sentence, *visiting England made him happy*? Using the ATN given in the Appendix, trace the parse of the sentence and show the recovery of whatever has been deleted.

Further reading

Most of the readings given for Chapter six, especially Winograd (1983) and Allen (1987), are relevant here, as are the several collections of papers on grammars and parsing: King (1983), Dowty, Karttunen and Zwicky (1985), Sparck Jones and Wilks (1985), Bolc (1987) and Reyle and Rohrer (1988). Woods (1970, 1973) proposed augmented transition networks as a method of capturing the phenomena described by transformational grammars; see also Bates (1978), Kaplan (1972) and Wanner (1978 and 1987). On augmented phrase structure grammars, see Heidorn (1975), Sager (1981) and Robinson (1982). On unification, Kay (1979 and 1985), Pereira (1985), Knight (1989) and Pulman (1990) are informative. Berwick and Weinberg (1984) explores the relation between theories of grammar and efficiency of parsing. On unbounded movement and "gaps," see McCawley (1988), Wanner and Maratsos (1978) and Stowe (1986). On the proposals to supplement or replace the transformational component, see Moravcsik and Wirth (1980), Johnson-Laird (1983) and Sells (1985). On lexical-functional grammar, see Bresnan (1978 and 1982) and Horn (1983). On generalized phrase structure grammar, see Sampson (1983), the papers in Jacobson and Pullum (1981) and Gazdar, Klein, Pullum and Sag (1985). Computational approaches are developed in C. Pollard (1988), Phillips and Thompson (1985), and Fisher (1989).

Appendix: the completed augmented transition networks

Sentence network:

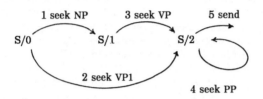

1 seek NP

con: CASE of * is not OBJECT

act: assign * to SUBJ
       set S-NUMB to NUMB of *

2 seek VP1

con: FORM of * is UNTENSED

ini: assign PRONOUN "you" to SUBJ
      assign MODAL "will" to AUX
      set SENT-TYPE to IMPERATIVE

4 seek PP

con: SENT-TYPE is not DEPENDENT

act: assign * to SENT-MODIFIER

Verbal phrase network:

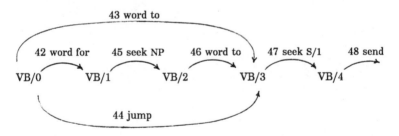

45 seek NP

Con: CASE of * is not SUBJECT

Act: assign * to HOLD

46 seek S/1

Ini: If HOLD is not empty
       assign HOLD to SUBJ
     If DIR OBJ↑ is not empty
       assign DIR OBJ↑ to SUBJ
     If SUBJ↑ is not empty
       assign SUBJ↑ to SUBJ
       assign [dummy] to SUBJECT
       set SENT TYPE to DEPENDENT
       set MAIN VERB to <u>be</u> / MODAL

Verb phrase network:

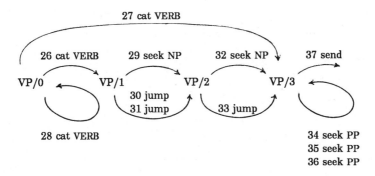

26 cat VERB

con: NUMB of S = NUMB of *

act: assign * to MAIN VERB
      set SUBCAT to SUBCAT of *

27 cat VERB

con: TYPE of VERB is <u>be</u>
      FORM of * is PAST PART
      SUBCAT is <u>eat</u> or <u>put</u>

act: append VERB to AUX
      assign * to MAIN VERB
      assign SUBJ to DIR OBJ
      assign [someone/thing] to SUBJ
      set VOICE to PASSIVE

28 cat VERB

con: If FORM of * is UNTENSED
      and TYPE of MAIN VERB is MODAL
      or TYPE of AUX is MODAL
      If TYPE of * is MODAL
      and TYPE of MAIN VERB
      is not MODAL
      If FORM of * is PAST PART
      and TYPE of MAIN VERB is <u>have</u>
      or TYPE of AUX is <u>have</u>
      If FORM of * is PRES PART
      and TYPE of MAIN VERB is <u>be</u>

act: append MAIN VERB to AUX
      assign MAIN VERB to *
      set SUBCAT to SUBCAT of *

29 seek NP

con: CASE of * is OBJ

30 jump

con: SUBCAT is <u>talk</u>

31 jump

con: SUBCAT is <u>eat</u> and not <u>put</u>

act: set DIR OBJ to [something]

32 seek NP

con: CASE of * is OBJECT
      if * is PRONOUN
      DIR OBJ is not PRONOUN

act: assign DIR OBJ to INDIR OBJ

34 seek PP

con: * is "to" or "for"

act: assign PREP-OBJ to INDIR OBJ

35 seek PP

con: * is "by"
      VOICE is PASSIVE

act: assign PREP-OBJ to SUBJ

Noun phrase network:

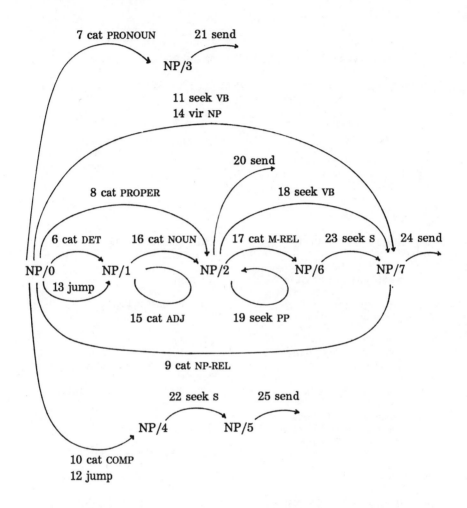

6 cat DET

act: assign * to DET
     set NP-NUMB to NUMB of *
     set NP-COUNT to COUNT of *

7 cat PRONOUN

act: assign * to NP-HEAD
     set CASE to CASE of *
     set NP-NUMB to NUMB of *

8 cat PROPER

act: assign * to NP-HEAD
     set NP-NUMB to NUMB of *

9 cat NP-REL

act: assign * to RELATIVE
     set REL-TYPE to NP

10 cat COMP

con: SUBJ is empty or SUBCAT is <u>say</u>
   ↑ is not PP

11   seek VB

act: assign * to NP-HEAD

12 jump

con: SUBCAT is <u>say</u>
   ↑ is not PP
   SUBJECT is not empty

14 vir NP

con: HOLD is an NP

act: retrieve HOLD

15 cat ADJ

act: append * to PRE-NOMINAL

16 cat NOUN

act: assign * to NP-HEAD
   set NP-NUMB to NUMB of *

17 cat M-REL

act: assign * to RELATIVE
   set REL-TYPE to MOD

18 seek VB

act: append * to POST-NOMINAL

19 seek PP

act: append * to POST-NOMINAL

22 seek S

ini: set SENT-TYPE to DEPENDENT

act: assign * to NP-HEAD

23 seek S

ini: set SENT-TYPE to DEPENDENT
       assign RELATIVE to HOLD ↑

act: if REL-TYPE is NP
   assign * to NP-HEAD
   if REL-TYPE is MOD
   append * to POST-NOMINAL

25 send

act: set NP-NUMB to SINGULAR

Prepositional phrase network:

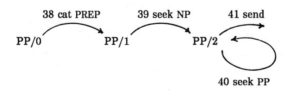

39 seek NP

Con: CASE of * is OBJECT

Chapter 8

Lexical Semantics

Section one: Meaning and Its Representation

1.1 Beginning with lexical relationships

The vocabulary of a language is more than an assemblage of lexical items each arbitrarily different from all others. Instead, as Ferdinand de Saussure first suggested, a vocabulary is "a system of interdependent terms in which the value of each term results solely from the simultaneous presence of others." In this respect the semantic component resembles other components of language. To recognize the phoneme /k/ in *kit*, we to perceive a contrast between its acoustic characteristics and those of similar phonemes, the /t/ in *tip* and the /g/ in *get*. To recognize the syntactic functions of *can* in *he can walk* or *the can spilled* requires that we know the relations into which *can* enters with *he* and *walk* or with *the* and *spilled* or, more generally, with nouns and pronouns and with verb forms. With meanings, it is much the same. The relational system of meanings determines how the meaning of one word resembles and differs from the meaning of another and determines how words can combine to form meaningful phrases and sentences.

Until recently, the study of semantic systems has been carried out within the paradigm of "structural" or "linguistic" semantics, which focuses on the relationships evident between words or within phrases and sentences, much as a chemist studies the composition of molecules. Though structural semantics has little to say about how meanings are mentally represented or about how language comprehension proceeds, it is reasonable to assume that relationships discoverable in language are reflected in meaning representations and that they play a role in language performance. Thus recently emerging "conceptual" approaches to meaning (largely the work of computational linguists and other cognitive scientists) build upon the structural research. Although these

258

new approaches seek to represent more fully the meanings of utterances, they begin from relationships evident among words.

The relationships are of several kinds. Words can share elements of meaning: along one dimension, *bachelor* and *husband* share the meaning male; along another dimension *husband* and *wife* share the meaning married. Large families of words may share meanings (*have, possess, own, give, donate, bequeath, lend, sell, buy, rent, lease, borrow,* and so on). Words that share an element of meaning may be further related in that they are incompatible with one another in certain specifiable ways. Some are related as contradictories: negating one affirms the other (*alive - dead, present - absent, same - different*), so that between them they exhaust the possibilities. Other words such as *buy - sell, parent - child, below - above* are related as converses; they describe a transitive or one-way relationship between entities such that reversing the order of the entities allows the converse to be substituted: *Joe is older than Jim* and *Jim is younger than Joe.* Many other words that share an element of meaning are related as contraries in that affirming one negates the other (*dog - cat, bus - truck*). Some contraries belong to closed groups which collectively exhaust all the relevant possibilities. Four-member groups are especially common (seasons of the year, points of the compass), but there are also groups of three (solids, liquids and gases) and groups larger than four (the days of the week or months of the year). Some groups of contraries, though finite at any given time, are open to expansion: for example the names of rooms in a house or utensils for cooking. Finally, there are the groups of words related as grades or degrees (*hot - warm - cool - cold, shout - speak - mumble - whisper*).

The relations mentioned thus far (and others like them) exist among words that might be substituted for one another. Thus we might say *the young man drove a bus* or, making two substitutions, *the old man drove a truck.* A second kind of semantic relationship exists between *young/old* and *man* and between *drove* and *truck/bus,* which permit those combinations, but not some others. Sentences like the following are anomalous:

> The old man drove a triangle.
> The deciduous man drove a truck.
> The female uncle drove a truck.
> The human man drove a truck.

What is at issue here is more than inappropriateness; the anomaly is not a slight incongruity that can be eliminated by substituting a synonym (for example, a different verb: *the tree died* for *the tree passed away*). Instead the anomaly inheres deeply in the meanings of the words. *Drove* in the sense that we are using it requires as its object a vehicle, not a geometric shape; *deciduous* requires that the word it modifies be a form of vegetation. Some of these anomalies are so clear-cut that they have been named. When one of the combinationally related words contradicts the other, as *female* partially contradicts *uncle*, the result is a paradox; when one partially repeats the sense of the other, as *human* does *man*, it is redundant.

With words that have multiple senses (like *drove*), the different senses enter into different combinational relationships. A convenient method of testing for ambiguity is to conjoin two relationships in a sentence, such as in *he drove a nail and his truck*. If the relationships pertain to different senses of the word, the resulting sentence will be anomalous. Substitutional and combinational relationships function cooperatively: the combinational relationships restrict the possibilities for substitution, whereas the substitutional relationships often generalize the possibilities for combination.

Though utterances may have several other kinds of meaning, those that inhere in lexical relationships are primary. This is not because they are more important than the others, but because the others emerge subsequently in the process of comprehension. Thus, the primary meaning is **literal** and distinguishable from non literal meanings. Non literal meanings are apparent when we metaphorically claim *the car is dead* (rather than *the car is inoperable*) or sarcastically declare *wonderful, it's sleeting* (instead of *it is bad that it is sleeting*). To grasp the intended meaning, we first work out the literal meaning and if it is in some way inappropriate, infer that the expression is not intended literally. Only animate beings can die, a *car* is not an animate being, so *dead* must be intended non literally. Similarly, sunshine or rain or snow may be greeted with pleasure, but few like sleet so *wonderful* is probably non literal. Other non-literal meanings emerge when speakers engage in overstatement (*nobody listens to me* probably means *not enough people*) or when they make substitutions, as of a writer for her works (*I've read all of Austen* for *I've read all Austen's writings.*)

The primary meaning is also **direct** and distinguishable from additional indirect meanings that some utterances may convey in some contexts. Were my son to hear me say *I think the dog needs to go out*, he might interpret my indirect meaning as "Please take the dog for a walk." Success in interpreting indirect meanings requires that we first interpret its primary meaning then decide whether that meaning is contextually appropriate. Thus interpreting an indirect meaning usually causes us to spurn the direct meaning, as when we politely respond to *would you mind telling me what time it is?* with *yes* rather than *no*. Sentences may have several possible indirect meanings; determining which is intended depends on appropriateness given the context. *Do you know what time it is?*, for example, may be intended to elicit a response such as *it is one o'clock* in one context, *time passes quickly when we are together* in a different context, and *I should be* *leaving* in a third. Thus we might entertain several indirect meanings until we find one that suits the context. However, no matter what the non literal or indirect meaning turns out to be, the primary meaning must usually be computed first then evaluated in the context, and that primary meaning is best approached via the relationships into which words enter.

Lexical relationships play a crucial role in language acquisition. Children learn the senses of words by overgeneralizing early words then restricting the sense of each word as they encounter its relationships to other words. *Ball* might be any round red entity until an edible ball is encountered which the child learns to call *apple*. Children also learn meanings by inference, using as their data the combinations into which words enter. Given a sentence or two such as *his glass of frit spilled* and *she drank her frit* a child will easily infer that *frit* is like *juice, water, milk*, that is a liquid and potable. Obviously these methods are very effective (children average about nine new words a day from ages one to six), but spontaneous learning is to an extent haphazard. We have not all had identical opportunities to generalize and to make inferences, and opportunities have not all come in the same sequence, so it is unlikely that our conceptual representations of the twelve- to fourteen-thousand words that comprise an average vocabulary for adults consist of exactly the same sets of relationships structured in exactly the same way. For this reason, we need only look for the simplest, the most general, and the most fully explicit ways of representing lexical relationships, and need not assume that the representation is identical to that possessed by any individual. Still better would be a way of modeling a child's capacity for spontaneous learning by forming then refining generalizations and by inferring the meanings of words from their contexts. Except in some experimental work, that is for the future.

1.2 The representation hypothesis

Linguistic structures and neural structures can both be investigated directly. Linguists can describe the multilevel systems of language symbols, as well as the rule-abiding ways that simple symbols combine to form complex lexical, syntactic, and semantic structures. Similarly, neuroscientist can study nerve cells in the brain, the circuits which connect them and the circumstances in which nerve cells propagate electrochemical impulses through the network. Between language structures and the brain, cognitive scientists postulate a level of explanation, something like what we call the "mind" and refer to with adjectives such as "mental."

Conceptual theories operate at this level, postulating a **representation hypothesis**, which says simply that representations of lexical and sentential concepts can be described. With the additional hypothesis that concepts are reflected in the properties of words and the relationships into which words enter, we have a way of investigating them. The nature of mental representations can be inferred from patterns observable in language, much as the properties of electrons, quarks, black holes, and the systems to which they belong are inferred (scientists have never seen any of them). Comprehension can be described as a set of procedures for operating on those representations. The representation hypothesis is so inviting as a level of explanation that it has been adopted not only for studying language comprehension but also for research into other cognitive activities as well. It is shared by researchers in all the cognitive sciences: cognitive philosophy, anthropology and psychology, as well as linguistics and artificial intelligence.

The representation hypothesis is not uncontroversial. Some argue that investigations in neuroscience and structural linguistics will eventually converge on an explanation of how language and meaning exist in the brain that requires no intermediate level of representation. After all, they argue, mental representations are not directly open to inspection or reliably available to introspection. No one can say just what they are. It is more profitable to study what can be observed: structures in the brain and structures of language. Mathematics, however, offers an encouraging analogy. Though no generally accepted theory exist as to just what a number is, we understand many of the properties of numbers and the relations into which they enter. We know that 1, 2, 3, 5, 7, and 11 are primes, divisible only by themselves and by 1; we know that 2 and 3 are related in such a way that their sum is 5 and their product is 6. If concepts also have their primes, their combinations, and so on; these should be identifiable and should be amenable to explicit representation. It should also be possible to model the processes that operate on them.

Others who distrust the representation hypothesis take the position of strict materialism, asserting that nothing goes on in the brain that is not a by-product of chemical and electrical events, of states of high and low activation. Therefore cognitive phenomena ought to be explained in terms of physical events and modeled, if at all, not by symbolic operations, but by a neurally inspired parallel distributed processing network. To accept the representation hypothesis is to side with the dualist against this strict materialism. Dualism respects our strong intuition that mental life is real and insists that the mind is its own place, partially autonomous and not reducible to physical explanation.

Computation offers an existence proof that autonomy is possible in symbolic processing and verifies, logically though not empirically, the meaning hypothesis. Though no computer program can execute without hardware, a given program can be instantiated on computers with very different circuitry and operating principles and yet remain the same program in its logic, its conceptual structuring of information its input and output. Whether the computer is of conventional serial processing architecture or a connectionist machine proceeding from state to stable state makes no difference; in principle, each is capable of emulating the other and both can execute any computable procedure. Explanations of programs can therefore be logically independent of the hardware that instantiates them, and the methods by which they process information can be fully described without recourse to their instantiation. This means only that the representation hypothesis affords a plausible level of description. Empirical verification of the hypothesis would require that concepts be fully and accurately encoded using a system of discrete symbols and that the generation and comprehension of language be reduced to rule-abiding processes.

Still others who distrust the representation hypothesis allow that it is a simplifying assumption appropriate to some cognitive phenomena, but not the meanings of words and sentences. It might, for example, be appropriate for syntactic processing, which is automatic (we cannot help but recognize the syntax of a sentence in a language we know) and always operates in the same way, unaffected by one's belief or knowledge. Thus syntactic knowledge might be fully and explicitly represented, and sentence recognition might be studied through computer modeling. With meanings, they argue, the case is different. Meanings do not exist in isolation and may be so inextricably bound to beliefs and intentions and emotions and immediate contexts and states of knowledge and cultural heritage and orientations toward the world that the simplifying assumption is not warranted. Indeed, the generation and comprehension of language may prove so complex or so ineffable that it is impossible either to verify or to falsify the representation hypothesis. It may turn out that mental representations of lexical meanings would become a cognitive Holy Grail, the object of perpetual quest. There can be no good answer to such an objection, except that the day is still early. If the quest leads into regions so labyrinthine or shadowy as to be unnavigable, then it must end. That time is not yet.

Even if a complete and fully satisfactory understanding of meaning is never reached, research into linguistic representations can yield some practical benefits. A dramatic example is machine translation. Consider, for example, a system for translating technical documents among eight languages. (Literary translation should probably remain a human enterprise.) One possibility would be to devise language-specific representations and procedures. Assuming they operate only in one direction, we would need seven sets of procedures and representations for each of the eight languages, for a total of fifty-six. If, instead, machine translation employs an intermediate form of meaning representation (an *interlingua*), only eight procedures are required to translate language into the interlingua and eight to generate language from it:

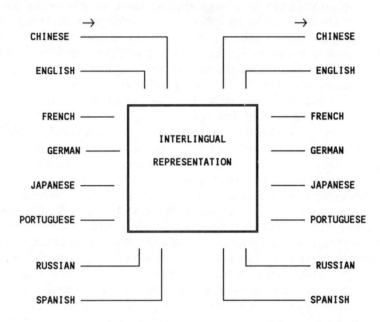

Also, interlingua-based systems are readily extensible to additional languages, an important facility for machine translation.

1.3 Iconic versus propositional representation

Once we accept as a level of explanation the representation hypothesis, we need to consider the form of meaning representations: whether they resemble images or consist of propositions.   Images are less amenable to computational representation and manipulation than are propositions.   That meanings exist "in the mind's eye" as images of things, scenes, and experiences is an old view, dating from ancient Greece.   Certainly we experience mental imagery as we think and speak, but is it likely that the mental representations are iconic? Imagery does play a role in young children's language acquisition and adults with eidetic or "photographic" memory continue to associate words with shapes, sounds, and even tactual sensations.   However, these circumstances do not necessarily support an image theory of meaning.   Eidetic memory may actually impede comprehension, flooding the mind with too much imagery. Also, in language acquisition, the role of imagery diminishes significantly as children learn to forget perceptible differences so that they can form the abstractions that are essential to learning.   Beyond these psychological considerations, Kant argues in *The Critique of Pure Reason*, that images are too particularistic to represent many conceptions. His example is the triangle.   What image could be sufficiently general to represent all triangles: those with three acute angles and those with one right angle, those that are equilateral and those that are not?

Theorists, particularly those who want to establish a single form of mental representation accommodating both perception and language, have scouted various ways around Kant's argument. Meanings might consist of characteristic attributes, perhaps iconic primitives like flatness, connectedness, and rigidity, together with procedures for deciding whether a perceived object meets enough criteria to fit the meaning.   But there is no generally agreed-upon theory and little empirical evidence on which to found one.   Even if an iconic theory could provide for the triangle, which has too many possible images, it would be defeated by abstractions and other meaningful expressions that do not appear to have any images associated with them. What, for example, is the image associated with *hello* or *truth* or *not*, and what image or combination of images would capture the relational meaning of *he considered the evidence and concluded she was guilty*? Research now centers on the hypothesis that there exists a mental component containing representations and processes dedicated to visual imagery and that this special-purpose component is not ordinarily involved in language comprehension.

The leading alternative to the image theory is propositional representation. Propositions are language-like forms of representation. Most simple declarative sentences express propositions, and **proposition** is often defined as what a declarative sentence expresses when it is used to make a statement. Propositions consist of **predicates** and **arguments**, with predicates asserting properties of arguments. The assertion is something that we can judge true or not true; and for this reason, propositions are assumed to be the simplest complete units of thought. In *she slept* and *he is a bird*, the predicates *slept* and *is a bird* complete propositions that may be either true or false of the entities *she* and *he*. Propositions typically capture relationships, such as the categorical relationship between *he* and *bird* or the stative relationship *John knows Mary*.

Phrases may also express propositions and can readily be converted into simple declarative sentences: *the red bus* expresses a proposition *the bus/ is red*, and *on the bus expresses* the location of something or someone. Single phrases and sentences may and commonly do express more than one proposition. *The big bad wolf destroyed the pig's house* might be paraphrased into at least four declarative sentences, each containing a proposition: *The wolf was big*; *the wolf was bad*; *the pig possessed a house*; and *the wolf destroyed that house*. Also, as the availability of these paraphrases suggests, different sentences may express the same proposition.

Words also express propositions, and ingredients of their meanings can be stated propositionally. Part of the meaning of *dog*, for example, is expressed propositionally as *a dog is an animal*, whereas *the person is not an adult* expresses two ingredients of the meaning of *child*. Indeed a major motive for adopting propositional representation is that it readily captures many important properties of sentence and word meaning. Another motive is that propositional representations facilitate the formal and informal reasoning (much of it unconscious) performed in language comprehension as well as the reasoning required to reach conclusions, find explanations, and in general to think.

Linguists originally adopted propositional representation because it is well understood and sufficiently expressive to capture word and sentence meanings; almost from the beginning computational researchers employed proposition representation because they are easily represented in knowledge structures and readily processed. In both cases the decision was fortuitous.

Abundant empirical evidence now exists that propositional representation plays a central role in comprehension. Speed of reading and accuracy of recall depend on the number of propositions in a sentence, even when the number of words is held constant. Tests of sentence recall show that subjects forget the syntax quite rapidly but remember the propositional content. In one classic experiment, subjects listened to paragraphs containing a sentence such as: *he sent a letter about it to John, his close friend*. The passages were then interrupted at a point 0, 40 or 80 syllables later, and subjects were presented either with the target sentence or with one of the following sentences:

1. He sent John, his closest friend, a letter about it.
2. To John his closest friend, he sent a letter about it.
3. John, his closest friend, sent him a letter about it.
4. He was sent a letter about it by John, his closest friend.

After 80 syllables subjects frequently thought that they had heard sentences 1 or 2, which express the same proposition in different syntax, but seldom thought that they had heard sentence 3 or 4, which expresses a different proposition. These findings strongly suggest that sentences are not stored verbatim in memory, but are instead translated into a different representation.

That sentences are not stored verbatim is hardly surprising given that listeners are interested in the gist of what they are getting and usually not the actual words or their syntactic form. Though the gist is apprehended very quickly (if only because short-term memory has limited capacity), apprehending it does require some processing. Reading time increases as a function of the number of propositions in a text even when the number of words is held constant. Empirical studies also show that propositions are either recalled in their entirety or not recalled at all, suggesting that meaning representations capture entire propositions. Subjects were presented with complete sentences, then asked to decide which of a list of words were in the sentences. Researcher found that when two words on the list came from the same proposition and not merely the same sentence, decisions on the second words were fastest and more reliable. In a sentence like,

> The skyscraper that contained the bureau overlooked the harbor,

overlooked is a better cue for recalling *skyscraper* than for *bureau* despite its proximity to *bureau*. These findings suggest that pieces of a proposition are stored together. Shadowing studies suggest that comprehension segments sentences into propositional units rather than phrase structures, when the two do not coincide. And sentences that contain one proposition with three arguments (such as *the friend wrote a letter to Mary*) tend to be remembered more reliably than sentences containing three propositions, each with one argument *(the tired friend complained frequently)*. That the arguments were unified presumably assisted their recall. Thus comprehension appears to focus on propositions. Though the precise form of their mental representations is not known, most computational representations of sentence meaning are based on propositional content.

To be sure, many forms of non linguistic material do not readily lend themselves to propositional representation. In particular it is difficult to imagine how the content of a visual scene might be translated into a set of propositions, how we come by the experience of mental imagery when we recall the scene, and how we can mentally shift perspectives and rotate objects. Musical and tactile experience presents similar problems. Another problem is that direct translation of sentences into propositions ignores the relative prominence that different sentences give to parts of a proposition. The sentences,

> Nancy wrote the letter to Jen yesterday.
> It was Nancy who wrote a letter to Jen yesterday.
> What Nancy did was write a letter to Jen yesterday.
> It was a letter to Jen that Nancy wrote yesterday.
> To Jen Nancy wrote a letter yesterday.
> It was yesterday that Nancy wrote a letter to Jen.

all express the same proposition but stress important or new information by giving different prominence to *Nancy, Jen, wrote, a letter,* and *yesterday*. And studies of lexical recall suggest that prominent constituents are more readily recalled than those that are not.

1.4 Predicate calculus and its network representation

The most commonly used method of representing propositions is **first-order predicate calculus,** which offers both a systematic method of specifying their internal structures and well-understood methods of generating (in effect, "calculating") new information from what is given. (Calculus in this instance has nothing to do with the mathematics of differentials and integrals, which also goes by that name.) Developed by Gottlob Frege in the late nineteenth century to capture properties of natural language and reasoning, predicate calculus serves as a standard notation for linguistic semantics. With propositions and other relationships encoded as semantic networks, it also serves computational linguistics, affording a uniform way of representing both lexical and sentence meanings and supporting the logical inferences that must be made in the course of computational interpretation.

That linguistic information can be represented in logical form does not mean that it should be. Some counsel despair, arguing that natural languages express meanings in untidy non-logical ways (one view) or in a logic that is subtler and more flexible than the predicate calculus can ever be (another view). Others concede that translation is possible and that the uniformity of the notation is useful, but they question whether it is worth the effort. Will it lead to any insight about the operation either of language or the mind? Nevertheless, translating simple sentences into propositional representation is quite straightforward, and the predicate calculus, sufficiently expressive to accommodate a great many meanings already, is being extended to encompass others, including information that is typically rather than necessarily true or possibly true, true only at certain times, or only believed to be true, as well as what is permissible, obligatory, and preferred. At the same time, work in "Montague grammar" (Richard Montague is an American logician) promises accurate, subtle, and complete translation of sentences into logical form, though Montague's method has been applied to only a fraction of the structures possible in English and other natural languages.

The propositions that English expresses as *the bad wolf* and *the wolf blusters*, would be in the notation of predicate calculus

bad (wolf1)

blusters (wolf1)

Wolf is numbered to specify an individual because the sentences have nothing to say about wolves in general, but instead predicate the badness and the blustering of one particular wolf whose existence is asserted by the utterance. (The numbers have no inherent meaning; any unique symbol would do.) As sentences are converted to logical form, each type is restricted to a token, representing a particular action or object existing in the world expressed by the sentence.

Within the proposition, the predicate asserts a property (bad) of an argument (wolf). *Bad* takes only one argument and is thus a one-place predicate, but predicates can also have two or more places. The verb *threaten* as in *the wolf threatens pigs* is a two-place predicate:

threatens (wolf1, pigs3)

Relational nouns and adjectives also express two-place predicates, for example *enemy* in the proposition *a wolf is an enemy of a pig* and *stronger* in *the wolf is stronger than the pig*.

enemy (wolf, pig)

stronger-than (wolf, pig)

Verbs such as *give* and *bring*, which take both a direct object and an indirect object, express three-place predicates. Sentences may contain more than one proposition and may include conjoined and nested propositions; *the big bad wolf tried to destroy the pig's brick house* has six, including a nested proposition, which can be simplified as

try6 (wolf1, (destroy4 (wolf1, house2))).

For present purposes, we can concentrate on the syntax of predicate calculus, but the expressions can also be given meaning via set theory, as we will see in section 3. Roughly speaking, the predicate expressed by a verb such as *sleeps* refers to the large set of all who sleep; the proposition expressed by the sentence *Jane sleeps* asserts that some individual Jane is a member of that set.

Though we can reserve discussion of the set theoretic semantics until section 3.3, when we consider how words refer to things in the world, we do need a way of representing plural nouns and compound NPs. Sets will be enclosed in curly braces, thus the sentence *the wolf and the pig ate supper* would be represented

ate ({wolf1, pig4}, supper)

The set {wolf1, pig4} is treated as is any other argument.

Propositions can readily be represented in semantic networks. The predicates and arguments become labeled links that connect concepts with the governing proposition. (See Figure 1 where brackets indicate nodes in the network and ←( )— is a labeled link.) The ←(is-a)— links point to a different portion of the network containing definitional information about words (for example, [ANIMAL] ←(is-a)— [wolf1]). The network is partitioned as represented by the heavy line in order to separate propositions specifying particular instances from such definitional information (as well as from other, unrelated propositions). The partition itself has a meaning that corresponds roughly to the English "there is" or "it is the case that." Though early versions of network theory did not provide for partitioning, the knowledge that

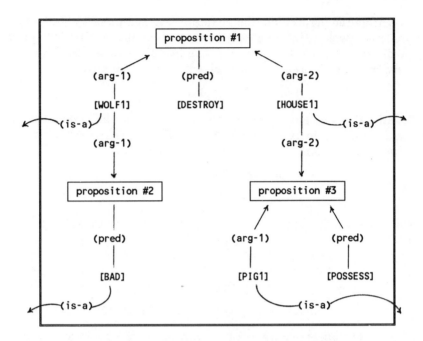

Figure 1. Network representation of the three propositions
asserted by *the bad wolf destroyed the pig's house.*

defines words of a language is different from the information expressed
by a particular sentence and should not be indiscriminately mixed.

Predicate calculus also provides for the combining of propositions by
means of certain logical connectives and quantifiers, which correspond
to expressions in natural language. The wolf's threat combines two
propositions: *if he huffs and puffs and blows, then the pig's house will
fall down*:

$$\text{blow2 (wolf1)} \supset \text{fall-down3 (house1)}$$

These propositions are connected by **material implication** (here
symbolized $\supset$). If (blow (wolf1)) is true then (fall-down (house1)) is
by implication also true. Though the relationship between blowing and
falling is causal, implication is "material" only and does not necessarily
involve causal connections. We could just as easily have

$$\text{blue(wolf3)} \supset \text{fall-down (house1)}$$

if it were somehow the case that when wolves are blue houses fall
down. Material implication is directional (blow implies fall-down and
not vice versa), but there is the connective **equivalence** ($\equiv$):

$$\text{fall-down (house1)} \equiv \text{collapsed (house1)}$$

With equivalence each proposition implies the other. In addition to specifying the relations between propositions, material implication and equivalence can also state the relation between terms.

The world of "The Three Little Pigs" is not quite so simple as our propositions thus far. Whether houses fall down depends crucially on what they are made of: *if it is the case both that the wolf blows and that the house is made of straw then the house will fall down*:

blow (wolf1) & made-of (house1 straw)

⊃ fall-down(house1)

Conjunction (symbolized by &) connects propositions in such a way that the resulting compound proposition is true if and only if both of the conjoined propositions are true. A second pig builds his house of sticks, only to discover that *if the wolf blows and either the house is made of straw or the house is made of sticks, then the house will fall down*:

low(wolf1)
& ((made-of (house1 straw)) ∧ (made-of (house2 sticks)))

⊃ (fall-down (house))

Disjunction (symbolized ∧) connects propositions, one of which must be true for the compound proposition to be true. In Figure 2, the partitions (again meaning "there is") separate disjunctive constituents. Finally, there is **negation**, which a third pig illustrates by building his house of brick: *it is not the case that if the wolf blows and the house is made of brick it will fall down*:

(blow (wolf1)
& ¬ (made-of (house3 brick))

⊃ fall-down (house3)

The negative symbol ¬ means *it is not the case that*; either an entire compound proposition (as here) or any constituent propositions can be negated.

Representing some meanings in natural language requires **quantified variables**. Quantification may be either **universal** or **existential**. Sentences that state generalizations, such as *Every pig builds a house* would be represented propositionally using the variable X and the universal quantifier:

∀ X,   (build (pigs X, houses))

∀ can be paraphrased "for all," thus "for all Xs if X is a pig then X builds a house." Other sentences do not generalize. *A pig built a house* would be represented

∃ X, Y (built (pig X, house Y))

∃ is the existential quantifier, and can be paraphrased "for some".
Using it, we can correct a small problem in the representation for *every
pig builds a house*. Unless the sentence means that every pig builds
every house, we need to restrict the quantification of *house*, representing it ∃ Y. Thus, with either form of quantification, the variables X
and Y help to represent the **scope** of the quantifiers, designating
exactly what is universally or existentially quantified. The "first-order"
predicate calculus allows quantification only of arguments, and
quantification of predicates and of certain other constructs that are
expressible in language requires a higher-order calculus. Nevertheless,
first order predicate calculus has sufficient expressive power for most
linguistic purposes.

In translating sentences into logical form, quantification needs to be
interpreted, and ordinary sentences are not always as clear as the
examples would suggest. For universal quantification, we often omit
all or *every* and simply use the plural: *wolves are predators*. But we
can also use the plural in other ways: *The wolves are hungry*
designates some group of *wolves* that are experiencing hunger, and
because it does not exclude the possibility that some other *wolf* or
wolves is or are well-fed, it should be translated into an existentially
qualified proposition. A very few plural sentences, such as *wolves are
nearly extinct*, are neither universally nor existentially quantified (try
translating it), but in general, the existential quantifier is assumed
when translating sentences into propositional representation, unless a
sentence explicitly asserts universal quantification with words such as
all, *every*, *no*, and *none*.

In network representation, existentially quantified propositions are
represented simply by partitioning. To distinguish existentially from
universally quantified propositions without inventing a different kind
of partition, we can use the fact that the negation of an existentially
qualified proposition yields the universal qualifier. That is,

> If it is not true that there must exist a wolf that is good,
> then it must be that all wolves are not good.

This strategy permits the nesting of propositions of any degree of
complexity, including sentences with preposterously embedded
universal quantifiers (for example, *every village has a house that has
been blown down by every wolf in the village*). Sketching the network
for every proposition would be cumbersome, so we will use an
abbreviated form that represents arguments as dependencies of
predicates. The network for *the wolf destroyed the house* can be
abbreviated:

> [destroy: #3]   ←(arg1)– [wolf1]
>   ←(arg2)– [house1]

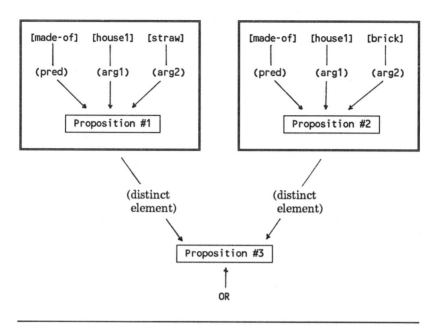

Figure 2. A semantic network partitioned for the disjunctive
propositions in *the house is made of brick or straw.*

Large brackets linked by the relation ←(or)— represent the partitioning
of disjunctive propositions in Figure 2:

$$
\begin{bmatrix}
\text{[made-of]} \leftarrow\text{(arg1)}-\text{[house1]} \\
\leftarrow\text{(arg2)}-\text{[brick]}
\end{bmatrix}
\overset{-\text{(or)}\rightarrow}{\underset{\leftarrow\text{(or)}-}{}}
\begin{bmatrix}
\text{[made-of]} \leftarrow\text{(arg1)}-\text{[house1]} \\
\leftarrow\text{(arg2)}-\text{[straw]}
\end{bmatrix}
$$

The full and abbreviated versions are only forms, and we have some
way to go before we can specify content that approximates the mental
representation of meanings. Specifically, we need a principled way of
deciding what lexical concepts are to be represented at the nodes and
represented by the labeled links connecting nodes. Predicators should
guide semantic analysis by anticipating the concepts or categories of
concepts that fill argument roles and words, phrases, or sentences with
the same meaning should have identical representations. Predicators
and arguments should belong to a system of concepts that captures
salient generalizations in the semantic structures of the language.
Better yet would be a small supply of primitive concepts that are also
linguistic universals, evident in the semantics of all natural languages.

Though it does not appear that language understanding requires much reasoning, logical form supports logical reasoning, which can in turn generate new information. An informal description of two kinds of reasoning, both of which computers can automate, will suggest some of the possibilities; section 3 will describe two other kinds, abductive and nonmonotonic reasoning.

Material implication supports reasoning by **deduction**: if we can establish that wolf1 indeed blows on house1 or house2, we can deduce that a house falls down. Deductive reasoning is at the heart of predicate calculus and is its chief reason for being, but other kinds of reasoning are possible as well. Before encountering the brick house, the wolf does some reasoning by **induction** from specific propositions to a general conclusion: *if the wolf blows on any house then the house will fall down.*

From: blow (wolf1 house1) ⊃ fall-down (house1)
       & blow (wolf1 house2) ⊃ fall-down (house2)

       house (house1)
       house (house2)

Induction: ∀ (house) blow (wolf) ⊃ fall-down (house)

Since the wolf had not yet encountered an example to the contrary, his conclusion was reasonable, and we would call it learning. As it happens, the wolf is wrong. When a contrary example does emerge (the brick house), it is still possible to deduce a conclusion, though the conclusion is somewhat weaker: *for some houses, if the wolf blows then the house will fall down.*

∃ (house)   blow (wolf1) ⊃ fall-down (house1)

When a large set of propositions is stored in a database, it is possible to ask if a given proposition can or cannot be inferred from the stored propositions. With deductive and inductive reasoning both available, information can be represented either as a set of interlinked propositions, with all the reasoning done inductively when the information is entered, or as a set of discrete propositions, with inferences deduced upon demand. (These strategies are known respectively as **forward chaining** and **backward chaining**). Computer databases employ disciplined versions of both strategies, though it is often more efficient to wait until there is a query and employ backward chaining to construct an answer. You do not know what you need to know until you are asked. For the same reason, plan analysis, a computational method for understanding multisentence discourse, employs backward chaining to infer a path from a goal state to initial state via a series of intermediate, propositionally represented actions. No one knows how the mind organizes and accesses information, but some of our thinking may consist of forward and backward chaining.

Section two: Lexical Concepts and Semantic Features

2.1 Hyponymy and meaning postulates

If the sense of a word exists in its relationships to other words, how might those relationships be captured in a meaning representation? One possibility would be simply to list them as attributes of the word. A lexical entry for *teenager* would assert that it is synonymous with *adolescent* and *juvenile*, that it is contrary to *adult* and to *grandparent*, that *human teenager* and *youthful teenager* are redundant, and that *floral teenager* and *hydraulic teenager* are anomalous. The lexicon would also list combinations into which *teenager* can enter: *the teenager spoke, the teenager will grow up*, and the like. All could be represented in a list of propositions:

> same (teenager, juvenile)
> not (adolescent, adult)
> speak (teenager)

Collectively, these facts may be represented in a semantic network of words with relationships as labeled links. Much as the identity of any point in space is given by its coordinates relative to other points in space, so the meaning of a word consists in its position relative to other words in the network, with each link making the word's meaning more fully explicit. (See Figure 3.)

Assuming it were possible, specifying all relationships among all words would impose an exorbitant burden on computer memory and entail implausibly long searches. What we need is a method of generalizing: something resembling the categories and subcategories of syntax. Offering just that is hyponymy, a hierarchical relationship among words. Though there are several other hierarchical relations among words, including part/whole and locative inclusion (for example, *neighborhood* is part of *town* which is part of *state* and so on), hyponymy has one special property. Two words are related by **hyponymy** if the meaning of one is included in the meaning of the other. Thus *woman* is a hyponym of the superordinating word *person*, but adds the meaning *female*. *Scarlet* is a hyponym of *red* and *murder* is a hyponym of *kill*. Though the term hyponym may be unfamiliar (it was coined on the analogy with synonym), knowledge of hyponymous relationships is part of our store of linguistic information, and sentences often presume that knowledge. It allows us, for example, to guess that the hyponym *murder* and its superordinate *kill* in *after murdering him, she was imprisoned for having killed an innocent man*, refer to the same act. The usefulness of hyponymy has long been recognized. Ordinary dictionary definitions often give a superordinating

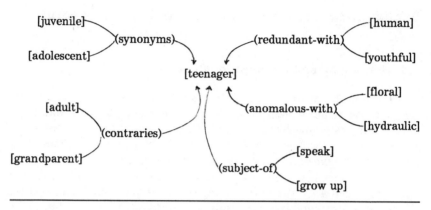

Figure 3. *Teenager* fragment of a semantic network of words.

word as the genus to which a word belongs; *person* is the genus of *teenager*, differentiated by adding "between the ages of thirteen and nineteen." And it is often possible to define a large number of words with a small vocabulary; the *Longman Dictionary of Contemporary English* employs only about two-thousand words in the definitions of its fifty-five-thousand entries.

As with all lexical relationships, it is ultimately the consent of language users that determines whether one word is a hyponym of another, but granted that consent, hyponymous relationships are founded in logic. A sentence asserting hyponymy is necessarily true (*a rose is a flower* or *scarlet is red*), and sentences that substitute superordinating terms for hyponyms are entailed; that is, the truth of one guarantees the truth of the second (if *that rose is scarlet* is true then *that flower is red* is necessarily also true). It should be stressed that hyponymous relationships are linguistic not empirical: they constitute part of our knowledge of words, and we do not need to check the world in order to verify them.

Hyponyms behave like their superordinates, inheriting the substitutional and combinational relationships in which the superordinates participate. Thus *teenager* is a hyponym of *person*: *human person* is redundant, *person* can be the subject of *spoke*, and so on. This means that we can generalize about large numbers of words, among them:

> ally, assistant, aunt, authority, carpenter, caucasian, crony, chauvinist, citizen, critic, driver, elder, fellow, flutist, genius, gentleman, grandparent, husband, infant, jerk, juvenile, liar, librarian, lover, opponent, madcap, matriarch, partner, pedant, pedestrian, person, preacher, professional, psychiatrist, quarterback, raconteur, reader, saint, scholar, smoker, spouse, statistician, sultan, sycophant, Syrian, tattletale, thug, tinhorn, trader, tramp, vampire, volunteer, warden, xenophobe, zealot

These words are diverse, characterizing by nationality, race, social role or vocation, by avocation, age, sex, kinship, behavior, and esteem; but all of them (and several hundred more) are hyponyms of *person* and therefore share important elements of meaning. In ordinary usage all are redundant with *human*, contradictories of *machine*, and potential subjects for *spoke*. Thus by associating a set of substitutional and combinational relationships with *person*, then allowing its multitude of hyponyms to inherit those relationships and other attributes, we generalize the meanings of the hyponyms. This does not mean that hyponymy and inheritance will exhaustively define the words, but they do capture important elements of meaning and assure parsimonious representation in the lexicon.

Unfortunately, matters are not quite so straightforward, because the residue of information that differentiates a hyponym from its superordinate may restrict the hyponym from certain relationships. *Person* can serve as the subject of the verb *speak* (or one of its hyponyms), and most of the hyponyms on our list enter into the same combinational relationship. But the list contains *infant* and infants do not speak (indeed the word derives from the Latin *infans*, meaning is "unable to speak"). This is a linguistic fact about *infant* and can be specified in the lexicon. It should not, however, be confused with extralinguistic facts. Suppose, for example, that in a moment of taxonomical enthusiasm we supply *persons* and *birds* as hyponyms of *biped*. Persons (or birds) that lose legs through accident or injury are no less bipeds, and their lexical entries would inherit that information, though the entry for the individual, *Long John Silver*, might include the information that one of his definitionally inherited legs is missing.

The relationship between a word and its hyponym (as well as other relationships between words) can be stated as an inference rule, known as a **meaning postulate**:

$$\forall X \quad teenager\ X \supset person\ X$$

Borrowed from formal semantics (a field in philosophy), meaning postulates are true by virtue of the meanings of words they link. Observation cannot prove them false, and if some *teenager*-like creature is found not to be a *person*, then that creature would not be a *teenager*. As with propositions that assert hyponymy, meaning postulates are entailed and support inferences. If a higher level of generality offers the meaning postulate

$$\forall X \quad person\ X \supset being\ X$$

(where *being* includes humans and other animals), we can infer

$$\forall X \quad teenager\ X \supset being\ X$$

And by implication *teenager* inherits any and all relationships associated with *being*. Meaning postulates can also represent the conjunction of two or more words in one:

$$\forall \ X \quad \textit{bachelor} \ X \ \supset \ \textit{person} \ X$$
$$\& \ \textit{male} \ X$$
$$\& \ \textit{adult} \ X$$
$$\& \ \neg \ \textit{married} \ X$$

The variables indicate unspecified individuals, in this case of the generic *person* or the generic *teenager*, and their repetition within a meaning postulate stipulates that the two words identify the same individual. (For words that make reference, the variable stands for the referent.) With logical negation, meaning postulates state incompatibilities, whether between contraries or between contradictories:

$$\forall \ X \quad \textit{teenager} \ X \ \supset \ \neg \ \textit{adult} \ X$$

$$\forall \ X \quad \textit{artifact} \ X \ \supset \ \neg \ \textit{nature} \ X$$
$$\& \ \textit{nature} \ X \ \supset \ \neg \ \textit{artifact} \ X$$

Transitive verbs and other relational expressions such as comparatives or spatial prepositions require multiple variables.

$$\forall \ X, Y \qquad X \ \textit{strikes} \ Y \ \supset \ X \ \textit{touches} \ Y$$

$$\forall \ X, Y, Z \quad X \ \textit{donates} \ Y \ Z \ \supset \ X \ \textit{gives} \ Y \ Z$$

$$\forall \ X, Y \qquad X \ \textit{larger than} \ Y \ \supset \ Y \ \textit{smaller than} \ X$$

$$\forall \ X, Y \qquad X \ \textit{above} \ Y \ \supset \ Y \ \textit{below} \ X$$

The relation is directional: X *loves* Y does not (alas) imply Y *loves* X.

Meaning postulates can be represented propositionally using special is-a predicates:

is a *(flower, rose)*

is a (*(strikes,* (X,Y)) *(touches* (X,Y)))

In a semantic network, ←(is-a)–links differ from links of other kinds in that they alone support inheritance; they allow any properties associated with the parent node to be associated also with the child node. When two or more ←(is-a)–links descend from the same superordinate, nothing more is implied than that they share the superordinate and its properties. They may be incompatible. Incompatibility, where it exists, is specified by ←(is-not-a)–links, which (among other uses) distinguish between potentially overlapping hyponyms (such as *flutist* and *grandmother*) and those that are disjoint (such as *grandmother* and *child*). Thus in the semantic network in Figure 4, all ←(is-a)– links descending from a given parent node are assumed to be overlapping and ←(is-not-a)–links establish which are disjoint.

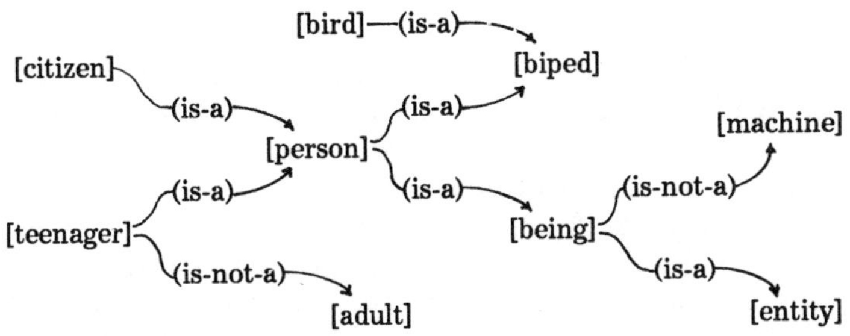

Figure 4. A semantic network of words incorporating hyponymy.

Whether meaning postulates afford a psychologically realistic theory of lexical meanings is open to question. Superordinates do not occur very often in slips of the tongue where we say one word but intend another. Often we slip with coordinates (*left* for *right*), opposites (*up* for *down*) and other close cousins, but seldom do we substitute superordinates. Moreover, many superordinating words do not occur so frequently as we might suppose if they were directly implicated in our understanding of words; *knives* and *forks*, *brothers* and *sisters* are common words, *cutlery* and *siblings* are not.

2.2 Toward a meta-language of lexical concepts

Because they relate words to words, meaning postulates depend entirely on the vocabularies of particular languages: a major disadvantage in capturing linguistic generalizations. Even English with its huge vocabulary does not lexicalize some very useful concepts. For instance, although the linguistic behavior of fluids and gases is similar, English has no word for "substances that flow"; similarly, though English has the superordinate *entity* (whose hyponyms are *being* and *thing*), English has no contrasting noun for what is non-entitative, including feelings, situations, and much more. Though the lack of superordinates pervades the lexicon, it is particularly felt at the upper reaches of the lexical hierarchy, because it is there that the broadest generalizations can be made.

That some other languages have the superordinates that English needs (but lack others) suggests a second problem. Depending entirely on lexicalized superordinates, on words not concepts, meaning postulates are necessarily language specific. Even languages closely related by culture and history (English and French are examples), do not have parallel vocabularies. Therefore no set of word-based meaning postulates can fully characterize a system of language (or cognitive) universals that underlies all human languages and is unique to them. What is needed instead is a meta-language, built of elements which, though founded on the conceptual relations that are evident in vocabularies, are themselves language neutral.

Recognizing these problems, some theorists have proposed a universal meta-language consisting of language-neutral concepts linked by meaning postulates. Concepts correspond virtually one-to-one with words, and the existence of a word in some natural language would justify adding the corresponding lexical concept to the meta-language. Each needs only a sub-set to compose the mental language ("mentalese" as it is often called) of its speakers and define its vocabulary. The meanings of concepts derive from the system of meaning postulates that connect them with other concepts. Thus the meta-language would have the lexical concept MAN, one sense of which is defined by the superordinating concepts PERSON and MALE. (Uppercase spellings will distinguish concepts from words.) In German the concept MAN is lexicalized as *mann*, in French as *homme*, and so on. Similarly, the lexical concept LIFT has the defining superordinates CAUSE and RISE and is realized by the words *erheben* and *lever*. Under this theory, comprehension consists first of translating utterances into mentalese, guided by the grammar of the language. *The man lifted the child* might be translated into the representation,

(s (np MAN) (vp (v CAUSED) (np (s (np CHILD) (vp RISE)))))

The representation is nearly isomorphic with the utterance because of the close correspondence between words and concepts. Though not as detailed and as fully explicit as the meaning representations that we will consider in the next two sections, it suffices to feed a second state of comprehension in which meaning postulates are used to derive such inferences as the CHILD is now UP.

A network of concepts defined only by meaning postulates cannot characterize all we know about the meanings of many words. Proponents of meaning postulates restrict the province of semantics to lexical relations and propose that finer-grained knowledge belongs somewhere else. Though this approach has not gotten beyond the proposal stage or stimulated much empirical research, it does offer something for computational systems because concepts can serve as labels for word meanings. Thus MAN would label *man* and its synonyms and serve, like an entry in an index, to link that set of words to the complex of information about adult human males. Labeling simplifies the extensive pattern-matching required to fit the words of a sentence into a coherent whole. The more ingredients to a meaning representation, the more cumbersome the processing and the more time that processing consumes. Early computational systems characterized the meanings in considerable detail and were notoriously slow. More recent systems have been equipped with facilities to expand labels (sometimes called "types") into full definitions and to contract definitions into labels. These facilities expedite processing without limiting the knowledge potentially available for comprehension.

2.3 Decomposition and semantic features

By giving the hyponym *person* as part of the meaning of *teenager*, we are beginning to decompose the sense of that word into smaller elements of meaning. *Teenager* has at least one additional element of meaning, which it shares with numerous other words. Consider the following group:

> adolescent, aurelia, baby, boy, brat, calf, chick, child, colt, chrysalis, cub, duckling, filly, fingerling, fledgling, foal, fry, girl, heifer, infant, junior, juvenile, kid, kitten, lass, minor, minx, mite, newborn, nestling, offspring, papoose, pullet, pup, pupa, sapling, schoolgirl, seedling, slip, smallfry, sprout, suckling, stripling, tadpole, toddler, tomboy, tot, tyke, urchin, weanling, whippersnapper, whelp, yearling, youngster, youth

All these words, whether signifying plants, insects, animals, and humans, also signify beings that are not fully grown or mature. All are redundant with *youthful*, incompatible with *elderly*, and acceptable subjects for *grew up*. However, English has no noun that is their superordinating word (some languages do). Representing the element of meaning that they share requires a lexical concept, something like -ADULT, an organic being that has not reached adulthood. Groups of verbs also share elements of meaning. Underlying a great many verbs is the transitive IMPAIR:

> afflict, batter, befoul, break, blight, burst, bust, chip, cleave, collapse, contaminate, corrode, corrupt, cripple, crumble, crunch, crush, dash, damage, debase, debauch, decay, deface, defile, deform, degrade, demolish, destroy, disable, disintegrate, erode, foul, fracture, fragment, fray, hamstring, harm, hurt, infect, injure, lame, mangle, mar, mutilate, pervert, poison, pollute, pulverize, rot, ruin, rupture, sabotage, sap, sever, shatter, shrivel, smash, splinter, split, spoil, sunder, taint, tatter, vitiate, wear, wilt, wither, wound, worsen, wreck

The lexical concept IMPAIR would capture the underlying similarity of these verbs, and additional concepts would discriminate impairments that are intentional or accidental, permanent or temporary, complete or partial, internal or external, and so on. -ADULT and IMPAIR are **semantic features,** smaller concepts into which words can be decomposed, and the meaning of a word or idiom consists of one or more features. For any method of semantic analysis that employs them, features are basic and indivisible particles of meaning, much as phonological features are indivisible particles from which allophones are formed. Much as allophones can be decomposed into phonological features, so meanings decompose into semantic features, though, of course, the sounds are physical events, whereas semantic features are mental phenomena. Semantic features permit analysis of a finer grain than do lexical concepts, each of which must correspond to a word in some language. In theory at least, it should be possible to specify for each word in a language a finite of semantic features that are necessary and collectively sufficient to distinguish the word from all others in the language. If the set is finite, then semantic features would not lead (as meaning postulates do) to the defining of words in terms of an endless web of other words.

Such is their promise that it is not surprising that semantic features have a long history. Aristotle posited a set of ten "categories" or primitive modes of being: a man is a substance, red is a quality, to kill is an action, and so on. In the thirteenth century Raimon Lully, a teacher of Arabic, proposed a mechanical contraption consisting of a set of concentric disks with features inscribed on them; rotating the disks would juxtapose inscriptions to compose thoughts. Four centuries later, the idea was to replace Latin as the universal language with a scientifically systematic artificial language built from primitive words, morphemes or sometimes ideographs. To reduce logical relationships to mathematical formulas, Leibnitz suggested that each primitive had as its symbol a prime number and that complex notions be represented by multiplying the primes. After the French Revolution, philosophers sought to analyze words into perceptual primitives so as to discover which ideas are sensible and therefore constitute a worthy foundation for a rebuilt society. Modern linguists have hypothesized systems of "semantic primitives," "markers," "components," or "nodes," "pre-lexicalized predicates" "semes" and "classemes."

Large sets of features have been adduced, and these have been applied to the analysis of substantial subsets of the vocabularies of English and other languages. No definitive set of primitives has emerged, however. Exhaustively decomposing words has proved difficult and, except in computational linguistics, interest in lexical decomposition has waned over the past several years. For such tasks as translation, paraphrase, and question-answering, many computational projects employ features, particularly the more general (and widely agreed-upon) features like -ADULT.

The essential idea is that word meanings consist of clusters of primitive components, some reflecting generalized lexical relationships

person	HUMAN: X
baby	ANIMATE: X ADULT: X
girl	HUMAN: X ADULT: X FEMALE: X
cub	-HUMAN: X -ADULT X
father	HUMAN: X MALE: X X PARENT OF Y
move1	X TRANSFER X
move2	X TRANSFER Y
bring	X CAUSE (Y TRANSFER)
take	X INTEND (X CAUSE (Y TRANSFER))
lose	X -INTEND (Y TRANSFER)

Figure 5. A lexicon built from clustered features.

and others capturing what is idiosyncratic about a word. By substituting the lexical concept HUMAN for the word *person*, supplying some opposites ADULT and -HUMAN (and while we are at it noting that some, though not all the words on the -ADULT and the *person* lists differentiate genders), we can begin to build a lexicon (see Figure 5). Note that move1 and move2 distinguish intransitive and transitive senses of *move*: transferring oneself and transferring someone or something else. Note also the verb features of intentionality and causation and the pattern of subordination in the entry for *steal*: CAUSE modifies TRANSFER, and INTEND modifies (CAUSE TRANSFER).

To add features for nominals (whether words or idioms) to our repertoire, we can pursue a line of superordinating concepts upward from HUMAN to ANIMAL (and for vegetative forms -ANIMAL), then upward to ANIMATE (and for inorganic entities -ANIMATE), then PHYSICAL-OBJECT and ABSTRACTION. Physical objects divide along other dimensions. At the level of ANIMATE and INANIMATE objects, we might also distinguish nominals with the feature COUNT and those with MASS (count nouns, such as *box* and *toe* cannot appear in the singular without a determiner). And among -ANIMATE entities we can have -ARTIFACT and ARTIFACT to distinguish those that are naturally occurring from those that are man-made.

As for verbs, one fundamental distinction is between those with the features ACTION and STATE: *buy* expresses an ACTION and *own* expresses a STATE. Each selects for certain contexts: stative verbs do not, for instance, typically occur in the imperative or progressive. *Own a house!* is slightly anomalous and *he is owning a house* is unlikely. Distinguishing other closely related verbs requires temporal features (for the difference between *see* and *glimpse*), spatial features (*see* and *sight*), and features of manner (*perceive* and *see*). Still other features distinguish verb meanings from meanings of other lexical categories:

an inchoative feature signifies the coming into existence of a state (to distinguish *hard* and *harden*), and a resultative feature does the reverse (*flatten* and *flat*).

Within computational linguistics, the best known set of verb features was proposed by Roger Schank and his colleagues as part of conceptual dependency theory. For their approach to language understanding, twelve conceptual "ACTs" suffice to describe many physical and mental events. Stative verbs are handled differently. Figure 6 lists the ACTs and paraphrases their meanings. As the neologisms imply, ACTs are conceptual rather than linguistic or empirical. They derive from analysis of the way we think about actions rather than how we express them in language or how they actually occur. Thus *we explained it to her and she listened* would be translated into a representation that says (roughly) we MTRANSed information to her from us by SPEAKing the information and she MTRANSed the information from us to her by ATTENDing her ears to us.

As with other representations of lexical meaning, there are problems with the ACTs. They are not irreducible primitives (PTRANS, INGEST, PROPEL have in common the idea of movement). It is not always easy to decide why these ACTs and not some others (ENCODE in place of SPEAK would encompass all encoding into language), and over the years different sets of ACTs were proposed. Also, they do not exhaustively represent the meanings of verbs and the often subtle differences between them (*chase* and *pursue* might be composed of the ACTs PTRANS and MOVE). But the object of *pursue* is more often pleasurable than the object of *chase*). These are, of course, problems for most decompositional theories, but the ACTs are shrewdly chosen and do achieve a useful level of abstraction. The combinations into which they enter, such as MTRANS with the instrumental ATTEND or SPEAK, aptly characterize the conceptual events described by a many sentences.

Semantic features describe meanings of words, but it is appropriate to ask whether any independent empirical evidence exists for their role in human sentence comprehension, and hence for computational projects that seek to model processes of comprehension. Devising controlled situations sensitive enough to detect decomposition and distinguish it from the application of meaning postulates or some other method of inference is very difficult, but several attempts have been made. If decomposition takes place, a "complexity effect" might be measurable: words with a complex of features (such as *murder* with, let's say, INTEND CAUSE BECOME -ALIVE) would take longer to comprehend than *die* (BECOME -ALIVE). But they do not. Since negatives often produce odd effects, researchers tried other decompositions, such as TRY (CATCH) for *chase*; but again there was no detectable complexity effect. Worse, there is no detectable difference between sentences like *Sue saw the window* and *Sue broke the window*, though more time should be required if the lexically complex verb, *broke*, decomposes

[MOVE]	To move a body part (for example, a hand or a foot) from one physical location to another.
[GRASP]	To seize and hold an object that must be of an appropriate size for humans and other creatures to grasp.
[PROPEL]	To apply physical force to an object with the object of moving it; is an instrument by which [PTRANS] is accomplished. Contained in such verbs as *throw* and *push*,
[INGEST] & [EXPEL]	To take something inside an orifice and to force something out an orifice.
[PTRANS]	To change the physical location of some object (which may include the actor) as in *shoving* or *throwing*.
[ATRANS]	To transfer (abstractly) the legal possession or control of something from one human to another.
[MTRANS]	To transfer information from one location to another. Locations include sense organs and long and short term memory, so as to represent *perceiving* and *remembering* as well as *telling* or *explaining*.
[MBUILD]	To combine or transform mental entities or to attempt that. Contained in such verbs as *conclude* and *consider*.
[SPEAK]	To utter with intonation a meaningful sequence of the phonemes of some language. Contained in verbs such as *talk*, *write*, *tell* and is the instrument of MTRANS.
[ATTEND]	To focus one or more sense organs so as perceive; underlies such verbs as *see*, *hear*, *smell*, *feel*, *taste*.
[DO]	To express the unspecified means by which some act is accomplished as, for example, in *he prevented her from going*.

Figure 6. The ACTs of conceptual dependency theory.

into two propositions, (*Sue* CAUSED (*the window* BROKE)). Though it may be that the assumed decompositions are wrong or that our processing of them is too fast to be measurable by current techniques, these experiments argue against decompositional theories of meaning.

Set-inclusion research, in contrast, supports the theory of decomposition. Subjects are asked to mark all instances of, for example, natural consumable liquids (-ARTIFACT CONSUMABLE AGGREGATE) in a list of words, then unexpectedly asked to recall the entire list. (AGGREGATE includes fluids and other substances such as salt and crushed rock that is capable of being poured.) If decomposition occurs, then recall for words sharing two of the features, say *coal* -ARTIFACT SOLID or *meat* -ARTIFACT CONSUMABLE, should be better than for those sharing none. It is, and in general recall seems to depend directly on the number of features shared with the target category. Set-inclusion demands analysis, however, and may not be relevant to lexical comprehension. Priming experiments come closer. Subjects are presented statements in which one feature of a word, for example the CONSUMABLE of *plum*, is primed (*he bit a plum*) or not primed (*he bought a plum*). Subject are then asked questions that stress primed and non-primed features (*are plums edible? are plums round?*) The response is quickest when both the statement and the question include the same primed feature, indicating that decomposition may play a role. Thus the empirical evidence for decomposition is at best mixed, and its role in human cognition has neither been demonstrated or firmly discredited.

2.4 Internal structures of words

Lexical entries may be more than simply clusters of features with no internal organization. Consider that the relationship between [-ADULT] and [HUMAN] in the entry for *child* resembles the dependency relationship between a modifier and a noun. One way of identifying the direction of dependency is to add an intensifier and ask what it modifies: *only young people were there* means *the only people there were young*, not *the only youthful ones there were people*. Thus we might represent the meanings of *child* and *boy* as a small network or **schema**, consisting of features connected by labeled links:

    child   [HUMAN:X] ←(attribute)— [-ADULT:X]

    girl   [HUMAN:X] ←(attribute)— [-MALE:X]
                          ←(attribute)— [-ADULT:X]

Concepts such as HUMAN and MALE are in brackets to show that they are nodes in the network. The ←(attribute)– is a **primitive relation** and unlike ←(is-a)– does not support inheritance.

Words such as *daughter* and *pet* have relational features, call them "progeny" and "companion" (possession?). They can be represented either propositionally or in schemata:

           ∀ X, Y (progeny-of (HUMAN X, HUMAN Y))
    son
           [HUMAN:X] ←(attribute)— [MALE:X]
                      ←(progeny)— [HUMAN:X]

           ∀ X, Y (companion-of (HUMAN X, -HUMAN Y))
    pet
           [HUMAN:X] ←(companion)— [-HUMAN:X]

Notice that the concepts linked by primitive relations are restricted. For *daughter*, the progeny relationship is between HUMANs and for *pet* between HUMAN and -HUMAN. The two primitive relations ←(progeny)– and ←(adversary)– are unilateral, oriented by the direction of the arrow. Other relations are symmetrical. These include ←(spouse)– a definitional feature for such words as *bride*, *groom*, *husband*, and *wife*, and ←(adversary)– for *foe*, *antagonist*, *opponent*, *competitor*, *nemesis* and host of other words. Symmetrical relations require double links, as in the schemata for *husband* and *foe*:

husband   [HUMAN:X]   ←(attribute)— [MALE:X]
                         ←(spouse)— [FEMALE:X]

foe   [ANIMATE:X]   ←(adversary)—
                          —(adversary)→   [ANIMATE:Y]

Another important relations specifies instances. Though ←(is-a)– is sometimes used indiscriminately for both subordinates and instances, those are not the same and we need an ←(instance)– relation. Thus my dog *Oliver* is an instance of the lexical concept DOG, and that concept has as part of its representation an ←(is-a)–relation, linking it to the superordinating lexical concept -HUMAN.

Verbs also require relations for their representation; the propositional representation and schema for one sense of *tell* might include the relations:

∃ X, Y, Z   (transfer (HUMAN:X, MESSAGE:Y, ANIMAL:Z))

[PERSON:X] —(subject)→ [TRANSFER]   ←(direct object)— [MESSAGE:Y]
                                     ←(indirect object)— [ANIMAL:Z]

The action of telling transfers a message from a human to some animal which may be human or nonhuman and if nonhuman may be an organization or a group. The discussion of sentence semantics will offer semantic relations that are more explicit than these grammatical functions.

Schemata specify general attributes and only enough of them to indicate the substitutional and combinational relationships into which the words can enter. They abstract away from the details of specific instances, so that we need not deal with the infinite number of attributes or instances of the concept. They thus avoid the problem of excessive particularity, which was Kant's criticism of image theories of meaning. Think what it would be like if every time *grape*, say, came up in conversation, it brought to mind all the information we share about even so simple a thing as a raspberry. The schema for *grape* might specify its being a fruit, edible, and an ingredient of wine; its being round, smooth-skinned, fleshy, seeded or seedless, and purple, red, or green; its manner of growing in clusters on vines, and much more.

2.5 Inheritance hierarchies and redundancy rules

We might continue for some time, happily supplying features and
compiling lexical entries, but eventually we will feel the need of some
systematic way of relating features to one another. We have not yet
specified that the set of all nominals with the feature HUMAN excludes
all those with the feature -HUMAN, and while it may be true that
snowball or *dream* (for example) are not human, we do not accomplish
much by giving them and several thousand words like them the feature
-HUMAN. A system that differentiates words that are to some degree
similar would make more sense. Features like MALE and FEMALE do
not apply to *snowball* or *dream*, or indeed to most words, thus we need
some way of establishing which features can co-occur in a word and
which cannot.

One answer is to provide an **inheritance hierarchy**, so named
because it is built of is-a links which support inheritance. As we saw
in Chapter 4 an inheritance hierarchy can be implemented computationally as a tree structure built of nodes and pointers. At any level in
the hierarchy, disjoint groups of nodes, such as HUMAN and -HUMAN,
may intersect with other disjoint groups (MALE FEMALE). Although
binary distinctions predominate at the higher levels of the inheritance
hierarchy, the lexical structure of natural languages appears to be such
that the lower one goes in the hierarchy the more bushy it becomes.
Descending through the hierarchy, we might encounter HAS-LOCATION
versus ABSTRACT, PHYSICAL-OBJECT versus SITUATION, ANIMATE versus
-ANIMATE and ARTIFACT versus -ARTIFACT, all of which are binary
divisions; but below ARTIFACT come multiple nodes, including TOOL
DOCUMENT, SHELTER (including clothing) and VEHICLE.

A different answer is to provide a set of inference rules, resembling
meaning postulates, to state these relationships:

$$\forall \; x \;\; \text{HUMAN} \; x \; \supset \; \text{ANIMATE} \; x$$

$$\forall \; x \;\; \text{HUMAN} \; x \; \supset \; \neg \; (\text{-HUMAN} \; x)$$

Such rules, because they capture generalizations and thus eliminate
duplications from the lexicon, are often called **redundancy rules**. If
we add rules that link words with features, the lexicon can be
represented as a semantic network. Thus we might have

$$\forall \; x \;\; \textit{person} \; x \; \supset \; \text{HUMAN} \; x$$

$$\forall \; x \;\; \textit{woman} \; x \; \supset \; \text{HUMAN} \; x \; \& \; \text{FEMALE} \; x$$

One advantage of providing rules of this sort is that they can represent
words that are not readily decomposed such as the conjunction *and*:

$$\forall \; x \, y \;\; x \; \textit{and} \; y \; \supset \; x \; \& \; y$$

The question remains open whether the human lexicon occupies a vast semantic network, which links every word to every other word, or consists of separate lexical entries perhaps structured as small, self-contained networks. Investigating the lexicon's structure is very difficult and it is as yet unclear what would constitute conclusive evidence. What follows in this section and the next assumes separate entries (mainly for the sake of clarity), but would not be precluded if the lexicon is an undifferentiated whole.

Decomposing the entire vocabulary of a language (assuming that were possible) would require a great many features, possibly including a unique feature for each member of every class. It might even require more features than there are words, though that is not a theoretical obstacle because the number of features would still be finite. There are, however, problems in decomposing words into features each of which is necessary and which collectively are sufficient to distinguish that word from every other word. Some words (such as terms for colors and temperatures) express gradations, boundaries between near synonyms are fuzzy, and judgments of language users differ. Some distinctions (as between a *duck* and a *goose*) are difficult to represent using features. Some words are best represented by inclusively disjunctive features. For example, *see* can mean either "gaze at" or "have visual experience of" or both, as the following sentences suggest:

> He saw the flag, but didn't notice it.
> He saw pink elephants.

Moreover, as we will see in section 3.1, many distinctions depend on what is typical as well as what is necessary. Computational projects usually employ just enough features to afford a unique signature for each word, to provide for substitutions (if the task is paraphrase or translation), and to state the combinational relations into which words possessing certain features can and cannot enter. They do not address the question of whether features are sufficient to define words. Note, for instance, that only nominals with ANIMAL can be the objects of CAUSE BECOME -ALIVE or the subjects when the main verb has the feature INTEND.

Nor is it necessary to suppose that decomposition always comes into play for sentence comprehension or that it is always exhaustive. It may be appropriate only in certain circumstances, as, for example, when one needs to verify that a word belongs to a set (for example to establish the antecedent of *he* in *I gave the man's dog a bone and he said thank you*). In other circumstances where only word recognition is required (*what is your name?*), decomposition need not occur. This much is reflected in the practice (mentioned in section 2.3) of expanding labeling concepts into configurations of features and contracting features into concepts with each word is represented both as a semantically unanalyzed lexical concept and as a cluster of features.

2.6 Selectional restrictions

One important motive for incorporating either meaning postulates or features in a semantic theory is that they help state the combinational relationships that pertain among the words in a phrase or sentence. Words do not combine at random, as we have noted; certain combinations are expected while others are anomalous. From phrases such as the following, it is clear that the adjective *articulate* anticipates a noun with the feature HUMAN or COMMUNICATIVE or with the superordinating terms *person* and *communication*:

an articulate person	? an articulate amoeba
an articulate child	? an articulate noise
an articulate speech	? an articulate purchase
an articulate novel	? an articulate trouble

Such expectations, when formulated as rules for combining words or phrases, are known as **selectional restrictions.** Not only adjectives but also most other modifiers select for what they modify. The prepositional phrase *in the corner* expects entities, and the relative clause *that shattered* expects brittle objects. In sentences, verbs select subjects, objects, and other functional NPs; *talk* selects subjects with the feature HUMAN or the superordinating term *person*, whereas *stood* is less particular, requiring only ENTITY or *thing*. Verbs may select several constituents, each for a different semantic role; *sell*, for example, presupposes a human seller, a human buyer, a non human entity to be sold, and money as the medium of exchange. As these examples suggest, selectional restrictions tend to be rather broad. Verbs for perception, rudimentary thinking, self-propulsion, and certain other actions require only that their subjects be ANIMATE *(the animal felt the warmth and crawled toward it)*, and their modifiers do likewise *(the vigilant animal)*. Verbs and modifiers for living, growing, and the like select a still more inclusive class of ORGANIC subjects *(the plant/ animal was alive and grew rapidly)*.

As with other semantic properties, selectional restrictions are inherited. This means that the restriction for a modifier or noun needs specify only the most general of the superordinating words or features, and lexical entries for nouns and other words need specify only the most specific hyponym or feature. The immature, non-human, animate, organic, solid entity called a *puppy* can be modified by *large*, which selects for entities, whether solid or not, organic or not, animate or not, human or not, and mature or not. Thus *large* requires only ENTITY as the selectional restriction, and -HUMAN in the lexical entry for *puppy* implies ENTITY.

When incorporated in systems for syntactic and semantic analysis, selectional restrictions serve several important purposes. They may

IF the preposition is *by*,

AND the voice is active

AND either

    the direct object and the object of the

    preposition are both LOCATIVE

       OR

    the direct object is COMMUNICATIVE and the object

    of the preposition is HUMAN

THEN the prepositional phrase modifies the direct object,

ELSE the prepositional phrase modifies the sentence.

Figure 7. Attachment rules for the preposition *by*.

resolve syntactic ambiguities that regularly baffle parsers. Consider, for example, the notorious problem of deciding what is modified by prepositional phrases occurring at the beginnings or ends of sentences. The only useful syntactic rules stipulate that if an adjective or a comparative immediately precedes the prepositional phrase, the phrase modifies it (*it is acceptable to him, it is the largest of the lot*). Parsing preferences will not guarantee the appropriate attachment. It is left to selectional restrictions to determine if the phrase modifies:

- the entire sentence (*he watched the house for four hours*)

- or the verb phrase (*he bought the dog for four dollars*)

- or the direct object (*he had a solution for the problem*).

Often it is the preposition's object that provides the relevant semantic information: when the object has a temporal feature (or is a hyponym of *time*), the phrase necessarily modifies the entire sentence (*he arrived home at six o'clock*). Sometimes the relevant information is in the verb: with stative verbs, for instance, the prepositional phrase always modifies the verb phrase (*he remained on the sidelines*). Principles like these can readily be stated as attachment rules. Figure 7 gives a set of rules for the preposition *by*. Applying these rules would establish that the prepositional phrase modifies the direct object in *he bought property by the sea* or *he read a novel by Austen*, but modifies the entire sentence in *he found the house by accident*.

For semantic analysis, selectional restrictions are virtually indispensable. As systematic constraints on the relationships into which words can enter, they limit the ways that phrases and sentences can be construed, usually allowing but a single interpretation. For example:

□   They distinguish between ambiguous senses of words. The words, *brazen* and *kid*, for instance, both have two senses, and without selectional restrictions *brazen kid* in *the brazen kid spoke out* might have four possible meanings. But *spoke* selects the sense "young person" (rather than "young goat") for *kid*, and *kid* selects the sense "impudent" for *brazen* (rather than "made of brass").

□   When the role played by a sentence constituent is unclear, selectional restrictions can help: in *he saw the eclipse with his kid*, the *with* phrase might identify either a co-agent or an instrument, or it might associate a location with an entity. Co-agents have the feature HUMAN, whereas the several instruments for enhancing eyesight–microscopes, telescopes, eye glasses and the like–all have OBJECT as a feature.

□   They also help picking out which part of a word's meaning is modified, clarifying, for example, the difference between *blond linguist* and *computational linguist*: a person who is blond and studies linguistics, versus a person who practices a kind of linguistics called computational. (*Organic chemist*, however, would still present difficulties.)

□   They can also help identify continuities within and between sentences by identifying words or phrases that are semantically compatible. Consider the noun phrases in the following sentences:

>   The girl had a kitten. But grandmother doubted that
>   such a young kid could care for an animal.

Using just the features FEMALE HUMAN and -ADULT, we could establish that of the three noun phrases in the second sentence only *kid* or HUMAN -ADULT is semantically equivalent to *girl* which has two of the same features and none that is incompatible with the third. *Grandmother* shares HUMAN and FEMALE, but also has the incompatible ADULT. *Animal* with the incompatible -HUMAN is also ruled out. (Semantic compatibility does exist between *kitten* and *an animal*; they share -HUMAN.)

□   Sometimes, selectional restrictions also help in identifying the antecedents of pronouns, though pronouns have little semantic content: in English only MALE, FEMALE and sometimes -HUMAN. If instead of *animal* in the second sentence, we have *it* (-HUMAN), then *kitten* in the first sentence is a plausible antecedent. If we have *she* instead of *young kid*, the antecedent could be either of the FEMALE nouns, *girl* or *grandmother*.

Selectional restrictions cannot, of course, resolve genuine ambiguities, but they can permit multiple separate analyses. An ambiguous sentence such as *he saw the fellow on the rooftop with a telescope* should have three separate analyses which attach *with a telescope* to *saw*, to *fellow*, and to *rooftop*. Selectional restrictions can be stated within lexical schemata. Thus *flow* and *heavy* might be represented:

[FLOW] ←(subject)— [AGGREGATE]

[ENTITY] ←(weight)— [HEAVY]

Sentence processing would attempt to match these entries with entries for words in the phrase or sentence and would succeed with *the river flows* and *a heavy rock*.

Language is not always so tidy as the examples so far would suggest. The verb *flow*, for example, ordinarily selects for a word or phrase with the feature FLUID or the superordinate *liquid*, but we can also speak of *information flowing freely* or *the flow of knowledge*. *Heavy* is another word that has acquired a meaning resembling, but different from its habitual meaning. Ordinarily an attribute (weight) of physical objects or substances: as in *a heavy object* or *a heavy cloud of gas*, it has come to enter relationships from which it had previously been restricted. Now it modifies activities and abstractions and means durable, intense, sustained, powerful, violent, important or large-scale:

a heavy responsibility	a heavy turnout
heavy taxes	heavy drinking
a heavy heart	heavy industry
heavy seas	heavy activity
a heavy investor	a heavy breakfast
heavy lines	a heavy thinker

Many content words, especially those for abstractions, came into the language by the adaptation of existing words to new situations, and a significant portion of those belong to a few dozen families of metaphor. Information as FLUID is one: we speak of conduits, streams and trickles of information, of plugging leaks and bottling up the outpourings. Others include financial metaphors for time *(spend, borrowed, budgeting)*, military metaphors for argumentation *(defensible, defeat, shot down)*, and fragile objects for adverse mental conditions and events (experiences are *shattering* and minds *break* under pressure). Metaphor is so frequent that it must be accommodated.

The computational interpreter cannot simply reject semantically anomalous input as the babbling of someone less well informed about language than it is, but must instead work on the assumption that the input contains a meaning. Dispensing with selectional restrictions for potentially metaphorical words, or making the restrictions so general as to encompass both metaphorical and literal senses will not help. We need FLUID, for example, to discriminate ambiguous senses of such words as *tear, solution, rapid, wave, punch* (all liquids in one sense). Two quite different approaches to metaphor have emerged. The first approach, pioneered by Yorick Wilks, is to specify selectional restrictions not as absolutes, but as **semantic preferences**. Thus the lexical entry for *flow* prefers a FLUID subject, but allows ABSTRACT subjects; the entry for *heavy* prefers ENTITY, but accepts ACTION. In effect the preferences say what is typical, but tolerate exceptions. By this approach, the most likely interpretation of a sentence is that which satisfies the largest number of preferences.

A different approach, advanced by Jaime Carbonell, has unfulfilled selectional restrictions trigger special procedures for the metaphoric families. Carbonell notes that speakers often sustain their metaphors; information *flows* and a *pipeline* is its path. Once it is invoked, the special procedure can look for extensions of the metaphor and thus avoid the awkwardness and inefficiency of shuttling too rapidly back and forth between literal and metaphorical analysis.

Section three: Prototypical and Referential Meanings

3.1 Lexical prototypes

Both meaning postulates and semantic features assert necessary ingredients of meaning; *woman* in one of its senses is necessarily a hyponym of *person* and *female*, or necessarily possesses the features HUMAN and FEMALE. However, arriving at a set of indispensable hyponyms or features that are collectively sufficient to capture the meaning can be very difficult even for common words. A frequently cited example is *bird*. A satisfactory lexical schema for *bird* would specify a small set of attributes. But some of the likeliest attributes for *bird* are only typical, not necessary. That neither an ostrich nor a penguin can fly does not mean they are something other than birds; they are simply atypical birds. That a penguin's feathers (lacking the double row of parallel filaments) resemble scales, and that a penguin's wings look and act like flippers does not invalidate our concepts of FEATHER and WING or the concept of BIRD that would depend on them for attributes. Typical attributes are assumed to pertain unless there is indication to the contrary.

When we are not always clear about whether a particular attribute is necessary or typical, we sometimes use a hedging expressions to suggest that we are aware of (and not particularly bothered by) the difference. If a given example has the necessary attributes, but lacks some that are only typical, then we might use the hedge *technically*: *technically a penguin is a bird*; if the example lacks necessary attributes, but shares some of the typical ones, we use *in a manner of speaking*: *in a manner of speaking a bat is a bird*. Typical does not, however, mean incidental, and lexical entries cannot exclude typical, if only because they often determine the combinations in which a word may appear. Such verbs as *fly*, *soar*, and *land* select for subjects capable of flight.

If only necessary attributes are permitted in lexical entries, the entries for some quite ordinary words would be uninformative and nearly useless. One example, as Wittgenstein pointed out, is the word *game*. Most games provide amusement, but war games do not; most involve competition with other players, but not solitaire; games can require physical skill (tennis), mental skill (chess), or just luck. No single attribute is shared by all, yet all are subsumed under the word *game* because of what Wittgenstein calls their "family resemblance." Each game has enough attributes in common with some other games to qualify.

That *game* has few or no necessary attributes might suggest that the lexicon need only associate *game* with the heterogenous family it subsumes. All are hyponyms, so *chess, patience,* and the others would each have an ←(is-a)- link pointing to *game*. This expedient raises some problems, however. Such attributes as amusement and competition, shared by many, perhaps most games, would be represented in the lexical entry for each game and make them partially redundant. What is worse, though hyponyms inherit from their superordinating terms, the process does not work in reverse. Associating competition and amusement with, say, chess would not permit the inference that games typically feature competition and amusement and thus would do little to supplement the threadbare definition of *game* or convey the family "resemblances." Other words present greater problems. *Game* is the superordinating term for a finite set of hyponyms that name various games, and the finite number of links to those games would at least circumscribe the lexical concept that unites them. But how would we define such words, as the noun *work*, which has no finite set of hyponyms? An answer to this problem has emerged from prototype theory.

Prototype theory originated in cross-cultural studies of shapes and colors conducted by Eleanor Rosch. People whose languages have no words for the geometrical shapes find circles and squares and triangles easier to re-identify than distorted examples of those shapes. For people whose languages have only two terms for colors (light and dark), focal reds and greens are more easily re-identified. Though other possibilities have since been advanced, one explanation is that certain examples of a conceptual shape or color are more typical than others, are more easily related to the concept, and are more easily remembered. These findings stimulated a considerable amount of research on typicality, much of it conducted by Rosch and her colleagues. Most subjects agree in typicality ratings, consistently identifying peas as typical vegetables and potatoes as less typical. These results could not be explained on the basis of word frequency; pajamas and bathing suits were typical clothes; shoe, hat and glove were less typical. Nor were judgments based consistently on appearance, which might afford reasonable identification criteria (typical vegetables also included carrots, but not onions) or on such knowledge as the use of the category (chair and bookcase are more typical instances of furniture than stools or benches). Also, as children acquire language, they tend to learn the more typical examples of a category first, and adults recall the typical examples more rapidly from memory. In category verification tasks, adults confirm the truth of a "typical" sentence, such as *a sparrow is a bird* more quickly than the truth of an "atypical" sentence, *a penguin is a bird*.

Prototype theory holds that for categorical words such as *clothing, vegetable, furniture, crime,* people have some exemplar in mind and decide whether something else is a member of the category by comparing it with that prototype. It helps explain how people deal with atypical instances: they judge them to be sufficiently like the prototype, although they do not share all of its characteristics. Qualifying damaged instances for a category (long a puzzle for linguists) occurs much the same way: a bird that is missing a wing and therefore unable to fly still shares enough characteristics to be a bird. The theory does not necessarily reject featural representations of meaning, it rejects only the claim that words have necessary features that collectively are sufficient to define them.

Though prototype theory is very attractive, some problems have emerged. Attributes of a prototype tend to be heterogeneous (identification criteria sometimes, use at other times) and sometimes inexplicable. Though for many words the prototype is a collection of attributes, for others, it is a central example: thus a person thirty-years old is closer to the prototype for adult than is an eighteen-year-old. Determining the relative importance of features is difficult; flight and feathers may be the most important attributes of *bird*, but what comes next in importance? And it is difficult to know when to stop specifying attributes. What information is in the mental lexicon and what is in the mental encyclopedia? (Indeed proponents sometime deny the existence of a semantic component that is separate from the mental encyclopedia.) In brief, the concept of a prototype is itself prototypical rather than criterial. It has fuzzy boundaries and is characterized by family resemblances and by typical rather than necessary and sufficient attributes. Therefore, it is not at all clear how one would set out to formalize prototypical representations or to employ them in a systematic account of the organization of the human lexicon.

3.2 Frames and nonmonotonic reasoning

Though prototype theory does not lend itself to any formal method of knowledge representation, it has led to a series of proposals that would incorporate typicality in lexical entries.   Some are probabilistic, assigning weights to components and qualifying an instance if it exceeds some threshold.   Other proposals invoke fuzzy set theory and the idea of membership to a degree–that is, not 0 or 1 but a value between 0 and 1. Fuzzy set theory defines precise rules for working with typicality, vagueness, and uncertainty. It can also accommodate degree words (*hot, warm, cool*) and intensifying or hedging adverbs like *very* and *somewhat*.

One of the simplest proposals comes from computational linguistics and is based on the idea of the **frame**. A frame may be simply a schema in which some values are defaults, assumed only until there is evidence to the contrary, or a frame may contain procedures for replacing defaults and perhaps accreting additional information. The frame for *bird* could thus contain, among other relations

[BIRD] ←(subject)— | defaults: [FLY] [WALK]

and that information need not be repeated in the entries for most species of birds. But the entry for *penguin* would contain the relation

[PENGUIN] ←(subject)— | defaults: [WALK] [SWIM]

and the frame for someone's pet penguin who never learned to swim might restrict the value to WALK.

During sentence processing, prototype frames serve as templates for new frames, showing the kinds of information that might be collected from an utterance. A prototype for *dog* might contain the following set of relations and values:

$$
\begin{array}{l}
\text{[DOG]} \ \leftarrow\text{(name)}-\ \text{[UNDEFINED]} \\[4pt]
\quad \leftarrow\text{(purpose)}-|\ \text{default:}
\begin{bmatrix}
\text{[GUARD]} & \leftarrow\text{(subject)}- \ \text{[DOG: X]} \\
 & \leftarrow\text{(object)}- \ \text{[RESIDENCE]} \\
\text{[AMUSE]} & \leftarrow\text{(subject)}- \ \text{[DOG: X]} \\
 & \leftarrow\text{(object)}- \ \text{[HUMAN]}
\end{bmatrix} \\[4pt]
\quad \leftarrow\text{(attribute)}-\ |\ \text{default: [WEIGHT: 20 to 50 pounds]} \\
\quad \leftarrow\text{(faculty)}-\ \text{[SMELL]} \ \leftarrow\text{(characteristic)}-\ |\ \text{default: [ACUTE]} \\
\quad \leftarrow\text{(faculty)}-\ \text{[HEARING]} \ \leftarrow\text{(characteristic)}-\ |\ \text{default: [ACUTE]} \\
\quad \leftarrow\text{(instance)}-\ \text{[UNDEFINED]}
\end{array}
$$

Encountering the (unusually informative) sentence, *my eighty-pound dog Oliver guards the house despite his loss of hearing*, the system would retrieve the prototype for DOG, together with information about

names, residences, and the like, then build a frame for this instance of
dog. The frame would include:

[DOG1]   ←(name)— [Oliver]
            ←(attribute)— [WEIGHT: 80 pounds]
            ←(purpose)— [GUARD] ←(subject)— [DOG1]
                                            ←(object)— [RESIDENCE]
            ←(faculty)—[HEARING] ←(status)—[-OPERABLE]

At the same time, the indexical DOG1 would be inserted in the instance
slot for DOG, in effect augmenting that lexical concept with information
about one instance.

The most useful lexical frames occupy a middle level in the
conceptual hierarchy, representing words like *dog, car,* and *table* rather
than their superordinates *animal, vehicle,* and *furniture* or their
subordinates *beagle, sedan,* and *buffet.* This is the level at which we
most frequently interact with the environment: we have mental images
to associate with *dog* but not with *animal* and specific motor skills for
using *chairs* and *tables,* but not for *furniture.* Children acquire words
at this level before they acquire the superordinates and subordinates.
It is the level at which we have the most extensive and readily
available information: one can say more about dogs than about
animals, and what one can say about beagles consists mainly of what
one can say about other dogs. Mid-level terms are also more frequent
in ordinary discourse than are their superordinates and their subordinates.

The typical values or defaults contained in lexical prototypes require
a third kind of reasoning, different from deduction and induction.
Returning briefly to the world of the three pigs, we want the wolf to
reason that typical houses fall down, the pigs' houses are typical, so
they will fall down. But we need to allow for an atypical pig's house
(made of brick) that does not fall down. Standard logics are monotonic
in that they work in one direction only; once an inference has been
established, it cannot be retracted. But common-sense reasoning often
employs some version of **nonmonotonic logic** for inferences that are
not ironclad. Nonmonotonic inferences are "defeasible"; that is, they
are tentative and, given better information, may be withdrawn. One
version of nonmonotonic logic employs propositions such as:

$\forall$ X house(X) & **CONSISTENT** (fall-down (house(X))
$\supset$ (fall-down (house(X))

That is, if X is a house and that it will fall down is consistent with
what we know, then X will indeed fall down or more generally 'infer
proposition P from the inability to infer not P.' That there exists the

brick house3, which will not fall down no matter how much huffing and puffing the wolf does, is represented

$$\exists \text{ (house3)} \ \neg \text{ (fall-down (house3))}$$

Technical considerations suggest that nonmonotonic logic may sometimes defy our intuitions of what can and cannot be inferred, producing anomalous results; but it is no less useful than the nonmonotonic reasoning we call common sense.

3.3 Reference and possible worlds

Substitutional and combinational relationships of words with other words will give us some understanding of how words and sentences can have meanings, but they will not explain how language operates as a symbolic system. We need also to understand how those meanings attach to entities, qualities, ideas, attitudes, actions, and states of being in the actual world. The attachment may seem direct. Words denote things, and when sentences combine words they are denoting relation-ships that inhere in the world. A more nearly adequate account, however, makes the attachment rather circuitously, via mentally represented models of possible worlds. To understand this indirection and the considerations that force it, we can begin with a simple reference theory of meaning, then refine it in light of some facts about languages and the mind.

For the present, a **referent** can be defined as an entity existing in the world or imputed by an utterance to exist. Speakers and writers refer and, if they succeed, their audiences will correctly identify the intended referent from among other possible referents. (Here we enter set-theoretic semantics, developed by Alfred Tarski to give content to logical formulas.) Sentences, in turn, assert that referents belong to sets of referents named in the verb phrase. A simple instance would be a sentence with a proper name as subject and an intransitive verb as predicate: *Wellington triumphed*. The referent of *Wellington* is an individual, the nineteenth-century British general whose army defeated Napoleon's army at Waterloo. The referent of *triumphed* is a set of individuals, a large heterogeneous set of people who in one way or another have triumphed. Sets may be identified either by giving criteria for membership or by naming the elements.

{those who triumphed}

{Van Cliburn, 1986 Boston Celtics, Corazon Aquino, Wellington, . . . }.

(The curly brackets denote a **set**, members of which are **elements**.) The referent of the sentence is truth. If and only if the entity referred to by its subject noun phrase is an element of the set referred to by the predicate, the sentence is true.

Other sentence constituents yield to the same analysis. *Blue* in the sentence, *the sky is blue* refers to the set of *blue* entities, and the sentence asserts that the sky is among them; in *the blue house*, the adjective is again the predicate and it places the house among the set *blue* entities. *The good house* would require a different analysis, which uses sets that are members of sets; presumably the house is good as a house, hence this particular house is being placed in the set of good houses, which is a subset of all houses. Sets within sets may also come into play with sentences like *the dog bit Mary*, which contains, among other referents, a *dog* that belongs to the set of creatures that have done some biting, as well as to the subset of those that have bitten Mary.

So far this analysis accords with our intuition that similar syntactic constituents should have similar semantic analyses. Syntax and semantics work hand in hand. If, however, we say that the subject NPs *Wellington, the sky,* and *the dog,* are all individuals, what are we to make of sentences such as *Everyone triumphs, Someone triumphs,* and *No one triumphs*? None of these subjects picks out individuals. We could work out a solution using quantified variables, but that would be treating these subjects in a manner different from the treatment of individuals. A better solution, at least from the perspective of those (such as Montague and his associates) who seek generalized methods for accommodating phenomena of natural language, is to treat all subject NPs uniformly, whether they refer to individuals or not, as **sets of sets** (sometimes called families of sets). Thus *Wellington* will have as its semantic value the family of sets containing a set of which *Wellington* is the only member and the semantic value of *something* would be the set containing all sets with just one member. The semantic value of *nothing* is a set of sets containing one empty set. By this view, the semantic value of *everything* could be the set containing every set, but another consideration enters. When we say *everything is hot*, the context usually implies some criterion of relevance; for example, we might say it of all the food for a meal. Often called the **domain of discourse**, this context allows us to restrict the set of sets to those that are relevant.

What we have thus far is a referential theory of word meaning. A long philosophical tradition equates the meanings of words with their referents. The equation works well for biological species and physical substances—so well that some have supposed that a scientifically accurate description of the sets and subsets of things existing in the world would yield a full and satisfactory semantic taxonomy. However, such theories of meaning fail to answer some important questions. Is the referential relationship pertaining between the word *dog* and the set of all dogs comparable to that between the word *blue* and the set of all things having that color? Is there a set that includes all examples of reasoning or imagining or loving, and if there is how do we scientifically describe it? What about cases in which the denotation may be either a set of entities or a set with no entities: intelligent life forms on other planets, for example? We just do not know which is the case.

Even if these perplexities could be resolved, it is by no means clear that the taxonomy should be based on a scientific description of the world. Language is, after all, a cultural phenomenon. As anyone who has learned a second language will know, denotations are not co-extensive from one language to another. If one language has a word denoting the class rats and mice, for example, another might have a word for rats and squirrels, and a different word for mice, cockroaches, and bedbugs. Should not the semantic taxonomy be based on a full and satisfactory account of the nature and roles that all denoted entities, processes, states, and properties have for the culture using the language? Some would press this point even further, asking what we as language users know as the world? Isn't it a conceptual structure, the world as it has been organized, automatically and unconsciously, by our minds?

Now consider that *Wellington* and *the victorious British leader at Waterloo* refer to the same individual, but pick out their referents in different ways: the first by naming him and the second by limiting the broadly referential noun *leader* to the point where the referent is unmistakable. Since the pairs of noun phrases are not identical, we must conclude that there exists some aspect of meaning that is not reference but contains information that our minds must grasp in order to identify a referent if there is any. This non-referential aspect of meaning is the **sense** of the word or phrase. Gottlob Frege, who first clarified the distinction between reference and sense, used the example of the *morning star* and the *evening star*, both of which have the same referent, the planet Venus, but differ as to sense. Since their referents are the same, it is necessarily the case that if the morning star is smaller than the sun, the evening star is also smaller than the sun. However, there are contexts in which we cannot substitute evening star for morning star without modifying the truth conditions of the statement: *Joe believes that Venus is the morning star* may be true, but *Joe believes that Venus is the evening star* may be false. To put it the other way around, the substitutional relationships among words belong to the sense rather than reference of words. We can substitute *Wellington* for *the victorious British military leader at Waterloo* even if we do not know that both refer to the same person. Combinational relationships also inhere in sense of a word rather than its reference: thus we can combine the set of qualifiers and understand the result even if no referent exists: *the victorious British military unicorn at Waterloo.*

Formal semantic theories employ sets of **possible worlds** as a device to make more fully explicit the notion of sense: worlds that are imaginable and expressible and which may or may not include the actual world. A name, we can assume, refers in all possible worlds to the referent bearing that name; but a set of possible worlds might exist in which that referent is *the nineteenth century British military leader vanquished by Napoleon at Waterloo*. It is imaginable. The sense of an expression is not limited to what occurs in the actual world, and in the possible worlds approach it is as if every sentence were prefaced by the phrase *it is possible that*.

As for a predicate, sense consists in what it takes to qualify for the set to which it refers. When we understand a sentence such as *violets are blue*, what we grasp is not so much the set of all blue things, but rather what something is like if it is blue and therefore qualifies for that set. For this reason the sense of a predicate is often called its **property**. Properties are the same in all sets of possible worlds, but the referents they pick out may differ. We can imagine a subset of possible worlds in which roses are blue and violets are red, though that subset does not happen to include the actual world.

The sense of a sentence is a proposition. It proposes (and describes) a possible world in which the sentence is true. The proposition may be either necessary *(Wellington is Wellington)* or contingent on the possible world. In the actual world, the referents of *birds* belong to the set of beings possessing the property of flight; so *Birds can fly* is also true. In a set of possible worlds, as *Pigs can fly* proposes, the referents of *pigs* belong to that set; thus the sentence is true of that set, though not of the actual world. This analysis has the advantage that it accords with our intuition that to understand a sentence is to know the circumstances in which it is true. Another advantage is that it explains the status of beliefs, desires and the like. A belief relates the believer to a proposition *(John believes that pigs can fly.)*, rather than directly to some non-extant relationship between referents.

3.4 Mentally represented models

With the notion of sense, semantic theory escapes a referential Scylla, but only to be engulfed by a Charybdis of sets representing worlds, some actual, others only possible, and all highly abstract. What is worse, the set of all possible worlds must be infinite in number and therefore incapable of being represented in a finite human mind. One answer, offered by Philip Johnson-Laird, is that language does not refer directly to the actual or possible worlds but rather to the entities, states and events in **mental models**. A speaker or writer has a mental model, some part of which is to be communicated using language. The listener or reader also has a mental model, some part of which comes into play in interpreting language. Interpretation builds a representation of the state of affairs communicated by the speaker, in effect investigating that state of affairs by modeling it.

If comprehension is model building, then an important attribute of the models is that they are tentative knowledge structures, readily expanded and revised as the discourse proceeds, and reconstructed or otherwise manipulated upon further reflection. Components of the model, deriving as they do from semantic analysis, are propositions about sets, families of sets, and properties of sets, and are composed in just the way semantic theory says they are composed. But at any one time, the model represents only a single possible world, that interpreted from the discourse, and it is therefore a finite structure. Reference specifies elements of the model and truth is relative to the current state of the model.

The idea of model building is more than an escape from the difficulties of possible world semantics. Several other lines of reasoning converge on the same idea. As we will see, in comprehending discourse, the mind does not simply record the events explicitly mentioned in the discourse; it provide connecting links, goals, likely preconditions and effects, and much more from its store of world knowledge. As Shakespeare's Theseus says, "if it would but apprehend some joy, / It comprehends some bringer of that joy." Different people, bringing to bear different information, build different models.

Model building helps explain the method by which humans prefer to reason. Instead of following rigidly logical inference rules, we prefer to accumulate information, then reach for a relevant conclusion that is not excluded by any piece of information in our store. Consider the reasoning of the third little pig. Before he went to the bother of using brick, he witnessed some fallen houses, thought about the propensity of wolves for blowing houses down, and reasoned backwards: *the fallen houses suggest that a wolf is blowing houses down.* He is reasoning by **abduction**, roughly as follows:

$$\forall \ (\text{house}) \ \text{blow} \ (\text{wolf1}) \supset \text{fall-down} \ (\text{house})$$
$$\exists \ \text{fall-down} \ (\text{house})$$

abduction: blow (wolf(1))

Abductive reasoning is not necessarily reliable (there may have been an earthquake or some other reason for the fallen houses), but the third pig's conclusion is nevertheless plausible. In effect, the third pig establishes one cause by eliminating the others, concluding either that the alternative causes do not exist or that they are improbable. We think this way every day and call it explanation; coping when the model is incomplete, we abductively "reach" for a explanation then we test that explanation against what we know or can infer from what we know.

Exercises

1. Which of the following sentences are false by virtue of the meanings of their constituent words and which simply happen to be untrue of the world as we know it?

My uncle is a grapefruit.	My uncle lifted eleven tons.
My sister is an only child.	All bachelors are married.
I stole it unintentionally.	All cats are black.

2. Using the notation in Section 1.4, represent the propositional meaning of the following lines from Shakespeare's plays:

> What fools these mortals be.
> I have no way and therefore want no eyes.

3. First, devise a series of meaning postulates to describe the hyponymous relations among the following words: *being, canine, coyote, dog, feline,* and *collie*; next devise a semantic network that will economically represent those relationships; finally, add to your network Lassie, the famous collie.

4. What semantic feature might distinguish such verbs as *walk, think, perceive,* and *talk* from verbs like *build, write, diagnose,* and *explain*?

5. Using the lexical features FEMALE, HUMAN, MALE, PROGENY and SIBLING devise lexical entries that represent accurately the internal structures of *aunt, parent, nephew,* and *son.*

6. What selectional restrictions associated with adjectives and verbs are violated to produce the semantic anomalies in *Deciduous automobiles speak tall lakes that read candy*?

7. Devise a prototype frame that represents useful information about of the meaning of *attorney* or *artist*. Briefly explain how you decided what to include.

Further reading

On semantic theory, see Lyons (1977) for an encyclopedic account, as well as Kempson (1977), Dillon (1977), Allan (1986), Cruse (1986), and the papers in Landman and Veltman (1984). Gibbs (1984, 1989) and Dascal (1987) debate the existence of literal meaning. On the lexical representation of semantic information, see Hüllen and Schulze (1988), Brugman (1988), and Evens (1989). Pylyshyn (1984) offers a thorough (but demanding) discussion of the representation hypothesis; for criticism of the hypothesis see Winograd and Flores (1986). Also see the collected papers in Eco, Santambrogio, and Violi (1988) and Kempson (1988).

Empirical studies supporting the psychological reality of propositional representation include Sachs (1967), Kintsch (1974), Ratcliff and McKoon

(1978) and Goetz, Anderson, and Shallert (1981). For an extensive account of their network representation, see Sowa (1984, 1990) and the papers in Brachman and Levesque (1985) and Brachman, Levesque, and Reiter (1989). On partitioning, see Hendrix (1979); Woods (1975) and Johnson-Laird, Herrmann, and Chaffin (1984) critique the earlier work. On the representation of semantic relations in formal logic see Allwood, Andersson, and Dahl (1977), or McCawley (1981). The original proposal for frames is Minsky (1975).

On meaning postulates, see Kintsch (1974) and Fodor, Fodor, and Garrett (1975); the approach is criticized in Katz and Nagel (1974). Katz and J. A. Fodor brought (1963) lexical decomposition into modern semantic theory; Kempson (1977) provides a clear, balanced introduction. Jackendoff (1983, 1989) presents a highly developed semantic theory employing semantic features. Nida (1975), Wierzbicka (1980), Dahlgren (1988), Dahlgren and Stabler (1989), and the papers in Chierchia, Partee, and Turner (1988) are additional sources. On the ubiquity of metaphor, see Lakoff and Johnson (1980) and Sweetster (1989); the two methods of handling metaphor are described in Wilks (1975) and Fass and Wilks (1983), and in Carbonell (1982). On semantic prototypes, see Rosch and Lloyd (1978), Rosch (1975), Smith and Medin (1981), Neisser (1987), Geeraerts (1989), and the papers in Lehmann (1988) and Tsohatzidis (1989). On the efforts to accommodate formal representations to natural language see Dowty, Wall, and Peters (1981), and on the uniform interpretation of subject noun phrases, Montague (1974) and Barwise and Cooper (1981). On possible world semantics, see Cresswell (1988) and on mental models, see Johnson-Laird (1975 and 1988), Webber (1978, 1979), Kamp (1981, 1990), Van Dijk and Kintch (1983), Garnham (1988), and Oakhill, Garnham, and Vonk (1989). Shafer and Pearl (1990) contains the seminal papers on uncertain reasoning.

Chapter 9

Phrase and Sentence Semantics

Section one: Relational Representation

1.1 Compositionality and conceptual relations

Most theories of semantics and language comprehension rest on the hypothesis that phrase and sentence meanings are **compositional**. That is, they are solely and systematically determined by the meanings of the words and idiomatic phrases that compose them and by the syntactic and semantic relationships into which the words and idioms enter. Compositionality is a fundamental virtue of language in that a finite number of words and idioms can be combined and recombined to form an infinite number of meaningful phrases and sentences. Were sentence meanings not compositional, we would need to carry in our brains a complete list of phrases and sentences with either their meanings or separate procedures to calculate each meaning—in either case an impossibility since they are infinite and brains are finite. An infinite number of possible phrases and sentences does not, however, mean that all sentences are possible.

Computational interpretation combines schemata for words into more complex schemata representing phrase meanings and sentence meanings. The underlying process is called **merging** or **joining** and is a variant of unification, a process in logic that consolidates formulas containing matching variables. The links are primitive relations, which express the roles that concepts play vis-á-vis one another. Let's stipulate, for example, that one meaning of the phrase *next to* (as well as *adjoining, contiguous, juxtaposed with*) and part of the meaning of *end to end* and *touching* is the primitive relation:

[ENTITY:] ←(adjacent)— [ENTITY:]

Then one way of interpreting *the car next to the house* is represented by the schema:

[VEHICLE] ←(adjacent)— [DWELLING]

Notice that even though each is adjacent to the other, the direction of the pointer preserves the subordination of the preposition's object to the head noun. If the phrase were the house next to the car, then the pointer would extend from VEHICLE to DWELLING.

Whereas graph notation stresses the relational nature of adjacency, formal logic offers a different perspective by expressing relations as functions. **Functions** assign values. Let's say, for instance, we have two sets, one consisting of names, the other of seven-digit numbers. We might define a "telephone number function" that assigns to each name a number:

telephone-number (name number)

That gives us a function from names to numbers or (in the locution of the logicians) a function that maps names into numbers. The transformations in a transformational grammar are functions in that they map deep structures into surface structures; for each deep structure entering the function there emerges exactly one structure. From this perspective, lexical relations are functions that assign properties or relationships to terms. Adjacency expressed as a function would be

(adjacent (ENTITY X ENTITY Y))

That is, the function assigns to each ENTITY represented by the variable X the relationship of being adjacent to another ENTITY (Y). Similarly, the property of having something as a part:

[ENTITY] ←(part)— [ENTITY]

can be expressed as a function that maps entities onto entities:

(part (ENTITY X ENTITY Y)

Several members of the first set may share an element of the second (but not vice versa); representing multiple parts of an entity would require multiple functions. The methods of semantic interpretation discussed in this chapter simply merge schemata, but "rule by rule" approaches (described in the next chapter) will pair syntactic and semantic rules, both stated as functions. The meaning of a constituent will be a function that maps the meaning of one constituent on another; thus, for example, the meaning of a sentence will be the meaning of a noun phrase mapped onto the meaning of a verb.

The relation or function for *next to* also specifies selectional restrictions. In this case selection is very broad; any entities, whether physical objects or even ideas, can be contiguous. *Car* and *house*, however, are of specific types. With merging, types resemble variables in that types can assume particular values. ENTITY X is a car, but

[ENTITY] ←(attribute)— [ENTITY]

    the young person
    [HUMAN #4] ←(attribute)— [-ADULT]

[ENTITY] ←(color)— [COLOR]

    the scarlet box
    [CONTAINER #14] ←(color)— [RED]

[ENTITY] ←(contains)— [ENTITY]

    person in the car
    [VEHICLE #9] ←(contains)— [HUMAN #3]

[ACT] ←(duration)— [TIME-PERIOD]

    I walked for an hour
    [GO #7] ←(duration)–[HOUR]

[ACT] ←(manner)— [CHARACTERISTIC]

    I walked carefully.
    [GO #6] ←(manner)— [CAUTION]

[ENTITY] ←(unique-part)— [ENTITY]

    Jim's liver
    [BODY #10] ←(unique-part)— [ORGAN #3]

[ENTITY] ←(part)— [ENTITY]

    Jim's toe
    [BODY #11] ←(part)— [APPENDAGE #3]

[HUMAN] ←(possession)–[ENTITY]

    Jim's house
    [HUMAN #22] ←(poss)— [DWELLING #2]

[ANIMATE] ←(progeny)— [ANIMATE]

    Jim's infant
    [HUMAN #6] ←(progeny)— [HUMAN #66]

Figure 1. A sampler of conceptual relations.

could be a cart or in some possible world, a unicorn. In interpreting *the car next to the house*, we need a way of narrowing the range of entities to just that car which is next to just that house. First, we can substitute ENTITY for VEHICLE and ENTITY for DWELLING, using the inheritance hierarchy to replace superordinates with more specific types. Substitution of the more specific for the less specific is known as **restricting**. Both merging and restricting are ways of specializing the representation and do not preserve truth, whereas generalizing does preserve truth (if a VEHICLE is next to a DWELLING, it is necessarily true that an ENTITY is next to an ENTITY). But that is what we want. Specialization makes truth contingent on whether the utterance is true, or to put it in terms of possible worlds, the specialized relation is true in the possible world of the utterance, but not necessarily in the actual world.

Figure 1 gives a sampler of relations, with their selectional restrictions and some examples. As the examples suggest, the relations may be realized as adjectives, adverbs, prepositional phrases, and possessives. They can even be promoted to the subject NP; *two days will finish the job* contains the relation

$$[\text{ACT: finish}] \leftarrow (\text{duration}) - [\text{TIME-PERIOD: two days}])$$

Most common relations are between two concepts, but triadic relations are also possible, notably:

$$[\text{ENTITY}] \leftarrow (\text{between}) - \begin{bmatrix} [\text{ENTITY}] \\ [\text{ENTITY}] \end{bmatrix}$$

No generally agreed-upon set of relationships has emerged, and for computational systems, relations tend to be specified *ad hoc*. Some generalizations are possible, however. As the following sets, of sentences suggest, locations and extents have temporal, spatial and conceptual manifestations:

Location: He finished the work **at noon.** (temporal)
He did the work **in Boston.** (spatial)
We wrote the programs **in computer science.** (conceptual)

Extent: He worked **between nine to six.** (temporal)
There are roads **between Boston and New York.** (spatial)
He did it all **from A to Z.** (conceptual)

Also, temporal and spatial locations can be either general *(at)* or more specific *(above, below, within; before, after, during)*. As these examples suggest, lexical relations belong to a hierarchy of relations, much as types belong to a hierarchy of types. Though the hierarchy of relations supports inheritance, it is shallow and quite bushy; therefore the generalizations it captures are less useful for linguistic knowledge representation than those for semantic features.

1.2 From grammatical functions to semantic cases

As we have already seen, verbs subcategorize for, and thereby predict, the direct objects, indirect objects, complements, and adverbials that can co-occur with them. Translating these functional structures into propositional representation offers a start on sentence meanings. For the intransitive and transitive senses of the verb *shatter*, the lexicon would list:

> SHATTER1 (subject X)
>
> SHATTER2 ((subject X) (direct-object Y) (indirect-object Z))

and sentence recognition would simply replace the three variables with a semantic representation of the named constituents. Synonymous sentences such as *Joe shattered the window* and *the window was shattered by Joe* would have identical representations and these would, at least in a loose way, represent the propositional content of the sentence: who did what to what.

Consider, however, these sentences, all of which could refer to the same act of shattering:

The window shatters.	SHATTER1 (subj WINDOW)
He shatters the window with a rock.	SHATTER2 ((subj JOE) (dir obj WINDOW))
A rock shatters the window.	SHATTER2 ((subj ROCK) (dir obj WINDOW))

The translation accurately reflects the functional structures of all three sentences, but nothing more. The three propositions do not systematically relate the intransitive sense of *shatter* in the first sentence to the transitive sense in the second and third. Moreover, although the semantic role of *rock* is essentially the same in the second and third sentences and *window* has the same role in all three, the three different propositions do not reveal that.

There are some connections, however. The intransitive sense of *shatter* requires that there be something brittle and hence capable of being shattered; the transitive sense requires in addition some animate force capable of action and hence of doing the shattering and may co-occur with some solid instrument by means of which the shattering is done. These roles are essentially the same, wherever they appear in the syntax, and they might be expressed as conceptual entities. The roles can be expressed as arguments in the predicate calculus:

> $\exists$ X SHATTER (X)   & (($\exists$ A (SHATTERER (X, A)) & (ANIMATE (A)))
> & ($\exists$ B (SHATTERED (X, B)) & (BRITTLE (B)))
> & ($\exists$ C (BY MEANS OF (X, C) & (PHYS OBJ (C))))

That is, for all instances (X) of the concept SHATTER there is implied an entity (A) that is SHATTERER and that same entity (A) is ANIMATE, and so on. The three arguments are connected by logical &, and collectively they label the constituents expected in a sentence whose verb is *shatter*.

Since the logical form is cumbersome to write out each time we need to represent a lexical entry, we can abbreviate using Pierce's graph notation, which has the additional advantage of resembling the semantic network that is its formal equivalent. Thus the transitive sense of *shatter* would be written:

[SHATTER]   ←(shatterer)–[ANIMATE]
              ←(shattered)–[BRITTLE]
              ←(by means of)–[PHYSICAL OBJECT]

This proposition asserts that there exists an ANIMATE being that is capable of acting as the cause, a BRITTLE object that is acted upon, and a PHYSICAL OBJECT that is the means.

The sequence of these constituents in the sentence and their grammatical role may be variable, but the underlying propositions are always the same: the something brittle is that which is shattered whether it appears in the syntax as the subject of the intransitive sense of *shatter*, the direct object of *shatter* in its transitive sense, or a complement in a sentence such as *it was the window that shattered*. The selectional restrictions or preferences guide the processing of sentences, helping to determine which sentence constituents perform what roles in the propositional representation. As with any other proposition, these roles can also be captured in a semantic network.

Expectations can be specified *ad hoc* for each verb and sometimes they are, especially for programs working with small vocabularies. Thus for one sense of *drive*, the lexicon might stipulate the predicate DRIVE and among its arguments (DRIVER HUMAN), and for one sense of *fly* (PILOT HUMAN), and so on. But each of these arguments is specific to a verb, probably too specific. DRIVER is partially redundant in that it repeats information that is already present in DRIVE, and PILOT has essentially the same role with respect to *fly* as DRIVER has to *drive*. What is needed is a way of generalizing the relationships, thereby reducing them to a finite set of frequently recurring roles.

The answer is to stipulate a set of **thematic roles** (θ roles) or **semantic cases**. Thematic roles are the semantic or conceptual parts that may be played by subcategorized arguments of verbs. One thematic role is the agent; it constitutes the element of meaning shared by DRIVER and PILOT. Another role is the semantic theme (performed in this case by the vehicles). Semantic cases are very similar and often go by the same names, except that they are not necessarily limited to arguments subcategorized by verbs.

Case analysis takes its cue from the elaborate sets of syntactic cases featured in many languages. These provide additional justification for generalizing. In English case is most evident in the forms that pronouns take as subjects (*she, we, who*), objects (*him, us, whom*), and possessors (*her, their, whose*). These are syntactic distinctions with important semantic or conceptual implications. English once had a more extensive set of cases, which identified subjects, direct objects, indirect objects, and so on; and distinctions were maintained by a set of inflectional suffixes. Other modern languages (German for example) still have suffixes to distinguish the direct and indirect objects, and some have suffixes to mark other cases. Russian has suffixes for six cases, including an instrumental case. Finnish also has a extensive set of cases, several of which have to do with location and movement; the suffix *-sta*, for example, designates an origin, and the suffix *-un*, a destination.   Japanese has the postpositions *ga* for subjects, *o* for objects, *de* for instruments and locations, and *ni* for destination. The markers are different, but many of the cases are the same. That many cases turn up in one language after another and involve the same relationships between noun phrase and verb suggests there might indeed exist a finite, relatively small and specifiable set of semantic cases underlying most of the world's languages. Thus case analysis promises not only to represent functional relationships within sentences, but also to correlate languages that mark case with inflections, with particular word orders, and with prepositions or postpositions.

Empirical evidence is accruing that themes or cases and the selectional restrictions on their fillers guide the processing sentences, overriding the parsing preferences when that is required. In the sentence *the man observed by the police escaped*, for example, right association leads to a garden path which although only momentary, is detectable by eye tracking.) However, the effect does not occur with *the van observed by the police escaped*, presumably because *observed* is associated with the thematic role or case, experiencer, and experiencers must be sentient beings. Experiments using sentences with syntactic gaps and fillers (such as would require a hold facility) also suggest that themes or cases play a role in sentence processing.

Well before the psychological evidence emerged, thematic or case analysis attracted computational linguists, because it generalizes semantic relationships, affording a finite set of recurring roles, and because the expectations exerted by verbs (together with selectional restrictions and preferences) can guide effective procedures. Lexical entries for the verbs *drive* and *break* would offer the **case frames**:

[OPERATE: drive] ←(agent)— [HUMAN]
                  ←(origin)— [PLACE]
                  ←(destination)— [PLACE]
                  ←(path)— [PLACE or DIRECTION]
                  ←(instrument)— [VEHICLE]

[BREAK: shatter] ←(agent)— [ANIMATE]
                  ←(patient)— [OBJECT] ←(attribute)— [BRITTLE]
                  ←(instrument)— [OBJECT] ←(attribute)— [HARD]

A case frame is a collection of functions or semantic relations. Some are mandatory, others optional (although at least one case must be present in the sentence). All associate verbs with noun and prepositional phrases and, whereas other relations (such as those expressing time and location) can occur with any verb, particular verbs predict particular constellations of cases.

1.3 Instantiating schemata and case frames

To interpret sentences, the computer instantiates representations, merging the verb's case frame with lexical schemata for noun phrases. For the sentence, *with a rock, the boy shattered the window*, we would have these additional lexical entries for *rock*, *boy*, and *window*.

[PHYS OBJ: rock] ←(attribute)— [HARD]

[HUMAN: boy] ←(attribute)— [MALE]
              ←(attribute)— [-ADULT]

[PHYS OBJ: window] ←(attribute)— [HARD]
                    ←(attribute)— [BRITTLE]

The object is to combine these schemata with the case frame to produce a representation of sentence meaning.

The interpreter would begin by looking for the agent predicted by the case frame. No noun phrase with the type ANIMATE presents itself, but ANIMATE is a superordinate of HUMAN. If ANIMATE in the case frame is restricted to HUMAN, *boy* meets the selectional restriction, and its entry can be substituted for HUMAN. The token for a generic noun phrase *the boy* is also represented by a unique number. (If instead we had a proper noun the token would be [HUMAN: boy #12] ←(name)– [Bob #12] or [HUMAN: Bob #12] in contracted form.) So far, we have:

[BREAK: #123] ←(agent)— [HUMAN: #234] ←(attribute)— [MALE]
                                       ←(attribute)— [-ADULT]
               ←(patient)— [PHYS OBJ] ←(attribute)— [HARD]
                                       ←(attribute)— [BRITTLE]
               ←(instrument)— [PHYS OBJ] ←(attribute)— [HARD]

Notice that all conceptual relations that are linked to the schema (in this case the attributes MALE and -ADULT) are carried over into the merged form.

Next the interpreter looks for a patient and finds two noun phrases with the type PHYS OBJs. They also share the attribute HARD, but only *window* has the attribute BRITTLE, so its entry is substituted for PHYS OBJ specified in the case frame. Finally, the interpreter fills the instrument role with the entry for *rock*; since no additional noun phrases need be accommodated, the representation is complete:

```
[BREAK1 #12]  ←(agent)— [HUMAN: #234]  ←(attribute)— [MALE]
                                       ←(attribute)— [-ADULT]
              ←(patient)— [PHYS OBJ: #35]  ←(attribute)— [HARD]
                                           ←(attribute)— [BRITTLE]
              ←(instrument)— [PHYS OBJ: #524]  ←(attribute)— [HARD]
```

Rarely is it this easy. More than one acceptable candidate for a role may be present, or candidates may be semantically ambiguous. Syntactic information is needed to guide the process. In section 2, we will see interpretation rules that use syntactic structures to guide the merge; Chapter 10 addresses the controversial questions of how much syntax is needed and when it should be applied.

If the sentence had been *the young hood broke the fragile object*, the noun phrases would need some interpretation before being merged with the case frame. The relevant lexical entries are:

young   [ANIMATE:] ←(attribute)— [-ADULT]

hood   [HUMAN: hood] ←(attribute)— [CRIMINAL]

fragile   [PHYS OBJ] ←(attribute)— [BRITTLE]

object   [PHYS OBJ: object]

Restricting [ANIMATE] to [HUMAN] and merging the schemata for *young* and *hood* and for *fragile* and *object* would produce the schemata:

```
[ANIMATE: #123] ←(attribute)— [-ADULT]
                ←(attribute)— [CRIMINAL]


[PHYS OBJ: #456] ←(attribute)– [BRITTLE]
```

In turn, these merge with the case frame for *break* to provide a representation for the meaning of the entire sentence. Since the processes are the same for sentences and for phrases, all that is required is a computational procedure that operates top down, interpreting the sentence by matching constituents against the case frame, and recursively interpreting phrases as needed to fill the roles.

Merging and restriction can also reduce information in multiple sentences to a single representation. Let's say we have the following sentences:

The boy shattered the window.

```
[BREAK #123]    ←(agent)— [HUMAN: #234] ←(attribute)— [MALE]
                                         ←(attribute)— [-ADULT]
                ←(patient)— [PHYS OBJ: #5] ←(attribute)— [HARD]
                                           ←(attribute)— [BRITTLE]
```

He broke it with a rock.

```
[BREAK1 #321]   ←(agent)— [ANIMATE: #311] ←(attribute)— [MALE]
                ←(patient)– [PHYS OBJ: #6]   ←(attribute)— [HARD]
                                             ←(attribute)— [BRITTLE]
                ←(instrument)— [PHYS OBJ: #24] ←(attribute)— [HARD]
```

The sentences presumably refer to the same act of breaking, though that presumption can in be difficult to establish with any certainty. (Chapter 12 will explore methods of establishing co-reference.) In all respects except for the tokens, the representations are not inconsistent. Compatible types occupy the roles of agent and patient, and no instrument is specified in the first sentence. Merging would produce the representation:

```
[BREAK #223]    ←(agent)— [HUMAN: #334]   ←(attribute)— [MALE]
                                           ←(attribute)— [-ADULT]
                ←(patient)— [PHYS OBJ: 452]   ←(attribute)— [HARD]
                                              ←(attribute)– [BRITTLE]
                ←(instrument)— [PHYS OBJ: #524] ←(attribute)— [HARD]
```

Notice that portions of the representation have been trimmed to eliminate redundancy: the representation for the pronouns *he* and *it*, being less specific and therefore less informative than the representation for *boy* and *window*, are removed.

Propositions may fill certain roles in case frames. Case frames for psychological verbs such as *know, think, decide,* and *believe,* for example, often have propositions filling the ←(patient)– role, as do performative verbs (that is, verbs that perform acts), including *concede, threaten, nominate,* and *predict*:

> I know that Tim broke the window.
> I concede that Tim broke window.

For such verbs, the case frame would specify an ABSTRACT role-filler or some more specific supertype of propositions and other objects of the psychological and performative verbs. Merging the case frames for the matrix and embedded sentences produces a representation for the whole:

[KNOW #2] ←(agent)— [HUMAN: #132]

←(patient)— $\begin{bmatrix} \text{[BREAK \#1]} & \begin{array}{l} \text{←(agent)— [HUMAN: \#3]} \\ \text{←(patient)— [PHYS OBJ: \#4]} \end{array} \end{bmatrix}$

Such representations can extend to any level of embeddings; I can know that he knows that I know, and so on.

Although interpretation is often conceived as a predictive or expectation-based process, in that schemata fulfill predictions made by case frames or other schemata, it can also be understood as a process of satisfying constraints. Case frames permit certain roles but not others, and they exercise selectional restrictions on potential role fillers. The difference is entirely in the processing. Predictive interpretation lends itself to conventional, serial computers, and to pattern matching. Constraint satisfaction, particularly when there are multiple, autonomous sources of constraints (from syntax and discourse, as well as from semantics), lends itself to connectionist and other parallel modes of computing.

1.4 Toward a taxonomy of cases

Case systems may be either linguistically or conceptually motivated. Linguistically motivated systems seek to describe the semantic relations which inhere between major constituents of a sentence. Most aim for a relatively small system of language-neutral cases that capture generalizations underlying multiple languages. Though no system has gained widespread acceptance, certain cases are proposed in many systems. We can look at these and at some of the reasons for proposing them, beginning with cases often filled by subjects of sentences. Figure 2 illustrates the case analysis of sample sentences.

An ←(agent)— possesses volition and instigates an action. *John* is the agent in *John built the table*. If an agent is present in an active sentence, it is necessarily the subject; in a passive sentence, the agent may be the object of *by*. Some systems distinguish sentences with compound subjects (*John and Mary built the table*) from those that explicitly subordinate the agent (such as *friends* in *Mary, together with her friends, built the table*) by allowing two agents for the former and a ←(co-agent)— for the latter. Presumably this is because the syntax makes such a distinction. (Similar subordinators are *with* and *as well as*.) A distinction that entails more difference exists between agent and ←(force)—. Forces (which include wind, rain, earthquakes and other natural phenomena) also initiate actions, but unlike agents they have no volition. Therefore, we would not say *the wind intentionally broke those windows in order to gain entry*: *intentionally* and *in order to* are appropriate only to beings that have volition. Some verbs such as *crawl* require an animate subject, hence an agent; the subject of others, such as *destroy*, may be either an agent or a force (*the storm destroyed our windmill*). Also, distinguishing agent from force helps maintain the heuristic (useful in specifying procedures for semantic analysis) that different cases cannot be conjoined; thus *Joe and the wind pushed open the door* is not semantically a well-formed sentence.

Some systems further distinguish the ←(experiencer)–, which is restricted to sentient beings and occurs with psychological verbs including verbs of perception. By this analysis, the sentence *Jack likes Mary* does not mean that Jack performs some action called "liking" on Mary, but only that Jack experiences some "liking" with respect to Mary. This helps explain why it is that experiencers but not agents can sometimes be either direct objects (especially for verbs with the prefix *in-*or *en-* as in *she entranced me*) or objects of spatial prepositions such as *to* (*the music is pleasing to me*). Another difference between agents and experiencers is that an experiencer does not act with intention: we would not say *he intentionally liked Mary* (or *was entranced by the music* or *remembered the book.*) Most of what we have discussed so far applies to verbs that in some way signify an action or a change of state. Some systems of case grammar also provide an ←(essive)– case for subject and object complements. Thus *governor* in *she became governor* or *we elected her governor* would be essives. As we noted in discussing the syntax of complements, only a relatively few verbs take subject complements and fewer still take object complements.

An ←(instrument)– is the means by which an agent performs an action or, more generally, an entity used to achieve some end. Some case systems limit instrument to concrete objects (*my key unlocked the door*), while others allow abstractions (*seeing the accident made me sick*). Some define instrument so broadly as to include the materials or ingredients employed in an act of making (*he used wood for the handle*). When the sentence mentions no agent, an instrument be the subject, though not with all verbs (*the brush painted the bookcase*).

With a few verbs the instrument may be the direct object (*I used a hammer*), and with others the object of the prepositions *with*, *by*, or occasionally *on* (*on foot*). Some verbs are also very specific as to kinds of instruments, allowing for narrowly stated selectional restrictions. Verbs of motion, for example, specify kinds of conveyance: trucks, buses, cars, and motorboats for *drive*, airplanes, gliders, dirigibles, and helicopters for *fly*. All these opportunities and constraints can guide semantic analysis.

The ←(patient)– undergoes a change of state as a result of the verb's action (*he broke the bicycle*) or exists in a state specified by the verb (*she owns a bicycle*). Although the original formulation (by Charles Fillmore) assigns only one case to each NP in a sentence, state changes and other actions suggest multiple simultaneous assignments.

John built a table.

[MAKE:#3] ←(agent)— [HUMAN: John2]
            ←(patient)— [PHYS-OBJ: table4]
            ←(instrument)— [TOOL:Z]

The key unlocked the door.

[UNLOCK:#2] ←(instrument)— [KEY: key9]
             ←(patient)— [LOCK: lock3]   ⎤
                                             ⎥
        [APERTURE #3: door] ←(part-of) ⎦

Joe went to Bangor.

[GO #33] ←(agent)— [HUMAN: Joe4]
          ←(patient)— [HUMAN: Joe4]
          ←(destination)— [CITY: Bangor1]
          ←(destination)— [PLACE:Z]

Joe gave the roses to Jack for Mary.

[GIVE #21] ←(source)— [HUMAN: Joe4]
            ←(patient)— [-ANIMAL: roses6]
            ←(recipient)— [HUMAN: Jack5]
            ←(beneficiary)— [HUMAN: Mary1]

Figure 2. Case analysis.

For example, if an agent changes its state (for example its location), then the agent and patient cases may be filled by the same entity: *Joe went to Bangor* means *Joe transferred Joe to Bangor.* Beyond those reasonably precise definitions the patient tends to be something of a catch-all for noun phrases that are not easily assigned to other roles. Usually, however, the patient is distinguished from the ←(beneficiary)–, the animate being for whose benefit an action is performed, in part because, both may occur in the same sentence. (Yet another useful rule of thumb is that two non-conjoined noun phrases cannot play the same role.) The beneficiary is usually an indirect object in a sentence that has the patient as direct object, but the beneficiary can also be the subject of certain specifiable verbs: in *the bicycle chain broke*, for example, it is the chain that undergoes the change of state. Interestingly, certain "ergative-absolutive" languages use the same inflectional suffix (the "absolutive") for the patient whether it is subject or object and different suffix (the "ergative") for subjects that are agents of change.

Systems which give special attention to verbs of motion may distinguish separate cases for locations, origins and destinations which many languages distinguish syntactically. Japanese has the postpositions *de* and *ni* to distinguish ←(location)– from ←(destination)– and many inflected languages, among them German, Finnish, Latin and Turkish, mark the same distinction with affixes. English has prepositions for ←(origin)– (*from* or *out, down from* or *out of*) and for ←(destination)–(*across, along, around*), in addition to those for location (*behind, below, by*) and for destination (*at, to, toward*), and distinguishes location from destination with such pairs as *in / into* or *on / onto*. Though native speakers of English do not consistently mark the location / destination distinction with prepositions (relying instead on the verb: *the roses sat in a vase* versus *I put the roses in a vase*), case frames for locational and movement verbs can reflect the distinction and thereby disambiguate the preposition. Similarly, destinations must sometimes be distinguished from beneficiaries as in *Joe gave the rose to Jack for Mary*. And case schemata supplied with default values can make sense of some sentences in which the location appears as the subject (*the room smells*). Such a sentence might be translated into the representation for *I smell something disagreeable in the room*.

The origin and destination cases can also represent abstract transfers of possession or responsibility (where physical movement is not necessarily implied), as well as transfers of information. Or the ←(source)– and ←(recipient)– cases may be specified for such verbs as *give, sell, report,* and *tell*. Once we begin to specialize cases, however, it is hard to know where to stop. Should we have ←(material)– and ←(result)– for transformations (such as *he converted the travelers' checks into cash*)? And what about changes in some value, such as temperature, time, or speed: ←(old-value)– and ←(new-value)– for *the car accelerated from fifty to seventy miles per hour*? Rather than letting cases proliferate in this manner, we can capture generalizations by establishing a set of directional cases: ←(at)–, ←(from)– and ←(to)– that can be modified by a set of descriptive cases: ←(loc)–, ←(poss)–, ←(state)– and ←(value)–. Three directive and four descriptive cases would allow for twelve possible combinations.

1.5 Conceptual structures for representing events

Adhering closely to the wording of sentences, linguistically motivated case analysis makes explicit the combinational relationships obtaining among major constituents of sentences and builds representations that consist of the predicator and only those cases actually present in the sentence. Conceptually motivated systems go much further, interpreting the events described in sentences by supplying more information than the utterance contains. This is because sentences are usually parsimonious, offering only new information and leaving it to the listener to supply what is common knowledge or easily inferred. For the sentence *Tim likes* (or *wants*) *coffee*, a listener would gather that it is coffee drinking that Tim likes or wants to be doing. Similarly, a listener might gather from *Jill sent John a book* that John received it and gather from *Beth left for Boston* that in due course Beth also arrived in Boston. In each case the listener is supplying additional pieces of information (often called **implications**), which are highly probable though not certain: Tim may be contemplating an investment in coffee, Jill might have mailed the book, and Beth could have changed her destination. Implications can often be identified by the "test of cancelability": they can be denied without contradicting the sentence. Thus we can say *Jill sent John a book but he never received it*. Meanings that are inherent, rather than implicative cannot be canceled without creating an absurdity: *Jim went to Boston, but did not depart*.

Several computational systems apply these supplementary implications to the task of sentence understanding; among them, the most fully developed is **conceptual dependency theory**, the source of primitive ACTs mentioned in Chapter 8. "Dependency" refers to the dependent relationship between an action and its causes and consequences or between an entity and its attributes; "conceptual" distinguishes this approach from approaches that seek only to interpret the combinational relationships among constituents of a sentence. Basic units of meaning (or thought) are "conceptualizations," pieces of network representation resembling case schemata in that they contain predicators drawn from among the twelve ACTs and cases selected from a small set of cases (actor, objective, directive, recipient, and instrumental). Conceptualizations may also contain temporal, spatial, causal, and attributive relations. All cases in a given lexical entry are mandatory, however, because they belong not to the utterance only, but also to the concept. (Writing implies an instrument for writing, giving implies a recipient, and so on.)

Syntactic functions, together with selectional restrictions and preferences, determine what constituents fill which cases. If case slots are not filled from the sentence at hand, they remain in the conceptualization, and the interpreter has special resources for finding the relevant information in subsequent sentences. Another difference is that conceptualizations contain much more information than do case schemata; most have at least two predicators and many have causal links that relate predicators to one another and to states or changes of state. The conceptualization for *Tim likes coffee* would causally link the lexical entries for *like* (containing a state change to pleased) and *coffee* (containing the INGEST primitive):

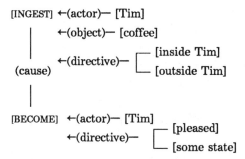

```
[INGEST]  ←(actor)— [Tim]
   |      ←(object)— [coffee]
   |                        ┌─ [inside Tim]
   |      ←(directive)—     │
(cause)                     └─ [outside Tim]
   |

[BECOME]  ←(actor)— [Tim]
          ←(directive)—  ┌─ [pleased]
                         └─ [some state]
```

That is, ingesting coffee causes Tim's state to change to pleased. If the
sentence were *Tim wants coffee,* the conceptualization would contain
the implications that Tim has mentally transferred (MTRANS) to the
speaker the intention that there should be either a physical transfer
(PTRANS) of coffee to him or of himself to a location (a place and
perhaps a cup) with coffee. The conceptualization will offer an
explanation if a subsequent sentence has Tim purchasing or drinking
or in new location.

Conceptual dependency theory achieves much of its expressive
power by explicating the relationships of instrumentality and causality.
Most acts have other acts as necessary instruments; thus INGEST
requires PTRANS, physically transferring either the food or the mouth
that ingests it, and an ATRANS of abstract possession or control of some
object requires either physical transfer of the object or a mental
transfer (MTRANS) via a verbal message or a document. A perceptual
event, in a sentence such as *Joe saw the crash,* decomposes into two
actions: the perceiving of the crash and the transfer of that information to the conscious mind:

```
[MTRANS]  ←(actor)— [Joe]
          ←(objective)— [crash]
          ←(instrument)— [ATTEND]  ←(actor)— [Joe]
                                   ←(objective)— [eye]
                         ┌─ [mind]
          ←(recipient)—  │
                         └─ [eyes]
                         ┌─ [Joe]
          ←(directive)—  │
                         └─ [location2]
```

Querying the system about Joe's knowledge of the crash, we would
need only look for an instance of MTRANS, and not for every conceivable
instruments of that transfer (being told by a friend, reading about it in
the paper, or whatever). Also it is often the case that utterances
concentrate on the central event and do not mention the instrumental
actions. When the exact nature of the instrumental action is not
explicit, as much as is known is specified. The sentence *Ann hit Bob,*
for example, does say what she propelled at him. Did she move her

hand against him or some other body part; did she swing a stick or bump him with her car?

[PROPEL] ←(actor)— [Ann]

       ←(objective)— [something]

       ←(directive)- ⌈ [Bob]
                  ⌊ [Ann]

       ←(instrument)- [DO] ←(actor)— [Ann]

                   ←(objective)— [something]

                   ←(directive) ⌈ [Bob]
                             ⌊ [Ann]

The dummy action [DO] as instrument affords a way of connecting events, and because PROPEL can have as instruments only MOVE, GRASP or PROPEL, the range of possibilities is constrained. Thus if the next sentence were *she apologized for the errant pitch*, the lexical entry for *pitch*

[PTRANS]   ←(agent)— [HUMAN]
            ←(object)— [ball]

provides a replacement for the [DO] and the connections among hitting, pitching and (eventually) apologizing become explicit.

In addition to instruments, conceptual dependency theory also stresses causal relations. Like implications, they are left unsaid but readily inferred. Both kinds can be informally identified using the test of cancelability: one event or state is implicit in another if inserting a *but* produces a sensible sentence;

Implicit: Jill's insult angered Lou **but** Lou did not become angry.
Inference: Jill left Boston for Milan **but** she did not get there.
Neither: Jill gave a ring to Lou **but** it did not rain.

The representation for *Jill's insult angered Lou* causally links the lexical entry for *anger* (a caused change of state) with the entry for *insult* (an act of MTRANS):

[MTRANS] ←(actor)— [Jill]

        ←(object)— [message]

        ←(recipient)— ⌈ [Lou]
                     ⌊ [Jill]

      — (cause)— [BECOME]   ←(actor)— [Lou]
                           ←(directive)— ⌈ [angry]
                                      ⌊ [some state]

Sometimes the conceptualization will make explicit what information is not available. For example, *Jim killed the fly* indicates that Jim performed some unknown causative act that resulted in the fly's undergoing a state change from alive to dead:

[DO] ←(actor)— [Jim]

└—(cause)— [BECOME]   ←(actor)— [fly]

←(directive)   ⎡ [dead]
                 ⎣ [alive]

If information about Jim's act becomes available, it can be substituted for the place-holding [DO]. Implications, however, are automatically generated when there is no evidence to the contrary; PTRANS, for example, generates the inference that Jill reached her destination:

[PTRANS]   ←(actor)— [Jill

| ←(object)— [Jill]

           ←(directive)   ⎡ [Milan]

(cause)   ⎣ [Boston]

|

[Jill] ←(location)— [Milan]

The problem, of course, is when to stop generating implications. Principled ways of determining what should and should not be part of a conceptualization are difficult to come by.

The examples thus far have all involved states or changes in states, but events can also cause events, and sometimes the causation is mutual. An example is the reciprocal transfer underlying such verbs as *buy, sell, purchase, vend*, and the like. *Jen sold a car to Tom* would be represented:

[ATRANS]   ←(actor)— [Jen]

| ←(object)— [money]

(cause)   ←(directive)—   ⎡ [Tom]
                           ⎣ [Jen]

|

[ATRANS]   ←(actor)— [Tom]

           ←(object)—[car]

           ←(directive)—   ⎡ [Jen]
                           ⎣ [Tom]

In addition to locally causal relations, there are other kinds of continuity. Sometimes speakers use surface cues (mainly temporal and causal conjunctives) to call attention to these, but speakers also rely on the listeners' experience of the connectedness of events, for example, the sequence of events in a restaurant: being seated, scanning the menu, ordering food, eating the meal, paying the bill, and so on. The next step for the developers of conceptual dependency theory was multi-sentence discourse and a theory of discourse comprehension based on scripts and plans, which afford chains of related events. Chapter eleven explores scripts, plans, and other representations of discourse continuity.

Section two: Semantic Interpretation

2.1 Modular processing with interpretation rules

The classical model for sentence processing, until recently assumed by most linguistic theory, has a syntactic module that parses the sentence then hands a representation of its structure to a separate semantic module for interpretation.   Syntactic and semantic processing are autonomous, and semantic information does not guide, alter, or in any way influence the parse. Semantics could not resolve local ambiguities, blocking, for example, the garden path in *the injury examined by the doctor was serious* by establishing that *injury* does not satisfy the selectional restriction for *examined*. For ambiguities that parsing cannot resolve, such as prepositional phrase attachment in *he ate the soup with a spoon*, the parser would hand two completed analyses to the semantics interpreter. These drawbacks make autonomous parsing an unlikely model for human sentence comprehension, but separating the parser from the interpreter simplifies both and allows us to investigate how interpretation might use syntactic information.

Interpretation requires two kinds of operations. One substitutes schemata and case frames for syntactic structures: the other merges those schemata and frames to build representations of sentence meaning. For the sentence, *children walk*, two **interpretation rules** would be retrieved from the lexicon:

children:

$$
\begin{bmatrix} \text{NP [HEAD: children]} \\ \text{[NUMBER: PLURAL]} \end{bmatrix} \rightarrow \begin{bmatrix} \text{[HUMAN: a]} \leftarrow\text{(attribute)} \text{— [-ADULT]} \end{bmatrix}
$$

walk:

$$
\begin{bmatrix} \text{S [VERB: walk]} \\ \text{[SUBJECT: ANIMAL]} \\ *\text{[P [PREP: from]} \\ \text{[POBJ: PLACE(x)]]} \\ *\text{[P [PREP: to]} \\ \text{[POBJ: PLACE(y)]} \\ *\text{[ADVERB: PLACE(y)]} \end{bmatrix} \rightarrow \begin{bmatrix} \text{[GO]} \leftarrow\text{(agent)— [SUBJECT]} \\ \leftarrow\text{(patient)— [SUBJECT]} \\ \leftarrow\text{(origin)— [PLACE(x)]} \\ \leftarrow\text{(destination)— [PLACE(y)]} \end{bmatrix}
$$

Resembling the rewrite rules of phrase structure grammars, interpretation rules specify how the syntactic structures on the left side of the rule can be mapped onto semantic structures on the right side if certain selectional restrictions (also specified on the left side) are met. The first rule stipulates a plural NP in which the head noun is the word children; it would substitute a schema in which the concept HUMAN is modified by the attribute relation to specify non-adult. The second rule stipulates a sentence in which the main verb is *walk* and the subject is ANIMAL. The sentence may optionally (as signified by the *) contain an origin or destination. An origin will be the object of the preposition *from*, and the destination will be either the object of *to* or an adverb of place (*home, there,* etc.). If the sentence meets these requirements, the case frame on the left side of the rule is applicable. The subject of the sentence becomes the agent and patient (when we walk we transport ourselves); a different sense of *walk* would have a direct object as patient, as in *I walked the dog*. Guided by the variables (x) and (y), any PLACEs of origin and destination are also assigned. The second operation merges the schema for *children* with the case frame for *walk* to produce:

[GO: #14] ←(agent)— [HUMAN: #7] ←(attribute)— [-ADULT]

←(patient)— [HUMAN: #7] ←(attribute)— [-ADULT]

←(origin)— [PLACE: #11]

←(destination)— [PLACE: #12]

Thus syntax directs the merging of semantic schemata, specifying the constituents that fill each of the slots.

2.2 An approach via heads and modifiers

Combining the case frame for *walk* with the schema for *children* does not require much syntactic information. For more complicated sentences, however, syntax must guide the interpreter step by step. This means that the parser should afford a representation of the syntax that is readable by the semantic interpreter. For our purposes we can assume a register structure resembling that in Figure 3. Shallower than a phrase marker, the tree has nodes descending from the sentence node which identify the major functional constituents of the sentence (subject, direct object, and so on.) As we saw in Chapter 7, such a structure is within the capabilities of an augmented transition network or augmented phrase structure grammar. Aside from some reordering of constituents, the only important difference from the register structure shown there is in the designation of "heads." Head and modifier representation predates phrase structures; the method of sentence "diagramming" that some of us learned in grade school is an

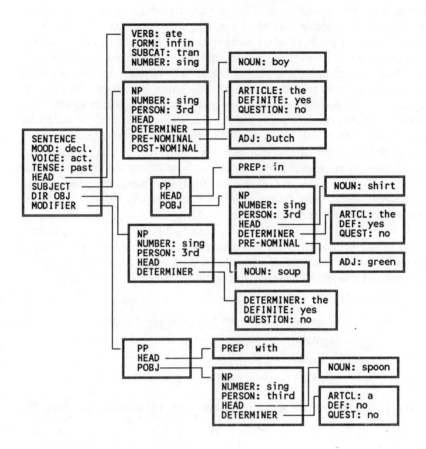

Alternative (non-minimal attachment):

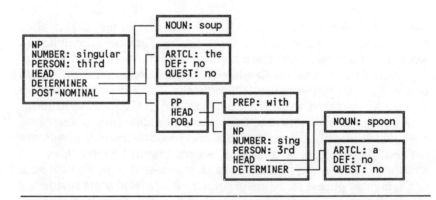

Figure 3. Register structure for *The Dutch boy in a green shirt ate the soup with a spoon*, with alternate attachments for the final PP.

example.   "Dependency grammars," sometimes used in question answering and machine translation, employ heads and modifiers for convenience in representing semantic relationships. For our purposes, the essential point is that each major constituent has a head, usually a single word for which a lexical entry may be retrieved. The main verb is the head of the sentence; a common noun, proper noun, or pronoun is the head of a noun phrase, and a preposition is the head of the prepositional phrase.

The interpreter traverses the tree, visiting first the head of the sentence, then the heads of its functional constituents in the order subject, direct object, indirect object or any sentence-level prepositional phrase. In the sample sentence *Eat* is the head, and the lexicon distinguishes two senses:

$$
\begin{bmatrix}
\text{S} & \text{[VERB: eat]} \\
& \text{[SUBJ: ANIMATE]} \\
& \text{*[DIR OBJ: EDIBLE]]} \\
& \text{*[MOD: [PP [PREP with]} \\
& \qquad\qquad \text{[POBJ UTENSIL]]]}
\end{bmatrix}
\rightarrow
\begin{bmatrix}
\text{[INGEST]} & \text{←(agent)— [SUBJ]} \\
& \text{←(patient)— [DIROBJ]} \\
& \text{←(instr)— [POBJ]}
\end{bmatrix}
$$

$$
\begin{bmatrix}
\text{S} & \text{[VERB: eat]} \\
& \text{[SUBJ: CORROSIVE]} \\
& \text{[DIR OBJ: PHYS-OBJ]}
\end{bmatrix}
\rightarrow
\begin{bmatrix}
\text{[DISSOLVE]} & \text{←(force)— [SUBJ]} \\
& \text{←(patient)— [DIR OBJ]}
\end{bmatrix}
$$

The left side of the first rule will match a sentence in which the main verb is *eat* and the subject ANIMATE; optionally it may contain an EDIBLE direct object and a UTENSIL as the object in an S-level prepositional phrase. If these conditions are met, the rule interprets *eat* as an act of ingesting, its subject as the semantic agent, its direct object as the semantic patient, and the object of *with* as the instrument. The second rule interprets *eat* as the act of dissolving, requires that its subject be a corrosive (such as an acid), and interprets it as a force. There being no way to choose between these senses until some of the NPs are interpreted, both case frames are attached to the S register, and the interpreter descends to the subject NP. The head of its NP is *boy* with the lexical entry:

$$
\begin{bmatrix}
\text{NP [NOUN: boy]}
\end{bmatrix}
\rightarrow
\begin{bmatrix}
\text{[PERSON: boy]} & \text{←(gender)— [MALE]} \\
& \text{←(attribute)— [-ADULT]}
\end{bmatrix}
$$

The left side of the rule matches the subject noun, so the noun register is rewritten as specified on the right side of the rule. Ascending back to the S level, the interpreter determines whether either case frame for the senses of *eat* matches an ANIMATE subject. Only the INGEST frame matches, so the DISSOLVE frame is discarded. The right side of the rule for *boy* is merged with the agent for INGEST.

Next the interpreter descends to the NP modifiers: *Dutch* has one adjectival sense, which requires an NP with a person or institution (superordinate HUMAN) as the HEAD.

$$\left[\begin{array}{ll} \text{NP} & \text{[ADJECTIVE: Dutch]} \\ & \text{[HEAD: HUMAN]} \end{array} \right] \rightarrow \left[\; \text{[HEAD]} \leftarrow\text{(nationality)}- \text{[Dutch]} \; \right]$$

Once the specified head, HUMAN, is restricted to PERSON, the representation for *Dutch* merges with the representation for *boy*. Next comes the prepositional phrase with the entries:

$$\left[\begin{array}{ll} \text{PP} & \text{[PREP: with]} \\ & \text{[POBJ: ALL]} \end{array} \right] \rightarrow \left[\; \text{[HEAD]} \leftarrow\text{(possession)}- \text{[POBJ]} \; \right]$$

$$\left[\begin{array}{ll} \text{NP} & \text{[NOUN: shirt]} \end{array} \right] \rightarrow \left[\; \text{GARMENT: shirt} \; \right]$$

In sequence, the entry for *with* merges with that for the developing NP, as does the entry for *shirt* and the appropriate entry for the ambiguous *green*, chosen through selectional restrictions from the following:

$$\left[\begin{array}{ll} \text{NP} & \text{[HEAD: PHYS-OBJ]} \\ & \text{[ADJECTIVE: green]} \end{array} \right] \rightarrow \left[\; \text{[HEAD]} \leftarrow\text{(attribute)}- \text{[COLOR: green]} \; \right]$$

$$\left[\begin{array}{ll} \text{NP} & \text{[HEAD: FRUIT]} \\ & \text{[ADJECTIVE: green]} \end{array} \right] \rightarrow \left[\; \text{[HEAD]} \leftarrow\text{(attribute)}- \text{[UNRIPE]} \; \right]$$

$$\left[\begin{array}{ll} \text{NP} & \text{[HEAD: PERSON]} \\ & \text{[ADJECTIVE: green]} \end{array} \right] \rightarrow \left[\; \text{[HEAD]} \leftarrow\text{(attribute)}- \text{[NAIVE]} \; \right]$$

Having exhausted the subject NP, the interpreter reascends to the S level, encounters the specifications for a patient, an EDIBLE as direct object. The schema for *soup* qualifies and is merged with the case frame.

Thus far the ambiguities have been semantic: two senses of *eat* and three of *green*, but the concluding phrase (*with a spoon*) presents a syntactic ambiguity in that it can attach either to the S (as a semantic instrument) or to the preceding NP (in a sentence such as *he ate the soup with barley* or *ate the bowl of soup*; see the alternative parse in Figure 3). This is a common ambiguity in part because prepositional phrases occurring in this position can specify not only instruments, but also beneficiaries and other relations as well:

> The boy ate the soup for his mother.
> The boy ate the soup for lunch.
> The boy ate the soup at noon.
> The boy ate the soup at home.
> The boy ate the soup with reluctance.
> The boy ate the soup with a grimace.

In the first of these, the object of the preposition is the beneficiary. The objects in the next three are circumstantial cases which, because they can attach to nearly every verb, are interpreted by rules for prepositions. For example, *at* specifies a time or a place:

$$\begin{bmatrix} \text{S MODIFIER} & [\text{PP [PREP: at]} \\ & [\text{POBJ: TIME]]} \end{bmatrix} \rightarrow \begin{bmatrix} [\text{VERB] } \leftarrow(\text{at time})- [\text{POBJ}] \end{bmatrix}$$

$$\begin{bmatrix} \text{S MODIFIER} & [\text{PP [PREP: at]} \\ & [\text{POBJ: PLACE]]} \end{bmatrix} \rightarrow \begin{bmatrix} [\text{VERB] } \leftarrow(\text{location})- [\text{POBJ}] \end{bmatrix}$$

If we suppose that the parser produces only one analysis at a time (reparsing the sentence to discover an alternative only if the first is rejected), we would want to consider first the possibility that the prepositional phrase proposes a case. Interestingly, this is precisely what syntax will give us. Minimal attachment would make the preferred parse attach the phrase to the verb. In this case, the interpreter will recognize that *spoon* is an instrument and will not need to consider the wide range of alternatives that could be attached to soup via the ←(accompanies)– relation specified by *with*. The interpreter has now accounted for the entire sentence and has built the following representation of its meaning:

[INGEST: #4] ←(agent)– [HUMAN: #3] ←(gender)– [MALE]
←(attribute)– [ADULT]
←(possession)–
[COLOR: green] —(attribute)→   [GARMENT: shirt]
←(patient)– [EDIBLE: #23] ←(attribute)– [FLOWSTUFF]
←(instrument)– [UTENSIL: #13]

If the prepositional phrase does not meet the selectional restrictions in the verb's case frame or those for one of the relations, semantic interpretation fails and the parser must attempt an alternative. In the example *with barley*, the prepositional phrase can (non-minimally) be attached to the preceding noun phrase. This semantic relationship may be captured by an interpretation rule for *with* that makes the preposition's object an attribute:

$$\begin{bmatrix} \text{NP} & [\text{HEAD: ALL]} \\ & [\text{PREP: with]} \\ & [\text{POBJ: ALL]} \end{bmatrix} \rightarrow \begin{bmatrix} [\text{NOUN] } \leftarrow(\text{attribute})- [\text{POBJ}] \end{bmatrix}$$

Because the number of cases is small, it is better to check for them before applying a rule this general. Even if, in place of the general rule, we employ rules that capture the specific relationships between NPs joined by *with* (or another preposition), the relationships expressed by non-minimally attached noun phrase modifiers are so numerous, that checking first for case will usually be more efficient. *With*, for example, can mean companion of (*Joe with his friend*), adjacent to (*flowers with ferns*), in control of (*she left the letter with me*), in support of (*are you with me*), part of (*the hand with the broken finger*), and so on. Thus the parsing preference for minimal attachment expedites semantic interpretation by giving precedence to the analysis that can be quickly confirmed or disconfirmed.

2.3 Sequences of semantic decisions

An important consideration in designing a parser, as we have seen, is the sequence in which decisions are made. Top-down, bottom-up, and mixed-mode approaches have their separate advantages in coping with local ambiguities. Because semantic ambiguities are equally problematic, the sequence in which the interpreter makes decisions is no less important. Although the essential idea is to make the most timely use of information, no principled strategy has yet emerged–only a few heuristics that facilitate interpretation of major constituents.

When more than one semantic rule might apply, the order in which they are tried is important. Using just functional specifications and selectional restrictions, the interpreter could decide between the two senses of *eat*. But as we have already seen (with *shatter*), agents, instruments, even patients, can serve as the subject. For this more challenging form of semantic ambiguity, one answer is in the "subject choice hierarchy," a very useful heuristic from Fillmore's seminal discussion of case.

- □ If there is an agent, it must be the subject.

- □ If there is no agent, but there are both an instrument and patient then the instrument must be the subject and the patient the object.

- □ If there is neither an agent nor an instrument, then the patient is the subject.

Fillmore's hierarchy suggests that the lexical entry for *shatter* should contain rules that look first for the agent as subject, then for an instrument as subject, and as a last resort for a patient as subject:

$$
\begin{bmatrix}
\text{S} & [\text{VERB: shatter}] \\
& [\text{SUBJ: ANIMATE}] \\
& [\text{DIR OBJ: PHYS-OBJ}] \\
& {}^*[\text{MOD: (PP PREP with}] \\
& \quad \text{POBJ PHYS-OBJ)}
\end{bmatrix}
\rightarrow
\begin{bmatrix}
[\text{BREAK}] & \leftarrow(\text{agent})- [\text{SUBJECT}] \\
& \leftarrow(\text{patient})- [\text{DIR OBJ}] \\
& \leftarrow(\text{instrument})- [\text{POBJ}]
\end{bmatrix}
$$

$$\begin{bmatrix} \text{S} & [\text{VERB: shatter}] \\ & [\text{SUBJ: PHYS-OBJ}] \\ & *[\text{DIR OBJ: PHYS-OBJ}] \end{bmatrix} \rightarrow \begin{bmatrix} [\text{BREAK}] & \leftarrow(\text{instrument})— [\text{SUBJ}] \\ & \leftarrow(\text{patient})— [\text{DIR OBJ}] \end{bmatrix}$$

$$\begin{bmatrix} \text{S} & [\text{VERB: shatter}] \\ & [\text{SUBJECT: PHYS-OBJ}] \end{bmatrix} \rightarrow \begin{bmatrix} [\text{BREAK} \leftarrow(\text{patient})— [\text{DIR OBJ}] \end{bmatrix}$$

Upon encountering a sentence with *shatter* as its HEAD, the interpreter would retrieve all three rules and attempt them in the order given. If the subject is not a potential agent, the interpreter moves on to the second rule. If, after satisfying the requirement for a subject in the second rule, the interpreter fails to find a direct object, it retrieves the third rule.

Where Fillmore's subject hierarchy does not apply, rules can be considered in the order of their likelihood. Consider, for example, that *flew* is ambiguous between GO and OPERATE. On the assumption that more sentences have people flying as passengers than as pilots, the rules for the GO sense might precede the rule for the OPERATE sense:

$$\begin{bmatrix} \text{S} & [\text{VERB: fly}] \\ & [\text{SUBJ: HUMAN}] \\ * & [\text{MOD: (PP PREP from}] \\ & \quad \text{POBJ1 PLACE})] \\ * & [\text{MOD: (PP PREP to}] \\ & \quad \text{POBJ2 PLACE})] \\ * & [\text{MOD: (PP PREP by}] \\ & \quad \text{POBJ3 VEHICLE}] \end{bmatrix} \rightarrow \begin{bmatrix} [\text{GO:}] & \leftarrow(\text{agent})— [\text{SUBJ}] \\ & \leftarrow(\text{patient})— [\text{SUBJ}] \\ & \leftarrow(\text{origin})— [\text{POBJ1}] \\ & \leftarrow(\text{destination})— [\text{POBJ2}] \\ & \leftarrow(\text{instrument})— [\text{POBJ3}] \end{bmatrix}$$

$$\begin{bmatrix} \text{S} & [\text{VERB: fly}] \\ & [\text{SUBJ: HUMAN}] \\ & [\text{DIR OBJ: VEHICLE}] \\ * & [\text{MOD: (PP PREP from}] \\ & \quad \text{POBJ1 PLACE})] \\ * & [\text{MOD: (PP PREP to}] \\ & \quad \text{POBJ2 PLACE})] \end{bmatrix} \rightarrow \begin{bmatrix} [\text{OPERATE: }] & \leftarrow(\text{agent})— [\text{SUBJ}] \\ & \leftarrow(\text{patient})— [\text{DOBJ}] \\ & \leftarrow(\text{origin})— [\text{POBJ1}] \\ & \leftarrow(\text{dest})— [\text{POBJ2}] \\ \\ \mathrel{\rule[-2ex]{0.4pt}{4ex}} \\ \llcorner(\text{cause})- & \begin{bmatrix} \text{GO:} \\ \text{as above} \end{bmatrix} \end{bmatrix}$$

The GO sense is assumed unless the interpreter encounters a VEHICLE in the register for direct objects. Trying rules in the order of their likeliness is simple common sense, but is especially useful when working with the "sublanguages" of limited domains such as might be employed in database retrieval or machine translation of technical documents. Because sublanguages are small and tend to be more highly constrained than the language at large, the probability that a

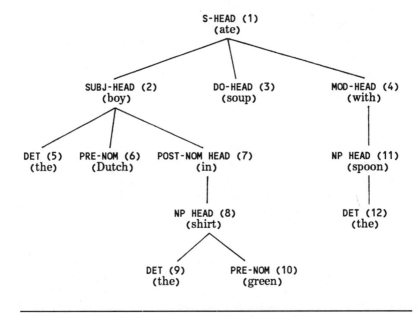

Figure 4: Traversal order for recursive interpretation

given word will have a given sense reliably determines the order in
which rules should be tried. Whether probabilities are sufficiently high
in the language at large is now an open question but may be decided
by the large corpora that are currently under study.

To decide between the second and third rules for *shatter* and the
two rules for *fly*, the interpreter visits the verb and subject nodes, then,
failing to find a direct object, it backtracks to the verb node to find a
different rule. By no means are these unusual instances, since it often
happens that the subject does not distinguish between senses of a verb.
Discharge is another example: selecting among its many senses
depends on whether the direct object is a person, a weapon, electrical
energy, a responsibility, and so on. In other cases, the subject will be
lexically ambiguous: *one* and *they* do not necessarily refer to HUMANs,
nor do nouns like *companion* and *group* (or, for that matter, *pilot*).
Indeed the case frame is often necessary to disambiguate the noun
phrase. One solution is to have the interpreter proceed with all possibilities in parallel (or pseudo parallel) and fill multiple case frames
until one proves viable, but that exacts a cost in memory and computational complexity.

Whereas the interpretive strategy described in the preceding section
builds composite schemata for entire noun and prepositional phrases
before attempting to merge them with the case frame, other interpreters employ a breadth-first strategy, seeking to fill the case frame
slots with heads of NPs, deferring any NP modifiers and qualifiers for

a second stage. Such a sequence is easily implemented using recursion. (Figure 4 gives the order of traversal for *the Dutch boy in a green shirt ate the soup with a spoon*.) The idea is that although modifiers are occasionally helpful in disambiguating the heads of noun and prepositional phrases, more disambiguation goes on at levels higher in the register structure, because heads guide the choice of case frames, and case frames choose among alternative heads. Yet another solution is to sequence the interpretation rules so that with such verbs as *shatter*, *fly*, and *discharge*, the interpreter gives priority to finding an appropriate patient in deciding between the candidate case frames, in effect letting semantics rather than syntax guide the interpreter. Chapter 10 looks into the advantages and disadvantages of giving privilege to semantics.

Though this breadth-first strategy will sometimes be more efficient, providing a timely decision on syntactic ambiguities, it may overlook some prospects for merging. Consider, for example, *the boy ate the bowl of soup*. Bowls cannot be eaten and failing to find an EDIBLE head of the NP, the interpreter would be blocked. Only after the interpreter builds a representation for the entire noun phrase, will it find a way of identifying a patient. One interpretation rule for *of* will identify the relationship between a container and its contents:

$$\left[\begin{array}{l} \text{NP[HEAD: CONTAINER]} \\ \text{*[[PREP: of]} \\ \text{[POBJ: PHYS-OBJ]]} \end{array} \right] \rightarrow \left[\begin{array}{l} \text{[HEAD] –(contains)}\rightarrow \text{[POBJ]} \end{array} \right]$$

Now the phrase can be merged via *soup* with the case frame for *eat*:

[INGEST: eat1] ←(patient)— [EDIBLE: soup1] ←(attribute)— [FLOWSTUFF]

[UTENSIL: bowl] ←(contains) ⌐

Thus neither depth-first and breadth-first interpretation has a decisive advantage; what does make a difference, as we will see in the next chapter is the timely application of semantic information to resolve syntactic ambiguities.

2.4 Capturing the salient generalizations

Thus far we have implicitly assumed that each verb entry in the lexicon will have several rules. For unambiguous verbs, such as *shatter*, separate and partially redundant rules will interpret sentences in which the subject is the agent, the patient, the instrument and so on. For ambiguous verbs (and the most frequently occurring verbs typically have many meanings), the number of rules multiply and interpretation becomes sluggish at best. Thus it is important to exploit regularities. The majority of verbs in English and all other languages describe physical actions and can be subdivided into those involving volition (hence requiring an agent) and those that do not (allowing either an agent or a force). In turn, each class divides into two subclasses depending on whether they take patients. Those that do take patients subdivide into four subclasses depending on whether they take instruments and beneficiaries. These classifications can be represented hierarchically; thus along one branch we would have:

AGENT

PATIENT

-INST -BENEF   -INST +BENEF   +INST -BENEF   +BENEF +INST

Sleep would be marked AGENT/FORCE, allowing only an agent; *admire* would be PATIENT; *destroy* would be marked +BENEF +INST because it allows all four cases. What is more, selectional restrictions can be specified for each of the cases. The majority would be defaults, applicable in most instances, but overridden in the lexical entries for certain verbs. Usually, the patient will be a physical object or a substance, but *shatter* and *boil* exert selectional restrictions that are more specific.

The hierarchy would also need to specify cases and selectional restrictions for other kinds of verbs expressing quite different relationships between sentence constituents. Consider, for example, that with the verbs we have considered thus far we can plausibly ask and answer:

> I shattered the window.
> What did you do to the window?   I shattered it.

But with many cognitive verbs we cannot:

> I knew the difference.
> What did you do to the difference?   I knew it.

A recent version of M.A.K. Halliday's systemic grammar promises a way of distinguishing kinds of verbs. The idea is to classify sentences into a conceptual types by the process or relationship expressed (usually by the verb). Whereas "material process clauses" correspond roughly to our sentences expressing physical actions, "mental process clauses" employ verbs of perception *(see, hear, smell, sense)*, cognition

| material process: | *The woman handed my sheepdog   a bone.* |
| | (agent)   (benefactive) (medium) |

The tourists took the wrong road.
(agent)   (range)

| verbal process: | *The suspect told the police   his story.* |
| | (sayer)   (addressee) (verbalization) |

| mental process: | *The audience noticed his mistake.* |
| | (cognizant)   (phenomenon) |

| equative: | *The woman is an inventor.* |
| | (identified)   (identifier) |

| attributive: | *The inventor is/becomes/remains persistent.* |
| | (carrier)   (attribute) |

| material-attributive: | *The carpenter got   the building   finished.* |
| | (agent)   (medium/carrier) (attribute) |

| verbal-attributive: | *The chair declared the meeting adjourned.* |
| | (sayer)   (carrier)   (attribute) |

| mental-attributive: | *Everyone   thought   him   rebellious.* |
| | (cognizant)   (carrier)   (attribute) |

Figure 5: process types and their participants

(understand, think, forgot), and reaction *(dislike, please, admire)* that do not change the state of the direct object, and "equative clauses" employ verbs (such as *equal* and *represent*) to assert the identity between subject and direct object. Each type has its own small set of cases (called **participants**), and verbs governing each type divide into subgroups that allow one, two, or more participants; *understand,* for instance, permits only a cognizant subject in the active voice and only a phenomenon in the passive, but *dislike* requires both in the active voice. Thus we have the makings of a hierarchy that would comprise all verbs. (The sample sentences in Figure 5 will suggest how this analysis works.) Note the useful distinctions among medium, verbalization, and phenomenon and between benefactive and addressee, as well as the distinctions among kinds of complements.

2.5 Interpreting modality

So far propositions have been couched as simple declarations, but natural languages have other ways of offering propositions, and these need to be interpreted. Consider, for instance the small, but important differences among these sentences:

> The leader saw Joe find Ted.
> The leader regretted that Joe found Ted.
> The leader believed that Joe found Ted.

Each consists of a matrix sentence and an embedded sentence and could be parsed into the register structure given in Figure 6. In the first sentence, the matrix and embedded sentences are both true of the same possible world and can be interpreted by the rule:

$$
\begin{bmatrix} \text{[VERB: saw]} \\ \text{[SUBJ: ANIMAL]} \\ \text{[DIR OBJ:} \\ \quad \text{PROPOSITION} \end{bmatrix} \rightarrow \begin{bmatrix} \text{[THINK]} & \leftarrow\text{(cognizant)}- & \text{[SUBJECT]} \\ & \leftarrow\text{(phenomenon)}- & \text{[DIR OBJ [SENT]]} \end{bmatrix}
$$

In the second sentence, the truth of the embedded sentence is presupposed, and it remains true whether the matrix sentence is true or not. In the third, the truth of the embedded sentence is independent of the truth of the matrix. To put this in terms of possible worlds, the two propositions belong to different possible worlds, either of which may be true or false of the real world without entailing anything about the truth or falsehood of the other proposition. The interpretation rule for *believe* resembles that for *see*, except that it identifies the embedded proposition as a belief:

$$\leftarrow\text{(phenomenon)}- \text{[DIR OBJ [SENTENCE]} \leftarrow\text{(belief)]}$$

The monadic relation ←(belief)– is a modal operator. Like AND and IMPLIES (sometimes called logical operators), a modal operator takes a proposition as its argument. Unlike the logical operators, the truth of the belief is not assured. It also differs from the modal operator [PROPOSITION] ←(known)–, which stipulates that a proposition is true, though only in the possible world of the utterance. Propositions that are believed must be partitioned in "belief spaces" dedicated to agents who do the believing; special circumstances may require additional layers of partitioning to account for beliefs about believing (*He believes that I believe*). Taking care with the modal operator and belief spaces is worthwhile, because logicians have developed special "epistemic logics," which extend the predicate calculus for reasoning with modes of belief and modes of knowledge. Representing beliefs is also important in interpreting certain performative verbs: the sentence *I promise to come home* has among other presuppositions the beliefs that I will be able to come home and that the person to whom I am speaking wants me to.

Natural languages have other ways of couching propositions for which extensions to the predicate calculus have been developed. Propositions can be expressed in terms of their necessity and possibility:

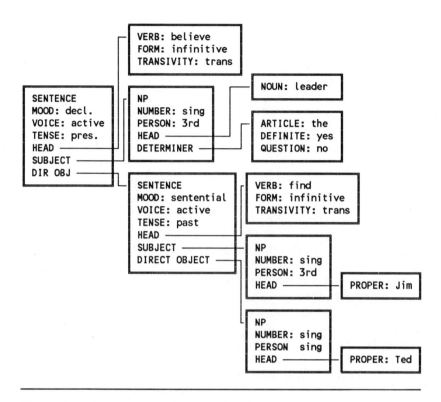

Figure 6:   register structure for an embedded sentence

> It is necessarily the case that Joe found Ted.
> Joe must have found Ted.
> Possibly, Joe found Ted.
> Joe could find Ted.

Since possibility and necessity are modes of truth, "alethic logics" accommodate them to the truth-preserving system of predicate calculus by mediating rules such as "anything that is true is possible" and "anything that is not possible is necessarily false."

Along a different dimension, natural language can stipulate that propositions are true only at certain times. To accommodate such sentences as

> Joe always (or sometimes or never) looks for Ted.
> Joe did (or will) look for Ted.

predicate calculus has been given temporal and tense extensions. Similarly, "deontic" extensions make it possible to represent and reason within modes of permission or obligation:

Joe may (or is permitted to) look for Ted.
Joe ought to (or is obliged to) look for Ted.

Beyond these are other modes in which the endless fertility of natural languages allows us to couch propositions:

It is probable that Joe looked for Ted.
It is generally known that Joe looked for Ted.
He doubted that Joe looked for Ted.
He agreed that Joe found Ted.
He preferred that Joe look for Ted.
He promised that Joe would look for Ted.

Extending the predicate calculus to incorporate more and still more of the modes expressible in natural language requires painstaking labor. In particular, logicians must carefully test for completeness (does the integrated system derive every proposition that is a true consequent of a given set of true premises?) and for consistency (will the system ever allow one to derive a contradiction in which a proposition and its negation are both true?).

Several of the modes are expressed by modal auxiliaries: *must have* for necessity, *may have* for possibility, *will have* for tense, *may* for permission, and *ought* for obligation. Generative grammars usually represent these as AUX, an abstract category that comprises tense and optional modals, forms of *have* and forms of *be*:

S → NP AUX VP

AUX → TENSE (MODAL) (have+) (be+) (NEGATION)

That is, tense is mandatory since every sentence has a tense, but the other modes are optional constituents. An augmented parser can build a special AUX register to hold them, and interpretation rules can consult that register immediately after they consult the verb register. Thus an interpretation rule for the verb *find* would first posit a case frame, then an interpretation rule for AUX:

$$\begin{bmatrix} \text{AUX} \\ \text{MODE: possible} \\ \text{TENSE: past} \end{bmatrix} \rightarrow \begin{bmatrix} [\text{[SENTENCE]} & \leftarrow\text{(possible)} \\ & \leftarrow\text{(past)} \end{bmatrix} \end{bmatrix}$$

will embed the proposition expressed by the case frame within a logical form indicating its modality then embed that logical form within another indicating its tense.

Exercises

1. Explain how semantic relations or cases would (or would not) help resolve the syntactic ambiguities in the following sentences.

> I worked for an hour.
> I bought it for Laura.
> He saw the molecule with a microscope.
> The plastic boxes decay.
> The dog sees a car and barks.

2. Using the taxonomy of cases in section 1.4, assign a case to each of the noun and prepositional phrases in the following sentences:

> Although John detested apple pie, he baked one for Mary.
> He was an experienced carpenter, but his hammer bent the nail.

3. Devise a schema that represents (and distinguishes) the meanings of the two possessives in the phrase:

> Donna's mother's house.

4. Using as models the linguistically motivated case frames in section 1.3 devise a representation for the sentence:

> Jack traded his bike for Jane's typewriter.

then using the conceptually motivated schemata in section 1.5, devise a schema representing the same sentence.

5. Devise interpretation rules for the intransitive verb *sleep* and the temporal sense of the preposition *for*. Assuming minimal attachment, show the steps by which the sentence *the boy slept for an hour* would be interpreted.

6. Using the case frames in section one as models, devise a pair of case frames that would distinguish two senses of the verb *run*: to move rapidly on foot and to operate a machine.

7. Show the steps by which your interpretation rules for run would analyze *He ran the machine on the table.*

8. Assuming minimal attachment, show the steps by which the locally ambiguous sentence *he ran the shredder for waste paper* would be interpreted.

9. What would be the consequence for the method of interpretation described in this chapter of using a parser that does not give preference to minimally attached prepositional phrases?

Further reading

The idea of compositionality derives from Gottlob Frege and is assumed by most semantic theories; see Frege (1952), Lyons (1981) and Fodor and Pylyshyn (1988). On conceptual relations and their representation, see Sowa (1984). The original proposal for case grammar is Fillmore (1968); see also Jackendoff (1972 and 1986), Carlson (1986) and the papers in Wilkins (1988). Bruce (1975) offers a survey of the case systems used in early computational projects; Charniak (1981) explores the relationship between cases and frames. On resolving semantic ambiguities, see Hirst (1987) and the papers in Gorfein (1989). Conceptual dependency theory was proposed in Schank (1972) and has since been substantially modified. For a more recent version, together with a lucid account of sentence processing, see Schank and Riesbeck (1981). Three alternatives, all highly developed, are "preference semantics" (Wilks 1975, Fass and Wilks, 1983), "conceptual graphs" (Sowa, 1984), and "word experts" (Small and Riegel, 1982 and Small, 1983). For more on semantic interpretation, see Hirst (1987), Allen (1987), D.L. Waltz (1989). For modal logic, a good starting point is Hughes and Cresswell (1968); see also Leblanc (1973) and the extended discussion in Lyons (1977).

Chapter 10

Integrating Syntactic and Semantic Processing

Section one: Only Syntax and Semantics

1.1 Advantages of timely semantics

Though it is profitable to separate syntax and semantics for purposes of study, few would propose that people perform a complete parsing of a sentence before undertaking to interpret its meaning. Introspective evidence suggests otherwise. Not only can we interpret sentences that are broken off in mid course:

> The dog walked over to . . . .

but we also have some clear semantic expectations of what will follow.

Integration of at least syntax and semantics is compelled by syntactic ambiguity. Local ambiguities are ubiquitous, and though some resolve themselves quickly, others persist much longer. A parser, whether operating top-down or bottom-up, would not disambiguate *can* in *the wealthy can eat soup* until it had seen the entire sentence. What is worse, many sentences have multiple parses, and syntax alone cannot choose between them. In *I saw the elderly man and child*, a parser cannot decide that *elderly* modifies only *man*. Nor can it decide whether the "squinting" prepositional phrase in *as he unlocked the door with his key the fire engine arrived* modifies *unlocked* or *arrived*. None of these ambiguities impede communication even for an instant because we know that cans are not wealthy, children are not elderly, and keys unlock doors. This suggests that semantics comes into play early in the process of sentence comprehension.

Timely semantic interpretation can also distinguish the quite different structures of *the child drew near the edge of the page* and *the plane drew near the edge of the tarmac*. Additional instances are legion.

341

Among the most frequently occurring words in most languages are conjunctions, and because they can join words or phrases of any kind or sentences, they engender notorious ambiguities.   Consider the pattern in *he has eaten the apple and orange*, then consider *he has eaten the apple and bought milk* (did he eat purchased *milk*?), *he has eaten the apple and the plastic wrapping can be discarded* (did he eat *plastic*? *wrapping*? *can*?).   Ellipsis presents equally formidable problems. Assuming that a parser can deduce that a verb is missing in *Joe said that the dog eats meat and the cat fish* (and that is no mean feat), it cannot, without semantic guidance, eliminate parses that have the cat saying "*fish*" or "*the dog eats fish.*" These ambiguities are not noticed, probably because of selectional restrictions (for semantic patient following *eat*, for instance, or for the agent of *speak*). Semantics can even function with incomplete information.   If someone unacquainted with French soups encounters *I ate the vichyssoise with a spoon*, she would effortlessly infer that *vichyssoise* is a liquid or semi-liquid food and she may store that information as an incomplete schema in the mental lexicon.

Disambiguation is rapid, as it must be to achieve the speed of language comprehension (four to six words per second) and it cannot rely on complete syntactic structures. Empirical research, using words than are ambiguous between noun and verb senses (such as *print* or *audit*), suggests that when an ambiguity is encountered, all of its senses known to the language user briefly become activated. Except in garden path sentences, however, those that are implausible become inactive, usually within the following three syllables and certainly before the clause boundary. This means that syntactically incomplete constituents must somehow be interpretable, so that when local syntactic ambiguity persists for more than a word or two, the semantically implausible alternative can be abandoned.

Impatient with syntactic ambiguities, we might consider dispensing with a parse and using only semantics. But that is no solution, because syntax resolves many semantic ambiguities. With the case frame,

$$[\text{Transfer: fly}] \leftarrow(\text{agent})- [\text{PERSON: a}]$$
$$\leftarrow(\text{patient})- [\text{ENTITY: b}]$$
$$\leftarrow(\text{origin})- [\text{PLACE: c}]$$
$$\leftarrow(\text{destination})- [\text{PLACE: d}]$$

if interpretation were exclusively semantic, a sentence like *Marie flew John from New York to Boston* would be ambiguous. A semantics-only interpreter would construe the sentence in four different ways. Either Marie or John could be agent; either New York or Boston could be the origin and the other the destination. To resolve these ambiguities we might incorporate some rudimentary information about word order and prepositions. However, that is to introduce syntax. *John was flown to*

Boston by Marie which inverts the order of agent and patient, would require more syntactic information, and sentences with two verbs *(The woman who flew John to Boston landed* or *the man flown to Boston landed)* would require still more. What is more, syntax can make a set of semantic roles harder or easier to comprehend. Most people, for example, have trouble when center embedding extends to two or more levels: *the plane that the man that Mary knew owned disappeared.* Though the difficulty diminishes only slightly when semantic cues are strengthened *the plane that the pilot that the owner bought flew crashed*, it disappears entirely when the syntax is altered: *the plane that was owned by the man that Mary knew disappeared.*

Another important consideration is that syntax can put words and phrases together in indefinitely many ways, and some of these express new meanings. Consider the advent of human flight, whether by hot air balloon or Icarus's wings. Syntax could put forth this new proposition: *Icarus flew toward the sun,* and though it overrode the then-pertaining selectional preferences that presumably allowed only avian agents for the verb *fly*, the sentence conveyed a meaning. For that matter, all selectional restrictions must be preferences and capable of being overridden by syntax. Though we may very well doubt the truth of *the airplane ate spaghetti and meatballs,* it cannot be denied that the sentence has a meaning.

That syntax and semantics must somehow cooperate was evident almost from the beginning. SHRDLU, developed by Terry Winograd in the early 1970s as the first linguistically principled system for interpreting language (its predecessors offer "engineering" solutions: using anything that worked) organized knowledge in such a way as to allow syntactic procedures to call on semantic procedures and vice versa. Extending this approach to incorporate a large amount of syntactic and semantic knowledge led to intractable issues of co-ordination and control, however, and most subsequent models have given precedence either to syntax or to semantics.

Conceptually oriented models, particularly those that implement conceptual dependency theory, give privilege to semantics. They use lexical schemata and case frames to predict phrase and sentence structures and build propositional representations of meaning. Though linguists have been slower to adopt integrative models, preferring to investigate the separate components more thoroughly before considering their interaction, several linguistically motivated models have emerged recently. These give precedence to syntactic rules, allowing them to anticipate constituents and show how they may combine. Though phrase structures may be implicit in the rules and the order in which they execute (much as a road map is implicit in a drive through the countryside), the only structure actually built is the propositional representation of sentence meaning. Direct translation accords with the empirical evidence. The click studies and other tests suggest that we implicitly recognize the phrase structures of sentences, but tests of sentence recall show that memory of syntactic structures decays very rapidly, and shadowing studies suggest that we build propositional representations as we proceed.

1.2 Modularity and language comprehension

A different and more difficult question is whether we should at this stage consider more information than might plausibly be associated with entries in the mental lexicon and more processing than is required for syntax and semantics. Clearly, such elements of syntax and semantics as nouns, verbs and adjectives, agents, patients, and attributes reflect our perceptions of a word in which things act, are acted upon, and have qualities and conditions. Although strong evidence shows that human cognition employs both a mental lexicon and a repository of general knowledge, a mental encyclopedia, it also suggests that they are separate. Those who lose language through brain damage do not lose their world knowledge, and the mental encyclopedias of the congenitally deaf are not fundamentally different from those of hearing and speaking persons. The mental encyclopedia covers more areas of experience than does the lexicon and may well be organized by categories that do not always correspond to words or other linguistic entities. Thus, in accessing the mental encyclopedia, the lexicon might function more nearly as an index than as a table of contents.

As for the lexicon, we can assume that for words we use (as opposed to those we only recognize), it incorporates all definitional attributes, together with enough information to distinguish non-synonymous words and enough to specify the combinations in which words can occur. But is there more? Exactly where do we set the boundary between lexical and world knowledge? To be sure, the more information contained in the lexical entry, the more sensitive the interpretation of, for instance, the nuances that distinguish synonyms.

Large structures, however, consume memory and are unwieldy to work with. Consider the many kinds of information we have about even a common word like *water*: its potability if the context is drinking, its buoyancy if the context is swimming, its many uses if the context is drought, and its appearance on a moonlit night if the context is romance. But only a small fraction of that information would come into play in interpreting *I drank a glass of water*. Then come problems with the level of detail. I drink the glass of water by first grasping the glass by partially encircling it with my hand, then moving it to my mouth by the complex interaction of arm muscles, then contracting muscles in my mouth and throat in such a way as to cause the liquid to move via my throat and esophagus to my stomach. Should these be

part of the lexical representation for *drank*? Finding principled ways
of determining how much is enough poses a serious problem for any
attempt to incorporate world knowledge in the comprehension of
sentences.

As for the processing, most theories of discourse comprehension
agree that as we move from sentence to sentence, we are integrating
sentences to construct a mental model of the developing discourse.
Integrating requires inferencing. Thus for the sentences,

> Joe saw Mary last night. He seemed very pleased.

The pronoun *he* and the consistency of tense allows us to map the
second sentence on a representation developed using the first and to
infer a causal connection. Sometimes knowledge from the mental
encyclopedia is required to make the connection. The sentences

> Joe had to decide between a hamburger and a steak.
> He chose the less expensive meal.

require knowledge of the relative cost of two kinds of meat in order to
interpret his choice. Contextual information can also disambiguate
sentences like *Landing planes can be dangerous*, judging one interpretation to be more plausible or more apposite than another:

> Don't walk too close to the runway. Landing planes can be dangerous.
> Pilots must be cautious. Landing planes can be dangerous.

Other examples are *Time passes quickly* (are we talking football?),
Visiting relatives can be fun (who's away from home?), and *the lamb
is ready to eat* (who does the eating?). The crucial question is whether
interpreting the sentence and building the mental model are temporally
discrete (and sequential) processes.   If they are, then sentence
processing would generate a propositional representation.   Does
knowledge of the world and of the prior discourse influence the
interpretation of sentences?   Or does it subsequently determine
whether their interpretation is plausible in light of world knowledge
and apposite in view of the prior discourse and, when necessary, force
a reinterpretation?

This question is brought into particularly sharp focus by the
modularity hypothesis, advanced recently by Jerry Fodor. Fodor
postulates the existence of reflexive "input modules," which handle
perceptual processing and the early stages of language comprehension.
There might be separate syntactic and semantic modules, or a single
module might combine syntactic and semantic processing, give privilege
either to syntax or semantics, and produce a propositional representation of sentence meaning (see Figure 1). The representation would be
turned over to the more reflective central processor, which makes
inferences, solves problems, and otherwise conducts our thinking. To

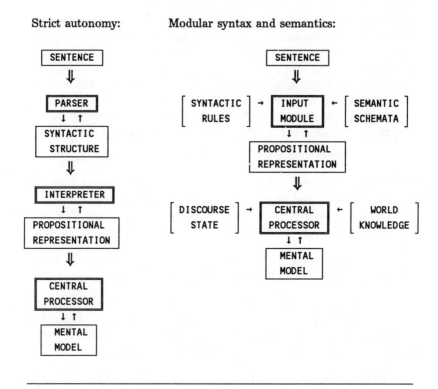

Figure 1. Models for sentence comprehension.

keep pace with rapid speech, input modules are fast, much faster than the deliberative central processor. Empirical research shows that more processing time is required in using world knowledge to determine a referent (as in the hamburger – steak example) than simply to comprehend a sentence that does not call for world knowledge. Moreover, input processing is mandatory. We cannot help but try to interpret as meaningful any utterance in a language we know, much as we cannot help but interpret visual stimuli as a scene. Input modules are domain specific. Phonology, syntax, and semantics may constitute domains, or they may be integrated to speed language comprehension. Modules are informationally encapsulated, having access only to their inputs and to a limited store of linguistic knowledge.

After presenting its interpretation to the general-purpose processor, however, the language module could obtain feedback that discredits one interpretation and favors another. The information would be available, but only as feedback. Teleological considerations suggest that a slow, inference-making central processor does not ordinarily guide the input modules. For language no less than for vision, organisms need to perceive quickly what is actually there and should not be prejudiced by what they expect to be there.

An alternative to Fodor's view is that mind operates as a general-purpose processor. Its various activities (whether interpreting perceptual information, comprehending language, making inferences, or solving problems) have access to the same seamlessly integrated store of knowledge:

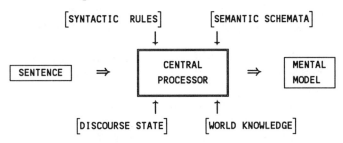

For sentence comprehension, that store would include not only the present sentence and information from the mental lexicon, but also any information that emerged previously in the discourse, together with anything and everything we know about the world. No relevant knowledge would, in principle, be excluded from the decision-making. By this view, our ability to distinguish between two phonologically similar words might depend on our knowledge of botany or baseball, and a decision between semantic senses of a verb might depend on how attentively we have followed the twists and turns of a conversation.

The question of whether sentence processing is modular, as Fodor contends, or centralized has stimulated considerable research, but with contradictory results. Studies using ambiguous noun phrases such as *landing planes* or *visiting relatives* suggest that discourse knowledge does intervene during sentence comprehension. Provided with the disambiguating context, subjects more quickly picked out the appropriate verb in such sentences as *Landing planes is/are.* . . . In another experiment, subjects were asked to listen to biasing narratives that conclude with an incomplete sentence:

> The police officer answered a call about a burglary in progress. While searching the building, she found a man lurking in the back room. Responding quickly,

> 1. she arrested [him / her.]   3. she confessed to [him / her.]
> 2. he arrested [him / her.]   4. he confessed to [him / her.]

Some of the narratives make a female the principal actor and object of focus; others focus on the male. Some of the incomplete sentences are plausible (as is 1 and 4 since police arrest and burglars confess), but world knowledge would judge others to be implausible. A completing word (in brackets) was presented visually to coincide with the pronounced last word in the incomplete sentence, and subjects were to name it as quickly as possible. Response times were measured to determine how fast the subjects were comprehending the completing sentence. The researchers hypothesized that if knowledge of the state of the discourse plays a role in sentence comprehension, response time would be slower if the incomplete sentence changed the focus. If world knowledge plays a role, responses would be slower with incomplete sentences that are implausible. The subjects' response times confirmed both hypotheses. Response was slightly slower when focus was shifted (as with 2 and 4) and slower still when inappropriate (as with 1 and 3). World knowledge and discourse knowledge did appear to influence processing time.

Though it is difficult to prove that knowledge of the world and of the present state of the discourse does not intervene in the early stages of language comprehension, the remarkable persistence of minimal attachment and the garden path phenomenon it engenders in sentences like *the horse raced past the barn fell* strongly suggest that syntactic processing resists the influence of prior discourse. The complex NP, *the horse raced past the barn,* presupposes some set of horses from which the modifier picks out one individual, whereas the simple NP, *the man,* does not. If knowledge of previous discourse plays a role in comprehension, two predictions should be confirmed. When prior context mentions several horses, the modifier should not send the reader down the garden path. When context mentions only one horse or none, the modifier should present a garden path. Repeated experiments in which subjects were presented with several kinds of minimal attachment and their eye movements were tracked and timed revealed no difference. Regardless of context, the garden path phenomenon persisted. Context that mentions several boxes did not override the preference for minimal attachment in

He loaded the boxes on the shelf onto the cart,

where *on the shelf* is misunderstood as the destination rather than the location of the boxes, nor did appropriate context prevent misreading of the conjoined clauses in

She told Tom and his sister did too,

where *his sister* is at first mistakenly conjoined with *Tom* rather than *she told Tom).* Garden paths also persist where world knowledge might preclude them. In each of the following pairs of sentences, for example, the first of the alternative head nouns should be more helpful than the second in avoiding the ensuing garden path:

The performer sent the flowers was pleased.
The florist sent the flowers was pleased.
The client provided the drawings was pleased.
The architect provided the drawings was pleased.

The help was not, however, effective; subjects were equally likely to follow the garden path with the helpful and non-helpful noun phrase, and there was equal perturbation upon reaching the disambiguating *was pleased*.

Besides offering a plausible (though unproven) account of how mental labor is divided, Fodor's modularity hypothesis has an important methodological advantage. Encapsulated, special-purpose systems are more easily studied, and theories of their operation are less susceptible to the notorious "frame problem" of how to delimit the information that needs to be considered in accomplishing any particular mental task. Differences in attentiveness and motivation, in experience and learning would need to be accommodated. It is no simple matter to characterize what knowledge of the present state of the discourse would be relevant to sentence comprehension, nor is it easy to identify the relevant world knowledge. In the absence of decisive evidence on either side, Fodor's hypothesis serves as a simplifying assumption. By assuming modularity, we can get on with the question of how syntax and semantics interact, and a better understanding of what they can accomplish will make other questions more tractable.

Section two: Giving Privilege to Semantics

2.1 Semantic cases and prediction

Semantic constructs are usually more specific than syntactic rules and often resolve syntactic ambiguities. So perhaps they should take the lead, predicting cases (*Eat* must have an ANIMATE agent and may have an EDIBLE as patient and a UTENSIL as instrument), as well as relationships (*Scottish* predicts a following ARTIFACT or a HUMAN). Operating top-down, the interpreter would build representations of sentence meaning directly from utterances and without any intermediate representation of phrase or functional structures. Though it could not ignore syntax entirely, the semantics-guided interpreter would use only local syntactic information such as the order of words in the utterance and grammatical properties of particular words, chiefly function words. Can this strategy succeed? Do the specificity and structural predictions of a semantics make parsing and phrase structural representation redundant? The answer, obtained from experience, is no. The past two decades have seen an evolving series of models (many built to implement conceptual dependency theory) in which semantic predictions and constraints guide interpretation, and at each stage in the evolution more and still more syntax has been incorporated.

The semantic interpreter employs rules or packets of affiliated rules, which it retrieves from the lexicon as it proceeds word by word through the sentence. It maintains both a simple list of the currently active rules or packets and, for the case frames and lexical schemata, a buffer. A buffer is a storage device where the input to or output from some process is temporarily stored and where some preliminary processing may take place.

The rules are not simple rewrite rules capable only of matching and merging structures, but more powerful and more flexible production rules. The production rules test for particular words and for word order. They can also look in the buffer for specified case frames and lexical schemata, for their parts and properties, and for their order.When tests succeed, several kinds of actions may ensue. Actions may add case frames or schemata to the buffer, or they may merge structures. They may activate or deactivate rules (including themselves), and they may prioritize rules.

To see how the interpreter operates, consider the sentence *John flew from Paris to Ankara at night*. Interpretation begins with an empty buffer and one active rule that recognizes the ends of sentences. Upon encountering the first word, *John*, it retrieves its rule, placing it one the list of active rules:

Buffer: **Active rules:**

< empty >   **If** current word is .
                                Then retrieve buffer

                                If True
                                Then add to buffer: [PERSON: John1]

(True means that the rule necessarily executes as soon as it is considered.) Rules are considered in the reverse order of their addition to the list, so that the most recently added rules are consulted first. This is one of a few, quite general heuristics that guide the interpreter. It applies to a substantial number of constructions. It guarantees, for example, that the relative clause in *Jim said that Mary left* will be correctly interpreted by building the structure:

[GO] ←(agent)— [PERSON: Mary1]

before attaching that proposition as a patient to

[SAY] ←(agent)— [PERSON: Jim1].

For some constructions, however, the heuristic needs to be overridden by having one rule prioritize another.

In this case the rule for *John* fires, placing [PERSON: John1] in the buffer then removing itself from the active list. The rule for sentence

If [VEHICLE] follows
Then activate: rule-packet #1

If [VEHICLE] does not follow
Then activate: rule-packet #2

rule-packet #1:

If true
Then add to buffer:

$$[OPERATE] \quad \leftarrow(agent) - [PERSON]$$
$$\leftarrow(patient) - [VEHICLE]$$
$$\leftarrow(origin) - [PLACE]$$
$$\leftarrow(destination) - [PLACE]$$

If [PERSON] precedes [OPERATE]
Then merge:

$$[OPERATE] \quad \leftarrow(agent) - [PERSON]$$

If [VEHICLE] follows [OPERATE]
Then merge:

$$[OPERATE] \quad \leftarrow(patient) - [VEHICLE]$$

If True
Then activate: Rule-packet #3

rule-packet #2:

If True
Then add to buffer:

$$[GO] \quad \leftarrow(agent) - [PERSON]$$
$$\leftarrow(patient) - [PERSON]$$
$$\leftarrow(origin) - [PLACE]$$
$$\leftarrow(destination) - [PLACE]$$
$$\leftarrow(instrument) - [VEHICLE]$$

If [PERSON] precedes [GO] in buffer
Then merge:

$$[GO] \quad \leftarrow(agent) - [PERSON]$$
$$\leftarrow(patient) - [PERSON]$$

If True
Then activate: Rule-packet #3

Figure 2. Case frames and associated rules for *flew*.

endings cannot execute, so the interpreter turns to the next word in the sentence. It is *flew* and its lexical entry consists of the rules and rule packets given in Figures 2 and 3. Notice that the sequence of rules is meaningful. The first two rules distinguish the two senses of *flew*. If a vehicle follows the verb as its direct object, indicating that if the sense is OPERATE, the rules in packet #1 are activated. Otherwise

rule-packet #3:

If current word is *from*
Then activate with priority:

> **If** [PLACE]
> **Then** merge:
>
> > [ACT] ←(origin)— [PLACE]

If current word is *to* or *into*
Then activate with priority:

> **If** [PLACE]
> **Then** merge:
>
> > [ACT] ←(destination)— [PLACE]

If [PLACE]
Then merge:

> [ACT] ←(destination)— [PLACE]

Figure 3. Rules for recognizing origins and destinations.

rules specific to GO are activated. A second general heuristic guiding interpretation is that rules are ordered so as to bring semantic constraints into play as early as possible. With this heuristic, the interpreter can resolve many local ambiguities in a timely manner. Notice also that neither set of rules is activated until sufficient information becomes available to decide between them. This means that structures will not be built only to be altered or discarded. In effect, interpretation will be deterministic.

Since no VEHICLE occupies the position of the direct object, rule packets #2 and #3 are activated. Rules for filling the agent and patient roles fire, as do the rules that activate packets #2 and #3, resulting in the following state of affairs:

Buffer:

[GO] ←(agent)— [PERSON: John1]
  ←(patient)— [PERSON: John1]
  ←(origin)— [PLACE]
  ←(destination)— [PLACE]
  ←(instrument)— [VEHICLE]

Active rules:

If current word is *from*
Then activate with priority:
  If [PLACE]
  Then merge:
    [GO] ←(origin)— [PLACE]

If current word is *to* or *into*
Then activate with priority:
  If [PLACE]
  Then merge:
    [GO] ←(destination)— [PLACE]

If [PLACE]
Then merge:
  [GO] ←(destination)— [PLACE]

Because every syntactic eventuality must be anticipated, a great many rules are required. Notice, for example, that for a destination, the tests look not only for the objects of *to* and *into*, but also for adverbs of place such as *there* or *home*. With every word that is input, the test for every active rule executes, checking either the word itself or the state of the buffer. If a word is ambiguous, all rules for all senses of the word must be active until the ambiguity is resolved. Moreover, since the sentence may be considerably more complicated than our sample, rules need to be more exacting. For example, the rules for finding the agent in both senses of *flew* cannot assume that any noun preceding the verb is the subject. It must exclude several syntactic possibilities:

If   [PERSON] precedes [OPERATE] in the buffer
            and it is not the object of a preposition
            and it is not attached to anything else preceding it
            and no other unaccounted for [PERSON] precedes [OPERATE]

Then   merge: [GO] ←(agent)— [HUMAN]

Continuing with the interpretation of *John flew from Paris to Ankara at night*, the next word is *from*, and although it has no schema, it does activate the rule for finding the origin. That rule is given priority over other rules, in particular the destination rule for adverbs of place. The next word is *Paris* with the rule:

If   True
Then   add: [PLACE: Paris]

Again the list of rules is considered, the rule for *Paris* places its schema in the buffer and the rule activated by *from* recognizes it as an origin. In much the same manner, *Ankara* is identified as the destination, and the rule for finding such destinations as *home* and *there*, discovers that that role is filled and deactivates itself. Unlike the origin and destination, the following phrase, *at night*, is not specifically anticipated by rules associated with *flew*. Since most acts can have times, locations, or manners, duplicating rules to capture these in lexical entries for every verb would fail to capture important generalizations. Instead, these rules are associated with prepositions and are given priority so as to pick up the prepositions's object. For *at*, the rule specifies temporal and locative alternatives:

If   True
Then   activate with priority:

            If [TIME] or [TIME-PERIOD]
            Then merge: [ACT] ←(temporal)— [   ]

            If [PLACE] or [PHYS-OBJ]
            Then merge: [ACT] ←(locative)— [   ]

With all three prepositional phrases, the strategy of looking first for a case guarantees the human preference for minimal attachment. If the preposition and its object are incompatible with the expected cases (as in *he flew to the city of two million people*), the interpreter has the option of attaching it as a modifier.

2.2 Interpreting noun groups

What we have so far is a straightforward method of predictive interpretation that correctly translates the sample sentence into propositional representation. Supplied with additional rules resembling those we already have, the interpreter will handle many, more complicated sentence structures and have little difficulty. However, any procedure that applies rules in a top-down sequence and is constrained only by recency will encounter problems with certain phrase structures, most notably the noun group–that is, a head noun and any determiners, adjectives, possessives, or attributive nouns that may precede it.

Consider what the interpreter would do with *John bought the large Dutch green apple pie*. Following *bought*, rules looking for a patient (the object purchased), a source (the seller), and a medium of exchange (as instrument, perhaps) would be activated and each would examine the five words of the noun group. The rule for finding a source would fire upon encountering *Dutch*, falsely interpreting it as a collective noun and the head of a noun phrase. Then the rule for finding a patient would fire upon encountering *green*, as another NP head, a place and hence a perspective patient. All the while *apple* is not yet in view, but upon reaching *apple* and eventually the actual patient, *pie*, the interpreter would have no way to account for them. Clearly, predictive interpretation needs to be constrained for noun groups, and the constraints must be syntactic if modifiers and nouns are to be distinguished and interpreted.

Within the confines of a noun group the interpreter must suspend its ordinary mode of operation and apply a different discipline, storing rules on a stack until the head noun is identified. The head will occur at the end of the noun group, so the interpreter must identify the boundary. Often this presents no difficulty. Because only a few lexical categories participate in a noun group, and the order in which they appear is rigidly fixed, the interpreter can identify the boundary when it encounters an unexpected word (a preposition, for example, or a finite verb) or an unexpected sequence (a determiner or adjective following a noun). In the example, the interpreter works through the several words in the noun group until it finally encounters the period ending the sentence. It now has a boundary and can begin popping items from the stack.

green1   **If** boundary
         Then add: [PLACE: green]

green2   **If** not boundary
         Then activate:

green3   **If** [FRUIT]
             Then merge: [FRUIT:] ←(attribute)— [-RIPE]

green4   **If** [HUMAN]
             Then merge: [HUMAN:] ←(attribute)— [-EXPERIENCED]

green5   **If** [PHYS-OBJ]
             Then merge: [PHYS-OBJ:] ←(color)— [GREEN]

green6   **If** true
             Then add: [PLACE: green]

Dutch1   **If** boundary
         Then add: [ORGANIZATION: Dutch]

Dutch2   **If** not boundary
         Then activate:

Dutch3   **If** [EDIBLE]
             Then merge: [EDIBLE] ←(manner of)— [NATIONALITY: Dutch]

Dutch4   **If** [HUMAN]
             Then merge: [HUMAN] ←(member of)— [ORGANIZATION: Dutch]

Dutch5   **If** [PHYS-OBJ]
             Then merge: [PHYS-OBJ] ←(made in)— [PLACE: Netherlands]

Dutch6   **If** true
             Then add: [ORGANIZATION: Dutch]

Figure 4. Rules for several meanings of *green* and *Dutch*.

The first two words are *the* and *large*, either of which could signal the beginning of a noun group:

large1   **If** [PHYS-OBJ]
         Then merge: [PHYS-OBJ] ←(size)— [GREATER THAN NORM]

the1   **If** [ALL]
         Then merge: [ALL] ←(reference)— [DEFINITE]

Though both rules apply to a large class of schemata, neither will execute until after the head is found and a concept is placed in the buffer. The next two words are *Dutch* and *green*, both of which have noun and adjective senses and several possible rules (see Figure 4). If after either word the boundary is encountered, the schema for that word goes into the buffer. The remaining rules recognize adjective and attributive noun senses. Note that the adjective rules are in the order of their specificity. Thus, the rules for *green* look first for the more specific senses "unripe" and "inexperienced" before looking for the color that can be an attribute of any physical object. This is another example in which the ordering of rules is significant, and again the idea is to favor semantic constraints. The order of decreasing specificity is a necessary heuristic given the number of modifiers that, like color, can apply to such broad categories as physical objects. The interpreter has not yet found the boundary, however, so all the rules go into the noun group stack. The next words are *apple* and *pie*:

> piel   **If** boundary
>   **Then** add: [EDIBLE: pie] and activate:
>
> pie2   **If** [FRUIT or MEAT or CHEESE]
>   **Then** merge: [EDIBLE: pie] ←(part)— [FRUIT/MEAT/CHEESE]
>
> apple1 **If** boundary
>   **Then** add: [FRUIT: apple]
>
> apple2 **If** not boundary
>   **Then** activate:
>
> apple3 **If** true
>   **Then** add: [FRUIT: apple]

Whereas the adjective rules for *green* and *Dutch* look to the right in the noun group for a noun that they may modify, the second rule for *pie* looks to the left for particular kinds of pie. This reflects the knowledge that pies in common with several other kinds of prepared food are identified by their ingredients, and because such leftward expectations are very specific, they have precedence.

Beyond *pie* is the end of the sentence, a boundary, so *pie* must be the head noun. Thus the rule for *pie* executes, placing [EDIBLE: piel] in the buffer. Then rules for *large* and *the* respond, producing the structure:

> [EDIBLE: piel] ←(reference)— [DEFINITE]
>   ←(size)— [GREATER THAN NORM]

Now that it has been established that *apple*, *green*, and *Dutch* are not the head nouns, the rules for their adjective and attributive nouns senses activate. Figure 5 shows the present state of the noun group stack. Moving downward through the stack, apple3 executes, then green3, which selects for [FRUIT], adds a modifier, producing the structure:

> [FRUIT: apple] ←(attribute)— [UNRIPE]

Still further down the stack, Dutch3 responds to the presence of [EDIBLE] in the buffer, producing:

Noun group stack:

pie2   **If** [FRUIT / MEAT / CHEESE]
          Then merge: [EDIBLE: pie] ←(part)— [FRUIT/MEAT/CHEESE]

apple3   **If** true
          Then add: [FRUIT: apple]

green3   **If** [FRUIT]
          Then merge: [FRUIT:] ←(attribute)— [-RIPE]

green4   **If** [HUMAN]
          Then merge: [HUMAN:] ←(attribute)— [-EXPERIENCED]

green5   **If** [PHYS-OBJ]
          Then merge: [PHYS-OBJ:] ←(color)— [GREEN]

green6   **If** true
          Then add: [PLACE: green]

Dutch3   **If** [EDIBLE]
          Then merge: [EDIBLE] ←(manner of)— [NATIONALITY: Dutch]

Dutch4   **If** [HUMAN]
          Then merge: [HUMAN] ←(member of)— [ORGANIZATION: Dutch]

Dutch5   **If** [PHYS-OBJ]
          Then merge: [PHYS-OBJ] ←(made in)— [PLACE: Netherlands]

Dutch6   **If** true
          Then add: [ORGANIZATION: Dutch]

Figure 5. State of the noun group stack for the phrase *the large Dutch green apple pie* after *pie* has been identified as the head.

[EDIBLE: pie1]   ←(reference)— [DEFINITE]
              ←(size)— [GREATER THAN NORM]
              ←(manner-of)— [NATIONALITY: Dutch]

The remaining rules for *apple, green* and *Dutch* deactivate, leaving only pie2, which merges the two structures in the buffer, producing

[EDIBLE: pie1]   ←(reference)— [DEFINITE]
              ←(size)— [GREATER THAN NORM]
              ←(manner-of)— [NATIONALITY: Dutch]
              ←(part)—[FRUIT: apple1] ←(attribute)— [-RIPE]

Thus the head is the key to noun groups; once the interpreter picks out the head, it can usually recognize the complete noun phrase without a misstep.

2.3 Accommodating post modifiers

So far we have considered only the pre-modifiers of the head noun, but we must also cope with prepositional phrases, verbal phrases, and relative clauses, any of which may follow the head noun. Though syntactically part of the noun phrase, these are best handled outside the noun-group mode, using rules that recognize their syntactic signatures. For prepositional phrases, the head noun predicts the preposition and its object. *Site, operator, problem, interpretation, practice, audit, psychology, harvest, education,* and *interior,* for example, predict *of* and contribute to its meaning. These require specific rules such as

> **If** *of* follows
> **Then** merge:
>   [PLACE: site]   ←(location)— [PHYS-OBJ or EVENT]
>
> **If** *of* follows
> **Then** merge:
>   [OPERATE: run] ←(agent)— [HUMAN]
>   ←(patient)— [VEHICLE/MACHINE/ORGANIZATION]

When a prepositional phrase is not expected, however, the interpreter resorts to generalized rules associated with prepositions. For example, the lexical entry for *of* would contain, among others, the following rules that express relationships between HUMANs and the preposition's objects:

> **If** [HUMAN] precedes
> **Then** activate:
>
> > **If** [PLACE]
> > **Then** merge: [PLACE] ←(inhabitant)— [HUMAN]
> >
> > **If** [ORGANIZATION]
> > **Then** merge: [ORGANIZATION] ←(member)— [HUMAN]

Verbal phrases and relative clauses are interpreted recursively. Among the rules for participles and for relative pronouns is the instruction to copy the most recent noun group in the buffer, put aside the buffer's remaining contents, and then proceed as if with a new sentence. The buffer must be cleared to avoid having two case frames with no way of deciding which constituents belong to which. Thus for the sentence, *they ate the pie bought from the bakery,* the rule for *bought* would look first for an unaccounted [HUMAN] to be agent and, finding none, activate the same case frame and rules employed when *bought* is the main verb. When that case frame is filled, it can be merged, via the common [EDIBLE: pie], with the case frame for *ate.* This strategy succeeds because the buffer contains no suitable agent.

When a potential agent is present, the interpreter can sometimes use other information in the phrase. If for instance a rule associated with *stuffed* (as past participle) looks for a following *with*, it could help decide that *stuffed* in the sentence *The boy stuffed with pie felt sick*, begins a reduced sentence with *boy* as the patient and is therefore not the main verb of the matrix sentence.

Often, however, information necessary to resolve an ambiguity is not locally available. Consider these sentences:

> Jill brought the man called John
> Jill knew the man called John.

In the first, the concluding phrase is a reduced form of the passive (*who was called* . . .) and *man* is the patient. In the second sentence, though the phrase is ambiguous, minimal attachment prefers the active reading, which has *man* as agent doing the calling. Capable of using only local information (the recursively explicated verbal phrase), the interpreter cannot decide between the passive and active possibilities. Although the verbs *met* and *knew* could decide the issue, they are not part of the phrase and cannot therefore be brought into play. This is one of many instances in which local information is insufficient. Similar problems occur with unbounded movement. It being difficult to specify distant words or structures by their locations, the interpreter views the sentence through a narrow window consisting only of the structures presently in the buffer and a word or two following the current word. A topicalized noun phrase, however, or the wh- word in a question can come from some distance away.

By now it will be obvious that giving privilege to semantics requires large numbers of rules. Rules associated with each sense of each word must not only anticipate the semantics of the word sense, the cases it predicts or relationships it may enter, but must also anticipate all the syntactic constructions in which that sense of the word may participate. Because rules depend on the output of other rules, all must function cooperatively, and devising a smoothly functioning system of rules is no trivial task. Anticipating all syntactic and semantic eventualities poses a different problem for the interpreter. As soon as it is a few words into the sentence, the interpreter is plodding through long lists of active rules, most of them irrelevant, applying every rule's tests to the contents of the buffer.

However, the main reason for the number and complexity of rules is that giving privilege semantics means that lexical entries cannot readily incorporate syntactic generalizations. For example, *bought*, *brought*, and *fought* behave in much the same way syntactically; they can be past tense main verbs, passive main verbs, or verbals. Though it would be convenient to employ general passive and verbal phrase rules (of the kind we saw in Chapter 7) for these verbs and the many others that act similarly, their differing semantics interfere:

> The squirrel brought a nut.
> ? The squirrel bought a nut.
> He brought the package home from the store
> ? He bought the package home from the store.

The agent for *brought* and *fought* is ANIMAL, but for *bought*, it is necessarily HUMAN; the patient of *bought* and *brought* is ALL, but for *fought* it is ANIMAL; *brought* may have a source and destination, but *bought* has only as source; and so on. Because the rules combine syntactic and semantic specifications, syntactic generalizations cannot be used. The reverse is also true. Semantic generalizations cannot be used because syntactic behavior differs. To be sure, when the goal is only to build an interpreter for a restricted vocabulary and syntax, proliferation of rules is not a serious problem. But achieving anything like the generality required for natural languages is impossible.

2.4 Privileged semantics with tandem parsing

One way of retaining the privilege given to semantics, but expanding somewhat the interpretive window and avoiding proliferation of rules is to have interpretation and parsing proceed in tandem. Although with tandem processing, syntactic and semantic processing remain largely autonomous in that neither component guides the other, there is provision for obtaining consent. One tandem model employs two buffers and three kinds of rules: interpretation rules, syntactic rules, and special interactive rules that mediate between components. Using a subset of ordinary phrase structure rules, a bottom-up parser assembles constituent structures (that is, the output of rules such as NP → DET NOUN) and places them in a syntactic buffer. It does not attempt the more difficult tasks of attaching them or identifying their functions. Proceeding apace, the interpreter accumulates schemata and case frames in its buffer and, applying semantic rules, proposes merges. Thus the interpreter initiates decisions which the parse must confirm. Each time a merge is proposed, the interpreter determines whether the result of that merge is grammatical by looking for an interactive rule capable of matching the present contents of the syntactic buffer. If the appropriate rule exists, its action performs the merge.

Consider how tandem processing would handle *Jill brought the man called John*, the sentence which revealed the inadequacy of local syntactic information. Semantics will not propose a merge until it has the verb and its case frame. Thus after encountering *brought*, the syntactic buffer contains an unattached NP and a verb capable of taking a direct object. The semantic buffer contains the representations for *Jill* and *brought*:

Syntactic buffer: **Semantic buffer:**

NP V(do/io)   [HUMAN: Jill1]

                       [TRANSFER]   ←(agent)— [ANIMAL]
                                       ←(patient)— [PHYS-OBJ]
                                       ←(origin)— [PLACE]
                                       ←(destination)— [PLACE]
                                       ←(beneficiary)— [ANIMATE]

At this point, the interpreter has three possibilities for *Jill*: agent, patient and beneficiary, with agent given preference, because its constraint is the most specific that *Jill* will meet. The interpreter evokes the interactive rules to determine if the syntax will support the agent assignment or one of the others. One rule recognizes the constituents in the syntax buffer:

If   NP V, V is active verb,
           and NP is not syntactically attached

Then   Syntactic assignment: NP is SUBJECT of V
           Semantic assignment: NP is ←(agent)— of V
           Remove NP

Jill qualifies as subject and agent and is so assigned; and the NP, having been accounted for, is removed from the buffer. Following the verb are an NP (*the man*) and beyond that a possible postmodifier, a reduced, passive relative clause (in unreduced form: *the man was called John*). But *called*, which is ambiguous between past participle and past tense, could also be the main verb of a sentential NP (as in *Jill knew John called the man*). Thus we have:

Syntactic buffer: **Semantic buffer:**

V(do & io) NP V2 / PPart.   [TRANSFER]   ←(agent)— [HUMAN: Jill1]
                                       ←(patient)— [PHYS-OBJ]
                                       ←(origin)— [PLACE]
                                       ←(destination)— [PLACE]
                                       ←(beneficiary)— [HUMAN]
                       [HUMAN: man]

                       [IDENTIFY] ←(patient)— [ALL]
                                     ←(patient)— [ALL]
                       or

                       [SPEAK] ←(agent)— [HUMAN]
                                 ←(patient)— [PROPOSITION]
                                 ←(beneficiary)— [HUMAN]

(The primitive IDENTIFY is one way of representing the relationship between something and its name.) Although the NP with postmodifier meets the constraints for beneficiary and patient (in that order of preference), syntax must eliminate the sentential possibility. Among the interactive rules are the following:

If	v(do & io) NP PPart

Then	Syntactic assignment:	RELATIVE CLAUSE (PASSIVE)
	NP is SUBJECT
	PPart is MAIN VERB

	Semantic assignment:	NP2 is patient of V2
	RELATIVE CLAUSE is attribute of NP

If	V (sentential do) NP V2

Then	Syntactic assignment:	SENTENTIAL NP (ACTIVE)
	NP is SUBJECT
	V2 is MAIN VERB

	Semantic assignment:	SENTENTIAL NP is patient of V

The first rule looks for the constituents of a reduced passive (that is, a past participle followed by a noun phrase). The second looks for the constituents of a embedded sentential NP, but also requires a verb capable of making that NP a direct object. Of the two rules, only the first rule applies to the sample sentence. It assigns as patient of *brought*, the IDENTIFY case frame with *man* as one patient and *John* as the other.

This tandem model has several advantages. Because the interpreter has the initiative, time is not wasted in exploring semantically unavailing parses. But global ambiguities are not ignored. Notice that rules for both the reduced passive and the sentential NP would match the constituents of the ambiguous *I knew the man called John*, there being no semantic basis for choosing between them. Also, the availability of the syntactic analysis as a last resort helps explain how we make some sense of semantically anomalous sentences, such as the famous *colorless green ideas sleep furiously*. Moreover, though the search for interactive rules is triggered by semantics, the test portion of the interactive rules specifies only syntactic constituents and can therefore embody syntactic generalizations. Consequently, the proliferation of rules is considerably reduced. (Note, however, that the example simplifies the syntactic possibilities: both rules would need to be extended so as to accommodate an indirect object preceding *the man called John*.) The interactive rules also afford a wide window in that they can scan whatever is in the syntactic buffer and are not limited only to local syntax.

Whether tandem processing offers a feasible model for human sentence comprehension will be difficult to establish empirically, though suggestive evidence has already emerged from an experiment which recorded subjects' eye fixation while they read sentences containing a syntactically or semantically anomalous constituent or spelling errors.

For syntactic anomalies in sentences that were readily interpreted using semantic information, subjects tended to linger on or return to those portions of the sentences containing anomalies, even though they did not recall having noticed them. Some amount of syntactic analysis appeared to be automatic even when it was not required for semantic interpretation.

Section three: Rule-by-Rule Interpretation

3.1 Giving precedence to syntax

Rather than giving privilege to semantics, a number of computational approaches have syntax guide the processing, but bring semantics to bear early enough to resolve ambiguities before they waste much time. These include **semantic grammars**, which incorporate semantic information within a syntactic formalism, often an augmented transition network. In place of such non terminal categories as NP and VP, semantic grammars employ semantic categories, usually categories that are tailored to the specific subject matter of a limited domain. A "baseball grammar" might have, among others, a statistics category of noun phrases (wins, complete games, home runs, hits, and so on) and a delimiters category of prepositional phrases (at home, against left handers, in his career, with men on base). Semantic grammars have many practical applications where only a limited number of sentence types and semantic constructs need be recognized: the "front ends," for example, which translate users' questions into the formal query language of databases. Semantic grammars are not readily extendible, however, and they sacrifice generalizations; the broader the syntactic generalization, the narrower the semantic category and vice versa.

   A different approach also having many practical applications employs **interleaved modules** for syntax and semantics. As the syntactic module parses each phrasal constituent, it turns its parse over to an appropriate semantic module. If that module can reach a plausible interpretation of the phrase, control returns to syntax and the parser proceeds deeper into the sentence. In this manner, control and information shuttle back and forth at each phrase boundary until interpretation is complete. The chief advantage is the modularity. Syntactic modules do not need to be rewritten for each new domain, but can be used with multiple semantic modules, each tailored to a specific application. A disadvantage is that the structures that pass between modules are large: complete noun phrases, prepositional phrases, sentential NPs, relative clauses, and the like. Though semantics is available to judge attachments, and therefore to eliminate one major source of ambiguity, it cannot block other false paths and, unless equipped with some special *ad hoc* rules, stumbles with long-distance dependencies.

Psychologically more plausible are the **rule-by-rule** approaches. Each syntactic rule has a corresponding semantic rule so that parsing and interpretation proceed incrementally, word by word, phrase by phrase. Though this approach was anticipated by early work on computer programming languages, its present impetus comes from Montague's work on the logic of natural languages. Montague grammar holds that the correspondence between syntax and logical form is much more direct than has been supposed. For each semantic type Montague grammar has a corresponding syntactic category, and for each semantic rule there is a corresponding syntactic rule.

In addition to the instantaneous judging of semantic plausibility, other considerations make this fine-grained approach very attractive. When syntactic and semantic operations interact, their combined operation can usually be judged locally; if something goes amiss, the problem is easier to diagnose. Moreover, the rule-by-rule approach may simulate sentence processing by humans. Empirical research on the persistence of ambiguities suggests that semantic interpretation does not await major syntactic boundaries but instead proceeds incrementally. If partially completed constituents are indeed interpretable, then the rule-by-rule approach demonstrates one way that interpretation might occur. Moreover, the incremental processing offers a useful byproduct in that nontrivial sentence fragments, which occur frequently in informal conversation, are also interpretable.

In a rule-by-rule approach, both syntactic and semantic rules are expressed as logical functions. The semantic rules are lambda functions (symbolized λ) that create new predicates by assigning values. These are not very different from the schemata and case frames that we have been using; thus the lambda function

$$\lambda \ (a) \quad ([\text{TRANSFER: move}] \ \leftarrow(\text{agent})- \ [a])$$

maps objects of the type a (the lambda variable) onto predications of which the predicator is TRANSFER and its argument is an agent represented by the variable (a). If we now have an object that is of the type over which the variable ranges (let's say a dog), we can apply it to the lambda function:

$$\lambda \ (a) \quad ([\text{TRANSFER: move}] \ \leftarrow(\text{agent})- \ [a]) \ * \ (\text{dog})$$

In effect, the property of ingesting that applies to a, applies also to dog. The next step is to reduce (some logicians say "convert") the formulae to produce:

$$[\text{TRANSFER: move}] \ \leftarrow(\text{agent})- \ [\text{dog}]$$

Selectional restrictions will specify the types over which lambda variables range, and the functions can contain multiple instances of a variable or multiple variables. Two senses of the verb *move* might be represented:

λ (a:ANIMAL) ([TRANSFER: move1] ←(agent)— [a]
                                          ←(patient)— [a])

λ (a:ANIMAL) (p:PHYS-OBJ) ([TRANSFER: move2] ←(agent)– [a]
                                                        ←(patient)— [p])

Lambda functions are logical equivalents of the expressions to which they will reduce when the substitution or substitutions are made for the lambda variables.

3.2 Isomorphic syntax and semantics

For syntactic rules that explicitly represent incomplete constituents, and thus are isomorphic with the semantic interpretation rules, some approaches, including Montague's, employ **categorial grammars**. These grammars have only two primitive elements: one to represent entities (call it N for name) and the other to represent assertions about entities (S for sentence). Everything else is derived. Let's say we wish to represent the syntax of the sentence *dogs eat*. *Dogs* as entities would be represented N. The intransitive *eat* would be S\N; that is, an S lacking an N or a function that forms an S by combining with an N (such as *dogs*) to its left. (More formally, the function S\N takes an N as its argument and by left concatenation produces the value S.) The function simultaneously expresses the category with which the present element can concatenate, the direction of concatenation, whether left or right, and the category formed by the concatenation. An example of right concatenation is the adjective (N/N), which concatenates with an N to its right and forms an N. Thus *small* (N/N) concatenates with *dog* (N) to produce N. The same function N/N also serves for determiners, because semantics will make the necessary distinctions between their roles:

the   N/N ←(reference)— [DEFINITE]

male   N/N ←(gender)— [MALE]

Since many adverbs (such as *only*) can concatenate either with an N or an S, both possibilities need to be represented: S/S or N/N. Notice that the direction of the slash signifies either left concatenation S\N or right concatenation N/N. Thus *dogs* and *only* would concatenate N * N/N. Most functions concatenate either to the left or to the right, but prepositions concatenate in both directions, attaching the preposition to its object and the resultant prepositional phrase to the structure that it modifies. Because the structure it modifies may be either an N (*the dog on the corner*) or an S (*the dog sat in the corner*), the preposition

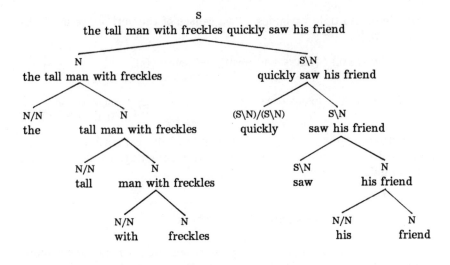

Figure 6. An analysis tree with categorial grammar.

function is ((N /N) \N or (S /N) \S). (Inner functions must execute first.)
Though left and right concatenation will suffice for our purposes,
categorial grammar can also be extended in various ways (for example,
by permitting two or more derived categories as arguments or values)
or augmented to accommodate unbounded movement.

Like phrase structure grammars, categorial grammar is recursive.
S and N categories are generated by functions composed from those
primitives. Thus the grammar does not impose any arbitrary limit on
the length of a sentence or the number of different sentences that can
be generated. Though the number of functions for any language is
finite, the number of possible derivations is infinite. Figure 6 gives an
analysis tree (the counterpart in categorial grammar of a phrase
marker) showing the generation of a simple sentence. Each parent
node is generated by a function in one of its branches. Thus, for
example, when the function N/N (for *tall*) is applied to N (for *man*), the
result is N (*tall man*); and when (S\N)/(S\N) representing *quickly*
concatenates with S\N, the resulting (S\N) represents the incomplete
verb phrase *quickly saw his friend*.

Processing takes place in parallel steps with syntax providing a map
to show how semantic representations should combine. Recognizing
our simple sentence is merely a matter of determining whether the
syntactic representations will concatenate and the semantic representations will convert. Thus, S\N concatenates with N to form an S and
[ANIMAL: dog] meets the selectional restriction stipulated for the
lambda variable, so the two structures reduce:

[INGEST: eat11] ←(agent)— [ANIMAL: dog1].

A simple shift/reduce mechanism of the sort used in Chapter 6 will manage these operations. The interpreter either shifts the lexical entry for a word, placing it atop the stack, or reduces the two top-most items on the stack by applying the syntactic and semantic functions. Consider, for example, the steps by which a shift-reduce interpreter would recognize *the boy ate soup with a spoon*. First, the representations for *the* and *boy* go on the stack:

boy shift   N   [HUMAN: boy1] ←(gender)— [MALE]

——   _____

N/N λ (r) [r] ←(reference)— [DEFINITE]

Then the interpreter attempts to reduce them and succeeds. The syntactic N will concatenate with N/N, and the lambda function will convert, reducing the representations to

N   [HUMAN: boy1] ←(reference)— [DEFINITE]

The interpreter next retrieves the lexical entry for *ate* and shifts it to the stack, which now contains:

shift   (S\N)/N λ (a:ANIMATE p:EDIBLE i:UTENSIL)

[INGEST: eat1]   ←(agent)— [a]
                 ←(patient)— [p]
                 ←(instrument)— [i]

——   _____

N   [HUMAN: boy1] ←(reference)— [DEFINITE]
                            ←(gender)— [MALE]

S\N permits left concatenation with N and the lambda function for *eat* will convert with the HUMAN as agent; therefore, the interpreter reduces the two to form the incomplete but (within the logic assumed here) viable representation:

S/N λ (p:EDIBLE i:UTENSIL)

[INGEST: eat1]   ←(agent)— [HUMAN: boy1]
                              ←(reference)— [DEFINITE]
                              ←(gender)— [MALE]
                  ←(patient)— [p]
                  ←(instrument)— [i]

A second reduce step adds the representation of *soup* to the evolving representation of the sentence. Then the interpreter shifts the entries for *with*, *a* and *spoon* to the stack, yielding:

N   [UTENSIL: spoon1]

N/N λ (r) [r] ←(reference)— [INDEFINITE]

(S/S\S) λ (y:PHYS-OBJ) [ACT] ←(instrument)— [y]
or   or
(N/N)\N λ (y:PHYS-OBJ) [PHYS-OBJ] ←(attribute)— [y]

S/(S/N) λ (i:UTENSIL)

    [INGEST: eat1] ←(agent)— [HUMAN: boy1]
                                   ←(reference)— [DEFINITE]
                                   ←(gender)— [MALE]
                ←(patient)— [EDIBLE: soup1]
                ←(instrument)— [i]

In keeping with minimal attachment, the representation for *with* offers first the possibility that the prepositional phrase attaches at the sentence level. Working downward through the stack, the interpreter reduces the representations for *a* and *spoon*, then the representations for *with* and *a spoon*, with the result that the representations for the prepositional phrase and for the remainder of the sentence remain on the stack:

S   [UTENSIL: spoon1] ←(reference)— [INDEFINITE]

S/S λ (i:UTENSIL)

    [INGEST: eat1] ←(agent)— [HUMAN: boy1]
                                   ←(reference)— [INDEFINITE]
                ←(patient)— [EDIBLE: soup1]
                ←(instrument)— [i]

These reduce to form a representation of the meaning of the complete sentence. When the only options are to concatenate or to wait, the processing is straightforward though not necessarily efficient.

3.3 Interpretive and phrase structure rules

Though isomorphic syntax and semantics has its appeal and categorial grammar simplifies certain issues in the logic of semantics (such as the specification of scope), this approach is not without its problems. One problem is the huge number of rules that need to be associated with each lexical entry if it is to describe every legal opportunity for left or right concatenation. Many rules are of daunting complexity in order to anticipate sequences of functions and to concatenate and reduce in precisely the right order. Rules must belong to a system of rules, delicately adjusted to function together, but for now the grammars are exploratory and address only a small subset of the English language.

Even supposing that enterprise were successful, there would still be empirical observations for which categorial grammar offers no explanation. Empirical research, as we have seen, suggests that phrase structures are psychologically real and play a part in sentence comprehension. Phrase structures also help explain the contours of intonation in spoken language, and they account for distributional and substitutional patterns (such as pronoun for a determiner and a noun) of which categorial grammar offers only a sketchy account. If, however, we borrow from categorial grammar the idea of stating rules as functions and add a method of manipulating the semantics of partially completed constituents, a rule-by-rule phrase structure grammar is feasible.

The first step is to convert the rewrite rules to functions. The rule NP → DET NP1 would become the function

$$\text{DET} * \text{NP} / \text{DET NP1}$$

When the DET is applied as argument (an operation symbolized by the asterisk), the function reduces to NP /NP1 (that is an NP lacking that portion of an NP that follows the determiner), with NP1 to be defined by additional functions such as NP1 /ADJ NP1 and NP1 /NOUN. Formulated in this way, syntactic rules can guide the parse, keeping track of what has been found and predicting what is to follow but without building structures.

Corresponding to each syntactic rule is a semantic rule that interprets the meanings of partial structures. For DET * NP /DET NP1, the corresponding semantic rule is

$$\text{NP-sem} = \text{NP1-sem} * \text{DET-sem}$$

That is, the semantics of the NP1, when it becomes available, is to be applied to the semantics of the determiner. For the determiners *a* and *an* the semantics would be

$$\lambda \ (\text{x:COUNT}) \ [\text{x}] \ \leftarrow(\text{reference})- \ [\text{INDEFINITE}]$$

The rule itself goes on the stack where it is available to execute as soon as syntax has parsed an NP1. Other semantic rules hand the value for one variable over to another:

$$\text{NP1 /NOUN} \qquad \text{NP1-sem} = \text{NOUN-sem}$$

The sentence *the wealthy can eat soup with a silver spoon* will pose interesting challenges for the rule-by-rule interpreter. *Wealthy* and *can* are both ambiguous as to lexical category, and the ambiguities would

| | Rule-by-rule |
Rewrite rule:	syntax and semantics:
S → NP VP	NP * (S /NP VP)
	S-sem = NP-sem * VP-sem
NP → DET NP1	DET * (NP /DET NP1)
	NP-sem = NP1-sem * DET-sem
NP1 → ADJ NP1	ADJ * (NP1 /ADJ)
	NP1-sem = NP1-sem * ADJ-sem
NP1 → NOUN	NOUN * (NP1 /NOUN)
	NP1-sem = NOUN-sem
VP → AUX VP1	AUX * (VP /AUX VP1)
	VP-sem = VP1-sem
VP → VP1	VP1 * (VP /VP1)
	VP1-sem = VERB-sem
VP1 → VERB	VERB * (VP1 /VERB)
	VP1-sem = VP1-sem * VERB-sem
VP1 → VP1 NP	VP1 /VP1 NP
	VP1-sem = NP-sem * VP1-sem
VP1 → VP1 PP	PP * (VP /PP VP1)
	VP-SEM = PP-sem * VP1
VP1 → VP1 NP PP	VP1 /VP1 NP PP
	VP1-sem = (PP-sem * (NP-sem * VP1-sem))
PP → PREP NP	PREP * (PP/(PREP NP))
	PP-sem = NP-sem * PREP-sem

Figure 7. A rule-by-rule grammar.

collude to mislead a parser (whether operating bottom-up or a top-down) into a false parse extending almost the length of the sentence. Neither parser could resolve the structural ambiguity of *with a silver spoon* and would instead generate alternative analyses in which that phrase is attached to the NP and the VP. Semantic information will resolve these ambiguities, and its availability in the course of interpretation, though no panacea will prove helpful.

The first three steps shift to the stack both the determiner and the only rule that specifies a determiner, then reduce them to represent an NP lacking the constituents that follow the determiner:

1. shift (DET → the)

DET   DET-sem = λ (x)
                                      [x] ←(reference)— [DEFINITE]

2. shift (NP → DET NP1)

NP /DET NP1   NP-sem = NP1-sem * DET-sem
―――――――   ―――――――――――――――――
DET   DET-sem (as above)

3. reduce

NP /NP1   NP-sem = NP1-sem * λ (x)
                                      [x] ←(reference)— [DEFINITE]

Two rules, equivalents of NP1 → ADJ NP1 and NP1 → NOUN, will accommodate NP1, but the interpreter has no way to decide between them. Though it can shift the lexical entry for the next word to the stack, that word, *wealthy*, is ambiguous between an adjective and a noun and both possibilities can be accommodated by rules. With nothing else to decide between them, the adjective sense has precedence. The following noun either allows or blocks the parse; were the noun sense given precedence, the interpreter could not apply selectional restrictions until much later. In this case the ordering of rules starts the interpreter down a false path, but later in the sentence, the same order will correctly interpret *silver* in *with a silver spoon*.

4. shift (ADJ → wealthy)

ADJ   ADJ-sem = λ (x: HUMAN)
                                       [x] ←(possessing)— [MONEY]
                                                 ←(amount)— [LARGE]
―――――――   ―――――――――――――――――
NP /NP1   NP-sem = NP1-sem * λ (x)
                                      [x] ←(reference)— [DEFINITE]

Wealthy can be predicated of a HUMAN, either a PERSON or a GROUP such as a family or nation, and that will prove helpful (*rich* would be less selective). Straying down the false path, the interpreter accommodates the adjective.

5. shift (NP1 → ADJ NP1)

NP1 /ADJ NP1   NP1-sem = NP1-sem * ADJ-sem
―――――――   ―――――――――――――――――
ADJ   ADJ-sem = λ (x: HUMAN)
                                       [x] ←(possessing)— [MONEY]
                                                 ←(amount)— [LARGE]
―――――――   ―――――――――――――――――
NP /NP1   NP-sem = NP1-sem * λ (x)
                                      [x] ←(reference)— [DEFINITE]

6. reduce

NP1 /NP1	NP-sem = NP1-sem * [λ (x: HUMAN)
	[x] ←(possessing)— [MONEY]
	←(amount)— [LARGE]]

NP /NP1	NP-sem = (as above)

The next word is *can*, either an auxiliary verb or a noun. The interpreter pursues the former possibility but is quickly blocked by the syntax, because the noun phrase must be completed before a verb can be parsed. Then it pursues the noun sense which, though allowed by syntax, is blocked by the semantics:

7. shift (NOUN → can)

NOUN	NOUN-sem = [CONTAINER: can1]

NP1 /NP1	NP1-sem = (as above)

NP /NP1	NP-sem = (as above)

8. shift (NP1 → NOUN)

NP1 /NOUN	NP1-sem = NOUN-sem

NOUN	NOUN-sem = (as above)

NP1 /NP1	NP1-sem = (as above)

NP /NP1	NP-sem = (as above)

9. reduce

NP1	NP1-sem = [CONTAINER: can1]

NP1 /NP1	NP1-sem = λ (x: HUMAN)
	[x] ←(possessing)— [MONEY]
	←(amount)— [LARGE]

NP /NP1	NP-sem = (as above)

The interpreter cannot reduce NP1 and NP1 /NP1, because a CONTAINER will not satisfy the selectional restrictions for HUMAN. With an ordinary bottom-up parser, without recourse to rule-by-rule semantics, the erroneous parse of *the wealthy can* as an NP would persist until, having completed the entire verb phrase, it discovers that *can* and *eat* do not agree in number. Thus although rule-by-rule semantics cannot eliminate the false paths that syntax offers, it does bring semantics to bear in a timely manner, making the false paths much shorter.

An alternative parse shifts to the stack the noun sense of *wealthy* (in step 4), then shifts NP1 /NOUN, reduces that function to NP1, then reduces NP /NP1 to NP, and thereby succeeds in interpreting the NP:

NP   [GROUP: wealthy1] ←(possessing)— [MONEY] ←(amount)— [LARGE]
                                        ←(reference)— [DEFINITE]

Because an NP is the first constituent specified by the rule for sentences and because incomplete representations are possible, the interpreter invokes that rule, then recognizes enough of the VP to allow a function that merges the agent NP with a VP lacking patient and instrument. Ordinarily a bottom-up parse requires that the entire VP be known before invoking the rule for sentences. Psychologically that is implausible. (Consider what one would know about the sense of *eat* in the interrupted sentence, *acid can eat. . . .*)

8b. shift (S → NP VP)

S /NP VP	S-sem = NP-sem * VP-sem
NP	NP-sem = (as above)

9b. reduce

S /VP	S-sem = (NP-sem above) * VP-sem

10. shift (AUX → can)

AUX	AUX-sem = λ (x:ACT)
	[x] (possible)
S /VP	S-sem = (NP-sem above) * VP-sem

11. shift (VP → AUX VP1)

VP /AUX VP1	VP-sem = AUX-sem * VP1-sem
AUX	AUX-sem = (as above)
S /VP	S-sem = (NP-sem above) * VP-sem

12. reduce

VP /VP1	VP-sem = VP1-sem * [λ (x:ACT)
	[x] (possible)]
S /VP	S-sem = (NP-sem above) * VP-sem

13. reduce

S /VP	S-sem = (NP-sem above) * (VP-sem-above)

14. shift   VERB → ate   governs = DO INSTR

VERB   VERB-sem = λ (a:ANIMATE p:EDIBLE i:UTENSIL)
governs = DO PP   [INGEST: eat1] ←(agent)— [a]
                                                           ←(patient)— [p]
                                                           ←(instrument)— [i]

                        or λ (f:CORROSIVE p:PHYS-OBJ)
                                 [CORRODE: eat1] ←(force)— [f]
                                                 ←(patient)— [p]

S /VP1   S-sem = as above

Notice that syntax specifies that *eat* takes a direct object, information
that step 15 will use to choose among possible rules. This slight
redundancy with the semantic entry would be avoided if the interpreter
could use semantic information to choose among syntactic rules. For
our purposes, however, the redundancy is convenient in that it
eliminates some backtracking, because the semantic information can
only come into play after the rules for S and VP execute.

15. shift (VP1 → VERB NP PP) governs = DO

VP1 /VERB NP PP   VP1-sem = NP-sem * VERB-sem
governs = DO PP

VERB   VERB-sem = as above

S /VP1   S-sem = as above

16. reduce

VP1 /NP PP   VP1-sem = PP-sem * [NP-sem * VERB-sem]

S /VP1   S-sem = as above

When these are reduced by applying the semantics for the subject NP
and for the AUX, we have S /NP PP and the semantic representation:

$$
\left[\text{PP-sem} * \left[\text{NP-sem} * \left[\begin{array}{l} \lambda \text{ (p:EDIBLE i:UTENSIL)} \\ \text{[INGEST: eat]} \leftarrow\text{(possible)} \\ \qquad\qquad \leftarrow\text{(agent)}— \text{[GROUP: wealthy1]} \\ \qquad\qquad\qquad \leftarrow\text{(possessing)}— \text{[MONEY]} \\ \qquad\qquad\qquad\qquad \leftarrow\text{(amount)}— \text{[LARGE]} \\ \qquad\qquad\qquad \leftarrow\text{(reference)}— \text{[DEF]} \\ \qquad\qquad \leftarrow\text{(patient)}— \text{[p]} \\ \qquad\qquad \leftarrow\text{(instrument)}— \text{[i]} \end{array} \right] \right] \right]
$$

That is, the interpreter has found a sentence consisting of a verb and
its agent, but lacking a patient, which is expected next, and a PP. The

NP *soup* is interpreted (via the functions NP1 /NOUN and NP /NP1), then the prepositional phrase *with a silver spoon.* (following the same sequence that misread *the wealthy can*: PP /PREP NP, NP /DET NP1, NP1 /ADJ NP1, NP1 /NOUN). This leaves us with an attachment for the prepositional phrase that is allowed by syntax and semantics.

NP	NP-sem = [UTENSIL: spoon1]
	←(made-of)— [METAL: silver]
	←(reference)— [DEFINITE]

PP /NP	PP-sem = NP-sem * [λ (y)
	[y:PHYS-OBJ) [ACT] ←(instrument)– [y]
	or λ (y)
	[PHYS-OBJ] ←(attribute)– [y]]

S /PP	S-sem =
	PP-sem * [λ (p:EDIBLE i:UTENSIL)
	[INGEST: eat1] ←(possible)
	←(agent)— [GROUP: wealthy1]
	←(possessing)— [MONEY]
	←(amount)— [LARGE]
	←(reference)— [DEF]
	←(patient)— [EDIBLE: soup]
	←(instrument)— [i]

Because an instrument is more specific than an attribute its rule is proposed first and it succeeds. A different method might associate with NOUN entries, the prospect of their being instruments. Representing two senses of *spoon.* we might have

NOUN-sem =   [INGEST, PREPARE] ←(instrument)— [UTENSIL: spoon]

        or [CATCH] ←(instrument)— [LURE: spoon]

The ordering of rules (specifically the choice at step 15) assures minimal attachment of the PP. If the prepositional phrase were *with barley*:

    PP   λ (x) [x] ←(accompanies)— [EDIBLE: barley]

semantics would block the attachment, forcing the interpreter to backtrack to the most recent choice point accommodating a phrase, and employ NP /NP1 PP instead of NP /NP1.

Though our illustration employs only a small grammar and simple shift-reduce parser, it is extendible in several directions. The grammar has all the flexibility of a phrase structure grammar and can be augmented to incorporate syntactic features for greater sensitivity to context and to accommodate bounded and unbounded movement. The parser could be any device which implements a phrase structure grammar: an augmented transition network, an active chart parser, even a look-ahead parser.

Exercises

1. In interpreting the following sentences, which would benefit from scheduling that encourages minimal attachment, which would benefit from timely semantics, and which would benefit from neither? In each case, explain your conclusion.

> They drove the car to the airport.
> They drove her home.
> They said they would go today.
> The experience of the passengers was frightening.
> They opened the door with the key.
> They decided on the plane.
> They put the book in a bag under the seat.

2. Assuming a system that gives privilege to semantics, devise a set of case frames and rules that would correctly interpret the subject, verb, and prepositional phrase in *he baked the cake for thirty minutes* and *the cake baked for thirty minutes*.

3. The sentences *they made her a cake* and *they made her president* might not be interpreted efficiently by a system giving privilege to semantics. Explain.

4. Give a rule of categorial grammar that would accommodate the adverb *rapidly* in *she walked rapidly*. Though that sentence can be accommodated, does the behavior of adverbs present a difficult challenge for categorial grammars? Explain.

5. One measure of the usefulness of rule-by-rule interpretation is its efficiency with lexical ambiguity. First, using the ATN in the appendix to Chapter 7, parse the sentence *Plastic balls hit people*; next, using the rule-by-rule grammar given in Figure 7, trace the parse and interpretation of the same sentence.

6. The categorial grammar described in Section 3.2 does not accommodate possessive personal pronouns in the attributive position; add the appropriate rule and trace the interpretation of *His mother wrote her letter*.

7. With the rules in Figure 7 and a shift-reduce interpreter, what would be the contents of the stack just before and just after encountering *eat* in *the young will eat supper*.

8. The rule-by-rule grammar given in Figure 7 does not accommodate prepositional phrases occurring within noun phrases. If the rewrite rule were NP → NOUN PP what would be the corresponding syntactic and semantic rules. Using a shift-reduce interpreter, apply your rules to the noun phrase *the corner of the house*, showing the state of the stack at each stage in the interpretation.

Further reading

On the modularity hypothesis and empirical research it has stimulated, consult J. A. Fodor (1983 and 1985) and the papers in Garfield (1987) by Clifton and Ferreira, Frazier, Altmann, and Marslen-Wilson. Also see Pulman (1986), Clifton and Ferreira (1989), Steedman and Altmann (1989), and Thompson and Altmann (1990). For arguments and empirical evidence that, at least on the first pass, parsing is autonomous see Rayner, Carlson, and Frazier (1983), Ferreira and Clifton (1986), Clifton and Ferreira (1989); also see Abney (1989) and Frazier (1990). Mitchell (1987, 1989) adduces evidence that not even information about verb subcategorizations can influence the parser's first pass through the sentence; see also Frazier, Clifton, and Randall (1983). On the other hand, Taraband and McClelland (1988), Carlson and Tanenhaus (1988), Stowe (1989), and Tanenhaus, Carlson, and Trueswell (1989) present evidence that thematic (case) information helps guide the first pass and will occasionally override the parsing preferences. According to Crain and Steedman (1985), Altmann and Steedman (1988) and Altmann (1988) even discourse analysis can influence parsing, specifically presuppositional information about the referents of anaphoric noun phrases.

On the conceptual dependency interpreter, see Schank and Riesbeck (1981) and Gershman (1982). Lytinen (1986) describes the tandem model. On categorial grammar, its extensions, and parsers to implement it see Steedman (1987), Haddock (1989), Pareschi and Steedman (1987), Wittenburg (1987), and the papers in Oehrle, Bach and Wheeler (1988). On Montague grammar, see Dowty, Wall, and Peters (1981), Partee (1975), and Halvorsen (1986); Hirst (1987) describes a rule-by-rule approach pairing Montague's semantics with a parser resembling Marcus's PARSIFAL. For rule-by rule approaches that translate sentences directly into logical form, see Rosenschein and Shieber (1982) and Schubert and Pelletier (1982). For ATN-based rule-by-rule interpreters, see Bobrow and Webber (1980), Ritchie (1980), and Woods (1980). Other incremental methods of combining syntactic and semantic analysis are described by Winograd (1972), Bobrow and Webber (1980), Robinson (1982), Mellish (1983, 1985), Lesmo and Torasso (1985), and Haddock (1989).

Chapter 11

Discourse Interpretation Using World Knowledge

Section one: Coherence and Implicit Knowledge

1.1 The coherence of discourse

Single sentences are seldom the basic units of communication. Even in conversations, communicative units are usually larger and have sentences (and sometimes fragments of sentences) as their constituents. To investigate these communicative units, their internal coherence, and their mental representation is to study **discourse**. Though the term discourse is sometimes restricted to extended, highly organized expositions of subjects, discourse may also be relaxed narrative or a sketchy description. It need not even be monologic; the give and take of conversations coalesce to form coherent units.

Discourse is presumed by the listener or reader to be coherent, to hang together in some more or less orderly fashion. If we encounter the sentences,

> The cat climbed a fence. He fell off.

we presume that *he* and *the cat* refer to the same animal. If the sentences are

> We are going to be in Boston. We will be visiting friends.

we presume that the friends are in Boston, because we are familiar with the general-particular ordering of sentences and presume that the ordering is operant here. Should we encounter,

> The burglar entered the house. Suddenly, the lights went on.

we presuming contiguity in space and time and never consider the possibility that whereas the entering occurs in Chicago on Wednesday, the lights went on in Detroit on the preceding Monday. Also, we may infer a causal connection between the events because we know that causes often precede results; certainly, we presume causality with

> The baby cried. His father picked him up.

The presumption of coherence is so strong that it operates in unpropitious situations. We are quite ready to interpret a murmur in such a way as to make it a relevant contribution to a conversation, even when it is made by an infant or by one who is gravely ill.

Languages offer many ways of explicitly expressing coherence; thus the speaker or writer could say,

The cat climbed the fence.	The same animal fell off.
We are going to Boston.	We will be visiting friends in the city.
The burglar entered the house.	Then the lights in the house went on.
The baby cried.	Therefore, the baby's father picked him up.

Although successive sentences could be explicitly connected, as these are, the connectives are often omitted, and that is significant. Speakers and writers know that coherence will be presumed and actively sought; consequently they reserve the explicit connectives for those occasions on which the relationship between successive utterances deserves special emphasis or might be misconstrued.

Since listeners and readers presume coherence, it is reasonable to suppose that they attempt to integrate propositions expressed by sentences, that their mental representations of the state of affairs presented in the discourse is something more than a simple list or cognitive inventory. The same participants and objects appear in successive sentences, so there should at a minimum be some linking of the arguments shared by propositions. Empirical studies suggest that at least this much does occur. The researchers presented subjects with series of sentences with iterated noun phrases or with sentences which connected some of them:

Series one:	Series two:
Some meat was on the table.	Some meat was on a table in a kitchen.
The table was in a kitchen.	The dog was hungry.
A dog was hungry.	The dog ate the meat and was punished.
The dog ate the meat.	
The dog was punished	

After a brief interval, the subjects were given unexpected recognition tests containing some sentences they had heard, and others which, though consistent with those they had heard, were not actually part of the series. *The hungry dog ate the meat* is an example. The subjects were to identify those that were part of the series and to rate their confidence in the identification. Not only were they unable to distinguish sentences they had heard from amalgams that they had not heard, but they tended to be more confident in identifying sentences with multiple propositions, including, for example, *The hungry dog ate the meat on the table in the kitchen and was punished.* Apparently, they had merged propositional representations via such shared arguments as:

[PHYS-OBJ: table122] ←(location)– [PLACE: kitchen43]

[PHYS-OBJ: meat89] ←(location) –[PHYS-OBJ: table122]

and therefore remembered a unified representation of the discourse.

That the table in the kitchen is indeed the same table holding the meat is not made explicit, but must instead be inferred. Such inferences, though not founded in logic and not guaranteed in the way that deduction guarantees a true conclusion from a true premise, are nonetheless plausible and we make them readily. The syntax helps, because definite noun phrases usually pick out some entity that has already been introduced, whereas new entities are nearly always introduced via indefinite noun phrases. But it is primarily the presumption of discourse coherence that lends credibility to the inference that both references are to the same table. Just as readily we infer connections when arguments, though not the same, are lexically related as parts and hyponyms:

> Joe bought a detective novel. When he got home, he
> read the first chapter.

That one sense of *novel* is a hyponym of *book* and one sense of *chapter* is a part of *book* is sufficient warrant for inferring that the first chapter that Joe read was of the detective novel that he purchased. Again there are no guarantees, but if discourse coherence is presumed, the inference is quite plausible.

1.2 Bridging Inferences

Combining the propositions in a discourse often requires inferences of a different sort. These **bridging inferences** connect entities, states, or events explicitly mentioned in the discourse by way of other entities, states, or events that are only implicit. Bridging inferences are founded not on linguistic knowledge, but on our experience, either direct or vicarious, of how things typically happen in the world. Consider, for example,

> Larry needed to be in Boston.
> He decided to take a train.
> He bought his ticket and boarded at South Station.
> The train got Larry to Boston by noon.

To connect the first sentence with the remainder of the discourse we infer a goal (being in Boston) that explains an ensuing action (taking the train.), though the discourse does not make that connection explicit. Integrating the third sentence requires another bridging inference: buying the ticket enables Larry to board the train. Though the ticket could have been for a lottery or a basketball game, train trips ordinarily require the prepurchase of tickets. When we subsequently hear that Larry enjoyed the view from his window, the window in question is part of the train and not a window somewhere else. Though they are not guaranteed in logic such inferences are highly probable, given the explicit indications and the presumed coherence of the discourse.

Another kind of bridging inference does bring to bear a knowledge of logical operations, but again the processing is largely unconscious. Consider, for example, what connects each of the following pairs of assertions:

> The Red Sox will win the pennant this year. That's because they've finally got good pitching.

> The Red Sox won't win the pennant this year. They traded away their pitchers.

> The Red Sox didn't trade their pitchers. So they must have decided that they are good enough.

The first two depend on an unspoken premise, something like:

> If the Red Sox have good pitching, then they will win the pennant.

and each depends on a familiar logical operation: affirming the antecedent also affirms the consequence, and denying the consequence also denies the antecedent. The third depends on an "exclusive or" premise, something like

> Either the Red Sox decided their pitchers were good enough or they traded them.

and an operation that affirms one by denying the other. Neither the premises nor the procedures that operate on them need be explicitly stated. In each case, what bridges the assertions, though unspoken, is readily inferable.

Bridging inferences are automatic and for the most part unconscious. Empirical studies suggest, but have not yet conclusively established, that the inferencing is done "on line" as we are comprehending the discourse and that the bridging entities, states and events are incorporated into the mental representation. Inferencing takes time and experiments show that subjects take a few milliseconds longer to read a sentence that requires a bridging inference to be coherent with the rest of the discourse. Once the discourse has been understood, however, verification of sentences expressing bridging propositions is equally quick whether that proposition is explicit in the text or requires an inference.

1.3 Constructive interpretation

Speakers or writers of discourse assume that bridging inferences can readily be made. They know how things happen in the world, can predict that their listeners or readers also know, and therefore need provide just enough information to evoke the relevant portion of the readers' or listeners' knowledge. After all, it is not as if the audience will be hearing of train trips for the first time. Because background information is an unexpressed part of the meaning of discourse and what is expressed is sketchy and full of gaps, discourse comprehension is necessarily constructive. Rather than simply stitching together the propositional representations of sentences, comprehension investigates the state of affairs presented in the discourse by building a mental model. Inevitably, some parts of the discourse receive special attention and others will be disregarded, some parts may be believed and others not. The information supplied by the listener or reader may be subtly or not so subtly different from that which the discourse omits.

This is hardly a recent insight; it originated in the 1930s with F. C. Bartlett's seminal research on memory. Bartlett read fairy tales to his subjects and, after some time elapsed, had them retell the stories. Consistently, the retellings were more orderly than the tales, and almost schematic as if reconstructed using a schema of how fairy tales usually proceed. The retellings omitted unusual or digressive elements and, what for our purposes is most interesting, they added bridging inferences and other information that could reasonably be expected given the situations and events in the tales. More recently, a series of empirical studies showed that knowledge of what usually happens also influences sentence recall. Subjects were given such sentences as,

> He slipped on a wet spot and dropped the delicate glass pitcher on the floor.
>
> (Johnson, Bransford and Soloman, 1973)

> Three turtles rested on a floating log and a fish swam beneath them.
> (Bransford, Barclay and Franks, 1972)

Then the subjects were given a recognition test containing sentences such as the following:

> He slipped on the wet floor and broke the delicate glass pitcher when it fell on the floor.

> Three turtles rested on a floating log and a fish swam beneath it.

The subjects were quite confident that they had heard these latter sentences, even though the sentences contain implications not explicitly mentioned in those they actually heard.

Clearly, comprehension requires vast amounts of "common sense" knowledge to supply for the discourse model what is taken for granted in the discourse. It is conceivable that comprehension builds the discourse model piece by piece, using whatever explicit connections present themselves and consulting long-term memory for connections and other information that is not explicit. By this view, memory could consist of one encyclopedic collection of knowledge. If that knowledge is arrayed as a vast semantic network, it might place mutually relevant information in the same region to enable priming, thus accounting for the rapidity of bridging and other inferences.

Though some early researchers adopted this view, it quickly became apparent that the organization of information is important not only for retrieval but for comprehension as well, and that processing would benefit from the partitioning of information into packets, each relevant to a discourse (or to some subsection). Each packet would consist of a distillation of prior experiences that retains regularities but omits incidental and non recurring detail. (That human minds exhibit an inborn propensity to expect regularities and to seek them out explains both how the packets come to be formed and why they are employed in interpreting discourse.) Functioning like a case frame, each packet would supply conceptual scaffolding and a series of expectations of particular participants, events, and results. Expectations which are satisfied by explicit propositions in the discourse would be instantiated; those remaining unfulfilled would constitute bridging inferences and would also be instantiated.

What empirical evidence there is also supports the latter view. One experiment presented measured reading times for target sentences following specific and generalized contexts. The specific context was sufficiently familiar to invoke a packet of relevant information:

> Title: In court
> Fred was being questioned.
> He had been accused of murder.
> Target: The lawyer was trying to prove his innocence.

The generalized context would not invoke the packet until the target sentence is reached:

> Title: Telling a lie.
> Fred was being questioned.
> He couldn't tell the truth.
> Target: The lawyer was trying to prove his innocence.
>   (Sanford & Garrod, 1981)

Reading times for target sentences presented in specific contexts were much faster and consistently so; recognizing a familiar context simplifies interpretation by predicting what will ensue. Other researchers have shown the strength of these expectations. They contrived passages that are ambiguous as to the activity taking place; making music or engaging in a game, for example, share enough words with multiple meanings (*play, score, exercise*) to make for passages that are pointedly ambiguous. Instead of noticing the ambiguity, subjects tended to invoke one domain or the other and to impose on the discourse a single interpretation.

At about the same time that psychologists were beginning to investigate the role of world knowledge in discourse comprehension, Roger Schank and his associates were developing their conceptually motivated theory of sentence comprehension. They wanted their representations of sentence meaning to include not only what was explicitly expressed but also any inferences that a listener or speaker would typically derive. But they encountered a problem. Each sentence gave rise to a large number of plausible inferences, each of which gave rise to further inferences, until very quickly the inferencing engendered a combinatorial explosion. Their answer was to use context to determine what inferences are useful and hence to consider the role played by each sentence in the developing discourse. Thus by a different route they were led to the packeting of information: packets constrain the number and kinds of inferences that need to be drawn.

That background knowledge should be brought to bear in packets rather than piecemeal leads to another set of questions. How is the appropriate packet selected? What are the properties of the packets and in particular should packets comprehend entire topics of discourse or subdivide knowledge into more frequently recurring units? If the latter, what should guide their integration into a unified interpretation of the entire discourse?

Section two: Scripts for stereotypical events

2.1 Scripted knowledge

Script-theory, developed by Roger Schank and Robert Abelson, provided an early and very influential model for constructive interpretation of narrative discourse. The essential idea is that much in discourse, as in life, is routine and unvarying or takes place within a routine context. Such stereotypical experiences are so readily invoked, that jokes can depend on them; the country music lyric, "My wife ran off with my best friend and I still miss . . . him" is an example. Schank and Abelson proposed that such routine experiences as visiting a restaurant, attending a movie, borrowing a book from a library, or getting somewhere by bus are mentally represented by prepackaged scripts. **Scripts** represent coherent sequences of the smaller events that compose routine experiences. Thus a restaurant script would include such events as being seated, reading a menu, ordering food, eating the meal, paying the bill, and so on in tedious enumeration. Such events occur during every visit to a restaurant, but only some of them might be mentioned in a narrative of the visit to the restaurant (mentioning them all would make the narrative as tedious as the script).

The script supplies motives and effects, context for the fragmentary information in the narrative, and causal or other connections between events. Some scripts include stereotypical variations on the ordinary course of events: what happens if some item on the menu proves not to be available or what occurs in a fast food restaurant. These are important in that they cope with what does not happen, and they can sometimes explain why. Scripts also bring context to bear on the problem of ambiguity. If one among multiple interpretations of an ambiguous sentence, such as *he went to the bank*, satisfies an active script (perhaps a fishing script or a financial transaction script), that interpretation is chosen.

Some empirical research supports the idea of scripts. When subjects are presented with narratives such as might be mentally represented as a script, and then asked to recall events in the narrative, they tended to recall events that had not been mentioned in the narrative. They also tended to recall that events occurred in what would be a plausible order for the script, rather than their actual order in the narrative. Another experiment measured reading times for sentences that might correspond to events in specific scripts. When the prior context was sufficiently specific as to activate a particular script, reading times were shorter than when prior context was less suggestive.

Scripts facilitate comprehension, and we consciously or unconsciously employ them, even when the topic is not a sequence of events. Asked about the spatial layout of their apartments, ninety seven percent of the respondents in one study did not proceed at random or present the most salient features first, but instead narrated a stereotypical walking tour; the tour began at the front door, just as it would if one were to visit the apartment for the first time, and moved from that natural starting point through a natural progression of rooms. The stereotypical narration provides a familiar conceptual framework within which the individuating details are more easily comprehended.

Scripts were never intended as a full solution to the challenge of continuous discourse, but rather as a first approximation of the knowledge structures and processing that discourse requires. By experimenting with script-based processing and determining exactly where and why it proves inadequate, their inventors thought, it should

Roles and props:

PATRON = [HUMAN: X]
LIBRARIAN = [HUMAN]
LIBRARY = [PLACE: A]
CATALOG = [PLACE: B]
CHECK-OUT = [PLACE: C]
BOOK = [PHYS-OBJ: A]
CARD = [PHYS-OBJ: B]
CALL NUMB. = [SYMBOL A]
KEYBOARD = [TOOL: A]
SCREEN = [TOOL: B]

Preconditions:

[WANT] ←(agent)— [HUMAN: X]
       ←(patient)— [PHYS-OBJ: book]

[HAS] ←(agent)— [HUMAN: X]
      ←(patient)— [PHYS-OBJ: card]

Effect:

[HAS] ←(agent)— [HUMAN: X]
      ←(patient)— [PHYS-OBJ: book]
      ←(location)— [PLACE: X]

1. [GO] ←(agent)— [HUMAN: X]
      ←(destination)— [PLACE: A]

2. [GO] ←(agent)— [HUMAN: X]
      ←(destination)— [PLACE: B]

3. [ASK] ←(agent)— [HUMAN: X]
      ←(patient)— [MESSAGE: X] ←(name)— [PHYS-OBJ: A]
      ←(instrument)— [WRITE] ←(agent)— [HUMAN]
                    ←(patient)— [MESSAGE: X]
                    ←(instrument)— [TOOL: A]

4. [TELL] ←(patient)— [MESSAGE: call number1]
      ←(instrument)— [WRITE] ←(patient)— [SYMBOL A]
                     ←(instrument)— [TOOL: B]
      ←(beneficiary)— [HUMAN: X]

5. [GO] ←(agent)— [HUMAN: X]
      ←(origin)— [PLACE: B]
      ←(destination)— [PLACE: C]

6. [MATCH] ←(agent)— [HUMAN: X]
      ←(patient)— [SYMBOL: A]
      ←(patient)— [SYMBOL: A]

7. [TAKE] ←(agent)— [HUMAN: X]
      ←(patient)— [PHYS-OBJ: A]

8. [GO] ←(agent)— [HUMAN: X]
      ←(origin)— [PLACE: C]
      ←(destination)— [PLACE: D]

9. [TRANSACT] ←(agent)— [HUMAN: Y]
      ←(patient)— [PHYS-OBJ: A]
      ←(recipient)— [HUMAN: X]
      ←(instrument)— [PHYS-OBJ: B]

10. [BRING] ←(agent)— [HUMAN: X]
      ←(patient)— [PHYS-OBJ: A]
      ←(origin)— [PLACE: A]

Figure 1. A library script.

be possible to gain some sense of how to proceed. That is what happened. Inadequacies of scripts pointed the way toward smaller, more adaptive structures and to a method of processing that combines the top-down, predictive operation of scripts with a bottom-up, more nearly inductive approach.

Each script consist of a header and a body. The header contains preconditions, effects, and sometimes roles and props: all of which can be useful in selecting one script over another similar script. **Preconditions** specify states of the world that exist prior to the enacting of the script and that must be true in order for the script to be enacted. **Effects** are states that necessarily exist as a consequence of the enactment of the script or those portions of the script that precede them. The **body** contains actions in the anticipated order of occurrence. Each action is a substep of the script that could plausibly be expressed by a single sentence. Each is to be matched against propositional representations of sentence meaning and those that are not explicit in the narrative are inferred to have occurred. (They are bridging inferences.) Actions may be simply listed or they may be connected by ←(is-next)– links; in either case they are interpreted as forming a chain. Chains may branch into separate tracks, with each track potentially leading to a different set of effects. In other respects, scripts resemble frames. Associated with each action are slots for the roles and props required by that action. Each slot would be constrained as to the values it will accept so that, for example, the eating is of food, but the paying is with money.

2.2 Script selection and instantiation

Reduced to its essentials, script-based processing consists of selecting the appropriate script then instantiating it by replacing variables in the script with entities from the sentence. The resulting representation is an instance as described in the narrative of the stereotypical course of events expressed in the script. The library script in Figure 1 is sufficient to explicate a brief narrative relating Louise's trip to the library:

> Louise wanted *Pride and Prejudice* or *Wuthering Heights*. The computer gave her the call numbers. Louise checked out *Pride and Prejudice*, and she brought it home.

The narrative leaves out most of what happened. It does not say that Louise went to the library, though the second and third sentences make that a strong probability. It does not tell us how she obtained the call number or, for that matter, how the narrative is advanced by obtaining it. Also, the verb in the third sentence is ambiguous among several senses, an ambiguity that information within the sentence can only partially resolve.

The first step is to select an appropriate script. In limited knowledge domains of the kind that many experimental systems employ, scripts are selected by keywords. Entities mentioned early in the narrative are be matched against roles in the script header. However, keyword matching can go drastically wrong—even in limited domains. One program for summarizing news stories selected a natural disaster script for a story headed "Pope's death shakes Western world," conjuring up an earthquake occurring somewhere in the Western world. When the number of scripts increases into the hundreds of thousands, as they would need to do if a computational 'scriptorium‛ is to represent the colossal variety of experience that adults possess, simple keyword matching would very frequently fail. Many are called, but few are chosen. Yet only rarely do humans go wrong in processing discourse. When we do, suddenly realizing that the subject is something other than we thought, we experience a conscious, effortful reconstruction of events to fit the new script.

A better method than keyword matching is to compare propositional representations of the narrative's sentence first sentence or two against preconditions in the headers. The first sentences in the library narrative might be represented:

[WANT] ←(agent)— [HUMAN: Louise1]
     ←(patient)— [PHYS-OBJ: book] ←(name)— [*Pride and Prejudice*]

Sentences, such as this, that express states rather than actions are especially helpful in script selection, because they can be matched against stative propositions given as preconditions and effects. In this case, the sentence expresses a goal. Nearly as helpful would be a statement that Louise possesses the book, since the state is assumed to be relevant either as a precondition to some event (such as her settling down to read the book) or as the effect of an event (a trip to the library or a bookstore). If, as often happens, neither roles nor preconditions avail, then representations for sentences must be matched against acts and effects in the body of the script. If the first sentence were *Louise got a ticket*, the vague *got* and ambiguous *ticket* would suggest TAKE-TRIP, ATTEND-EVENT, BECOME-CERTIFIED, RECEIVE-SUMMONS, LABEL-MERCHANDISE, and perhaps other scripts, each of which must be matched against the representations for subsequent sentences. Working with actions rather than states can be more difficult. Scripts typically contain many more actions than preconditions or effects, and many more actions than are mentioned in the narrative. Actions at the beginning of the narrative may come somewhere in the middle of the script, so script selection may require tedious amounts of pattern matching. Actions can also be vague, ambiguous, or both.

Precondition:

[WANT] ←(agent)— [HUMAN: Louise1]
   ←(patient1)— [PHYS-OBJ: book] ←(name)— [*Pride and Prejudice*]
   ←(patient2)— [PHYS-OBJ: book] ←(name)— [*Wuthering Heights*]

Actions:

1. [GO] ←(agent)— [HUMAN: Louise1]
   ←(destination)— [PLACE: library1]

2. [GO] ←(agent)— [HUMAN: Louise1]
   ←(destination)— [PLACE: catalog]

3. [ASK] ←(agent)— [HUMAN: Louise1]
   ←(patient)— [MESSAGE1: "*Pride and Prejudice*"]
   ←(name)— [PHYS-OBJ: book]
   ←(instrument)— [WRITE] ←(agent)— [HUMAN: Louise1]
           ←(patient)— [MESSAGE1]
           ←(instrument)— [TOOL: keyboard]

4. [TELL] ←(patient)— [MESSAGE: call number1]
   ←(instrument)— [WRITE] ←(patient)— [MESSAGE: call number1]
           ←(instrument)— [TOOL: screen1]

Figure 2. The partially instantiated library script.

For the library narrative, even knowing the goal is not sufficient to select one script. A reasonably complete collection of scripts (scriptorium?) would offer more than one way of satisfying Louise's goal: she might, for example, be about to go to a bookstore. Hence the goal only narrows the search for the relevant script. Bookstore and library scripts would be retrieved, but neither would be selected until, with the second sentence, there is a basis for deciding between them. The verb *gave* could express several kind of TRANSFERs, but with MESSAGE as patient, TELL is the relevant subtype. The appropriate propositional representation is generated and it matches subaction #4 in the library script. Perhaps the bookstore script also has a computer TELLing customers whether the book is in stock (some bookstores do), but the library script with its mention of a call number would afford a more specific match. Were there no reference to a call number, the more specific of the meanings of *checked out* would identify the library script. When specificity will not decide among scripts, selection uses other heuristics which compute the number and kinds of correspondence between narrative and script.

The selected script is instantiated using information from the narrative (mainly roles and props) to fill the slots. In Louise's narrative, the first action corresponds to the fourth step so instantiation can proceed up to that point (see Figure 2). And we now have useful information on how to proceed. Action #4 is a "now-point," the location within the script from which to start matching propositional representations of the remaining sentences in the narrative. The now-point will be continuously updated as events in the narrative are matched against actions in the script. There may also be a limit on the number of future actions that are accessible from the now-point so as to limit the number of actions against which each propositional representation is matched.

The next sentence is *Louise checked out Pride and Prejudice*, with its ambiguous verb. Semantic interpretation can eliminate only some of the possible meanings of the phrasal verb *checked out*. It does not refer to the acts of vacating (as of a hotel or motel room) or testing (as of a spacecraft), because the sentence does not fill slots in the case frames for those senses of the verb. Two other senses remain, however. Louise may either have investigated the book or she may have transacted a loan. A script-based system would simply tentatively accept the latter, because the most specific sense meeting the constraints has priority, but what clinches that interpretation is the final sentence. Checking out a book enables one to remove the book from the library, and because the final sentence says that Louise brought the book home with her, *checked out* must denote the transaction. Successfully traversing the script disambiguates the phrasal verb.

Assuming an appropriate mechanism for retrieving information from the instantiated script, the following dialogue is possible:

Query:	Did Louise go to the library?
Answer:	Yes
Query:	What enabled Louise to get the call number?
Answer:	Louise typed the book title.
Query:	Did the library have what she wanted?
Answer:	The library had *Pride and Prejudice*.
Query:	What book did Louise not get.
Answer:	Louise did not get *Wuthering Heights*.

This may seem a modest accomplishment, but consider that the narrative never explicitly said that Louise went to the library or that she obtained the call number by typing the title. That enabling and instrumental actions were executed required bridging inferences warranted by Louise's success in executing subsequent actions. The inferences that the library had a copy of *Pride and Prejudice* and that Louise did not get *Wuthering Heights* also depend on the coherence of the script and are obtained by comparing the WANT precondition with the successfully completed actions. With the instantiated script as context, the final question is not answered inappropriately by listing every book that Louise did not obtain.

2.3 Some emerging problems

As Schank and his colleagues anticipated, experience with scripts and script processing showed them what to try next: smaller, more flexible structures would be computationally more tractable and would better model the processes by which people explicate discourse. Script selection is difficult and, especially when the first sentence or two do not decide the question, it consumes a psychologically implausible amount of time. Yet people do not wait until they are confident they know the specific topic of the discourse before they begin building a model of its content. Because scripts are inherently specific to particular experiences, slightly different experiences would require different scripts: for libraries and bookstores, for supermarkets and convenience stores, on the one hand, and for appliance and furniture stores on the other, for visits to a doctor and a dentist.

Yet most of those thousands of scripts would be partially redundant, with actions and combinations of actions appearing in many scripts. How many differences are there between visiting a doctor and a dentist, between taking a trip by bus and by train? What is known about other aspects of human cognition (sentence recognition for example) suggests that we use and reuse a limited set of knowledge structures, flexibly deploying them to perform in many different contexts. Also, psychologists have documented memory confusions between stories that enact similar, but different scripts, confusions that should not happen if scripts are separately stored knowledge structures.

Another problem is that no script can provide for situations that offer an unbounded number of ways to achieve a given state. For example, the connection between these sentences:

> Jim wanted to impress Marie. Jim prepared Beef Wellington
> for dinner.

is not much more difficult to understand than the connection between Louise wanting a book and going to the library. Understanding it does not even require that one know what Beef Wellington is, though that information will reinforce the point. Yet it is highly unlikely that we have an IMPRESS script, enumerating all the ways that one person might go about impressing another. Finally, structures that capture routines (and routine variations on the routine) cannot cope with the unexpected, except to recognize that it indeed is unexpected. If during Louise's visit to the library, the electric power were suddenly to fail, no action specified in the script would account for it or for Louise's response. Yet the unexpected is often the most important event of a narrative and the reason it is told.

2.4 Adaptive representations

What is required is a more adaptive set of knowledge structures. These should include not only episodic structures corresponding to scripts but also smaller structures—call them **scenes**—consisting of actions and serving as building blocks for episodes. Scenes have three defining characteristics:

  □ The actions of which they are composed are collocational and frequently co-occur in different contexts.

  □ The actions combine to accomplish instrumental goals, which in turn help accomplish the higher-order goals of episodes.

  □ Scene are context free and, as building blocks for episodes, they can be tapped over and over as needed.

When these criteria are applied, the ten actions in the library script readily divide into four groups: GOTO, QUERY, FETCH, TRANSACT (see Figure 3). Clearly, the first three groups would qualify as scenes in that their actions frequently co-occur. Each of the groups accomplishes an instrumental purpose, and each group occurs in many other episodes. Perhaps the fourth would qualify as well, although the particular collocation of actions involved in checking out a library book is idiosyncratic.

One advantage of this scheme is its efficiency. Scenes are context free, so they need not be stored one place in memory and can be accessed via pointers from the episodes. Most of the redundancies in scripts are wrung out of the representations. Another advantage is that scenes can be borrowed from familiar episodes in order to understand episodes that are entirely unfamiliar or contain novel variations. Say, for example, that we have this brief narrative about Louise's job:

> Louise read the part number on the order form. She went to the shelf and compared the part number with those on the bins. Then she picked up the part and took the part over to the shipping clerk.

Even if the computer has no parts-warehouse episode, the intervening event between the reading of the part number and picking up the part is familiar; it enacts the FETCH scene.

```
┌                                                                        ┐
│   GOTO SCENE                                                           │
│                                                                        │
│   Precondition:                                                        │
│   [PHYS-OBJ: X] ←(location)— [PLACE: X]                                │
│                                                                        │
│   Action:                                                              │
│   [GO]   ←(agent)— [ANIMAL:X]                                          │
│          ←(origin)— [PLACE: Y]                                         │
│          ←(destination)— [PLACE: Z]                                    │
│                                                                        │
│   Effect:                                                              │
│   [PHYS-OBJ: X] ←(location)— [PLACE: Y]                                │
└                                                                        ┘

┌                                                                        ┐
│   QUERY SCENE                                                          │
│                                                                        │
│   Preconditions:                                                       │
│   [HUMAN: X] ←(location)— [PLACE: X] —(location)→ [TERMINAL]           │
│                                                                        │
│   [KNOW]  ←(agent)— [HUMAN]                                            │
│           ←(patient)–[MESSAGE: X] —(name)→ [PHYS-OBJ: A]               │
│                                                                        │
│   Actions:                                                             │
│   [ASK]   ←(agent)— [HUMAN]                                            │
│           ←(patient)— [MESSAGE: X]                                     │
│           ←(instrument)— [WRITE] ←(agent)— [HUMAN]                     │
│                                   ←(patient)— [MESSAGE: X]             │
│                                   ←(instrument)— [TOOL: keyboard]      │
│                                                                        │
│   [RESPOND]  ←(patient)— [MESSAGE: X]                                  │
│              ←(instrument)— [WRITE] ←(patient)— [MESSAGE: X]           │
│                                     ←(instr)— [TOOL: screen]           │
│   Effect:                                                              │
│   [KNOW]  ←(agent)— [HUMAN: X]                                         │
│           ←(patient)— [MESSAGE: Y]                                     │
└                                                                        ┘

┌                                                                        ┐
│   FETCH SCENE                                                          │
│                                                                        │
│   Preconditions:                                                       │
│   [KNOW]  ←(agent)— [HUMAN]                                            │
│           ←(patient)— [MESSAGE: Y]                                     │
│                                                                        │
│   [HUMAN: X] ←(location)— [PLACE: X] —(location)→ [SHELVES]            │
│                                                                        │
│   Actions:                                                             │
│   [MATCH]   ←(agent)— [HUMAN]                                          │
│             ←(patient)— [MESSAGE: Y]                                   │
│             ←(patient)— [MESSAGE: Y]                                   │
│                                                                        │
│   [TAKE]   ←(agent)— [HUMAN]                                           │
│            ←(patient)— [PHYS-OBJ: X]                                   │
│                                                                        │
│   Effect:                                                              │
│   [HAS]   ←(agent)— [HUMAN]                                            │
│           ←(patient)— [PHYS-OBJ: X]                                    │
└                                                                        ┘
```

Figure 3. Three recurring scenes.

Like scripts, scenes represent preconditions and effects as states, and the relationship between states and the events that connect them can be formally stated in the **situational calculus**. A situation is an interval during which the truth value of a state does not change; collocations of actions effect transitions between situations and may change the truth values of states. The situation calculus requires some simplifying assumptions, however, and these limit its applicability. All states must be discrete, and changes in state cannot be continuous; every state in the situation remains the same except those that are explicitly changed; and, finally, each old situation is succeeded by exactly one new situation. If the domain allows these simplifications and may do, logically secure inferences can be made. The state that Louise is in the library is true of the situation resulting from Louise's going to the library. Abductive reasoning is also available, though it still has its attendant risks: if Louise has a library book and we have no evidence to the contrary, Louise must have fetched that library book.

The successors to script theory, notably Robert Wilensky's theory of **plans** and **plan inferencing**, and Schank's theory of **memory information packets (MOPs)** and **dynamic memory**, employ knowledge structures corresponding to scenes. Plans and MOPs correspond to the episodes, and both theories have counterparts of scenes and actions. Wilensky's focus is on the connections that explain how actions participate in scenes and scenes participate in episodes. Assuming purposive behavior, planning systems perform means-ends analysis to determine how actions enable the completion of scenes and scenes help accomplish the goals of episodes. (Planning on various scales and in various domains has been extensively studied since the early 1970s when Allen Newell and Herbert Simon introduced it as a method for computational modeling of mental processes; it underlies work in several disciplines of artificial intelligence, among them automated theorem proving and robotics.) Many computational linguists have adopted the plan-based approach, and the account of discourse processing in the next section derives from Wilensky's work. Schank's focus is complementary. He is primarily interested in the cognitive processes that acquire, store, and retrieve knowledge structures. In his view, memory is dynamic rather than static; it is capable of learning new MOPs from a few exposures to the kind of event they represent. Dynamic memory can also adapt scenes and MOPs to accommodate minor variations, and (most importantly) it can abstract away any minor discrepancies so as to create generalized scenes and MOPs. Thus understanding a narrative about a dental appointment would require a generalized visit-professional-office MOP together with a visit-dentist MOP containing events particular to that experience.

Section three: Planning and Interpretation

3.1 Comprehending by inferring plans

To comprehend narrative and explanatory discourse is to infer how
events explicitly mentioned in the discourse are part of a plan to
accomplish some goal. That is the central idea of plan-based interpretation, an approach inspired by computational research in non linguistic
problem solving. (A major subfield of artificial intelligence, problem
solving research addresses such questions as how a robot might
program itself to accomplish assigned tasks). Plan-inference systems
use information about the goals that people commonly have and about
the plans by which people achieve their goals. Typical goals include
procuring ownership or physical possession, changing physical location
or proximity, acquiring information or skills, obtaining authority to
perform a certain action or freedom to perform any action, and
delegating agency from oneself to someone else. Some goals may be
instrumental to other goals; a delegation of agency, for example, by
which one instructs or persuades another to execute a plan, might not
be an end in itself but rather a precondition to procuring ownership or
achieving information. Plan-based interpretation also copes with
hitches, interruptions, and other unexpected events and with the
potentially conflicting goals of multiple participants. Though it is
difficult to represent certain kinds of actions, notably repetitive actions
and cyclical sequences of actions, in any straightforward way, planning
does offer a coherent way of interpreting most kinds of narrative.

   Plans organize events in terms of the goals that they accomplish.
These links can be stated as rules. A rule of the general form
<state> → <goal> specifies that particular goals arise from particular
states, thus we might have a state of wanting a physical object as
leading to a goal of possessing that object:

   [WANT] ←(agent)— [HUMAN]   →   [HAS] ←(agent)— [HUMAN]
          ←(patient)— [PHYS-OBJ]   ←(patient)— [PHYS-OBJ]

The rule <goal> → <plan> links a particular plan with a goal; if the
goal is to obtain a book, for example, this rule would evoke bookstore,
library and other plans for obtaining a book. It is equally possible that
something is wanted for its intended use (a hammer to pound a nail),
and that its use is the substep in a plan. Thus, we can have inference
rules of the form <state> → <act>:

   [WANT] ←(agent)— [HUMAN]   →   [ACT] ←(agent)— [HUMAN]
          ←(patient)— [PHYS-OBJ]   ←(instr)— [PHYS-OBJ]

and <act> → <plan> identifies a plan of which a particular act is a constituent. Some plans may be instrumental in the execution of others. In order to GOTO the library or bookstore, for example, one must have a suitable means of transport. So we also need rules of the general form <plan1> → <goal <plan2 > > to specify plans that have as their goals the satisfaction of prerequisites of higher-order plans.

The plans themselves contain substeps for accomplishing the goal and sometimes alternative ways that the goal might be accomplished, each with its substeps (see Figure 4). The substeps correspond in their scope to our scenes. Both plans and substeps may have **preconditions**, which determine when they are applicable. The preconditions resemble those for scripts except that they are sometimes divided into preconditions that an agent can plan to satisfy and those that are out of the agent's control. (If, for example, it is precondition to obtaining a library book that one know the title of the book, then there may be a plan for obtaining the title.) Plans and substeps also have **effects** that will result from their execution. Some but not all effects are goals. For instance, when physical objects are obtained by purchasing them, possession of the object is a goal, but non possession of the money expended for the object is an effect but (ordinarily) not a goal.

The plan for borrowing a library book looks very much like the corresponding script (though there will be differences in processing), because the requisite substeps and their sequence can be choreographed. Plan inferencing does not ignore the insight that much experience is routine. Of a much higher level of generality, the plan for obtaining a physical object suggests the flexibility of plan inferencing. The HAS effect is precondition to countless higher-order plans, and the alternative BORROW, PURCHASE, and STEAL substeps represent alternative ways of carrying out the plan.

3.2 Predictions and chaining

The chief difference between plan-based and script-based systems is in the processing. Rather than simply matching events against a prepackaged script, plan inferencing might begin with an action and look for a substep of which the action is part. Or it might begin with a state and look for that state as the precondition or effect of some substep. Once a substep is identified, the processor continues upward looking for a plan of which that substep is a part. This repetitive inferring of wholes from parts is called **decomposition chaining**.

Once a plan or (as often happens) several plans are identified as candidates for interpreting the narrative, there is a second way of making connections. Plans also predict substeps and substeps predict actions. Thus top-down **predictions** must supplement the bottom-up

BORROW LIBRARY BOOK PLAN

Roles and props: Preconditions:

PATRON = [HUMAN: X]   [WANT] ←(agent)— [HUMAN: X]
LIBRARIAN = [HUMAN: Y]   ←(patient)— [PHYS-OBJ: A]
BOOK = [PHYS-OBJ: A]
CARD = [PHYS-OBJ: B]   [HAS] ←(agent)— [HUMAN: X]
LIBRARY = [PLACE]   ←(patient)— [PHYS-OBJ: B]
TITLE = [MESSAGE]
CALL NUMBER = [SYMBOL]

                              Effect:

Substeps: [HAS] ←(agent)— [HUMAN]
                               ←(patient)— [PHYS-OBJ: Y]

[GOTO] PATRON = [HUMAN: X]
         LIBRARY = [PLACE: Y]

[GOTO] PATRON = [HUMAN: X]
         CATALOG = [PLACE: Y]

[QUERY] TITLE = [MESSAGE: X]
          CALL NUMBER = [MESSAGE: Y]

[GOTO] PATRON = [HUMAN: X]
         SHELF = [PLACE: Y]

[FETCH] [CALL NUMBER] = [MESSAGE: Y]

[GOTO] PATRON = [HUMAN: X]
         CHECK OUT = [PLACE: Y]

[TRANSACT] LIBRARIAN = [HUMAN: X]

OBTAIN PHYSICAL OBJECT PLAN

Roles and props: Precondition:

ACTOR = [ANIMAL: X]   [WANT] ←(agent)— [ANIMAL: X]
OBJECT = [PHYS-OBJ: X]   ←(patient)— [PHYS-OBJ: X]
LENDER = [HUMAN]   Effect:
SELLER = [HUMAN]

                        [HAS] ←(agent)— [HUMAN]
Alternative substeps: ←(patient)— [PHYS-OBJ: X]

       [BORROW] ACTOR = [HUMAN: X]
               LENDER = [HUMAN: Y]
               OBJECT = [PHYS-OBJ: X]

Or   [PURCHASE] ACTOR = [HUMAN: X]
                  SELLER = [HUMAN: Y]
                  OBJECT = [PHYS-OBJ: X]

Or   [STEAL] ACTOR = [ANIMAL: X]
             OBJECT = [PHYS-OBJ: Y]

Figure 4. Specific and general-purpose plans.

method of decomposition chaining. These predictions are important in limiting the search space, which otherwise would include any plan to which a given action might contribute. The candidate plans, even if there are several, make a bounded number of predictions and these are fewer than the number of possible paths for decomposition chaining. Equally important, predicted actions help choose among alternative interpretations of an ambiguous sentence. The influence exerted by candidate plans is only predictive, however. If the action of a given sentence is not predicted, decomposition chaining is still available and can generate additional substeps and plans to be connected to those already present.

If we think of the plans, substeps, and actions as occupying a tree, decomposition chaining probes upward through the tree, whereas predictions propagate downward (see Figure 5). Thus, although the next sentence belongs to a GOTO scene and, with shelf as destination, could be part of a bookstore plan, a tidying-up plan, or perhaps some other, decomposition chaining would not pursue those possibilities. The BORROW-LIBRARY-BOOK plan is predicting that in pursuit of her goal, Louise will next GOTO a shelf.

Linguistic cues can help determine the relationships among events and between states and events or at least limit the number of possibilities that need to be considered. Coordinating and subordinating conjunctions, as well as transitional phrases, often connect sentences and specify relationships relevant to the planning. These include temporal sequence *(now, then, next, immediately, eventually, later, subsequently)*, causation *(hence, so, thus, because, consequently, in order that, so that, provided that)*, and instrumentality *(by, by means of, in order to, in the process of, with a view to, with the intention of)*. Negatives and such connectives as *but, however, lacking, except* can signal precondition failures, modal verbs *(can, could, may, might, would)* may relate preconditions to actions or actions to effects, and tense shifts may move the discourse forward (and sometimes backward) in the plan. From the perspective of plan-inferencing, such linguistic cues are only epiphenomena of the underlying coherence of discourse, and indeed they do not appear to be indispensable to the process of understanding. They are only intermittently available, often ambiguous and sometimes (especially tense shifts) misleading. But they are deployed by careful speakers or writers at precisely the points where connections might otherwise be unclear, and we need to supplement the generalized rules with lexical rules. We might, for example, have rules of the form

$$<state> + [causal\ connective] \rightarrow <plan>$$

where [causal connective] represents the category of transitional words and phrases that denote enablement or causation.

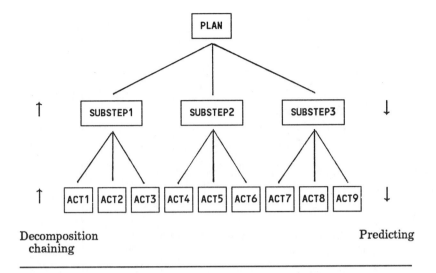

Figure 5. A goal tree.

3.3 Cooperative inferencing

For some idea of how the top down and bottom up inferencing cooperate, we can use a narrative that enacts a familiar episode, but poses two challenges:

> Louise requested the call number and she went to the shelf. When she had the book in hand, Louise borrowed Barbara's library card. Louise checked out the book.

The narrative begins in the middle of things and includes an unexpected borrowing of a library card. The propositional representation for the first sentence matches the [ASK] action in the QUERY substep, and that substep is instantiated as a token of the substep type QUERY. In turn, the QUERY substep with call number as patient matches the BORROW-LIBRARY-BOOK plan; thus decomposition chaining has led upward to a likely plan, and it too is instantiated. Rarely, of course, is it this easy to select a plan. Often it is necessary to go a sentence or two further into the narrative before deciding among specific candidate plans or settling for a generic plan such as OBTAIN-PHYSICAL-OBJECT.

In this case the plan is quite specific and its predictions will be tried. Some of the most useful predictions are of effects, because they support abductive inferencing from effects. In the absence of information to the contrary, a sentence describing the effect of some substep is taken to be sufficient evidence that the substep has been performed. The next sentence offers an example. In the BORROW-LIBRARY-BOOK

OBTAIN PHYSICAL OBJECT

Roles and props:
ACTOR: [HUMAN: Louise]
OBJECT = [PHYS-OBJ: library card]
LENDER = [HUMAN: Barbara]

Precondition:

[WANT]   ←(agent)— [HUMAN: Louise]
         ←(patient)— [ENTITY: library card]

[HAS]   ←(agent)— [HUMAN: Barbara]
        ←(patient)–[PHYS-OBJ: library card]

Effect:

[HAS]   ←(agent)— [HUMAN: Louise]
        ←(patient)— [ENTITY: library card]

BORROW SUBSTEP

Actions:

[REQUEST]   ←(agent)— [HUMAN: Louise]
            ←(patient)— [ACT: TRANSFER]

[TRANSFER]   ←(agent)— [HUMAN: Barbara]
             ←(patient)— [ENTITY: library card]
             ←(source)— [HUMAN: Barbara]
             ←(recipient)— [HUMAN: Louise]

Figure 6. Instantiated OBTAIN-PHYSICAL-OBJECT plan.

plan, the state of having the book is an effect of FETCH. Even though the narrative never mentions how it came to be in her hand, the sentence is accounted for by Louise's having FETCHed the book and the FETCH substep is instantiated. Predictions also supply the necessary context with which to resolve ambiguities. Had the sentence been *Louise located the book on the shelf*, predictions would choose "to find" rather than "to put" as the contextual meaning of the ambiguous *locate*.

Their ability to proceed either by predictive interpretation or by decomposition chaining gives planners the necessary flexibility to succeed with discourse that would thwart simple script-based analysis. Recall that a major problem with scripts is they cannot cope with events that are not specified in the script. The next sentence in our narrative, to the effect that Louise borrowed Barbara's library card, offers an example. Though unexpected, this step is instrumental to her plan, but no plan can anticipate every event that plausibly could further its goal. No borrow-a-library-card substep is to be found in the library plan, but that plan can help explain Louise's action in either of two ways. By decomposition chaining, the processor can find a plan of which borrowing is a substep and instantiate it (see Figure 6), then determine if its effect is a precondition of the present plan. In this case the result of Louise's having borrowed Barbara's card is indeed a precondition of the library plan. If preconditions to the plan had not yielded a match, preconditions of the substeps of the present plan would be consulted. Though substeps will have many more preconditions than does the plan itself: too many to be sorted through in the ordinary course of things, the already-established context should not be disregarded, and the search can start at the now-point and proceed forward.

A different method of accomplishing the same end is to have any failure to meet a precondition make the prediction that some way will be found of overcoming that failure. Failure of a LOCATION precondition, for example, would invoke a GOTO substep. Similarly, failure of a HAS precondition would invoke the OBTAIN-PHYSICAL-OBJECT plan and predict BUY, BORROW, and perhaps STEAL substeps, together with their constituent actions. Thus, upon encountering an explicit precondition failure *(Louise did not possess a library card)*, the context would offer an explanation of what ensues *(Louise borrowed Barbara's library card)*.

In addition to unexpected events, plan-inferencing must cope with failed plans and alternative ways of reaching a goal even when, as often happens, the narrative is not fully explicit. Consider, for example, the relationships implied by successive sentences in this narrative:

> Late one night, Allison wanted to know when Columbus landed.
> First, she asked her father then she looked in a dictionary. She felt
> tired and went to bed.

The first sentence expresses as a goal the acquisition of a piece of information. Several plans would have [WANT] information as preconditions and from among those plans, the second sentence selects CONSULT-BOOK. When the third sentence invokes the competing ASK-PERSON plan, the implication is that CONSULT-BOOK has failed. To record explicit failures (and successes) and to recognize those that are only implicit, plan inferencing needs to track the states achieved or changed through the execution of a given plan.

One solution is to maintain a list of states that are known to exist at each stage of the narrative. Each plan would contain explicit instructions to write to that list its preconditions and, if the plan succeeds, to delete certain preconditions and add effects. If the narrative proceeds from a substep or plan to another substep of the plan it enables, the implicit success of the substep or plan is recorded.

Thus if Allison's looking in the dictionary had been followed by a sentence such as *she wrote it down*, [WANT] would be deleted from the list and [KNOW] would be added. If the narrative proceeds from one plan to a second plan with the same goal, the implicit failure of the first plan is recorded. If, however, the narrative moves from one goal to another (as when Allison tires and goes to bed) the list remains unchanged.

3.4 Planning and speech acts

Thus far the sentences that we have considered describe actions, but a different kind of sentence can perform an action. When Louise says, *I promise that I will go to the library*, for example, she performs the act of placing herself under an obligation. Promising is one of many ways that a sentence can perform a communicative action. The following list of verbs, each of which has at least one sense in which it is performative, will suggest some others:

> accuse, acknowledge, admit, agree, apologize, applaud, arrest, assign, assert, baptize, bet, bless, claim, commend, compliment, concede, concur, congratulate, criticize, dare, declare, defy, demand, deny, dispute, dissent, explain, extol, fine, hypothesize, invite, insist, name, nominate, predict, protest, remind, request, resign, sentence, speculate, suggest, pledge, thank, threaten, theorize, warn, welcome

(One can tell whether a verb sense is performative by asking if it can co-occur with the adverb *hereby: I hereby remind you of your decision*). When sentences with these verbs and others like them perform actions, the actions are **speech acts**. To understand discourse containing performative verbs (which is virtually any discourse in which communication plays a part), we need to understand sentences as acts. For that purpose, plan-based analysis is especially well suited. The goals, preconditions, effects, and substeps of plans provide a sufficiently rich formalism to represent speech acts, and there is considerable advantage in making their representation consistent with the representations of other kinds of actions.

Speech acts have conditions for their appropriate use (sometimes called "appropriacy" or "felicity conditions") which can be incorporated as preconditions. The speech act, REQUEST, in which a speaker asks a hearer to perform some action, has two conditions. The speaker wants the hearer to perform the action and believes that the hearer can perform it. Speech acts also have effects on the addressee; the effect of REQUEST is that the hearer believes the speaker wants her to do what has been requested. In speech act theory, this is called the "perlocutionary force" of the act; perlocutionary contrasts with "locutionary" (which has to do with the uttering of a sentence) and "illocutionary" (the intention to request, promise, or whatever). Similarly, an INFORM speech act has the preconditions that the speaker knows a proposition and intends for the hearer to believe the speaker believes the proposition to be true. INFORM has two effects: the hearer knows the proposition and believes that the speaker intended the hearer to believe it true. If the sentence represents either speech act as having occurred, we can infer that the preconditions and effects are operative and add them to our store of knowledge.

With some speech acts, these inferences are well worth having. Consider, for example, what can be inferred from a speech act PROMISE to perform some action: the speaker wants to put herself under the obligation, knows that the hearer wants her to go perform the action, believes that she can perform it, and would not be performing the action in the ordinary course of things. Similarly, ACCUSE (of some act of omission or commission) has the inferable preconditions that the speaker believes the one accused responsible for the action and believes that the action in question is bad. None of this needs to be explicit in the narrative, because it can be inferred from performance of the speech act. That preconditions and effects are often beliefs that speakers and hearers have about the world and about each other means that they must be partitioned from other knowledge obtained from the discourse. Beliefs are not necessarily true or shared, so the planner must maintain spaces for each participant in the discourse, partition them from shared knowledge, and label them with the modal operator, [concept] ←(belief).

With the performative verbs, interpretation is straightforward. The speech act is functioning as a substep and the planner attempts to reconstruct a plan to which it contributes an enabling link. Other speech acts are more challenging because they are indirect and must be interpreted from the context. For example, INFORM is commonly performed indirectly, either by stating one of its preconditions (*I believe he is here*) or by asking about its effect (*are you aware that he is here?*). As an indirect speech act a REQUEST is often posed in the form of a yes/no question. Asking about one's capacity to perform an action (*can you pass the salt?*) can be a request for that action, asking about a possession can be a request for the possession (*do you have a match?*), and asking the state of one's knowledge can be a request for information (*do you know the time?*).

Conceivably, indirect speech acts are understood as idioms with no ffort made to interpret the direct meaning, reject it, and look for an indirect meaning. A few speech acts (such as the greeting *how do you do?*) probably are idioms. But empirical evidence suggests that most are not. Sentences containing negatives require slightly more processing than those that do not. Thus, if interpretation takes place, speech acts containing negatives should take longer to comprehend, and several studies have shown that they do.

```
┌                                                                          ┐
│  Roles:                        Precronditions:                           │
│                                                                          │
│  ASKER = [HUMAN: X]            [WANT]  ←(agent)— [HUMAN: X]               │
│  INFORMANT = [HUMAN: Y]                ←(patient)— [KNOW]                 │
│  QUESTION = [PROP: A]                            ←(agent)— [HUMAN: X]     │
│  INFORMATION = [PROP: B]                         ←(patient)— [PROP: B]    │
│                                                                          │
│                                [KNOW]  ←(agent)— [HUMAN: Y]               │
│                                        ←(patient)— [PROP: B]              │
│                                                                          │
│                                Effect:                                   │
│                                                                          │
│                                [KNOW]  ←(agent)— [HUMAN: X]               │
│                                        ←(patient)— [PROP: B              │
│  Substeps:                                                               │
│                                                                          │
│  REQUEST    ASKER = [HUMAN: X]                                           │
│             QUESTION = [PROP: A]                                         │
│                                                                          │
│  INFORM     INFORMANT = [HUMAN:Y]                                        │
│             INFORMATION = [PROP:B]                                       │
└                                                                          ┘
```

Figure 7. An OBTAIN-INFORMATION plan.

To identify an indirect speech act and determine, for example, whether the question is indeed a request depends first on the assumption, shared by participants in a dialogue, that each intends purposeful and effective communication. The assumption, called the **cooperative principle**, serves as a condition of appropriacy for all utterances and is sometimes reduced to **conversational postulates**: "be simple," "be helpful," "be relevant," "be perspicuous," and so on. It is therefore reasonable to ask of any yes/no question whether the REQUEST meaning is relevant, and that is where plans come in. Consider, for example, this narrative:

> Rus wanted a library book. Rus went to the catalog terminal and he asked Louise, "Do you know how to obtain call numbers?" She responded, "I believe you just type in the title you want."

Even before we reach Louise's response, Rus's question is interpretable as a request for information. The first two sentences select the BORROW-LIBRARY-BOOK plan, and the QUERY is a substep in that plan. Rus does not, however, ask for a call number. If his question is relevant, it must be to part of a generic OBTAIN-INFORMATION plan that is instrumental to enacting the QUERY substep, much as Louise's plan for borrowing the library card was instrumental to the transaction substep. Louise's response, in turn, is not just a statement of her beliefs, but instead an instance of INFORM that completes OBTAIN-INFORMATION (see Figure 7).

Not all indirect speech acts yield so readily to plan-based analysis. Often it is difficult to decide whether the direct or indirect meaning is intended. Speech acts can also be ambiguous between two or more indirect meanings or can be embedded in ambiguous contexts. What is worse, one sentence can perform multiple speech acts or several sentences can combine to perform a single speech act. But plan-based analysis does go some way toward answering what is the most difficult question for speech act theory: how it is that certain sentences in certain contexts come to receive particular interpretations.

Exercises

1. What bridging inferences would be required to comprehend the following brief narrative? Would they be better supplied using a script or a series of plans? Explain.

> She got in the car and turned the key, but there was only a
> clicking sound. So she decided to walk.

2. Devise a script that would help comprehend narratives of attending a movie, a play, a concert, and a sporting event. The object is to specify all and only the subevents that would occur in narratives of all four.

3. Explain how a set of plans might connect events and disambiguate words in the following brief narrative.

> Needing a new car, Seymour found one in the classified ads.
> He got a check from the bank and bought it.

4. Devise a set of plans that are sufficiently general to interpret narratives of both attending a concert and watching a parade.

5. One challenge for discourse analysis is to identify the antecedents to which pronouns refer. Using the OBTAIN INFORMATION plan in Figure 7 and any subsidiary plan that is required, show how it can be established that both instances of he in the following brief narrative refer to Chuck.

> Chuck needed her phone number. He asked Bill for it. He
> used it to call her.

6. Devise a plan for recognizing the direct speech act in *I fine you $100 for speeding* and the indirect speech act in *That will cost you $100* when spoken by a judge.

7. It has been observed that if we indeed use scripts or plans in interpreting discourse, it is surprising that discourse contains as much information as it does. Comment.

Further reading

An excellent introduction to discourse and its interpretation is given in Brown and Yule, *Discourse Analysis* (1983). See also Stubbs (1983), Leech (1983), and the papers in Joshi, Webber, and Sag (1981) and Grosz, Sparck Jones, and Webber (1986). On constructive interpretation see Bartlett (1932), Barclay, Bransford, and Franks (1972), Bransford and Johnson (1972), Johnson, Bransford, and Solomon (1973), Thorndyke (1977), and the review of early empirical research in Spiro (1980). Subsequent work includes Sanford and Garrod (1981) and Stenning (1986). Also see, Hobbs (1990) and Kegl (1990). Morgan and Sellner (1980) argue that discourse structure is epiphenomenal of the "world" it conveys. On the integrative nature of discourse processing, see Bransford and Franks (1971), Scholtz and Potts (1974), Mani and Johnson-Laird (1982), McKoon, Ratcliff, and Seifert (1989) and Oakhill, Garnham, and Vonk (1989); and on discourse coherence, see Garnham, Oakhill, and Johnson-Laird (1982), Black, Freeman, and Johnson-Laird (1986), and Kintsch (1988). Also see the discussions of discourse models, cited in Chapter 8. On bridging and elaborative inferencing and the question of what kinds of inferences are made on line during discourse processing, see Haviland and Clark (1974), Corbett and Dorsher (1978), Garrod and Stanford (1981), Singer (1981), Garnham (1982), and Rickheit and Strohner (1985). From the burgeoning literature on discourse analysis, deBeaugrande (1980), Tannen (1985), Petröfi (1985), and Reilly (1987) are recommended.

On scripts and script processing, see Schank and Abelson (1977) and Schank and Riesbeck (1981); the latter also contains an account of plan-inferencing. Bower, Black, and Turner (1979) and Abbott, Black, and Smith (1985) describe relevant empirical research. For systems that apply scripts, see DeJong (1982) and Cullingford (1981). The primary source for the linguistic role of plans is Wilensky (1983); on the psychology of planning, see Hoc (1988). Charniak and McDermott (1985) and Allen (1987) offer extensive and complementary discussions of the computational issues. Dyer (1983) describes a fully developed system using plans; others are presented in Litman and Allen (1987 and 1990), Wilensky, Chin, Luria, Martin, Mayfield, and Wu (1988), Grosz, and Sidner (1990), and Carberry (1990). The idea that sentences can be performative originated with Austin (1962) and was extended and formalized by Searle (1969 and 1975). Levinson (1983) provides a comprehensive survey of work in speech act theory. On the computational approach to speech acts using plans, see Cohen and Perrault (1979), Allen and Perrault (1980), Carberry (1983 and 1988), and Sidner (1985).

Chapter 12

Knowledge about Discourse

Section one: Anaphora and Segmentation

1.1 Anaphora and its resolution

The essential insight of script-based and plan based processing is that listeners or readers come to discourse with experience in the world. Constructively interpreting the discourse, they build a mental model that synthesizes information in the discourse with the knowledge of how things typically happen in the world. Listeners and readers also have experience with discourse and apply unconscious expertise to following its twists and turns, suspensions and resumptions. Though it is not easy to model this expertise computationally, considerable progress has been made along two lines: the resolution of anaphoric expressions and the segmentation of discourse. These are, as it turns out, closely related in that resolving anaphora helps identify segments and identifying segments helps resolve anaphora.

An **anaphor** is an expression that takes part of its meaning from some entity, state, or event mentioned nearby (that mention is its **antecedent**). In the simplest case, the anaphor is a definite noun phrase and its antecedent precedes it. For example, the representations for the sentences, *I saw the boy get hit. The kid suffered a broken leg,* where *the kid* is an anaphor and *the boy* its antecedent would share [HUMAN: #123] ←(gender)– [MALE]. In effect, both the anaphor and its antecedent co-specify the same **antecedent concept**.

Locating antecedents has proved to be one of the classic hard problems for computational linguistics. Part of the difficulty is that the search space can be substantial, especially for anaphors that are not pronouns. Though most antecedents occur in the sentence with the anaphor or in the sentence immediately preceding, some may be further back, and when there is a digression in the discourse, the antecedent may occur before the digression and therefore be several sentences away. Within the search space, there may be several NPs, among them more than one that would plausibly serve as antecedent, so the challenge is to find the optimal antecedent, that NP which most nearly agrees with the anaphor.

The difficulty posed by a large search space is compounded by the superabundance of potentially relevant information for identifying antecedents. Sometimes anaphora is resolved simply by finding an antecedent that agrees in number: for example, the antecedents of *they* and *it* in *some boys found a dog and they took it home*. Other cases are far more challenging. Consider, for example, that the antecedent of *he* in *the car was going nearly eighty miles an hour; he did not see the curve in time*, is the mandatory, but unmentioned agent of a case frame for the verb *drive* (also unmentioned). Though script- or plan-based systems, equipped with lists of expected participants and roles, can make some headway, they also require content-independent methods of limiting the search space, locating antecedent concepts, and making the best match when more than one candidate presents itself.

Search space can be narrowed because discourses are not unpartitioned wholes. Instead utterances tend to aggregate into differentiated parts or **segments**. Each is a coherent whole, though it may be partially dependent on context for its interpretation. Segments, in turn, combine to form discourse structures. **Structure**, as the term is used here, does not refer to some externally imposed set of norms for well-formed discourse, though there have been enough pedagogical or editorial efforts to legislate structure. Rather it refers to the organization or outline of the discourse, which may be planned in advance or may simply evolve in an orderly fashion as the discourse proceeds. Structure is as much an attribute of spontaneous conversations as it is of carefully contrived exposition or argumentation. Though segmentation and structure are determined largely by the content of the discourse, there are reliable ways of determining segment boundaries and discourse structure that apply whatever the content. Computational approaches to discourse made little use of this knowledge until quite recently, when it was recognized that content-independent methods of determining boundaries and structure can simplify the instantiating of plans and guide decomposition chaining.

Much of what follows concerns significant regularities derived from large samples of written and tape-recorded discourse. The regularities hold for many, but not all cases; hence they afford heuristics, but not rules. Discourse does not lend itself to the formulation of explicit rules. It offers no equivalent to the finite, quite small set of phonemes or phonological features whose systematic behavior can be specified as phonological rules. Nor does discourse offer any counterpart the well formed sentence whose generation can be specified by a finite set of syntactic rules, or to the substitutional and combinational relations on which semantic rules depend. The basic units for discourse linguistics are propositions, sentences or sometimes "t-units" (groups of words that could be punctuated as sentences), and far from belonging to a small set, these are infinite in number.

1.2 Two approaches to ellipsis

Though the world's languages exhibit many different kinds of ana-phora, two are particularly challenging for computational linguistics. The first is **ellipsis**: the omission of a word or phrase:

> Someone did the work for him. But I don't know who.

The elided (omitted by ellipsis) element is a noun or verb phrase, or one of their constituents, that would be expected in a full, syntactically well-formed sentence. What is omitted leaves a void or "null element," resembling the gap left when wh-words are fronted in relative clauses and wh-questions. With ellipsis, however, no completing word or phrase occupies the hold register. Instead, the null element is anapho-ric, and the antecedent concept is the same element occurring in the immediately preceding sentence or (in the case of dialogue) a sentence or two earlier. That ellipsis is an anaphor distinguishes it from other cases in which something is left unsaid or a sentences is not fully formed: the anaphoric null element is as much a constituent of the sentence as any word or phrase would be. Though especially pervasive in conversation, ellipsis occurs in all kinds of discourse. The gap or null element left by ellipsis signifies only that something is "under-stood," so the challenge is to determine just what has been omitted: a word, part of a phrase, or what.

Much of the computational work on ellipsis has focused on information-seeking dialogue. With natural language query systems, for example, the object is to generate well-structured queries from fragmentary questions:

1. User: How many went to Richmond last month?
2. User: How many to Durham?
3. User: To Fairfax this month?

Since queries are predictable and readily divided into semantic classes, systems can employ templates that correspond to sequences of those classes and match substrings in the input. There might be templates for [QUANTITY], [ENTITY], [TRANSFER], [DESTINATION] and [TIME-PERIOD], each matching the syntactic ways of expressing those concepts. The next step employs patterns that match sequence of templates and convert them into complete queries, reconstructing whatever is missing:

	[QUANTITY]	[ENTITY] [TRANSFER]	[DESTINATION]		[TIME]
1.	| how many |	[ENTITY] [TRANSFER] |	Richmond |	|	March |
2.	| how many |	[ENTITY] [TRANSFER] |	Durham |	|	March |
3.	[QUANTITY]	[ENTITY] [TRANSFER] |	Fairfax |	¦	April |

The interpretation of elliptical questions is thus a two step exercise in pattern matching: substrings against templates, then template sequences against query patterns.

With unconstrained languages, however, patterns cannot be predicted *a priori*; there are infinitely many sentence structures and many varieties of ellipsis. Consider the following pairs of sentences:

Bill likes sheepdogs, and Jen 0 dachshunds.   0 = likes
No one wanted to take the dog. So I agreed 0.   0 = to take the dog
Where are the records? 0 The books?   0 = Where are
We listened to four records. The last two 0 were good.   0 = records

Sometimes *so, do*, or both are supplied:

He feels he should have a rest. And so he should 0. 0 = have a rest
He wants a vacation. They do 0 too. 0 = want a vacation
He made coffee yesterday. She did so 0 today. 0 = made coffee

Prespecified patterns will not work, but prior context offers something almost as good: the syntactic structure of the preceding sentence. Some portion of that sentence will parallel the elliptical expression, and the remainder will supply what is missing.

The procedure for interpreting ellipsis begins with a failure to parse. The parser recognizes one or more substrings but reaches a state from which no rule (or arc) allows it to proceed further. When the parse fails, the substring can be made into a template to be matched against the parse of the preceding sentence. The template incorporates the syntactic structure of the substring and any function words (except for *so* and forms of the auxiliary verb *do*), but replaces content words either with "wildcards" that will match any word of the same lexical category or with their semantic types (see Figure 1). Function words are retained because they will often decide between syntactically parallel structures in the preceding sentence. If, for example, *did the man bring a friend?* is followed by *a colleague?*, the latter is probably elliptical for *did the man bring a colleague?* But if it is followed by *the woman?*, then *did the woman bring a friend* is more likely. Semantic types may also restrict the range of possible matches. Thus, if *did the man* [HUMAN] *bring the fish* [ANIMAL or EDIBLE]? is followed by *the*

Bill owns the sheepdogs,   Jen the dachshunds.

S: decl. active, pres   Template:

  Subject   Subject
    NP sing 3rd   →   NP sing 3rd
      Head: Proper: [HUMAN]   Head: Pronoun: [HUMAN]

  Verb: infin. trans. pres.
    Head: [POSSESS]

  Direct Object   Direct Object
    NP plural 3rd   NP plural 3rd
      Head: Noun: [ANIMAL]   →   Head: Noun: [ANIMAL]
      Det: Article: *the*   Det: Article: *the*

Figure 1. Pattern matching for ellipsis.

chicken? [ANIMAL or EDIBLE], then *did the man bring the chicken* is a more likely interpretation than *Did the chicken bring the fish?* Sometimes the template will be too specific. Should no match be found, the template must be generalized first by replacing certain function words with their lexical categories, and then, if that does not avail, by deleting any modifiers. Replacing function words would succeed with *did you put the book on a shelf? in the closet?*: [PREP] [DET] *closet* and stripping modifiers would find in *do you want dessert?* a match for *lemon sponge cake with fudge sauce?*: *do you want dessert = cake.* Though nothing guarantees that most specific matching template is the antecedent, stripping the modifiers usually succeeds.

1.3 Finding NP anaphors and their antecedents

The brief discussion of pronouns and their antecedents anticipates the second major kind of anaphora in English: an explicit anaphor and its antecedent co-specify an antecedent concept. The following trivial tale, in which anaphors are italicized, will illustrate some of the varieties and properties of anaphoric expressions:

> The small boy walked home. *He* wasn't happy. *The kid* had been playing with his friends, but *it* got boring. It was also hot and *that* spoiled the fun. *No one* wanted to play any longer. When *she* heard the door open, *his* mother went to greet *him* with a large glass of milk. *She* got a small *one* for *herself*.

In the second sentence the pronoun *he* is an anaphor with *a young boy* as its antecedent. The pronoun is connecting the sentences, but without repetition because the anaphoric relation allows us to associate the attribute -ADULT with *he*. Like pronouns, reduced definite noun phrases (such as the abbreviatory *the kid* in the third sentence) are usually anaphoric, but indefinite noun phrases (*a young boy*) typically introduce new entities into the discourse and are not. The remainder of the narrative illustrates the diversity of anaphoric expressions. In addition to being heads of noun phrases, they can be also be modifiers; *his* in the first sentence is an example. Although most of the remaining pronouns (including *his*, *it*, *that*, *him*, *she*, and *herself*) are anaphoric, some (such as the indefinite pronouns, *no one*, and the second *it*) are not. Anaphoric expressions usually precede their antecedents, but *she* does not. Though antecedents are often entities, they can be events or states. The antecedent of the first *it* is the preceding sentence, and the antecedent of *that* is *too hot*.)

Information of several different kinds may be required to locate antecedents. Often syntactic constraints come into play, particularly when the antecedent occurs within the same sentence. These range from relatively simple constraints on reflexive pronouns (*himself*, *itself*) and reciprocals (*one another*, *each other*) to sophisticated "precede and command" constraints which appeal to both the linear and hierarchical structures of sentences in determining, for example, that *he* can have *Joe* as antecedent in *Joe thinks he is a doctor*, but not in any of the following:

> He thinks Joe is a doctor,
> Next to Joe, he saw a doctor.
> Joe, whose car he bought, came along.

Empirical studies show that where there is a choice between possible antecedents, certain principles are employed to resolve the anaphora. **Parallel function**, for example, chooses an antecedent that plays the same syntactic role as the anaphor. Thus the likeliest interpretation of *because Joe liked Tom he gave him a ride*, has *Joe* as antecedent of *he* and *Tom* as antecedent of *him*.

Semantic compatibilities can also be helpful. In *the dog came to the door and it ate the food we offered*, the selectional restriction for *eat* determines that *it* must refer to some animate being and therefore to *dog* rather than *door*. Empirical studies also suggest that we use semantic information about the verb in a sentence to predict whether its subject or object is likely to be referred to in a subsequent sentence. For verbs such as *buy* or *ask*, the subject is more likely, and for others, including *envy* and *punish*, it is the object that is more likely. Finally, world knowledge can sometimes influence the decision among possible antecedents. Consider the difference that the second verb makes in the following sentence:

The city council refused to grant the women a parade permit

$$\text{because they} \left\{ \begin{array}{l} \text{feared} \\ \text{advocated} \end{array} \right\} \text{violence.}$$

Where world knowledge influences the choice, script- or plan-based processing will sometimes supply the relevant information, as it does, for example, for this brief narrative:

> I went to buy a ring. The store sold jewelry and silver and
> offered a good discount. Besides they let me take it with me.

A GO-TO-A-STORE script would help identify *ring*, as the likely antecedent of *it*, despite the intervening jewelry, silver and discount, because one ordinarily leaves stores with the object purchased.

1.4 Heuristics and the history list

A simple but not always reliable strategy for finding antecedent concepts is to look first in the sentences containing the anaphor for NPs of the same number and semantic type, those being the most useful criteria. The logical form for the anaphor is compared with the logical form for the head of the NP, and if they match, the procedure succeeds. Or if the NP head is a set, a matching anaphor is a member of that set. If no antecedent is found, however, the same appropriateness criteria are applied to a history list containing NPs collected from previous sentences and ordered as to the likeliness of their being antecedents.

Certain heuristics may assist in the intrasentential search. Though the heuristics are *ad hoc* and not motivated by any direct evidence that they play a role in human cognition, they are algorithmic and can therefore be implemented in computational systems where frequently succeed in locating the antecedent (see Figure 2). For example, reciprocal and reflexive pronouns occurring as indirect or direct objects necessarily take the heads of the subject NP as antecedent, but other pronominal objects do not. Thus *each other* must pick out *they* in *they wrote to each other*, and *himself* must specify *Chuck* in *Chuck gave himself a gift*, but *him* cannot refer to *Tom* in *Tom gave him a gift*. When reflexives occur within NPs that also contain possessives, the pronoun refers to the nearest appropriate antecedent. Thus *himself* in *Tom's opinion of himself is quite high* refers to *Tom*, as does *him* in *Tom's father's opinion of him is low*. Another useful heuristic specifies that if the same pronoun occurs previously in the sentence it is a likely antecedent. These heuristics apply only to intrasentential anaphors that are personal pronouns, and at that they do not always succeed

- If * is a reflexive pronoun or a reciprocal pronoun and is a direct or indirect object, then the subject is the antecedent.

- If * is a reflexive pronoun and a constituent of an NP modified by a possessive, the nearest appropriate head or possessive is the antecedent.

- If * is a personal pronoun but not it or they, and the same pronoun occurs previously in the sentence, it is the antecedent.

- If * is a definite NP or a definite non-reflexive pronoun and is a direct or indirect object, then the antecedent is not the subject.

- If * is an indefinite NP or an indefinite pronoun, then instantiate it as a new entity.

Figure 2. Heuristics for intrasentential NP anaphora.

with the undiscriminating *it* or *they*: *he put the money in a bag; but because it had a hole in it, it fell out*). But it is reasonable to look first in a bounded space, especially when the possibilities within that space are subject to constraints.

If the sentence containing the anaphor does not also contain an appropriate antecedent, the next step is to consult a **history list** containing the heads of all NPs in the preceding sentences. Recency of sentences and prominence within sentences determine the sequence of NPs on the history list. All NPs from the immediately preceding sentence come first, then NPs in the sentence before that, and so on–a sequence that is readily achieved by making the history list a stack. Within each sentence, NPs go on the history list in the reverse order of a top-down breadth-first traversal of the register structure. Subjects are more likely antecedents than are direct and indirect objects, so they precede them; in turn the object NPs precede subordinated NPs, including any possessives, attributive nouns, and objects of prepositions, as well as the NP constituents of relative and other subordinate clauses. Following the sentence, *Lorena's daughter got a spoon from the drawer*, the history list stack would be:

[HUMAN: daughter] ←(gender)— [FEMALE]

[UTENSIL: spoon]

[HUMAN: Lorena] ←(gender)— [FEMALE]

[CONTAINER: drawer]

If the following sentence is *she knew it was clean*, the representation for *she* [HUMAN: X] ←(gender)– [FEMALE] would pick out the schema [HUMAN: daughter], and [PHYS-OBJ: X] for *it* would (following restriction) pick out [UTENSIL: spoon].

Many antecedents are entities expressed as NP heads, but not all. "One" anaphors, which include *one, those, some, a few*, and sometimes *it*, refer not to entities, but to descriptions. Consider the following sentences:

> He has a large box of Nancy's books and he has a small one of mine.

> I met two of my friends in the parking lot and saw some in the hall.

The antecedent of *one* is probably the pattern:

$$[\text{CONTAINER: box}] \quad \begin{array}{l} \leftarrow(\text{size})- \; [x] \\ \leftarrow(\text{possessor})- \; [y] \end{array}$$

rather than simply *box*, and the antecedent of *some* in the second sentence is certainly not *two*, but instead the pattern:

$$[\text{HUMAN: \{friends\}}] \quad \leftarrow(\text{quantity})-[x]$$

In the same vein, the antecedent of certain demonstrative pronouns and *it* is sometimes a preceding verb phrase or sentence:

> Joe brought Mary. But that was a mistake.

Notice that we cannot simply substitute *I*, or *brought*, or *Mary*; what we need to represent *that* is instead the pattern:

$$[\text{ACT: X}] \quad \leftarrow(\text{agent})- \; [Y]$$

Finally, consider:

> The fish which he caught, he then scaled and filleted. Next he put it in the oven.

Does *it* refer to *the fish* or to *the fish which he caught* and if the latter, is *it* the same entity after the scaling and filleting? Clearly not. Given these examples, the history list must contain representations for entire noun and verb phrases, or (since antecedents for both forms of anaphora are in the immediately preceding sentence) a separate procedure should retain and consult the propositional representations of predecessor sentences.

Figure 3. Problems in determining antecendent concepts.

If the history list is to be of manageable length, there must be some provision for removing the least recent NPs. Sometimes a maximum length (in the number either of NPs or of sentences) is arbitrarily set, but a better method is to clear the history list at segment shifts in the discourse. The next section explores segmentation and focus in discourse and describes an alternative approach to pronoun anaphors.

1.5 Focus and potential for pronominalization

Study of the circumstances in which pronouns appear in many samples of naturally occurring discourse–of what can and what cannot be pronominalized–has yielded a remarkable double benefit: help in identifying pronoun antecedents and help in locating the often elusive boundaries between discourse segments. The researchers discovered that, in a given stretch of discourse, pronouns (but not other anaphors) obey constraints, and these are sufficiently explicit and reliable to be stated algorithmically:

  □ if a sentence contains a single pronoun, that pronoun's antecedent must be the entity, state or event that is the focus of the segment;

  □ if the sentence has two or more pronouns, then one of them must refer to the focus, and the other refers to some entity, state or event in the preceding sentence.

Note that **focus**, a term that linguists and psychologists use in several different ways, here has a particular meaning; it refers to that element (entity, state, or event) that may or must, depending on the number of pronouns in the sentence, be pronominalized. Only one element can be the focus at a time, though the focus may be explicitly changed as the discourse proceeds.   Once the focus is changed, the element previously in focus has no distinguished status.

Speakers or writers can explicitly change the focus in several ways. Each of the following sentences foregrounds *sheepdog(s)*, making it the focus and until a new focus is established, subsequent pronouns (the pronoun could be *he, him, she, her,* or *it*) or "close" deictic anaphors (*this, these* or *here* rather than *those* or *there*) will necessarily refer to *sheepdog(s)*.

> It is the sheepdog(s) that I have.
> What I have is/are the sheepdog(s).
> The sheepdog(s) I like.
> There entered the sheepdog(s).

These sentences respectively illustrate clefting, pseudoclefting, topicalization, and *there* insertion (terms that derive from transformational grammar). In each case, the sentence gives prominence to the constituent in focus by **foregrounding** it: moving it from its accustomed place in the sentence either to the beginning or the end. (Other languages use explicit markers to foreground constituents; Japanese, for example, uses the marker *wa*.) Yet another way of establishing focus in English is to use the proper name of an element that has previously been referred to by a description: using *San Diego*, for example, where previous references have been to *a city*. Focus can also be established by making the focused element the subject of the sentence. Though this method is weaker than the moving or naming, because non focused agents can also be subjects, it is common–inconveniently common when the purpose is to track focus.

There are, however, ways of recognizing that the focus has changed. Chief among them are the failure to pronominalize an element previously in focus and the employment of a pronoun that is incompatible (in number, person, or gender) with the element previously in focus. When either occurs, it is usually the case that focus was unobtrusively altered (as by placing the focused element in the subject position). Though it is possible to force a change by pronominalizing or failing to pronominalize, that is rare and the result can be confusion for listeners or hearers, who are anticipating that pronominalization constraints will be observed.

Focus is important both because pronouns are very frequent (about 7/100 words in the Brown Corpus) and because they have less semantic content than do other anaphoric expressions. Some pronouns, such as *it*, have hardly any content. Selecting antecedent concepts from the history list can therefore be very difficult. We might consider adding a mechanism for recognizing explicit changes in the focus, as well as the signs that focus has been changed, so that the element currently in focus can be accorded distinguished status on the history list. A more resourceful use of focus, however, exploits its close correlation with discourse segmentation. As we will see, focus is one of several criteria for determining the segmentation of discourse, and changes of focus constitute evidence that a segment boundary has been traversed. Identification of discourse segments, in turn, will limit the search space for antecedent concepts of nonpronominal anaphors.

The discovery that focus determines pronominalization and nonpronominalization comes from computational work on speech recognition, specifically from Barbara Grosz's seminal research on task-oriented dialogues. The tasks that Grosz investigated divide into subtasks, and those have subtasks; not surprisingly, the structure of each dialogue mirrors the hierarchical structure of the task. It consists of a matrix containing both conversation about the overall task and embedded subdialogues; the subdialogues contain conversation about the subtask and may lead into further levels of embedding. At each level, a particular antecedent concept is in focus. This much is not surprising, since the candidate for pronominalization is, roughly speaking, the entity, state, or event that is being talked about in a given segment. But Grosz discovered that with suspensions and resumptions focus behaves in a very systematic way. When a subdialogue begins, the present focus can be suspended; the focus is not forgotten, however, even if the subdialogue is quite long or itself has subdialogues. When the subdialogues are completed, the prior

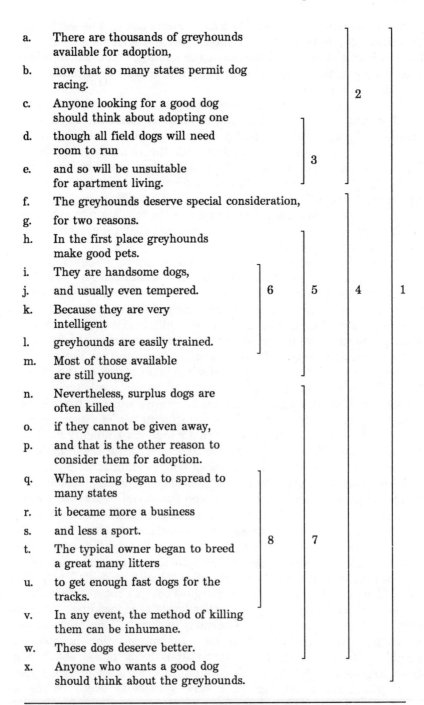

a. There are thousands of greyhounds available for adoption,

b. now that so many states permit dog racing.

c. Anyone looking for a good dog should think about adopting one

d. though all field dogs will need room to run

e. and so will be unsuitable for apartment living.

f. The greyhounds deserve special consideration,

g. for two reasons.

h. In the first place greyhounds make good pets.

i. They are handsome dogs,

j. and usually even tempered.

k. Because they are very intelligent

l. greyhounds are easily trained.

m. Most of those available are still young.

n. Nevertheless, surplus dogs are often killed

o. if they cannot be given away,

p. and that is the other reason to consider them for adoption.

q. When racing began to spread to many states

r. it became more a business

s. and less a sport.

t. The typical owner began to breed a great many litters

u. to get enough fast dogs for the tracks.

v. In any event, the method of killing them can be inhumane.

w. These dogs deserve better.

x. Anyone who wants a good dog should think about the greyhounds.

Figure 4. Discourse segments in the student's essay.

focus is automatically restored as if there had been no interruption. In one case, the antecedent of minimally informative *it* was clear, even though sixty utterances intervened with no focusing syntax to restore it explicitly. Each of the segments, whether matrix or an embedding, whether suspended or not, is a coherent whole. A subdialogue can therefore be removed from a matrix with no loss of coherence, but removing non-embedded parts of a matrix or removing parts of the subdialogue does sacrifice coherency.

Section two: Discourse Segments and Structure

2.1 Segmentation and hierarchy

The phenomenon of focus, controlling whether an antecedent can be pronominalized, leads directly to a hierarchical view of discourse structure. Though segmentation is necessarily linear, given the constraint that allows only one utterance at a time in the production and perception of language, the relationship among segments is hierarchical and allows for resumptions of suspended superordinate segments. The structure that Grosz found in task-oriented dialogues where the subject discussed is inherently hierarchal, has also been found in many other kinds of discourse, and the pronouns behave in much the same way. Hierarchies with suspensions and resumptions have been found in narrative, descriptive, explanatory, and argumentative discourse, in therapeutic dialogue, classroom instruction, even the Watergate transcripts.

Figure 4 shows the segmentation and the structure of a brief essay written for a college composition course. Though some utterances close to boundaries serve as transitions and might be assigned to either segment (proposition m is an example), the segmentation and structure are for the most part quite clear:

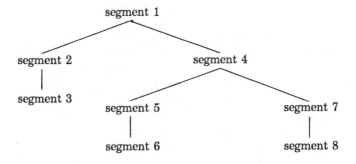

To proceed through the discourse is to execute a depth-first traversal of the tree. Suspensions and resumptions move downward in the tree then back up; segment 7, for example, is interrupted by the account (in segment 8) of how it is that there are dogs to be killed and is resumed via the transitional "in any event," so that utterances belonging to a given segment need not be contiguous

Though discourse structure is always hierarchical and each subordinate segment has one and only one superordinate, the exact topography of the tree and method of traversal depends on the writer/speaker. Favored topographies and traversals vary from culture to culture. In Western discourse, of which the essay on greyhounds is an example, the hierarchy tends to have several levels and the traversal visits most of the subordinate node only once, In contrast, there appear to have two different ways of constructing discourse in Chinese. One resembles the Western paradigm; the other has a tree with fewer levels. It is traversed in a reiterative, descending spiral that partially develops a subsegment, leaves it for a while, and then returns to develop it further.

Within the discourse hierarchy, each subordinate segment contributes to its superordinate, and that contribution (what the subordinate is in aid of) is therefore an aspect of the segment's meaning. Segment 6 of the essay on greyhounds, is offered not simply as a description of greyhounds, their appearance, temperament and intelligence, but as support for the assertion in the superordinating segment 5 that "greyhounds make good pets." In turn, segments 5 and 7 (about the surplus greyhounds' fate), are embedded within segment 4, where they support the assertion that "greyhounds deserve special consideration." This linking of assertion and support is perhaps the most common relation between discourse segments; it pervades all genres of discourse, though it may be phrased as elaboration or explanation rather than as argument.

Other relationships bind subordinate sections to their superordinates. Segment 5, for example, which is immediately subordinate to segment 1, supplies motivation for "people should think about adopting them." Similarly, segment 3 (on the constraints of apartment living) qualifies and segment 8, though somewhat digressive, explains why so many greyhounds are available. On other occasions, a segment might present the plan for achieving a goal introduced in its superordinate or describe some entity that the superordinate singles out. Conversations in which two or more speakers disagree offer still more possibilities, including several ways of rebutting or deflecting the claim initiated in a superordinating segment. Whatever the relationship, whether of support, motivation, qualification, explanation, or description, the subordinate segment cannot be fully comprehended in isolation. A significant portion of its meaning consists in the contribution it makes to its superordinate.

Transitional words or phrases may signal the beginnings of new segments *(now, next, first, finally, moreover)*. Digressive sections may begin with *incidentally, by the way, that reminds me, speaking of* . . . or *parenthetically* and end with *anyway, at any rate, in any case,* or *now back to.* Such phrases make little or no contribution to the meaning of the sentences that contain them and serve only as boundary markers. Some transitional words and phrases specify relationships between segments. English has many temporal indicators, for example. These include *earlier, previously, a while ago* for segments set in the past; *meanwhile, simultaneously, at the same time* for concurrent settings; and *subsequently, afterwards, sooner or later* for futurity. Other transitional phrases indicate logical or topical relationships between segments. *as a result* or *because of this* signify implications, *in particular* or *specifically* introduce details, and *in other words* or *once more* add summaries or reformulations. Spoken English marks segment boundaries with additional tags such as *right, ok,* or *good* and uses intonation as well. Pitch is lowered somewhat at the ends of declarative sentences, but lowered still more at the ends of sentences that conclude segments.

The student's essay also illustrates some of the ways that focus interacts with segmentation and the hierarchy of segments. If the focus has not explicitly been established within a given segment, then the focus of the superordinating segment prevails. Thus, for example, the first sentence of the student's essay places in focus the antecedent concept

$$[\text{DOG: } \{x\}] \; \leftarrow\!(\text{type})\!- \; [\text{greyhound}]$$

and it allows pronominalization *(them)* in proposition c. The representation for the intervening *states* is not in focus and therefore not a candidate. *They* is possible in segment 3, because it is the focus of the superordinating segment 2. Once the focus changes, the element previously in focus has no distinguished status and must be specified by a full definite noun group *(the dogs* or *those greyhounds* rather than *them)*. As Grosz discovered, the focus of the superordinating segment does not need to be explicitly restored. Thus, *them* in proposition x can refer to the antecedent concept of *surplus dogs,* the focus of segment 7, because that segment is resumed once the digressive explanation in section 8 is completed. Also, within a subordinate segment the focus of either the present segment or the superordinate segment can be specified by a "close" deictic: *this* or *these* rather than the distanced *those.* *These dogs* in proposition y, which resumes segment 7 is an example.

Though not as strictly constrained as pronominalization, other forms of anaphora are sensitive to segmentation and the discourse hierarchy. Absent an explicit shift to a different topic, if an antecedent concept is not in the present segment, its most likely location is the superordinating segment even if that segment is some distance away. When taken together with the focus constraints, this behavior of anaphors suggests a selective attention on the part of participants in a discourse and probably reflects limitations either of short-term memory or of the cognitive processes that use it. We are not very proficient at working with more than a few discrete entities at any one time: no more than, as George Miller, suggested, "seven, plus or minus two."

Tense and tense change are also constrained. Discourse segments either maintain the same tense or vary the tense in certain predictable ways, as for example from a basic tense to its progressive form (marked by a form of *to be* together with the present participle)

> Bill walked at a fast pace. He was getting some exercise.

or from a perfect form (marked by a form of *to have* plus the past participle) to the basic tense:

> Bill had walked four miles. He slowed his pace.

Any changes in tense other than these may indicate segment shifts. For example, segment 3 of the student's essay shifts to the future tense then maintains that tense throughout the segment, and segment 8 shifts to and maintains the past tense. (Shifts from the progressive to the basic tense or from the basic tense to the perfect are even more reliable as indicators of segment boundaries.) Empirical studies have shown that when a tense shift or an indication of the passage of time intervenes between an antecedent and a pronoun, the time required to find pronoun's antecedent increases. This suggests that the subjects recognized a segment boundary and knew that the previous focus might not be sustained. Tense and focus are also connected in that, just as focus is restored when the superordinating segment resumes following a interrupting subsegment, tense also is restored.

2.2 Determining discourse structure

The most natural representation for discourse structure, as for many other linguistic structures, is a simple stack. The stack holds a separate record for each segment, and the top-most can be updated for each utterance. Segment records contain such context sensitive information as the focus and tense of the segments, together with potential foci from the sentence immediately preceding and any antecedent concepts other than the focus and potential foci. When segment boundaries are crossed, a record representing the new segment is pushed on the stack, displacing downward its superordinating segment. Completed subsegments are popped from the stack.

Figure 5 gives the content of the segment stack preceding and following proposition v of the students' essay. For convenience, antecedent words and phrases are given rather than their antecedent concepts. The slot for ALTernatives holds the antecedents from the immediately preceding proposition, which are candidates to replace the current focus; when ALT is updated, those antecedents are moved to the HISTory list. Previously, several segment records have been placed on the stack, including segments 1 (superordinate for the entire essay) and 4 (to the effect that greyhounds deserve special attention). Some have been popped from the stack, including segments 2 (on the attributes that make greyhounds good pets) and 3 (on city living). Four segments remain on the stack, each the superordinate of the one above it. However, proposition v contains evidence that a segment boundary has been crossed (the tense shift) and that the previous segment is now closed (the transitional phrase *in any event* indicates a return from a digression), so segment 8 is popped from the stack. Therefore, segment 7 becomes active and its tense and focus are restored.

Routines for tracking focus, anaphors, and tense maintain the segment stack. These examine each proposition in the discourse for evidence of segment boundaries and, depending on what they find, may update the present segment record, push a new segment on the stack, or pop the present segment.

- If the pronoun is compatible with FOCUS in the active record, then the present proposition is a continuation, assign FOCUS as the antecedent concept of the pronoun.

- Else if the pronoun is compatible with one of the potential foci ALT, in the active record then the present proposition is a continuation, assign ALT as the antecedent concept of the pronoun.

When no compatible antecedent is found in the active record, the FOCUS and ALT in slots in records for the superordinating segments are consulted and, as with the history list, the first qualifying noun phrase is accepted. A parallel routine looks for antecedent concepts of potential non pronoun anaphors

- If the anaphor is compatible with an element in ALT or HIST in the active record, then the present proposition is a continuation, assign the element as the antecedent concept of the anaphor.

ALT and HIST of superordinating segments on the stack are consulted if those in the active segment do not afford a match. The third routine looks for the same or a compatible tense:

Before proposition v: After proposition v:

```
┌ SEGMENT 8                              ┌ SEGMENT 7

  FOCUS   = typical owner                  FOCUS   = surplus dogs

  ALT     = many litters                   ALT     = adoption
          = fast dogs                              = other reason
          = tracks
                                           HIST    = <empty>
  HIST    = racing
          = many states                    TENSE   = present
          = business
          = sport                        └ SEGMENT 4

  TENSE   = past                           FOCUS   = greyhounds
┌ SEGMENT 7
                                           ALT     = special
  FOCUS   = surplus dogs                            consideration
                                                   = two reasons
  ALT     = adoption
          = other reason                   HIST    = <empty>

  HIST    = <empty>                        TENSE   = present

  TENSE   = present                      └ SEGMENT 1
┌ SEGMENT 4
                                           FOCUS   = greyhounds
  FOCUS   = greyhounds
                                           ALT     = anyone
  ALT     = special                                = good dog
          consideration                            = one
          = two reasons                            (greyhound)

  HIST    = <empty>                        HIST    = adoption
                                                   = many states
  TENSE   = present                                = dog racing
┌ SEGMENT 1
                                           TENSE   = present
  FOCUS   = greyhounds

  ALT     = anyone
          = good dog
          = one
          (greyhound)

  HIST    = adoption
          = many states
          = dog racing

  TENSE   = present
```

Figure 5. Segment stack during and after a digression.

- If the tense is the same as TENSE, then the proposition is a possible continuation.

- If the tense is progressive form and TENSE is its basic form in the active record, then the proposition is a possible continuation, set TENSE to the tense of the proposition.

- If the tense is a basic form and TENSE is its perfect form, then the present proposition is a possible continuation, set TENSE to the tense of the proposition.

The tense routine also identifies incompatible tense sequences, that is those that do not allow continuation.

- If tense is a basic form and TENSE is its progressive form, then the proposition is not a continuation.

- If tense is a perfect form and TENSE is its basic form, then the proposition is not a continuation.

- If the tense is a progressive form and TENSE is its perfect form then the proposition is not a continuation.

One additional routine looks for transitional phrases and distinguishes those that explicitly indicate a resumption (*anyhow, at any rate*) from the majority, which do not specify whether the current proposition is part of a resumption or a new section.

2.3 Planning and structure

These routines will help discern the structure of the discourse, but they cannot locate every boundary and will not always establish the pattern of subordination. The problem is not so much that the routines are fallible (though they are), but that they can be indecisive. Segment boundaries, especially those between superordinating and subordinate segments, may not be marked. The subordinate may and often does continue the same tense, the same focus, the same history list. One answer is to employ the routines in conjunction with content-dependent plan inferencing, allowing knowledge about discourse to supplement knowledge about the world. Thus another set of routines would determine whether the present proposition is a plausible continuation or subplan of the currently active plan.

As a first approximation, we might stipulate that the duration of a plan or subplan dictates the extent of a segment. The status of a plan, whether continuing, suspended, or complete, helps determine segmentation and structure. This suggests a processing model that would maintain in the current record of the segment stack a pointer to the currently active plan and another pointer to its now-point. The pointers are set as soon as the plan is identified, and the segment is popped from the stack as soon as the plan is completed.

Among the possibilities for a given utterance, the likeliest is that it continues the present segment and plan. Thus the first step is to match its propositional representation against the expected action, as indicated by the now-point, then against actions subsequent to the now-point. If a match succeeds, the now-point and history list are updated. For example, preceding the final utterance in the following narrative fragment, the relevant plan and segment register would be as represented in Figure 6.

> Louise walked from her office to the Harbor Campus Library. She looked up the call number for Jane Austen's *Pride and Prejudice*, then went to the shelf.

The plan anticipates as the next act a GOTO with shelves the destination, and that indeed is borne out in the narrative, so the sentence is accepted as a continuation of the present segment. Following the GOTO are FETCH and TRANSACT, together with additional GOTOs, but if the sentence following her excursion to the shelves were something like

> She had to read the book for a course she was taking.

it would not be accepted as a continuation of the segment. When no match is found (as would be the case here), three possibilities remain:

- □ the utterance resumes a segment and plan that have previously been suspended,

- □ the utterance begins an interruptive segment following which the present segment and plan may resume,

- □ the present segment is complete and the utterance begins a new segment and a new plan.

Only the first of these possibilities can be directly investigated, so even when there is not an explicit indication (such as *at any rate* or *anyhow*) that a segment is being resumed, the search is extended downward in the segment stack to an interrupted segment at or beyond the now-point that refers to an act of reading.

Unless there is a transitional phrase (such as *incidentally* or *by the way* for an interruption; *now, next,* or *then* for a subsequent plan) the remaining possibilities are impossible to distinguish. Interruptions can occur at any point in the discourse, and segments can end precipitously, with the remaining actions to be filled in as bridging inferences. To allow for the possibility that the utterance is only an interruption, the

$$
\begin{bmatrix}
\text{SEGMENT X} & \\
\text{FOCUS} & = \text{[HUMAN: Louise1]} \\
\text{ALT} & = \text{[SYMBOL: call number]} \\
& = \text{[HUMAN: Jane Austen]} \\
& = \text{[MESSAGE: } Pride\ and\ Prejudice\text{]} \\
\text{HIST} & = \text{[PLACE: office]} \\
& = \text{[PLACE: Harbor Campus Library]} \\
\text{TENSE} & = \text{past} \\
\text{PLAN} & = \text{OBTAIN-LIBRARY-BOOK} \\
\text{NOW} & = \text{[GOTO-3]}
\end{bmatrix}
$$

$$
\begin{bmatrix}
\text{OBTAIN-LIBRARY-BOOK PLAN} & \\
\textbf{Substeps:} & \\
\text{[GOTO-1]} & \text{PATRON = [HUMAN: X]} \\
& \text{LIBRARY = [PLACE: Y]} \\
\text{[GOTO-2]} & \text{PATRON = HUMAN: X]} \\
& \text{CATALOG = [PLACE: Y]} \\
\text{[QUERY]} & \text{TITLE= [MESSAGE: X]} \\
& \text{CALL NUMBER = [MESSAGE: Y]} \\
\text{[GOTO-3]} & \text{PATRON = [HUMAN: X]} \\
& \text{SHELF = [PLACE: Y]} \\
\text{[FETCH]} & \text{[CALL NUMBER] = [MESSAGE: Y]} \\
\text{[GOTO-4]} & \text{PATRON = [HUMAN: X]} \\
& \text{CHECK OUT = [PLACE: Y]} \\
\text{[TRANSACT]} & \text{LIBRARIAN = [HUMAN: X]}
\end{bmatrix}
$$

Figure 6. Segment record with pointers to the current plan.

present segment is not popped from the stack. Instead a new segment record is pushed on the stack and a search is launched for a new plan.

The search is not entirely blind. Interruptions are usually relevant to the present plan; sometimes they fill in steps in the plan that were previously omitted from the discourse, or they attach to preconditions or effects of the plan; in either case they may be prefaced by meta-statements about the discourse such as *I forgot to mention* or *You should know*. A succeeding, noninterruptive segment may introduce a new plan for which the preceding plan supplies an enabling precondition; or because the order of segments is less constrained than the order of actions within segments, that sequence may be reversed.

2.4 Toward a grammar of discourse

So far we have a way of handling continuations, resumptions, interruptions and new beginnings; but there are other regularly recurring relationships between segments in a discourse, and these too are content independent. Attempts to generalize the possible relationships between segments go by the name of **discourse grammars**. The grammars propose that discourse structures resemble sentence structures in that they consist of constituent segments, drawn from a finite "vocabulary" of constituent kinds (analogous to lexical categories) or a hierarchy of kinds (phrase structures as well as lexical categories), that constituent kinds are precisely relatable to utterances or groups of utterances, that constituents combine with one another in regular ways, and that some combinations are impossible.

Though a discourse parser cannot, upon encountering a particular constituent, anticipate the constituents to follow with anything like the assurance that a sentence parser anticipates that following a determiner there will perhaps be an adjective but eventually a noun, the parser can make certain predictions. Consider what can follow a segment containing a claim that something is true or valuable or appropriate. The ensuing segment can support the claim, deny the claim, make a competing claim which if true invalidates the initiating claim, and so on. Another possibility is that the ensuing segment fulfills no prediction and is a digression, but that too is information worth having.

Our familiarity with the usual relations between segments makes it easier to follow the twists and turns of discourse. Proponents of discourse grammars do not deny the relevance of goals, plans, beliefs to the understanding of discourse nor do they dismiss the role played by bridging inferences founded on world knowledge. But they are adding content-independent knowledge about the constituents of discourse and relations among those constituents, knowledge that may be sufficiently systematic to be formulated in data structures and algorithms. These, in turn, guide comprehension and constrain the inferences that can be made at any point in the discourse.

Some discourse grammars describe constrained, highly structured conversation, such as would occur in a schoolroom or a doctor's office; they have only a few very general kinds of constituents and concentrate on quite local connections (for example, the elicitation-response-feedback sequence used to instruct children.) Other grammars focus on global structures and their substructures. Among these are grammars for simple stories (see Figure 7) and for argumentative

Story grammars specify a small number of constituent structures together with rules for combining them. Some use context-free rules such as

STORY	→	SETTING EPISODE
EPISODE	→	EVENT EPISODE
EPISODE	→	EVENT RESPONSE.

And as with sentence grammars, the rules generate hierarchical structures:

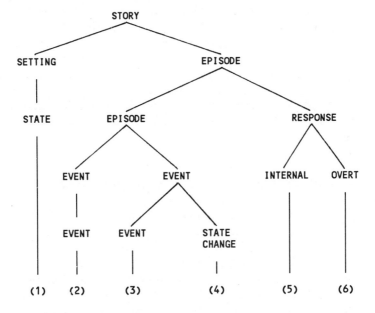

(1) Samson was a strong man and Delilah was an enemy Philistine. (2) Samson slept with Delilah. (3) When she cut his hair, (4) he lost his strength. (5) He was enraged and (6) smote the Philistines.

Other story grammars supplement the context-free rules with more powerful transformational rules that delete constituents (bridging inferences, for example) or move them (as for flashbacks). Some also have rule-by-rule semantics; an interpretation rule corresponding to the "syntactic" rule EPISODE → EVENT RESPONSE would specify the predication INITIATE (EVENT, RESPONSE).

Figure 7. Story grammars.

discourse. Though story grammars are theories of competence and do not explain how stories are produced or comprehended, some empirical findings have been cited in their support. Information at nodes high in the hierarchy (the gist of the story) is more easily recalled. Subjects spend more time reading the same sentence if it is high in one story rather than low in another, and jumbled versions of stories are more difficult to understand and remember than are the original versions, even which anaphoric continuity is maintained.

Most discourse grammars, however, have one serious flaw. In place of the words that serve as terminals in syntactic grammars, most use propositions, t-units, or sentences; but this is to ignore important differences between words and these discourse terminals. The words of a sentence grammar can be listed in a finite lexicon and classified according to a small set of lexical categories. The set of all propositions or t-units or sentences is infinitely large, however, so there can be no equivalent of the lexicon to list them. Moreover, there is no evident way of determining categories to which these units belong. A grammar can be imposed on a discourse by assuming that the propositions, t-units, or sentences are members of the apposite categories, but without independent evidence as to the existence and nature of those categories, this procedure is merely circular, and the grammar has none of the explanatory power that validates sentence grammars.

2.5 Context spaces and conversational moves

More recently Rachel Reichman has offered an account of "context spaces" and "conversational moves" that derives from careful observation and applies to a broad range of discourse ranging from informal conversation to forensic debate. Like the discourse grammars, Reichman's account offers a taxonomy of discourse constituents and their relations. Reichman's terminals are segments rather than propositions, and her rules specify the contexts and sequences in which given segments can occur. Her account is more explicit than other discourse grammars, offering both a processing model (formulated as an augmented transition network) for generating discourse structures and an account of the requisite knowledge representation.

Context spaces are aggregates of utterances; they correspond to discourse segments and exhibit the same focusing phenomena. Discussion is initiated with autonomous "issue" spaces that make some claim. The claim may be epistemic (the truth or necessity of some state of affairs), evaluative (its worth or lack of worth), or deontic (its appropriateness or inappropriateness). For example, segment 5 of the student's essay (about the merits of greyhounds as pets) makes an evaluative claim, and segment 4 (to the effect that greyhounds deserve special consideration) makes a deontic claim. Typical predications help identify issue spaces and the issues themselves; *x should y* or *x is unfair*, for example, characterize deontic issues.

Subordinated to issue spaces are "non-issue spaces," each performing a "conversational move" with respect to a prior issue or non-issue space. A conversational move can, for example, support or challenge the claim in a superordinating issue space. The tone need not be debative; support, for example, can be couched as elaboration or explanation, but when it is elaborating or explaining a claim, it is at the same time supporting it. Speakers and writers choose from a finite repertoire of conversational moves, and are constrained in their choices by rules that determine which moves can occur in what contexts and sequence (see Figure 8). Their listeners or readers are also familiar with the repertoire and the rules. Knowing what is and is not possible at any point in the discourse, and aided by transitional words or phrases, they recognize the conversational move and hence the relationship between the context spaces.

The speaker's or listener's model of a particular discourse consists of a hierarchy of frame-like pieces of knowledge representation. Each represents a context space and consists of labeled slots to be filled, updated, and sometimes revised as the discourse proceeds. Like a segment record, each frame has slots for the current focus and for other antecedent concepts; however, it contains many other slots with constraints for what may fill each slot. There are slots for the nature of the context space (deontic issue space, say, or supportive non-issue space), for links with superordinating and subordinate context spaces, for the conversational move that is underway, for the specific strategy (citing an authority, for example, or arguing from an if/then premise), and so on. At any one point in the discourse, the hierarchy of frames represents the participant's understanding of what has already occurred in the discourse and what is underway.

Among the slots, one of the most important contains the status of the concept space. Status determines the focus, the accessibility of other antecedent concepts, and the available conversational moves. To follow the twists and turns of discourse requires frequent updating of the status slot with fillers determined by rule. Reichman distinguishes several fillers, but only four need concern us here: active, closed, controlling, and generating. A context space is active when the present utterances are contributing to that space. A conversational move may either close an active space (and open a new one) or it may consign the space to controlling status. For some idea of how this works, we can recast the essay about greyhounds as a conversation.

The discourse structure will be the joint product of the contributions of two participants. The first participant will begin as the student did by urging (in an issue space) the adoption of greyhounds and contending (in a non-issue support space) that greyhounds make good pets. The relation between an issue and a support space is such that when the move is made to support, the issue space is controlling and the support space is active. From within the active space, it is possible to use a close deictic (*these dogs*) to specify an antecedent concept in the controlling space. Now let's say that the second participant offers a direct challenge, that cats make better pets. The effect of a challenge

Support A subordinate segment may support the claim initiated by its superordinate by appealing to analogy, if/then inferencing, and certain other argumentative schemata. Support moves are sometimes introduced by *like* or *like when* or *because*.

Restatement Once a claim made in a superordinating segment has been supported, there may be a return to the superordinate segment and the initiating claim may be restated, expanded, or modified. Restatements are sometimes signalled by *so*.

Direct challenge A subordinate segment may explicitly deny a claim made in its superordinate and may produce evidence that directly invalidates the claim. The challenge may be introduced by *but* or *no but*.

Indirect challenge A subordinate segment may indirectly discredit a claim in its superordinate by offering a competing claim, which if borne out implies that the first claim is not true. These challenges are sometimes introduced by *yes but* or *right but*.

Subargument concession A subordinate segment may concede the force of an aversive segment immediately preceding, but continues the discourse by initiating or resuming discussion of a different claim that has not yet been resolved. Such concessives may begin with *all right* or *ok*.

Prior logical abstraction A segment may be closed by shifting the discourse from the present issue to another issue that engenders or subsumes the present issue. (For example, the issue of whether there should be capital punishment subsumes the issue of how it should be carried out.) This move may be signalled by *but look* or *but listen* or *but you see*.

Interruption A segment may be temporarily suspended by a shift to some related but tangential matter. Such temporary suspensions may be signalled by *incidentally, by the way*, or *oh, I forgot to mention*.

Return A temporarily suspended segment is returned to and the return may be indicated by *anyway* or *in any case/event*.

Figure 8. A repertoire of conversational moves.

is to reduce the controlling context space (adopt greyhounds) to a generating space and make the support (dogs make good pets) into the controlling space. At this point the first participant might choose either of two conversational moves. She can challenge the challenge (making it the controlling space):

ISSUE = generating
(adopt greyhounds)

     ↘

      SUPPORT = closed
      (greyhounds make
      good pets)

        ↘

           CHALLENGE = controlling
           (cats make better pets)

             ↘

                CHALLENGE = active
                (no they don't)

Or she can explicitly concede the subargument (perhaps saying *all right but*) whereupon the challenge is closed, the generating space regains controlling status, and a new support (greyhounds will be killed) can be opened. If she chooses the latter option, we have:

ISSUE = controlling
(adopt greyhounds)

     ↘

      SUPPORT = closed   SUPPORT = active
      (greyhounds make   (greyhounds will
      good pets)   be killed)

        ↘   ↗

           CHALLENGE = closed
           (cats make better pets)

Once a context space is closed, it cannot be reopened, its focus remains unavailable for pronominalization, and its antecedent concepts are not available for anaphora. If a speaker reverts to the same topic (sometimes called a "semantic return"), a new context space must be created.

Reichman does not claim that her collection of moves and analysis of the occasions on which they can be made is exhaustive. Her supporting, interrupting, and contesting moves need to be expanded to include moves with expository functions, including situation-setting, question-answering, exemplification, qualification, exception, inclusion or exclusion, differentiation, and summary. The eventual aim is to arrive at a more complete categorization of the ways in which discourse moves relate to one another, as well as reliable heuristics for recognizing each move from the utterances that initiate it.

Exercises

1. How would an ellipsis-recognizing template need to be generalized in order to succeed with:

Can he work on the car? Change its flat tire?

2. If the noun phrases in the final paragraph of this chapter were marked for gender and number, would a history list successfully identify the antecedents of the pronouns *her, they, her,* and *it* in the final paragraph above? Demonstrate your conclusion.

3. Explain why it is usually quite simple to find the antecedents of relative pronouns.

4. Give the contents of the segment stack for the essay on greyhounds (see Figure 4) before and after segment m.

5. Draw and label a tree that represents the hierarchical structure of the following brief discourse.

   (1) New England was settled by the Puritans in the seventeenth
   century. (2) They were seeking a refuge from religious intolerance.
   (3) Its weather was harsh, however, and (3) its soil was not fertile.
   (4) Many of the Puritans died in the first winter.

With reference to your tree explain the pattern of pronominalization and non-pronominalization in (2) through (4).

6. Using Reichman's taxonomy of conversational moves, explain the relationships between issue and non-issue spaces in the following brief conversation between speakers A and B.

   A: I wouldn't want to live in Boston. It has a long cold winter and
   a very brief, rainy spring.

   B: You're right about the winter, but it doesn't rain that much in
   the spring. I was in Boston last March for a meeting. You remember, the CLA where I gave my paper on discourse. Anyway it was
   sunny. Besides Boston has lots of other attractions, including a great
   symphony orchestra.

   A: That's right, but most people would be put off by the climate.

7. Describe the subtly different relationships between the following pairs of sentences.

   The plane for Boston was late. So I missed the meeting.
   I arrived in Boston in time for the meeting. I attended it.

Explain why it might be useful to distinguish the relationships. Are the connectives different? The relationships between plans or substeps in plans?

Further reading

On linguistic approaches to anaphora, see Lyons (1977), Perlmutter and Soames (1979), Reinhart (1983), and Green (1988). Several studies, including

Clark and Sengul (1979) and Daneman and Carpenter (1980), demonstrate that distant pronoun antecedents are more difficult to recognize. The source of the difficulty may be shifts in focus rather than distance *per se*: see Lesgold, Roth, and Curtis (1979) and Clifton and Ferreira (1987) or the difficulty may arise from the nature of the intervening material (Garnham, 1987). On the importance of parallel function, see Grober, Beardsley, and Caramazza (1978), Caramazza and Gupta (1979), and Frederiksen (1981); on foregrounding and other mechanisms that improve access, see Ehrlich and Rayner (1983) and Gernsbacher (1989). On the psychological importance of number and gender as cues, see Vonk (1984) and Garnham and Oakhill (1985); and on the influence exerted by verbs, see Caramazza, Grober, Garvey, and Yates (1977) and Vonk (1985). On whether anaphor resolution occurs on-line as sentences are being interpreted, see Marslen-Wilson and Tyler (1980), Sanford and Garrod (1989), and Oakhill, Garnham, and Vonk (1989). Grosz (1977) describes her seminal work on focus and segmentation; for subsequent research see Linde (1979), Sidner (1981 and 1983), Grosz (1981), Grosz, Joshi, and Weinstein (1983), Anderson, Garrod, and Stanford (1983), and Bosch (1988); Marslen-Wilson, Levy, and Tyler (1982) demonstrate that focus is less important in resolving anaphoric noun phrases than it is in resolving anaphoric pronouns.

Hirst (1981) surveys the early computational approaches to anaphora. On history lists and their implementation, see Hobbs (1978). See also Clark and Marshall (1981), Goodman (1986), Strzalkowski and Cercone (1986), and Carter (1987). For ellipsis resolution, some approaches are primarily syntactic (Weischedel and Sondheimer, 1982), some are primarily semantic (Carbonell, 1983), and others employ plans (Litman, 1986 and Carberry, 1988). Grosz and Sidner (1986) offer a comprehensive and subtle account of the role of focus and purpose in determining (or recognizing) discourse structure. On the interaction of segment shifts and tense shifts, see Webber (1987); and the papers in Tedesci and Zaenen (1981), Dowty, Karttunen and Zwicky (1985), as well as the special issue on *Tense and Aspect* of the journal *Discourse of Linguistics and Philosophy* (1986).

On story grammars, see Lakoff (1972) and Rumelhart (1975); for critiques of the approach, see Black and Wilensky (1979) and Garnham (1985). Reichman (1985) presents an account of conversational moves and context spaces; see also Polanyi and Scha (1983 and 1986), Cohen (1987) and Alvarado (1990). On the constraints governing conversation, see Polanyi (1989). The earlier work, focused on structured encounters, is described in Coulthard and Montgomery (1981). For related research, see Van Dijk and Kintsch (1983), Van Dijk (1985), McKeown (1985), Sperber and Wilson (1986), and the journals *Discourse Processes* and *Advances in Discourse Processes*.

Bibliography

Aarts, J. and W. Meijs, eds. *Corpus Linguistics. Recent Developments in the Use of Computer Corpora in English Language Research.* Amsterdam: Rodopi, 1984.

Aarts, J. and W. Meijs, eds. *Corpus Linguistics II. New Studies in the Analysis and Exploitation of Computer Corpora.* Amsterdam: Rodopi, 1986.

Aarts, J. and T. van den Heuvel. "Computational Tools for Syntactic Analysis of Corpora." *Linguistics* 23 (1985), 303-35.

Abbott, V., J. B. Black, and E. Smith. "The Representation of Scripts in Memory." *Journal of Memory and Language* 24 (1985), 179-89.

Abney, S. "A Computational Model of Human Parsing." *Journal of Psycholinguistic Research* 18 (1989), 129-44.

Adams, V. *An Introduction to Modern English Word-Formation.* London: Longman, 1973.

Aho, A. V., J. E. Hopcroft, and J. D. Ullman. *Data Structures and Algorithms.* Reading, MA: Addison-Wesley, 1983.

Aho, A. V., R. Sethi, and J. D. Ullman. *Compilers: Principles, Techniques, and Tools.* Reading, MA: Prentice-Hall, 1986.

Aho, A. V. and J. D. Ullman. *The Theory of Parsing, Translation and Compiling.* 2 vols. Englewood Cliffs, NJ: Prentice-Hall, 1972, 1973.

Aitchison, J. *Words in the Mind: An Introduction to the Mental Lexicon.* Oxford: Basil Blackwell, 1987.

Aitchison, J. *The Articulate Mammal: An Introduction to Psycholinguistics.* 3rd Ed. Winchester, MA: Unwin Hyman, 1989.

Akmajian, A. and F. Heny. *An Introduction to the Principles of Transformational Grammar.* Cambridge, MA: MIT Press, 1975.

Allan, K. *Linguistic Meaning.* London: Routledge, 1986.

Allen, J., M. S. Hunnicutt, and D. Klatt. *From Text to Speech: the MITalk System.* Cambridge: Cambridge University Press, 1987.

Allen, J. F. *Natural Language Understanding.* Menlo Park, CA: Benjamin/ Cummings, 1987.

Allen, J. F. and C. R. Perrault. "Analyzing Intentions in Utterances." *Artificial Intelligence* 25 (1980), 143-78.

Allport, A., D. MacKay, W. Prinz, and E. Scherer. *Language Perception and Production.* New York: Academic Press, 1987.

Allwood, J., L-G. Andersson, and Ö. Dahl. *Logic in Linguistics.* Cambridge: Cambridge University Press, 1977.

Altmann, G. T. M. "Ambiguity, Parsing Strategies and Computational Models." *Language and Cognitive Processes* 3 (1988), 73-97.

Altmann, G. T. M. ed. *Cognitive Models for Speech Processing: Psycholinguistic and Computational Perspectives.* Cambridge, MA: MIT Press, 1990.

Altmann, G. T. M. and M. Steedman. "Interaction with Context During Human Sentence Processing." *Cognition* 30 (1988), 191-238.

Alvarado, S.J. *Understanding Editorial Text: A Computer Model of Argument Comprehension.* Boston, MA: Kluwer, 1990.

Anderson, A., S. C. Garrod, and A. J. Sanford. "The Accessibility of Pronominal Antecedents as a Function of Episode Shifts in Narrative Text." *Quarterly Journal of Experimental Psychology* 35A (1983), 427-40

Anderson, J. A. and E. Rosenfield, eds. *Neurocomputing: Foundations of Research.* Cambridge, MA: MIT Press, 1988.

Anderson, S. R. *Phonology in the Twentieth Century.* Chicago: University of Chicago Press, 1985.

Arib, M. A., D. Caplan, and J. C. Marshall. *Neural Models of Language Processes.* New York: Academic Press, 1982.

Aronoff, M. *Word Formation in Generative Grammar.* Cambridge, MA: MIT Press, 1976.

Atwell, E. "Constituent-likelihood Grammar." In R. Garside, G. Leech and G. Sampson, eds. *The Computational Analysis of English.* London: Longman, 1987.

Austin, J. L. *How to Do Things With Words.* Oxford: Oxford University Press, 1962.

Barclay, J. R., J. D. Bransford, and J. J. Franks. "Sentence Memory: A Constructive versus Interpretive Approach." *Cognitive Psychology* 3 (1972), 183-209.

Baron, R. J. *The Cerebral Computer: An Introduction to the Computational Structure of the Human Brain.* Hillsdale, NJ: Lawrence Erlbaum, 1987.

Bartlett, F. C. *Remembering: A Study in Experimental and Social Psychology.* Cambridge: Cambridge University Press, 1932.

Barwise, J. and R. Cooper. "Generalized quantifiers and natural language." *Linguistics and Philosophy* 4 (1981), 159-219.

Bates, M. "The Theory and Practice of Augmented Transition Networks." In L. Bolc, ed. *Natural Language Communication with Computers.* New York: Springer-Verlag, 1978.

Bear, J. "A Morphological Recognizer with Syntactic and Phonological Rules." *Proceedings of the 11th International Conference on Computational Linguistics* (1986), 272-6.

Becker, J. D. "Multilingual Word Processing." *Scientific American* 254 (1984), 96-107.

Berry-Rogghe, G. L. M. "The Computation of Collocations and their Relevance in Lexical Studies." In A. J. Aitken, R. W. Bailey, and N. Hamilton-Smith, *The Computer and Literary Studies.* Edinburgh: Edinburgh University Press, 1973.

Berwick, R. C, and A. Weinberg. *The Grammatical Basis of Linguistic Performance.* Cambridge, MA: MIT Press, 1984.

Bever, T. "The Cognitive Basis for Linguistic Structures." In J. Hayes, ed. *Cognition and the Development of Language,* New York: Wiley, 1970.

Bever, T., J. Carroll, and L. A. Miller, eds. *Talking Minds: The Study of Language in the Cognitive Sciences.* Cambridge, MA: MIT Press, 1984.

Bever, T., M. Garrett, and R. Hurtig. "The Interaction of Perceptual Processes and Ambiguous Sentences." *Memory and Cognition* 1 (1973), 277-86.

Biber, D. *Variations Across Speech and Writing.* Cambridge: Cambridge University Press, 1988.

Biber, D. "A Typography of English Texts." *Linguistics* 27 (1989), 3-43.

Black, A., P. Freeman and P. N. Johnson Laird. "Plausibility and the Coherence of Discourse." *British Journal of Psychology* 77 (1986), 51-62.

Black, J. B. and R. Wilensky. "An Evaluation of Story Grammars." *Cognitive Science* 3 (1979), 213-30.

Bobrow, D. G. and A. Collins. *Representation and Understanding: Studies in Cognitive Science.* New York: Academic Press, 1975.

Bobrow, R. J. and B. L. Webber. "Knowledge Representation for Syntactic/ Semantic Processing." *Proceedings of the American Association for Artificial Intelligence* (1980), 316-23.

Boguraev, B. and T. Briscoe, eds. *Computational Lexicography for Natural Language Processing.* New York: Longman, 1989.

Bolc, L. ed. *Natural Language Parsing Systems.* Berlin: Springer-Verlag, 1987.

Bosch, P. "Representing and Accessing Focused Referents." *Language and Cognitive Processes* 3 (1988), 207-31.

Bower, G. H., J. B. Black and T. J. Turner. "Scripts in Text Comprehension and Memory." *Cognitive Psychology* 11 (1979), 177-220.

Brachman, R. J. and H. Q. Levesque, eds. *Readings in Knowledge Representation.* Palo Alto, CA: Morgan Kaufmann, 1985.

Brachman, R. J., H. Q. Levesque, and R. Reiter, eds. *Readings in Knowledge Representation and Reasoning.* San Mateo, CA: Morgan Kaufmann, 1990.

Brady, M. and R. Berwick, eds. *Computational Models of Discourse.* Cambridge, MA: MIT Press, 1985.

Bransford, J. D. and J. J. Franks. "The Abstraction of Linguistic Ideas." *Cognitive Psychology* 3 (1971), 331-50.

Bransford, J. D. and M. K. Johnson. "Contextual Prerequisites for Understanding: Some Investigations of Comprehension and Recall." *Journal of Verbal Learning and Verbal Behavior* 11 (1972), 717-26.

Bresnan, J. W. "A Realistic Transformational Grammar." In M. Halle, J. W. Bresnan, and G. A. Miller, eds. *Linguistic Theory and Psychological Reality.* Cambridge, MA: MIT Press, 1978.

Bresnan, J. W., ed. *The Mental Representation of Grammatical Relations.* Cambridge, MA: MIT Press, 1982.

Briscoe, E. J. "Garden Path Sentences or Garden Path Utterances." In F. Nolan, G. Harrington, P. Warren, and E. J. Briscoe, eds. *Cambridge Papers in Phonetics and Experimental Linguistics*, Vol. I. Cambridge University: Department of Linguistics, 1982.

Briscoe, E. J. "Determinism and Its Implementation in PARSIFAL." In K. Sparck Jones and Y. Wilks. *Automatic Natural Language Parsing.* Chichester: Ellis Horwood, 1983.

Brown, G. and G. Yule. *Discourse Analysis.* Cambridge: Cambridge University Press, 1983.

Bruce, B. "Case Systems for Natural Language." *Artificial Intelligence* 6 (1975), 327-60.

Brugman, C. *The Story of Over: Polysemy, Semantics and Structure in the Lexicon.* New York: Garland, 1988.

Bryan, M. *SGML: An Author's Guide to the Standard Generalized Markup Language.* Reading, MA: Addison-Wesley, 1988.

Burrows, J. F. *Computation into Criticism: A Study of Jane Austen's Novels and An Experiment in Method.* Oxford: Clarendon Press, 1987.

Butler, C. S. "Poetry and the Computer: Some Qualitative Aspects of the Poetry of Sylvia Plath." *Proceedings of the British Academy* 115 (1979), 291-311.

Butler, C. S. *Computers in Linguistics.* Oxford: Basil Blackwell, 1985.

Butler, C. S. *Systemic Linguistics: Theory and Applications.* London: Batford, 1985).

Byrd, R. J. "Word Formation in Natural Language Processing Systems." *Proceedings of the Eighth International Conference on Artificial Intelligence* (1983), 704-6.

Caramazza, A. and R. S. Berndt. "A Psycholinguistic Assessment of Adult Aphasias." In *Handbook of Applied Psycholinguistics.* Hillsdale, N.J.: Lawrence Erlbaum, 1982.

Caramazza, A., E. H. Gruber, C. Garvey, and J. Yates. "Comprehension of Anaphoric Pronouns." *Journal of Verbal Learning and Verbal Behavior* 16 (1977), 601-9.

Caramazza, A. and S. Gupta. "The Role of Topicalization, Parallel Function and Verb Semantics in the Interpretation of Pronouns." *Linguistics* 17 (1979), 497-518.

Carberry, S. "Tracking User's Goals in an Information Seeking Environment." In *Proceedings of The National Conference on Artificial Intelligence* (1983), 1-59.

Carberry, S. "Modeling the User's Plans and Goals." *Computational Linguistics* 14 (1988), 23-37.

Carberry, S. "A Pragmatics-Based Approach to Ellipsis Resolution." *Computational Linguistics* 15 (1989), 75-96.

Carberry, S. *Plan Recognition in Natural Language Dialogue.* Cambridge, MA: MIT Press, 1990.

Carbonell, J. G. "Metaphor: an Inescapable Phenomenon in Natural-language Comprehension." In W. G. Lehnert and M. H. Ringle, eds. *Strategies for Natural Language Processing.* Hillsdale, NJ: Lawrence Erlbaum, 1982.

Carbonell, J. G. "Discourse Pragmatics and Ellipsis Resolution in Task-Oriented Natural Language Interfaces." *Proceedings of the Twenty-First Annual Meeting of the Association for Computational Linguistics* (1983), 164-68.

Carlson, G.N. "Thematic Roles and Their Role in Semantic Interpretation." *Linguistics* 22 (1984), 259-79.

Carlson, G. N. and M. K. Tanenhaus. "Thematic Roles and Language Comprehension." In *Syntax and Semantics 21: Thematic Relations.* London: Academic, 1988.

Carlson, G. N. and M. K. Tanenhaus, eds. *Linguistic Structures in Language Processing.* Dordrecht, Netherlands: Kluwer, 1989.

Carter, D.M. *Interpreting Anaphors in Natural Language Text.* Chichester: Ellis Horwood, 1987.

Catford, J. C. *A Practical Introduction to Phonetics.* Oxford: Oxford University Press, 1988.

Cercone, N. and G. McCalla. *The Knowledge Frontier. Essays in the Representation of Knowledge.* Berlin: Springer-Verlag, 1987.

Charniak, E. "The Case-Slot Identity Theory." *Cognitive Science* 5 (1981), 285-92.

Charniak, E. and D. McDermott. *Introduction to Artificial Intelligence.* Reading, MA: Addison-Wesley, 1985.

Chierchia, G., B. Partee, and D. Turner, eds. *Property Theory, Type Theory, and Natural Language Semantics.* Dordrecht, Netherlands: Kluwer, 1988.

Chomsky, N. *Syntactic Structures.* Gravenhage, Netherlands: Mouton, 1957.

Chomsky, N. "Formal Properties of Grammars." In R. D. Luce, R. Bush, and E. Galanter, eds. *Handbook of Mathematical Psychology.* New York: Wiley, 1963.

Chomsky, N. *Aspects of the Theory of Syntax*. Cambridge, MA: MIT Press, 1965.

Chomsky, N. *Rules and Representations*. Oxford: Blackwell, 1980.

Chomsky, N. *Some Concepts and Consequences of the Theory of Government and Binding*. Cambridge, MA: MIT Press, 1982.

Chomsky, N. *Knowledge of Language: Its Nature, Origin and Use*. New York: Praeger, 1986.

Church, K. W. *Phonological Parsing in Speech Recognition*. Boston, MA: Kluwer, 1987.

Church, K. W. "A Stochastic Parts Program and Noun Phrase Parser for Unrestricted Text." *Proceedings of the Second Conference on Applied Natural Language Processing* (1988).

Church, K., K. W. Gale, P. Hanks, and D. Hindle. "Parsing, Word Associations, and Typical Predicate-Argument Relations." In *Proceedings of the DARPA Speech and Natural Language Workshop*. San Mateo, CA: Morgan Kaufman, 1989.

Churchland, P. M. *Matter and Consciousness: A Contemporary Introduction to the Philosophy of Mind*. Rev. Ed. Cambridge, MA: Bradford/MIT Press, 1988.

Churchland, P. S. *Neurophilosophy: Toward a Unified Science of the Mind-Brain*. Cambridge, MA: MIT Press, 1986.

Clark, H. H. and C. R. Marshall. "Definite Reference and Mutual Knowledge." In A. Joshi, B. L. Webber, and I. Sag, eds. *Elements of Discourse Understanding*. New York: Cambridge University Press, 1981.

Clark, H. H. and C. J. Sengul. "In Search of Referents for Noun Phrases and Pronouns." *Memory and Cognition* 7 (1979), 35-41.

Clifton, C. and F. Ferreira. "Discourse Structure and Anaphora: Some Experimental Results." In M. Coltheart, ed. *Attention and Performance XII: The Psychology of Reading*. London: Lawrence Erlbaum, 1987.

Clifton, C. and F. Ferreira. "Modularity in Sentence Comprehension." In J. L. Garfield, ed. *Modularity in Knowledge Representation and Natural Language Processing*. Cambridge, MA: MIT Press, 1987.

Clifton, C. and F. Ferreira. "Ambiguity in Context." *Language and Cognitive Processes* 4 (1989), 77-103.

Cluett, R. *Prose Style and Critical Reading*. New York: Columbia University Teachers College Press, 1976.

Cohen, P. R. and C. R. Perrault. "Elements of a Plan-Based Theory of Speech Acts." *Cognitive Science* 3 (1979), 177-212.

Cohen, P. R., J. Morgan, and M. E. Pollack, eds. *Intentions in Communication*. Cambridge, MA: MIT Press, 1990.

Cohen, R. "Analyzing the Structure of Argumentative Discourse." *Computational Linguistics* 13 (1987), 11-24.

Cole, R. A. *Perception and Production of Fluent Speech*. Hillsdale, NJ: Lawrence Erlbaum, 1980.

Collins, A. M. and E. F. Loftus. "A Spreading Activation Theory of Semantic Processing." *Psychological Review* 82 (1975), 407-28.

Coombs, J. H. A. H. Renear and S. J. DeRose. "Markup Systems and the Future of Scholarly Text Processing." *Communications of the Association for Computing Machinery* 30 (1987), 933-47.

Corbett, A. T. and B. A. Dorsher. "Instrumental Inferences in Sentence Encoding." *Journal of Verbal Learning and Verbal Behavior* 17 (1978), 479-91.

Cotrell, G. W. *A Connectionist Approach to Word Sense Disambiguation*, Palo Alto, CA: Morgan Kaufmann, 1989.

Coulmas, F. *Writing Systems of the World*, Oxford: Basil Blackwell, 1989.

Coulthard, R. M. and M. Montgomery, eds. *Studies in Discourse Analysis*. London: Routledge & Kegan Paul, 1981.

Cowan, J. D. and D. H. Sharp. *A Primer on Neural Nets*. Cambridge, MA: MIT Press, 1989.

Crain, S. and M. J. Steedman. "On Not Being Led Up the Garden Path: The Use of Context By the Psychological Syntax Parser." In Dowty, D. R., L. Karttunen, and A. M. Zwicky, eds. *Natural Language Parsing: Psychological, Computational and Theoretical Perspectives*. Cambridge, Cambridge University Press, 1985.

Cresswell, M.J. *Semantical Essays Possible Worlds and Their Rivals*. Dordrecht, Netherlands: Kluwer, 1988.

Cruse, D. A. *Lexical Semantics*. New York: Cambridge University Press, 1986.

Cruttenden, A. *Intonation*. Cambridge: Cambridge University Press, 1986.

Cullingford, R. "SAM." In R. C. Schank and C. K. Riesbeck, eds. *Inside Computer Understanding: Five Programs Plus Miniatures*. Hillsdale, NJ: Lawrence Erlbaum, 1981.

Dahlgren, K. *Naive Semantics for Natural Language Understanding*. Boston, MA: Kluwer, 1988.

Dahlgren K. and E. Stabler. "Knowledge Representation for Commonplace Reasoning with Text." *Computational Linguistics* 15 (1989), 149-70.

Daneman, M. and P. A. Carpenter. "Individual Differences in Working Memory and Reading." *Journal of Verbal Learning and Verbal Behavior* 19 (1980), 450-66.

Dascal, M. "Defending Literal Meaning." *Cognitive Science* 11 (1987), 259-81.

de Beaugrande, R. *Text, Discourse and Process. Toward a Multidisciplinary Science of Discourse*. Norwood, NJ: Ablex, 1980.

Dell, G. "A Spreading Activation Theory of Retrieval in Sentence Production." *Psychological Review* 93 (1986), 283-321.

DeRose, S. J. "Grammatical Category Disambiguation by Statistical Optimization." *Computational Linguistics* 14 (1988), 31-39.

Dillon, G. *Introduction to Linguistic Semantics*. Englewood Cliffs, NJ: Prentice-Hall, 1977.

Dowty, D. R., L. Karttunen, and A. M. Zwicky, eds. *Natural Language Parsing: Psychological, Computational and Theoretical Perspectives*. Cambridge: Cambridge University Press, 1985.

Dowty, D. R., R. E. Wall, and S. Peters, eds. *Introduction to Montague Semantics*. Dordrecht, Netherlands: Reidel, 1981.

Durbin, R., C. Miall, and G. Mitchison. *The Computing Neuron*, Reading, MA: Addison-Wesley, 1989.

Dyer, M. *In-depth Understanding: A Computer Model for Integrated Processing for Narrative Comprehension*. Cambridge, MA: MIT Press, 1983.

Eco U., M. Santambrogio, and P.Violi, eds. *Meaning and Mental Representations*. Bloomington, Indiana: Indiana University Press, 1988.

Ehrlich K. and P. N. Johnson-Laird. "Spatial Descriptions and Referential Continuity." *Journal of Verbal Learning and Verbal Behavior* 21 (1982), 296-306.

Ehrlich, K. and K. Rayner. "Pronoun Assignment and Semantic Integration During Reading: Eye Movements and Immediacy of Processing." *Journal of Verbal Learning and Verbal Behavior* 22 (1983), 75-87.

Erdman, L. D., F. Hayes-Roth, V. R. Lesser, and D. R. Reddy. "The HEARSAY-II speech-understanding system: integrating knowledge to resolve uncertainty" *Computing Surveys* 12 (1980), 213-53.

Evens, M. W. ed. *Relational Models of the Lexicon. Representing Knowledge in Semantic Networks*. Cambridge: Cambridge University Press, 1989.

Fallside, F. and W. Woods, eds. *Computer Speech Processing*. London: Prentice-Hall, 1985.

Fass, D. and Y. Wilks. "Preference Semantics, Ill-formedness, and Metaphor." *Computational Linguistics* 9 (1983), 178-87.

Feldman, J. A. and D. H. Ballard. "Connectionist Models and Their Properties." *Cognitive Science* 6 (1982), 205-54.

Ferreira, F. and C. Clifton. "The Independence of Syntactic Processing." *Journal of Memory and Language* 25 (1986), 348-68.

Fillmore, C. J. "The Case for Case." In E. Bach and R. Harms, eds. *Universals in Linguistic Theory*. New York: Holt, Rinehart and Winston, 1968.

Fillmore, C. J. "The Case for Case Reopened." In P. Cole and J. Sadock, eds. *Syntax and Semantics 8: Grammatical Relations*. New York: Academic Press, 1977.

Findler, N. V. ed. *Associative Networks: Representation and Use of Knowledge by Computers*. New York: Academic, 1975.

Fisher, A. J. "Practical Parsing of Generalized Phrase Structure Grammars." *Computational Linguistics* 15 (1989), 139-48.

Flores D'Arcais, G. B. and R. J. Jarvella. *The Process of Language Understanding*. New York: Wiley, 1983.

Fodor, J. A. "The Psychological Reality of Linguistic Segments." *Journal of Verbal Learning and Verbal Behavior* 4 (1965), 414-20.

Fodor, J. A. *The Modularity of Mind: An Essay on Faculty Psychology*. Cambridge, MA: MIT Press, 1983.

Fodor, J. A. "Precis of *The Modularity of Mind* and Peer Commentary." *The Behavioral and Brain Sciences* 8 (1985), 1-42.

Fodor, J. A., M. Garrett, and T. Bever. *The Psychology of Language*. New York: McGraw-Hill, 1974.

Fodor, J. A., J. D. Fodor, and M. Garrett. "The psychological unreality of Semantic Representations." *Linguistic Inquiry* 6 (1975), 515-31.

Fodor, J. A. and Z. W. Pylyshyn. "Connectionism and Cognitive Architecture." In S. Pinker and J. Mehler, eds. *Connections and Symbols*. Cambridge, MA: Bradford/MIT Press, 1988.

Fodor, J. D. and L. Frazier. "Is the HSPM an ATN?" *Cognition* 8 (1980), 417-59.

Forster, K. I. "Accessing the Mental Lexicon." In R. J. Wales and E. Walker, eds. *New Approaches to Language Mechanisms*. Amsterdam: North Holland, 1976.

Foss, D. "Decision Processes During Sentence Comprehension: Effects of Lexical Item Difficulty and Position on Decision Times." *Journal of Verbal Learning and Verbal Behavior* 8 (1969), 457-62.

Foss, D. and D. Hakes. *Psycholinguistics: An Introduction to the Psychology of Language*. Englewood Cliffs, NJ: Prentice-Hall, 1978.

Francis, N. and H. Kučera. *Frequency Analysis of English Usage: Lexicon and Grammar*. Boston: Houghton Mifflin, 1982.

Frazier, L. "Parsing Modifiers: Special Purpose Routines in the HSPM?" In Balota, D.A., G. B. Flores d'Arcais, and K. Rayner. *Comprehension Processes in Reading*. Hillsdale, NJ: Lawrence Erlbaum, 1990.

Frazier, L. "Theories of Language Comprehension." In J. L. Garfield, ed. *Modularity in Knowledge Representation and Natural Language Processing* Cambridge, MA: MIT Press, 1987.

Frazier, L., C. Clifton, and J. Randall. "Filling Gaps: Decision Principles and Structure in Sentence Comprehension." *Cognition* 13 (1983), 187-222.

Frazier, L. and J. D. Fodor. "The Sausage Machine: A New Two-Stage Parsing Model." *Cognition* 6 (1978).

Fredericksen, J. R. "Understanding Anaphora: Rules Used by Readers in Assigning Pronominal Referents." *Discourse Processes* 4 (1981), 323-47.

Frege, G. *Translations from the Philosophical Writings of Gottlob Frege*. P. T. Geach and M. Black, eds. Oxford: Basil Blackwell, 1952.

Fry, D. B. *The Physics of Speech*. Cambridge: Cambridge University Press, 1976.

Ganong, W. F. "Phonetic Categorization in Auditory Word Perception." *Journal of Experimental Psychology: Human Perception and Performance* 6 (1980), 110-25.

Garfield, J. L. ed. *Modularity in Knowledge Representation and Natural Language Processing*. Cambridge, MA: MIT Press, 1987.

Garnham, A. "Testing Psychological Theories about Inference Making." *Memory and Cognition* 10 (1982), 341-9.

Garnham, A. *Psycholinguistics: Central Topics*. London: Methuen, 1985.

Garnham, A. "Understanding Anaphora." In A. W. Ellis, ed. *Progress in the Psychology of Language*, Vol 3. London: Lawrence Erlbaum, 1987.

Garnham, A. *Mental Models as Representations of Discourse and Text*. Chichester: Ellis Horwood, 1988.

Garnham, A. and J. Oakhill. "On-line Resolution of Anaphoric Pronouns: Effects of Inference Making and Verb Semantics." *British Journal of Psychology* 76 (1985), 377-84.

Garnham, A. and J. Oakhill. "Anaphoric Islands Revisited." *Quarterly Journal of Experimental Psychology*. 40a (1989) 719-35.

Garnham, A., J. Oakhill, and P. N. Johnson-Laird. "Referential Continuity and the Coherence of Discourse." *Cognition* 11 (1982), 29-46.

Garrod, S. C. and A. J. Sanford. "Bridging Inferences and the Extended Domain of Reference." In J. Long and A. Baddeley, eds. *Attention and Performance IX*. Hillsdale, N.J. Lawrence Erlbaum, 1981.

Garside, R. "The CLAWS Word-Tagging System." In R. Garside, G. Leech, and G. Sampson, eds. *The Computational Analysis of English: A Corpus-based Approach*. New York: Longman, 1987.

Garside, R. and G. Leech. "The UCREL Probabilistic Parsing System." In R. Garside, G., Leech, and G. Sampson, eds. *The Computational Analysis of English*. New York: Longman, 1987.

Garside, R., G. Leech, and G. Samson. *The Computational Analysis of English: A Corpus-based Approach*. New York: Longman, 1987.

Gazdar, G. "Computational Tools for Doing Linguistics." special issue of *Computational Linguistics* 23 (1985).

Gazdar, G., E. Klein, G. K. Pullum, and I. Sag. *Generalized Phrase Structure Grammar*. Oxford: Basil Blackwell, 1985.

Geeraerts, D. "Introduction: Prospects and Problems of Prototype Theory." *Linguistics* 27 (1989), 587-612.

Gellerstam, M. ed. *Studies in Computer-Aided Lexicology*. Stockholm: Almqvist and Wiksell, 1988.

Gernsbacher, M. A. "Mechanisms That Improve Referential Access." *Cognition* 32 (1989), 99-156.

Gershman, A. V. "A Framework for Conceptual Analyzers." In W. G. Lehnert and M. H. Ringle, eds. *Strategies for Natural Language Processing.* Hillsdale, NJ: Lawrence Erlbaum, 1982.

Gibbs, R. "Literal Meaning and Psychological Theory." *Cognitive Science* 8 (1984), 275-304.

Gibbs, R. "Understanding and Literal Meaning." *Cognitive Science* 13 (1989), 243-51.

Goetz, E. T., R. C. Anderson, and D. L. Shallert. "The Representation of Sentences in Memory." *Journal of Verbal Learning and Verbal Behavior* 20 (1981), 369-81.

Goodman, B. A. "Reference Identification and Reference Identification Failures." *Computational Linguistics* 12 (1986), 273-305.

Gorfein, D. S., ed. *Resolving Semantic Ambiguity.* New York: Springer-Verlag, 1989.

Greach P. and M. Black, eds. *Translations from the Philosophical Writing of Gotlob Frege.* Oxford: Basil Blackwell, 1952.

Green, G. M. *Pragmatics and Natural Language Understanding.* San Mateo, CA: Morgan Kaufmann, 1988.

Greenbaum, S. "The International Corpus of English." *ICAME Journal* 14 (1990), 106-8.

Greene, B. B. and G. M. Rubin. *Automatic Grammatical Tagging of English.* Providence, RI: Brown University Department of Linguistics, 1971.

Grishman, R. *Computational Linguistics: An Introduction,* Cambridge: Cambridge University Press, 1986.

Grober, E. H., W. Beardsley, and A. Caramazza. "Parallel Function in Pronoun Assignment." *Cognition* 6 (1978), 117-33.

Grosjean, F. "Spoken Word Recognition Processes and the Gating Paradigm." *Perception and Psychophysics* 28 (1980), 267-83.

Grosjean, F. and J. P. Gee. "Prosodic Structure and Spoken Word Recognition." *Cognition* 25 (1987), 135-55.

Grosz, B. J. "The Representation and Use of Focus in a System for Understanding Dialogues." *Proceedings of the International Joint Conference on Artificial Intelligence* (1977), 67-76.

Grosz, B. J. "Focus and Description in Natural Language Dialogues." In A. K. Joshi, B. L. Webber, and I. A. Sag, eds. *Elements of Discourse Understanding.* Cambridge: Cambridge University Press, 1981.

Grosz, B. J., A. K. Joshi, and S. Weinstein. "Providing a Unified Account of Definite Noun Phrases in Discourse." *Proceedings of the Association for Computational Linguistics* (1983), 44-50.

Grosz, B. J. and C. L. Sidner. "Attention, Intentions, and the Structure of Discourse." *Computational Linguistics* 12 (1986), 175-94.

Grosz, B. J. and C. L. Sidner. "Plans for Discourse." In P. R. Cohen, J. Morgan and M.E. Pollack, eds. *Intentions in Communication*. Cambridge, MA: MIT Press, 1990.

Grosz, B. J., K. Sparck Jones, and B. L. Webber. *Readings in Natural Language Processing*. San Mateo, CA: Morgan Kaufmann, 1986.

Haddock, N. J. "Incremental Interpretation and Combinatory Categorial Grammar." In *Proceedings of the Tenth International Joint Conference on Artificial Intelligence*. (1987), 661-63.

Haddock, N. J. "Computational Models of Incremental Semantics." *Language and Cognitive Processes* 4 (1989), 337-68.

Halle, M., J. W. Bresnan, and G. A. Miller. *Linguistic Theory and Psychological Reality*. Cambridge, MA: MIT Press, 1978.

Halliday, M. A. K. *An Introduction to Functional Grammar*. London: Arnold, 1985.

Halliday, M. A. K. and R. Hasan. *Cohesion in English*. London: Longman, 1976.

Halvorsen, P. "Natural Language Understanding and Montague Grammar." *Computational Intelligence* 2 (1986), 54-62.

Handel, S. *Listening: An Introduction to the Perception of Auditory Events*. Cambridge, MA: Bradford/MIT Press, 1989.

Harris, M. and M. Coltheart. *Language Processing in Children and Adults*. London: Routledge, 1986.

Haviland, S. E. and H. H. Clark. "What's New? Acquiring New Information as a Process in Comprehension." *Journal of Verbal Learning and Verbal Behavior* 13 (1974), 512-21.

Heidorn, G. "Augmented Phrase Structure Grammars." In R. C. Schank and B. L. Nash-Webber, eds. *Theoretical Issues in Natural Language Processing*, Association for Computational Linguistics, 1975.

Hendrix, G. G. "Encoding Knowledge in Partitioned Networks." In N. N. Findler, ed. *Associative Networks: Representation and Use of Knowledge in Computers*. New York: Academic Press, 1979.

Hinton, G. E. and J. A. Anderson. *Parallel Models of Associative Memory*. Updated Edition. Hillsdale, NJ: Lawrence Erlbaum, 1989.

Hirst, G. *Anaphora in Natural Language Understanding*. New York: Springer-Verlag, 1981.

Hirst, G. *Semantic Interpretation Against Ambiguity*. Cambridge: Cambridge University Press, 1987.

Hobbs, J. R. "Resolving Pronoun References." *Lingua* 44 (1978), 311-38.

Hobbs, J. R. "World Knowledge and Word Meaning." In Y. Wilks, ed. *Theoretical Issues in Natural Language Processing*. Hillsdale, NJ: Lawrence Erlbaum, 1990.

Hobbs, J. R. and D. A. Evans. "Conversation as Planned Behavior." *Cognitive Science* 4 (1980), 349-77.

Hoc, J. M. *Cognitive Psychology of Planning*. New York: Academic, 1988.

Hockey, S. *A Guide to Computer Applications in the Humanities*. Baltimore: Johns Hopkins University Press, 1980.

Hockey, S. and I. Marriott. *Oxford Concordance Program: Users' Manual*. Oxford: Oxford University Computing Centre, 1980.

Hopcroft, J. E. and J. D. Ullman. *Introduction to Automata Theory, Languages and Computation*. Reading, MA: Addison-Wesley, 1969.

Hopfield, J. J. "Neural Networks and Physical Systems with Emergent Collective Computational Abilities." *Proceedings of the National Academy of Sciences* 79 (1982), 2554-58.

Horn, G. M. *Lexical Functional Grammar*, New York: Moulton, 1983.

Hughes, G. E. and M. J. Cresswell. *An Introduction to Modal Logic*. London: Methuen, 1968.

Hüllen, W. and R. Schulze. *Understanding the Lexicon: Meaning, Sense and World Knowledge in Lexical Semantics*, Tübingen, Germany: Niemeyer, 1988.

Hultin, N. C. and H. M. Logan. "The *New Oxford English Dictionary* Project at Waterloo." *Dictionaries* 6 (1984), 128, 183-98.

Hyman, L. M. and C. N. Li. *Language, Speech and Mind*. New York: Routledge, 1988.

Jackendoff, R. *Semantic Interpretation in Generative Grammar*. Cambridge, MA: MIT Press, 1972.

Jackendoff, R. *Semantics and Cognition*. Cambridge, MA, MIT Press, 1983.

Jackendoff, R. *Semantic Structures*. Cambridge, MA: MIT Press, 1989.

Jacobson, P. and G. Pullum. *The Nature of Syntactic Representation*. Dordrecht, Netherlands: Reidel, 1982.

Jakobson, R. *Six Lectures on Sound and Meaning*. Cambridge, MA: MIT Press, 1978.

Jaynes, J. T. "A Search for Trends in the Poetic Style of W. B. Yeats." *ALLC Journal* 1 (1980), 11-18.

Johansson, S. *Computer Corpora in English Language Research*. Bergen, Norway: Norwegian Computing Centre for the Humanities, 1982.

Johansson, S. and K. Hofland. *Frequency Analysis of English Vocabulary and Grammar*. 2 Vols. Oxford: Clarendon, 1989.

Johnson, M. K. J. D. Bransford and S. Solomon. "Memory for Tacit Implications of a Sentence." *Journal of Experimental Psychology* 98 (1973), 203-5.

Johnson-Laird, P. N. "Models of Deduction." In R. J. Falmagne, ed. *Reasoning: Representation and Process in Children and Adults*. Hillsdale, NJ: Lawrence Erlbaum, 1975.

Johnson-Laird, P. N. *Mental Models: Toward a Cognitive Science of Language, Inference and Consciousness*. Cambridge: Cambridge University Press, 1983.

Johnson-Laird, P. N. "How Is Meaning Mentally Represented." In U. Eco, M. Santambrogio, and P. Violi, eds. *Meaning and Mental Representations.* Bloomington, Indiana: Indiana University Press, 1988.

Johnson-Laird, P. N. *The Computer and the Mind.* Cambridge, MA: Harvard University Press, 1988.

Johnson-Laird, P. N., D. J. Herrmann, and R. Chaffin. "Only Connections: A Critique of Semantic Networks." *Psychological Bulletin* 96 (1984), 292-315.

deJong, G. "An Overview of the FRUMP system. In W. G. Lehnert and M. H. Ringle, eds. *Strategies for Natural Language Processing.* Hillsdale, NJ: Lawrence Erlbaum, 1982.

Joshi, A. K., B. L. Webber, and I. A. Sag, eds. *Elements of Discourse Understanding.* Cambridge: Cambridge University Press, 1981.

Kamp, H. "A Theory of Truth and Semantic Representation." In J. A. G. Groenendijk, T. M. V. Janssen, and M. B. J. Stokhof, eds. *Formal Methods in the Study of Language.* Amsterdam: Mathematical Centre Tracts, 1981.

Kamp, H. *From Discourse to Logic.* Vol.1, Boston, MA: Kluwer, 1990.

Kanal, L. H. and V. Kumar. *Search in Artificial Intelligence.* Berlin: Springer-Verlag, 1988.

Kaplan, R. M. "Augmented Transition Networks as Psychological Models of Sentence Comprehension." *Artificial Intelligence* 3 (1972), 77-100.

Kaplan, R. M. "A General Syntactic Processor." In B. Rustin, ed. *Natural Language Processing.* New York: Algorithmics Press, 1983.

Kaplan, R. M. and J. W. Bresnan. "Lexical-functional Grammar; a Formal System for Grammatical Representation." In J. W. Bresnan, ed. *The Mental Representation of Grammatical Relations.* Cambridge, MA: MIT Press, 1982.

Karttunen, L. "KIMMO: A General Morphological Processor." *Texas Linguistics Forum 22.* Austin, Texas: University of Texas, 1983, 165-86.

Karttunen, L. and K. Wittenburg. "A Two-level Morphological Analysis of English." *Texas Linguistics Forum 22.* Austin, Texas: University of Texas, 1983, 217-28.

Katz, J. J. and J. A. Fodor. "The Structure of a Semantic Theory." *Language* 39 (1963), 170-210.

Katz, J. J. and R. Nagel. "Meaning Postulates and Semantic Theory." *Foundations of Language* 11 (1974), 311-40.

Katz, J. J. and P. Postal. *An Integrated Theory of Semantic Descriptions.* Cambridge, MA: MIT Press, 1964.

Kay, M. "Functional Grammar." *Proceedings of the Fifth Annual Meeting of the Berkeley Linguistics Society.* 1979, 142-58.

Kay, M. "Parsing in Functional Unification Grammar." In D. R. Dowty, L. Karttunen, and A. M. Zwicky, eds. *Natural Language Parsing: Psychological, Computational and Theoretical Perspectives.* Cambridge: Cambridge University Press, 1985.

Kaye, J. *Phonology: A Cognitive View.* Hillsdale, NJ: Lawrence Erlbaum, 1989.

Kean, M. L. "The Linguistic Interpretation of Aphasic Syndromes." In E. Walker, ed. *Explorations in the Biology of Language.* Hassocks, Sussex: Harvester, Press, 1978.

Kegl, J. "The Boundary between Word Knowledge and World Knowledge." In Y. Wilks, ed. *Theoretical Issues in Natural Language Processing.* Hillsdale, NJ: Lawrence Erlbaum, 1990.

Kellerman, K., S. Broetzmann, T. Lim, and K. Kitao. "The Conversational Mop: Scenes in the Stream of Discourse." *Discourse Processes* 12 (1989), 27-62.

Kempson, R. *Semantic Theory.* Cambridge: Cambridge University Press, 1977.

Kempson, R., ed. *Mental Representations: The Interface Between Language and Reality.* Cambridge: Cambridge University Press, 1988.

Khanna, T. *Foundations of Neural Networks*, Reading, MA: Addison-Wesley, 1990.

Kimball, J. "Seven Principles of Surface Structure Parsing in Natural Language." *Cognition* 2 (1973), 15-47.

Kimball, J. "Predictive Analysis and Over-the-top Parsing." In J. Kimball, ed. *Syntax and Semantics*, Vol. 4. London: Academic, 1975.

King, M. "Transformational Parsing." In M. King, ed. *Parsing Natural Language.* London: Academic, 1983.

Kintsch, W. *The Representation of Meaning in Memory.* Hillsdale, NJ: Lawrence Erlbaum, 1974.

Kintsch, W. "The Role of Knowledge in Discourse Comprehension: A Construction-Integration Model." *Psychological Review* 95 (1988), 161-82.

Kjetsaa, G., S. Gustavsson, B. Beckman, and S. Gil. *The Authorship of "The Quiet Don."* Atlantic Highlands, NJ: Humanities Press, 1984.

Knight, K. "Unification: a Multidisciplinary Survey." *Computing Surveys* 21 (1989), 93-124.

Knuth, D. E. *The Art of Computer Programming*, Volumes 1 and 3. Reading, MA: Addison-Wesley, 1968, 1973.

Kohonen, T. *Content Addressable Memories.* 2nd Ed. Berlin: Springer-Verlag, 1987.

Kowalik, J. S., ed. *Parallel Computation and Computers for Artificial Intelligence.* Boston, MA: Kluwer, 1987.

Krishnamurthy, E. V. *Parallel Processing.* Reading, MA: Addison-Wesley, 1989

Kučera, H. and W. N. Francis. *Computational Analysis of Present Day American English.* Providence, RI: Brown University Press, 1967.

Lachter, J. and T. G. Bever. "The Relation between Linguistic Structure and Associative Theories of Language Learning: A Constructive Critique of Some Connectionist Learning Models." In S. Pinker and J. Mehler, eds. *Connections and Symbols.* Cambridge, MA: Bradford/MIT Press, 1988.

Ladefoged, P. *A Course in Phonetics*. 2nd Ed. New York: Harcourt, Brace, Jovanovich, 1982.

Lakoff, G. "Structural Complexity in Fairy Tales." *The Study of Man* 1 (1972), 128-90.

Lakoff, G. and M. Johnson. *Metaphors We Live By*. Chicago: University of Chicago Press, 1980.

Landman, F. and F. Veltman. *Varieties of Formal Semantics*. Dordrecht, Netherlands: Foris, 1984.

Lea, W. A. ed. *Trends in Speech Recognition* Englewood Cliffs, NJ: Prentice-Hall, 1980.

Leblanc, H. ed. *Truth, Syntax and Modality*. Amsterdam: North-Holland, 1973.

Leech, G. N. *Principles of Pragmatics*. London: Longman, 1983.

Leech, G. N. and M. H. Short. *Style in Fiction: A Linguistic Introduction to English Fictional Prose*. London: Longman, 1981.

Lehmann, W. P. ed. *Prototypes in Language and Cognition*, Ann Arbor, MI: Karoma, 1988.

Lehnert, W. G. and M. H. Ringle, eds. *Strategies in Natural Language Processing*. Hillsdale, NJ: Lawrence Erlbaum, 1982.

Lesgold, A., S. Roth, and M. Curtis. "Foregrounding Effects in Discourse Comprehension." *Journal of Verbal Learning and Verbal Behavior* 18 (1979), 291-308.

Lesmo, L. and P. Torasso. "Weighted Interaction of Syntax and Semantics in Natural Language Analysis." *Proceedings of the Tenth International Joint Conference of Artificial Intelligence* (1985), 772-78.

Levelt, W. J. M. *Speaking: From Intention to Articulation*. Cambridge, MA: Bradford/MIT Press, 1989.

Levine, D. S. *Introduction to Neural and Cognitive Modeling*. Hillsdale, NJ: Lawrence Erlbaum, 1989.

Levinson, S. C. *Pragmatics*. Cambridge: Cambridge University Press, 1983.

Liberman, M. "Text on Tap: the ACL/DCI." In *Proceedings of the DARPA Speech and Natural Language Workshop*. San Mateo, CA: Morgan Kaufman, 1989.

Linde, C. "Focus of Attention and the Choice of Pronouns in Discourse." In T. Givón, ed. *Syntax and Semantics 12: Discourse and Syntax*. New York: Academic, 1979.

Linggard, R. *The Electronic Synthesis of Speech*. Cambridge: Cambridge University Press, 1985.

Litman, D. J. "Understanding Plan Ellipsis." In *Proceedings of the Fifth National Conference on Artificial Intelligence* (1986).

Litman, D. J. and J. F. Allen. "A Plan Recognition Model for Subdialogues in Conversations." *Cognitive Science* 11 (1987), 163-200.

Litman, D. J. and J. F. Allen. "Recognizing and Relating Discourse Intentions and Task-oriented Plans. In P. R. Cohen, J. Morgan, and M. E. Pollack, eds. *Intentions in Communication.* Cambridge, MA: MIT Press, 1990.

Lovins, J. B. "Development of a Stemming Algorithm." *Mechanical Translation* and Computational Linguistics. 11 (1968), 11-31.

Lyons, J. *Semantics.* Cambridge: Cambridge University Press, 1977.

Lyons, J. *Language, Meaning and Context,* London: Fontana, 1981.

Lytinen, S. L. "Dynamically Combining Syntax and Semantics in Natural Language Processing." *Proceedings of the American Association for Artificial Intelligence* (1986), 574-78.

Mackin, R. "On Collocations: Words Shall Be Known by the Company They Keep." In P. Stevens, ed. *In Honour of A. S. Hornby.* Oxford: Oxford University Press, 1978.

Mani, K. and P. N. Johnson-Laird. "The Mental Representation of Spatial Descriptions." *Memory and Cognition* 10 (1982), 181-87.

Marcus, M. *A Theory of Syntactic Recognition for Natural Language.* Cambridge, MA: MIT Press, 1980.

Marslen-Wilson, W. D. "Speech Shadowing and Speech Comprehension." *Speech Communication* 4 (1985), 55-73.

Marslen-Wilson, W. D. "Against Modularity." In J. L. Garfield, ed. *Modularity in Knowledge Representation and Natural Language Processing.* Cambridge, MA: MIT Press, 1987.

Marslen-Wilson, W. D. "Functional Parallelism in Spoken Word Recognition." *Cognition* 25 (1987), 71-102.

Marslen-Wilson, W. D. ed. *Lexical Representation and Processing.* Cambridge, MA.: MIT Press, 1989.

Marslen-Wilson, W. D., E. Levy, and L. K. Tyler. "Producing Interpretable Discourse: The Establishment and Maintenance of Reference." In R. J. Jarvella and W. Klein, eds. *Speech, Place, and Action.* Chichester: John Wiley, 1982.

Marslen-Wilson, W. D. and L. K. Tyler. "The Temporal Structure of Spoken Language Understanding." *Cognition* 8 (1980), 1-71.

Matthews, P. H. *Morphology: An Introduction to the Theory of Word Structure.* Cambridge: Cambridge University Press, 1974.

McCawley, J. *Everything That Linguists Have Always Wanted to Know about Logic.* Chicago: University of Chicago Press, 1981.

McCawley, J. *The Syntactic Phenomena of English.* Chicago: University of Chicago Press, 1988.

McClelland, J. L. and J. Elman. "Interactive Processes in Speech Perception: The TRACE model." In J. L. McClelland and D. E. Rumelhart, eds. *Parallel Distributed Processing: Explorations in the Microstructure of Cognition.* Vol. 2. Cambridge, MA: MIT Press, 1986.

McClelland, J. L. and D. E. Rumelhart. "An Interactive Activation Model of Context Effects in Letter Perception: Part 1: The Basic Findings." *Psychological Review* 88 (1981), 60-94.

McGregor R. J. *Neural and Brain Modeling*. New York: Academic, 1987.

McKeown, K. R. *Text Generation: Using Discourse Strategies and Focus Constraints to Generate Natural Language Discourse*. Cambridge: Cambridge University Press, 1985.

McKoon, G. and R. Ratcliff. "The Comprehension Process and Memory Structures Involved in Anaphoric Reference." *Journal of Verbal Learning and Verbal Behavior* 19 (1980), 668-82.

McKoon, G., R. Ratcliff, and C. Seifert. "Making the Connection: Generalized Knowledge Structures in Story Understanding." *Journal of Memory and Language* 28 (1989), 711-34.

McTear, M. *The Articulate Computer*. Oxford: Basil Blackwell, 1987.

Meijs, W. ed. *Corpus Linguistic and Beyond*. Amsterdam: Rodopi, 1986.

Mellish, C. S. "Incremental Semantic Interpretation." In K. Sparck Jones and Y. A. Wilks, ed. *Automatic Natural Language Parsing*. Chichester: Ellis Horwood, 1983.

Mellish, C. S. *Computer Interpretation of Natural Language Descriptions*. Chichester: Ellis Horwood, 1985.

Meyer, D. M. and R. W. Schvaneveldt. "Facilitation in Recognizing Pairs of Words: Evidence of a Dependence Between Retrieval Operations." *Journal of Experimental Psychology* 90 (1971), 227-34.

Miller, G. A. "The Magical Number Seven, Plus or Minus Two." *Psychological Review* 63 (1956), 81-94.

Miller, G. A. "Dictionaries of the Mind." *Language and Cognitive Processes* 1 (1986), 171-85.

Miller, G. A. and S. Isard. "Some Perceptual Consequences of Linguistic Rules." *Journal of Verbal Learning and Verbal Behavior* 2 (1963), 217-28.

Millic, L. T. *A Quantitative Approach to the Style of Jonathan Swift*. The Hague: Mouton, 1967.

Milne, R. "Resolving Lexical Ambiguity in a Deterministic Parser." *Computational Linguistics* 12 (1986), 1-12.

Minsky, M. "A Framework for Representing Knowledge." In P. H. Winston, ed. *The Psychology of Computer Vision*. New York: McGraw-Hill, 1975.

Mitchell, D. C. "Lexical Guidance in Human Parsing: Laws and Processing Characteristics." In M. Coltheart, ed. *Attention and Performance XII: The Psychology of Reading*. London: Lawrence Erlbaum, 1987.

Mitchell, D. C. "Verbal Guidance and Other Lexical Effects in Parsing." *Language and Cognitive Processes* 4 (1989), 123-54.

Mitchell, T. F. "Linguistic 'Goings-on': Collocations and Other Lexical Matters Arising on the Syntagmatic Record." *Archivum Linguisticum* 2 (1971), 35-69.

Montague, R. "The Proper Treatment of Quantification in Ordinary English." In R. Thompson, ed. *Selected Papers of Richard Montague*. New Haven, CT: Yale University Press, 1974.

Moravcsik E. A. and J. R. Wirth. *Current Approaches to Syntax*. New York: Academic, 1980.

Morgan, J. and M. Sellner. "Discourse and Linguistic Theory." In R. Spiro, B. Bruce, and W. Brewer, eds. *Theoretical Issues in Reading Comprehension*. Hillsdale, NJ: Lawrence Erlbaum, 1980.

Mosteller, F. and D. L. Wallace. *Inference and Disputed Authorship: The Federalist*. Reading, MA: Addison-Wesley, 1964.

Moyne, J. A. *Understanding Language Man or Machine*. New York: Plenum, 1985.

Neely, J. H. "Semantic Priming and Retrieval from Lexical Memory: Roles of Inhibitionless Spreading Activation and Limited Capacity Attention." *Journal of Experimental Psychology: General* 106 (1977), 226-54.

Neisser, U. *Concepts and Conceptual Development. Ecological and Intellectual Factors in Categorization*. Cambridge: Cambridge University Press, 1987.

Newell, A. and H. A. Simon. *Human Problem Solving*. Englewood Cliffs, NJ: Prentice-Hall, 1972.

Nida, E. *Componential Analysis of Meaning*. The Hague: Mouton, 1975.

Nilsson, N. *Principles of Artificial Intelligence*. Los Altos, CA: Morgan Kaufmann, 1980.

Norris, D. "Word Recognition: Context Effects Without Priming." *Cognition* 22 (1986), 93-136.

Oakhill, J., A. Garnham, and W. Vonk. "The On-Line Construction of Discourse Models." *Language and Cognitive Processes* 4 (1989), 263-86.

Oakman, R. L. *Computer Methods for Literary Research*. Rev. Ed. Athens, GA: University of Georgia Press, 1984.

Oehrle, R. T., E. Bach, and D. Wheeler, eds. *Categorial Grammars and Natural Language Structures*. Dordrecht, Netherlands: Reidel, 1988.

Pao, Y. *Adaptive Pattern Recognition and Neural Networks*. Reading, MA: Addison-Wesley, 1989.

Pareschi, R. and M. J. Steedman. "A Lazy Way to Chart Parse with Extended Categorial Grammars." In *Proceedings of the 25th Annual Meeting of the Association for Computational Linguistics*. (1987).

Partee, B. H., ed. *Montague Grammars*. New York: Academic Press, 1976.

Partee, B. H., A. ter Meulen, and R. E. Wall. *Mathematical Methods in Linguistics*. Boston, MA: Kluwer, 1990.

Pereira, F. C. N. "A New Characterization of Attachment Preferences." In D. R. Dowty, L. Karttunen, and A. M. Zwicky. *Natural Language Parsing: Psychological, Computational and Theoretical Perspectives*. Cambridge: Cambridge University Press, 1985a.

Pereira, F. C. N. "Structure-sharing Representation for Unification-Based Grammar Formalisms." *Proceedings of the Association for Computational Linguistics* (1985b), 137-44.

Perlmutter, D. M. and S. Soames. *Syntactic Argumentation and the Structure of English*. Berkeley, CA: University of California Press, 1979.

Peterson, J. L. "Computer Programs for Detecting and Correcting Spelling Errors." *Communications of the Association for Computing Machinery* 23 (1980), 676-87.

Petrick, S. R. "Transformational Analysis." In R. Rustin, ed. *Natural Language Processing*. New York: Algorithmics Press, 1973.

Petröfi, J. S. ed. *Text Connectedness from a Psychological Point of View*. Hamburg, Germany: Buske, 1985.

Phillips, J. D. and H. S. Thompson. "GPSGP–A Parser for Generalized Phrase Structure Grammars." *Linguistics* 23 (1985), 245-61.

Pinker, S. "On Language and Connectionism: Analysis of a Parallel Distributed Model of Language Acquisition." In S. Pinker and J. Mehler, eds. *Connections and Symbols*. Cambridge, MA: Bradford/MIT Press, 1988.

Polanyi, L. *Telling the American Story*. Cambridge, MA: MIT Press, 1989.

Polanyi, L. and R. J. H. Scha. "The Syntax of Discourse." *Text* 3 (1983), 261-70.

Polanyi, L. and R. J. H. Scha. "Discourse Syntax and Semantics." In L. Polanyi. *The Structure of Discourse*. New York: Ablex, 1986.

Pollack, J. J. and A. Zamora. "Automatic Spelling Correction in Scientific Scholarly Text." *Communications of the Association for Computing Machinery* 27 (1984), 358-68.

Pollard, C. *Generalized Phrase Structure Grammars, Head Grammars, and Natural Languages*. Cambridge: Cambridge University Press, 1988.

Potter, R. G. "Literary Criticism and Literary Computing: the Difficulties of a Synthesis." *Computers and the Humanities* 22 (1988), 91-97.

Pulman, S. G. "Grammars, Parsers, and Memory Limitations." *Language and Cognitive Processes* 1 (1986), 197-225.

Pulman, S. G. "Unification and the New Grammatism." In Y. Wilks, ed. *Theoretical Issues in Natural Language Processing*. Hillsdale, NJ: Lawrence Erlbaum, 1990.

Pylyshyn, Z. W. *Computation and Cognition: Toward a Foundation for Cognitive Science*. Cambridge, MA: Bradford/MIT Press, 1984.

Quillian, M. R. "Semantic Memory." In M. L. Minsky, ed. *Semantic Information Processing*. Cambridge, MA: MIT Press, 1968.

Quirk, R. S., Greenbaum, G. Leech, and J. Svartvic. *A Comprehensive Grammar of the English Language*. New York: Longman, 1985.

Radford, A. *Transformational Syntax: A Student's Guide to Chomsky's Extended Standard Theory*. New York: Cambridge University Press, 1981.

Ratcliff, R. and G. McKoon. "Priming in Item Recognition: Evidence for the Propositional Structure of Sentences." *Journal of Verbal Learning and Verbal Behavior* 17 (1978), 403-17.

Rayner, K., M. Carlson, and L. Frazier. "The Interaction of Syntax and Semantics During Sentence Processing." *Journal of Verbal Learning and Verbal Behavior* 22 (1983), 358-74.

Reed, A. "CLOC: A Collocation Package." *ALLC Bulletin* 5 (1977), 169-83.

Reichgelt, H. *Knowledge Representation: An AI Perspective.* Norwood, NJ: Ablex, 1990.

Reichman, R. *Getting Computers to Talk Like You and Me.* Cambridge, MA: Bradford/MIT Press, 1985.

Reilly, R. *Communicative Failure in Dialogue and Discourse.* Amsterdam: North-Holland, 1987.

Reinhart, T. *Anaphora and Semantic Interpretation.* London: Croom Helm, 1983.

Renouf, A. "Corpus Development." In J. M. Sinclair, ed. *Looking Up: An Account of the COBUILD Project in Lexical Computing.* London and Glasgow: Collins ELT, 1987.

Reyle, U. and C. Rohrer. *Natural Language Parsing and Linguistic Theories.* Boston, MA: Kluwer, 1988.

Rich, E. *Artificial Intelligence.* London: McGraw-Hill, 1983.

Rickheit, G. and H. Strohner. *Inferences in Text Processing.* Amsterdam: North-Holland, 1985.

Ritchie, G. D. *Computational Grammar.* New York: Barnes and Noble, 1980.

Ritchie, G. D, S. G. Pulman, A. W. Black and G. J. Russell. "A Computational Framework for Lexical Description." *Computational Linguistics* 13 (1987), 290-307.

Roberts, D. D. *The Existential Graphs of Charles S. Peirce.* The Hague: Mouton, 1973.

Robinson, J. J. "DIAGRAM: A Grammar for Dialogues." *Communications of the Association for Computing Machinery* 25, 1 (1982), 27-47.

Rosch, E. "Cognitive Representations of Semantic Categories." *Journal of Experimental Psychology: General* 104 (1975), 192-233.

Rosch, E. and B. Lloyd, eds. *Cognition and Categorization.* Hillsdale, NJ: Lawrence Erlbaum, 1978.

Rosch, E. "Coherence and Categorization: A Historical View." In F. S. Kessel, ed. *The Development of Language and Language Researchers.* Hillsdale, NJ: Lawrence Erlbaum, 1988.

Rosenschein, S. J. and S. M. Shieber. "Translating English into Logical Form." *Proceedings of the Twentieth Annual Meeting of Association for Computational Linguistics* (1982), 1-8.

Rumelhart, D. E. "Notes on Schema for Stories." In D. Bobrow and A. Collins, eds. *Representation and Understanding.* New York: Academic, 1975.

Rumelhart, D. E. and J. L. McClelland. *Parallel Distributed Processing.* 2 vols. Cambridge, MA: MIT Press, 1986, 1987.

Rumelhart, D. E. and J. L. McClelland. "An Interactive Activation Model of Context Effects in Letter Perception: Part 2: The Contextual Enhancement Effect and Some Tests of the Model." *Psychological Review* 89, 1 (1981), 60-94.

Rumelhart, D. E. and J. L. McClelland. "Learning the Past Tenses of English Verbs: Implicit Rules or Parallel Distributed Processing." In B. MacWhinney, ed. *Mechanisms of Language Acquisition.* Hillsdale, NJ: Lawrence Erlbaum, 1987.

Sachs, J. S. "Recognition Memory for Syntactic and Semantic Aspects of Connected Discourse." *Perception and Psychophysics* 2 (1967), 437-42.

Sager, N. *Natural Language Information Processing: A Computer Grammar of English and Its Applications.* Reading, MA: Addison-Wesley, 1981.

Salasoo, A. and D. B. Pisoni. "Interaction of Knowledge Sources in Spoken Word Identification." *Journal of Memory and Language* 24 (1985), 210-31.

Salton, G. *Automatic Text Processing: The Transformation, Analysis, and Retrieval of Information by Computer.* Reading, MA: Addison-Wesley, 1989.

Salton, G. and M. J. McGill. *Introduction to Modern Information Retrieval.* New York: McGraw-Hill, 1983.

Sampson, G. R. "Context-Free Parsing and the Adequacy of Context-Free Grammar." In M. King, ed. *Parsing Natural Language.* London: Academic, 1983.

Sampson, G. *Writing Systems: a Linguistic Introduction,* London, Hutchison, 1985.

Sanford, A. J. and S. C. Garrod. *Understanding Written Language: Explorations of Comprehension Beyond the Sentence.* Chichester: Wiley, 1981.

Sanford, A. J. and S. C. Garrod. "What, When, and How?: Questions of Immediacy in Anaphoric Reference Resolution." *Language and Cognitive Processes.* 4 (1989), 235-62.

Scarborough, D. L., C. Cortese, and H. S. Scarborough. "Frequency and Repetition Effects in Lexical Memory." *Journal of Experimental Psychology: Human Perception and Performance* 3 (1977), 1-17.

Schank, R. C. "Conceptual Dependency: A Theory of Natural Language Understanding." *Cognitive Psychology.* 3/4 (1972) 552-630.

Schank, R. C. *Dynamic Memory A Theory of Reminding and Learning in Computers and People.* New York: Cambridge University Press, 1982a.

Schank, R. C. "Reminding and Memory Organization: An Introduction to MOPs." In W. Lehnert and M. Ringle, eds. *Strategies for Natural Language Processing.* Hillsdale, NJ: Lawrence Erlbaum, 1982b.

Schank, R. C. and R. Abelson. *Scripts, Plans, Goals and Understanding.* Hillsdale, NJ: Lawrence Erlbaum, 1977.

Schank, R. C. and C. K. Riesbeck. *Inside Computer Understanding: Five Programs Plus Miniatures.* Hillsdale, NJ: Lawrence Erlbaum, 1981.

Schatz, C. "The Role of Context in the Perception of Stops." *Language* 30 (1954), 47-56.

Scholtz, K. and G. R. Potts. "Cognitive Processing of Linear Orderings." *Journal of Experimental Psychology* 102 (1974), 323-26.

Schubert, L. K. and F. J. Pelletier. "From English to Logic: Context Free Computation of Conventional Logical Translation." *Computational Linguistics* 8 (1982), 165-76.

Searle, J. R. *Speech Acts: An Essay in the Philosophy of Language.* Cambridge: Cambridge University Press, 1969.

Searle, J. R. "Indirect Speech Acts." In P. Cole and J. Morgan. *Syntax and Semantics 3: Speech Acts.* New York: Academic, 1975.

Seidenberg, M. S., G. S. Waters, M. Sanders, and P. Langer. "Pre- and Postlexical Loci of Contextual Effects on Word Recognition." *Memory and Cognition* 12 (1984), 315-28.

Sejnowski, T. J. and C. Rosenberg. "Parallel Networks That Learn to Pronounce English." *Complex Systems* 1 (1987), 145-68.

Selkirk, E. O. *The Syntax of Words.* Cambridge, MA: MIT Press, 1982.

Sells, P. *Lectures on Contemporary Syntactic Theories: An Introduction to Government-binding Theory, Generalized Phrase Structure Grammar, Lexical Functional Grammar.* Stanford, CA: Center for the Study of Language and Information, 1985.

Shafer, G. and J. Pearl, eds. *Readings in Uncertain Reasoning.* San Mateo, CA: Morgan Kaufmann, 1990.

Shieber, S. M. "Sentence Disambiguation by a Shift-Reduce Parsing Technique." *Proceedings of the Twenty-first Annual Meeting of the Association for Computational Linguistics* (1983), 113-8.

Shieber, S. M. "Evidence against the Context-Freeness of Natural Language." *Linguistics and Philosophy* 8 (1985), 333-43.

Shieber, S. M. *CSLI Lecture Notes. Volume 4: An Introduction to Unification-based Approaches to Grammar.* Chicago: University of Chicago Press, 1986.

Sidner, C. L. "Focusing for Interpretation of Pronouns." *American Journal of Computational Linguistics* 7 (1981), 217-31.

Sidner, C. L. "Focusing in the Comprehension of Definite Anaphora." In M. Brady and R. C. Berwick, eds. *Computational Models of Discourse,* Cambridge, MA: MIT Press, 1983.

Sidner, C. L. "Plan Parsing for Intended Response Recognition in Discourse." *Computational Intelligence* 1 (1985), 1-10.

Simpson, J. A. and E. S. C. Weiner, eds. *The Oxford English Dictionary.* 2nd Ed. Oxford: Oxford University Press, 1989.

Sinclair, J. M. ed. *Looking Up: An Account of the COBUILD Project in Lexical Computing.* London and Glasgow: Collins ELT, 1987.

Singer, M. "Verifying the Assertions and Implications of Language." *Journal of Verbal Learning and Verbal Behavior* 20 (1981), 46-60.

Smadja, F. A. and K. R. McKeown. "Automatically Extracting and Representing Collocations for Language Generation." *Proceedings of the Twenty Eighth Annual Meeting of the Association for Computational Linguistics* (1990), 252-59.

Small, S. "Parsing as Cooperative Distributed Inference: Understanding Through Memory Interactions." In M. King, ed. *Parsing Natural Language.* London: Academic, 1983.

Small, S., G. Cotrell, and M. Tanenhaus. *Lexical Ambiguity Resolution.* San Mateo, CA: Morgan Kaufmann, 1988.

Small, S. and C. Rieger. "Parsing and Comprehending with Word Experts (A Theory and Its Realization)." In W. G. Lehnert and M. H. Ringle, eds. *Strategies for Natural Language Processing.* Hillsdale, NJ: Lawrence Erlbaum, 1982.

Smith, E. and D. Medin. *Categories and Concepts.* Cambridge, MA: Harvard University Press, 1981.

Smith, P.D. *An Introduction to Text Processing.* Cambridge, MA: MIT, 1990.

Sowa, J. F. *Conceptual Structures: Information Processing in Mind and Machine.* Reading, MA: Addison-Wesley, 1984.

Sowa, J. F. *Principles of Semantic Networks.* San Mateo, CA: Morgan Kaufman, 1990.

Sparck Jones, K. and Y. Wilks eds. *Automatic Natural Language Parsing.* Chichester: Ellis Horwood, 1983.

Sperber, D. and D. Wilson. *Relevance: Communication and Cognition.* Cambridge: Cambridge University Press, 1986.

Spiro, R. J. "Constructive Processes in Prose Comprehension and Recall." In *Theoretical Issues in Reading Comprehension*, R. J. Spiro, B. C. Bruce and W. F. Brewer, eds. Hillsdale, NJ: Lawrence Erlbaum, 1980.

Standish, T. A. *Data Structure Techniques.* Reading, MA: Addison-Wesley, 1980.

Steedman, M. "Combinatory Grammars and Human Sentence Processing." In J. Garfield, ed. *Modularity in Knowledge Representation and Natural Language Processing.* Cambridge, MA: MIT Press, 1987.

Steedman, M. and G. T. M. Altmann. "Ambiguity in Context: A Reply." *Language and Cognitive Processes* 4 (1989), 105-22.

Stenning, K. "On Making Models: A Study of Constructive Memory." In T. Meyers, K. Brown, and B. McGonigle, eds. *Reasoning and Discourse Processes.* London: Academic, 1986.

Stowe, L. "Parsing Wh-constructions: Evidence for On-line Gap Location." *Language and Cognitive Processes* 1 (1986), 227-45.

Stowe, L. "Thematic Structures and Sentence Comprehension." In G. N. Carlson and M. K. Tanenhaus, eds. *Linguistic Structures in Language Processing*. Dordrecht, Netherlands: Kluwer, 1989.

Strzalkowski, T. and N. Cercone. "A Framework for Computing Extra-Sentential References." *Computational Intelligence* 2 (1986), 159-80.

Stubbs, M. *Discourse Analysis: The Sociological Analysis of Natural Language*. Oxford: Blackwell, 1983.

Svartvik, J. and R. Quirk. eds. *A Corpus of English Conversation*. Lund Studies in English 56. Lund, Sweden: Gleerup/Liber, 1980.

Sweetster, E. V. *From Etymology to Pragmatics: The Mind-as-Body Metaphor in Semantic Structure and Semantic Change*. Cambridge: Cambridge University Press, 1989.

Tanenhaus, M. K., G. N. Carlson, M. S. Seidenberg. "Do Listeners Compute Linguistic Representations?" In D. R. Dowty, L. Kartunnen, A. M. Zwicky, eds. *Natural Language Parsing: Psychological, Theoretical and Computational Perspectives*. Cambridge: Cambridge University Press, 1985.

Tanenhaus, M. K., G. N. Carlson and J. C. Trueswell. "The Role of Semantic Structures in Interpretation and Parsing." *Language and Cognitive Processes* 4 (1989), 211-34.

Tanenhaus, M. K., J. Leiman, and M. Seidenberg. "Context Effects in Lexical Procession." *Cognition* 25 (1987), 213-34.

Tannen, D. ed. *Coherence in Spoken and Written Discourse*. Norwood, NJ: Ablex, 1985.

Taraband, R. and J. L. McClelland. "Constituent Attachment and Thematic Role Assignment in Sentence Processing: Influences of Content-based Expectations." *Journal of Memory and Language*. 27 (1988), 597-632.

Taylor, J. *Linguistic Categorization. An Essay in Cognitive Linguistics*. Oxford: Oxford University Press, 1989.

Tedesci, P. and A. Zaenen, eds. *Syntax and Semantics 14: Tense and Aspect*. London: Academic, 1981.

Teskey, F. N. *Principles of Text Processing*. Chichester: Ellis Horwood, 1982.

Thompson, H. S. and G. T. M. Altmann. "Modularity Compromised – Selecting Partial Hypotheses." In G. T. M. Altmann, ed. *Cognitive Models for Speech Processing: Psycholinguistic and Computational Perspectives*. Cambridge, MA: MIT Press, 1990.

Thorndyke, P. W. "The Role of Inference in Discourse Comprehension." *Journal of Verbal Learning and Verbal Behavior* 15 (1976), 437-46.

Thorndyke, P. W. "Cognitive Structures in Comprehension and Memory of Narrative Discourse." *Cognitive Psychology* 9 (1977), 77-110.

Tomita, M. *Efficient Parsing for Natural Language*. Boston, MA: Kluwer, 1986.

Tsohatzidis, S. L. ed. *Meanings and Prototypes: Studies in Linguistic Categorization*. London: Routledge, 1989.

Turing, A. M. "Computing Machinery and Intelligence." *Mind* 59 (1950), 433- 60.

Tyler, L. K. and W. Marslen-Wilson. "The Resolution of Discourse Anaphora: Some On-line Studies." *Text* 2 (1982), 263-91.

van Dijk, T. *Handbook of Discourse Analysis.* 4 Vols. London: Academic, 1985.

van Dijk, T. and W. Kintsch. *Strategies of Discourse Comprehension.* New York: Academic, 1983.

Vonk, W. "Eye Movements During the Comprehension of Pronouns." In A. G. Gale and F. Johnson, eds. *Theoretical and Applied Aspects of Eye Movement Research.* Amsterdam: North-Holland, 1984.

Vonk, W. "The Immediacy of Inferences in the Understanding of Pronouns." In G. Rickheit and H. Strohmer, eds. *Inferences in Text Processing.* Amsterdam: North-Holland, 1985.

Waibel, A. *Prosody and Speech Recognition.* San Mateo, CA: Morgan Kaufmann, 1988.

Waibel, A and K. Lee, eds. *Readings in Speech Recognition.* San Mateo, CA: Morgan Kaufmann, 1990.

Walker, C. H. and F. R. Yekovich. "Activation and Use of Script-based Antecedents in Anaphoric Reference." *Journal of Memory and Language* 26 (1987), 673-91.

Walker, D. E. ed. *Understanding Spoken Language.* New York: Elsevier/ North-Holland, 1978.

Waltz, D. L. ed. *Theoretical Issues in Natural Language Processing 2.* New York: Association for Computational Machinery, 1978.

Waltz, D. L. ed. *Semantic Structures: Advances in Natural Language Processing.* Hillsdale, NJ: Lawrence Erlbaum, 1989.

Wanner, E. "The ATN and the Sausage Machine." *Cognition* 8 (1980), 209-25.

Wanner, E. "The Parser's Architecture." In F. Kessel, ed. *The Development of Language and Language Researchers: Essays in Honour of Roger Brown.* London: Lawrence Erlbaum, 1987.

Wanner, E. and M. P. Maratsos. "An ATN Approach to Comprehension." In M. Halle, J. W. Bresnan, and G. A. Miller. *Linguistic Theory and Psychological Reality.* Cambridge, MA: MIT Press, 1978.

Warren, R. M. "Perceptual Restoration and Missing Speech Sounds." *Science* 167 (1970), 393-95.

Webber, B. L. "Description Formation and Discourse Model Synthesis." In D.L. Waltz, ed. *Theoretical Issues in Natural Language Processing 2.* New York: Association for Computational Machinery, 1978.

Webber, B. L. *A Formal Approach to Discourse Anaphora.* New York: Garland, 1979.

Webber, B. L. "Discourse Model Synthesis." In M. Brady and R. Berwick, eds. *Computational Models of Discourse.* Cambridge, MA: MIT Press, 1985.

Webber, B. L. "The Interpretation of Tense in Discourse." *Proceedings of the Twenty Fifth Annual Meeting of the Association for Computational Linguistics* (1987), 147-54.

Weiner, E. S. C. "The New Oxford English Dictionary." *Journal of English Linguistics* 18 (1985), 1-13.

Weischedel, R. and N. K. Sondheimer. "An Improved Heuristic for Ellipsis Processing." *Proceedings of the Twentieth Annual Meeting of the Association for Computational Linguistics* (1982), 85-88.

Whitelock, P., M. M. Wood, H. L. Summers, R. Johnson, and P. Bennett. *Linguistic Theory and Computer Applications.* New York: Academic Press, 1987.

Wierzbicka, A. *Lingua Mentalis: The Semantics of Natural Language.* New York: Academic Press, 1980.

Wilensky, R. *Planning and Understanding: A Computational Approach to Human Reasoning.* Reading, MA: Addison-Wesley, 1983.

Wilensky, R., D. N. Chin, M. Luria, J. Martin, J. Mayfield, and D. Wu. "The Berkeley Unix Consultant Project." *Computational Linguistics* 14 (1988).

Wilkins, W. ed. *Syntax and Semantics 21: Thematic Relations.* San Diego, CA: Academic Press, 1988.

Wilks, Y. "A Preferential Pattern-seeking Semantics for Natural Language Inference." *Artificial Intelligence* 6 (1975), 53-74.

Wilks, Y. "An Intelligent Analyzer and Understander of English." *Communications of the ACM* 18 (1975), 264-74.

Winograd, T. *Understanding Natural Language.* New York: Academic Press, 1972.

Winograd, T. *Language as a Cognitive Process.* Vol 1, Reading, MA: Addison-Wesley, 1983.

Winograd, T. and F. Flores. *Understanding Computers and Cognition.* Norwood, NJ: Ablex, 1986.

Winston, P. H. *Artificial Intelligence.* 2nd edn. Reading, MA: Addison-Wesley, 1984.

Witten, L. H. *Principles of Computer Speech.* London: Academic Press, 1982.

Wittenburg, K.W. "Predictive Combinators: A Method for Efficient Processing of Combinatory Categorial Grammars." In *Proceedings of the 25th Annual Meeting of the Association for Computational Linguistics* (1987).

Wittgenstein, L. *Philosophical Investigations.* New York: Macmillan, 1953.

Woods, A., P. Fletcher, and A. Hughes. *Statistics in Language Study.* Cambridge: Cambridge University Press, 1986.

Woods, W. A. "Transition Network Grammars for Natural Language Analysis." *Communications of the Association for Computing Machinery* 13 (1970), 591-606.

Woods, W. A. "An Experimental Parsing System for Transition Network Grammars." In R. Rustin, ed. *Natural Language Processing.* New York: Algorithmics Press, 1973.

Woods, W. A. "What's in a Link: Foundations for Semantic Networks." In D. G. Bobrow and A. Collins, eds. *Representation and Understanding: Studies in Cognitive Science.* New York: Academic Press, 1975.

Woods, W. A. "Cascaded ATN Grammars." *American Journal of Computational Linguistics* 6 (1980), 1-12.

Zipf, G. K. *Human Behavior and the Principle of Least Effort.* New York: Hafner, 1965.

Index

Equi-NP deletion, 223

Equivalence (logical), 270-1

Ergative-absolutive languages, 318

Essive (case), 317

Exchange sort, 71-2

Existential quantification, 271-2

Experiencer (case), 317

Extraposition, 223, 227

F-structure, 251

Factor analysis, 82

Features, printed characters, 15, 139-41; phonological, 28, 38-9, 141-2; semantic, 29, 67, 95-6, 281-6; syntactic, 66-7, 205-7

Fillmore, C., 330

Finite-state device, 158-9, 163, 167-8

Finnish, 7, 312, 319

Flap (speech sound), 42

Focus (discourse), 416-9, 431-2

Fodor, J.A. 169, 345

Force (case), 316-7

Foregrounding, 416-7

Formant, 38-9, 42

Formative, 21-2

Forward chaining, 274

Frame, 101-2; for lexical proto-types, 297-9; case frame, 312-6, 350, 383

Frame problem, 349

Frege, G. 301, 340

French, 35, 52, 75, 82

Frequency, of characters, 15-6; of words, 75, 79-81, 82-4, 85-6, 109-11, 126-7, 342

Frequency domain sampling, 44

Function (logical), 307-9; Lambda, 364-5

Function words, 50, 65, 79, 82-5, 327, 411

Functional structures, 158, 173-4, 212-3, 220-1, 249, 310-1

Fundamental frequency (of speech), 37-8

Fuzzy set theory, 297

Gap (left by unbounded movement), 234-5, 246; distinguished from ellipsis, 409

Garden path sentence, 156, 193, 202, 324-5, 348

Gazdar, G. 243

German, 22, 25, 82, 312, 319

Government and binding theory, 225

Grammar, defined, 162; case, 67-8, 311-20; categorical, 365-8; context free, 168-171, 174-180; context sensitive, 206-7, 209-18; dependency, 327; discourse, 428-30; generative, 162; generalized phrase structure, 243-7; lexical functional, 247-52; phrase structure, 170-1, 174-9, 368-76; semantic, 100, 363; story, 429; systemic, 335-6; transformational, 224-8; unificational, 218-20

Graph notation, 68, 311

Greek, 15, 21

Grosz, B. 417

Halliday, M.A.K., 334

Hashing, 116-20, 122

74143